# A Time of Crisis

*Japan, the Great Depression,
and Rural Revitalization*

Harvard East Asian Monographs 191

# A Time of Crisis

## Japan, the Great Depression, and Rural Revitalization

Kerry Smith

Published by the Harvard University Asia Center
and distributed by Harvard University Press
Cambridge (Massachusetts) and London 2001

© 2001 by the President and Fellows of Harvard College

Printed in the United States of America

The Harvard University Asia Center publishes a monograph series and, in coordination with the Fairbank Center for East Asian Research, the Korea Institute, the Reischauer Institute of Japanese Studies, and other faculties and institutes, administers research projects designed to further scholarly understanding of China, Japan, Vietnam, Korea, and other Asian countries. The Center also sponsors projects addressing multidisciplinary and regional issues in Asia.

Library of Congress Cataloging-in-Publication Data

Smith, Kerry.
   A time of crisis : Japan, the great depression, and rural revitalization / Kerry Smith.
   p.  cm.
   Includes bibliographical references and index.
   ISBN 0-674-00370-5 (cloth : alk. paper); 0-674-01277-1 (paperback : alk. paper)
    1. Sekishiba-machi (Kitakata-shi, Japan)--History. 2. Kitakata-shi (Japan)--History. 3. Sekishiba-machi (Kitakata-shi, Japan)--Economic conditions. 4. Kitakata-shi (Japan)--Economic conditions. 5. Depression--1929--Japan--Kitakata-shi (Japan). 6. Sekishiba-machi (Kitakata-shi, Japan). I. Title.

DS897.S3923 S65 2000
952'.117--dc 21
                                                                                   00-046093

Index by the author

♾  Printed on acid-free paper

Last figure below indicates year of this printing
12  11  10  09  08  07  06  05  04  03

First paperback edition, 2003

*For Alyssa*

# Acknowledgments

THIS BOOK IS ABOUT SEKISHIBA because of good luck and the kindness of strangers. In 1990, I arrived at the University of Tokyo's Institute of Social Science as a graduate student, visiting researcher, and Fulbright recipient. Professor Nishida Yoshiaki graciously agreed to serve as my advisor and helped me arrange to meet with a graduate student "tutor" from time to time to go over the texts and documents I was working with in the early stages of my research on the Great Depression in rural Japan. My tutor, Kimitsukasa Tasaki (now Professor Tasaki of the Osaka University of Commerce), mentioned after several months that he was involved in helping edit and write a local history of Kitakata city in Fukushima, and asked whether I would like to come and have a look at the materials there. He had close family and personal ties to the community, and as one of the few students from the area to have made it to Tokyo University, his professional interests in Meiji history, as well as his personal ones, brought him back to Kitakata on a regular basis. Tasaki invited me to join him on one of those trips home to spend a few days in the archives and in the city. He understood even then I'm certain something that it took me longer to realize. His offer was only in passing about the archive, as rich as it turned out to be. It was in a more personal and important way an invitation to a particular community and its particular past.

Most villages and towns have done a haphazard job of preserving the paperwork and chronicles that document their past, even as relatively recent a history as I was interested in. The incentives to preserve are few, and there are often compelling reasons to get rid of old records. In the last days of the

Pacific War, it was common practice to destroy some if not all official documents to keep them from falling into the hands of the occupiers. Fire, neglect, and the imperatives of storage space have done their share of damage as well. Sekishiba was different, and I owe a special debt to Professor Tasaki. His patient advice and deep knowledge of Japanese history have been invaluable assets. I am particularly thankful for his help.

In the course of researching and writing this book, I have relied on the guidance and assistance of many others. Let me begin by thanking the librarians and archivists who made this study possible. The staff of the Tokyo University Economics Library, the Agricultural Science Library, and the Institute of Social Science Library were always friendly and helpful. The National Research Institute of Agricultural Economics provided access to periodicals that were otherwise hard to find. I would especially like to thank the staff of the Office for the Compilation of Municipal History of the Kitakata Municipal Library. Together they made it possible for me to have unrestricted access to the materials on Sekishiba Village and the communities nearby. They gave freely of their time, resources, and friendship. Members of the Editorial Committee also provided useful advice and tremendous hospitality.

I received financial support from several sources. As a graduate student in residence at Harvard, a series of Foreign Language and Area Studies Fellowships allowed me to pursue my research interests. As a researcher in Japan, the Japan–United States Educational Commission Fulbright program (1990–1991), the Department of Education Fulbright program (1991–1992), and the Edwin O. Reischauer Institute of Japanese Studies, Harvard University (1992–1993) provided generous support at important stages in the development of the dissertation. The Institute of Social Science Research at Tokyo University provided me with an affiliation, library access, and good company for many years. The Institute's scholars and staff provide a tremendous service to Western scholars of Japan. A National Endowment for the Humanities Fellowship for College Teachers and Independent Scholars supported the completion of the manuscript (1998–1999), as did a Northeast Asia Council Association for Asian Studies Travel Grant to Japan. Keio University was generous with its assistance and facilities.

Professor Albert Craig helped shape this project in many ways. His advice, careful analysis, and patience have been invaluable over the years it took to complete this study. Professors Harold Bolitho, Carol Gluck, Andrew

Gordon, and James L. McClain gave freely of their time and ideas. Professor Stephen Vlastos read and commented on early drafts of several chapters; Laura Hein and Thomas Havens were also generous with suggestions and guidance. A. Michelle of Brown Graphic Services deserves recognition for her skillful preparation of the maps. Victoria Scott's careful editing improved the manuscript considerably. An anonymous reader's suggestions were invaluable in shaping the book's final form.

I am equally indebted to scholars in Japan. I am especially grateful to Professor Nishida Yoshiaki of the Institute of Social Science, Tokyo University, for his kindness. He not only found the time to answer my many questions but also arranged to travel with me to Kitakata to look over the documents that went into this study. His advice then and at all other times was invaluable; his insights shaped my research in more ways than I can count. Professor Kase Kazutoshi, also of the Institute of Social Science, shared the results of his ongoing research on unemployment policy with me, read an early draft of the chapter on farm debt, and was always willing to help me to better understand interwar Japan. Professors Nakamura Masanori and Ōishi Kaichirō provided guidance early in my research on the depression; Professor Ōishi continued to do so through his involvement with the writing of the *Kitakata-shi shi*. I am grateful as well for the comments and encouragement of Professors Mori Takemaro and Ōkado Masakatsu. Professor Kawai Takao of Keio University was generous with his time and advice.

Friends in Japan and in the United States were sources of ideas, welcome criticism, and help. Barbara Brooks, Sandra Wilson, and Tak Matsusaka shared their experiences of writing about the 1930s. Larry and Tae Fouraker clarified my thinking on any number of topics. My classmate Louisa Rubinfien helped me better understand the goals and scope of my research through her own careful work on the depression era; she, too, read and commented on parts of this study. Michael Molasky, Nancy Abelmann, and Jeffrey Lesser's support in my own times of crisis was unwavering. In Kitakata, the Anazawa and Takazawa families opened their homes to me on several occasions. In Tokyo, Tony Hind and his family provided friendship, hospitality, and encouragement time and again. The Tsuji family, too, was always more than generous with their kindness.

K.S.

# Contents

|   |   |   |
|---|---|---|
| *Tables, Maps, and Figures* | | xv |
| *Abbreviations* | | xvii |
| 1 | Japan in a Time of Crisis | 1 |
| | A Land of Milk and Honey 6/ Sekishiba 10/ Revitalization and the Modern Countryside 12 | |
| 2 | Locations | 19 |
| | The Tōhoku 20/ Fukushima and Aizu 24/ Kitakata 27/ Sekishiba 32 | |
| 3 | The Rural Depression | 42 |
| | The Crises of the 1920s 44/ The Great Depression: Crises of Farms and Finances 50/ The Crises of Community 68/ The Crises of State and Nation 80 | |
| 4 | Rescuing the Countryside | 84 |
| | Yesterday's Countryside 87/ Putting Farmers First: The Agrarianist Campaign for Relief 94/ The Agrarianist Legacy 110/ Managing Debt 113/ Debt Arrangement in Practice 129/ Conclusions 132 | |
| 5 | Crafting Rural Relief | 135 |
| | Public Works as Relief 137/ Relief at the Village Level 146/ Assessing Rural Relief 152/ The Limits of Relief 155/ The Military and Rural Relief 166/ Conclusions 170 | |

| | | |
|---|---|---|
| 6 | Revitalization | 172 |

Local Reform 174/ Self-revitalization on the National Stage 188/ Development of a National Self-revitalization Program 192/ Self-revitalization, the Ministries, and the Sixty-third Diet 196/ The Framework of Revitalization 206/ The Popular Culture of Reform and Revitalization 214/

| | | |
|---|---|---|
| 7 | Revitalization in a Famine Year: Sekishiba, 1934–1935 | 224 |

Embracing Revitalization 225/ Revitalization Strategies 239/ The 1934 Famine 241/ Surviving the Famine 251/ A Village Plans 259/ The Best-Laid Plans 266/

| | | |
|---|---|---|
| 8 | The Village Economy, 1935–1939 | 269 |

Organizing for Recovery 271/ Community Infrastructure 277/ Farm Production 281/ Family and Village Finances 284/ From Recovery to War: The Village Economy at the End of the Decade 286/

| | | |
|---|---|---|
| 9 | Reconstructing Community: Sekishiba, 1935–1937 | 288 |

The Mayor, the Businessman, and the Committee 291/ Harmony, Culture, and Discipline 303/ Yabe and the Hōtoku Societies 304/ The Hamlet Assemblies 312/ The Reform of Daily Life 319/ Conclusions 321

| | | |
|---|---|---|
| 10 | Sekishiba in Wartime | 325 |

Revitalization, the Rural Economy, and the Early Years of the War 329/ Mobilizing the Village 335/ Village Mainstays 339/ Emigration and Revitalization 345/ Mobilization and the Modern Countryside 349

| | | |
|---|---|---|
| 11 | The Elusive Revitalized Village | 353 |

Occupation Reforms 353/ Creating the Prosperous Countryside 358/ City and Country 361/ The Elusive Revitalized Village 366/

## Appendix

Membership of Sekishiba's Economic Revitalization Committee, 1934 — 373

## Reference Matter

Notes — 379
Works Cited — 451
Index — 469

# Tables, Maps, and Figures

## Tables

| | | |
|---|---|---|
| 1 | Agricultural production in Sekishiba, 1925–1939 | 54 |
| 2 | The yen value of agricultural production in Sekishiba, 1925–1939 | 55 |
| 3 | Local conditions in Sekishiba, 1924–1934 | 59 |
| 4 | Sekishiba Economic Revitalization Debt Survey, 1934 | 66 |
| 5 | Status of farm households in Sekishiba, 1926–1938 | 77 |
| 6 | Japanese government spending on relief projects by agency, 1932–1934 | 144 |
| 7 | Projected results for 1939 of economic revitalization for sixteen households in Komatsu Hamlet, Sekishiba | 232 |
| 8 | Rice farming in a famine year in the six Tōhoku prefectures, 1934 | 244 |
| 9 | Rice crop losses and farmland in Sekishiba, 1934 | 246 |
| 10 | Famine effects and farmland in Sekishiba, 1934 | 248 |
| 11 | Harvests under Sekishiba's Economic Revitalization Plan, selected crops, 1935–1940 | 282 |
| 12 | Sample lectures from Sekishiba's first year of hamlet assemblies, 1934–1935 | 316 |

## Maps

| | | |
|---|---|---|
| 1 | Northeastern Japan | 21 |
| 2 | The Aizu basin | 25 |
| 3 | Sekishiba village | 33 |

## Figures

| | | |
|---|---|---|
| 1 | The major sources of farm poverty and distress | 182 |
| 2 | The effects of diligence and the family farm | 184 |
| 3 | Village-level revitalization materials | 186 |
| 4 | *Sekishiba Industrial Cooperative Newsletter*, 1936 | 274 |
| 5 | Map of Special Assistance revitalization projects in Sekishiba, 1937–1938 | 279 |
| 6 | Sekishiba village leaders with Mayor Satō Sakichi, September 1932 | 292 |
| 7 | Zenbei and Tsuneko Yabe, 1933 | 295 |
| 8 | Structure of the Sekishiba Economic Revitalization Committee, 1934–1935 | 298 |
| 9 | Sekishiba's monthly village newspaper, the *Sekishiba sonpō*, October 1938 issue | 338 |

# Abbreviations

The following abbreviations are used in the text and notes.

KST   Kitakata shiritsu toshokan shi-shi hensan shitsu (Office for the Compilation of Municipal History, Kitakata Municipal Library). Repository of Sekishiba village document collection in Kitakata city, Fukushima prefecture.

NSS   Takeda Tsutomu and Kusumoto Masahiro, eds. *Nōsangyoson keizai kōsei undō shi shiryō shūsei* (Collected Documents of the Farm, Mountain, and Fishing Village Economic Revitalization Campaign), Parts 1 and 2.

SMY   Sekishiba mura yakuba (Sekishiba village office).

TGT 63   Teikoku gikai shūgiin. *Dai 63 teikoku gikai shūgiin giji tekiyō* (Summary of the proceedings of the 63rd Session of the Lower House of the Imperial Diet).

TGT 64   Teikoku gikai shūgiin. *Dai 64 teikoku gikai shūgiin giji tekiyō* (Summary of the proceedings of the 64th Session of the Lower House of the Imperial Diet).

# A Time of Crisis

*Japan, the Great Depression,
and Rural Revitalization*

# 1 Japan in a Time of Crisis

THE DILEMMAS OF THE EARLY 1930S were so unlike any that modern Japan had encountered before that a new vocabulary was necessary to describe them. "Recession" and even "depression," the usual terms for periods of economic collapse, were tried and found wanting. Average men and women spoke instead in a more powerful language of unparalleled difficulties, of a national emergency (*jikyoku*), and of lives "deadlocked" (*yukizumari*), trapped like the nation itself by circumstances beyond their control. Setbacks abroad and at home left citizens reeling, certain only that Japan had entered a new era in its long history. Taken separately, any one or two of the problems that confronted the country in the early 1930s would probably have been easy to overcome. Unfortunately, dealing with them separately was never an option. Japan faced multiple crises on several fronts at once—so many and so often that commentators despaired of ever escaping the burdens they imposed. This moment in modern Japan's diplomatic, economic, and social histories became for many citizens simply *hijōji*, a time of crisis.[1]

If there had been no war in the Pacific, the Great Depression in Japan would likely be remembered today much as it is in the United States—as a time of economic collapse, political unrest, and profound social change. The events of the early 1930s were unprecedented in the history of modern Japan and deeply unsettling to those who experienced them. That we remember the war and the Occupation rather than the Great Depression as the transforming experiences of a generation and of an era speaks to the utter destruction wrought by Japan's aggression in the late 1930s and 1940s. The historical memory of modern Japan is thus one in which narratives of the depression era are often absent, or are subsumed by the national and personal tragedies that followed.

When historians have looked at the 1930s, it has been to explain the ascendancy of authoritarian rule and the origins and course of the war in China and the Pacific. The result has been the construction over the years of a useful map of the road to war—a map that does a good job of describing significant events in Tokyo and the decisions made by those in the upper echelons of the government, the military, and business. This portrayal is less reliable when it comes to understanding what was happening in other parts of Japan and to Japanese who were not among the elite.[2] This is not to say that the map is flawed. It is, however, limited in what it seeks to describe.

This study suggests that there is more to the experiences of the 1930s than a foreshadowing of the coming war. My focus is on developments outside of the halls of power in Tokyo, and on the particular importance of community life and the economics of farming. This is an approach familiar to scholars in Japan, where both the economic crisis and its effects on rural communities have long been the subject of careful study.[3] Their interest in the countryside—and mine—stems from rural Japan's importance to the nation's economy and its role as a site of political and social change. Rural Japan responded to the Great Depression and its aftermath with a wide range of dynamic and innovative efforts to repair the immediate economic damage to farm families and create long-term solutions for the community as a whole. Farmers had to use petitions and public appeals to force the government to make a package of rural relief and reform policies available to them.[4] Yet the average citizen did not react to the economic downturn with violence; even the sharp upswing in labor and tenancy disputes during the depression encompassed but a small fraction of the working and farming populations. By revealing some of the ways in which the state and communities provided alternatives to despair and violence, this study brings us closer to a grass-roots perspective on the meaning of Japan's time of crisis.

By the 1930s Japan had already been through several periods of rapid and significant social change in a relatively short span of time. The nation was no stranger to economic collapse, natural disasters, or popular unrest. The end of the First World War and the economic boom that accompanied it, the death of the Meiji emperor in 1912, and two military victories, one against China in 1894–1895 and the other against Russia a decade later, were among the events that in some way marked moments of transition. Each had sparked government efforts to simultaneously accommodate the needs of its citizenry and maintain social order, just as each had signaled the rise of new forms of public culture and discourse.

The crises of the early 1930s were different. Citizens old enough to remember the years on either side of the 1868 Meiji Restoration, when the dismantling of the old regime and the creation of a new one began Japan's transformation into a modern, powerful state, found in the 1930s a similar combination of outside threats and domestic upheaval. There were diplomatic catastrophes, as the nation's relations with the West and with China entered uncharted territory in the 1930s. Japan had formal colonies in Asia (Korea and Taiwan among them, with several lesser possessions as well), but it was its powerful and informal interest in China that caused the most difficulty.[5] Japan's position there was unique among the world powers; Japanese companies had far more invested in China than any Western nation and much more to lose should doors long open begin to close. Yet Japan's uncompromising presence in China—to say nothing of the visible disdain that many Japanese expressed toward China and the Chinese people—only made its interests the target of choice for anti-colonial protests by students, workers, and political activists of all stripes. After officers of the Kwantung Army, charged with the security of Japan's treaty interests in Manchuria, launched a carefully planned offensive against Chinese forces there in 1931, international criticism of Japan's policies reached new heights. The willingness of the Western powers to compromise their positions in China, when Japan would not, isolated Japan even further and marked the beginnings of the widely held belief among many Japanese that they were alone, vulnerable, and constantly under threat.

Political issues at home compounded entanglements abroad. Parties had been a part of the political landscape since before the turn of the century but had not begun to exercise power publicly and consistently until after the First World War. From then until 1932, it had become almost the regular practice to allow the party with the majority in the lower house of the Diet to form the cabinet. Moreover, the electorate was sharply expanded in 1925 to include almost all adult males. The lower house elections of 1928 were the first to test this new body politic. The decade before the Great Depression thus marks a high point in popular participation in the political process.

The economic collapse and problems in Manchuria, however, increasingly called the parties' effectiveness into question. Democracy and the social arrangements that went with it were similarly challenged. Japan's circumstances seemed to many observers to demand new, perhaps more authoritarian responses than Western-style democracies were able to provide. The two mainstream parties, the Seiyūkai and the Minseitō, ultimately did little to defend their positions. Although often more alike in their policies than otherwise, of the two the Minseitō in particular had been slow to react to the depression's impact at home, and neither party was thought to be very good at protecting Japan's interests abroad. Both could also be indifferent to the voters, and when the balance of power within the government began to shift away from the parties and toward the military and the bureaucrats, few protested the parties' demise.[6] The transition from an era of party-led governments to one in which bureaucrats and the military held power was marked by several coup attempts and shocking acts of violence, which only fueled elite and popular anxieties about Japan's future. The nation's "new" non-party leadership after 1932 promised unity and a clear direction, but the relationship between Japan's government and its citizens had changed significantly.

Social unrest reached new levels in the 1930s, mirroring upheavals in diplomacy and politics. Disputes between landlords and tenants and between workers and employers skyrocketed throughout the 1920s and showed no signs of abating in the early 1930s. Both workers and tenants increasingly turned to unions and other forms of social activism to shape the environment in which they labored; such confrontational tactics were deemed anathema to the wonderful qualities of Japanese paternal practices, sparking crackdown after crackdown on even relatively mild displays of resistance. That women played an increasingly varied and visible role in public life in the 1920s and 1930s only complicated matters. Not a few observers saw in these changes further evidence of Japan's cultural decay and rushed to shore up what they feared was the crumbling façade of Japanese tradition.

Finally, it is worth noting that popular culture was an important component of the crises of the depression era. The 1920s in Japan, as in many

Western states, saw a blossoming of new modes of entertainment and leisure, ones that celebrated the erotic, the grotesque, and the nonsensical.[7] A mass media capable of creating and sustaining a popular culture took shape in the interwar era and promoted a growing sensationalism that exacerbated the urban/modern and rural/traditional divide.[8] New technologies, radio, and a much more vigorous media and publishing industry reached out to the listening and reading public as never before. The crises of the 1930s were shared by a national public to an extent previously impossible. Citizens were better informed (within the limits of state censorship), but they were also more susceptible to campaigns to organize them, sway their opinions, and shape their actions. Radio first reached into average homes in the 1920s and took off as a broadcast medium in the 1930s.[9] Popular magazines and journals reached record levels of circulation by the mid-1930s, as they found readers eager to consume the fiction, commentary, and cartoons they provided—and experienced in understanding the world outside their communities as filtered through the lens of the press and the state. Movies, too, emerged as an important medium for the dissemination of images and ideas.[10]

For many average Japanese, the overlapping crises made the late 1920s and early 1930s a period of profound uncertainty, an almost liminal moment in their lives, when established patterns of social relationships and structures were breaking down with nothing to replace them.[11] It is precisely during such moments that long-standing practices can be called into question, and new and sometimes unexpected relationships and structures can be created to accommodate the changed circumstances.

One reason therefore to look carefully at what was happening in the countryside is that these attempts to confront the specific problems of the depression shed new light on how average Japanese dealt with some of the most basic questions of the modern age. How could rural communities retain what was best about their past and still have a future? When did tradition have to surrender to new practices and beliefs? What was the role of agriculture in a modern economy? Where was the boundary between city and country and where should it be? The economic and social crises of the 1930s forced farmers, and the towns and villages in which they lived, to address these issues publicly and repeatedly. Their discussions clarify the range of possible answers to these questions and suggest the direction of popular social and ideological change in the aftermath of the depression. The countryside was actively engaged in re-creating itself on many levels before the war directed those efforts and the enthusiasm with which they had been pursued down other roads.[12]

## A Land of Milk and Honey

Efforts to describe how rural communities were transformed in the 1930s, however, face several obstacles. At the time, few communities thought to document what was happening to them, and the national government was little better at keeping careful track of how towns and villages fared under its programs. One of the most influential contemporary accounts of the rural crisis, Kagawa Toyohiko's (1888–1960) novel *The Land of Milk and Honey* (*Chichi to mitsu no nagaruru sato*), in fact, deliberately blurred the line between fact and fiction. That novel is worth describing in some detail for two reasons. First, it is a work that many farmers would later identify as having inspired and impressed them deeply.[13] As such, it offers a window on how rural citizens viewed their changing circumstances in the early 1930s. Second, both Kagawa's novel and this book focus to a considerable extent on developments in a single community; *The Land of Milk and Honey* reveals some of the strengths and shortcomings of such an approach. The first installment of Christian social activist and former labor organizer Kagawa Toyohiko's novel appeared in the January 1934 issue of the popular journal *Ie no hikari*, the twentieth and final segment in December 1935. The respected publishing house Kaizō issued *The Land of Milk and Honey* in book form that same year.[14] Though widely read and enthusiastically received by its primarily rural audience, it is not one of the world's great works of literature. Contrived and melodramatic, as a novel it has ample weaknesses. Part adventure story, part romance, and very much a polemic on behalf of Japan's Industrial Cooperative movement, the book moves from one crisis to another with dizzying speed.[15] And yet, in the midst of all this, Kagawa renders the countryside's dilemmas with clarity and passion. The struggle to overcome the effects of the Great Depression, the drama at the heart of the novel, was one even then being played out in towns and villages throughout Japan.

His story begins in 1931, with twenty-four-year-old Tanaka Tōsuke's decision to leave his family's small farm in the village of Ōshio, which, like all the named locations in the novel, is a real community. This one lies along the eastern edge of the Aizu basin, nestled in the mountains that separate that region from the rest of Fukushima prefecture. Tōsuke's decision is driven both by a desire to lessen the burden on his family, which had been forced by the collapse in the silk market to forage for grasshoppers and bulbs in order to survive, and by Tōsuke's belief that he could discover a means to rescue his village and his family. From Ōshio, Tōsuke begins a series of journeys that blend adventure and apprenticeship in the methods and values of the industrial cooperative movement. He learns to sell fish and other goods via a cooperative in Urazato village in Nagano, is rescued from the wilderness by a mountain man who teaches him to survive on nature's bounty, and helps run a consumers' union in Tokyo's Kōenji neighborhood before collapsing from overwork and disease. While he recovers in a union-run hospital, kindly doctors and nurses provide a sort of mini-seminar on how to provide medical care to rural communities.

By the time Tōsuke makes his way back to Fukushima, he is well-prepared to begin the revitalization (or *kōsei*) of his village. But his troubles are hardly over. Opposition to his endeavor is strong and cunning. Led by a landlord's son and a Diet representative (of the "Minyū" party), local elites at first undermine Tōsuke's every effort and, through malicious rumor, false accusations, and outright fraud, for a time succeed in turning the community against him and his plans. Only then does Tōsuke realize the error of his ways. In his zeal to transform the village, Tōsuke had focused only on what he himself could do for the community, on the projects that he could lead and the goals that he thought important. The lessons that Kagawa has Tōsuke draw from this setback are simple ones: the village must change in order to survive, but strong leadership alone won't bring this about. Revitalization can truly succeed only when everyone in the community supports it.

His first attempt at reform failed, Tōsuke decides, not because he had tried to do too much but because he had tried to do too little. Villagers clearly longed for something more than a piecemeal response to their problems, and for more than pie-in-the-sky proposals drawn up in distant Tokyo. The rural Japan Kagawa describes is one in which farmers sought a better future, but only if they could help decide its shape. Tōsuke thus renewed his struggle against the local elites and the status quo armed with proposals for a sweeping transformation of rural life. This time he takes care to enlist the ideas and energies of the entire village, and in short order turns the table on his opponents. The landlord's son is sent off to jail, found guilty of a crime of which he had falsely accused Tōsuke, while the wily politician simply slips away. Tōsuke and his allies arrange for the cooperative to buy all the landlord's land at fair prices, distributing some to local tenants and using the rest as the site for a local sanitarium-resort where women returning from the textile factories can recover from the illnesses they so often brought back with them.

These and other reforms transform the village. Farmers learn under Tōsuke's guidance to raise goats (the source of the village's milk; the honey comes from local hives, also introduced by Tōsuke), rabbits, and new crops to supplement their income and their diets. By the end of the story, which brings the narrative into the mid-1930s, Ōshio has recovered sufficiently to prepare to dispatch its own delegation of young women to Okinawa to assist in the revitalization of communities there. In the novel's final scene, Tōsuke is a featured speaker at a national convention of industrial cooperative activists. They embrace his proposals for rural reform wholeheartedly. As he leaves the stage, the audience's cheers still ringing in his ears, Tōsuke vows to use what he has learned in Ōshio to save not only his village but all villages and ultimately the nation itself.

*The Land of Milk and Honey* reflects in fiction some basic realities about rural life in the 1930s. That the countryside and the nation needed to be rescued there was no doubt, neither for Kagawa nor for his readers. *The Land of Milk and Honey*'s publication coincided with the worst famine in Japan's modern memory, which itself followed closely on the heels of the Great Depression's harshest years. Chapter after chapter of the book described the devastation in detail, drawing on events, places, and issues that were instantly familiar to its audience. Poor medical care, the impoverishment of rural communities in the wake of the depression, famine, police crackdowns on the left, prostitution, and the misdeeds of local elites and politicians—are all related in a matter-of-fact and credible manner.[16] As unlikely as it was that one poor farmer would experience all the things that Tōsuke did, the novel doesn't stoop to imagining a countryside that was better off than its readers knew to be true.

Yet *The Land of Milk and Honey* documents more than just a litany of rural despair. In its insistence that the countryside could be changed for the better and that the power to do so was in the hands of average citizens, the novel maps the extent of Japan's transformation by the crises of the early 1930s. Kagawa depicts farm families and their villages as profoundly changed not just by the Great Depression, but by the nature of their responses to it. Here, too, the context was familiar to rural readers. By the time the novel first appeared in Ie no hikari, the countryside had been the target of an unprecedented national campaign of rural revitalization for more than a year. Communities throughout Japan were actively re-creating themselves in the depression's wake, experimenting with local variants of economic and social reforms. Tōsuke's goals and methods in Ōshio owed everything to these real-life examples. His predicament was never simply how to restore the village to what it had been like before the depression. Tōsuke's dilemma, and ultimately his greatest success, was finding a future for Ōshio that promised more than its past.[17]

Kagawa's novel makes at least one other important if unintentional observation about its subject matter, and that is that many of what were ultimately the national crises of the early 1930s are best understood locally. The qualities that set the early 1930s apart in the social history of modern Japan, namely, the tremendous damage done by the Great Depression, the unprecedented efforts to revitalize the countryside that followed, and the first signs of new relationships between citizens and the state in the depression's aftermath, are evident most tangibly at the village level. Any attempt to address the questions raised earlier about the tensions between past and present, farm and factory, rural and urban, it seems to me, begins there.

Kagawa had some advantages in his telling of Ōshio's story; not having to stick to the facts was one of them. As a work of fiction, *The Land of Milk and Honey* made the distance between Kagawa's imaginary revitalized village and the depression-ravaged ones his readers lived in seem almost negligible. In Tōsuke's land of milk and honey, good intentions and revitalization carried the day unconditionally. But as farmers everywhere else discovered, the struggle to recover from the Great Depression would prove far more complex, the future much less secure, than the novel's happy ending promised. The revitalized village remained elusive for most.

This book shares *The Land of Milk and Honey*'s focus on the village but has found a different solution to the problem of scarce sources and documentation, one that doesn't rely on fiction. It turns instead to the example of Sekishiba, one of a handful of villages that has preserved a richly detailed archival record of its experiences with revitalization.[18] This study draws extensively on that record and the experiences it relates.

## Sekishiba

The village of Sekishiba is quite literally right down the road from Ōshio, the site of Tanaka Tōsuke's fictional revitalization efforts. The two communities are only kilometers apart. The main route connecting Ōshio to Kitakata, the largest local town and closest train station, descends out of the mountains and passes through Sekishiba, flanked by paddy fields and irrigation ditches. Sekishiba's borders nestle against the mountains at the northeastern end of the Aizu basin, but most of the village lies within the flat, fertile expanse of the plain.

In the early 1930s, Sekishiba was home to several thousand residents, most of them farmers, most of them also rice producers, and almost all of them badly off as a result of the depression. Residents likely would have considered themselves luckier than the characters inhabiting Tōsuke's Ōshio, but they might equally well have been struck by the commonalities between the two communities and have taken heart at Tōsuke's successes. "If one just sits by and does nothing," wrote Sekishiba's mayor in 1934, "then with every year the beautiful customs of the past will fall into the shadows, and every day that passes will hasten the desolation of the village."[19] At the time, Sekishiba was four years into the Great Depression, months away from the country's most serious famine in generations, and desperately in search of solutions. The story of Tōsuke's imagined revitalization went to press just as Sekishiba's quest for a real one was beginning.

Sekishiba is a fairly unremarkable place. There were no recorded disputes between tenants and landlords, or between residents and the authorities, for much of the prewar era. Nor is there any sign that radical political parties, tenant unions, or nationalist bodies ever established a foothold in the village. By all accounts the village fit squarely in the ranks of the average. It was home to several hundred farming families in the 1930s, most of whom relied on rice and silk cocoons for their incomes. Their experiences during the depression appear to have been no better and no worse than those of farmers in nearby communities and were certainly comparable to the ones shared by farmers throughout Japan. In most ways that can be measured, Sekishiba and its residents were as ordinary as can be.

Of course if asked, residents of the region near Sekishiba have a list of qualities that distinguish them from Japanese of other regions. The local dialect is one such quality, the area's unique handicrafts are another, and its history of resistance to the "new" government in Tokyo, yet another.[20] All of these help distinguish the region from the rest of the prefecture and from the rest of the country. At the same time, though, there was much that Sekishiba had in common with other villages in the 1930s. Sekishiba and the communities near it were fully incorporated into the prefectural and national political administration and into the state's education system. Voters cast their ballots for mainstream parties more often than not, and the spread of newspapers and magazines (not to mention radio) meant that by the 1930s people throughout Japan shared in something like a national culture. The region's economy was built on a combination of agriculture and some light manufacturing; both benefited from the rail line that linked the Aizu area to Tokyo and to points north. Towns like Kitakata and nearby Wakamatsu provided access to markets, hospitals, and other urban amenities. In these ways the area was much like many other rural regions in Japan.

Sekishiba's enthusiasm for the process of reform is one of the few ways that the village stands apart. The village did win an award from the prefecture and a measure of media attention for its successes with the state's most important reform programs. This alone was enough to distinguish it somewhat from its immediate neighbors, but the gap was neither deep nor very wide and seems not to have lasted very long. Sekishiba went back to being just another village once the opportunity to pursue reform had ended. Its overall normalcy is important. Many of the studies of depression-era villages have concentrated on communities that were clearly unusual, either because of what local leaders tried to accomplish or the methods they chose to employ. It has been hard to judge whether the ideas and goals that emerged from their struggles to survive the depression are at all indicative of what happened elsewhere.

Sekishiba provides a useful counterpart to those cases and suggests that even average communities were home to rich and varied lives. Our assumptions about what the depression may have done to communities—and even about how ordinary people came to support an increasingly authoritarian state—rest on a sketchy understanding of how those communities worked. Although no single case study can provide all the answers, it is clear that in Sekishiba we have the chance to observe ordinary lives in extraordinary times.

This study draws on Sekishiba's experiences to shed light on a brief but important period in Japan's modern history. Three domestic developments in particular are associated with the social landscape of the 1930s: the Great Depression, the long struggle to revitalize the countryside, and the insidious course of mobilization for war together transformed the nation. The next sections of this chapter locate those developments alongside other significant tensions in Japanese society of the 1930s.

## Revitalization and the Modern Countryside

The search for solutions to Japan's economic and social crises in the early 1930s was more far-reaching than is generally recognized. Unprecedented government spending on the military was only the most obvious part of a collection of programs designed to fix what was wrong with the country, and with the countryside in particular. Over the course of the depression and in the years after its official conclusion, state and private efforts to overcome the effects of the economic crisis changed the way millions of Japanese lived and worked.[21]

Large-scale programs to provide work relief to the urban unemployed and eventually to cash-hungry farmers ran for several years. In the countryside new laws helped farmers cope with debt, gain access to low-interest credit, and participate in local agricultural cooperatives. The summer of 1932 ended with the state committed to a three-year spending program for the countryside that was huge by past standards. The state planned to spend approximately 800 million yen to run public works programs, and to help defray the cost of local participation in the projects. In addition, planners hoped to pump another 800 million yen into the countryside through debt refinancing loans and other forms of "relief" credit. The three-year total came to roughly 1.6 billion yen in cash and loans—a substantial amount and one that indicates the seriousness with which the government took the village problem. The Ministry of Agriculture and Forestry, which administered many of these new programs and spearheaded official efforts for rural reform, saw its funding grow by more than 80 percent between 1931 and 1932. The ministry's 1934 budget was more than double what it had been in 1930, and almost three times as large as its 1926 allocation.[22] The countryside had clearly become a priority for the government.

The state's spending policies for rural Japan were joined by other more sweeping efforts at reform. In 1932 the Farm, Mountain, and Fishing Village Economic Revitalization Campaign, or *Nōsangyoson keizai kōsei undō*—

arguably the state's most significant single response to the crisis in the countryside—got under way. The campaign promised sweeping reforms not only in the local economy but also in education, farm management, rural culture, and social life. For the thousands of towns and villages that participated in it, the campaign as well as the other programs of relief and reform became an integral part of community life in the 1930s.

Plans resembling rural Japan's introduction of new approaches to social organization, economic management, and private life can be found in many of those countries most affected by the Great Depression. Professor Nasu Hiroshi, a well-respected scholar of agricultural science and member of the committee providing oversight to the Economic Revitalization Campaign, at one point recounted for the other committee members his experiences in the United States during a trip there in the summer of 1933. Nasu had met with officials in the Department of Agriculture in Washington, D.C., where they discussed ongoing recovery efforts in the United States as well as Japan's own Economic Revitalization Campaign. Nasu said that he found the U.S. officials to be very impressed by what Japan was trying to accomplish. "They showed great respect for our nation's [Economic Revitalization] Campaign," he related, "and will pay close attention to its future," adding that

> In the United States the "Agricultural Adjustment Act" is starting to have a large effect on farming, and in Russia part of the five year production plan is having an effect on farming. But I wonder if it isn't all right to put the Farm Village Economic Revitalization plan up there alongside the American and Russian plans. I think that it is one of the three biggest movements in this field in the entire world.[23]

Nasu clearly found common ground between Japan's efforts at rural reform and what he understood the Americans (and the Soviets) to be attempting. There are interesting parallels as well with Germany's efforts under the National Socialists to control farm debt—a high priority for Japan and the United States, too.[24] In each of these states, governments intervened in new and aggressive ways to counteract the depression's effects and made the recovery and improvement of rural communities one of the nation's priorities.

Japan's experiences in developing and implementing relief and revitalization policies do differ from what we know about the process elsewhere, however, and are revealing on several levels. Nasu believed, for example, that America's great size and widely dispersed farm households would prevent reformers there from accomplishing as much as might be possible in rural Japan, where life and farming centered on small villages, and few rural communities were truly remote.

Perhaps the simplest observation is that there was nothing new about the Japanese state intervening aggressively in the lives of its citizens or in the economy. The government had a long history of using social and economic policies to do so. Unlike the case of the United States, for example, depression-era relief in Japan was another in a series of efforts to alter the circumstances of its citizens' lives and not a major departure for a previously hands-off government. Citizens had every expectation that the state would be involved in helping them cope with the depression's effects.

This makes possible another observation. As Sheldon Garon and others have pointed out, one of the ongoing challenges for historians of modern Japan is teasing out where the initiative lies in the creation of policies to guide and shape society. Do they originate with the state, with the parties, with extremists from the Right or from the Left?[25] This study offers some answers to those questions so far as rural relief is concerned, suggesting that bureaucratic imperatives and those of rural reformers and spokesmen for average farmers shared a common perspective about the causes of and solutions to Japan's problems. These joint interests encouraged both bureaucrats and reformers to move ahead with the revitalization of the countryside and with reforms of rural life, the farm economy, and village institutions. Such practices—both the coming together of local and state initiatives and campaigns to reform private and community life—have clearly continued into the postwar era. Efforts to abolish prostitution, to shape the discourse on gender and gender roles, and the seemingly ever-present campaigns to get citizens to be frugal and save—all these reflect similar patterns of state and private cooperation.[26] This book examines some of the ways in which these patterns persist in rural reform as well.

It has been easier, I think, to identify the ways in which depression-era outsiders in America and in Europe expressed their anger and their agenda (when they had one) than it has been in Japan. Huey Long, Father Coughlin, and even the Southern Tenant Farmers' Union embodied distinct and usually articulate alternatives to the state's policies.[27] Fascist parties and their leaders played similar but crueler roles in Europe. In Japan, however, the search for the source of political and societal change has more often than not, begun and ended within the state. When scholars have tried to explain how Japan got from where it was in the early 1930s to what it became by the start of the next decade, there were few credible alternatives to officialdom as the key actor. The military and the bureaucrats provided more than sufficient evidence that they had a firm grip on the actions and ideas that would guide Japan.

Yet the more we learn about what was happening in rural and in urban communities in the 1930s, however, the less complete that grip has come to seem. A diverse array of social activists, leaders of mainstream farmers' organizations, and private citizens was responsible, along with like-minded bureaucrats, for bringing rural relief and revitalization to the countryside. Ideas and practices with at least one foot outside the government's camp were widely popular with regular farmers, and many eventually found concrete expression in the relief programs approved by the state. For a time, the seriousness of the economic crisis created opportunities for activists to take part publicly in a national debate on relief—opportunities that diminished once relief legislation was passed. The stage was thus set for ongoing efforts at the local level, which had been the goal of most of the lobbyists and activists in the first place.

The farmers and their spokespersons focused the nation's attention on the problems of the countryside by describing the damage to the rural community. The solutions they advocated insisted on the importance of action at the local level and defining success in local terms. People who would have agreed about very little else seem to have had this in common. What they shared was not an identical set of opinions about the particulars of the economic crisis or about the path to recovery so much as a common way of looking at the social and economic landscape of rural Japan. Some sense of that can be had in the early debates over rural relief and the rapidity with which the crisis was defined as one that community-based economic reforms could solve.

The language of relief, and eventually of revitalization as well, fell quickly into patterns with which agrarianists, landlords, and farmers were all comfortable. The only group that remained consistently outside the framework of shared language and viewpoint was the far Left, whose members' insistence on putting the debate on a very different footing meant that their ideas and their solutions would not be heard. For almost everyone else, however, the domestic crises of the 1930s were best understood through the twin lenses of the agricultural economy and the community. Both points of view included—and allowed wide ranges of opinion about—what type of economy was appropriate, and how the rural community should participate in modern Japanese society. In that sense farmers had a lot of latitude in how they chose to think about the depression and its consequences. At the same time, this particular set of crises seems to have convinced many Japanese that it was very important to bring the two points of view together and see the countryside through a single lens that merged the farm economy and the community. This particular combination was new, and it made the problems of the 1930s seem familiar, even as it made the answers to those problems harder to find.

By their very nature relief and reform policies touched on concerns shared by many citizens. Some of those worries were fundamental ones of survival. Whether or not the state provided aid—or the right kind of aid at the right time—mattered a great deal to the many Japanese who were out of work in the cities or out of money in the countryside. Other concerns belonged to the long-term. Questions about the state's responsibility to its citizens, the nature of communities, and how society was supposed to work were also caught up in the creation and implementation of depression-era relief and reform.

Revitalization thus spoke to two of modern Japan's most persistent dilemmas. The first was that both the economy and patterns of employment, residence and lifestyle were in the midst of a sea change in the 1930s, when the farm and the countryside were replaced by the factory and the city as the most familiar environments for a majority of the Japanese people. The economic components of this process had been under way for many years, as light industry had supplanted agriculture as the engine of growth. From the early 1930s on, however, heavy industry and the large corporation were increasingly dominant. One consequence of these developments was a sharp widening of the gap between standards of living in the countryside and in the cities: Factory employment, and especially employment in heavy industry, was concentrated in urban centers, which meant that rural Japanese could seldom benefit from the higher wages and other benefits associated with local economic development. The relatively high tax burden imposed on farmland, compared to corporate and business profits, convinced many farmers and landowners that they were in fact bearing too much of the burden and seeing too few of the returns. The best schools, the best medical care, and the clearest signs of Japan's transformation into a modern nation were only to be had in the cities. Farmers and their spokespersons in the early 1930s viewed what was happening to their communities as unprecedented, and worthy of unprecedented solutions.

The second factor that added to the liminal quality of the 1930s was that many of the impulses toward modernity that characterized the Meiji (1868-1912) and Taishō (1912-1926) periods were alive and well during the time of crisis. Modernity's importance and meaning to farmers and their families are reflected in their pursuit of revitalization. Popular interest in education and culture, in civic life, and in the pursuit of a more rational, even scientific way of life in the home and in the workplace all characterized late Meiji and Taishō society. They were evident as well in a burgeoning public discourse about modernity and in tangible efforts to gain access to better schools, more participation in the political process, and active engagement in public and private efforts at reform.[28] This study suggests that these same impulses were very much a part of the popular, rural response to the depression and its attendant crises.

The history of the decade leading up to the start of the Pacific War is often related in terms that emphasize its regressive, oppressive tendencies, which were indeed considerable, but that downplay the persistence of a dynamic popular culture and the pursuit of reform at the local level. There can be no doubt that the country as a whole took a turn toward authoritarianism by the late 1930s. This should not, however, be allowed to obscure developments at the level of the neighborhood, the village, and the workplace, which reveal how average citizens and their communities negotiated these changes in ways that were not always traditional or simplistic. As local solutions to national problems began to take shape, citizens drew on their desire for better standards of living, and for more "modern" answers to long-standing concerns. These included efforts to strengthen and expand existing village and farm institutions, and to broaden participation in them. Farmers pursued new agricultural technologies, drafted detailed economic plans and tried to improve basic community infrastructure in the form of better roads, sanitary facilities, and cooperative work areas. Finally, revitalization extended into the home as well. Punctuality, frugality, bookkeeping and family budgeting were just a few of the many areas of private life that reformers tried to reach. They were often successful.

Much of the analysis to date of the Revitalization Campaign has lumped the rhetoric and practices of rural reform together with those of the wartime state, thus painting a picture of the campaign as essentially regressive, as authoritarian if not fascist, and as having little bearing on an understanding of either the period leading up to the depression or of the long postwar era.[29] This study takes a different approach, and can be located among the recent works that have attempted to trace continuities between prewar, wartime, and post-surrender society.[30] In rural communities like Sekishiba, the modern components of revitalization—stronger farm organizations, more efficient farming practices, advanced training for qualified farmers, and so on—were all beneficial steps forward in the eyes of many village residents. However, many of these same reforms and "steps forward" ultimately facilitated the state's mobilization of the populace on a variety of levels and across several years. Cooperative unions, strengthened to pull farmers out of the depression, were ready tools of mobilization; improvements in farm technology (also intended to give farmers a fighting chance in a competitive market economy) were easily adapted to produce more of what the military wanted later in the decade. Similarly, the insistence on community solidarity as a prerequisite for prosperity could readily be used to help silence dissent. In other words, there were many ways in which the modern ideas and practices of revitalization merged seamlessly with those of a nation mobilizing for total war.

Modernity's ambiguities were everywhere in Japan's time of crisis. That some of the tenets of revitalization surfaced again in the immediate post-surrender era, when rural communities were once again in search of economic stability and a secure place in an increasingly urban nation, suggests that this condition was hardly unique to the 1930s.[31]

## 2   Locations

TWO HUNDRED TWENTY-FIVE KILOMETERS north of Tokyo, trains pass through the outskirts of Kōriyama before turning west into the mountains toward Aizu. These trains are smaller and slower than the streamlined expresses on the main routes and better suited to the winding curves and tunnels ahead. The tracks negotiate a path between Lake Inawashiro (Japan's fourth largest) to the south and Mount Bandai on the right and to the north. The lake can be seen only in brief glimpses, but the mountain's steeply wooded slopes rise away from the tracks, gradually at first and then much more sharply toward distant summits.[1]

There used to be more of Mount Bandai to admire; a third of it has been missing since the volcano's most recent and highly unexpected eruption on July 15, 1888. The explosion left behind a spectacular double peak, a chain of small lakes in a beautiful wooded plateau, and more than five hundred dead in nearby communities. Quiet since, the mountain punctuates one end of the broken circle of peaks that surround the Aizu basin, a flat and fertile expanse of land some thirteen kilometers across and almost three times as long. The former village of Sekishiba and Kitakata, the city of which it has been a part since 1954, are at the basin's northern end.

As the train moved past the foot of the mountain on my first trip to the area, snow covered the ground in a thick blanket, swirling and eddying outside the windows and along the tracks. The sounds of the railroad crossings' warning bells were muffled as the train moved into the basin, past the mountains, far from Tokyo.

## The Tōhoku

The northeast occupies a special place in Japan's social and cultural landscapes, its distance from the center measured as much in time as in space. Frontier for many centuries after the pacification of the western provinces, the northeast remained remote if not contested territory well into the early modern era. Though the area was largely integrated into the Tokugawa system of rule, the seventeenth-century poet and traveler Bashō nevertheless conveyed a clear sense of what it meant to leave Edo behind and cross the Shirakawa Barrier into the north.[2] It was not a journey to be taken lightly. His poems reminded readers, then as now, of the rugged beauty of the part of Japan sometimes referred to as Michi-no-oku, or "the End of the Road" (see Map 1).[3]

Some of the differences that set the northeast apart from the rest of the country in the seventeenth century were still evident in the early twentieth. The region was relatively sparsely settled. The six Tōhoku prefectures together accounted for almost 20 percent of Japan's area, but in 1930 were home to just a tenth of the population. Only the northernmost island of Hokkaido was less densely populated, and of all Japanese, only the residents of that island were less likely to live in a city than northeasterners.[4] By far the largest single region in Japan (bigger than the Kantō and Kinki districts combined), the northeast was also among the most rugged. The Ōu mountain range stretches from Aomori south to the Kantō plain, while other lesser ranges divide the region further, into distinct and often isolated subdistricts. Forests and mountains claimed large parts of the landscape, more so than was common in other parts of the country, so that only a relatively small share of the land was arable.[5]

To further complicate matters, what farmland there was proved hostage to the weather. Most of Japan was well suited to growing rice, with ample water, a temperate climate, and plenty of sun. The northeast was not. It stayed cold longer and got cold sooner, and the region as a whole was far more likely than the rest of the country to suffer from the overcast, wet, and cool summers that could devastate rice crops. The 1934 famine, discussed in Chapter 7, was only the latest in a long series of crop failures there.[6]

Despite such disadvantages, agriculture was central to the economy of the northeast. In 1929, just under half the value of all production in the region

Map 1  Northeastern Japan

came from agriculture; its share nationally was less than a quarter.[7] There were more farming than non-farming households in the six Tōhoku prefectures, something that was no longer true of the nation as a whole by the early 1930s. And while there were individual prefectures with higher shares of farmers in the population (Okinawa, for example), generally speaking the northeast did not keep pace with the transformation in industry and employment that began in the interwar era.[8] People were more likely to stay on the farm than find employment in other sectors, not least because of the paucity of job opportunities close at hand. Mining was an important source of income and employment (especially in Fukushima), and there were numerous small factories scattered throughout the region, but large-scale employers of skilled industrial workers were few and far between. Heavy industry was slow to take advantage of the northeast's comparatively low wages; light industry in the form of textile factories was common (again mostly in Fukushima), but employees there were often short term and never well paid. Though work away from home (*dekasegi*) was a common strategy employed by both men and women to supplement incomes from farming, it was no substitute for diversification of the local economy.[9]

The northeast stood out in other ways as well. Landlord and tenant relationships were so unlike those seen elsewhere that scholars described them as a unique "Tōhoku type" characterized by a sense of "traditional" mutual obligation and responsibility. More commercial, contractual arrangements between landlords and tenants were gaining ground during the 1910s and 1920s in those parts of the country closest to urban centers and with ready access either to markets for farm products or to non-farm employment. Such changes came slowly to the north, where observers continued to use terms like "master and servant" when referring to the persistence of almost feudal patterns of deference and social control in farm communities.[10]

Many of Japan's largest landlords lived in the northeast and had managed to hold on to what were huge tracts of land by Japanese standards. Landlord power was demonstrated by the relatively high rents they were able to obtain, by the anecdotal but persistent tales of landlords' involvement in the lives of their tenants at a level unthinkable (by the 1920s, that is) in more developed areas, and by what were until the 1930s very low rates of landlord-tenant disputes.[11] An organized tenant movement was slow to take root in the northeast—yet another sign that rural society there was on a different, or at least slower, course than elsewhere.

The region's reliance on agriculture, its remoteness and other handicaps had clear costs for the people who lived there, costs that were only exaggerated by the depression. Per capita incomes in the early 1930s were significantly lower in the northeast; with one-tenth of Japan's population, the northeast reported only a twentieth of the nation's income. Families devoted a larger share of household spending to necessities than the national average; 51 percent of spending in the northeast went for food alone, as compared to 42 percent nationally.[12] Women tended to marry earlier, and families were generally larger than national norms despite cruel infant-mortality rates. The latter can be attributed at least in part to the scarcity of doctors; the number of villages in the region without a physician actually increased in the late 1920s, from 550 in 1927 to 598 in 1931. Of all Japanese living in a community without a doctor that year, a fifth were residents of the northeast.[13]

Education stands out as one of the few areas in which the region met or exceeded national standards. Attendance rates for the compulsory years were very high, and farm families in the northeast were much more likely than similar families elsewhere to have sent at least one member for technical education in agriculture. Family spending on education and training was at or above the national average in the early 1930s. The seriousness with which education was taken seemed to be reflected in the diligence of local students. In country-wide tests administered in 1933, Tōhoku schoolchildren scored higher than the national average. Despite the persistence of local dialects, or perhaps because of it, the children did especially well on Japanese, scoring 69 and again besting the national average, which was only 57.[14]

A trivial yet telling indicator reveals something more about the (widening) gap between city and country, northeast and center. In 1930, 90 percent of all households in Japan had at least one electric light. Since billing was usually on a per-bulb basis, the number of lights is known with some certainty: There were 57 for every hundred Japanese that year. The comparable figures for the Tōhoku region show that 80 percent of households had electric lighting (a good showing considering the predominance of rural communities), and that the region had on average 34 light bulbs per hundred residents. At the risk of getting ahead of the narrative, it is worth pointing out that between 1930 and 1935, while the rest of the country was busy adding lights at a rapid pace (5.9 million new bulbs, a 16 percent increase), the northeast barely held its own. There were only 6 percent more lights in the northeast in 1935 then there had been in 1930; since the population grew at a faster rate there, the share of households with at least one electric light actually declined over the same period. In Fukushima the situation was worse; power companies dimmed 18,652 bulbs between 1930 and 1935, resulting in a 6 percent drop in the number of households with lights. Where there had been 34 lights per hundred people, in 1935 there were only 32.

The contrast with the bright lights of the big cities couldn't be clearer. In Tokyo, where 98 percent of all households had at least one bulb lit in 1930, there were more lights than people (113 for every hundred residents). By 1935, a typical Tokyoite was surrounded by almost four times as much illumination as his Fukushima neighbor to the north.[15]

## Fukushima and Aizu

For a short time after the collapse of the Tokugawa shogunate in 1868, the Aizu district was a prefecture unto itself. It wasn't until 1876 that Aizu and two neighboring districts to the east were combined to create Fukushima, the nation's third largest prefecture and the southernmost of the six Tōhoku districts. Folding Aizu into Fukushima was part of a broader process of creating citizens out of a population that in the past had not been encouraged to think in national terms. Aizu's physical as well as its political landscape made such an integration especially important. Aizu was big. The domain was among the largest in the Tokugawa system and had been administered by the Matsudaira clan from its castle town at the southern end of the basin for much of the early modern era. Related by blood to the Tokugawa household, the Matsudaira remained staunch supporters of the regime even in its final days, and Aizu samurai held out against imperial forces much longer than most. Sites in and around Aizu-Wakamatsu city, the former seat of the domain, today celebrate the warriors' idealized loyalty more than their resistance to central authority, a good indication that the Meiji oligarchs' program of nation-building accomplished what it was intended to (see Map 2).[16]

There are two urban centers in the Aizu basin. Once past Mount Bandai, the train heads first to Wakamatsu city. Located at the basin's southeastern edge, Wakamatsu was in the 1930s the region's largest city and most important commercial hub; a dozen miles to the north, the town of Kitakata ran a distant second. Wakamatsu's population of more than forty thousand occupied itself in trades that reflected both the community's past as a castle town

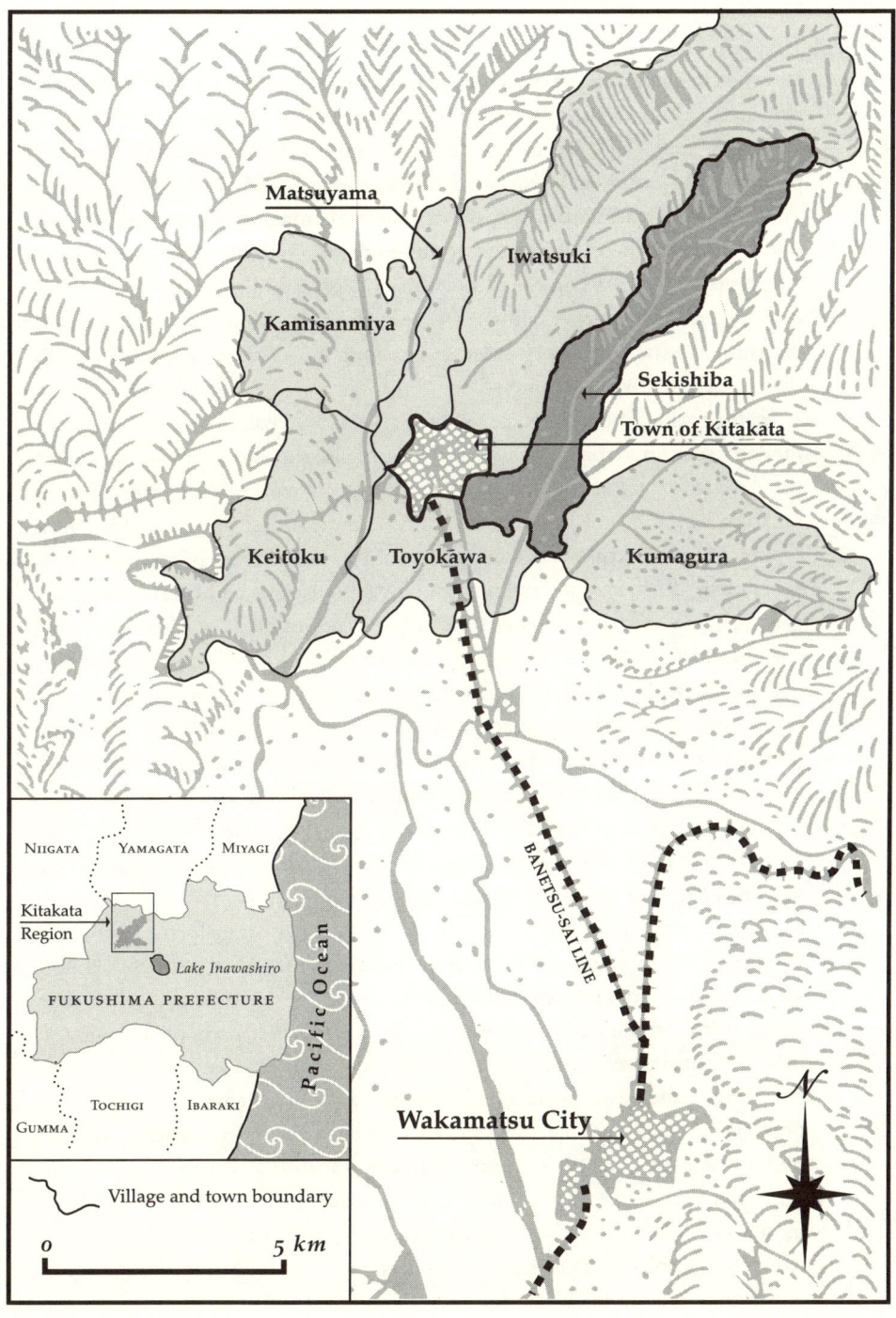

Map 2   The Aizu basin

and the continued importance of the goods and services that the Aizu basin provided. The Matsudaira family had protected its interests by controlling as best it could the sale of the domain's most marketable cash crops and products. As Stephen Vlastos has noted, the domain's administrators also discouraged farmers from transferring land or making other changes that might threaten their willingness or ability to produce rice, the most important crop by far.[17] When the old regime collapsed and a new, modern economy began to develop within the framework of the Meiji state, farmers and craftsmen in the region expanded the production of those goods for which they already had some affinity.[18]

Rail provided new links and new markets and made the transition to a modern economy that much easier. The main transportation networks of the Tokugawa era largely bypassed the region in favor of more direct routes north or to the Sea of Japan coast.[19] The completion of the rail line between Tokyo's Ueno Station and Kōriyama in 1887 (and to Sendai later that same year) opened up new possibilities, and local politicians and businessmen began lobbying hard for a connection to their communities. Rail service along the new Banetsu line between Kōriyama and Wakamatsu city began in 1899 and was extended to Kitakata five years later. By 1917, the line stretched east to the Pacific Coast and west to the Sea of Japan. Though still a lengthy journey, travel from the Aizu basin to Tokyo and other major cities was by the early part of the twentieth century measured in hours, not in days.[20]

Both Wakamatsu and Kitakata did well in their roles as intermediaries between local farmers and other producers and the national market. Aizu lacquerware, once a luxury, became common enough for daily use in households near and far, while local pottery kilns slowly transformed much of their production to meet the electrical industry's need for insulators.[21] The local sake brewers first expanded their share of the prefectural market, then began to ship more and more of their product to other parts of the country. Silk and cotton were similarly an important part of the city and the region's economy in the 1930s, as they had been half a century before. Having lost its political and military role, Wakamatsu managed to retain a hold on its economic usefulness for many years. Still, the transformation of Japan's economy from the 1930s on has not gone unnoticed in the basin. Silk, sake, and lacquerware are not today growth industries, and local rice growers have their own problems. Tourism has begun to make up for losses in other areas, but it, too, faces an uncertain future.

As the train leaves Aizu-Wakamatsu and heads north to Kitakata, clusters of farmhouses and other, smaller homes out beyond the local stations and rice fields pass in and out of sight. Some of the dwellings have clearly served their owners for many years, though a fair number are of recent construction and design. The blurring of the line between farm and town, residence and business, is as evident in Fukushima as it is in the rest of the country, but here, as in much of the northeast, there are fewer people around to notice.[22] In the 1930s, the differences in population density between Fukushima and the country as a whole were apparent but not profound; there were 169 people per square kilometer in Japan proper, and 109 in Fukushima.[23] (Of the more than one hundred communities in the Aizu region in the early 1930s, there were only two with populations in excess of ten thousand; Wakamatsu was one, Kitakata the other.) By 1995, the gap had grown considerably, to the point that the nation was on average more than twice as densely populated as Fukushima.[24] It is also clear that the differences between urban and not-so-urban Japan have widened sharply. In 1930, the nearby Kantō region was roughly four times as densely populated as Fukushima; in 1995, there were on average twelve times as many people in a single square kilometer of Kantō real estate as in the same area in Fukushima. Aizu's contemporary appeal to harried urbanities is a little easier to understand when we know that these differences are real and not entirely imagined.

## Kitakata

Aizu's other city, and the rail stop closest to Sekishiba, is about a dozen miles to the north of Wakamatsu. Until the Meiji era, "Kitakata" was a term that applied to most of the territory north of the castle town, and it was in fact written with two characters that mean "northern direction." When the cluster of five villages at the northern end of the basin was consolidated to form a single town, residents reportedly resented the idea of their community's name and identity being based on how people in Wakamatsu viewed them, so characters with the same pronunciation but different meanings were substituted. These five villages had grown in size and importance during the Tokugawa era, attracting a mix of handicraft producers and small commercial enterprises. Roads linking the domain with Yonezawa and points west passed close by, and as time passed the communities began to host regular markets as well as a local administrative office.²⁵ The early Meiji creation of a town where there had been only villages before reflected the already changed makeup of the population and also accelerated the growth of local business.²⁶

Kitakata has a somewhat unusual place in Meiji history, though it is not a past that the community makes much effort to publicize. In 1882, the new governor of Fukushima prefecture announced his intention to complete a series of major road projects in the Aizu region to improve access to Yamagata, Niigata, and eventually Tokyo and the south as well. Those projects would come at considerable cost to Aizu residents, however, and over the summer local resistance to the taxes and to the process of planning and approving the road construction solidified. As Roger Bowen has pointed out, the tax boycott and other protests were part of a broader, often national struggle by leaders of the Freedom and People's Rights movement to challenge the authority of the central government.²⁷

Some of the leaders of the opposition lived in and around Kitakata, and as the state escalated its efforts to suppress the movement, police arrested several local activists and incarcerated them in the town police station. In late November 1882, efforts by a crowd of supporters to protest these arrests and the removal of some of the prisoners to Wakamatsu (among them Sekishiba's Uda Seiichi, a member of the prefectural assembly and an important figure in the local anti-government campaign) erupted into violence. The police killed at least one of the protesters and wounded others before the crowd fled. Thousands were arrested in the weeks that followed, and many prosecuted for crimes ranging from "inciting to riot" to treason. Although the courts reduced many of the charges and overturned convictions on appeal, there is little doubt that the Kitakata Incident led to a considerably weakened movement for Freedom and People's Rights.²⁸

It did not, however, foster a radicalized polity in or around the town. Some of those charged, including Uda Seiichi, went on to have impressive careers as local politicians. Uda was mayor of Sekishiba from 1905 to 1917, and Hara Heizō was mayor of Kitakata from 1893 to 1917, then again from 1921 to 1925.²⁹ With the exception of some minor unrest during the 1918 Rice Riots, Kitakata and the surrounding communities were seldom again sites of overt political or social unrest. Hara's successors as mayor in Kitakata generally served lengthy terms; between 1926 and 1946, there were only two.

Voting patterns in the 1920s and 1930s reveal a similarly stable and unsurprising relationship with the national mainstream parties. Some years the Minseitō had the edge, while in others the Seiyūkai prevailed. The balance seldom tipped very far one way or the other, even after voting rights were expanded in the 1928 elections.[30] Politicians courted local votes assiduously, visiting the town and nearby villages for stump speeches and rallies, or just to voice their criticism of the other party.[31] Hatta Sōkichi, a Seiyūkai stalwart and consistently one of the most popular candidates in the county in the 1920s and 1930s, made Kitakata a regular stop. His Minseitō opponents did much the same; in the five elections between 1928 and 1937, the last before the parties disbanded themselves, the Minseitō and Seiyūkai split the district's Diet seats thirteen to ten (two independents also won election). In Kitakata, 42 percent of the votes in those elections went to Seiyūkai candidates, 44 percent to the Minseitō. In nearby villages voters tended to favor the Minseitō over the alternatives by a slight margin. Sekishiba's residents, for example, gave slightly more than half their votes to the Minseitō, 35 percent to the Seiyūkai, and the remainder to independent candidates.[32] Although individual politicians like Hatta could and did count on local support, no one party dominated local politics.

Kitakata's fortunes improved in other ways once the Incident was over and done with. The completion in 1904 of the rail station was a boon to businesses and to farmers as well. Several textile factories opened in town to take advantage of local silk-cocoon production and inexpensive rural labor; sericulture and the factory work associated with it remained a part of the town's economy until the end of the Pacific War. A prefectural survey in 1933 established that the two largest local factories employed some 570 people in their spinning operations, 529 of whom were women.[33] As in Aizu-Wakamatsu, however, there were few of the smokestacks associated with modern manufacturing in Kitakata, with one notable exception. The sprawling and grim "Shōwa Tekku" (formerly Shōwa Denkō) industrial complex is located just across from Kitakata station on the south side of the tracks. Construction on the site didn't start until 1942, though planning for it began in the late 1930s as part of a national effort to disperse the manufacturing infrastructure. The aluminum production that had been hoped for wasn't realized until well after the end of the war, however, and there was little other heavy industry in or around the town.[34]

Perhaps as a result, the area was not a target for U.S. bombers during the war, and local neighborhoods and roads were spared any direct damage. Most have not been especially displaced by progress since, so in many parts of the city the relationships of home to garden, businesses to street fronts, and so on are not unlike the ones revealed in maps and photographs of the 1930s. That the aluminum plant disappears from view almost as soon as one leaves the train station helps sustain the illusion that little of importance has changed.

The business of the town in the years leading up to the depression was divided among the manufacturing and sale of goods long produced in the area and the commercial activities that supported the community and nearby villages. Exact figures are hard to come by, but most estimates agree that sericulture, sake, and lacquerware constituted the three major moneymakers in the town in the immediate prewar era. Soy sauce and miso sold consistently also, but not as well.[35] About a fifth of all town households in 1913 (the last pre-surrender year for which reliable data are available) described themselves as primarily farmers; another fifth were involved in manufacturing.[36] The remainder engaged in commercial enterprises, of which there were a wide variety in town. Local businesses arranged for the sale and transportation of local goods, sending silk to Yokohama, rice to Tokyo, and silk cocoons to Nagano, and brought in the raw materials, foodstuffs, and other materials that sustained the community. Kitakata's streets were lined with all the establishments one would expect to find in a reasonably prosperous small town: fish shops, clothing stores, greengrocers, doctors' offices,[37] restaurants, and, of course, banks.

The first bank established in the area was a Kitakata branch of the Aizu Bank, which opened its doors in 1900. (This branch was overseen by Yabe Zenbei, a powerful local businessman; his son and namesake played a major role in local efforts at recovery during the depression; see Chapter 9 below.) The Yasuda Bank and Fukushima Commercial Bank established branches soon after, and several Kōriyama banks had offices in town by the mid-1920s. Most weathered the financial problems of the depression era reasonably well. An exception is the 107th Bank, which opened a local branch in 1915 only to close it suddenly in the wake of the 1927 financial crisis, never to reopen. The town, and presumably individual depositors as well, lost much of the money they had entrusted to the bank; whether officials ever made good on their promises to pay them back over time is not clear.[38] There were in addition to the banks several other financial institutions in Kitakata. The public pawnshop established by the town in 1931 and nicely tucked away down a narrow lane, not to mention the local credit union and a handful of non-bank lenders, could count among their clientele those area residents whom the banks could not or would not serve.

Kitakata was home as well to much of the official and semi-official administrative apparatus for the northern part of the basin. Local branches of national organizations like the Imperial Agricultural Association were based in town, although much of its membership lay in outlying villages. The county office was housed in town, in a large, Western-style two-story building until 1926, when the state eliminated the county as a separate administrative layer. The police were a consistent presence; the Kitakata station was responsible for supervising Kitakata, two other nearby towns, and more than thirty other villages in the area.[39] The police could and did make their presence felt in the affairs of these communities, though quelling the sort of violence that erupted during the Kitakata Incident was not a regular part of their activities.

Kitakata was also home to many of the area's higher educational institutions. The local two-year higher elementary school was in town, and construction of the Kitakata Middle School was completed in 1920, after years of lobbying and fundraising by local officials and community leaders. Prior to its opening, there had been only one middle school serving the entire Aizu region, so the addition of the new facility was a major victory for the town. By the late 1920s, students also had access to a girls' high school and a commercial vocational school, thus rounding out the local educational opportunities.[40]

In the years leading up to the depression, there were thus reasons to be optimistic about the town's future and the fortunes of the communities nearby. At the end of the 1920s, more than thirty-four thousand people lived in neighboring villages and in Kitakata itself. Though small in comparison to Wakamatsu city, which had about forty-six thousand residents in 1929, there were enough people and businesses in and around Kitakata that it mattered economically and politically.[41] While the local economy remained tightly linked to agriculture and to a lesser extent to sericulture, the northern end of the basin was home to a reasonably sophisticated network of financial and social institutions. These promised a commitment to opportunity for young people, economic growth, and the possibility of an even brighter regional role for Kitakata. The depression years would make clear how tenuous some of those gains had been.

The town did eventually become a city, though not until 1954. As often happened elsewhere, the transformation in Kitakata came not by virtue of growth from within but by administrative fiat from without. The town's limits were expanded in 1954 to encompass the seven villages on its borders, uniting what had been distinct communities under a single administration.[42] In many ways this was the culmination of a process of amalgamation that had been under way nationally since the late nineteenth century. When the Tokugawa regime collapsed, there were hundreds of small farming communities in the area around what would become the town of Kitakata. By the early 1890s, the town itself and the seven villages of Matsuyama, Iwatsuki, Sekishiba, Kumagura, Toyokawa, Keitoku, and Kamisanmiya were all that were left, the others having been consolidated within these eight new communities. Bringing these last seven villages within the new city's borders in 1954 marked the final stage in a long relationship between town and country.

## Sekishiba

Four rivers shaped the lay of the land. From west to east, the Tatsuki, Ubadō, Minomori, and Ōshio rivers flow down from the mountains and toward the center of the Aizu basin. Broad fan-shaped deposits accumulated as the rivers gathered and joined larger waterways farther along, leaving behind fertile and readily farmed surfaces. Though the rivers long since have been confined to well-crafted channels, with much of their water borrowed for irrigation or pooled within the village's many reservoirs, the long and narrow band of land that is modern-day Sekishiba still seems to follow these older markers of the landscape.[43]

The village's boundaries stretch from the foot of Mount Kōzone in the northeast to the banks of the Tatsuki River in the southwest (see Map 3). At its widest point the village is only 3.5 kilometers wide, and from one end to the other the community spans slightly less than 11 kilometers. If one were to begin at the southern end of the village and walk north along any of the dozens of narrow paths and wider roads that crisscross the countryside, several features would likely catch the eye. First, most of the land in the village is low and flat; the southern and central sections of the community are roughly 270 meters above sea level, and account for three-fifths of the village's 24

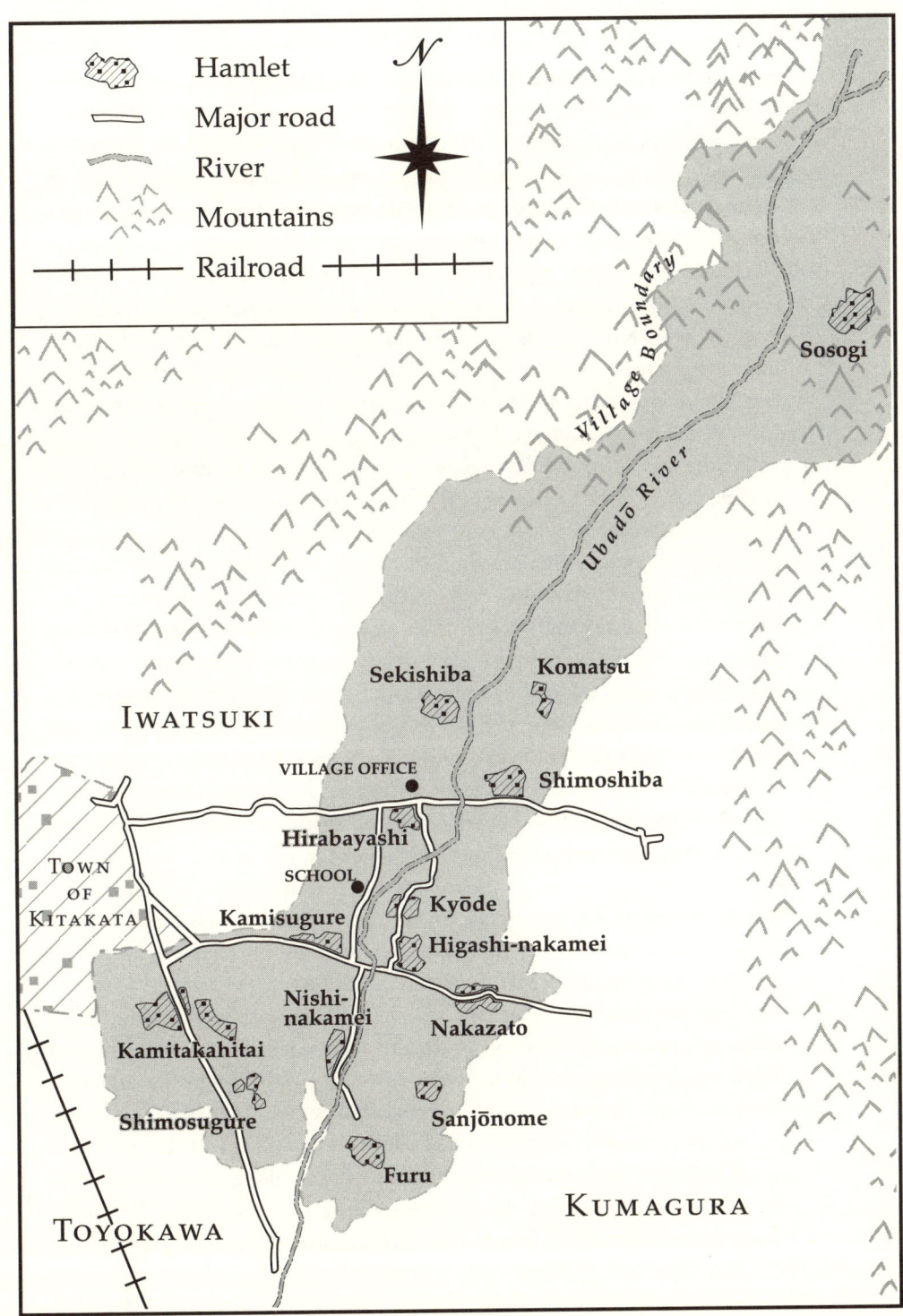

Map 3  Sekishiba village

square kilometers.[44] Much of this land is still given over to rice paddies, each section contained within earthen barriers and an intricate network of interlocking irrigation ditches. One is seldom out of sight of a field of some sort, and though there was once more planted land—and fewer obstructions to looking out across the paddies—it is easy to imagine that a scene much like this greeted villagers in the 1930s.

As one approaches the northern third or so of the village, the ground starts to incline upward and wooded hills encroach on the paddies. On average, the northern sections of Sekishiba are sixty to one hundred meters higher above sea level than the land below, and it isn't long after the slow rise begins that one starts to see fewer irrigation ditches and more dry fields. Most of the paddies in the village are just slightly below the level of the roads and paths that surround them; here in the north there is a difference of several meters, so that the homes at the crest of the hills look out across vistas of green in the spring.

These differences within the village are important, if only because changes in microclimate, soil type, and access to irrigation had a direct impact on the quantity and variety of farm products that villagers could hope to harvest from the land. It also matters that the forests were close. The hills in the north are blanketed by different varieties of beech, cedar, *keyaki* (zelkova), and horse chestnut and are rich in other plant and animal life. The contrast with the rest of the village is marked; walking here, it seems as if the village comes to an end long before the maps say it does. Though signs of habitation are few and far between at its northernmost reaches, Sekishiba's borders reach the feet of the mountain range that defines this part of the rim of the Aizu basin. Access to the forests that surround the lower-lying fields was important to farmers in the 1930s. The woods and hills could provide important resources to the villagers, and proximity to them was an advantage that communities deeper in the basin didn't have.

The two main roads that cross the village from east to west offer quick and easy access to Kitakata or, in the other direction, either to the town of Shiokawa or up into the plateau behind Mount Bandai. Highway 121, which intersects the village at its southwest edge, follows the route of a Tokugawa-era roadway north to Yamagata and south through Aizu-Wakamatsu and on to Nikkō. A few small stores and shops cluster along the roads near the middle of the village, but most of the commercial activity belonged to the neighboring town, as it does today. Kitakata was within easy walking distance for most villagers, and for those who were so inclined, bicycles brought the town's shops and services even closer. After 1927, regular bus service shortened the trip even more.

Travel within the village is facilitated by a gridlike pattern of paths and narrow roads that also allow easier access to farmers' fields. In contemporary Sekishiba, the roads and paths are generally straight and well maintained, but maps from the 1930s suggest that such was not always the case. Paddy borders were much less regular then, and the paths among them meandered accordingly. Postwar rationalizations of landholdings made the straighter roads possible, whereas in the 1930s, maintaining and sometimes extending the existing network was a common and difficult undertaking.

People have been living in and around Sekishiba for a long, long time. Evidence places humans in the area during the Jōmon era (10,000–300 B.C.E.), and although the written record doesn't commence in any meaningful way until the sixteenth century or so, it is certain that people lived there in the intervening years.[45] By the early Tokugawa era, there were a dozen or so small farming villages in the area, each distinct in the eyes of the local administration, and ranging in size from a few dozen inhabitants to several hundred. A glance at a map of Sekishiba in the 1930s reflects the legacy of these earlier patterns of living and farming. The modern village lacks a center; there isn't a single collection of homes or structures that can be identified as the obvious locus of power or population. Rather, what one sees are small clusters of households, each with at least some access to a small road or path, but for the most part surrounded by farmland. Each cluster is one of fourteen separate hamlets, or *buraku*, within Sekishiba. Most of these were once small villages in their own right, often close enough to be within shouting distance but nevertheless possessing separate shrines, tax burdens, and social and political structures.

The same process of consolidation and amalgamation that created the town of Kitakata helped craft the village of Sekishiba out of these communities, as it did the same for thousands of other villages. By the late 1880s, the Meiji government had cut the number of towns and villages by nearly 80 percent from levels earlier in the same decade.[46] By 1877, the twelve communities that would become Sekishiba had been combined into seven; the final consolidation into the single village of Sekishiba was complete by 1889.

Amalgamation was pursued so assiduously for several reasons, most of them having to do with the new burdens that the Meiji state planned to foist upon local administrations. Compulsory education was too costly an enterprise for small villages to undertake, and there was a long list of similarly expensive and complex tasks that bigger organizations would be better able to handle.[47] The state could also exert more control over a small number of large villages than over a large number of small ones. Financial and political oversight was strong. The newly formed villages collected taxes and elected local officials to a village council (which in turn elected a mayor), but in each instance they did so largely at the discretion of the Home Ministry and authorities of the prefectural government. As Tadashi Fukutake observed, the Meiji government "was not recognizing the right of residents democratically to control their own affairs; it was imposing a system which it was the duty of the people to operate."[48]

The state's desire to deconstruct local loyalties and redirect them toward the center was also at work. Merging villages was probably far less significant in this process of creating citizens of a modern nation than were compulsory education and conscription, which had much more profound effects on how citizens understood their relationships with the state.[49] Nevertheless, overcoming parochial attitudes would remain a regular and elusive goal for the makers of rural policy in the modern era.

One reason for the persistence of local identity in the face of such sweeping change is the survival of the older communities in different guises. Merging them into a single village didn't wipe the slate clean; in Sekishiba, as elsewhere, the original villages remained the basic building blocks of social life and economic activity in the newly constituted community. Residents kept local identities alive by continuing to use the old village names to describe parts of the new village. That meant that Sekishiba in the 1930s was divided into seven ōaza, or major districts, and fourteen hamlets. Some of these districts were mapped on top of a single older village, while others contained several of the original communities. The seven ōaza, and fourteen hamlet names are: Sekishiba (and Sekishiba hamlet), Shimoshiba (Shimoshiba, Sosogi, Komatsu), Hirabayashi (Hirabayashi), Mitsui (Kyōde, Higashi-nakamei, Kamisugure), Kamitakahitai (Kamitakahitai), Nishisugure (Shimosugure, Nishi-nakamei), and Toyoashi (Nakazato, Sanjōnome, and Furu).

Forty years after the merger, many families continued to live in the hamlets their ancestors had called home, and their houses remained clustered around and within the original communities. Sekishiba and Kamitakahitai were the largest of these, with 66 and 53 farm households, respectively, but most were about half as big. Komatsu, for instance, in the northernmost section of Shimoshiba, was home to only 18 households. Between 1925 and 1929, Sekishiba was home to an average of 426 households, and 433 for the next five-year period.[50] As might be expected, land and to some extent wealth were also divided unequally among the various hamlets.

Something like urban sprawl has taken place in recent years in the community, as newer homes have grown in number and blurred the edges of what was once a more clearly defined and smaller collection of dwellings. For the most part, though, there is still no mistaking where a hamlet begins and where it ends. The surrounding farmland acts as a border between communities. Some of the smaller hamlets, of which Komatsu is a good example, define themselves even more distinctly through the use of neighborhood maps posted at key intersections near hamlet boundaries. These maps display the homes and family names of the owners, orienting visitors—and perhaps residents as well—to the layout and even the genealogy of the hamlet. In Komatsu's case, I recognized in the early 1990s many of the same family names that had been associated with the hamlet in the 1930s.

Within the hamlets, homes and farm buildings are close together, a mix in recent years of old, sprawling wood-and-plaster farmhouses and the occasional contemporary-looking two-story, single-family home. The older homes were once well suited to farming and extended families, and the addition of a big-screen television and other modern conveniences may continue to tip the balance in their favor. The local storehouses, or *kura*, though still plentiful, are now less likely to be filled with grain or food and more likely to house farm implements, bicycles, and the other tools of daily life.

Sekishiba's landscape has a few other features worth pointing out. In this village, as in others, hamlets and sometimes the farmland as well are dotted with small growths of very old and very tall trees. These often mark out the precincts of the local Shinto shrines, an accessible and public reminder of community and a holdover from the days when each of the older original villages had its own such space. The Meiji government tried and failed in the early part of the century to eliminate all but one shrine in any given village as part of its effort to unite allegiances and break down local ties. In Sekishiba, as elsewhere, the hamlets were reluctant to let them go, and they remain welcoming islands of shelter in an otherwise open space.

A similar though more sustained effect is evident near Chūzenji Temple in the northwestern part of the village, perhaps best known in recent memory as the place where Freedom and People's Rights activists met on the eve of the Kitakata Incident. The temple may or may not be as old as the Kamakura-era sculpture it houses (sources are uncertain), but the building and the many trees that surround it are clearly ancient. The large pond that abuts the temple attracts geese and other wildlife, and on my visits there was little evidence that the temple grounds had been affected by the changes that had swept the surrounding village.

The community's other public spaces have been less permanent but more centrally located. The first village office served Sekishiba from 1889 until the early 1930s. Arguments within the village council over cost delayed the decision to build a new office until 1931, and construction on the new site in Hirabayashi wasn't completed until early 1933. The new building, located just north of the main road to the Bandai plateau, continued in service until the village was absorbed by Kitakata. After that, the offices were used for a variety of official purposes before being sold to the public in 1978.[51] The local police office has a similar history. Built down the road from the first village hall in 1899 and then relocated in late 1936 to another site in Hirabayashi, the thousand-square-foot building remained in use by the police until another site was developed in 1978. The original building was then adopted by the residents of Hirabayashi as a meeting hall.

Sekishiba's schoolchildren were for many years dispatched to several different and distant elementary schools. It wasn't until 1906 that the village opened the Sekishiba Elementary School (like the village office and police box also in Hirabayashi), allowing students from the various hamlets to attend school together. The addition of a higher elementary curriculum to the school in 1926 made it possible for those who could afford to do so to continue beyond the compulsory six-year program. Attendance rates for the compulsory part of the system were reportedly very high. In the mid-1930s the village claimed that 98 percent of school-age children were in school, which at the time meant that there were almost seven hundred students being taught by a dozen or so full- and part-time teachers.[52]

Elementary school graduates in the 1920s and 1930s could continue on to middle school in Kitakata, if they passed the difficult examination, but many ended up attending the local vocational school instead. The organization of this part of the village's educational system was in almost constant flux for many years, suggesting an ongoing commitment to post-elementary training but a dissatisfaction with the results. Changes were still under way in the 1930s; what had been the village's "supplementary technical school" became in 1932 the Public Vocational School (Kōmin jitsugyō gakkō), which was renamed the Sekishiba Agricultural Public School (Sekishiba nōgyō kōmin gakkō) the following year.[53] As Richard Smethurst notes, by this time most vocational schools were dedicated to agricultural education, though they also provided coverage (which varied by gender) of Japanese language, some history and ethics, and other technical training.[54] Male students of the vocational school were, after 1926, also likely to attend the local Youth Training Center, where they received additional instruction in military drill and ethics.

The Training Center and the Agricultural School were merged in accordance with a new nationwide policy in 1935 to create the Sekishiba Youth School. The new curriculum combined aspects of practical, vocational training with instruction in moral and patriotic subjects, as well as military drill for the boys and the equivalent of home economics courses for female students. It was the state's goal to ensure that every educable child be enrolled in one of the village's schools, and Sekishiba's officials at least claimed to have achieved this in the 1930s.[55] Postwar reforms in education that did away with the youth schools left Sekishiba with one elementary and one middle school, which were made part of the larger Kitakata education system after the merger.

The permanence of some of the institutions and landmarks of contemporary Sekishiba hints at commonalties with the community as it was in the 1930s. It was reassuring to be able to walk the village's roads and paths and have a sense of how the physical reality of the place related to the social landscape that was revealing itself in my archival work. At the same time, the similarities between the two communities—Sekishiba in the 1930s and the one I encountered in the 1990s—did not extend very far. While residents may well think of themselves and the community as having a connection to the past, what was once the village is not at all a living museum of rural life from days gone by. As many observers of the countryside have noted, rural life has undergone a fundamental reworking in the past sixty years.[56] Land reform, mechanization, and a series of other changes in the ways rural agricultural society has been incorporated into the mainstream have had a profound effect on places like Sekishiba.

In the 1930s, most of the people who lived in Sekishiba farmed the land. Nine-tenths of the working population in the late 1920s and throughout the 1930s listed their occupation as "farming," while only a handful were employed in other areas. Commerce accounted for about 50 people (about 3 percent of the working population) during this period; the "other" category, which included day laborers, fell from more than 80 people in 1928 to closer to 60 after 1931.[57] A household-by-household survey in 1933 showed that there were 371 full-time and 25 part-time farming families, only 2 full-time manufacturers, and 10 full-time merchants.[58]

Farming has since become, for most families, a part-time enterprise and is often the responsibility of the old. Younger people who have stayed in the area work in nearby offices and factories and may venture out into the fields only occasionally. Many others have left the region entirely in search of opportunities elsewhere; the decline in Kitakata's population over the years is in part testimony to this phenomenon. These arrangements are possible and common because farming itself is a more stable, profitable, and regularized activity than it ever was in the 1930s. The local agricultural cooperative, or Nōkyō, located just across from the elementary school, oversees the purchase and sale of rice and other crops to the government at highly subsidized prices, helps mediate state payments to farmers not to grow certain crops, and defends farmers' interests against any and all challenges. Roughly half the farmland in the village was rented at the end of the war, but by the end of the land reforms, only 8 percent was.[59] Skyrocketing prices for land have made many a farmer wealthy, at least on paper, while laws put in place to protect farmers have generally discouraged them from selling their land. As a result of these relatively new and benevolent policies, farm families have for the most part managed since the 1960s to share with their urban counterparts in Japan's economic successes.

The outlines of the countryside's postwar recovery were only dimly visible in the 1930s. As the crises of that era unfolded in Sekishiba, local activists and farm families sought to reshape the social and economic landscape to match their visions of a stronger and more viable community. No one called publicly for the sort of sweeping changes that eventually proved necessary to bring some measure of stability and prosperity to rural Japan. The solutions of the 1930s were, of necessity, narrower in focus. Still, the search for any solution to the problems of the countryside brought into play some fundamental questions—ones that continue to have resonance in contemporary

Japan: How would rural communities negotiate their participation in the economic and social changes sweeping the rest of the country? How would farmers, divided by distance and class status, organize themselves to best serve their interests and those of their families? The chapters that follow explore the countryside's efforts to come to terms with these issues, to save itself in a time of crisis.

3   *The Rural Depression*

THE REMAINS OF THE FIRST local soldier killed in Manchuria arrived at Kitakata station on a mid-December Saturday in 1931. In a scene repeated in towns and villages across the country, local schoolchildren and their teachers turned out to mark the return of Keitoku native Corporal Yamazaki Masami, who had survived his twenty-second birthday by only a few months.[1] The solemn occasion on the cold railway platform was a stark reminder of how events outside the village manifested themselves locally, sometimes with tragic consequences.

For residents of Sekishiba and surrounding communities, the Manchurian Incident was one of several slowly unfolding dramas that lent the early 1930s their particular sense of a headlong rush into crisis and uncertainty. As elementary schoolchildren in Sekishiba took up collections of money in support of soldiers dispatched to the mainland, their parents struggled with a long and seemingly unending slide in farming's fortunes and became convinced that Tokyo could not set things right.[2] Even as Corporal Yamazaki's remains reached the station, the countryside was fast becoming the theater in which the nation's hopes and fears were acted out.

The depression that began in 1930 and was all but over by 1935 hit rural Japan unlike any other before it. Crises overlapped in time and in context to such an extent that no clear solution to any one of them ever seemed within reach. In September 1931, officers of the Kwantung Army launched a series of offensives in Manchuria, "liberating" it from Chinese control and installing a puppet government. The civilian leadership in Tokyo proved powerless to control the course of events and would soon be forced to realign the country's relationships with the West to reflect this new reality.

It would not be the last time this happened, and Corporal Yamazaki was but the first of many local soldiers to pay the price. Politicians and business leaders, already suspect for their poor handling of Japan's economic and diplomatic goals, became the targets of stunning terrorist violence in the early 1930s. Two prime ministers, a former finance minister, the director general of Mitsui, and Tanaka Gorō, a policeman assigned to the prime minister's residence, were among those who died at the hands of terrorists in the first two years of the decade. Party-led government ended with the last in this cycle of incidents, which took place on May 15, 1932.

The participation of young farmers alongside army and navy officers in that attack revealed three other developments that set this depression apart. The first was this: the economic crisis in the countryside was spread across several fronts at once. Rice prices and silk prices plummeted together and remained at rock-bottom levels for years—and this after a decade of ups and downs (mostly downs) in agriculture that had raised expectations but lowered returns. The simultaneous collapse of the urban-industrial economy amplified the harm to rural communities, as did the persistence of burdensome rural debt and roller-coaster years of record-setting rice yields followed by harvests smaller than any in recent memory. Any one of these economic misfortunes would have brought hardship to some families; together, they were that much more harmful. Many farm families quickly lost the ability to balance income and expenditure, with potentially serious consequences for their solvency, their health, and the stability of their communities.

The widening gap between city and country was a second issue of considerable importance. By the start of the depression, rural life had grown increasingly distant from what was going on (or what was imagined to be going on) in Japan's cities. Demographic change had something to do with this. In 1920, one in eight Japanese lived in a city of a hundred thousand or more; by 1935, one in four did. More than 80 percent of the population growth in that fifteen-year period was absorbed by urban centers, so that whereas in 1920 there had been only sixteen communities with populations of a hundred thousand or more, by 1935 there were thirty-four such cities.[3] With the growth of cities came a vibrant urban culture which to many rural observers embodied a frivolity and decadence that they found distasteful, not least because it was also extremely attractive to rural youth. Industrialization was more an urban than a rural phenomenon; higher wages and improvements in standards of living tended to accrue in cities first. The countryside was slow to get modern medical facilities (or doctors, for that matter), electric lights, telephones, or radio. The newest medium of mass communication, radio reached a million listeners in 1930, but city dwellers were far more likely to have access to a radio than those in rural communities.[4] The depression only heightened fears that the city's gains in wealth and in the trappings of modernity were the countryside's losses.

The emergence of articulate spokespersons for rural causes is a third development of consequence. Tenancy produced one cohort of activists; agrarianism (or *nōhonshugi*) another. Both grew in strength and numbers in the 1920s, although the former group frequently came under attack by the state and lost much of its earlier strength by 1930.

As Ann Waswo and others have argued, these two streams of rural thought and activism shared a great deal. Both attracted a generation of young leaders at the national and local levels, and both sought resolutions of fractious economic problems that neither local elites nor the state seemed willing to address.[5] Young farmers coming of age in the late 1920s and early 1930s had experiences and training that were vastly different from those of the generation then in positions of power in most communities. The thirst for knowledge and self-improvement that characterized the rising generation made it that much harder to stand by and do nothing as the depression worsened or to defer to the advice of local leaders less anxious or prepared for change. The agrarianists who participated in the May 15 Incident were one expression of these strains; local activists pursued the possibility of reform in other guises throughout Japan with much less fanfare, and without bloodshed. Rural women were often part of this dynamic as they sought to create new roles for themselves within local society and, in so doing, often challenged the state's ongoing efforts to define and restrict women's lives.[6]

## The Crises of the 1920s

The problems that harried farmers most in the early 1930s weren't all new. Falling prices, fixed expenses, and fears of insolvency stood out as common concerns well before the depression struck. The countryside's problems in the early 1930s were foreshadowed by a decade of economic uncertainty and by a slow shift in agriculture's standing as the cornerstone of the nation's wealth.

Years of spectacular business successes around the time of the First World War had reshaped the economic landscape from one made up primarily of farming and light industry into one that was more technologically sophisticated, modern, and diverse. Japan transformed itself from a debtor into a creditor nation, and for the first time its nascent heavy industries began to do well without the careful protection of the state. The war kept foreign competition out of domestic markets and allowed Japanese companies to challenge Western producers abroad. Industrial output grew by more than 70 percent during the conflict, triggering a sharp rise in employment and massive capital investments in production capability. The nation's shipyards, which had completed only 8 vessels in 1915, christened 174 in 1918.[7] Other sectors showed similar growth, and at least some of these gains made their way to factory workers in the form of higher wages and job opportunities. At the same time, wages in heavy industry began to outstrip those available in other areas, mirroring a broader shift of wealth and capital into the hands of big business through the interwar years.[8]

For farmers, the boom years were a mixed blessing. There were increased opportunities for employment off the farm, and many young men and women took advantage of the demand for new workers. The expanding economy also fueled the demand for some farm products. Factory workers and the growing urban population kept their taste for rice, and farmers were happy to supply it to them, especially at the higher prices that their crops began to command as the war went on.

At first the cost of rice kept pace with the general upward trend in almost all consumer-item prices, but then it began to run further and further ahead. Consumers in August 1918 paid three times as much for rice as they had three years before, as compared to a rough doubling of other consumer prices over the same period. For growers, the surge in rice prices between 1917 and 1918 was the largest year-to-year increase in the nation's modern history. Cocoon prices jumped by almost half between 1915 and 1916, rose by another 45 percent the following year, and continued their upward spiral for another two years. By 1919 cocoons (like rice) were worth more than three times what they had sold for in 1915.[9]

These increases, which eventually applied to almost all the products farmers grew, were unparalleled. In a rare display of conspicuous consumption, farmers in Sekishiba, giddy from their good fortune, reportedly took to tossing around 5- and 10-yen notes as if they had money to burn, behavior unusual enough to merit notice in the official records.[10] Their elation is certainly understandable. Nothing in recent experience or memory could have prepared farmers for the quick change in farming's fortunes that accompanied the boom.

Even while the economy remained robust, however, there were signs of problems ahead. In the last year of the war, the very rapid increase in rice prices outpaced the ability of many families to keep up purchases of this most basic of staples, and by the summer of 1918, rumors of hoarding fueled the public's anger, triggering massive and sometimes violent riots throughout the country.[11] In Kitakata a crowd estimated at seven hundred strong spent an evening in August attacking rice merchants and the homes of the wealthy, "encouraging" them to donate money and grain. The same scenes were acted out elsewhere in Fukushima, throughout the countryside, and in numerous urban centers across Japan.[12]

One issue for residents of many rural communities was that they were both producers and consumers of crops like rice. Households often chose to sell all or most of the rice they harvested in order to meet an immediate need for cash. Families that did so could then supplement whatever rice had been set aside by buying more later; those in areas where sericulture or other cash crops were the primary source of income might not grow any rice, or very little, and thus be almost totally dependent on the market to meet their dietary needs.

To the extent that this system worked, it did so because less well-off farmers could anticipate the difference in prices from peak to trough over the course of a year. Large shifts in the price of rice could play havoc with a family's ability to feed itself, and very sharp increases in prices were thus not in the best interests of all farmers. Tenants in particular often were stuck selling near harvest time, when prices were lowest, and buying rice again later in the year, after prices had risen. Landlords and others with the wherewithal to store rice in anticipation of higher prices later on realized more profit, more often. For tenants, the newly buoyant economy helped make this difference between their potential earning power and the realities of their relationships with landowners seem less and less acceptable. One of the legacies of the boom years was the emergence of a proactive and sometimes successful farmers' movement that took as one of its goals the creation of a more equitable arrangement for tenants.

The bust that followed the boom was for farmers not just one setback but a series of them. The first and most obvious casualty of the recession that began in 1920 was crop prices. Prices worldwide for agricultural products slumped after the war in Europe, but this was of little comfort to farmers in Japan. Rice prices, which had risen or at least stayed constant in seven of the ten years from 1910 through 1920, fell in eight of the next ten.[13] To make matters worse, the costs of sustaining a farm and a family tended not to drop as dramatically as prices for farm goods did. This, too, was a new set of circumstances for most farmers. In the three decades leading up to 1920, in all but four years changes in crop prices had either kept pace with or risen faster than the consumer price index for farm families. This pattern broke down in the post–World War I era. Farmers' expenses outran crop prices in five of the ten years from 1920 through 1929, and in ten of the fifteen years from 1920 through 1934.[14] The last time expenses and farm prices had been at odds for any length of time had been in the mid-1880s, during the Matsukata deflation, and even then the gaps had closed much more quickly than they did in the interwar era.[15]

The volatility of the boom and busts was another feature of the period that farmers could easily have done without. Between 1876 and 1940, from one year to the next farm commodity prices either rose or fell by 20 percent or more on only eleven occasions, but six of the largest shifts came between 1913 and 1920. Silk prices changed by 10 percent or more from year to year in all but four years between 1915 and 1935; they rose or fell by more than 20 percent in thirteen of those years, and by more than 40 percent in eight of them. The largest percentage increase in rice prices in the prewar era occurred between 1917 and 1918; the largest drop, between 1929 and 1930. One has to go back to 1876 to find an increase in the value of silk cocoons larger than the one that took place between 1915 and 1916, while the free fall between 1929 and 1930 was without modern precedent.[16]

Some of the blame for the agricultural recession can be attributed to the state's own policies. In the aftermath of the Rice Riots, local leaders in Kitakata had responded with plans to sell rice cheaply to residents; nationally, a new cabinet under Prime Minister Hara Kei began pursuing similar plans on a broader scale.[17] One aspect of those plans was the promotion of colonial exports of rice to the home islands. By reducing import tariffs and promoting, if not forcing, the export of rice from Korea and Taiwan, policymakers hoped to ensure that domestic supplies stayed high and consumer prices low. Rice imports shot up from 0.25 million metric tons in 1916–1917 to almost 1.7 million metric tons a decade later. By the 1930s, a sixth of the rice supply originated abroad, most of it from Korean and Taiwanese fields.[18]

Farmers' organizations had not been in favor of encouraging these imports. They feared—correctly, as it turned out—that an influx of grain from abroad would drive domestic prices down. That this might happen wasn't yet fully evident in the first half of the 1920s; prices were sometimes up and sometimes off from one year to the next. After a brief upswing in the market in 1924, the trend toward lower prices was clear. In 1925, and every year for the next six, rice prices fell.

Attempts by the state and by farmers' organizations to find a way to intervene in fluctuations in the markets for farm goods were unsuccessful. A framework for these efforts began to take shape in 1921 with the Rice Law, which in theory gave the state the ability to control the volume of rice on the market at any one time through government purchases.[19] Coming so soon after the Rice Riots, policymakers were still concerned about guaranteeing an adequate domestic supply of rice at low prices; it took until the mid-1920s for the Imperial Agricultural Association (Teikoku Nōkai) and other spokespersons for the countryside to win revisions to the law that committed the state to trying to keep prices not only from getting too high but also from sinking too low.[20] Even with the changes, however, the government couldn't buy enough rice to stabilize prices. Rice that had sold at the end of the First World War for close to 50 yen a *koku* (180 liters) went for about half that in 1929, when prices hit a twelve-year low.

The market for silk fared little better. The silk industry, though far better organized and a more successful lobby than rice producers, similarly was unable to find a formula to keep prices high, or at least stable. Part of the problem was the nature of the trade in silk; Japan's farmers supplied cocoons that ended up, more often than not, in silk sold in the U.S. market. There was very little that producers in Japan could do to influence markets overseas, save to try to keep enough silk off the market to drive prices up. That wasn't a simple proposition; in 1925, a record year, silk and silk products alone were responsible for over 1 billion yen in export earnings, or 45 percent of the value of all exported goods. In the United States, Japanese products made up four-fifths of the silk brought into the country; nine-tenths of the silk that Japan exported went to the United States.[21] Japan exported more silk in 1929 than it ever had and generated near-record earnings by doing so.[22]

On the eve of the Great Depression, more people were involved in producing more cocoons and more silk thread than ever before in the country's history. Even though prices had been unstable for much of the 1920s, cocoon production increased as farmers tried to make up for potential losses in income by selling more and more cocoons. The average cocoon yield per producer in 1915 was close to 235 pounds; by the end of the 1920s, this had risen to over 400 pounds.[23] The 1929 cocoon crop nationwide was more than 60 percent larger than in 1920, while rice harvests that decade fluctuated within a much narrower range.[24]

Accompanying the increase in yields was a geographic expansion of cocoon production. At the end of the Meiji period, almost two-thirds of cocoons had been produced in eastern Japan, but by the start of the Shōwa era, eastern and western Japan had almost equal shares.[25] The wider distribution meant that changes in the U.S. market affected farm families throughout Japan and that a downturn had an especially devastating effect on those communities that relied extensively on sericulture for income. These effects were not evenly distributed. Nationally, about 40 percent of farm households grew cocoons, the sale of which accounted for 12 percent of farm income.[26] In Nagano in 1929, however, four-fifths of the farm households were involved in sericulture, and 70 percent of farm income came from the sale of cocoons. Fukushima is another example of a prefecture in which sericulture was an important part of the local economy. Seventy percent of its farm households grew cocoons, and income from their sale accounted for a quarter to a third of income in the most sericulture-intensive parts of the prefecture.[27]

Attempts to stabilize the market for silk in the 1920s were usually unsuccessful. These efforts relied on the purchase and storage of thread to help keep prices high, but it was hard to enforce compliance and harder still to buy up enough silk to make a difference. By the end of the decade, the state was providing incentives to encourage exporters to keep their silk off the market, but even then the impact was limited. Rural cocoon producers, meanwhile, were left to their own devices. The state's efforts on their behalf were similar to the steps taken for exporters—namely, the provision of limited low-interest loans and programs to encourage long-term storage of cocoons, but all on a much smaller scale.[28] That the programs existed at all was a tacit acknowledgment by officials that rural families were in need of help; that support was limited and ineffective was a common characteristic of rural relief policies.

The problem of prices was compounded by the Shōwa banking crisis that began in 1927. Though it directly affected few farmers, the shakeout in banking did have some important side effects for rural communities. In Fukushima, the most notable of these were a rapid dwindling in the number of locally owned banks and the disappearance of key institutions linked to the local textile industry. Of the forty-four banks operating in the prefecture before 1927, thirty-three disappeared at some point during the Shōwa crisis.[29] As Ōishi Kaichirō has argued, this rapid decline was a product of the weakness of many of Fukushima's banks, which were late in joining a national trend toward mergers. Local entrepreneurs in Fukushima were still creating new banks in the 1920s, even as the Ministry of Finance was pushing hard for consolidation in the financial sector.

The collapse of so many banks allowed institutions from outside the prefecture to get a foothold in the late 1920s; outside banks accounted for only 11 percent of deposits in 1927, but by 1931 had more than half.[30] As banks closed their doors, depositors often lost savings either for good or for long periods as creditors negotiated partial repayments. In the long term, the reduction in the number of lending institutions—and particularly of lenders with local connections—meant that borrowing became even more arduous. Banks from outside the community were less likely to provide credit to borderline borrowers, and after 1929, there were very few who did not fall into that category.[31]

## The Great Depression: Crises of Farms and Finances

Reporting from New York in late 1929, a Foreign Ministry commercial secretary wrote home that there was "no need to be especially pessimistic" about America's burgeoning economic problems.[32] He was wrong to be so cavalier, but he was also writing at a time when many Japanese desperately wanted to believe that their troubles were almost over. After a decade of recession and uncertainty, in 1929 it finally looked as if the economy were going to be put back on the right track. A new government promised stability through austerity and a return to the gold standard, and an eventual return as well to more prosperous circumstances. While little the new government proposed seemed directed toward the problems of rural Japan, farmers in 1929 had no reason to believe that their situation could get much worse. They were wrong, too.

The Minseitō cabinet's decision to return to the gold standard, a step announced in 1929 and taken in January of the following year, began Japan's spiral into economic collapse. The decision had been expected for some time, and there were sound reasons for it. A return to gold at the very least meant an end to constant fluctuations in the exchange rate, and easier borrowing from international lenders.[33] Some measure of international prestige was also attached to participation in the gold standard, a point not overlooked by the Minseitō and Finance Minister Inoue Junnosuke. These factors also had a role in the government's decision to return to the rate of exchange that had been in place in 1917, the last year Japan was on the gold standard.

In the twelve years that had passed, fluctuations in the exchange rate had made the yen less valuable in dollar terms; returning to the old rate was bound to make Japanese products more expensive abroad and lead to deflationary pressures at home. Critics of the plan argued that the damage to the economy would outweigh expected benefits.[34]

Prices began slowly declining in mid-1929, on the heels of the announcement of the planned return to the gold standard; at the same time, the Hamaguchi cabinet initiated sharp cuts in government spending to help deflate the economy further. By the time the implications of Wall Street's collapse were clear in Tokyo, it was too late to lead the economy down a different and less dangerous path. Between 1929 and 1931, the nation's GNP declined by almost a fifth, and the Tokyo stock market lost half its worth as the value of the nation's exports fell by more than 40 percent.[35] Unemployment soared as factories either closed or sharply cut back on production.

The textile industry was hit especially hard, and its experience offers one of the clearest indications of the global market's effects on the domestic economy and on the countryside in particular. Japanese silk that had sold in New York for $5.25 a pound in September 1929 went for $2.50 thirteen months later.[36] Silk prices continued to fall for the next three years. Producers kept on making the thread, and exporters kept on selling it abroad, but they made far less money doing so than they had before the start of America's depression. The dollar value of silk thread exports to the United States fell by almost a third between 1929 and 1931 and by 1934 was less than 25 percent of what it had been five years before.[37] Domestic prices for silk cocoons followed suit, with obvious consequences for the many Japanese farm households that relied on sericulture for some or all of their income.

Rural Japan was vulnerable in other ways as well. Rice markets also tumbled in the early 1930s, but here the blame lies closer to Tokyo than to Wall Street. The government's farm policies in the aftermath of the Rice Riots had helped increase the production of rice both domestically and in the colonies, pushing prices down at home. In 1929, rice prices were roughly three-quarters of what they had been in 1925 and were just above half their 1919 peak.[38] Early in 1930, the return to the gold standard sent prices down slightly, but to the relief of the countryside, by July prices were back up to where they had been in July of the year before. That summer's excellent weather and their own skill conspired against farmers, however. The 1930 harvest was the largest in the nation's history. Initial estimates predicted a crop of 66.9 million *koku* of rice, or 12 percent more than the average harvest over the previous five years.[39] The government's October announcement of its crop estimate for 1930 sent prices tumbling, and this time they kept falling. The price of a *koku* of rice fell by a third between September and October alone, and farmers learned after the New Year that their rice would fetch only about half as much as it had in the years leading up to the depression.[40]

The drop in prices wasn't confined to rice; just about everything farmers produced was affected.[41] In some cases good harvests contributed to the downward pressure on prices, but the general drop in wages, in consumer spending, in available credit, and in some cases in prices overseas all contributed to what was happening to farm goods. Cocoon prices fell early and furthest, spurred by the poor export situation for silk thread and by the record crop on the market in 1930. In 1929 a standard unit of cocoons had fetched roughly 7 yen; the same volume of cocoons brought in only 3 yen a year later, and by 1931, cocoons were selling for slightly more than a third of their 1925–1927 value. Wheat, barley, and buckwheat prices all fell by more than 40 percent between 1929 and 1931; chicken and egg prices slumped to half their pre-depression levels by 1932.

All in all, agricultural commodities lost about 45 percent of their value in the two years between 1929 and 1931, even as farmers struggled to compensate by producing more rice and more cocoons.[42] The record rice harvest of 1930 was surpassed in 1933 (and once more in 1939). Cocoon growers beat the record they had set in 1929 the very next year and came close to doing so again in 1933.

Some sense of how these developments affected farm communities and farm families is evident in Sekishiba's situation in the early years of the Great Depression. Farmers there grew a diverse collection of crops that became more varied as the decade wore on. When the depression began, local fields were regularly planted with rice, barley, persimmons and other fruits, soybeans, and a variety of vegetables. Farmers also raised chickens, collected their eggs, and tended silkworms in spring, summer, and fall for their cocoons. As Table 1 suggests, farmers in Sekishiba maintained a very high level of production throughout the 1930s, especially in rice. Yields were higher after the depression began than in the years leading up to it. Ironically, the disastrous 1934 season came on the heels of the biggest rice harvest in the history of the village and was itself followed by years of above-average output. It wasn't until 1943 that Sekishiba's rice crop dropped back to the lower levels that had been normal in the 1920s. The same upward trend is evident in the volume of barley, silk cocoons, persimmons, and other cash crops produced by local farmers.[43] During and after the worst years of the economic downturn, farmers were able to coax more out of the land than they had in the past.

However, as Table 2 suggests, huge harvests could not compensate for the lower prices caused by the depression. Prices for rice, cocoons, and other farm products plummeted so far in 1930 that just growing more couldn't begin to make up for lost income, with the result that farmers produced more only to earn less. It wasn't until 1937 that the prices farmers received for a *koku* of rice were back to where they had been on average in the 1920s. Prices for silk cocoons, meanwhile, stayed below their 1925–1929 levels until 1939.[44] On average, it took until 1935 or 1936 for income from farming to reach a level equivalent to what it had been before 1930 in Sekishiba.

Table 1
Agricultural Production in Sekishiba, 1925–1939

| Commodity | 1925–1929 average | 1930 | 1931 | 1932 | 1933 | 1934 | 1935 | 1936 | 1937 | 1938 | 1939 |
|---|---|---|---|---|---|---|---|---|---|---|---|
| Rice | 11,008 | 12,801 | 12,905 | 12,783 | 14,585 | 5,817 | 12,698 | 12,698 | 13,918 | 12,557 | 14,383 |
| Index | 100 | 116 | 117 | 116 | 132 | 53 | 115 | 115 | 126 | 114 | 131 |
| Barley | 778 | 1,125 | 826 | 1,163 | 1,439 | 630 | 1,189 | 1,189 | 1,107 | 466 | 1,031 |
| Index | 100 | 145 | 106 | 150 | 185 | 81 | 153 | 153 | 142 | 60 | 133 |
| Silk cocoons | 4,304 | 5,186 | 5,652 | 4,898 | 6,704 | 5,112 | 5,712 | | 5,588 | 4,701 | 5,424 |
| Index | 100 | 120 | 131 | 114 | 156 | 119 | 133 | na | 130 | 109 | 126 |

NOTES: Rice and barley production are measured in *koku*, cocoon production in *kan* (1 *koku* = 180 liters; 1 *kan* = 3.75 kilograms). No data are available for spring silk-cocoon production for 1928 or for rice and barley production in 1929.
SOURCE: Kitakata-shi hensan iinkai, ed., *Kitakata-shi shi*, vol. 6, pp. 796–799.

Table 2
The Yen Value of Agricultural Production in Sekishiba, 1925-1939

| Commodity | 1925-1929 average | 1930 | 1931 | 1932 | 1933 | 1934 | 1935 | 1936 | 1937 | 1938 | 1939 |
|---|---|---|---|---|---|---|---|---|---|---|---|
| Rice | ¥313,088 | ¥205,198 | ¥194,339 | ¥245,146 | ¥283,972 | ¥145,425 | ¥318,794 | | ¥405,232 | ¥392,912 | ¥582,360 |
| Index | 100 | 66 | 62 | 78 | 91 | 46 | 102 | na | 129 | 125 | 186 |
| Mugi | 7,607 | 7,834 | 4,977 | 5,798 | 10,723 | 5,322 | 9,348 | | 13,703 | 6,392 | 16,893 |
| Index | 100 | 103 | 65 | 76 | 141 | 70 | 123 | na | 180 | 84 | 222 |
| Silk cocoons | 32,577 | 14,767 | 15,987 | 15,695 | 34,272 | 10,446 | 19,243 | 13,580 | 26,433 | 19,768 | 44,089 |
| Index | 100 | 45 | 49 | 48 | 105 | 32 | 59 | 42 | 81 | 61 | 135 |
| Yen value subtotal | 392,617 | 261,934 | 252,109 | 309,113 | 368,243 | 195,208 | | | 492,067 | 483,783 | 754,731 |
| Index | 100 | 67 | 64 | 79 | 94 | 50 | na | na | 125 | 123 | 192 |
| Yen value per farm household | 922 | 609 | 588 | 716 | 843 | 448 | | | 1,093 | 1,095 | 1,705 |
| Index | 100 | 66 | 64 | 78 | 91 | 49 | na | na | 119 | 119 | 185 |

NOTES: All figures except the indexes are village office estimates of the yen value (at current prices) of local production. Local officials also divided the total yen worth of production by the number of farm households; this figure appears as the "yen value per farm household." The "yen value subtotal" includes categories not listed separately in the table (e.g. lumber, chickens and eggs, charcoal, and so on). Listed categories account for between 80 and 90 percent of the total value of farm production in Sekishiba during the period in question. The only figures available for 1929 are the yen value subtotal and the yen value of production per household; no data exist for that year for specific crops.
SOURCE: Kitakata-shi shi hensan iinkai, ed., *Kitakata-shi shi*, vol. 6, pp. 796-799.

## INCOME AND SPENDING

How did these changes in the economy affect farm households? Did standards of living decline markedly during the depression, or were falling prices for rice and other farm products offset by lower spending on fertilizer and other expenses? Those important questions are surprisingly complicated ones to answer, in part because of the nature of the available evidence but also because of the scope of the questions themselves. If our interest is in a broad measure of the effects of the depression, for example, the evidence is that although Japanese farm households did less well than they had in the 1920s, on average they may have weathered the depression years reasonably well. Richard Smethurst has argued that for most of Japan's farmers the period "from 1930 to 1934 was a straitened time for rural Japanese" but not an especially desperate one, given what the statistical evidence suggests about income, expenditure, and other indicators of financial well-being.[45] The average cost of fertilizer, for example, fell as far or farther than did prices for agricultural products.[46] As Smethurst has pointed out, farmers did not reduce their use of commercial fertilizers during the early 1930s and in fact may have used more of it to help boost crop yields as prices dropped.[47]

Other data support the idea that farm families were able to cut back on their household spending as their incomes declined. One interpretation of the national Farm Household Surveys (Nōka keizai chōsa) conducted by the Ministry of Agriculture and Forestry suggests that, with the single exception of 1931, farmers spent less than they brought in every year from 1921 through the 1930s.[48] In other words, the aggregate data—or the "big picture"—can be read to suggest that the rural depression did not cause long-term, severe economic dislocation for farm families.

This is an approach to the data that Richard Smethurst has taken in his analysis of tenancy in the interwar period, and there is some merit to it. It is clear, for example, that productivity in farming did increase in the 1930s, and that farmers were aggressive in their pursuit of crop diversification and other improvements during that decade. The data indicate that the setbacks experienced by most farmers were not permanent. Moreover, although the relationship between tenancy disputes and the depression is complex, the argument that some tenants may have used the economic downturn to win better terms from landlords is, on the surface, a reasonable one.[49]

Why then, if the statistical evidence suggests that the rural depression did not do significant harm to rural families, have so many argued for so long that it did?[50] Much of the scholarship about rural Japan in the 1930s draws on the same data described above, yet arrives at a quite pessimistic assessment that sees the economic crisis as more severe and more widespread than indicated by the quantitative data alone and that views the depression as a watershed in the lives of most rural Japanese. Such divergent conclusions are possible in part because of serious shortcomings in the statistical evidence. Scholars have long recognized that the household surveys, as valuable as they are in some contexts, don't tell the whole story. The Farm Household Surveys that reported relative stability and balanced income and expenditures through much of the depression years were supervised by the Ministry of Agriculture and Forestry and are a unique and valuable resource, but it would take a powerful imagination to conclude that they are a representative cross-section of the rural experience. The survey sample was quite small; it included 210 households in 1928 and 334 in 1931, years when the total number of farm households was close to 14 million. Participants in the survey tended to be at the upper end of the ranges of landholding and land use. Thus the reported results offer insight into the circumstances of a relatively better-off segment of rural society. Participation was skewed in other ways as well, because completing the surveys required a knowledge of record-keeping and other skills not evenly distributed among the farming population. Problems in data collection and with changes in the survey contents further complicate matters and make comparisons across time problematic.[51]

And even if the quantitative evidence weren't suspect, contemporary narratives are clear and compelling in their descriptions of the very hardship and fear that the overall statistics mask. This body of qualitative evidence includes journalistic and semi-fictional accounts of the rural depression, official reports generated at all levels of government, privately commissioned surveys and studies, and, by 1932, a plethora of local appeals and petitions for relief and reform. There is no lack of material; the public and the state were awash in it for much of the depression, more so once relief efforts fully were under way.

One of the side effects of efforts to provide rural relief was the careful documentation of the depression's effects. With a level of detail seldom seen before the 1930s, mayors and other local leaders began to record both what had happened to their communities and their efforts to overcome the crises at hand. Journalists provided moving accounts of local conditions in rural and sometimes remote villages. Their presence in any numbers in the countryside was a new phenomenon, and their writings reveal their own expectations as well as the discoveries they made.

In Sekishiba, local analysis of the depression's economic effects revealed serious problems. Toward the end of September 1934, village officials in Sekishiba drew up one in a series of reports in which they attempted to gauge the effect of the depression on local households (see Table 3). Their estimates were based on data gathered earlier in the month and thus are too early to reflect the full effects of that year's famine. Even so, they clearly show that farmers in 1934 were far worse off than they had been in 1929 or in 1924. Spending had overtaken income, average household debt was considerably higher (it had quintupled), and dozens of Sekishiba's young people had left home in search of survival elsewhere.

Leaving the village to look for work in local cities or factories was not a new phenomenon, but during the depression years its implications for the community changed. For one thing, the economic collapse extended to Japan's cities and to factories, putting thousands of urban dwellers out of work and sharply narrowing the ability of rural Japanese to find non-farm employment in the early years of the depression.[52] To make matters worse, many of the newly unemployed originally came from the countryside, and as they made their way from the factories back to the family farm, they became yet another mouth to feed.[53] Wages that daughters and sons had earned working away from home were lost to their families in the aftermath of firings and plant closings that began in 1930.

Officials had other problems to worry about as well. Farm income was down, debt was rising, and so was the number of village households reporting a shortage of eating rice between harvests. Table 3 shows that, from just under half of all farm families in 1924, in 1929, and again in 1934, slightly more than half of Sekishiba's farm families ran out of rice in the interlude between one harvest and the next. The increase involved an additional thirty or so families. Though it may seem unlikely that a farm family would run out of the very crop it produced, tenant farmers often paid out a substantial portion of their rice harvest as rent, in addition to selling at least some of what remained to pay for necessities and, as the depression wore on, to cover

Table 3
Local Conditions in Sekishiba, 1924–1934

| Year | Income | Expenditure | Households with insufficient eating rice | Debt per household | Young men leaving the village | Young women leaving the village |
| --- | --- | --- | --- | --- | --- | --- |
| 1924 | 1,263 | 1,263 | 203 (48%) | 300 | 23 | 16 |
| 1929 | 870 | 727 | 232 (55%) | 1,000 | 32 | 22 |
| 1934 | 715 | 935 | 236 (54%) | 1,500 | 67 | 23 |

NOTES: "Households with insufficient eating rice" refers to those that were expected to run out of the staple in the period between harvests. Only those young people who left the village for economic reasons are included in the final two categories of the table. A review of the eight remaining individual reports from the village's hamlets suggests that conditions varied sharply from one to the next. Income and expenditure were almost balanced in Shimoshiba's report, for instance, while spending in Kyōde in each of the reported years outweighed income by two to one. Predicted shortages of food were subject to similar variations; Shimoshiba, Furu, and Nakazato reported that less than 10 percent of their households would run out of rice, whereas Kyōde and Shimosugure expected that more than half of their farm households would.
SOURCE: SMY, "Nōsakubutsu sakujō chōsa ni kansuru ken," September 28, 1934. *Kangyō kankei shorui 1934*, KST.

interest payments on back debt. The lower that rice prices dropped, the more rice a farm family had to sell to earn the same amount of money as the year before, or the year before that, which helps explain why more farmers were running out of rice.

Between 1933 and the harvest of 1934, some 236 families, or more than half of Sekishiba's farm families, found that their supply of rice was insufficient. These figures reflect the number of families that ran out of the staple after the record 1933 harvest, not those facing shortages as a result of the greatly reduced 1934 crop. The persistently high level of rice shortages despite a hugely successful growing season is good evidence of how quickly local farmers had to dispose of their rice once it was harvested. Higher yields did not translate into either a larger cushion of stored rice for personal consumption or greater security for farm families in Sekishiba. The situation in 1934 was particularly troubling to local officials because the harvest that fall was almost certain to be one of the worst in recent memory. If half of Sekishiba's families didn't have enough rice after a spectacularly successful harvest, it wasn't hard to imagine what would happen after a spectacularly bad one.

More detailed surveys of local conditions revealed the full extent of the depression's impact. The rough comparison between income and expenses that appears in Table 3 was supplemented by the so-called Basic Survey (Kihon chōsa). Conducted by village officials in 1934 as part of the preparations for economic revitalization, the Basic Survey was meant to provide a baseline of information about family finances and other conditions from which to create a plan of reform and recovery. It did so by asking every farm family in the village to remember and record developments about the year before, 1933. For example, one of the questions called on farm households to estimate how much they had made from farming and other sources that year, and how much they had spent to raise their crops, on living expenses, and so on.

Completed surveys were collated at the hamlet level and then turned in to the village office, where a single report was generated for the entire community. Village officials then simply put the figures of 1933 income and expenses side by side, added them up, and estimated that the village as a whole had ended the year 54,875 yen in the black. That averaged out, according to the survey, to 126 yen in surplus per Sekishiba household.[54] The existence of such a surplus suggests that farmers had adjusted to hard times by managing to strike a balance between reduced income and what they had to spend to keep production and their families going.

Yet village leaders did not conclude from their survey results that all was well; far from it. They remained convinced that their community was in jeopardy. Some feared the survey results were not accurate. Later efforts by local officials to introduce bookkeeping to villagers indicated that few households were familiar with accounting methods or concepts and thus had been unlikely to have kept detailed records of spending and income in 1933. Local officials recognized the limits of their data and also had the benefit of access to individual and hamlet survey results, which told stories often at odds with the single broader narrative.

The Economic Revitalization Plans filed by the residents of Komatsu, explained in detail below, also can tell us about the state of the family coffers in that particular part of the village. To begin with, a comparison of total income and total spending reveals that only five of Komatsu's eighteen households reported income in excess of expenses. In fact, the remaining thirteen households spent 4,190 yen more than they made in 1933, or just under 300 yen on average.[55]

The survey further categorizes households according to how much money they paid in Special Household Tax (*kosūwari*) in 1933. The Special Household Tax is a rough gauge of relative wealth because it generated a considerable share of rural communities' tax receipts by levying tariffs on property and other assets, and was often used as a marker with which to rank households in a village.[56] The Basic Survey divides the families in Sekishiba into three groups: the highest-ranking families are those that paid more than 25 yen in household taxes, the middle are those paying between 10 and 25 yen, and anyone paying less than 10 yen is a member of the "bottom" group.

In Sekishiba in 1933, only 34 households, or less than a tenth of all village families, belonged to the "upper class." The middle range was made up of 104 families, or about a quarter of the community as a whole. The remaining 282 households—two-thirds of all families in Sekishiba—were at the bottom of the heap.[57] Komatsu's families fared somewhat better than the village as a whole. Of the 18 households in the hamlet, 8 belonged to the lowest tax bracket, 6 were in the middle, and 4 were at the top in 1933. Although Komatsu did have a higher share of households in the middle and upper brackets than the village as a whole, the largest collection of households was still at the lower end of the tax scale.[58] In Komatsu, 7 of the 8 lowest-ranking households were in the red, with an average deficit in 1933 of 203 yen. Of the 6 mid-level families, 3 reported spending more than they brought in; their average deficit was 191 yen. And 3 of the 4 highest-ranked taxpayers in Komatsu were also running deficits, although their average was only 162 yen per household. Those families who earned the least were the ones hit hardest in 1933, and while increased income seems to have softened the blow by degrees, it did not prevent losses.[59]

Of the five families with surpluses, three were from the middle tax bracket and one each came from the lower and upper classes. The highest surplus in Komatsu in 1933 belonged to the mid-ranking Uda household, which according to its own estimates ended up with 46 yen left over at the end of the year. Mayor Satō Sakichi, one of the other middle-class householders who spent less than he earned, ended up with a 29-yen surplus, while Hara Masaru had an almost perfectly balanced budget and earned only about 0.1 yen more than his family spent.[60] Satō Chōta's family of eight paid just over 4 yen in taxes, were thus at the low end of the tax scale, and ended the year with less than 1 yen left over after expenses. Watanabe Hikoe, the second highest taxpayer in the hamlet, came away just under 19 yen in the black.

The surplus that Sekishiba seemed to enjoy at the end of 1933 was not evenly distributed across the village. On balance the community was bringing in more money than it was spending, but no one in the village office concluded that those indicators alone were worth much. The Basic Survey seems to have confirmed rather than challenged the locally held belief that the village was in dire straits.

Three years into the depression, most families in Komatsu had not yet managed to compensate in any consistent way for what had happened to farm prices. Even though fertilizer and other prices had fallen, and even though farmers were harvesting more of their key crops than ever, households of widely disparate economic standing were having the same difficulty keeping spending in line with income. If it was happening in Komatsu, it was surely happening elsewhere in the village. Though local officials had no way of knowing whether the situation revealed in the survey results was getting better or worse, since the Basic Survey did not ask respondents to consider circumstances prior to 1933, they assumed the worst. There were few reasons not to.

### DEBT

Although it may appear that farmers had less of everything during the depression, there is one thing they had in abundance: debt. Rural indebtedness concerned bureaucrats within the Ministry of Agriculture and Forestry and officials of the Imperial Agricultural Association throughout the 1920s, in part because no one had a clear sense of how much money farmers owed, or to whom. Available estimates were based on reports generated by official lenders, among them banks, credit unions, and other above-board potential sources of credit. The problem was that no one thought for a moment that those lenders represented the sum of all sources of money in the countryside; private lenders of all sorts were a huge pool of potential credit, and their loans were almost certain to go unreported. As a result, at the start of the depression neither the state nor farmers' organizations had a solid estimate of how deeply in debt farmers were, nor could they begin to guess how the economic downturn would affect that aspect of rural household finances.

Village-level surveys conducted once the economic crisis had begun confirmed what farmers already knew and what officials had only feared: rural communities were mired in debt, and the sharp drops in prices and household income meant that growing numbers of families were unable to pay back their loans. They were at great risk of losing their land (if they had land to lose), their possessions, and their livelihoods.

By 1930, farmers' organizations and commentators on rural policy had raised the alarm about farm debt, even if there were few who paid it much heed.[61] The sharp drops in prices and farm income quickly transformed what had been acceptable levels of debt into crushing burdens much too heavy for farm families to support. Households that might have been able to make interest and principal payments when rice was selling for about 40 yen a *koku* (as it did in the mid-1920s) were hard-pressed when prices fell to less than half that. To make matters worse, the recession made it that much more difficult to get new loans. Banks were carrying too much of their own bad debt to be interested in making additional risky loans to the agricultural community. Consequently, when loans were available, they were likely to come from local moneylenders and merchants, who charged high rates of interest. Yet, farmers who needed cash for seed and fertilizer often had no one else to turn to, and as long as prices continued to tumble, there was no end in sight to the spiral of rising debt and falling income.

By 1932, petitioners and others were demanding that the state step in. Those demands were based on firsthand observations of the problems associated with debt, and to a lesser extent on estimates of the size of the debt burden. More useful for their shock value than for any clues as to how to deal with debt, nationwide surveys nevertheless gave policymakers a rough idea of the scale of the crisis. What officials found when they looked at conditions in the countryside in the early 1930s was that the nation's farm families owed a tremendous amount. Estimates suggested that farmers were between 4 and 6 billion yen in debt to banks, credit unions, and private lenders. That was enough for every farm family in the country to owe between 800 and 1,000 yen.

Debt had not been a serious enough problem to merit many surveys prior to the economic downturn. The estimate cited above came from a survey conducted by the Imperial Agricultural Association in 1929, which was one of the first to look carefully at farm indebtedness.[62] Other surveys followed; Agriculture Minister Gotō dispatched authorities to Nagano, Iwate, Niigata, and Hyōgo to perform debt surveys in June 1932. Results released in July established that farm debt across the country was indeed over 4.7 billion yen, or an average of 837 yen per farm household.[63] A similar survey in 1935 concluded that total farm debt was about 4.9 billion yen.[64]

These national surveys were supported by several studies at the prefectural and village levels, which painted an even bleaker picture of local conditions. Average household debt in Niigata in 1932, for instance, was estimated at more than 2,300 yen; in Yamanashi it was just over 1,200 yen, and in Fukushima, where 86 percent of the seventeen thousand households surveyed had at least some debt, the average was 1,590 yen.[65]

By 1932, when many of these surveys were released to the public, it was already obvious that the farm crisis was a serious problem. The debt figures reinforced that conclusion and gave some sense of the scale of what had happened to farmers. Because there had been little attention paid to debt prior to the start of the depression, newspaper readers could not help but be shocked by the amount that farmers owed: In 1932, 4.7 billion yen was more than twice the value of all farm production that year, almost 2.5 times the size of the government's budget, and more than a third the size of the GNP. And although the comparison was seldom made explicit, average farm-household debt in some cases was equivalent to between two and three years of that household's income from farming.[66] Like national deficits in a more recent day and age, there could be little doubt that farm debt was too big a problem to ignore.

Sekishiba faced several debt-related problems in the early 1930s. First and foremost, the village simply lacked adequate financial institutions to meet residents' needs. In 1934, the village was home to one credit union, five moneylending businesses, and twelve farm households that loaned money on the side. Although this might seem like a large number of potential creditors, village officials pointed out that a general lack of access to credit kept annual interest rates hovering between 12 and 20 percent—more than double the rates that favored borrowers got from banks. "Borrowing at these high rates year after year," wrote one official, "leads to distress."

The situation was made worse by the tendency of local farmers to deposit their money in banks and in postal savings accounts rather than in the local credit union. Since only the latter institution was willing to make loans without collateral, the village's poorer families found themselves turned away from official institutions and had to borrow at usurious interest rates from private lenders. Thus it was imperative that the community do something not only about the burden of debt but also about local credit practices in general.[67]

Sekishiba tried several times to determine how much residents had borrowed and from whom. There was at least one debt survey done in the late summer of 1932, and others in 1934, in conjunction with the Economic Revitalization Campaign. The surveys approached the problem of farm debt from slightly different angles, however, which makes direct comparisons problematic. In 1932, village officials estimated that Sekishiba's residents owed a total of 600,260 yen, or an average of 1,500 yen for each household, to banks, moneylenders, and credit unions.[68] In 1934, the Economic Revitalization Debt Survey (see Table 4) recorded only the actual amount of debt reported by residents. Thus the 1934 survey was more precise but more dependent on residents coming clean about exactly how much they had borrowed from banks, businesses, and each other. In their final estimate of village indebtedness, however, Sekishiba's officials revised the survey results sharply upward. They concluded that the actual debt level of the village was around 800,000 yen—higher than it had been back in 1932, and more than twice as high as residents admitted to owing in 1934. The average household's share of that sum was thus 1,839 yen, which was more than four times as much as the village estimated a typical family would earn through farming in 1934. Their estimate paints a picture of a community falling deeper into debt with each passing year.[69]

This survey revealed as much to Sekishiba's leaders about the scale of the village's debt as it did about where the money was coming from and where it went. There were 109 households that had loaned at least some money to borrowers—far fewer than the 297 households that admitted to being in debt. Close to half of the borrowed money went to the costs of everyday life. Residents took out loans to pay for food, clothing, and other necessities far more often than for any other reason. Business credit accounted for less than a third of all borrowed funds, while another fifth or so fell into a category simply called "other," which may have included expenses such as weddings, taxes, and medical bills (i.e., expenditures that might be expected to fall through the cracks between "business" and normal "living" expenses).

Table 4
Sekishiba Economic Revitalization Debt Survey, 1934

| Creditors/ Purpose of the loan | Business | Living expenses | Disaster recovery | Other | Total | Percent |
|---|---|---|---|---|---|---|
| Individual (within Sekishiba) | ¥21,700 | ¥39,150 | ¥3,000 | ¥25,200 | ¥89,050 | 27% |
| Individual (outside Sekishiba) | 18,600 | 61,850 | 2,300 | 21,500 | 104,250 | 32% |
| Banks, unions | 46,800 | 32,300 | 1,100 | 19,843 | 100,043 | 31% |
| Others | 4,100 | 30,000 | | | 34,100 | 10% |
| Total village debt | ¥91,200 | ¥163,300 | ¥6,400 | ¥66,543 | ¥327,443 | 100% |
| Average debt per farm household | ¥210 | ¥377 | ¥15 | ¥153 | ¥755 | |
| Percentages | 28% | 50% | 2% | 20% | 100% | |

NOTES: The Basic Survey calculates total village debt at 341,190 yen, but the math is in error. The smaller total in the table reflects what I believe to be the correct sum. A December 1934 survey provided the following breakdown of borrowing within Sekishiba: 14 percent of the loans were at interest rates of less than 7 percent; 27 percent, at rates of between 7 and 10 percent; 38 percent, at rates of between 10 and 15 percent; and 17 percent was at rates of more than 15 percent interest. See SMY, Satō to Fukushima ken keizai buchō, "Nōsangyoka fusai chōsa ni kansuru ken," Kangyō kankei 1935, KST.
SOURCE: *Keizai kōsei keikaku kihon chōsa*, 1934, KST.

The survey confirmed Sekishiba's residents relied greatly on individual lenders. In the 1932 survey, a little over 20 percent of all village borrowing came from banks, credit unions, or the state, whereas the 1934 Economic Revitalization Survey suggests that a little over 30 percent came from those sources (see Table 4). Individual lenders, meanwhile, accounted for almost 60 percent of the money borrowed in Sekishiba by the end of 1933. Much of that, or almost a third of the total, had been borrowed from someone outside the community. The surveys drew a distinction between local and "outside" lenders, perhaps to gauge how relationships within the village might be governed by creditor-borrower relationships. By the time the Basic Survey was conducted in Sekishiba, local leaders also were thinking about how best to "adjust" (*seiri*) existing debt, in which case it mattered a great deal where the money had come from. Local creditors were usually easier to negotiate with than those outside the community.

There were clear connections between the stated purpose of the loan and its likely source. About half of all the money loaned by banks, unions, and the government was spent on business-related projects, and only a third or so on living expenses. A little more than half of all the money borrowed from individuals, in contrast, went to cover some sort of "living-related" cost. Business loans came in third, after lending for "other" purposes. This pattern is more or less what one might expect, given that banks and other institutional lenders often had funds that were targeted for specific farming-related projects and that would thus be lent to farmers who could put up land or other assets as security. For people who needed the money for something other than business, private sources, and higher interest rates, were their only alternative.

Sekishiba's residents thus were involved in a complex set of credit relationships. Borrowing was widespread, lending commonplace, and interest rates high. The village reported that banks and credit unions charged a uniform 11 percent on their loans, while private moneylenders were able to demand 15 percent. Only the pawnshop was higher, and it carried but a small amount of debt. Assuming that all the borrowing from private sources in the survey falls into this 15 percent category (and the figures are quite close), it is easy to see why local debt was a serious problem. Sekishiba's borrowers had to pay 28,995 yen annually in interest charges alone on the money they borrowed from individuals, and another 11,000 or so to the banks and credit unions.[70]

Those were significant sums, but little in Sekishiba's debt picture was out of the ordinary for Fukushima, or for rural communities more generally. Farmers outside the prefecture tended on average to borrow more often from institutional sources and thus at slightly lower interest rates than had become the norm in Sekishiba and in Fukushima, but the overall level of indebtedness in the village was typical of rural communities nationwide.[71]

Debt thus was one reason that falling commodity prices could have such a devastating impact on farmers even when most expenses also declined. Not only was the loan principal unaffected by the economic downturn, but interest rates remained tenaciously high. Like taxes, interest payments and the burden of debt remained a constant in farmers' lives even as everything else around them adjusted to the new reality of lower prices.

One has some sense of the frustration associated with personal efforts to cope with these burdens in the diary of Nishiyama Kōichi, a young tenant farmer in neighboring Niigata prefecture. Nishiyama's father had over the years accumulated considerable debt, and as Kōichi assumed control of the family, it became his responsibility to cope with it. By 1933 he was several thousand yen in debt to twenty-five different creditors, many of them relatives or well-to-do neighbors in the village. His diary in 1932 and the following year is almost consumed by the burden and full of accounts of his borrowing 10 or 20 yen from one creditor to pay back what he owed to someone else.[72] Some of what Nishiyama had borrowed went to fund his efforts to start a small business (and thus supplement the family's failing prospects from agriculture alone); some of it was caught up in purchasing necessities for farming; and as in Sekishiba, much of his borrowing went simply to sustaining his family from one day to the next.

It was several years before Nishiyama was able to free himself and his family from the vigilance that the loans demanded. His experiences, though atypical in some respects, speak to the importance of credit to farm families and the extent to which the relationships associated with borrowing were woven into farm communities. Debt was an inescapable and potentially destructive component of modern farming, and efforts to lessen its impact on rural communities became one of the first ingredients of the relief package that the state created to rescue villages from the depression.

## The Crises of Community

The mayor's fears that "with every year the beautiful customs of the past will fall into the shadows, and every day that passes will hasten the desolation of the village" rested on a belief that the community was at risk. Falling prices and rising debt were concrete problems that threatened farm families; as much as Mayor Satō may have worried about these families' private misfortune, his attention was transfixed by the damage the depression was doing, and might yet do, to the village as a community and as an institution.[73]

By 1933 and 1934, Satō could point to a long list of issues that confronted

Sekishiba, from tax delinquency to unpaid teachers' salaries to the collapse of hamlet and community associations. These ate away at the sense of stability so important to local elites and fueled concerns about other, more serious divisions within the village. Tenancy and class issues were never far from the surface in official narratives of the depression and its impact but were covered over with frequent allusions to the need to protect village harmony and cooperation from the forces that threatened them, combined, eventually, with a series of measures to shore up a faltering sense of community. This inability to confront tenancy and class conflict in any meaningful way at the village level only made the ongoing economic crisis all the more troubling, especially as farmers' unions and tenancy disputes began to spread throughout the northeast. One reads seldom in the 1930s of the "farm problem" or the "farm household problem," but the "problems of rural villages" was a phrase on everyone's lips.

## CIVIC LIFE

Sekishiba relied on the taxes its officials collected to pay for the services and facilities provided to village residents. The central government provided very little in the way of regular subsidies or support, which meant that most of the costs of schoolteachers' salaries, social services, public works projects, and the like were shouldered by the village. Local budgets had skyrocketed during the interwar years as town and village governments paid for a growing collection of programs and projects, and for the expanding education system.[74] Teachers' salaries and other costs associated with education consumed between 40 and 50 percent of Sekishiba's budget, which grew from less than 8,000 yen in 1918 to more than 25,000 in 1928; the average over the next five years was close to 21,000 yen.[75]

Despite revisions to the tax system in the mid-1920s, spending outran tax revenues even before the economic downturn later in the decade. Towns and villages tried to close the gap by borrowing (local indebtedness nationally grew more than twenty-one times between 1913 and 1929), but that was hardly a permanent or fiscally healthy solution.[76] At the start of the depression local officials tried to reduce spending where they could, but they soon discovered that the relatively high share of expensive fixed costs, such as education and other centrally mandated programs, made it very difficult to cut budgets sufficiently. As the economic situation deteriorated in the countryside, Tokyo made matters worse by ordering local administrations to support an even heavier burden of public works and social welfare projects than they had in the past.

In Sekishiba and villages like it, the depression made tax collection difficult and sometimes impossible. Farmers and other residents stopped paying what they owed (a third of all village taxes were unpaid in Fukushima by 1932) or delayed payment as long as they could. Since village finances were already in a precarious condition, even a relatively minor drop in revenue could make it impossible for communities to continue to provide basic services. Local civic groups were in a similar situation; many formerly active unions and service organizations stopped functioning once their members became unable to contribute operating funds, which meant that both the official civic infrastructure and its private counterpart were weakened by the depression just when they were needed most.[77]

The press and government commentators gave considerable weight to these problems as indicators of the extent of the decline of local order and often focused on one aspect of community life in particular to gauge rural distress: schools. Education was one of the last expenditures that rural families cut back on, and few people seem to have pulled their children from school even during the leanest years of the depression. Thus local institutions remained open and full, a visible symbol of the community's future.[78] At the same time, however, town and village schools were open windows on the state of rural life, and as the depression deepened, they began to show the strain.

Local teachers were paid primarily out of town and village budgets, of which their salaries accounted for a significant share. As the guardians of the nation's children, teachers deserved the respect of the communities they served, and under normal circumstances their wages were accepted as a burden the community would bear. Yet teachers were paid well (if not extravagantly by rural standards) and did not necessarily have close ties to the communities in which they taught, so perhaps it should come as no surprise that, under the abnormal circumstances of the depression, teachers' salaries were early casualties of local budget shortfalls. In Fukushima roughly half of all towns and villages owed money to local teachers as of 1932, with some reporting delays in payment of more than nine months.[79]

Although commentators acknowledged scattered instances of unpaid wages in the past, never before had the problem been so widespread and the amounts involved so large. By the end of August 1934, Fukushima's communities had the dubious distinction of owing more money to teachers than any other prefecture in the country. In Aizu, where the newspaper *Fukushima minpō* took to reporting the rare cases in which salaries had actually been paid, close to half of all communities admitted to being behind in what they owed their teachers in late 1934.[80] Similar situations were commonplace throughout the country. The national and local press reported on them regularly in tones that were appreciative both of teachers who continued to teach class though they had been unpaid for months and of the apparently intractable problems facing local communities.[81]

Sekishiba itself had reached a point earlier, in the 1920s, when it had to take out short-term loans to pay its teachers' salaries. By the start of the depression, though, the village was on firmer fiscal ground. One of the first things Mayor Satō had done when he took office in 1924 was cajole tax deadbeats in the village into paying what they owed.[82] The tax unions he helped establish afterward kept payments coming into the village coffers regularly and probably helped prevent delinquency from becoming so severe that it led once again to unpaid teachers' salaries.

Even so, the number of people whom village officials dunned for back taxes rose dramatically during the first few years of the depression, more than doubling between 1927 and 1930. By the end of 1930, village officials were threatening to seize the property of 340 delinquent taxpayers, more than two and a half times as many as in 1927.[83] Such seizures, when thoroughly pursued, resulted in an official inventory of the family's possessions, a public display of that inventory, and a public auction to recoup the amount owed to the village. Sekishiba's records include long lists of clothing, furniture, bicycles, and other household items made ready for sale. Some families went through the process again and again, staving off outright sale of their goods only at the last minute.

Some communities seized the items outright, as journalists described in this scene from a village office in Tottori prefecture in 1932:

In the night watch room, ten or more clocks are hung on the walls so that it looks just like a clock store. They are all dirtied with smoke and very old and look strange where they are. In one corner of the room, *tatami* are piled deep. In the opposite corner lie stacks of *fusuma* and *shōji*. The *fusuma* speak of times when they were once pristine but are now black; the *shōji* have suffered at the hands of children. In another corner there is a small suitcase, a small desk that looks like a child practiced writing on it up until yesterday, pots, a *hibachi*, and so on, like a store for old cheap things.[84]

Reports on teacher salaries and tax delinquency often were coupled with troubling ones about the lives of rural children. Although they continued to come to school, it was clear to teachers and other observers that children were not as well fed or supplied with necessities as they had been before the economic crisis.[85] For example, the decline in the quality and quantity of the food children brought to school for lunch was marked. In one village in Gifu prefecture, teachers responded to rumors that some of their students were not being properly fed by conducting an impromptu survey of the contents of children's lunchboxes, only to have several dozen students refuse to open them up on the grounds that they weren't really hungry. Once the teachers finally looked inside, they found that the majority had brought only barley mixed with rice and a bit of bamboo shoot on the side.

It is hard to know how many of the two hundred thousand children whom the Ministry of Education eventually estimated were going hungry in mid-1932 were chronically underfed and how many were only recently so, because the ministry had up to that point not studied the problem, on the grounds that deeply ingrained local practices of mutual assistance would ensure that children received enough to eat. Clearly something had changed, if only the state's willingness to acknowledge that a problem existed. Anecdotal evidence certainly suggests that teachers and others treated the issue of underfed schoolchildren as another aspect of the broader depression crisis.[86]

Hungry children, unpaid teachers, delinquent taxes, the slow collapse of local civic organizations—all were side effects of diminished rural income, and all testify to the multiple ways in which the economic downturn undermined social structures and the conduct of everyday life. Even if a community avoided some aspects of the problem, as Sekishiba was able to do, few were immune to it. Barter had become commonplace in some cash-strapped villages, and one Nagano resident reported that even the dead were affected by the economy. People in his village used every possible excuse to avoid having to attend local funerals so as not to have to provide the customary gift to the bereaved. When they did go, he said, people wrote "30 sen" or "50 sen" on a piece of paper as an IOU, took the intended recipient aside, and explained, "I'm very sorry, but when I sell some cocoons, or when the economy gets better, at that time I will certainly bring the money."[87]

## SOCIAL DIVISION

If rural families were united in their shared experiences of hard times, they were also divided in some fundamental and potentially disruptive ways. In 1933, the 34 families in Sekishiba's "upper" tax bracket reported spending, on average, 855 yen on general expenses (food, clothing, shelter, medical care, education, transportation, and entertainment). The 104 families in the middle bracket spent an average of only 345 yen on the same items, while the majority of households (the 282 in the lower tax category) spent only 196 yen on average.[88]

In most spending categories, the gap between the 34 upper-level taxpayers and everyone else was much more pronounced than that between lower- and mid-level households. Upper-level households spent around 247 yen on food and drink, compared to only 88 yen for a middle-class family and 79 yen for those in the lowest tax bracket. In 1933, families in the latter category spent around 22 yen on education and another 11 on health-related costs, while their wealthiest neighbors spent 69 and 205 yen, respectively.[89] The only category in which the upper-level households did not spend much more than everyone else was entertainment, which included such diversions as short trips, tobacco, plays, and so on. Middle-level families reported spending around 25 yen a year, lower-level families only 5, and the wealthiest households 15 yen in this area.

In addition to the costs of everyday living, families had to pay for the occasional wedding, funeral, or childbirth, and here, too, the upper and lower groups of taxpayers in the village varied widely in what they could afford. A typical upper-class funeral, for instance, cost 107 yen, compared to the 67 yen that a middle-status family would spend, or the 35 yen that it cost to bury a member of the lower tax bracket. The gap was less pronounced on spending for childbirth (12, 13, and 9 yen, respectively), and for the cost of ceremonies for newly conscripted soldiers (60, 45, and 41 yen). Members of the village's poorer families spent almost as much (12 yen) on Buddhist memorial services as did their wealthier neighbors, who spent only one yen more.[90]

Because these data about spending are available in Sekishiba only for 1933, there is no way to get a sense of how, or if, those patterns changed over the years. Nor is there any way to know for certain that the depression exacerbated the gaps between those at the upper and lower ends of the economic spectrum, though it is hard to imagine that it did not. Despite these limitations, the differences that the survey identifies are worth noting, if only because they help point out that divisions in the countryside were more than ideological constructions. A 35-yen funeral was not the same event as one that cost 107 yen; a family that could afford 11 yen a year for medical expenses did not receive the same level of care as one that paid six times as much, or twenty times as much. Standards of living varied greatly not just between city and country but also within rural communities. How or whether to address this issue was one question that rural policymakers and communities themselves had to consider in deciding how best to overcome the depression's effects. Was it enough to keep farmers from abject poverty and starvation, providing emergency relief as had been done time and again, or did this crisis require a different response?

Other differences and potential divisions lurked close to the surface as well. Land was a fundamental problem. Not all the real and potential conflicts in rural communities in the early 1930s were rooted in land and its ownership, but these were certainly the most visible and concrete of the countryside's internal struggles. Battles between landlords and tenants had raged throughout the 1920s in unprecedented numbers, and they had an impact even where they didn't spill over into the public eye. For the first time, as Ann Waswo has suggested, tenants began to believe that they could work and negotiate their way out of poverty and toward a better standard of living for themselves and their families.[91] As the rural economic crisis worsened, many observers worried that such gains would prove elusive and that when tenants and other poor farmers fell farther behind their wealthier neighbors, they would rise up in anger and bring their communities crashing down with them. Although such apocalyptic tenant uprisings never occurred (save in the nightmares of local elites and the dreams of radical rural activists), the depression did bring with it a significant shift in the scope and nature of landlord-tenant conflict.

Tenancy was a particularly difficult issue, even for those villages, like Sekishiba, that were not sites of large public disputes. Throughout the 1920s, tenants and landlords in the more commercially developed centers of central and western Japan had been caught up in often lengthy and contentious struggles, usually over tenant demands for lower rent. The first wave of disputes peaked in 1926, when more than one hundred fifty thousand tenants clashed with almost forty thousand landlords in 2,751 disputes.[92] While still involving only a fraction of the entire farming population, such open expressions of discontent over such a long period were signs that rural Japan had entered a new phase in its history. The burgeoning tenant union movement played a key role in facilitating those struggles and defining their goals, but so did a more volatile market economy, a better-educated tenant class, and changing state policies toward agriculture.[93] Something similar was happening in factories as organized labor began its own push for better terms and better status. Unlike strikes, however, landlord-tenant conflicts tended to be local events that involved neighbors and hence called into question long-standing patterns of deference and service at a very personal level.[94]

As disputes spread in western Japan in the 1920s, Sekishiba's farmers showed few public signs of similar unrest, and in this they were typical of their counterparts throughout the northeast. Unlike Gifu, Osaka, and Hyōgo, all centers of tenant activity, the six northeastern prefectures were relative backwaters when it came to organizing tenants and initiating disputes. Between 1917 and 1931, there were altogether only two thousand recorded disputes there, or less than a tenth of the national total.[95] That does not mean landlord-tenant relations in the region were free from strain. "Even if there is a famine, rents are not reduced by so much as a single grain," wrote a Sekishiba official in 1919. "In cases where rent payments are late by a single day," he continued, "[renters] are immediately pressed very hard for payment."[96]

Sekishiba's landlords appear to have been no more or less lenient than their counterparts in other local villages. They were strict and demanding but did from time to time allow tenants leeway when absolutely necessary, as they would do later, during the 1934 famine.[97] In explaining why there were relatively few disputes in the northeast in the 1920s, scholars have emphasized both the absence of an effective movement to organize tenants there and the lack of well-developed commercial centers as found in western Japan. Northeastern tenants had fewer employment options and less organizational support, and northeastern landlords appear to have been more likely to remain in the village and close to the land than their counterparts in Osaka, Gifu, and other developed areas, where absentee landlords were increasingly common.[98] The landlord-tenant relationship in the northeast was thus widely described as more traditional and personal than the increasingly contractual and businesslike ties thought to be commonplace in the western part of the country.

As the rural economy worsened, tenancy disputes took on new forms, and the northeast's immunity from them quickly eroded. Between 1932 and 1941, the Tōhoku region experienced a sixfold increase in the number of reported landlord-tenant conflicts. Its prefectures accounted for more than a quarter of all struggles over that period, helping push the national total to a new record in 1935 of 6,824 disputes—more than three times as many as had occurred in 1928 and twice as many as in 1929.[99] In 1930, Fukushima ranked thirty-third nationally in terms of the number of its tenancy disputes; in 1932 it was eighth, and it was among the top ten prefectures almost every year from 1932 to 1937.[100] Between 1920 and 1929, the government had catalogued a total of only 89 tenancy disputes in Fukushima. By 1932 Fukushima was experiencing 82 incidents in a single year, peaking at 471 in 1936. The Aizu region saw disputes there increase from just 7 in 1928 to 75 in 1936; in Yama county over the same period, the number of conflicts more than doubled, from 5 to 11. Tenant union membership in the prefecture swelled from negligible numbers to about four thousand in more than eighty unions by 1935, yet another indication that rural society in the northeast was in the midst of unprecedented changes.[101]

Although there was no single underlying cause for the increase in disputes in the northeast during the depression, the most frequently cited problems were attempts by landlords to take land back from tenants to farm themselves and the sale of land by its owner to someone other than the tenant. Although it was common for tenants to rent from more than one landlord, the loss of even one parcel of farmland could have serious consequences for tenant farmers.

The willingness of some tenants to contest land seizures (bearing in mind that many more probably acquiesced to landlord demands without a public struggle) and their desire to somehow secure a continued right to cultivate particular parcels were responsible for the increase in so-called defensive tenancy disputes in Fukushima and throughout the Tōhoku region. In 1935, almost 70 percent of all tenant disputes in the northeastern prefectures started over tenancy rights or landlord attempts to take land back; in about two-thirds of the cases, tenants demanded to be allowed to continue their status as renters. The experiences of Fukushima's tenants were similar.[102] The sharp rise in disputes and the nature of the forces driving them gave pause to those who had long considered the northeast immune from such disruptions.

Table 5
Status of Farm Households in Sekishiba, 1926–1938

|      | Owner farmer | Owner tenant | Tenant | Other | Total |
|------|--------------|--------------|--------|-------|-------|
| 1926 | 101 | 171 | 114 |   | 386 |
| 1928 | 90  | 156 | 123 | 1 | 370 |
| 1933 | 86  | 161 | 124 |   | 371 |
| 1934 | 83  | 160 | 137 |   | 380 |
| 1935 | 80  | 163 | 140 | 7 | 390 |
| 1938 | 83  | 170 | 147 |   | 400 |

NOTES: Figures are not always consistent across sources. The 1933 Economic Revitalization Survey, for example, provides slightly different estimates of household status.
SOURCES: Kitakata-shi shi hensan iinkai, ed. *Kitakata-shi shi*, vol. 6, pp. 239–240, 270, 495; vol. 8, p. 670.

Sekishiba avoided the public tenancy disputes that accompanied the depression elsewhere in the northeast, but not the underlying issues that produced them. Local officials were convinced that the balance of farmers and land in their community was ultimately inefficient, a sentiment shared by like-minded bureaucrats and observers of the countryside.[103] Land was expensive, heavily taxed, and the source not only of food but also of social and economic standing. Although more farmers in Sekishiba owned land than did not (in 1933 about two-thirds of the village's farm households owned at least some land), tenant families made up a larger share of the village's farmers than was common in the rest of the prefecture or in the nation more generally (see Table 5).[104] They relied on fellow villagers to rent them most (close to 60 percent as of 1947) of their farmland (paddy and upland fields together).[105]

The village's detailed 1923 land survey and depression-era studies conducted as part of the Economic Revitalization Campaign support the conclusion that there were within the village a small number of large landlords and a much broader group of people who rented out small plots. Although these surveys must be interpreted with caution, they seem to reveal patterns of ownership and borrowing common in the Japanese countryside. Most landlords rented out plots of less than a *chō* (slightly less than one hectare) of land (in 1923; later figures are unavailable), and most tenants borrowed from several different landlords.[106] The surveys suggest also that landlord-tenant relationships defy any single stereotype: people leased from neighbors and also from landlords in neighboring hamlets and villages, so that at any given moment Sekishiba's farmers were involved in a very complex collection of associations and obligations that extended beyond a simple dichotomy of poor tenant and rich landlord.

As for rich landlords, there were seven Sekishiba residents who owned 10 or more *chō* of land in 1936. Since the average-sized farm required only 2 or at most 3 *chō*, these men clearly rented out what they didn't farm. Endō Gengō, a Kamitakahitai farmer and landlord, owned the most, 54 *chō* of paddy and 11 *chō* of upland fields. Indeed, his paddy holdings alone were bigger than several of the village's hamlets. The average paddy holding of the remaining six men was about 15 *chō*, still a large amount of land. Much of what they held was within village boundaries. Altogether, Sekishiba landlords claimed ownership of only 50 or so *chō* of paddy land in other communities, as opposed to the more than 130 *chō* of Sekishiba paddy land that belonged to outsiders, most of which was farmed by tenants.[107]

Some absentee owners may have lived close by, as did Yabe Zenbei, a Kitakata businessman and landlord to many Sekishiba residents. Yabe was closely involved with his tenants and with the village and during the depression played a leading role in the pursuit of various types of reform there (see Chapter 9 below). The distinction between resident and non-resident landlord is thus a complicated one, but clearly local tenants also had to contend with some owners who were not personally familiar with local conditions and needs. In other settings, the tenant–absentee-landlord relationship was often seen as particularly vulnerable to disputes.[108]

Tenancy became more common in Sekishiba over the course of the late 1920s and early 1930s. Such a development was in sharp contrast to the conditions described by the government's figures for the nation as a whole, which showed very little change in tenancy's share of the rural population. A closer look reveals that shifts out of tenancy and into landholding status in parts of western Japan masked increases in tenant numbers in the northeast. The balance between tenants, landholders, and the various stages in between remained in flux despite the illusion of stability. Certainly farmers in Sekishiba would have thought so: there were twenty-nine fewer owner-cultivators and owner-tenants there in 1935 than there had been in 1926, and twenty-six more tenant households (see Table 5). By 1935 there were thus close to 10 percent fewer farm households with at least some land to their name in Sekishiba than there had been in 1926.[109] A reasonable conclusion is that some of the people who had been landholders had slipped into tenancy.

The status of land in the village reflects a similar shift out of the hands of owners and into the hands of tenants. In 1925 more than 60 percent of all paddy land was farmed by the family who owned it; by 1934 only about half was. In absolute terms, owner-farmed paddy acreage declined by 20 percent over the same period. Although the ratio of tenanted to owned land was still lower in Sekishiba (and in Fukushima) than the national average, this was little consolation to local farmers.

Who owned the land and who had access to it—and at what cost—were vital considerations in village life and seldom more so than during the depression. Ironically, the state's best efforts to deal directly with tenancy ground to a halt just as the depression got under way. Attempts to provide a stronger legal framework for tenancy and thus to head off landlord-tenant conflict, in a pattern similar to that employed by those developing policy toward labor and unions, had come to a standstill by the end of 1931, after repeated failures in the Diet. A program dating from the mid-1920s to provide loans to those wishing to purchase farmland was on paper a worthwhile venture, but in practice it had proved unwieldy and unfavorable to tenants. Nothing much would come of it until very late in the decade, and even then the number it served made up only a small fraction of the tenant population.[110] Rural communities thus began the economic crisis with no new tools for dealing with the problems of tenancy.

This mattered, even in as apparently peaceful a place as Sekishiba. Disputes were only part of the reason that landownership was a concern for both local elites and tenants. Landlord-tenant relations could vary widely from place to place and from personality to personality, but generally speaking, land-rich farmers and landlords in many communities had come to dominate local offices and politics and could often involve themselves in their tenants' lives in ways that would never have been accepted by an independent landowner. The depression called into question more forcefully than before the continued value of such guidance and control from above. The new economic realities of the countryside seemed to require a new approach to leadership and to farming, one in which landlords were not necessarily the best qualified.

One reason such challenges were possible was that the spread of education, conscription, and other practices had evened out the differences between tenants, landowners, and landlords on many levels. Technological know-how and access to better farming methods were by the late 1920s no longer the domain of the landlord or the rich farmer. Nor were the ambition and the experience necessary to lead; both were widespread.[111] Qualified to serve in every way, and kept from doing so only by their status as tenants or land-poor farmers, rural youth had good reason to challenge the status quo.

Fault lines of educational attainment, gender, generation, and politics mapped out a complicated set of relationships among landlords and tenants, family members, older local elites, and younger, ambitious farmers in the early 1930s. The depression threatened to further disrupt village society by accelerating the pace of change, whether in the form of a sharp rise in tenancy disputes or through more subtle challenges to local authority and hierarchies. These changes promised no stable transition from whatever the countryside had been to whatever it might become; no new model of post-depression rural society had yet been constructed. As the crises continued, many communities began to construct their own.

## The Crises of State and Nation

On May 15, 1932, groups of armed men made up of young army and navy officers and civilian agrarianists attacked a series of preselected targets in Tokyo. Their goal was to bring chaos to the city, overthrow the government of Prime Minister Inukai, and somehow construct a new polity out of the vacuum they hoped to create. They succeeded only in killing the prime minister and a police officer and wounding several others; the agrarianists' goal had been to knock out several power stations, but as Stephen Vlastos notes, "They failed to dim even one offensive neon sign."[112]

The first of the trials of those charged with insurrection and murder began in July the following year. Army and navy officers were tried in separate military proceedings; Tachibana Kōzaburō and the others from his Aikyō-kai farm cooperative movement were tried in criminal court. All proceedings were open to the press, allowing the public its first clear glimpse into the motives and characters of those involved. As much spectacle as formal judgment, the trials were never really about determining guilt or innocence.

The questions before the courts had more to do with how to strike a balance: the defendants had to be punished, yet few seemed to doubt that the officers had acted unselfishly and with the purest possible motives. The military—the army more than the navy perhaps—reinforced this image of its overzealous but sincere young officers by making sure that they had the appropriate uniforms to wear for their public appearances and by transporting them to and from the courtrooms in comfortable sedans, as befit their celebrity status. The judges were solicitous and allowed the men ample opportunity to hold forth about their concerns, their motives, and their vision of a better Japan, which the press reported at length and in breathless detail. Tachibana's opening address alone took three weeks.[113]

No clear blueprint of what the young officers thought would happen after they acted ever emerged from their testimony, but their words resonated with the public nevertheless. The officers and to a lesser extent the civilians spoke of the injustice of the London Naval Conference, of their fears of a weakened military and a corrupt political system, of Manchuria, and of their strong desire to rescue rural Japan. "One reason for our action," testified one officer, "was to help the families of the soldiers from the Tōhoku. A peasant uprising was sure to occur if that state of affairs was allowed to continue."[114] Another defendant moved the spectators to tears (a not infrequent event during testimony; the judges and lawyers often succumbed as well) as he recounted the destitution of rural villages.[115]

The trial fascinated in part because, like the Incident itself, it brought together in a single arena what were nominally distinct problems: the rural crisis, political and ideological corruption, fears of military weakness, Japan's international standing, and Manchuria.[116] The conspirators' efforts to resolve all these issues at once suggested that somehow they could all be solved and that the nation's lingering sense of uncertainty could end. The participation of Tachibana Kōzaburō and his fellow agrarianists in the May 15 plot may have come as a shock to many farmers, for their causes were usually not so violently promoted. Yet few would have doubted the need to focus attention on rural communities, or that agrarianism might play a role in defining a future course for the countryside.

Agrarianism in its various forms had established itself as a force to be reckoned with even before the economic downturn. It was well organized, possessed eloquent and persuasive spokesmen, and was not without supporters in the government. Its rural-centric message, as developed by Tachibana, Gondō Seikyō, and others, was not simply backward-looking and regressive. In their hands the progressive, rational, and modern aspects of agrarianism made it a viable and popular approach to thinking about the countryside and its problems.[117] The depression thus provided both a means and an end for rural activists. Desperate farmers were more receptive than ever to agrarianist proposals for change and helped build their organizations in the early 1930s. Ironically, the agrarianists' stated goals of fundamental reform, economic self-sufficiency, and social rejuvenation seemed possible precisely because the rural crisis was so profound and so few alternatives existed.

As of early 1932, very little had been done for the countryside despite the persistently bleak situation there. The Minseitō cabinets, whose budget-cutting and return to the gold standard were widely blamed for the depression, had made halfhearted stabs at emergency public works projects but had accomplished little else. A new Seiyūkai government led by Inukai came to power in December 1931, promising to take Japan off the gold standard as quickly as was feasible, but made no commitment to do anything about the countryside one way or another. By the time of the trial, the outlook for the countryside was quite different.

Still, the sense of crisis, of liminality, had not dissipated entirely. Well before the inevitable guilty verdicts were announced later that summer (the civilian verdicts came in February 1934), letters and petitions in support of the May 15 defendants began pouring into government and media offices. By the end of December 1933, the state had reportedly received 1,148,000 signatures (many written in blood, and many with urban return addresses) on tens of thousands of petitions.[118] The *Tōkyō asahi shinbun* reported receiving letters from as far away as Seattle, Los Angeles, and Oakland, California. Some were clearly the product of well-organized campaigns by right-wing organizations and reservist groups, but a large share, and especially those from rural areas, were sent privately. Perhaps most surprising were the ones that arrived from certain parts of Okayama prefecture; even the people who had voted for Inukai in his home district time and again added their names to the long list of those asking for leniency for his murderers.[119]

The army's prosecutors called for sentences of only eight years for its officers, but the navy was much harsher. It demanded the death penalty for three, indefinite imprisonment for another three, and prison terms of between three and six years for the others. At the trial of the civilians, which ended well after the military hearings, the public procurator asked for indefinite imprisonment for Tachibana and for terms varying from seven to fifteen years for his followers.[120] The army's sentences were announced on September 19; the navy's followed in November. The army officers received prison terms of just four years, far less than the fifteen years that the leading conspirators on the navy's side were ordered to serve.

In some respects the campaigns for leniency clearly worked; none of the officers was punished as severely as the law allowed. Not so lucky were the civilians; lawyers for those defendants were heard to exclaim in surprise as the sentences were handed down. They were almost exactly what the procurator had asked for. The civilians were shown far less mercy than that accorded to those in the military proceedings.[121]

By the time Tachibana was released from prison in 1940, pardoned with many others on the occasion of the twenty-six-hundredth anniversary of the founding of Japan, the crises that had driven him to act had long since passed.[122] Others would take their place soon enough. The countryside he came back to, though, was a very different place than the one he had left. Chapter 4 explores the efforts of rural activists and local citizens to shape the course of rural relief, and thus the future of their communities.

# 4   Rescuing the Countryside

AKUTAGAWA SHINKICHI WAS AN unlikely spokesman for an unlikely collection of farmers. From a family of moderate means in a village just west of Kitakata, Akutagawa had been chosen in late 1931 by a group of his fellow farmers to act as their representative.[1] The assembly was a temporary one, but not unlike similar ad hoc coalitions which had started appearing in other towns and villages across the country that autumn. This one called itself the Yama County Depression-Policy People's General Meeting (Fukyō taisaku mintaikai), and by the end of the gathering those in attendance had drafted a list of ten steps they hoped the government and local leaders would take to set things right. The farmers asked for surveys of local debt, for low-interest loans and lower taxes, for the state to help them buy the fertilizer they'd need for next year's crops, and for other steps to stabilize the local economy.[2] Akutagawa helped present the group's resolutions to the most logical audience, the County Association of Mayors of Towns and Villages. The association, however, promptly refused to have anything to do with their requests, leading to what one newspaper account described as "extreme indignation" among local farmers.[3]

Ten months later Akutagawa tried again, this time with a new petition quite unlike the first. He had upped the ante: not only was the petition more specific about the steps they wanted the state to take, but it also linked those steps to a potentially sweeping set of changes in rural life. Akutagawa's petition asked explicitly for policies that would lessen the burden of farm debt, for a reduction of fertilizer prices by half, for the state to assume all the costs of local compulsory education, and for the state to commit to substantial local relief spending and address rural overpopulation (presumably via emigration). The petition also articulated a broader goal of rural recovery—namely, the pursuit of "fundamental revitalization and self-realization on the part of each citizen."[4] Sometime between October 1931 and July 1932, Akutagawa and the farmers he spoke for had turned a rather tentative collection of ideas about relief into a focused list of demands with important implications for rural communities. More important, Akutagawa had managed to make allies of the same group of local leaders that had once shunned his approach to recovery.

This time, members of the Yama County Association of Mayors of Towns and Villages not only agreed to look them over but borrowed liberally from Akutagawa's draft when they wrote out their own petition to higher authorities in the summer of 1932. Their version begins with an almost word-for-word copy of the preamble used by Akutagawa; thus, like Akutagawa, the mayors are on record as being in favor of the "fundamental revitalization" of the countryside. There are other signs that the association copied freely from the farmers' draft, although the mayors seem to have toned down some of its ideas in the process. Instead of asking that fertilizer prices be cut in half, for instance, the association asked only that they be reduced. Other items, such as the request for a debt adjustment policy and for the state to take over paying for compulsory education, are the same in both documents; so, too, are requests to return management of state-owned forests to the local government, initiate relief projects in the villages, and reform the education system.

The association did come up with a few new proposals of its own, such as those for a three-year extension on loans from some state banks, support for commodity prices, and an end to state-run charcoal production, but the tone and direction of its appeal clearly mimicked Akutagawa's original. Ideas that had once been beyond the pale for local leaders became the subject of their public policies in the span of only a few months.[5] A similar process was under way across the country.

The depression's second summer began with an unprecedented effort by farmers and rural activists to reshape the countryside's future; it ended with an emergency session of the Diet and passage of a sweeping and expensive package of relief policies. The timing of these developments reflected both a boiling over of rural dissatisfaction after almost two years of hard times and a changed political landscape. The new Seiyūkai cabinet was understood to be more likely to spend money than its Minseitō predecessors, in keeping with Seiyūkai tradition and the stated objectives of the new finance minister, Takahashi Korekiyo. As of early May, however, rural relief had yet to surface in public policy or budget discussions, and that spring's session of the Diet was poised to end without offering any solutions to farmers' problems.

Two developments transformed the countryside's prospects. The first was the involvement of Tachibana Kōzaburō and his followers in the May 15 Incident (see Chapter 3 above). There was no mistaking the role that rural distress had played in prompting them to act. And although Tachibana had certainly imagined a different outcome, one of the effects of his actions was to draw the attention of the public, the press, and the state to the countryside.

For obvious reasons, the government—meaning the police as well as bureaucrats and politicians—sought to head off other forms of rural social unrest before they, too, got out of hand. With so much of the state's resources dedicated to containing leftist organizations and ideas, threats from other quarters were harder for the security forces to predict (and, before May 15, perhaps even to imagine).[6] After Prime Minister Inukai's death, however, in every village there lurked the potential of dark and dangerous acts. The press and its audiences picked up on the change and found in the post–May 15 countryside stories and images that demonstrated the depression's impact in no uncertain terms.

A second development that spring was the coming together of formerly disparate voices into a handful of organized campaigns, all demanding help from the state for farmers and their families. Though less dramatic than Tachibana's approach, agrarianist petitioners, worried landlords, and mainstream farmers' organizations inundated politicians, the press, and bureaucrats with pleas for help, proposals for reform, and thinly veiled threats about the perils of doing nothing. From May into August, the various camps lobbied for their particular visions of rural reform both in Tokyo and in villages across the country.

The agrarianists were the first to act and were in many ways the impetus for what was to follow. Their petition campaigns demanded a lengthy moratorium on the repayment of farm debt, which appealed powerfully to beleaguered farmers. The broader message of the campaigns, however, had less to do with old loans than with a new vision for rural Japan; the agrarianists offered the petitions as a first step toward a radically transformed, autonomous countryside, and every signature they received represented a farmer who was at least potentially in agreement with that vision. As the number of signatures climbed past ten thousand and then grew to ten times that number, the petition campaign rode a wave of discontent that grew larger with every passing day. These campaigns laid bare the failure of existing institutions, and of the ideas that informed them, to respond to the depression in any meaningful way. New structures and new approaches were essential.

More mainstream spokespersons for farmers seized the opportunity that the agrarianists had created and began proposing reforms that reflected a very different understanding of what the countryside could become. The Imperial Agricultural Association (Teikoku Nōkai) set the tone for many of the debates in the Diet over whether and how to provide relief to the countryside. More than those of the agrarianists, its proposals most closely resembled the final versions of relief policies. Like the agrarianists, these groups embraced popular participation in the form of local rallies, locally drafted proposals for relief, and direct lobbying efforts by their members. Where the agrarianists hinted at the possibility of sweeping political and social change alongside economic recovery, the Imperial Agricultural Association offered a more conservative blueprint. By August 1932, its proposals for debt management and *keizai kōsei* (economic revitalization) were at the center of state and public discourse about the future of the countryside.

In their rhetoric and their demands, the countryside's spokespersons challenged the public and the government to rethink commonly held assumptions about rural Japan. The interaction of farmers, the organizations that represented them, and policymakers in the early 1930s eventually set in motion a series of changes in the rural economy and community life. Those changes helped reshape the countryside's relationships with the state, with its own past, and with its place as part of a modern nation. This chapter and the next explore rural Japan's demands for reform, and investigate the political and social meanings of the relief policies that took shape that summer.

## *Yesterday's Countryside*

That common citizens went to uncommon lengths to enlist the state's help testifies to the sharp sense of dislocation that the depression brought, although the rise of such practices speaks as well to the failure of the resources and structures already in place to assure and guide farmers and their families. By the start of the depression, the ways in which rural communities were organized, the civic bodies common to most villages, and many of the policies designed to encourage and sustain agriculture were decades old. As useful as those approaches and institutions might once have been, the countryside they served best no longer existed. Rural communities found themselves having to respond to the problems of the early 1930s with policies from the 1890s. It wasn't a good match.

Modern state and private efforts to reform and strengthen the countryside had been under way since early in the Meiji era, and policymakers and activists had struggled since then to keep pace with rapid changes in the economic and social realities of rural life. Debates about rural life and policies tended to dwell on areas of recurring concern: self-government and local leadership, farming practices and the modern economy, and class tensions and land use. These same issues remained paramount in discussions of how best to respond to the depression.

Self-government, or *jichi*, not only invoked a degree of autonomy in the management of local affairs but implied as well the construction of stable and vibrant rural communities. Meiji state-builders had helped promote the idea of self-government as a local reflection of the national polity, thus strengthening and stabilizing the social fabric while maintaining the state's oversight of it.[7] One aspect of this process was the creation of several layers of civic organization at the village level, beginning with groups like the local industrial cooperatives (*sangyō kumiai*), agricultural associations, Hōtoku societies (discussed below), and, eventually, reservists (*zaigō gunjinkai*) and young men's (*seinendan*) and sometimes young women's associations. Depression-era villages were home to a bewildering variety of these groups; the histories of the industrial cooperatives, agricultural associations, and Hōtoku societies in particular reveal how questions of economic reform, social stability, and local leadership were intertwined at the local level.

The industrial cooperatives got their start at the hands of Hirata Tōsuke and his colleague Shinagawa Yajirō, both bureaucrats and associates of the oligarch Yamagata Aritomo. The two were typical in their advocacy of legislation to protect farmers while at the same time creating new connections both among them and with the state. The first step in the direction of a more organized village came with a proposal to allow farmers to form credit unions, legislation that failed to pass the Diet in 1891. Hirata went on to write the Industrial Cooperatives Law, which passed in 1900, and he founded the Central Union of Cooperative Societies in 1905. Hirata found much of value in providing for villages and villagers that could fend for themselves, and he trusted the industrial cooperatives to perform that role. "Spiritual cooperation and unity," explained Hirata, "plus material cooperation and help are the inner meaning of cooperatives."[8]

The cooperatives were, by design, largely independent of state assistance and were meant to facilitate low-interest financing, provide for group purchases of raw materials, and eliminate the middlemen in bringing local produce to market. Membership was open to all and participation encouraged, and although membership levels fell far short of the ideal in the years leading up to the depression, the cooperatives themselves were widespread.[9]

Local agricultural associations, in contrast, were from the start more common and less inclusive. Passage of the Agricultural Association Law (Nōkaihō) in 1899 created local branches of the Imperial Agricultural Association in every town and village, provided state subsidies to keep them going, and required large landowners to join.[10] Landlords and their interests thus were overrepresented in the associations, both at the local level and nationally via the Imperial Agricultural Association. The associations' local role was to disseminate agricultural technology and methods, and many local chapters paid for all or part of the services of a local agricultural technician to oversee this process and to keep members abreast of the newest advances in farm practices. In Tokyo, the national association lobbied for landlord interests; it had, for example, pushed for years for changes that would shift some of the tax burden from landowners to industry.

Meiji bureaucrats and well-off farmers found expression for their beliefs in other ways as well. The teachings of Ninomiya Sontoku (1787–1856) and the nation's Hōtoku societies had been a part of rural life much longer than had the Meiji government. Hirata was instrumental in finding ways for the state and Hōtoku organizations to help each other achieve their respective goals in the countryside. Both the ideas and the organizations had important roles to play in the development and implementation of economic revitalization in the 1930s, and thus they deserve a brief examination here.

The life work and teachings of Ninomiya Sontoku provided abundant raw material for his disciples, who collected, commented on, and publicized his approach to rural life, which was known as "Hōtoku" (one translation of which is "returned/returning blessings"). Ninomiya was renowned for his skill at taking destitute communities and returning them to sound economic health, a process that he insisted began with the cultivation by farmers of a set of personal qualities—namely, honesty in one's dealings with others, diligence ("Work much, earn much, and spend little!" Ninomiya advised), sound financial management, and a willingness to yield to others or sacrifice one's own needs for the greater good.[11] The secret of wealth, Ninomiya taught, had more to do with attitude and self-discipline than one's circumstances. "The way to live a peaceful life," he explained, "is to carry wood from the mountain today to boil tomorrow's rice, and this evening to make hay rope to mend the fence tomorrow."[12] Ninomiya's teachings put the responsibility for success firmly on the shoulders of the individual farmer, while at the same time affirming the rural order. The Hōtoku solution to poverty was harder work, not changes in the balance of power between the haves and the have-nots.

The appeal of Ninomiya's approach to rural problems lay not only in its content but also in the way his methods were transmitted to farmers. Hōtoku beliefs encompassed more than a collection of sayings and philosophical commentary; they also promoted self-government (*jichi*) through the creation of hamlet- and village-level societies known as "Hōtokusha." Late Tokugawa landlords and others anxious to reform their communities were the first to organize these societies, and almost a thousand were still in place in the early years of the Meiji era. Most were in the Tōkai region, where Shizuoka emerged as the home prefecture of the most successful societies. These local associations were governed by a set of rules that defined proper conduct for members and outlined the group's goals for the community. Members attended the society's monthly meetings, which featured practical discussions and lectures on "industrial, educational, hygienic, or ethical subjects."[13] The didactic role of the local society was joined with a more practical one as well, in that members were expected to save at least one-fourth of their annual income. Members would contribute the local surplus to funds for use in personal or community projects.[14]

Two organizations provided national exposure to Ninomiya's movement. The Dai Nihon Hōtokusha (Greater Japan Hōtoku Society) served from 1924 as an umbrella organization for most of the country's local Hōtoku societies,[15] while the Chūō Hōtokukai (Central Hōtoku Association) worked since 1906 to popularize Ninomiya's teachings and promote research into Hōtoku thought. Founded in the aftermath of Japan's victory in the Russo-Japanese War, its members included many prominent bureaucrats, businessmen, and intellectuals who shared an interest in Ninomiya's methods and a desire for a stable countryside. Founding members Hirata Tōsuke, Ichiki Kitokurō, Okada Ryōhei, Sawayanagi Masatarō, and others like them were deeply involved in the development of prewar state-led social policy initiatives, including the creation of the Local Improvement Campaign.[16]

The Local Improvement Campaign (Chihō kairyō undō) was a Home Ministry plan to bring rapid change to several facets of village administration and village life. Bureaucrats hoped to shift the political and social focus of rural communities away from the hamlet (or *buraku*) to the larger village level. Not only would steps like shrine amalgamation make it easier for the central government to pursue administrative control of villages and the people who lived in them, but it was hoped the movement would foster a stronger sense of attachment to the national state. Training programs targeted local leaders to serve as links between the countryside and the central government.[17] Moreover, since economic success was thought to be another way of assuring continued loyalty to the government, the Home Ministry also encouraged villages to take a rational approach to that aspect of rural life. A campaign of local surveys and plans for specific improvements in farming (known as *chōson-ze*) got under way in 1901. That program was linked to efforts to have local farming organizations, agricultural associations among them, take the lead in bringing technological improvements to the villages.[18]

Official interest in the movement faded by the end of the First World War. By then bureaucrats had accomplished some of their administrative goals, although they were not at all overwhelmed by success in other areas. The state's enthusiasm for certain types of reform did not transfer very well to local communities, especially when those reforms imperiled local prerogatives. Even *chōson-ze* economic planning failed to catch on, despite its apparent potential for improving the lot of many in rural communities.[19] Local Improvement's legacies were significant, however. It left behind a strengthened Hōtoku movement, one with a more visible national presence. Home Ministry bureaucrats helped found the aforementioned Chūō

Hōtokukai and hoped to use it to shape the activities of local societies. In doing so, bureaucrats and civilian activists spent less time talking about the particular attributes of Hōtoku-ism and chose instead to emphasize the way Ninomiya's teachings helped create a "harmony between morality and economics." The appeal of such a promised solidarity is clear even if the mechanisms of its achievement were not. Home Ministry policymakers and local elites alike who were trying to imagine how to head off social unrest found in Hōtoku-ism the comforting image of an obedient, hardworking farmer untouched by radical thought.[20]

One result of these ongoing efforts to nurture "local government" and social harmony was that rural communities in the early 1930s were home to a dense network of official and semi-official associations and societies. None proved particularly effective in staving off the effects of the depression. A partial list of the key organizations in Sekishiba includes a Young Men's Association, a Reservists' Association, a Young Women's Association, a Women's Association (Fujinkai), a branch of the Patriotic Women's Association (Aikoku Fujinkai), the village-level agricultural association, an industrial cooperative, and a village fire brigade. Membership in local civic societies in theory overlapped and complemented one another, so that a farmer could be active in several and serve the community in many ways at once.

Affiliations of one kind or another also typically followed the life course of villagers, so that younger men and women left their respective youth groups only to begin participation in some other association better suited to their new, more mature status.[21] Such membership tied individuals to the community and to their peers and at some level provided a connection to the world outside. The local agricultural association, the industrial cooperatives, and so on possessed dual identities as village-level bodies and as local branches of a national organization. Sekishiba was hardly unique in featuring so many layers of belonging; such complexity was commonplace, the result of years of state-sponsored organization-building at the local level.[22]

Although the government responded institutionally to many of the concerns raised about rural life and farming at the turn of the century, the quarter century between the start of the Local Improvement Campaign and the summer of 1932 was more than enough time for those programs to lose their luster. As organized (or overorganized) as the countryside was, villages and village associations were not very well equipped to respond to the crises of the early 1930s. The uncertain decade leading up to the depression already had taken a toll, so that Sekishiba and many villages like it ended the 1920s with the bulk of their civic bodies intact but inactive. As already described in Chapter 3, unpaid dues and a dearth of cash kept people at home and limited the ability of resource-strapped associations to do more than just keep up appearances.

The state had little to offer, and the lack of local leadership was also an issue. The sharp rise in tenancy disputes clearly signaled that local elites had failed to prevent unrest from surfacing. In contests with tenant unions, agrarianists, and other activists, local leaders and the institutions they controlled could no longer be sure of holding the high ground, and the state provided little in the way of new programs or policies in response to the changing realities of rural life after World War I.

Conflicts over community life were also influenced by the emergence of a new generation of local leaders. By the late 1920s, young men born after the turn of the century were moving into their roles as village leaders. For these rural youth and for some of their elders, years of state-run education and time in the military had made them more aware of their role in the nation-state than any generation before them and more confident of their capacity to lead. In the eyes of many younger farmers, the organizations that had traditionally provided order and guidance in times of crisis were slow to respond to the challenges of the late 1920s and early 1930s, hampered by old-fashioned agendas and leadership. As of early 1932, neither the Imperial Agricultural Association nor any of the established spokespersons for the countryside had formulated a coherent response to the rural crisis. In the years leading up to the depression, the association's leaders had campaigned for lower land taxes and higher state subsidies for its own experts but had offered little in the way of a more long-term vision of the countryside's future. Asked by the government in 1930 to recommend steps for farm families to take in response to the recession, the association's leaders replied only that farmers had to learn to be more self-sufficient and frugal. Farmers, the association advised, should do what they could to develop "a spirit of self-help and self-empowerment."[23] Since the state was similarly silent about what it might do to help struggling farmers and their families, they returned to their fields that spring against a background of almost overwhelming uncertainty.

### Putting Farmers First: The Agrarianist Campaign for Relief

During the depression years, agrarianism (*nōhonshugi*) took on a larger role in shaping the state's policies toward the countryside and rural Japan's perception of itself than at any time in its long history as a constant but usually unobtrusive feature of the ideological landscape. Agrarianists, as Stephen Vlastos puts it, "imagined the Japanese farm village as (the only) social space within Japan's capitalist modernity capable of transcending class divisions" and advocated the preservation of its special qualities against a rising tide of industrialization and urbanization since before the turn of the century.[24]

Yet there was no single dominant discourse of agrarianism; several coexisted. Yamazaki Nobuyoshi, Okada Atsushi, Tachibana Kōzaburō, Gondō Seikyō, Gondō's associate Nagano Akira, and Katō Kanji—the men most closely associated with agrarianist thought and action in the depression era—varied widely on key issues. Although they would likely have agreed that society's fundamental and ideal form was one based on farming and farm life, opinions diverged over the extent to which agriculture could coexist with industry, and farming communities with cities. Capitalism, city life and city culture, the central state and bureaucrats were all held in varying degrees of contempt, but proponents of agrarianism also argued over how best to achieve their respective visions; most preferred slow change, with a small minority advocating more radical action. Tachibana's tactics were thus out of character for the rural activists of his generation, although his pursuit of a blend of socially conservative policies with a modern, scientific approach to rural life and farming reflects some of the ambiguities common in agrarianist ideology of the early 1930s—not to mention the difficulties of putting them into practice on anything but a modest scale.[25]

If the agrarianists had difficulty in realizing their goal of a more prosperous and stable countryside, they had at least succeeded by the start of the depression in defining many of the key issues in rural reform. Yamazaki and Okada were probably the best known of the agrarianist ideologues and the closest to the mainstream. Yamazaki, in addition to serving in the Imperial Agricultural Association, was a regular contributor throughout the late 1920s to *Ie no hikari*, the journal of the industrial cooperatives and the most widely read of any magazine directed at a rural audience in the pre-surrender era. The magazine revisited his ideas repeatedly in the 1930s. Yamazaki's advocacy of strong farm families and hardworking, autonomous rural communities was accessible and pragmatic, and it spoke to the long decay of village leadership and prosperity. Okada was equally influential as secretary of the Imperial Agricultural Association and adamant in his arguments in favor of protecting rural communities from the inroads of capitalism. Yamazaki and Okada's straightforward message of villages strengthened from within found ready audiences and seemed relevant during the depression, although communities had little to show for agreeing with their doctrines. The two men had defined the problems of the countryside in more sophisticated ways than had their predecessors, but their continued emphasis on harmony and self-help had done little to free farmers from the depression's grasp.[26]

Katō Kanji, meanwhile, was less visible in the early years of the depression than later, when he emerged as a popular and effective advocate of emigration as a solution to farming's problems at home and as a stepping stone toward the creation of ideal rural communities abroad. Few could match Katō's credentials and practical mastery of farming (his Nihon kokumin kōtō gakkō [Japan National Higher Level School] in Ibaraki kept him closer to the realities of rural life than any of his agrarianist counterparts). A graduate of Tokyo University's Faculty of Agriculture, Katō had formed close friendships with people like Nasu Hiroshi and Ministry of Agriculture and Forestry bureaucrat Kodaira Gonichi, both of whom went on to play key roles in shaping depression-era farm policies.[27]

Gondō remained an ideologue apart. His particular brand of agrarianism posited an ideal form of Japanese society made up of self-sufficient and self-governing farming communities, each maintaining its bonds to the land, to nature, and to the imperial institution. Modern society no longer possessed the wholesome qualities of cooperation and solidarity ascribed by Gondō to Japan's past, but he argued that it was still possible for rural communities to regain what had been lost. To return agriculture and rural communities to their proper places in the economic and cultural life of the nation, Gondō said, the central government, the bureaucracy, the established parties, and the self-interest that guided all of them would have to be abandoned. These drastic steps alone would permit the autonomous villages of Gondō's imagined past to flourish.[28]

Despite the radical changes he advocated, Gondō was not a firebrand. Official reports characterized his approach as one that expressed ideals without doing much to put them into effect, and as "unrealistic."[29] He was willing to let change develop for itself from within villages rather than try to impose leadership from outside. As economic conditions deteriorated over the course of the depression, Gondō hoped that farmers would take steps to protect themselves, but his own beliefs about the need for self-sufficiency and freedom from outside control prevented him from taking a direct role in fomenting change.

The appeal of his vision for rural change was powerful, however, and inspiring to many who encountered it. Although he was never charged, the police were concerned that Gondō had lectured some of those involved in the murders of Inoue Junnosuke and Dan Takuma in early 1932 and the abortive coup attempt of May 15; they took interest also when Nagano Akira, a Gondō confidante, emerged at the head of the petition campaigns of that spring. Nagano had managed by then to pull together a temporary alliance of agrarianists and rural activists from several different camps, an unusual achievement given the suspicion and outright hostility that usually characterized relationships among them. The rural crises and Nagano's skills together encouraged a more cooperative stance.

Operating from his home in Tokyo, Nagano brought important skills to the agrarianist campaigns of the early 1930s. As a long-time associate of Gondō, Nagano was both well versed in the rhetoric of the movement and skilled in the realities of organizing it. Nagano was a graduate of the Tokyo military academy, a close follower of Japan's growing role on the mainland, and, as his military career drew to a close, a man in search of a cause at home. He became friends with radical nationalist Ōkawa Shūmei while still in the army and, through Ōkawa, had contact with influential ideologue Kita Ikki as well. Nagano's understanding of Japan's domestic problems, however, owed less to Ōkawa or Kita than to Gondō. The two Fukuoka natives met for the first time in 1920, when Nagano was in his early thirties and Gondō fifty-two; Nagano left the army the next year with a captain's rank, and by the end of the decade was working alongside his mentor promoting their visions of a better Japan.[30]

Nagano shared many of Gondō's ideas without necessarily agreeing with him on how best to make them come true. Nagano imagined a countryside in which the modern amalgamated villages of the Meiji era were eliminated and the original villages, or hamlets, were restored to political and cultural autonomy. To keep such a step from plunging communities back into a primitive standard of living, Nagano proposed that modern industry be redistributed piecemeal throughout the countryside, thus assuring villages of access to modern goods and services. Factories too large or production too complicated to be dispersed within the villages would exist apart from them, administered separately. Such an approach would avoid the exploitation and exorbitant profit-taking that Nagano felt characterized modern commercial activity. He described this process as "moving from today's profit-first economics to the economics of public welfare"—a process in which production would be directed first and foremost at providing for the people's needs. Politically, the self-ruling communities he described would make most of the functions of the central government obsolete. Prefectural governors would be the sole point of contact between the self-ruling communities and the state. That would leave "only five or six" ministries still functioning, and Nagano reasoned that the resulting huge cut in bureaucratic spending would substantially reduce the financial burden on citizens.[31]

Where Gondō was content to describe the ideal society, Nagano wanted to take an active role in creating it.[32] And unlike Tachibana, Nagano didn't expect success overnight. His was an incremental vision, one that grew out of his skills as an organizer and a lobbyist. Nagano spent late 1931 and early 1932 trying to piece together a nationwide organization of agrarianist and local autonomy activists. Early efforts met with little success; most of the groups they organized collapsed after only a few months. The Japan Village Rule Alliance (Nihon sonjiha dōmei), founded in 1931 by Nagano, Tachibana, Ibaraki politician and legislator Kazami Akira (of the Kokumin dōmei, or National League), Gondō, and several others in an attempt to bring together agrarianist activists from throughout the country, is one example of just such a group. With slogans like "Overcome material culture," "Establish agrarianist culture," and "Create an autonomous society," the alliance displayed what the authorities at the time considered the characteristic ideas of "agrarianist local autonomy-ism." Organizations like the alliance sought to bring that message to the countryside, organize the farmers there, and with them somehow reshape the country along the lines described in the group's manifesto.[33]

This was easier said than done, not least because of differences of opinion among the would-be leaders of the movement. Questions about how to organize the countryside fed concerns about what the group would do if it won the support of the farmers. The alliance dissolved soon after it was formed. Part of the problem was that no two leaders shared the same vision of what ought to be done in the countryside. Gondō, for instance, reportedly did not want to pursue a political movement to further his views, whereas Tachibana and Nagano were both anxious to do so. The presence of people like Miyagi Shinichirō, an anarchist and advocate of the destruction of Japan's cities, testifies to the diversity of opinion within the agrarianist camp and also gives some idea of how hard it was to reach a consensus on the hows and the whys of a broad-based organization.

Nagano tried again after the demise of the Village Rule Alliance, this time via the Agrarianist Federation (Nōhon renmei). Formed in March 1932, the federation, like its predecessors, quickly fell victim to internal squabbling over issues such as whether or not to form an agrarianist-led political party and was defunct by May.[34] Even before its members went their separate ways, Nagano Akira was thinking about his future plans. An answer was provided by one of the activists the federation had attracted to Tokyo. Wagō Tsuneo, from just outside Nagano prefecture's Matsumoto city, was reportedly the first of the Agrarianists to speak of a petition drive.

Nagano prefecture was home to a good part of the country's silk-cocoon production, and many households also sent their daughters to work in its spinning mills. In a pattern that was repeated elsewhere, families thus lost two important sources of income when silk prices collapsed. No longer able to make a profit on their cocoons, and no longer able to count on their daughters to bring in extra cash from the factory, local farmers and their plight became matters of great concern to Wagō Tsuneo.[35] Wagō had come home to the Matsumoto area after graduating from Tokyo University (his studies there had focused on Nichiren Buddhism) and spending several years at Katō Kanji's model village in Ibaraki. Wagō combined the aggressive proselytizing of the Nichiren sect with an agrarianist bent, urging farmers to stand up and demand better treatment at the hands of the government. By the end of 1930 he was holding public rallies, and the following year he and his supporters started publication of *The Farmer* (*Hyakushō*) as a forum for their views.[36] Wagō ran for a seat in the Nagano Prefectural Assembly in 1931 on a platform that focused on farm debt, taxes, prices, and other pocketbook issues.[37] Wagō argued that only by lowering taxes and reducing debt would the average farmer be able to survive the depression.[38] "Farmland to the farmers!" "Rescue the villages from the grasp of the cities!" and "Lower debt and taxes in accordance with prices!" became rallying cries for his candidacy.

Wagō garnered twenty-four hundred votes in a race dominated by candidates from the mainstream parties—not a poor showing for a candidate who came late to the race, but not enough to win a seat.[39] Undaunted, Wagō and his supporters continued to clamor for change and expanded their contacts with activists in Tokyo. Wagō met Gondō Seikyō for the first time in the fall of 1931 and arranged for him to come to Nagano to speak directly to farmers there.[40] At their first large rally, held in Matsumoto in mid-March, Wagō first began toying publicly with the idea of a petition campaign as an organizational tool and as a lever to use against the government. Having tried and failed to change the state's lackadaisical attitude toward the countryside from within, Wagō was more than willing to see what could be done from the outside.[41]

A national petition movement began to take shape at Nagano Akira's Harajuku residence in early April 1932. Nagano brought together an unusual mix of activists, many of them veterans of the earlier agrarianist organizations. They included Wagō, Tachibana (who did not participate after the May 15 Incident), Inamura Ryūichi from the leftist Zennō in Niigata, and anarchist Miyagi Shinichirō of the Kokumin Kaizō sha.[42] (Gondo's role in the petition movement was indirect at best. He appears to have played no role in the planning of the petitions themselves, and at one point reportedly said that, under the circumstances, the petition movement itself was a bad idea.)[43] Together they settled on a name for their new organization: the Local Autonomy Farmers' Conference (Jichi nōmin kyōgikai).

One of the conference's first acts was to draft the text of a petition for farm relief[44] that included three items:

1. A three-year deferment of farm family debt
2. A fertilizer subsidy for all farmers
3. Fifty million yen in assistance for emigration to Manchuria[45]

Explanatory text accompanied the petitions when they were sent to villages. In it the conference laid out the reasoning behind each item, often citing the severity of the crisis in the countryside as proof of the need to act. Also included were comparisons between the relatively modest needs of the farmers and the huge amounts of money that the government was already distributing to big business, thus reinforcing the message to readers that the depression was not the same for everyone and that the situation in the countryside was different from that of urban, industrial Japan. Special steps were necessary if the nation's villages were to regain their strength and resume their rightful place at the center of the country's economic and cultural life.

The moratorium on debt collection, explained the text, was simply a step to prevent farm families and rural communities from breaking down; if debt collections were allowed to continue apace, the petitioners implied, there was no telling what might happen. By linking the health of the villages to that of the nation at large, the petitioners avoided any charges that self-interest had prompted their demands. Nagano and the others were also careful to find precedents for their demands in programs already in place to aid big business. As the notes accompanying the petition pointed out, in 1929 the government had agreed to defer the Kokusai Steamship Company's 29-million-yen debt for a ten-year period. For farmers to ask for "just three years" of deferment seemed reasonable in comparison.[46]

Similar arguments were offered for the other elements of the petition. Falling prices for rice and silk cocoons had left farmers with so little income that they could not buy the goods they needed to survive. Fertilizer, always a major expense for farm households, was rapidly becoming a luxury that few could afford. A vicious cycle ensued: The less fertilizer they used, the smaller their harvests and the lower their income from farming. The situation was so dire that soldiers stationed in Shanghai had been forced to take up collections of money to help out their families at home, while domestic fertilizer producers and other big companies received 150 million yen a year in subsidies from the government (or so the petitioners argued). Pointing once again to the state's willingness to bend over backward to help business while abandoning farmers to their own devices, the conference estimated that just 60 of the 150 million yen already paid to big business would be enough to give every farmer a substantial fertilizer subsidy.

The money to help people emigrate to Manchuria could also be found in the coffers of state support for business. Thirty of the 50 million yen should come from the state's subsidies for industry, argued the conference, while the other 20 million could be taken from the dividends paid by the Southern Manchurian Railway. The money would go to families willing to settle in

Manchuria; by going, they would help solve the problems of urban and rural overpopulation even as they strengthened Japan's diplomatic position.

The inspiration for these three appeals came at least in part from Wagō's earlier campaigns in the Matsumoto area. His organization had been advocating emigration for some time and had also been discussing steps to reduce the burden of farm debt. These issues clearly interested farmers. Moreover, the promise of subsidies, cash from the state, and a moratorium on the repayment of debt was a combination that was certain to have solid support in the countryside; this appeal was a factor in the conference's embrace of the petition. Getting farmers to respond to rhetoric about the benefits of local autonomy and sweeping reforms had never been easy. The depression had hurt farmers, but it had yet to cause a groundswell of interest in agrarianism. If Nagano Akira and his colleagues were ever going to reach a wider audience with their message, they first had to find a way to attract the attention of the countryside. The petitions did just that.

The practice of petitioning and making direct appeals to authorities in order to redress injustice (or simply to bring bad management to the attention of higher-ups) has a long history in rural Japan. Some of the country's more spectacular peasant revolts were linked to the failure of local administrators to heed peasant demands, as were the best-known stories of rural martyrs.[47] Japan's most famous peasant hero, Sakura Sōgorō, saved his village by presenting his appeal for help directly to the Tokugawa shōgun. He and his fellow village leaders had been ignored by local officials despite repeated attempts to draw official attention to the crisis in the countryside. Sakura's final appeal to the very top got the villagers the help they needed, even though Sakura and his wife and children were executed for having broken the rules governing the proper procedure for petitions.[48]

Less personally costly examples of interaction between ruler and ruled through written appeals can be found in the widespread use of petition boxes by domain officials during the Tokugawa period. Open to both samurai and commoners, the boxes gave a voice to people who otherwise would not have been heard by administrators. Officials paid close attention to the appeals and suggestions that appeared in the boxes and incorporated some of them into domain policy.[49]

The petition boxes disappeared soon after the Meiji government came to power, and with them most opportunities to make oneself heard by those in high office. A few formal channels did exist. One could, for example, petition the Diet. Such a petition would normally be introduced by a sitting legislator to the Petitions Committee, which would vote whether to send the petition on to the Diet. If it was sent on, the Diet itself was given the opportunity to indicate its approval of the petition; a successful petition was then forwarded to the cabinet or other government office. The state, however, was required by the Constitution only to accept the petition and was under no compulsion to act on its contents.

Despite its limited efficacy, it was not uncommon for farmers to make use of the right, especially in times of distress. In 1922 and 1923, for example, farmers used petitions in an unsuccessful bid to persuade the government to lower taxes and provide aid to the countryside. Appeals continued to be sent in small numbers throughout the rest of the decade and in the first few years of the next. The Diet session of April 1930 received three petitions having to do with problems in the countryside and farm relief. As the sense of crisis in the rural economy grew, so did the pace of petitioning. By the December 1930 session, the number had risen to 124. It is telling that the Sixty-second Diet session, which met in June 1932, soon after the appointment of the Saitō cabinet, received 407 petitions related to farm relief; the next session, later that summer, brought in almost 300.[50] Many were the direct product of the conference's efforts in Nagano.

After the organizational meeting in April 1932, Wagō and the others printed up their petitions and mailed them to supporters, who circulated them locally, collected signatures, and sent them back to Tokyo. Conference members were under a tight deadline: they needed to submit as many of the signed documents as possible to the Petitions Committee if they were to have any chance of getting a reaction out of the larger legislature, and the Diet session scheduled for early June was likely to last only a few weeks. There wasn't much time.

Local media interest helped; in Nagano prefecture the papers covered the movement from early on, and on May 3 the entire text of the three-clause petition appeared in the *Shinano mainichi shinbun*. The newspaper also kept the public informed about the schedule of the general meetings and lectures held to gather support for the petitions. Although the first series of public assemblies took place in early May, a busy time for farmers, they were all well attended and enthusiasm for the petitions ran high.[51] The reception was milder in Ibaraki, in Niigata, and in the other prefectures represented in the conference. The grassroots organizations there were not as developed as the ones in Nagano prefecture, where Wagō could count on solid support. Tachibana's group had been expected to make a strong showing in Ibaraki, but was unable to do much in the aftermath of the May 15 Incident. Local activists still made every effort to gather at least a few signatures so as to represent as many prefectures as possible.

Conference members went back and forth between their home prefectures and Tokyo, where Nagano Akira coordinated lobbying efforts. By the end of May, Wagō's group and others under the Local Autonomy Farmers' Conference umbrella had collected more than thirty thousand signatures—a very large number by petition drive standards, although conference members were still having a hard time making themselves heard in the capital. Access to the Diet was one problem, since they needed a legislator to see the petition safely through committee and on to discussion. Reaching a larger rural audience was another concern. Despite the petition's success, that almost 90 percent of the signatures came from Nagano prefecture showed that their organizational base was still narrower than they would have liked it to be.

Finding a political ally turned out to be relatively easy. Wagō worked hard to win over legislators elected from Nagano, and the others in Tokyo did the same with the politicians from their prefectures. Conference members did their best to meet with both Gotō Fumio, the newly appointed head of the Ministry of Agriculture and Forestry, and Finance Minister Takahashi. Both claimed to be too busy to see them, although they did manage to discuss their views with people like Ministry of Agriculture and Forestry Vice Minister Ishiguro Tadaatsu.[52] As it turned out, however, it was Gondō's influence that got them their strongest ally in the Diet. He helped introduce Wagō to the Seiyūkai's Takeshita Fumi (Okinawa), an admirer of Gondō.[53] Takeshita agreed to present their petitions to the Diet and do whatever was required to rally support for village relief.

Winning over the national press was harder. Despite good media coverage in Nagano prefecture, the major newspapers in Tokyo had shown little interest in the petition campaign. In an attempt to persuade editors to take them more seriously, groups of seven or eight of the conference activists in Tokyo went from one newspaper office to the next carrying bundles of the signed petitions on their backs.[54] They had little luck at first, and as of the start of the Diet session on June 1, 1932, the three-clause petition had not been discussed in the nation's most influential media.

That soon changed. The *Tōkyō asahi shinbun* began its coverage of the petition movement on June 3, in an article that described how the agrarianists had collected some thirty-two thousand signatures in sixteen different prefectures. The piece also discussed the links between the Local Autonomy Farmers' Conference and its immediate predecessors, the Japan Village Rule Alliance and the Agrarianist Federation, but did so without mentioning Tachibana or Gondō.[55] Diet member Takeshita was quoted as saying that the problems raised in the petitions were ones for the whole country and not just for the parties, and were thus worthy of careful study. Nagano was much more forthcoming:

> I came today to hand over all of the petitions. Of course, the signature collecting is continuing in some areas, so there will probably be more. The spirit of the farmers is incredible, and some regions have gone so far as to send petitions on to the Upper House. What is interesting is that in many places [people] have resolved not to cast a single vote for any Diet member who opposes us on this issue in the legislature. So while we have high hopes in the progress of the Diet, the preparations for this Extraordinary Session were insufficient and may end up adding fuel to the fire.[56]

Nagano made it clear that the petitioners were a force to be reckoned with, and one that was likely to continue playing a role in national politics. The people who signed the petitions were paying close attention to what was going on in the Diet, he pointed out, and were willing and able to hold the politicians responsible for what came next. This comment may have been as much for the benefit of the reading public as for any politicians, because any farmer who read what Nagano had to say would no doubt have been pleased to find himself talked about as part of such a powerful political force. The rest of the public was left to wonder about old images of the docile countryside and about what Nagano Akira had in mind with his talk of "feeding the fire."

By the time the agrarianists had attracted the attention of the national press, other advocates of rural reform had begun to make their presence known. On June 6—the same day that the Diet's Petitions Committee voted to consider the three-clause petitions presented by Takeshita—press coverage expanded to include detailed discussions of the various campaigns for rural relief; the agrarianists were commonly presented as one alternative, and the Northern Shinano Depression-Policy Association (Hokushin fukyō taisakukai) as another. The contrasts are interesting: Although, like the agrarianists, the members of the association hailed from Nagano prefecture, they represented not the imperiled farmer but the worried elite. Local landlords and established local leaders were prominent in the association; they expected to be taken seriously by the press and policymakers, and they were.[57] Once in the capital, they enjoyed ready access to high officials: Minister of Agriculture and Forestry Gotō Fumio, the chiefs of the ministry's Regional Bureau and the Finance Ministry's Banking Bureau, and the president of the Development Bank all met with them.

On the day they left for home, the group took time to meet with journalists from the *Tōyō keizai shimpō* in a roundtable discussion that covered both their petition and what they thought about conditions in the countryside. The magazine published the results the next week. Association members huddled as well with the three Diet members from their electoral district as well as with Kamei Kaichirō, a representative from Fukuoka. These Diet members, along with Kazami Akira and Sugiyama Motojirō, helped get their petition presented to the Diet.[58]

That petition, echoing what had been the agrarianist's refrain, placed the treatment of debt at the heart of rural recovery:

1. In consideration of current economic problems, issue an order suspending payments [of debt].
2. Reduce debt in proportion to the fall in commodity prices.
3. Reduce taxes significantly.
4. Revise the Interest Limitations Law so that loans in villages are at rates of no more than 3 percent interest a year; make it legally possible to convert old debt.
5. When losses occur as a result of the production of significant agricultural products, the government should provide guarantees.[59]

The Depression-Policy Association collected almost five thousand signatures from seventeen villages in the Chisagata, Hokusaku, and Hinashina regions of Nagano before coming to Tokyo. Though this was only a fraction of the number of signatures the agrarianists would eventually turn in, the association's impact had less to do with support for its petitions than with the dire warnings that came with them.[60] In their statements to the press and in discussions with policymakers, association spokesmen were forthright in explaining why they thought these steps were necessary. Without them, these men explained, the countryside was certain to erupt in violence. Spokesmen referred to the huge burden of debt that many families bore and to the sharp drops in income that made repayment next to impossible.[61] Existing institutions had failed them; neither the credit unions, the agricultural associations, nor any government-sponsored program had helped in any meaningful way, they complained.[62] These men shared a belief that the countryside was on the verge of revolt. In meetings with politicians and the press, they did an effective job of describing not only what had already befallen their communities but also their estimates of what might happen next. Given what they had seen back home, and given the lack of action in Tokyo, they feared the worst.[63]

The combined effect of the agrarianists' show of force and the spirited pleas for help from local elites left legislators with little room to maneuver. On the afternoon of June 6, 1932, Takeshita made his case with the Diet's Petitions Committee. With tears rolling down his cheeks, he argued for immediate acceptance of the three-clause petitions:

The impoverishment of the villages has reached the point where notice must be taken. The rapid decline in income has destroyed the very foundations of farm household life. The accumulation of debt has shaken the nucleus of everyday life. It is hard to look on this pitiful sight, and it cannot be witnessed without tears. Voices calling out for help are even now like a flood tide across the country. It is pitiful for those farmers who are caught in a life or death predicament to fall into despair. Our nation, built on farming, faces a future of unbearable sorrow. I hope you will adopt this proposal straightaway.[64]

The committee lost no time in agreeing unanimously to accept the petitions, and called on the government to seek ways to implement the proposals put forth in them. According to press accounts, it was as if "the cries of the farmers, cries squeezed from them by the difficulties in their lives," had driven the committee members to act.[65]

Yet despite growing public support for village relief and the enthusiasm of some members of the Diet, it seemed less and less likely that the sixty-second session would produce any meaningful help for the farms. The Saitō cabinet had only just come to power, and neither the new cabinet nor the parties were ready with any well-developed relief programs. The petitioners' and other proposals flowing into the Diet were too raw and sometimes too radical to make reasonable policies. As an alternative, politicians began to discuss calling a special session of the Diet committed solely to the village crisis. The agrarianists and other spokespersons for the countryside quickly seized on this idea and waited anxiously to see if it would actually happen.

The vote to approve such a special session came on June 13. "The day was muggy and hot," Nagano Akira remembered, "and the inside of the Diet chambers was so unpleasant as to be stifling, but there was no room to stand in the visitors' gallery. [People] were spilling over outside. When the bill was presented, everybody sat up and listened carefully, so as not to miss anything."[66]

Both the Seiyūkai and the Minseitō had fielded bills calling for a special session; the Minseitō urged the government to call an emergency Diet to develop policies on finances, debt, control of production and sales, and public works on behalf of both the agricultural community and small businesses. The Seiyūkai's version, which was the one eventually adopted in an unanimous vote, read:

In light of the mission of the current cabinet, and to enable the government to put into place emergency policies of appropriate economic facilities and policies to reassure the people, an Extraordinary Diet should be called quickly. Bills and budget matters to be discussed include the harmonious distribution of currency, debt arrangement in the villages and elsewhere, thorough undertaking of public works, and the control of agricultural production and other important areas of production.[67]

In a long speech interrupted repeatedly by applause, the Seiyūkai's Shimada Toshio (representing Shimane) explained the reasoning behind his party's requests. "Unless we put into practice a thorough and effective emergency relief policy," he warned, "in the future—and this may not be the distant future—one cannot say that we will not see unexpected calamities in our society. (Applause)."[68] Representatives of the other major parties indicated their support, Prime Minister Saitō followed suit, and the entire lower house voted unanimously to adopt the Seiyūkai's resolution.[69]

Thus assured that sometime within the next few months the government and the parties would meet to deal exclusively with rural relief, Nagano and the agrarianists' supporters began planning another petition campaign to build on the success of the first one. This time they were not alone; the combination of a heightened public interest in the problems of the countryside, the apparent success of the earlier petitioners, and the prospects held out by the Sixty-third Diet convinced would-be spokesmen for farmers and their communities to try to make themselves heard. What had been a trickle of proposals and pleas soon grew into a flood of petitions and petitioners, all pursuing help for the countryside.

With the Diet set to reconvene in late August, Wagō, Nagano Akira, and the others tried to make the best use of the remaining time. Their earlier successes complicated matters; the first petitions had done so well that as the group prepared to draft the next one, conference members who had earlier been willing to let Nagano and Wagō shape the content demanded more input. Thus the uneasy alliances within the conference began to fray at the edges even as the petition's content expanded from three items to five.

The new petition, instead of calling for a general moratorium on debt repayment, asked that the government defer only loans that the government itself had made. There were good reasons to take this approach. The original demands had not been specific about what sort of debt was to be deferred and could thus have been interpreted to mean that debts between individuals or from credit unions and banks would be subject to the moratorium. The new clause made it clear that only loans that came from the government were subject to deferral—a much more realistic prospect.

Also dropped were the calls for subsidies for fertilizer purchases and for emigration to Manchuria. In their place were demands for funds to pay for land development projects; for 100 yen in assistance for any rural family leaving a village, regardless of destination; and for an equivalent amount for anyone moving into a village. Wagō would elsewhere make explicit appeals to the unemployed and to urbanites to return to the villages and pursue a better life there. Wagō's brand of agrarianism made him "the opponent of the city" but left room for him to be "the friend of the city dweller." Wagō wrote, "Our brothers, the unemployed, the workers: Throw away the cities, where all is dark before you, and turn toward the sun in our blue sky!"[70]

Nagano Akira's contribution was a section of the new petition that called on the state to limit how much of a household's assets could be taken away as a result of legal seizure procedures. His goal was to ensure that farmers would never be pushed below minimum levels of access to land—or minimum levels of ownership of the basic necessities of farm life—in the aftermath of any legal procedure against them. Similarly, under Nagano's proposal tenants could not be prevented from farming land that they needed to cultivate in order to survive. Nagano went to the extra effort of having a specialist write draft legislation to this effect; Kazami Akira duly submitted it to the Diet, where it was sent to committee and shelved.[71] Nagano described these measures as an attempt to provide security to the typical farm family by guaranteeing them some minimum level of sustenance. Doing that, he said, would make the country stronger and give farmers the support they needed to carry on. Nagano believed that it would also "create, for the first time, a basis for the self-revitalization (*jiriki kōsei*) of farmers."[72]

The new five-clause petition asked for:

1. A three-year deferment on loans from the state with assistance on interest;

2. Guarantees of a farmer's right to survive through revisions in the Compulsory Process Law (Kyōsei shikkō hō);

3. Three hundred million yen in funding for land development, and an expansion in the scope of land-opening assistance;

4. Appropriate education for emigration; bonuses of 100 yen per emigrant and 100 yen per domestic relocation; and 4 *sho* [ 1 *shō* = 1.8 liters] of rice for three years for each person who returned to the farm;

5. Adjustments to salaries in accordance with the rise and fall of prices, and a revision of the salary decree.[73]

The final clause, which called for revisions in salaries in accordance with changes in commodity prices, reflected concerns about the imbalance between city and country, agriculture and industry. Although farm households had seen their incomes plummet since 1930, not everyone in the community had been in the same boat. Those in salaried positions, and especially those in official salaried positions (state and local officials, for instance, and certainly local teachers), had not been subject to the same drastic cuts in income. The conference hoped that the fifth provision in the petition would rectify the imbalance. Nagano described its importance this way:

This shows the sentiments of the nation's farmers toward those living on salaries.... There are two feelings tied up in the farmer's attitudes toward revision of the Official Salary order. First is that the various types of people in the community should lead the same type of life. That is, it is selfish to want to live with special rights or characteristics, and that only leads to the creation of bureaucrats and the *zaibatsu*. As a rule they should live with the masses and like the masses. In that sense it is a reaction to the high living that only those on salaries can enjoy. In the village, a person earning 100 yen a month has the same income as a landlord with 1,000 bales of rice in rent.

The second point is opposition to official politics. Farmers are strongly opposed, and increasingly so, to bureaucratic politics with its control over everything, and to the corruption of officials.[74]

This was in keeping with Nagano's long-held anti-bureaucratic beliefs and with his argument that supporting the costs of the central government had placed a huge burden on farmers. Note, too, that as Nagano interpreted this clause, it meant more than just cutting back on salaries to save money. In his words, it was also about equalizing standards of living, about making sure that there were no huge gaps between the rich and the poor in a single community, and about allowing each community to manage its own affairs.

By early August 1932, the conference was ready, and on August 11 it mailed out copies of the new petitions. The course of events after that was largely a repeat of those in the spring; by the end of the month, the conference had collected 38,829 signatures on the second, five-clause petition.[75] In the countryside, local rallies stirred up interest in the petitions and in the group's ideas about self-rule, while in Tokyo, Nagano lobbied bureaucrats and politicians. (During a brief stop in the Kitakata area on his way from Tokyo to Niigata in July, Nagano observed local conditions and held at least one lecture. Prefectural security officials reported that his speech had helped local supporters collect only 50 or so signatures. Home Ministry sources confirm that figure, although they note that just under 200 signatures were collected on the earlier, three-clause version of the petition.)[76] Their former ally in the Diet, Takeshita, was sick and unable to help them much, but the Kokumin dōmei's Kazami Akira took over. Kazami arranged for Nagano and Wagō to meet with the vice chairman of the Diet, which made it possible for them to present their petition to him personally.[77] The Petitions Committee voted in late August to report favorably on the petitions, and the full Diet accepted the committee's decision the next day.[78]

## The Agrarianist Legacy

After August 1932, Nagano and the members of the Local Autonomy Farmers' Conference no longer played any public role of significance in shaping rural relief. Their brief moment in the public eye had passed. Nevertheless, the petition campaign led by the conference played an important role in convincing the government to act on behalf of farmers, and to act quickly. Not only did the conference help attract the public's attention to conditions in the countryside, but its specific demands helped prompt other organizations to offer solutions of their own. The call for a moratorium on debt repayments, for example, had a powerful impact on the more established farmers' organizations. The Imperial Agriculture Association and others moved quickly to offer less radical responses to the problem of farm debt. Their versions of farm relief policies were much closer to what the state eventually agreed to implement than anything the conference had called for.

Nagano Akira was neither surprised nor upset by that outcome. In a series of post-petition appearances in national journals, Nagano looked ahead to his next project and looked back on the importance of the petition movements. He was very clear about why the conference had chosen the demands that it had, and made it equally clear that the demands themselves were secondary to the conference's true goals.[79] The timing of the petition process itself had much to do with the conference's demands. The "three-year debt moratorium" came about "more than anything else because debt was the most worrisome thing for farmers at the time." The three-clause petition was drawn up early enough in the planting cycle that farmers were more worried about being able to pay for fertilizer than about selling what they grew. In 1932, many farmers didn't have enough money to buy the fertilizer they needed, so fertilizer subsidies had become part of the petition, while the funding for emigration had been included to reflect the strong interest in emigration on the part of farmers in the Nagano and Tōhoku regions.[80]

By the time the second, five-clause petition was ready for distribution, farmers were further along in the yearly crop cycle. The season for fertilizer use had passed, and fertilizer subsidies were no longer of immediate interest. There was growing concern about instability in Manchuria, so the conference decided to play it down in favor of more general emigration assistance.[81] The call to revise official salaries, explained Nagano, had to do with how farmers felt about the salaried class and with the need to adjust officials' standard of living to levels that were equivalent to those of the non-salaried members of their communities.

Nagano tried to make it clear that he and his colleagues neither expected nor really wanted to have the petition's demands to become actual policy. The two bills they drafted and had Kazami Akira submit to the Diet—revisions of the Civil Suit and Tax Collection laws—were the group's only venture into concrete policymaking. The petitions themselves were supposed to stimulate discussion in the Diet, attract attention, and help the conference win support in the countryside. Even the moratorium on debt repayments, wrote Nagano, was questionable as an actual policy. "If it had been put into effect, there is room for thought about whether or not its effects would have been beneficial to the general farm family," he maintained, and continued, "Thus anyone who considers these three clauses as actual plans for action is mistaken, given what we intended."[82]

According to Nagano, the petition drives had two goals. The first was to bring the villagers together, to unite them in defense of their communities, and to make them aware of their own power.[83] The petitions were a way of focusing the attention of the farmers; Nagano spoke in terms of "waking the farmers from a deep sleep." Organizers relied on the call for a debt moratorium to provide the clamor that would force the farmers to open their eyes. The second goal of the movement was to warn the government and the rest of the country about conditions in the villages. Nagano explained:

> That the villages are heavily burdened and the cities lightly so is well known. The representatives are elected with votes from the countryside and become the cat's paw of the *zaibatsu*. The institutions of speech are also subordinated to the cities and do not take notice of the villages. The villages have to pay huge amounts of interest to the financiers, commissions and handling fees to the merchants, while they sell their raw materials to industry for very little and buy back the finished goods at a high price. The promising youth of the villages are sucked in by the cities and the balance of the sexes is destroyed when young women leave the countryside. The autonomy of the village is snatched away to the center, and the burden of supporting a large number of useless officials is increased. There is no way to warn the world about the villages except through some sort of action.[84]

Writing about the same topic some thirty years later, Nagano repeated his argument that no one outside the villages had been aware of the actual conditions in the countryside prior to the spring and summer of 1932. The newspapers and the magazines wrote nothing about the problems of the farmer, he said, while the government and parties acted as if it didn't matter whether the farmers lived or died. He was sure that the petition movements had helped change all that.[85]

That much was almost certainly true. The summer of 1932 marked a watershed in the public's understanding of "the village problem." The press responded energetically not only to the various petition campaigns but also to a new sense of crisis in the countryside. On June 2, the day Nagano delivered the petitions to the Diet, the *Tōkyō asahi shinbun* began a series of almost daily articles on conditions in rural villages. The first described bleak conditions in Nagano prefecture, and the articles that followed featured reports on the northeast, on Ibaraki, Kanagawa, and elsewhere. Journalists wrote about the tenancy problem, low-interest loans, suicides, and the sale of daughters into prostitution as part of their attempt to portray rural life.[86] The *Tōkyō nichi nichi shinbun* sponsored a roundtable discussion about the village problem on June 11, a forum attended by several dozen politicians, academics, and activists, and published the contents of their wide-ranging discussion the following month as a small pamphlet entitled "What Should Be Done to Rescue the Villages?"[87] Although local papers seem to have been better at covering village conditions before June, it is clear that many of them put a great deal more effort into reporting on the issue after the petition campaigns became news.[88]

If one of the agrarianists' accomplishments was a degree of strategic success, in the sense that they were able to draw attention to the countryside at a time when it needed it most, they also helped set the stage for a broader reconsideration of the scope and meaning of rural reform in several other ways. The agrarianists and groups like the Northern Shinano Depression-Policy Association, for example, clearly helped shape the state's response to farm debt. Prior to May 1932, rural debt was a non-issue for public policymakers; after the petitions started coming in, finding a solution to the problems that farm debt was causing became a priority for the Ministry of Agriculture. The petitioners' role in this was both to bring to light the seriousness of the problems and to force the issue by proposing their own remedies. The idea of a sustained moratorium on debt was clearly impractical, as Nagano Akira himself recognized, but with so many farmers grasping at the possibility, what could the state do but provide some comparable remedy of its own?

## Managing Debt

The agrarianists neither invented rural debt nor proposed a particularly effective method for dealing with it. What they did do was dramatize a problem that until 1932 had been largely ignored outside the very narrow circle of those interested in farm finance. As noted earlier, estimates that summer placed farm debt at between 4.7 and 4.9 billion yen, with individual households reporting outstanding loans of anywhere between 1,590 yen (Fukushima) and 2,300 yen (Niigata), often borrowed at usurious rates. Although borrowers found new ways to pay off their debts and new ways to reach an accommodation with their creditors as long as there had been loans, the agrarianists' petition campaigns drew attention to the fact that no systematic or effective program existed to deal with those debts; farm families had no recourse against seizures of land or other assets, an event that anecdotal evidence suggests was becoming increasingly commonplace as the depression worsened.

A government study established that by late 1931 twelve prefectures sponsored efforts to reduce rural debt; private programs (run by agricultural associations, for instance) were operating in another eleven, and several other prefectures were considering putting plans into effect.[89] But even among those prefectures that actually had policies in place, only three (Osaka, Fukuoka, and Kagawa) had gone so far as to help debtors financially. The others limited their efforts to providing advice.[90] No serious initiatives were on the table to expand these programs beyond their local borders.

All that changed in the aftermath of the petition campaigns and decision to hold an Extraordinary Diet. Policies to deal with debt took center stage in planning sessions that summer, and then again during the Diet itself, and though none was as radical as the agrarianists' proposals, all offered new approaches to old problems. At the heart of what eventually were labeled "debt arrangement" (*fusai seiri*) policies was a vision of stronger rural communities, ones in which cooperative institutions worked to subvert conflicts between creditors and borrowers. This vision was most evident in the proposals put forth by the Ministry of Agriculture, but it was one the political parties and mainstream farmers' organizations endorsed as well. As a result, the tools that rural communities eventually used to deal with the problem of farm debt reflected more than an attempt to address their financial failings; debt arrangement became one element of a broader endeavor to shore up the rural economy and rural communities alike.

The actors in this part of the effort to rescue the villages were no longer outsiders, as the agrarianists had been, but regular participants in the political process. Imperial Agriculture Association spokespersons and Ministry of Agriculture bureaucrats took the lead in defining the range of possible responses to the debt crisis and in shepherding their proposals through the Diet. These initiatives shared a common, communal approach to debt arrangement but differed in how they planned to pay for it and who they thought should participate. The Imperial Agriculture Association sought very large amounts of low-interest funding but wanted it to go to a narrow range of relatively well-off borrowers. The Ministry of Agriculture, in contrast, argued in favor of a much more inclusive but less expensive plan.

The legislature was the squeaky wheel in this arrangement, refusing again and again to pass a debt arrangement bill unless it included provisions that Seiyūkai politicians in particular demanded—namely, a reasonably large spending commitment and measures to shift the burden of borrowing from local governments to other institutions. The lower house's intransigence prevented passage of the bill in its original form; the cabinet was forced to repropose a modified version in early 1933, which eventually did win approval in the Diet. Both the debt arrangement proposals themselves and the process of making them into law are interesting for what they reveal about the convergence of bureaucratic and popular views of the rural crisis and the countryside's future.

Kodaira Gonichi (1884–1976) was the Ministry of Agriculture and Forestry's leading authority on farm finance, debt, and a wide range of other economic and social issues. Kodaira was probably unique among his colleagues in his ability to make policies and write intelligently about them; he published extensively both in academic and popular journals.[91] As a graduate of the First Higher School and Tokyo University (where he took two consecutive degrees in agricultural studies and law), Kodaira came to the Ministry of Agriculture and Commerce in 1914 with a solid education and wide circle of promising friends. At university Kodaira studied tenancy issues and farm finance; his classmates included Nasu Hiroshi, later a professor at Tokyo University and an influential voice in rural policy, and Katō Kanji, whose impact on the way people felt about the countryside was also considerable. (Later in their careers, Kodaira and Nasu took to donating parts of their salaries to Katō's school.) Kodaira stayed close to the two throughout his life and also reportedly developed a friendship with Gotō Fumio on the basis of their shared university experiences.[92]

After entering government service, Kodaira filled a series of major posts before appointment to the head of the Ministry of Agriculture's important Agricultural Affairs Department in late 1931.[93] It was during his short tenure in that job (he left to run the Economic Revitalization Department in September 1932) that the Diet began deliberations on his ministry's Debt Arrangement Union bill. By that time, he and his mentor in the ministry, Ishiguro Tadaatsu, had helped draft a series of important policies for the countryside—covering everything from tenancy, rice pricing, and promotion of the industrial cooperatives—and Kodaira himself was well versed in the nuances of rural finance, having conducted his own extensive research on the topic. His recommendations can be briefly stated.[94]

Kodaira argued that there was simply too much farm debt to ever consider relying on normal channels to refinance it. Even if the state chose to provide low-interest funding, he suggested, there was every likelihood that it would end up in the hands of only a few farm families. Nor could the government be expected to come up with enough money to cover the several billion yen that seemed necessary, despite the demands of groups like the Imperial Agricultural Association that it do just that. Luckily there were alternatives to refinancing; Kodaira outlined an approach in which creditors would have to make concessions to allow borrowers to repay all or most of what was owed. Those concessions might include agreeing to a longer repayment period or lower interest rates. The borrower, for his part, would have to make every effort to correct the situation that had led to his being in so much debt and to do everything within his power to make good on his existing obligations.

Kodaira linked this emphasis on cooperation to proposals for a system of agricultural finance designed specifically for the needs of the farmer. Such a system would emphasize the importance of short- and medium-term credit and allow borrowers to take out loans using something other than land as collateral. By eliminating real estate ownership as a precondition for access to credit at reasonable interest rates, Kodaira's plan both expanded the potential pool of borrowers and reduced the risk that those farmers who did own land would lose it during hard times.[95] He also proposed that debtors and creditors together enter into debt arrangement unions to facilitate negotiations and, when necessary, to channel low-interest loans to borrowers as part of the repayment process.

Finally, Kodaira stressed that neither all debts nor all borrowers were equal. To him it was more important to do something about the debts of those households that were at greatest risk of losing their land; less vulnerable families would have lower priority. Kodaira also made it a point to differentiate between those debts that were the result of attempts to improve production and ones that went to pay for emergencies, educational expenses, ceremonial occasions, and the like. Borrowing to expand one's landholdings or to improve farming methods would likely pay for itself in time, whereas the other variety would have no effect at all on farm income. It was this latter category of debt that would become a tremendous burden on farm households and that must be given priority in management policies, he reasoned.[96]

The Ministry of Agriculture's planning for debt management began in late 1931, although no definitive steps were taken until the Sixty-second Diet.[97] While legislators were still in session, spokesmen announced that the ministry would pursue extensions on the repayment of some forms of government loans and that it planned to introduce a bill on debt arrangement unions (*fusai seiri kumiai*) to the upcoming Diet. The ministry estimated that of the roughly 6 billion yen in farm debt, only about 2.5 billion had been loaned at high interest rates, and that it was these loans that should be the target of any debt arrangement program. Kodaira's influence was clear as Gotō and other ministry officials announced their intention to request only 100 million yen in low-interest funding for the debt management unions they would create.[98]

Signs that debt management might have a hard time in the Diet were there to see as early as June 1932. A few days before the end of the sixty-second session, the Seiyūkai submitted its own bill to create debt arrangement unions, preempting the state's promise to do the same later that summer.[99] Under the provisions of the bill, the state would provide not 100 million yen in funding, as Gotō had promised, but ten times as much—a billion yen for the unions over a period of five years. These funds would flow as low-interest loans through the unions and into the hands of farmers and small businessmen, allowing them to borrow as much as 20,000 yen for those with collateral, or 2,000 yen for those without. Interestingly, one clause of the bill also allowed the union to impose a settlement on reluctant lenders that deferred debt for three years and established a thirty-year repayment plan at 5 percent annual interest.[100]

The Seiyūkai proposal was thus far more expensive and potentially coercive than the one that Gotō had fielded. It was also opposed by the Minseitō, the minority party, which argued that the bill left too much up in the air (who precisely was eligible to join, which debts were subject to negotiation and refinancing and which were not) and that it came too late in the session to make it through the upper house and into law and might thus cause panic among creditors.[101] The Seiyūkai went ahead with the bill anyway and, as predicted, saw it die in the upper house when the session ended.

Even so, the Seiyūkai was effectively on record as supporting not only a debt arrangement policy but one that would send very large sums of low-interest credit to the countryside. There was much there for farmers to be hopeful about.

The Imperial Agricultural Association, for its part, valued both the state's apparent willingness to do something about debt and the Seiyūkai's goal of spending large amounts of the government's money on it. Along with the National Association of Mayors of Towns and Villages and the industrial cooperatives, the Imperial Agricultural Association had in 1930, and then again in 1931, repeatedly and unsuccessfully presented debt arrangement plans to the Minseitō government. "Arrangement" as these organizations understood it consisted of methods to help debtors refinance or renegotiate the terms of existing loans. To make the whole process easier, debt arrangement proposals focused on credit unions, the local agricultural association, or another community-level organization that could provide support, counseling, and money to those involved. Households and villages would draft debt repayment plans based on careful surveys of outstanding loans, and in at least one proposal a Farm Household Debt-Arrangement Planning Committee, staffed by local leaders, would oversee the implementation of those plans. By mid-summer the Imperial Agricultural Association also suggested ordering the Development Bank and the Agriculture and Industrial Bank to ease up on repayment and interest conditions on its loans. These institutions were important sources of credit to local governments and respectable rural borrowers, which explains the association's interest.[102]

The resolution of debt problems would thus involve the farming community to the greatest extent possible; every effort would be made to prevent divisive and disruptive conflicts between debtors and creditors, while simultaneously ensuring that private creditors were paid back. The local credit union—and, in some instances, cooperative associations set up specifically to deal with outstanding loans (i.e., debt arrangement unions)—would be responsible for bringing the two sides together, drafting repayment plans, obtaining low-interest loans for those who needed them, and overseeing the repayment process.[103] The union alternative was especially attractive to the local agricultural associations, which unlike local industrial cooperatives could not oversee funding or credit for farmers.

The Imperial Agricultural Association's vision of debt unions was a narrow one, however, and unlike the agrarianists' moratorium or the state's proposals, its policies were clearly designed to rescue creditors, not borrowers. The association's original conception of the unions was one in which members borrowed money at low interest rates from the state to pay back existing loans; the original creditor was thus assured of complete repayment while the state and the debt union assumed liability for any new borrowing.[104] The borrower was still in debt for as much as before, only it would be the government coming to collect and not the local lender. Under the original plan, union membership would also have been limited to those farmers with enough collateral to make them safe credit risks; tenants and many others would be excluded.

Although the Imperial Agricultural Association had some success in promoting local attempts at debt arrangement on a trial basis, there were neither government funds available specifically for that purpose nor legal protection for anything like a "debt arrangement union." Unfortunately for those in need of assistance, neither the state nor the parties had shown any consistent signs of addressing the debt problem before 1932.[105] That, of course, changed once the petition movements got under way and the national association, by then under considerable criticism for its failure to act, redoubled its efforts to shape debt management policy.[106]

Lobbying began in earnest in June 1932 and coincided with a series of scheduled conferences of local and national association leaders. Resolutions and policy outlines discussed at these meetings became the basis for parallel discussions at the local level, where chapters were urged to ratify proposals for debt management (similar to those outlined above) and to make their wishes known to their representatives in the Diet. In Fukushima, for example, where communities had little involvement with the agrarianist-led petition movements, interest in the Imperial Agricultural Association's proposals ran high.[107] The prefectural agricultural association, county associations, and village associations all held meetings to review policy guidelines.[108]

Through these sessions, farmers were kept up to date on the progress of events in Tokyo and informed about the national organization's stance on key issues.[109] Some local groups, like the 5,500-member Nankō Agricultural Association, eventually sent representatives to Tokyo to meet with policymakers; two members of the chapter traveled to the capital in June 1932 to make a direct appeal to Fukushima's representatives in the Diet. "We hope to move quickly to rebuild the economy of the farm household," they wrote, "under the protection of the [Debt Arrangement Union Law]."[110] In making their appeal, this group explicitly contrasted themselves with advocates of a moratorium on repayment of farm household debts. They noted that "although we have recently heard talk of a village debt moratorium, we are worried that the moratorium will not stop with the villages but will bring about the collapse of the entire financial structure of the nation." Theirs was clearly a better alternative.[111]

Efforts to persuade legislators to implement debt management continued throughout the summer. In early July, representatives of the prefecture's local agricultural associations met with Okada Atsushi, and at various times the Seiyūkai and Minseitō offices, Minister of Agriculture and Forestry Gotō, the Home Minister, and Prime Minister Saitō himself received association delegations.[112] Politicians like the Seiyūkai's Hatta Sōkichi (Fukushima) attended association conferences and went with delegates on some of their visits, while bureaucrats from the Ministry of Agriculture and Forestry, Kodaira Gonichi prominent among them, also held discussions with association representatives over the summer.[113]

Lobbying efforts redoubled once the Sixty-third Diet got under way. The Imperial Agricultural Association's general meeting opened in Tokyo just as the session was beginning, and the two thousand members in attendance were given specific instructions about how best to further their agenda with legislators. Politicians persuaded to agree with the association's proposals were given badges to wear indicating their support for the countryside, while small groups of delegates pushed for bills of particular concern to the association. One group, for instance, met repeatedly with the Special Subcommittee on Debt Arrangement, while others pressed for association causes with high officials and party leaders.[114]

Policymakers were thus confronted with reasonably consistent sets of requests for help with debt arrangement that summer. The industrial cooperatives and the National Association of Mayors of Towns and Villages pursued debt arrangement policies of their own, but they were generally similar to Imperial Agricultural Association proposals in their emphasis on repayment, limited deferrals, and the need for a form of local union to oversee the management process.[115] The appeal of such proposals to policymakers should be clear: Not only did they offer an alternative to the agrarianists' moratorium, but they did so with the promise of widespread popular support. The groups of farmers waiting outside Diet offices and in ministry hallways testified to the desire for a specific type of relief, one that was far more palatable than an outright end to debt repayment. Of course, all their travels would have been for naught had policymakers been opposed to the framework that the association and other organizations proposed or to its likely outcomes. As proposals for debt management policies made their way toward Diet passage, though, it was soon clear that key bureaucrats shared many of the association's goals for rural reform.

Four bills dealing either directly or indirectly with debt were proposed by the government during the Sixty-third Diet. Of these, the Law for Special Financing of the Industrial Cooperative Central Bank and Indemnification for Losses and the Law for Credit on Immovables and Indemnification for Losses were both measures to assist the Industrial Cooperative Central Bank and other official financial institutions. The Deposit Bureau was to provide 100 million yen to the Central Bank and up to 500 million yen to other financial institutions to free up capital that would otherwise remain locked up in real estate. To further assist both institutions and to ensure that the funds made it back into circulation, the state would cover part of any losses on those loans.[116]

Two other bills dealt more directly with the problems of rural debt. One, the Justice Ministry's Monetary Claims Temporary Conciliation Law (Kinsen saimu rinji chōtei hōan), provided a framework for negotiations between debtors and creditors. The law continued a pattern, begun with the 1924 Farm Tenancy Conciliation Law, of moving first contentious social issues and eventually all civil conflict out of the realm of litigation and into state-mandated mediated settlements.[117] Debt seemed especially well suited to such an undertaking. Like tenancy, debt was a threat to social stability, and as with tenant-landlord disputes, it was possible to invoke a "tradition" of social harmony in order to make conciliation seem reasonable.

The basic provisions of the law allowed either creditors or debtors to appeal to local courts to oversee negotiations involving debts of up to 1,000 yen, provided that the loans had been made before the end of July 1932. Once asked, the court could step into the negotiation process and, if necessary, issue a compulsory settlement. However, banks and other state-supervised lending institutions could claim exemption from a compulsory settlement if "there was fear of damage to the structure of that business."[118]

The proposed law was thus somewhat vague about what types of debt might be covered and what types would not be, a failing legislators seized on as soon as the bill was introduced. Concerned also about the 1,000-yen limit on the debts that the law addressed, the Seiyūkai-controlled committee responsible for vetting the bill modified it, eliminating the upper limit on the law's scope and clarifying the bill's language in other areas. The upper house promptly removed those amendments, returning the bill to its original language, and sent it back to the lower house. The two houses would face a similar situation when it came time to deal with the Debt Arrangement Union Law, but in this instance the lower house elected to take the path of least resistance and passed the Monetary Claims Temporary Conciliation Law, with all the original limitations in place, on September 7, 1932.[119]

The second of the rural debt laws, the Farm Village Debt Arrangement Union Law (Nōson fusai seiri kumiai hōan), had a much more complicated passage. In his introductory remarks to the Diet, Agriculture and Forestry Minister Gotō stressed that the Debt Arrangement Union bill was a key element in the state's self-revitalization program and one more way to foster the spirit of neighborly cooperation in rural communities. The debt unions his ministry proposed, Gotō said, "are organized with the people who live in the hamlet . . . to arrange their debt and to plan for their economic recovery."[120]

The bill promised to help farmers draw up plans for debt repayments; to help borrowers and lenders negotiate amounts owed, interest rates, repayment periods, and methods of repayment; and to provide funds to union members.[121] The unions themselves were to be organized at the hamlet level; only in special cases would village-wide unions be permitted. The bill also included a provision for appeals to the village's Debt Arrangement Committee, which could be asked to arbitrate when negotiations within the union were unsuccessful.

Kodaira's influence is clear, since the bill envisioned a more inclusive and long-term approach to debt management than had any farm organizations so far. Rather than just flood the countryside with low-interest loans bound for agricultural association or industrial cooperative members, Kodaira wanted to ensure that the solution to the debt problem was less dependent on the state, more likely to leave financially sound households in its wake, and available to more than just a few members of the farming community. Thus he insisted that unions include both sides of the credit equation, thus ensuring a community-wide commitment to a resolution of the debt problem. Limiting membership to debtors, as the farming organizations and the parties were content to do, would only serve to further marginalize those households.

It was clear from what was not mentioned in the bill that funding would take a back seat to the union's other activities. Planning, negotiations, and the pursuit of cooperative solutions at the hamlet level were obviously preferred to more borrowing. Unfortunately for Agriculture and Forestry Minister Gotō, who had to field legislators' questions in the Diet, not everyone shared his and Kodaira's vision of what was best for the villages. The problem lay not in relying on what Gotō called the "spirit of mutual assistance" as in the logistics of doing so. Legislators quickly realized that the bill had almost nothing to say about where funding was going to come from, how much would be available, or how it would be used. When it was clear that Gotō, too, had nothing to say on the issue, legislators took it upon themselves to make the changes they thought necessary.

Miyasaki Hajime (Seiyūkai, Saitama) responded to Gotō's opening statements with his own lament. He suggested that the state might have been deceived by prefectural governors who painted rosy pictures of conditions in the countryside when in fact people were desperate. Had they been able to, many of those people would have come to Tokyo and told the Diet how things really were, Miyasaki said. Even the petition groups were under considerable pressure (from the police), all of which suggested that the "truth" about the situation in the countryside had not yet been heard. "Gentlemen," Miyasaki exclaimed, "the night before the storm is very quiet, but I beg each of you to consider the terrible events that will befall this great country if nothing is done, if those of us in the government give no consideration to the danger."[122]

Miyasaki's concern stemmed from his feeling that the government's proposal didn't do enough for the villages. He explained that although he agreed with the spirit of the bill, he had doubts about its ability to accomplish what it was supposed to. The key points of Miyasaki's criticism, and the crux of the ensuing struggle between the Seiyūkai and the state, were these: How much money would the state provide to the unions, and where would it come from? The Seiyūkai, as Miyasaki made clear, wanted Gotō and the government to accept at least two major changes to the original conception of the bill. First, the party wanted the state to create a centralized financial body to handle the funding process for the unions. Second, the Seiyūkai was anxious to hear a firm figure for the amount of funding available to the unions. No one had a definite idea about how much would be necessary, but legislators could be counted on to decide how much was too little.

There was little Gotō could do to address these concerns. He responded that although he expected funding to come from the Deposit Bureau, he couldn't be sure of the amount. Nor was the ministry considering the creation of a separate funding institution for the unions, Gotō explained, while nevertheless insisting that he had complete confidence in the measure as it stood. Miyasaki was not at all satisfied with the minister's responses and drove home his and his party's reluctance to follow the state's lead. He asked Gotō:

Did you hear why we called an Extraordinary Session? We called the third Extraordinary Session of the Diet because we couldn't wait until this winter. Even though you've produced that bill, it is just a bill, and you haven't thought about how much money to provide. What will that accomplish? What can you do about the destitution of the farmers with something as stupid as that? The government doesn't understand what this crisis means, and I have no further questions to pose.[123]

Once the bill was sent to committee, the Seiyūkai's legislators were free to make any changes they saw fit. The party had already introduced its own Debt Arrangement Union Central Treasury Law, which they incorporated into the government's proposal, and Fukushima's Sukegawa Keishirō proposed the other amendments eventually adopted by the committee. They began by renaming the state's bill and didn't stop until the new version of the law included the items they thought the original draft had lacked. (The original bill had sixteen clauses, the amended one, thirty-four.)

Major changes included the division of the unions into three types: one whose members had unlimited responsibility for the debts of the union, one that only required limited responsibility, and a secured (hoshō) responsibility union.[124] The advantage of a limited-liability option to those with assets at risk was clear: they could lose only as much as they chose to invest in the union.[125] On the key issue of the amount of funding that would be available to the unions, the Seiyūkai revisions were specific. A central financial treasury would be created to assist the debt unions by providing them with the loans needed to arrange member debt. The treasury would have the ability to issue up to 600 million yen in bonds and lottery tickets.[126] This was apparently enough money to reassure Seiyūkai legislators that union members who wanted to borrow money would be able to do so.

In his report to the Diet, committee chairman Oguchi Kiroku (a veteran Seiyūkai politician known for his financial acumen) summed up the key points discussed by the committee. On the issues of the source and amount of funding to be provided to the unions, he noted that, when questioned, the government's spokesmen had been able to reply only that the Deposit Bureau would provide low-interest funds without citing a specific amount. Takahashi himself had been asked to appear before the committee, but even he could only repeat what the committee already knew—that the government intended the Deposit Bureau to come up with funding.[127] There just hadn't been enough time for negotiations with other ministries on the amount, and until there was, no one would be able to give an honest answer to the question. The government's explanations left many committee members unsatisfied.[128]

When the speeches were over, the Seiyūkai-controlled lower house voted to amend the bill along the lines proposed by Sukegawa. The Debt Arrangement Union bill was then sent on to the upper house, where the peers promptly removed all of the Seiyūkai's amendments and returned the bill, now identical to the government's original draft, to the lower house. The two houses came together in joint committee meetings to try to resolve their differences, but with no success. The bill in its Seiyūkai-amended form was sent once again to the upper house, where the peers treated it exactly as they had the first time. When the session ended in mid-September, Diet members left the capital without a debt union bill to show for their efforts.

There were a number of factors at work in this dispute. Inter-ministerial fighting had prevented the Ministry of Agriculture and Forestry from fielding a more fully developed funding proposal.[129] Gotō's statements on behalf of the government suggest that while the bureaucrats expected funds to be available to the unions, he had been unable to get a commitment from the Finance Ministry. The Seiyūkai, for its part, wanted to be sure that someone other than its rural supporters would bear the brunt of financing the unions. As long as the responsibility for funding remained local and not with the state or a central treasury, it was doubtful that people with assets would participate in an organization that put what they owned at risk. This may also explain the committee's decision to add limited-liability unions to the bill—unions that might be more attractive to the upper echelons of the community.

The Seiyūkai and the Ministry of Agriculture (and the Minseitō) were clearly far apart on a number of issues. The Seiyūkai, as had been its wont, pursued a spending-based solution to the debt crisis, one that was willing to use one type of debt (the government's) to fight another (the average citizen's). The Minseitō and the government were much less willing to put a price tag on their support for debt relief, and less willing still to create another financial institution to oversee the process. With the Ministry of Agriculture and Forestry and the Finance Ministry at odds over spending, it is unlikely that Gotō would risk trying to win support for such an institution, knowing that Finance Ministry bureaucrats would strongly oppose the creation of any financial body not under their control. The best Gotō could do was present a vague bill and hope to fill in the blanks after it passed. When that gambit failed, the Ministry of Agriculture and Forestry began to weave parts of the failed debt union program into the newborn self-revitalization campaign and to prepare for another round of debate in the Diet.

The state's failure to pass a debt arrangement measure was definitely a setback to the countryside's recovery, one that the Ministry of Agriculture tried to correct at the earliest possible opportunity. By early January 1933, ministry planners had a draft in hand that they were ready to share with the rest of the government, although not yet with the Diet. Their new proposal addressed some of the issues raised by the Seiyūkai and also established clear funding levels and sources. The ministry proposed that a total of 300 million yen in state low-interest funds be made available to the debt unions over a five-year period (with funding in the first year to reach 60 million yen).[130] The money would be channeled to the unions through prefectural governments. The problem this time was less with the Seiyūkai than with the Ministry of Finance, and with Finance Minister Takahashi Korekiyo in particular. Gotō took a draft to Takahashi on January 13 for consultation, but Takahashi was emphatic in his opposition to any plan that made the state explicitly responsible for private debts. Even President Hoover, noted Takahashi, preferred to deal with debt through compromise and extending the period of repayment. If Hoover hadn't seen the need to pay for other people's debts, why would Japan? Takahashi commented to reporters:

Where is there a country where someone gets compensation from the government after a loan is due? If someone is having difficulty with debt, people around should help.... Unless it is done in the manner of the so-called self-revitalization, [by] extending the repayment period, or compromising so that both creditors and debtors benefit, it will be worthless.[131]

Other setbacks followed. In a meeting on January 23, 1933, the Finance Ministry made it clear that the Deposit Bureau was unable to provide all of the 300 million yen in loans that the Ministry of Agriculture and Forestry had sought, and that it opposed the idea of additional state bonds to close the gap. Instead, the Finance Ministry proposed making the prefectural governments responsible for the loans, thus shifting the burden from the central government to those regions that pursued debt policies most aggressively. The catch, of course, was that those regions most in need of debt adjustment would likely be those least able to raise more loans.[132]

The Home Ministry had its own suggestions, including provisions for the prefectures to split losses with the central government (and thus avoid crippling burdens if loan losses exceeded 30 million yen), for Deposit Bureau loans to bypass prefectural offices and go directly to unions (another measure to protect the prefectures from potential bad loans), and for the prefectures to establish offices to supervise the unions.[133] The Home Ministry's constituency included prefectural governments, and it was unwilling to further burden their already shaky financial systems. Home Minister Yamamoto reportedly shared Takahashi's belief that the state need not intervene to assist in the arrangement of privately held debt.[134]

The three-way deadlock lasted for more than a month, while Gotō tried to fend off questions in the Diet about the government's failure to field a bill.[135] In early March, Saitō himself stepped in and chaired a meeting attended by Takahashi, Home Minister Yamamoto, Gotō, and the head of the Legislative Bureau. The compromise solution proposed during this meeting was of the "Don't raise the bridge, lower the river" variety. Because the Finance Ministry wouldn't budge on its upper limit of 30 million yen in loan guarantees, and because the Home Ministry insisted on limiting the potential risk to local finances of those losses, the only viable solution was to lower the amount of money that would be loaned. A smaller loan package meant that the ratio of loans to loan guarantees was much lower, thus addressing the worries of the Home and Finance Ministries. That the political solution to the problem was not necessarily the most practical or the most beneficial to farmers goes without saying, but the compromise proved acceptable to all concerned.

The Farm Village Debt Arrangement Union bill that was sent to the Diet on March 11, 1933, featured funding levels of 200 million yen in loans over four years and a funding route that began with the Finance Ministry's Deposit Bureau, flowed through the prefectural government to towns and villages, and finally arrived at local debt arrangement unions. The burden of defaulted loans would be shared among the state, prefecture, and local community in a ratio of 2:1:1.[136] The new government proposal also incorporated at least some of the revisions demanded by the Seiyūkai, including a clause that allowed one union member to borrow money via the union to purchase land being sold by another member for the purpose of debt arrangement. Two types of unions—unlimited responsibility and secured (hoshō) responsibility—were to be permitted, but no attempt was made to create a central treasury.[137]

The bill had a number of developments in its favor. It came very late in the session, which left representatives little time to haggle or to build a consensus on an alternative proposal. During the last session it must have been in the back of legislators' minds that, as important as the bill was, they would have another shot at it later in the year. The Diet and the government no longer had that luxury; once the regular session closed, it was not likely that another emergency session would be called. In addition, the government had met several of the key demands of the parties.

Finally, there was the knowledge that Gotō had struggled hard for the concessions he had won from the Home and Finance Ministries, a process that had been covered thoroughly in the newspapers. In the face of the Finance Ministry's strong resistance to demands for more money, few Diet members could reasonably expect to get more for the bill than had Gotō. As Nishikata Toshima (Seiyūkai, Yamagata) said in his statement of reluctant support for the bill, it was better to have something than nothing.[138] The bill passed both houses without amendment and became law on March 29, 1933.

Public commentary after the bill passed reflected some of the same concerns that had been raised in the Diet. An article in the *Tōkyō asahi shinbun*, for example, featured some simple calculations comparing what the government had said farmers owed and the resources the new policy would bring to bear on the problem. It pointed out that a 1932 Ministry of Agriculture and Forestry survey had estimated village debt at 4.5 billion yen. The state had assumed that of the twelve thousand villages in Japan, half were farming communities in need of debt arrangement, and that those six thousand communities would be the main target of the debt arrangement program. On a yearly basis each community could expect, on average, only 6,600 yen in low-interest loans, although the survey suggested that the combined debt of the residents of each of those villages was 750,000 yen. "One can only say," concluded the article, that the new policy was little better than "administering eye drops from the second floor."[139]

## Debt Arrangement in Practice

As a practical matter, the critics were right: the debt arrangement unions proved neither popular nor effective. Ministry planners had predicted that twenty-five thousand unions would be created three years after the law's inception. By the end of January 1939, almost six years after the law went into effect, farmers had formed fewer than nine thousand unions and had borrowed less than a quarter of the hard-won 200 million yen in government loans. The unions' 245,000 members represented only about 4 percent of the farm population, and the 280 million yen that had been adjusted by then accounted for only 7 percent of total farm debt.[140] Farmers offered a long list of reasons they didn't rush to make use of debt arrangement: Complicated and time-consuming bureaucratic procedures deterred some, as did a general reluctance on the part of many borrowers and creditors to make private financial matters public.

Ministry of Agriculture and Forestry bureaucrats thought debt arrangement would work as follows. Debtors would first develop a repayment and economic recovery plan under the union's guidance, after which the union would mediate between the debtor, now with a plan in hand to strengthen his position, and the creditor. The final step was for the union to obtain the loans necessary to support the negotiations. As laid out by the ministry, "According to this system, the special funding [low-interest loans from the Deposit Bureau] is not to be loaned for the purpose of replacing the entire debt amount, but will be loaned to make the conditions for negotiations of the terms of the debt easier."[141] The best scenario was one in which no loans at all would be necessary, although the bureaucrats admitted that in some cases the union might have to use the special funding to provide money up front before a creditor would consent to negotiations.[142]

Debt unions required full community participation to work:

If you're sick, you cannot be made well relying on your own strength. When someone is sick in your family, is there anyone who says that the reason you are sick is that you are unhealthy, that it is your fault, and that you should heal yourself? The hamlet is one big family. The village and the nation, too, are one big family. It would be better if those who didn't understand this weren't in the community. The more people there are in difficulty because of debt in a community, the more they add to the material and spiritual burden of those who are not that way. Thus the revitalization of the hamlet ought to be everyone's responsibility. But that isn't all that should be done by everyone. Truly, debt liquidation is also done by the whole hamlet.[143]

That the debt arrangement process was not an end in itself was something that Kodaira repeated again and again. Managing debt was only a part of the economic redevelopment of the village. The burden of debt in many communities was so large that repayment of the principal had become impossible and interest payments alone were enough to consume whatever surplus a farm family might generate.

Kodaira cited one example of a family with 1,000 yen in loans paying 12 percent interest on what was owed. The family owned a small amount of paddy land and had used the land as security to take out the loan. Their yearly surplus income was 120 yen, which meant that, after interest payments, they would have nothing remaining to repay the principal. Kodaira proposed that the family obtain an interest reduction down to 10 percent and use the paddy as security for another loan, this one from the debt arrangement union, for 330 yen (one-third the amount of the original debt, the maximum amount the union could loan). There would be no interest due on the loan from the union for the first three years. The money from that loan would be paid to the creditor, thus reducing that debt to 670 yen. While the total debt was still 1,000 yen, the reduction in the interest rate meant that total yearly payments would be less, and that at the end of the repayment period the debtor would have paid out considerably less (1,542.98 yen under the new arrangement, compared to 1,660 if nothing had changed). With careful planning, Kodaira estimated that at the end of five years the family would have saved more than 100 yen, and at the end of ten years, when they made their final payment on the original loan, almost 350. By the time the low-interest loan was paid off at the end of seventeen years, the family could have as much as 1,279 yen in savings.[144]

Although one role of the debt arrangement process was to ensure that as many people as possible paid their debts, Kodaira and others went out of their way to emphasize that the goal was not to put money in the pockets of creditors but to limit the effects of debt on farmers. As economic revitalization planning took hold, farmers could expect to boost their income, or at least reduce their expenditures. For the many farmers who were in serious debt, adjustment was the only reasonable way to hold on to as much of this increase as possible.

As reasonable as this sounds, the debt unions were not as popular as the government had hoped. By the end of 1936, only 4,500 unions in 1,651 villages had been formed throughout Japan, and only a fraction of the allocated funding was on its way to union members.¹⁴⁵ As noted above, the situation improved only marginally over the next few years. In Sekishiba, organized attempts to do something about local debt were discussed early in the depression years, but there is little evidence that much came of them. It took until 1937 for the village to set up an official Debt Arrangement Committee, although it had selected nominees for one as early as 1932. By the end of the decade, only one hamlet in the whole village (Furu) had gone so far as to establish a Debt Arrangement Union. Sekishiba was one of the many villages that put much more energy into boosting income (and cutting costs) than into taking care of old loans.

As Kodaira admitted in 1937, the laws dealing with debt arrangement had not been fully understood. "Looking at these [results], and at popular opinion," Kodaira and Furuse Denzō, a leading figure in the industrial cooperatives, wrote, "one cannot avoid the criticism that the system's results have been insignificant."¹⁴⁶ There was plenty of blame to go around. The application process was widely acknowledged to be difficult, and funding was often hard to come by; local communities were unwilling or unable to take on the extra risk that funding entailed, and reports of creditors interfering with the arrangement process were not uncommon.

At a 1939 meeting about debt arrangement, a farmer from Miyagi prefecture described his experience trying to establish a debt union in his fifteen-person hamlet. Droughts in 1918 and 1919 and low prices in the early Shōwa period, explained Hoshi Tozaburō, had left him and his neighbors deeply in debt. Their hamlet was known as the most diligent in the village and was the first in the area to try to set up a debt union. The village officials did not know what they were supposed to do and were of no help. Hoshi and others went to the nearest village with a debt union they could find to learn how to set one up. Although it seemed very difficult, Hoshi and his neighbors wrote out economic revitalization and debt repayment plans and sent them via the village administration to the prefectural government for approval. After some corrections, they were granted permission to form a union.

Their troubles had just begun, however, for when they applied for funding from the Deposit Bureau, they were told that because the village owed back taxes, the bureau would not release funds to them. Hoshi continued:

To put it bluntly, the reason for the Deposit Bureau's policies is that they have never had the unpleasant experience of chewing *tarako* root or eating *daikon* leaf soup. We were in great difficulty, and I felt that if we couldn't pay back our debts we weren't really men. The government's plan was to loan money to make it possible to repay debt, and I wanted to borrow some and asked to do so, but contrary to what I expected, I was terribly disappointed. I went to see the head of the village and said to him, "The reason the Deposit Bureau won't loan us any money is that you didn't make enough of an effort. Can't you talk to them or something?" But he owns 20 *chō* of land and had never eaten a *tarako* root himself, so he wasn't very enthusiastic. (Laughter.) Boy, were we in trouble.[147]

Forming and funding a union were no simple matters. Local officials sometimes lacked the know-how or enthusiasm, while officials at the state and prefectural levels, where the money came from, found that regulations made it hard to lend to the communities in greatest need. In the example described by Hoshi, most of the money owed by union members had been borrowed from banks, primarily the Hypothec Bank; negotiating with institutions over debt was notoriously difficult. Union members had originally intended to borrow 9,800 yen from the Deposit Bureau, but it wasn't until late in the summer of 1938 that they were able to borrow a smaller amount, not from the Deposit Bureau but from the Industrial Cooperative Central Treasury.[148] The union also applied for, and received, owner-cultivator funding to buy some land that they had been farming cooperatively.

The difficulties faced by this small group of farmers may help explain why the program did not perform as well as the government had hoped. For all those who stuck with it, as Hoshi and his neighbors did, there must have been many others who did not. Yet it is worth noting the extent to which the state's programs appealed to many in the agricultural community. Farmers at the lower end of the economic ladder were well aware of the options available to them and looked to the state's programs as potential solutions to at least some of their problems. To access the full benefits of these programs, they pushed local authorities where they could and, as Hoshi pointed out, recognized that the points of views of the village elite and the central government were very different from their own.

## Conclusions

Debt arrangement's shortcomings aside, several aspects of the policy and the process that created it stand out. On the one hand, the state was clearly reacting to the upsurge in public criticism and organized protest around the issue of farm debt when it decided to go ahead with a national program of debt arrangement. On the other hand, this was clearly not a case of top-down policymaking: As is even more evident in the discussion ahead of the Economic Revitalization Campaign, the boundaries between state and what might be thought of as popular initiatives were blurred where depression-era relief policy was concerned. Actors and organizations other than bureaucrats and political parties played key roles in shaping relief policy. As far as the Imperial Agricultural Association was from representing the entire countryside, its roots in rural communities were deep and wide, allowing it to claim a legitimacy that few others could match.

That so many organizations developed agendas quite similar to those pursued by the association lends credence to the idea that there was widespread if sometimes vicarious participation in the policymaking process that summer. Not many farmers went to Tokyo to meet with the prime minister, but a great many made their hopes known in other guises—as signatures on a petition, votes for or against particular policies, or simply as an audience member in the many local rallies held to consider rural relief. By the time debt arrangement took form as legislation, it had in many ways become the policy of choice by and for those who had joined the debates over relief.

That debt arrangement looked to the community, and to the hamlet in particular, as the starting place for financial rebirth is interesting. The introduction of another layer of organization to an already highly organized social landscape may seem redundant, but the choice seems to have been deliberate. As it would with the Economic Revitalization Campaign, the Ministry of Agriculture and Forestry was reaching out to farmers by reaching around existing institutions like the agricultural associations. Yesterday's countryside was being modified, tentatively, with the introduction of new structures and new approaches to problems like rural debt. Placing the debt unions at the hamlet level and invoking practices of mutual assistance, as Gotō did, was at once a practical step and a symbolic one. It made sense to organize around the hamlet, since it was there that many of the social and economic relationships in farming communities originated, but it also went against the grain of the state's (and particularly the Home Ministry's) approach to the countryside.

Ever since the pursuit of self-government had begun, the practice had been to elevate the village above the hamlet, decrying the hamlet as a haven of parochial behavior and backward belief. The Ministry of Agriculture's approach turned that judgment on its head, naming the hamlet as the key to social stability and economic recovery. At the same time, neither Kodaira nor other policymakers involved envisioned this as a step backward toward a more harmonious past, but rather as a rational step forward toward a modern future. It was possible, they implied, to bring the rhetoric of mutual assistance together with the mundane realities of long-term, low-interest loans and make them work.

To farm debt, the agrarianists and other petitioners eventually added other concerns: emigration, the need to provide minimum standards of land and property for farmers, and, of course, the pursuit of "self-revitalization." Each issue pointed to the countryside's inability to sustain itself on its current course. There seemed no denying that financial chaos, a wide and growing gap between the standards of living in city and country, and the potential for social unrest were endemic in rural communities. Even taken separately, these were problems that offered no quick solutions; taken together, as the agrarianists implied must be the case, it was hard to imagine what resolution might be possible. Nagano Akira and like-minded activists offered what was at best an unlikely scenario—that of fully autonomous villages in a drastically reconstructed economic and political landscape. Few in the countryside, and fewer still among policymakers, were willing to countenance such a radical vision of the future of the countryside.

What emerged in its place was a set of policies and ideas about rural Japan that embraced at least the vision of the re-created community, one that was better led, stronger economically, culturally vibrant, and free from strife. In the months between the decision to convene an extraordinary session of the legislature and the first day of Diet deliberations, policymakers and rural activists gradually transformed the rhetoric of rural relief into something more concrete. This chapter has traced the rise of one of relief's three key components: For all its shortcomings, debt arrangement was an important part of the recovery process in many communities, as later chapters discuss. Chapters 5 and 6 explore in more detail the discourse of relief as reflected in the creation of relief's remaining parts: emergency public works and loan programs, and the Economic Revitalization Campaign.

# 5 Crafting Rural Relief

ON A WARM WEDNESDAY EVENING in July 1932, Prime Minister Saitō took to the airwaves and spoke to the nation about the rural crisis and the state's response to it. He assured his radio audience that the countryside was of great concern to his government. Public works programs and legislation to reduce the burden of farm debt were already being contemplated; those proposals and more would be ready when the Village Rescue Diet session began in August. But, he went on, for farm families and their communities truly to recover clearly required more help than the state alone could or should provide. The nation could neither afford nor countenance a countryside dependent on handouts. What the government could do was help farmers help themselves. By introducing them to economic and social reforms that built on rural traditions even as they embraced modern techniques, the prime minister suggested, the countryside would soon overcome its many crises. Saitō himself had heard the "strong voices of those who will use their own strength to eliminate the problems that have arisen" and had been moved by their sincerity and impressed by the efficacy of the approach.[1] The prime minister urged those listening to pursue a similar path of "self-revitalization," even as he promised to place it at the heart of the state's emerging program of rural relief and recovery.

Only a month before Saitō's speech, the government and most farmers' organizations had been scrambling to come up with viable responses to the countryside's troubles. Spurred on by Nagano Akira's bold petition campaign and a growing chorus of discontent from farmers (Akutagawa Shinkichi among them; his group from the Kitakata area presented its second set of relief proposals to local mayors at about the same time as the prime minister's radio appeal), policymakers moved quickly. By early July the outlines of several key policies were already visible; they received a final going-over during the Sixty-third Diet in August and September, and with one or two exceptions were ready for implementation soon after the end of that session. Different from any previous efforts to help the countryside in both scale and scope, the state's rural relief program was a complicated and often contradictory collection of policies, touching on everything from how to set a national price for rice to how to build a better outhouse. As Saitō's speech suggested, however, the question of what the state could do to help the countryside was very much contingent on what policymakers believed the state should do. The prime minister was inclined to think that less was more, and he was joined in this opinion by, among others, Finance Minister Takahashi.

Part of the summer's tension over how best to help rural communities was thus played out in debates over budgets. As already seen in the case of debt arrangement, finding funding for relief was sometimes problematic; the parties wanted it, farm organizations wanted it, and sometimes even Ministry of Agriculture and Forestry bureaucrats wanted it, but the Finance Ministry was almost always reluctant to give it up without a fight. The discourse of relief reflected these fault lines quite clearly, especially where spending on public works was concerned. Public works projects had been a mainstay of relief efforts for many years and were commonly understood to be the quickest way to channel money into the hands of needy workers or farmers. The severity of the rural depression, however, made it unlikely that public works on any reasonable scale could begin to compensate farmers for lost income.

Decisions about how much to spend and how to spend it were thus enormously complicated and quickly politicized. One of the outcomes of these debates, for example, was that the military was forced to take steps to strengthen its relationship with the countryside after its budget demands were blamed for stripping rural communities of their relief funding in 1933 and 1934. Though army rhetoric did little to help families still trying to escape the grip of the depression, the fact that the military bothered with a public relations campaign testifies to the importance of rural relief. The parties, meanwhile, were largely absent from the key debates over how to keep money flowing to farmers.

Against this background of concern over what relief said about the character of Japan's farmers and what it might cost, self-revitalization stood out as a beacon of sound thinking. Though hardly a new approach to the countryside's problems, the idea that rural communities could somehow pull themselves up by their own bootstraps was immensely appealing to people like the prime minister, who saw in self-revitalization an affirmation of their own preconceptions about farm life—and a less costly alternative to the expensive aid projects demanded by many farmers' groups. Revitalization was aggressively marketed as a broad solution to the rural crisis first by local agricultural associations and eventually by national organizations, including the Imperial Agricultural Association, before being adopted as the central component of the state's program of depression-era rural relief. This chapter begins to trace the course of the adoption of self-revitalization as a national policy alongside the rise and fall of the state's commitment to spending on more direct forms of relief.

## Public Works as Relief

Public works projects were not only the most visible sign of the state's commitment to the countryside but also the biggest draw on the government's budget. Between 1932 and 1934, the Finance Ministry allowed the Home and the Agriculture and Forestry ministries to oversee a wide variety of projects and spend almost 420 million yen on them (enough to pay for the Ministry of Agriculture and Forestry's entire 1931 budget more than five and a half times over). For a short while at least, the legislature and ministries were able to put their money where their rhetoric said it should be and offer cash when it was needed most.

Such largesse, however, did not last long. The struggle among Gotō Fumio, Finance Minister Takahashi, and the military over who would get how much of the 1934 budget ended badly for the Ministry of Agriculture and Forestry and for farmers.[2] Although some spending went on under other guises, sharp cuts in the funding for public works projects after 1934 marked the end of short-term rural relief, and the end of any significant direct support for the nation's farmers as well.[3] Debates over how much to spend on public works and how to spend it reveal both deep-seated concerns about the efficacy of relief and changing perceptions of the nature of the rural constituency.

From the start, it was clear that public works would play a role in rural relief; projects were a time-tested method of putting cash in the hands of the able-bodied but out-of-work.[4] The problem was deciding how much money was enough and how to spend it. A Home Ministry spokesperson reported in early June 1932 on its plans to spend 350 million yen on road and other projects over the next several years.[5] Though a substantial increase over previous years' spending, the proposal immediately came under fire from the Diet. "I would like to ask the government," one Seiyūkai legislator commented, "if they think doing that much—spending 350 million in public works over three years—will be sufficient to rescue those people right before our eyes who are in the hell of unemployment, the hell of trying to find work. (Applause.)"[6]

Politicians, governors, and others who stood to benefit from the flow of cash into the countryside kept up the pressure all summer as parsimonious bureaucrats from the Finance Ministry did everything they could to limit the state's commitments. In the middle were Ministry of Agriculture planners, who both wanted the cash the projects offered and preferred longer-term solutions to the countryside's problems, and local administrators, who needed the projects but feared the costs they were expected to bear. Saitō and Finance Minister Takahashi's support for economic revitalization only complicated matters further because it allowed the Finance Ministry to justify spending less on the countryside than might otherwise have been the case.

Neither state assistance for public works nor using those projects as a form of relief was a new concept in 1932. Land development projects had been funded by the state before the turn of the century, while some forms of repairs and improvements on bridges, roads, and other facilities had been eligible for help since 1908. In most instances state assistance was limited to low-interest loans that could be used by the sponsors of the projects to cover a percentage of the costs. Initially most projects had been the doing of local landlords, but by the mid-1920s more emphasis was placed on the role that local governments could play as project sponsors.[7] Similarly, using employment on a public works project as a limited form of assistance for the unemployed was not without precedent. In the aftermath of the 1918 Rice Riots, government-sponsored advisory bodies had recommended that both urban and rural projects be encouraged to help ease the threat of unemployment.[8] This didn't actually begin until 1925, and then only in the cities; as late as

1932, there was still nothing like a national effort to provide employment on projects.

Aid directed specifically at villages was even less common. Indeed, urban unemployment project managers went out of their way to keep farmers and the like out of the ranks of those employed in public works programs. Under pressure from the Imperial Agricultural Association, the Hamaguchi cabinet announced a plan in the late summer of 1930 to provide 70 million yen in loans to help with rural relief projects. The association's response was that adding more debt on top of that already burdening local governments wasn't likely to do much good and would probably make things much worse. What the countryside needed, the association argued, was grants, not loans.[9] That advice was not heeded by the Minseitō cabinet, and it wasn't until the summer of 1932 that steps were taken to go beyond a strictly loan-based approach to rural relief.

Planning for public works and for local funding to go with it began in earnest in early July, at roughly the same time that the contours of debt policy and the Economic Revitalization Campaign were taking shape.[10] Knowing how they were going to cope with debt and other long-term issues made it easier to decide what to do about direct relief.[11] Ministry of Agriculture proposals from mid-summer featured both large-scale credit packages for local governments and direct government spending on public works. On the surface there was little new about either approach, but a closer look revealed that the ministry was in fact moving in new directions. The loans, for example, made it possible for local communities to sponsor public works projects on a small scale; the ministry would help town and village administrations or other qualified sponsors borrow the necessary money, much as the Minseitō had proposed earlier. Unlike the earlier scheme, however, the state was also offering to assume between one- and two-thirds of the cost of these local projects, thus lessening considerably the burden on village budgets. This willingness to pay directly for locally run relief projects is an important shift in the relationship between the central and local governments, and one that reflects a growing dependence of town and village administrations on direct subsidies from the state.[12]

In addition, the ministry offered to make more loans directly available to farmers via local industrial cooperatives (channeling the money at first to the Industrial Cooperative Central Bank), which would approve small-scale borrowing for things like the purchase of fertilizer or seeds—precisely the sort of short-term funding at reasonable rates that was missing in rural communities. It was the absence of reliable creditors that drove farmers to borrow at usurious rates from local private lenders; ministry planners could thus kill two birds with one stone.

Finally, a third loan program would pump 200 million yen into industrial cooperative coffers to refinance their outstanding and possibly unrecoverable loans. These funds would be repaid at low interest over twenty years, the hope being that the cooperatives would take the borrowed money and loan it back to the community.[13] Kodaira's hand is evident in these details, since it had long been his complaint that the countryside's debt problem was inextricably tied to the utter absence of reliable sources of low-interest funds for mundane but necessary expenses. Providing such a source was a key element in the debt arrangement policy that he was helping to shape as well.

Public works projects were also redesigned to better serve local needs. In planning documents from early July 1932, the ministry first pointed out that projects had to be ones that a community could reasonably undertake—in other words, nothing too complicated or too expensive. Digging a ditch was one thing, building a bridge another. It was also important, planners noted, for projects to put cash directly into farmers' hands, and for the projects themselves to have some lasting impact on the community. Prefectural governors had already made known their worries about money being diverted to contractors, who had in the past brought in their own, usually low-paid workers on projects, something that neither the governors nor policymakers wanted to see happen again.

Finally, the ministry's planners wanted to be certain that as large a share as possible of the total costs of the project went toward wages. That meant defining the ministry's goals in ways that favored labor-intensive projects over those that demanded spending on cement, steel, or other costly materials.[14] (As a rule, the Home Ministry's approach allowed much more leeway in the proportion of the budget that could be spent on materials, reflecting its interest in infrastructural improvement. This is covered in more detail below.) Land-opening projects, irrigation, mulberry field redevelopment, and even some work on harbors for fishing villages were all eligible for funding, but the overall emphasis in each was on small-scale undertakings. The ideal project was one that could be completed relatively quickly by employing large numbers of farmers. Land-opening projects, for example, were divided into those that involved more than 5 *chō* of land and those that involved less, with the latter receiving higher levels of support from the state. In the past, the government had not been willing to involve itself in this sort of very small-scale, almost household-level project. The Ministry of Agriculture and Forestry's plan suggests that bureaucrats were trying to think of new ways to make contact with the individual farmer and to ensure that relief reached those who needed it.[15]

The question for planners and farmers alike was how big a relief budget they could expect. Those decisions, however, were largely divorced from any consideration of need, being based instead on wrangling within the cabinet. Vice-ministerial meetings on village relief were soon supplemented by ones among the ministers themselves. Those sessions brought together the Home, Finance, Commerce and Industry, Agriculture and Forestry, and Rail ministers in a series of eight often-contentious sessions beginning on June 17. Although the policy groundwork had almost certainly been laid by their underlings—Home Minister Yamamoto, for instance, had very little interest in the issue of farm relief—the ministers themselves did discuss how the state should proceed and where its money should be spent.[16] By early August they had come up with a number of proposals that the cabinet would support in the Diet; emergency public works for the countryside was the first on their list.[17]

The cabinet took a revised version of these proposals to the Diet session later in August. The combination of spending (new credit, public works, other funding programs) and reform (economic revitalization, village planning, debt arrangement) seemed to be a credible approach to the problems that had been raised by the petitioners. However, some of the policies, and especially the spending programs, were only as effective as the size of their budgets would permit. Even though the relief budget that the cabinet took to the Diet in August 1932 far outdid any previous spending on the countryside, in what would become a familiar refrain over the next several years, both the Home and the Agriculture Ministries found that there was a considerable gap between what they wanted to spend on relief and what the Finance Ministry was willing to let them have.

Government loans were an important part of the relief package, and Takahashi's ministry did give the go-ahead to an impressive expansion of credit for the countryside.[18] By the end of 1934 it expected to have made available almost 1 billion yen in credit. A little more than 200 million of that was designated for use by local communities to help pay for public works projects. The bulk of the remaining almost 800 million yen was earmarked for loans to allow regional banks and industrial cooperatives to refinance existing debt.[19] In what was the closest the government came to approving a debt deferral of any type—and the closest it would come to meeting the demands of those petitioners who were after a deferral of state funding—the Finance Ministry allocated roughly 200 million of the 800 million yen to the Deposit Bureau.

This funding would provide additional credit to a class of borrowers who had already taken out loans originating with the Deposit Bureau, but who had clearly "found it difficult to pursue recovery unassisted." In other words, funds would be targeted at those marginal borrowers who were about to default. Refinancing would allow borrowers to continue paying back the loan at the same time that it prevented the government from having to write off the debts entirely. Since the Deposit Bureau was not known for making risky loans in the first place, recipients of both the original loan and the aid package for temporarily indisposed borrowers were likely to be relatively well off.[20]

Although the cabinet's credit proposals eventually passed, legislators were quick to challenge Takahashi on their efficacy. Many suspected that in the end the funding was far more likely to help troubled banks than farmers, a point made again and again from the floor of the Diet. How, Takahashi was asked, did the government expect such a paltry amount to have any effect on the average farmer?[21] Takahashi's response that the money would "permeate widely" was not convincing. As one lower house member put it, "Your answer confirms that it is as I had imagined: the primary purpose of this bill is to rescue the banks, which is quite regrettable." Nevertheless, the committee assigned to consider the bill that would provide loans to regional banks sent it back to the lower house unchanged, where it received the support of both major parties.

In his speech approving the bill, Kazami Akira summed up what many likely felt about this particular program. "According to our understanding of this bill, only a very few of the citizens of this country will benefit from it," Kazami pointed out, noting that his own approval was based on the fact that in a time of crisis it was necessary to make do with measures that were less than perfect. He and others in the legislature were willing to take what they could get, and both houses approved the bill early in September. It was soon joined by its counterpart credit package for the industrial cooperatives.[22]

From the point of view of the many petitioners who asked the state to provide their villages and towns with public works projects, the credit packages were of less immediate interest than the promise of direct spending in the form of project wages. Of particular importance were the final form the spending would take and the balance between local and state contributions. Saitō spoke to these points in his opening address to the Sixty-third Diet, emphasizing the importance of the public works programs as a means of putting money into the hands of farmers as quickly and directly as possible. In Saitō's words, the purpose of the state's public work projects was to "provide opportunities for employment directly to those farmers and fishermen who are in difficulty, and to open the door to wage earning throughout the country."[23]

Table 6 helps describe where the government spent its relief money. As the figures illustrate, most of the funds that the government allocated to relief were channeled through either the Home Ministry or the Ministry of Agriculture and Forestry. Roughly four-fifths of the Home Ministry's relief outlays and almost three-quarters of the Ministry of Agriculture's were for public works; together the two accounted for more than three-quarters of the state's relief budget between 1932 and 1934, and their public works spending alone made up 60 percent of all state relief outlays.[24]

The two ministries took different approaches to public works as relief. The Home Ministry's budget for public works in 1933, for instance, estimated that towns and villages running projects would have to cover only one-third of the total cost of their projects, an amount they would likely borrow at low interest rates (prefectural governments had to pay 75 percent of the expenses of their projects).[25] Home Ministry projects, however, spent no more than half of their budgets on wages, whereas the Ministry of Agriculture and Forestry spent a relatively larger share—as much as four-fifths in the case of some public works projects. Yet the Ministry of Agriculture was less forthcoming with money for local governments than the Home Ministry because it could generally subsidize only about half the cost of its projects, though it, too, could sometimes make low-interest loans available.[26]

The projects differed in other ways as well. While the Home Ministry concentrated its efforts and its budget on road improvements, the bureaucrats in the Ministry of Agriculture and Forestry made sure that its money was being spent in the villages themselves, on projects related to farming. In

Table 6
Japanese Government Spending
on Relief Projects by Agency, 1932–1934
(000 ¥)

| Ministry | 1932 | 1933 | 1934 | Total |
|---|---|---|---|---|
| Home Ministry | | | | |
|   Public works | ¥48,818 | ¥99,958 | ¥49,842 | ¥198,618 |
|     Waterways | 13,253 | 28,568 | 19,842 | 61,663 |
|     Harbors | 1,904 | 8,944 | 5,850 | 16,698 |
|     Roads | 33,661 | 62,446 | 24,150 | 120,257 |
|     Other | 11,961 | 20,706 | 14,531 | 47,198 |
|     Total | 60,779 | 120,664 | 64,373 | 245,816 |
| Finance Ministry | 3,687 | 6,123 | 4,459 | 14,269 |
| Army | 18,500 | 0 | 0 | 18,500 |
| Navy | 18,440 | 0 | 0 | 18,440 |
| Justice Ministry | 951 | 1,493 | 1,453 | 3,897 |
| Education Ministry | 12,520 | 14,511 | 14,576 | 41,607 |
| Agriculture Ministry | | | | |
|   Public works | 37,483 | 48,416 | 24,514 | 110,413 |
|   Nōson keizai kōsei | 3,368 | 3,355 | 3,051 | 9,774 |
|   Grain storage | 0 | 5,000 | 19,500 | 24,500 |
|   Other | 1,873 | 1,234 | 2,720 | 5,827 |
|   Total | 42,724 | 58,005 | 49,785 | 150,514 |
| Industry and Commerce Ministry | 396 | 439 | 256 | 1,091 |
| Communications Ministry | 2,398 | 6,943 | 4,630 | 13,971 |
| Colonial Ministry | 2,821 | 5,602 | 5,869 | 14,292 |
| General account totals | ¥163,216 | ¥213,781 | ¥145,401 | ¥522,398 |

SOURCE: Ōkurashō Shōwa zaisei shi henshūshitsu, *Shōwa zaisei shi*, vol. 5, p. 264.

a description of what the projects were supposed to accomplish, planners quoted the prime minister's speech about "providing job opportunities" word for word, then went on to add two more goals to the list. Harking back to the ministry's earlier designs on developing public works that would have a lasting impact, bureaucrats wrote that, in addition to putting wages into farmers' hands, their projects would boost farm production and lower production costs on the farm.[27]

Planners designed the Ministry of Agriculture's projects accordingly. There were three categories: land development, drainage and irrigation, and small-scale facilities, which included farm roads, embankments, sluices, and the like. Within the first two categories there were divisions between small- and large-scale projects, so that someone who wanted to improve his small plot of land received a slightly higher level of assistance than someone doing the same to a large piece of farmland. For the irrigation projects, the rate of assistance was the same (at 50 percent of project costs) for both large- and small-scale jobs, but the ministry compensated by calculating the costs for the projects in such a way that the smaller ones received more money. Work on drainage culverts, or on the small roads that crisscrossed the paddy fields, received a standard 50-percent subsidy.

What made these public works projects so different from what had come before was that for the first time the state was actively providing assistance to very small-scale undertakings. Most land or farm development projects before the relief program had been something that landlords or others with substantial landholdings might attempt. Small farmers and tenants were generally excluded from access to assistance and had been forced to rely on private sources of funding for their attempts to improve their farms. By making the scale of the projects smaller, the Ministry of Agriculture and Forestry expanded the range of people and farmland involved in local improvement efforts and increased the number of potential beneficiaries.[28]

Once the projects got under way, the ministry reported that there had been almost thirty-five thousand individually sponsored, small-scale land development projects in 1932 alone and that altogether more than ninety-three thousand public-works projects under Ministry of Agriculture and Forestry jurisdiction began that year. By the end of fiscal year 1933, more than 116 million days of work had been provided via the projects, at an average daily wage of about 0.7 yen.[29] By reaching down past landlords and large landholders to average farmers, public works projects were designed to share in the broader agenda of rural reform—an agenda that sought to protect producers, to foster community, and to defuse farmers' discontent all at the same time.

## Relief at the Village Level

Sekishiba's experiences with local relief projects were by and large positive ones. "Construction projects for the relief of the poor were undertaken in various places," says a 1932 report on village conditions, "and the benefits were quite substantial."[30] From late 1932 on, the village administration oversaw three years of road work and other local improvements funded in part by the state's rural relief programs. During the winter months, when farming was at a standstill, villagers made repairs to local roads, worked on irrigation facilities, and spent time making other improvements to the community's infrastructure. To the extent that these projects made transportation a little easier or water control a little more reliable, they brought useful long-term benefits to the village. In the short term, the projects did what the state had said they were supposed to do: give farmers who needed outside income chances to work. Wages were paid in cash, usually within a few days of the actual employment. It isn't hard to see why local commentators felt that the relief projects had been good for the community.

The projects came with a price tag, however, and local officials had to balance the potential benefits of any given project with its cost to the village. The 1932 projects were initially budgeted at just over 7,000 yen, but that figure was soon adjusted upward to more than 9,800; the village spent roughly the same amount for each of the next two years.[31] The central government, via the prefecture, paid approximately three-quarters of the total cost of the road repair projects and half of what it cost to undertake the irrigation-pond projects. This meant that the state picked up close to 60 percent of the total cost of relief projects in Sekishiba.

The roughly 2,900 yen that Sekishiba had to cover was paid for in two ways. First, residents of the hamlets that would benefit most from the improved facilities were asked to pay the balance of the costs of those projects. Sekishiba hamlet, for instance, was assessed 450 yen, money that presumably came out of the pockets of hamlet farmers. The road repair projects were less directly burdensome; a single anonymous donor provided the 25-yen local assessment, and the village took out a 600-yen loan from the prefecture to pay for the rest. Interest on the twenty-year loan was only 4.2 percent a year, with three years of assistance on the interest charges and a five-year deferment on repayment of principal.[32]

This combination of debt, contributions, and state grants continued into 1933, although the balance among them changed. The village administration chose to concentrate exclusively on road repair projects, in part because those came with a grant level considerably higher than that for irrigation work. Three-quarters of the total cost of 5,400 yen was covered by the state, as opposed to the roughly 50-percent level of support under the Ministry of Agriculture and Forestry's program of farm-village public works. Shifting to the Home Ministry's projects was one way to reduce the cost of relief to the village itself. Program rules made it relatively easy for the community to borrow enough to cover the rest of their relief-project expenses, and the village took on another 1,300 yen loan. Road repair had another advantage over the other alternatives, in that its benefits were spread more widely than the small-scale irrigation projects sponsored by the Ministry of Agriculture and Forestry, which by definition were of limited scope. The benefits of those projects accrued to a tiny part of the community, so there was no good reason to have the whole village foot the bill.[33]

Three-quarters of the money that the village proposed to spend on relief projects in 1932 and the first few months of 1933 was for wages. In accordance with state guidelines, different types of projects came with different rules about how much money had to be spent on workers and how much administrators were free to spend on materials and other costs. Thus less than half of the 1932 budget for road work projects went into wages, whereas 94 percent of the 4,600-yen allocation for "small projects" (under the Ministry of Agriculture and Forestry) was supposed to be paid out to workers.[34] At the going wage rates, that was enough to provide more than 8,700 worker-days of employment for the village.

The 1932 and early 1933 projects were responsible for almost a thousand jobs: road repair was responsible for almost half of all the hiring (478 jobs); the "small facilities" projects employed another 250 or so; and the farming association's mulberry field work hired 260 men and women. A man working on one of the road repair projects received a standard wage of 0.65 yen a day (a woman earned slightly less), while the supervisor-contractor might make 1.5 yen for a day's work. According to a report put out by the prefecture, the going rate for day laborers in the silk-producing part of the prefecture in 1933 was 0.60 yen a day for men and 0.45 yen a day for women. Relief wages in Sekishiba were slightly better than that, although still less than a "regular employee" could expect.[35] Women accounted for about a fourth of all workers and were most evident in the mulberry field work, where they made up more than 40 percent of the work force. They were least likely to be found on the irrigation projects; only 27 women were hired to work beside 227 men. Women made up about a quarter of the road-repair work force.

Farmers outnumbered non-farmers working on the projects by more than three to one. Project administrators hired a total of 75 "unemployed" people and 147 individuals classified as "other"—both relatively small numbers compared to the 770 men and women from local farms who were given jobs.[36] The large number of farmers employed on the projects is reassuring, in that it makes it less likely that the supervisor-contractors brought in many of their own workers; unfortunately, however, it remains difficult to determine exactly where these farmers and non-farmers resided. It seems likely that most if not all came from within Sekishiba itself, given that the village had to pay a substantial part of the cost of the projects and that residents would not have been happy about putting money into the pockets of outsiders.

There is no indication that the administration went out of its way to distribute the jobs equally within the community.[37] (Village records of wage payments in this period do not include information on where recipients lived.)[38] The project sites themselves, however, were located throughout the village, which may have rendered unnecessary any special effort to share the work equally. There were six different sites for irrigation-pond projects, and road work was not confined to any particular area. The longest-running project involved the repair, and in some places the building, of a road connecting Furu, in the southern part of the village, to Sekishiba hamlet in the north. Work on the road actually began in 1931, before the state-funded relief projects got under way, and was completed in 1933. The north-south route not only brought the community a little closer together but also meant that a good part of the village was within easy walking distance of the construction.

Another way to look at the effects of the relief program is to remember that the projects provided 992 jobs in a village with a population (in 1933) of just under 3,000. Given the likelihood that at least some of those hired worked on more than one project, the minimum number of people actually employed was probably close to the number hired to work on road repair, or around 500.[39] Comparing the number of farmers who worked on road repair with the total number of farmers in the village suggests that 39 percent of the male farmers (more than one in three) and 12 percent of the female farmers in the village (about one in nine) had been hired to work on a road repair project at least once.[40] If all the men who worked on other projects were drawn from the pool of people who worked on the roads, then 39 percent represents the maximum proportion of male farmers involved in relief projects in the village in 1932 and early 1933. For women, the figure is closer to 15 percent (one in seven), since there were 110 women hired to work on the mulberry field projects (28 more than worked on the roads).

The more workers there were on the irrigation and mulberry field projects who had not been involved in road repair, the higher the overall rate of participation. For example, if there were no overlap in hiring for each type of project (road, irrigation, and mulberry field), then a total of 560 male and 210 female farmers—or 86 and 30 percent of all male and female farmers, respectively—participated in village relief. These rough estimates provide some idea of how likely it was that the average farmer worked on a relief project. If what the village told the prefecture about its running of the relief programs is true, then it is clear that a good part of the farming community participated in some way in village relief.

Another way to assess the impact of these programs on the community is to ask how much the average farmer might have earned working on road repair or irrigation improvement or a mulberry field project. The various categories of projects committed a total of 5,776 yen toward wages. That much cash was worth more than either the 1932 soybean crop or the vegetable crop, considerably more than farmers got for their chickens and chicken eggs, and almost as much as all the barley harvested in 1932.[41] By those yardsticks, the projects were a significant source of income for the community.

On the individual level, however, the results are less impressive. Bear in mind that if each project category's wage budget and the number of days of work it provided are divided by the number of people it hired, on average, a road project employee worked just under 4 days over the five- or six-month span of the project to earn 2.4 yen. People who were hired to do the work on the irrigation ponds brought home more. They worked, on average, 25.5 days and earned 17 yen doing so.[42] It is, of course, true that some people would have worked for only a day or two, while others might have managed to get hired on a more regular basis, so that their relief-project income varied accordingly.

There are thus several points to consider when thinking about the value of the projects to the community, and specifically about the importance of relief-project wages. One is that wages were low, and so, too, were wage earnings. Farmers would not get rich doing relief work, and the short-term nature of the projects meant that it was impossible to sustain a family on what a person could earn doing road work or repairing irrigation ditches. Similarly, relief wages were a drop in the bucket compared to the almost overwhelming burden of debt facing many farm families. (As noted above, one village estimate put average household debt at 1,500 yen in August 1932.) And given that the average value of farm production per household in Sekishiba fell by more than 170 yen between 1927 and 1932, it is apparent that a few months of work on the prefectural payroll would not return farm income to where it had been.

That, of course, was never the purpose of the relief projects. The state had no desire to supplement every farmer in the country, and bureaucrats shied away from defining an acceptable standard of living for the farming community. Since the state made no commitment to maintain families at some minimum level of food, shelter, and clothing, emergency relief might best be thought of as little more than another type of part-time job, the difference being the source of the funds. Like other part-time jobs (and other employers), the market and not individual needs determined the wage level. Unlike other jobs, the neediest applicants were supposed to be hired before less needy ones and be given more opportunities to work. This is not to say that the neediest were helped to maintain a particular standard of living, only that they were given the opportunity to earn a cash wage. If other employers had been willing to provide these jobs, the state would have been happy to have them do so, but it was clear that no one else would.

In Sekishiba, though, there were no guarantees that the people who were hired were in fact the neediest. Decisions about who would work and who wouldn't were left in the hands of local authorities. Construction on a road between Shimoshiba and Komatsu in late 1934, for instance, employed a number of householders from the latter hamlet. Wage payment records reveal that those hired included some of the hamlet's larger taxpayers. In fact, three of Komatsu's top four household taxpayers in 1934 worked on the relief project in November and December. Hara Haruji (the top taxpayer) worked only 2 days in November 1934, Watanabe Hikoe (who ranked second) reportedly worked 5 days in November and another 10 the following month, while Utsumi Haruki (fourth in tax payments) worked 28 days over that two-month period. Mid-level taxpayers were also part of the work force that winter. Both Watanabe Shinta, who worked for 22 days in two months, and Watanabe Masaichi, who worked for 40, made ample use of the opportunity provided by the relief projects. At the lower end of household tax rankings, Satō Chōta worked some 20 days in November and 9 in December.[43]

Because the Shimoshiba-Komatsu project happened to coincide with the 1934 famine, crops and farm incomes were at their lowest levels in recent memory when Komatsu residents were hired to work that winter. The wages they earned were thus even more valuable than they would have been in an average year. At the standard rate of 0.65 yen a day (for male workers), Satō Chōta earned a total of almost 19 yen for road work during November and December, while Watanabe Masaichi received the large sum of 26 yen for his efforts over the same period. Comparing those amounts with figures for spending and farm income included in their Economic Revitalization Plans (discussed in Chapter 7), a better picture of the importance of the relief income to their households emerges. (The plans report conditions as they were in 1933, not 1934.)

For a mid-level taxpayer like Watanabe Masaichi, who farmed almost 2 *chō* of paddy land, 26 yen would not in a normal year have made much difference in the family's fortunes. Such an amount pales in comparison to the more than 1,000 yen the family earned farming in 1933, and would have paid for only a tenth of the fertilizer they used that year, or less than half of their prefectural taxes. The other middle- and upper-level farmers in Komatsu were in the same boat, in that farming brought in far more than they could make by working on the relief projects. For those members of the community with smaller farms and smaller incomes, however, relief-project wages could change the shape of family finances. Satō Chōta, for instance, reported a farm income of 210 yen in 1933. His 19 yen in relief wages was thus almost one-tenth the value of what the family made from farming. It was also more than Watanabe paid in prefectural taxes, more than he paid for light and heat for a year, and enough to purchase two-fifths of the fertilizer his family bought in 1933.[44] In other words, it was not an inconsiderable sum compared to the family's other sources of income and to their level of spending.

That village council members and the relatively well-off can be found on the rolls of one of the village's relief projects suggests that social status was not much of a barrier to employment. There is nothing here to suggest that people of means shunned the work as an admission of poverty or second-class citizenship. On the contrary, the presence of so many of the hamlet's top taxpayers in the ranks of the relief workers makes it clear that the jobs had wide appeal. As low as the wages were, the willingness of people like Utsumi Haruki and others like him to work as often as they did suggests that the income was welcome.[45]

Sekishiba's approach to "relief" was thus one that encompassed the entire community, not just the village's poorest residents. Working on the projects did not taint one as a ward of the state or as someone who was unable to provide for his or her family. Some of the least well-off of the farmers in Komatsu hamlet, for instance, worked alongside some of the richest. Thus when local officials spoke of "relief projects for the poor" in their reports, they were being a bit disingenuous about the scope of the projects' reach in the village. The state's public-works relief program did not require officials or residents to make concrete and public divisions within the village between those who were eligible for help and those who were not. Avoiding that step provided further support for the idea of the village as a harmonious community, working together to solve a set of problems shared by all.

## Assessing Rural Relief

Sekishiba's largely positive assessment notwithstanding, the government's public works programs were early and easy targets for critics. As soon as the public works budget was announced, complaints began that it was too little, too late.[46] Once the projects were under way, there were other problems to contend with, as local politicians and administrative shortcomings combined to put relief in a bad light. Newspaper reports described numerous cases in which contractors were running projects that ought to have been under local control; their presence meant that they could bring in their own workers, pay them less than they would have to pay local residents, and pocket the difference. (Home Ministry projects seemed especially prone to this sort of activity.) Similar incidents—and worse—were widely reported.[47]

Public works programs bore the brunt of the criticism. Commentators complained that too much was being spent on materials and not enough on wages, that not everyone had equal access to jobs, or that, as had happened in at least one community, people were being compelled to work on projects. According to one man from Yamagata prefecture, "Officials, scholars, and others might think that the villages have really been rescued by these projects, but in reality the results are of little value." In one village he knew of, local officials took back taxes and other charges out of the day wages for the people hired to work on projects, while paying themselves twice the going rate for "supervising" the job. Officials in another village charged every employee a 10 *sen* per day "tool charge" but in reality used the money to go drinking, while also paying themselves an exorbitant wage. A Mr. Kubota from Kanagawa prefecture pointed out what seemed to be a common ploy among cash-strapped communities: the government provided towns and villages enough subsidies for their projects to cover, for example, 70 percent of the costs, always on the assumption that the community would come up with the remaining 30 percent through borrowing or some other means. What was actually happening, said Mr. Kubota, was that those communities wouldn't bother to pay their share but would simply spend what the government gave them and let it go at that.[48]

These individual reports were supplemented by more comprehensive criticisms. Among the better known of these was commentator Inomata Tsunao's *Kyūbō no nōson* (The Impoverished Village), which appeared in late 1934. This popular book was based on Inomata's observations on the state of the village during the depression and included sharp and insightful analyses of relief policies. Economic revitalization came under the strongest attack, but Inomata also dealt with the shortcomings of public works. In doing so he took care to emphasize the role of the projects in maintaining the gap between the poor and the powerful within the village. When benefits did accrue from public works, he argued, they went overwhelmingly into the hands of the landlords and local elite. In at least one village he knew of, local planners had padded the payroll with so-called shadow workers and then collected their wages for use as they saw fit.

Inomata described a handful of examples in which low wages, overworked laborers, and the poor design of the projects themselves kept the projects from being of much use to anyone but landlords, who profited by selling their land at higher than normal prices to make way for road projects. At least some local residents were aware of what was happening; Inomata quoted comments by farmers in Nagano who told him that "the landlords, supervisors, cement companies, and steel suppliers were the ones who benefited from rural relief projects."[49]

Some of the first scholars to write in the postwar period about the depression and the state's response to it shared Inomata's assessment.[50] They pointed to the huge gap between what had been spent on wages under the public works programs and the state's own estimates of how far farm income had fallen over the same period. Such calculations make it clear that it was impossible for farmers to rely on public works jobs to make up either for wages lost from other employment or for income lost because of the drop in rice and silk prices. More recent calculations by Teruoka Shūzō suggest that the amount an average farmer could earn by working on public works projects between 1932 and 1934 was equal to only about 3 or 4 percent of his annual income, or just under 26 yen a year. That was enough to buy about 150 kilograms of rice at Tokyo prices but would not have gone very far toward helping the average farm family get back on its feet.[51]

Those negative assessments have been modified by more recent analyses that put relief spending in a somewhat more positive light. Common sense suggests that if the government spent several hundred million yen on rural relief over a short period of time, at least some of it must have made its way to the villages and into farmers' pockets. This macro-level approach ignores the problems of precisely who benefited from the state's largesse and whether the budget was big enough and instead describes the effects of spending in much broader terms. Miwa Ryōichi's careful study of Takahashi's budget programs (including relief) suggests not only that relief projects were helpful in stimulating the economy, but also that in 1932 and 1933 they were at least as important as new spending on the military. It wasn't until the sharp cuts in the 1934 relief budget that the size of the military budget completely overshadowed relief allocations.[52]

Nakamura Takafusa has taken a closer look at the overall impact of spending on the countryside, and he, too, suggests that public works were likely helpful if not valuable to many communities and individuals. He concludes that even though the average farm household could have earned only 17 yen a year in wages from the projects (considerably less than the 26 yen that Teruoka uses), the extra money would have been more than welcomed by small farm households, especially during the off-season, when other sources of income were unavailable.

There seems to be no denying that, on the whole, public works spending gave the economy a welcome shot in the arm. Whether the countryside in general or the neediest farmers in particular benefited at least as much as the cities or the landlords is another question and one that cannot be answered with any certainty. Public works projects that were run for relief were probably no more corrupt or inefficient than their regular counterparts, the difference being that the stated goals of relief (to put money into the hands of farmers, and to do so fairly) guaranteed that they were held to higher standards. The state's commitment to relief was thrown into doubt every time a case of fraud appeared in the press. That—and the fact that decisions about how much to spend (and, after 1933, whether to spend anything) seemed so removed from any consideration of actual conditions in the countryside—certainly cast the relief programs in a negative light.

It is also worth noting, however, that it was the short-lived nature of the huge boost in spending that made it possible for the Ministry of Agriculture and Forestry and the Home Ministry to get as much as they did for public works. The prime minister and certainly Takahashi were not at all willing to make guarantees about sustaining a high level of funding for any length of time. Fears of rendering able-bodied citizens dependent on the state were common among legislators and bureaucrats alike, which is one reason that both groups were willing to differentiate between expensive policies for the short term and those for the long term, which addressed more fundamental problems than just a lack of ready cash. The debate over how much the countryside needed, and for how long, simmered during the summer of 1932 and finally boiled over during negotiations over the 1934 budget.

## The Limits of Relief

Saitō's government was in office for more than two years, ruling until the Imperial Rayon corruption scandal implicated several high-ranking officials and brought the cabinet down in July 1934.[53] By then the fate of rural relief had been set, those decisions made against a background of growing concern over Japan's international vulnerability and domestic political infighting. The Lytton Commission released its report on the Manchurian Incident in October 1932, and although hardly hostile to Japan, the report did refute Japan's narrative of the events surrounding the Incident. Once the League of Nations accepted the report in February 1933, Japan's delegation walked out, and soon afterward Japan withdrew from the League altogether. Concerns over trade barriers and the gradual collapse of the Washington Treaty system only heightened worries about Japan's economic and strategic position in Asia. Military and some civilian planners began articulating proposals for a more mobilized nation, better prepared for the challenges that lay ahead. These concerns helped sustain the nation's sense of crisis.

In the meantime, struggles within the mainstream political parties kept them from presenting a viable alternative to non-party cabinets. The Seiyūkai leadership, which held a majority in the lower house, expected to regain the prime ministership and had supported the cabinet during the Sixty-fourth Diet in the belief that its return to power was imminent.[54] However, on his way back from reporting Japan's withdrawal from the League of Nations at the Ise Shrine, Prime Minister Saitō met with the still-influential Saionji Kinmochi to discuss the fate of the cabinet.[55] Apparently convinced by Saionji of the need to continue rather than turn the reins over to someone else, Saitō managed to persuade Takahashi to remain in the cabinet (and did the same with Yamamoto, who also expressed a desire to leave), thus delaying one potential scenario of a return to party rule. Saitō maintained that the crisis was still with them both domestically and internationally, areas in which Takahashi's advice was essential. In the late summer of 1933, to placate Seiyūkai leaders, Saitō began negotiations with the party to win its support for cabinet policies.[56] His insistence that the cabinet and the party saw eye to eye on general policy matters wasn't enough for party leaders, and from that point on the Seiyūkai was at best only conciliatory toward the cabinet's proposals.

In its earlier encounters with rural relief, the government had been able to count on a measure of unanimity among the various camps, as reflected by the record-setting relief budgets of 1932 and 1933. This unanimity—and Takahashi's willingness to pursue deficit spending in the short term to rebuild the economy—meant that for a few years both relief and military spending grew side by side. However, the commitment to rural relief was due for reconsideration as discussion began on the 1934 budget, and by then there were few signs of unanimity. Not only were the parties, and the Seiyūkai in particular, feeling less than charitable toward the cabinet, but it was also clear that the military's role would loom larger in budget discussions than it had in many years. In the aftermath of the Manchurian Incident, the army and to some extent the navy had enjoyed huge boosts in spending, and both were loath to see their share of the budget pie reduced. Spokesmen for the services were thus increasingly vocal in 1933 about the need to prepare for the next security crisis, which many predicted would arise no later than 1936.

The problem they and others in search of funding faced was that the budget pie was no longer growing. Based on cabinet decisions reached in the early summer, the Finance Ministry had drawn up its own rules for the coming budget negotiations. Takahashi and ministry bureaucrats desperately wanted to rein in the snowballing budgets of the past two years, and in July they decided that debt levels and total spending in 1934 would go no higher than they had been in 1933. Requests for new spending would also, to the extent possible, be limited to 1933 levels.[57]

Meetings of key ministers to set budget priorities began in early October 1933 and were quickly dominated by military and diplomatic concerns. Army Minister Araki Sadao led this shift in focus and, together with his counterpart from the navy, used the meetings to make as powerful a case as possible for a significant boost in defense spending.[58] Araki was a skilled and forceful negotiator, timing the release of public statements of support from other elite officers to strengthen his case and using other means to put Saitō and, increasingly, Finance Minister Takahashi on the defensive.[59] By the time the ministers' meetings ended in late October, Takahashi had been placed in the unenviable position of having to justify his reasons for not giving the army and navy what they wanted. The finance minister's insistence on the primacy of diplomacy did not sit well with his opponents and lacked the visceral pull of the military's "strong defense" campaign.

Most requests for funding were in line with what they had been the previous year. The exception was the military, which accounted for more than half of the 1.4 billion yen in spending that the Finance Ministry was asked to approve. Takahashi made an initial announcement of budget decisions on November 17, revealing that the army had received more than 60 percent of its initial requests for new funding (the highest rate of any ministry) and that the navy, which had demanded 440 million in new funding, had been given only 170 million, or less than 40 percent of its original request.[60] Spokesmen for the navy made no mystery of their dissatisfaction, and at several points during the budget discussions Takahashi's refusal to be flexible in the face of strong demands from the military cast doubt on the future of the cabinet.

The tension reached its peak at the end of November, when Saitō negotiated a compromise solution. The navy was demanding an increase of at least 15 million yen over what it had already been offered. After Takahashi showed some flexibility and agreed to add another 10 million to the budget,

Army Minister Araki also agreed to free up 10 million from the army budget for Manchuria for use by the navy. Takahashi split the 10 million in new funding down the middle, giving half to the navy (thus meeting its demands) and making the rest potentially available to the Ministry of Agriculture and Forestry.[61] This solution was the best that Saitō could do, and it seems to have left most participants happy.[62]

Gotō was the exception. His ministry and his requests for more funding for the countryside had been hard hit by the newly parsimonious Finance Ministry.[63] Only 14 percent of his requests for new funding had been approved, the lowest rate of any ministry and well below the average approval rate of 46 percent. Gotō fared no better in a second round of requests in early December.[64] Such budget cutbacks seemed to threaten the ministry's ability to continue providing substantive aid to the countryside, and at the very least represented a sharp shift in the state's commitment to direct relief in the form of public works, loans, and credit programs. In part at Araki's urging, the cabinet had earlier agreed to hold a series of Domestic Policy Conferences (Naisei kaigi) to address some of the issues that hadn't come up during the ministerial meetings in October; once the outlines of the budget were known, the conferences quickly became a forum to allow Gotō to make a case for expanded relief and farm-reform funding prior to the Sixty-fifth Diet and finalization of budget plans for the coming year. (The Diet session began on December 26.) A total of eight meetings were eventually convened, the first on November 7, 1933, the last on December 22. In addition to the prime minister and the Home, Agriculture, Commerce, and Colonial ministers, all of whom were present from the start, Army Minister Araki and Rail Minister Mitsuchi attended from the second session on, and Finance Minister Takahashi joined in late as well.[65]

Several factors were working against Gotō during negotiations over the budget. He and Army Minister Araki had developed a close working relationship in the months leading up to the conferences, so much so that Takahashi began to associate Gotō with the military and their causes.[66] Takahashi made no bones about his opposition to the military's attempts to discredit the parties, to its expansion plans, and occasionally, to some of the comments that Araki was prone to make in cabinet meetings. After Takahashi repeated for the benefit of the cabinet a story about a visit he had received from some village headmen (see below), Araki made some comment about their "spirit," to which the finance minister replied:

Whatever is said you jump in and start talking about "spirit" this and "spirit" that, but what does that mean? Isn't spirit a mental attitude about hard work? It is enough to have an attitude of hard work; this is what is most important. But no one has any idea what you're talking about if you just talk randomly about "spirit."[67]

The problem for Gotō was that while Araki proved an outspoken ally in the cabinet, his support for the Ministry of Agriculture and Forestry's demands only strengthened Takahashi's opposition to more spending for the villages. A contemporary described Takahashi's impression of Gotō as "extremely bad." In an attempt to come to Gotō's defense, one observer suggested to Takahashi that it wasn't Gotō who was stirring up the villages but the army. Takahashi responded, "No, what he has done is no different from what the army has done." The finance minister clearly felt that Gotō had aligned himself and his ministry with the military.[68]

Gotō and Takahashi were also far apart in how they viewed the countryside and solutions to its problems. Gotō was anxious to get the state fully involved in supporting rural relief and reform; Takahashi was convinced that farmers needed less help, not more. The finance minister's attitude did not go unnoticed by Gotō, who said, "I've talked to Takahashi about many different things, but since it seems that our ideas about the villages are fundamentally different, it's quite difficult. I can't be very optimistic [about the budget]."[69] Takahashi had this to say about Gotō's budget aspirations:

As for the village problem, the Minister's requests are extremely large. At present, even without spending any money, if we think in terms of reducing burdens, avoiding frivolous spending—or, rather, cutting back on spending—there are methods [that are effective]. It is not a bad thing not to give the villages money.[70]

Takahashi then offered a personal example to illustrate where he stood. In early November, a group of some two or three hundred village headmen had arrived and asked to meet the finance minister. He refused and sent a vice minister in his place, whom the villagers turned away, repeating their demand to meet Takahashi face to face. Relenting, Takahashi invited a group of fifty representatives into his residence and ended up talking with them for two hours. In what was apparently a very frank discussion, he chastised the group, saying:

On the one hand you talk about pursuing national defense to the utmost, so that the Japanese have all come to feel like soldiers, while on the other hand you say time and again that the villages can't get on their feet and "Can't you do something?" Taken together, these demands invite ridicule from abroad. You must stop thinking like that and take on a mental attitude of proceeding with self-revitalization.[71]

The finance minister was pleased to find that, after having been given the runaround by bureaucrats, the local officials were favorably impressed by some straight talk. They left happy, Takahashi reported.

It is easy to see how important the self-revitalization approach had become for Takahashi. Putting fiscal realities aside for a moment, he seems to have genuinely respected the values promoted under its auspices. Hard work, frugality, and local or individual initiative had a strong appeal for the finance minister, as he made clear to the visiting headmen. Takahashi was probably also less willing than many to accept the fact that the villages were truly in need. Shortly after the close of the Sixty-third Diet, he had opined that it might be possible to make cuts in the relief budget based on his belief that a slight increase in rice and silk prices had improved conditions in the villages. The same day, Prime Minister Saitō talked with reporters about how he hoped to "get results while spending as little money as possible"; people who had actually been to the countryside, he said, reported that conditions there were really not that bad.[72] Both men were dismayed by the appearance during the summer of so many petitioners asking for handouts from the state. Their subsequent advocacy of self-revitalization and the Economic Revitalization Campaign had as much to do with their personal attitudes toward the idea of state aid as it did with the realization that there was no way the state could afford to please everyone.

Still, Gotō tried during the Domestic Conferences to convince if not Takahashi then other cabinet members of the need to continue and to expand rural relief.[73] After describing the ongoing crisis in the countryside, Gotō outlined his ministry's proposals for new programs to address it. Referring regularly to the need to better "control" the farm economy, Gotō advocated an expanded role for the industrial cooperatives, closer coordination between the production and sale of farm goods, and implementation of a tenancy law to stabilize tenant rights. He mentioned local financial reform, better balance between rural and urban tax burdens, and more state funding for schools. On the ideological front, he wanted to train village "mainstays" to help them provide local leadership and to instill loyalty, patriotism, and the spirit of mutual assistance in rural communities.[74]

Most of Gotō's proposals would have been familiar to those active in rural reform, and each item on the agenda probably had its own supporters within the cabinet and in groups like the Imperial Agricultural Association. Under normal circumstances, those points might have worked on the minister's behalf, but these were not normal times and the Domestic Policy Conferences were themselves an unusual venue for negotiation. The conferences cried out for the bold, the colorful, the unusual. Unfortunately for Gotō (and, one assumes, for the villages), it was clear that he had not risen to the occasion. Gotō brought little that was new to the negotiating table, and nothing in his list of farm policies was capable of exciting the passion of any but the most dedicated bureaucrat. After Araki's fiery rhetoric and bold visions, Gotō's suggestions about what the state needed to do in the countryside were colorless and bland.

Finance Minister Takahashi attended his first conference in early December, and though he quickly agreed with Gotō about the issues plaguing the countryside, the two wasted no time in disagreeing about solutions. After listening to a summary of what had transpired in the first two meetings, Takahashi began his reply by referring to Maeda Masana's 1884 *Kōgyō iken* (Advice on Promoting Enterprise), a document that had described local economic conditions in great detail and suggested ways the government might best use its scant resources in developing the country. Although focused on industrial development, the work did not ignore farmers and identified several areas in which the state could help the countryside, provided that farmers did their part by not living beyond their means.[75] He tended to agree with the agriculture minister's comments, said Takahashi, but he still felt that the initiative for recovery ought to remain in local hands, as the *Kōgyō iken* had so clearly stated: "I am certain that, even today, the spirit of what was done in 1882 and 1883 is not inappropriate."[76]

Later, Takahashi added to this in discussions with reporters, noting that Gotō's explanations of the countryside's problems had only deepened his belief in the need for self-revitalization in rural communities. While the state might need to provide farmers with a hint or two about how to take on the job of recovery themselves, the government clearly should not be in the habit of handing out money. That would only "bring on dependency," Takahashi complained, and no one wanted that.

The lines were drawn even more sharply at the next meeting, held on December 7. Takahashi reportedly blamed the lack of recovery in the villages on the farmers themselves, who, he said, spent too much on frivolous things. Weddings were too ornate, people paid too much for education (especially for women, he noted), and they used too much chemical fertilizer when compost worked just as well. Takahashi was supported by Rail Minister Mitsuchi, whose argument was that middle-level landlords had in fact been hardest hit by the depression in agriculture. Though they made as much now as they had ten years ago, Mitsuchi complained, these landlords hadn't bothered to adjust their lifestyle to economic realities and were thus living beyond their means.[77] As before, Takahashi emerged as a strong advocate of individual change and local initiative, short-circuiting Gotō's plans for broader state efforts. The best Gotō could do was get attendees to express support for the idea that "the fundamental problem of village reform is the development of simple, vigorous, land-loving farmer's spirit."[78]

Having apparently abandoned his earlier focus on economic and fiscal reform in favor of spiritual recovery, Gotō agreed to provide specific policy recommendations at the next session. By then, other cabinet members and the press had concluded that whatever the conferences might once have been about, they had become nothing but a face-saving effort for Gotō. Education Minister Hatayama, who had finally been asked to attend a meeting, refused to participate in such a pointless exercise. The same day, the *Chūgai shōgyō* made similar comments, describing the conferences as little more than a sop to Gotō to help make up for his failure in regular budget negotiations.[79]

The other consensus that was emerging from the meetings was that advocates of self-revitalization, Takahashi and Mitsuchi among them, would probably come out ahead. Home Minister Yamamoto told reporters that Gotō, Araki, and Takahashi were in agreement on the need for self-revitalization and ready to move ahead on a budget that reflected this newfound common ground. Exactly what that budget might support wasn't clear, but Yamamoto was quick to caution farmers against getting their hopes up. The Finance Ministry had no money to spare, and farmers would certainly be disappointed if they "expected a tiger to appear" and got a pussycat in its stead. Gotō lived up to his billing, offering at the remaining conferences only watered-down versions of his earlier proposals for rural reform and focusing instead on "the development of farmer's spirit" and "the implementation of cooperative organization"—both clearly in line with Takahashi's emphasis on self-revitalization.[80]

Although this left open the door to certain types of funding in association with the Economic Revitalization Campaign, the conferences were clearly a setback for Gotō and to some extent for the countryside as well. Land issues, which had at least been mentioned early in the conferences, were dropped from discussion—as was the better part of a long list of plans for "stabilization of village life," which had included rural medical facilities, local industrialization efforts, and boosting the state's share of compulsory education costs.[81] Saitō and others assured the press that consideration of these topics had not been abandoned, only postponed. The Domestic Policy Conferences were to continue in the spring, he insisted, at which time these subjects would be given the attention they deserved.[82] The press was skeptical, noting that Gotō and Araki were the only officials who seemed enthusiastic about pursuing rural reform and concluding that the cabinet kept alive the fiction that the meetings would continue only to reassure the Diet and the public that they were doing something about domestic problems and to avoid embarrassing Gotō and Araki any further.[83]

The conferences sharply narrowed the scope of Gotō's vision for the countryside and, in so doing, made the cabinet appear unwilling to address rural problems head on. Part of the problem was that Gotō's policies were seen at the time as a collection of dated and rather feeble responses to the needs of the countryside. It is questionable whether they would have won funding even under less stringent budgetary conditions. In addition to the problems with the policies themselves, Araki's support for them and for Gotō was clearly a liability. Takahashi's personal feelings were more than enough reason for him to block Gotō at every turn, knowing that eventually at least some of the blame for the lack of funds would stick to the military like glue.

The Sixty-fifth Diet provided the first testing ground for the results of the Domestic Policy Conferences. In his opening speech to the upper house of the Diet, Saitō was cautiously optimistic about the state of the economy and mentioned each of the conferences' rural policy items at least once without going into detail.[84] Takahashi took a similar approach: upbeat about the economy, tight-lipped on funding for the Ministry of Agriculture. Legislators responded with vigor to the budget and raised the village problem in discussions about it, but it was clear that they, too, found the countryside's concerns less pressing than before.

Politicians concerned about rural relief turned their energies toward garnering as big a piece as they could of a much smaller budget pie. The major parties expressed regret about what had happened to the relief budget, but they tempered their statements carefully. They agreed that the villages needed help but were not necessarily of one mind about how best to provide it. In a refrain common to the major parties, the Seiyūkai's Azuma Takeshi pointed out that, according to his calculations, more than half of the 1934 budget was given over to military use. Without directly challenging the need for such spending, Azuma pointed out that Japan was spending relatively little on its rural communities. He referred to the serious steps under way in Germany to protect farmers and noted that the U.S. government had allocated a billion dollars to the Agricultural Recovery Act. Why was Japan, which had more farmers as a percentage of the population than either of these countries, seeing fit to spend so little? he asked.[85] As for Gotō, Azuma expressed admiration for the way he pressed his case in the Domestic Policy Conferences, but didn't really grasp what the fuss was about. There was no chance for funding, and Gotō should have known as much. What was worse, said Azuma, the policies Gotō presented to the conferences appeared to have been sitting around in someone's desk for years, only to be renamed and presented as "emergency" policies.[86]

Similar charges were raised by Minseitō legislators. Former bureaucrat and legislator Den Akira could talk with some authority about how Gotō's "shopworn stock" had failed to motivate anyone in the Finance Ministry. He also pointed out that Takahashi, Yamamoto, and Mitsuchi had good connections within the Ministry of Agriculture and were well informed about exaggerations in that ministry's budget requests. Like Azuma, Den was not at all surprised by what had happened in the budget meeting and was as dubious as his Seiyūkai counterpart about Gotō's hopes for the conferences. "As everyone expected," there had been little chance of Gotō getting the funds he needed out of the meetings.[87]

Even the Imperial Agricultural Association, which might have been expected to complain the loudest about the budget fiasco, suggested that at least some of the blame was Gotō's. Writing about the policies that the agriculture minister had proposed, one commentator said, "There are no new flavors in them. It doesn't seem as if there were any good ideas worthy of the crisis." The fact that the policies were not new eliminated the need to discuss them. Of course it would be nice to have them implemented, but whether they were the best treatment at this time for the ills of the countryside was in doubt.[88] In other words, Gotō hadn't raised enough of a fuss—or asked for enough money—to be taken seriously by Takahashi and the others.

One bright spot in the aftermath of the conferences and the budgeting process was the successful fight by the Seiyūkai for funds for agricultural association technicians. For years, both the parties and the association had been calling for increased state support for the local technicians. The nascent Economic Revitalization Campaign relied heavily on the guidance of the technicians, and if the conferences had done nothing else, they had made it clear that Takahashi supported at least some aspects of revitalization. Past efforts to convince Takahashi to release funding for the technicians had been rebuffed; at one point he had suggested that—unlike local experts in the United States, who were serious about their work—their Japanese counterparts were far less competent.[89]

The Ministry of Agriculture asked for 3 million yen during the 1934 budget negotiations, and the Imperial Agricultural Association kept up its lobbying efforts. In mid-November, Viscount Makino Tadayuki visited the finance minister and presented him with a written description of the progress made by Kawahara Saburō, a local technician in the Shikoku village of Sawachi. The materials had been prepared hastily and were probably intended only to supplement Makino's attempts at persuasion. Makino's report of the meeting was that it had gone rather badly, with Takahashi saying it was unlikely that the Finance Ministry would be able to do anything to help. As they were about to go their separate ways, Makino remembered that he had brought some documents and handed them over to Takahashi to read at his leisure.[90] For many months that seemed to be the end of it. Observers predicted that the Ministry of Agriculture might see at most a few hundred thousand yen for training efforts in the countryside; 3 million yen seemed out of reach.

What happened next must have surprised almost everyone. At a budget committee meeting in late January 1934, Takahashi pulled from his briefcase the materials Makino had given him months before and began to read aloud. He read about how Technician Kawahara had spent the last six years ceaselessly working, helping the villagers help themselves. At his urging they had formed dozens of farm practice associations and had shifted production to cucumbers, which could be sold profitably. When other communities copied their example and prices for cucumbers dropped, Kawahara got seeds for peas from all the seed wholesalers in Japan and led the search for the "right" variety. The "Sawachi pea" soon attracted enough of a following that merchants began to buy directly from the village. Income was well above what it had once been, and Kawahara was exploring other ways of making the community a better place in which to live.

Although Kawahara's exploits don't seem to have changed Takahashi's mind about relief in general, his approach to recovery was close enough to Takahashi's own to make the finance minister rethink his attitude toward local technicians. "Just relying on the state to provide aid to help the villages will not have any result. When there are people like this, the villages will prosper for the first time," Takahashi told the assembled committee. "More than anything else, I would like the government and you (pointing at the legislators) to nurture people like this and make full use of them."[91] The finance minister was sticking to his guns on the importance of self-revitalization; luckily for the Imperial Agricultural Association, Kawahara's efforts played right into Takahashi's idea of what every village should be doing, and all without any help from the state.

The association and its allies in the Seiyūkai still had a tough road ahead of them, however, for Takahashi's new attitude was no guarantee of funding. Only last-minute negotiations between Takahashi and a Seiyūkai contingent made up of Azuma, Hatta Sokichi from Fukushima, other representatives with rural constituencies, and Rail Minister Mitsuchi convinced him to yield the money they wanted. In late February 1934, a supplementary budget provision gave 200,000 yen toward the support of association technicians.[92]

## The Military and Rural Relief

Shortly after the key decisions on the 1934 budget were reached, the army released a "Declaration Concerning the Estrangement of the People and the Military." Stinging from sharp criticism over its role in helping decimate the village relief budget, army spokesmen insisted:

Like [statements] that suggest that the village problems have been sacrificed to the military budget, . . . the movement to split apart the people and the military means to destroy the links between the people who have the defense of the nation at heart. As for the village problem, based on the fact that it is a general problem of national governance, it cannot be separated from national defense. As everyone knows, it is of the utmost concern to the military.[93]

When asked what had prompted the release of this statement, the army and navy ministers told Prime Minister Saitō that they had been concerned about a series of incidents in which anti-military manifestos had been sent to military units throughout Japan in October and November 1933. Army Minister Hayashi (who replaced Araki in January 1934) later laid the blame for these incidents on foreign agitators, whom he said were trying to weaken the country's defense by causing problems in the relationship between the military and the people.[94] Hayashi insisted that not only were foreigners responsible for the propaganda but that they had even mailed it from abroad. He thus removed any possible connection between domestic events and the "Declaration" and rather clumsily played on national anxieties about foreign enemies.

Since the press had been quick to link the declaration to problems associated with the 1934 budget, it is not clear whom Hayashi thought he might fool. Military leaders were obviously concerned about the impact of their ballooning budgets on public perceptions and worked hard to offset the public's anger with symbolic and concrete steps on the countryside's behalf. Both during and after the late 1933 meetings about the budget, General Araki had made it clear that rural policy was one of his concerns and that he felt it was well within his rights as the army's spokesman to comment on it. After all, domestic unrest and the nation's defense were not unrelated. It was Araki who went to Saitō immediately after the end of the ministers' conferences to request cabinet-level discussion of domestic policies.[95]

Minister of Agriculture and Forestry Gotō might have challenged Araki's prerogatives, but he seems to have welcomed the general's intrusions into his domain. The links between the two men were probably strengthened by Gotō's participation in a conference of army officers in Fukui city, held in conjunction with the military maneuvers there. The so-called Farm Village Policy Federation Conference (Nōson taisaku rengō kyōgikai) featured discussions among Araki, Gotō, and general staff officers on farm policy; also in attendance were high officials in the Industrial Cooperative movement.[96] Newspaper reports also describe meetings between Araki, Gotō, Rail Minister Mitsuchi, and local leaders on the subject of village conditions, suggesting a consistent effort on Araki's part to participate—and to be seen participating—in discussions of rural relief.

In published reports, Araki's opinions on farm policy were strongly influenced by his own concerns with national security in a broad sense, which included assurances about an adequate food supply and a healthy industrial base. Thus he could help negotiate with the Ministry of Commerce and

Industry to lower domestic fertilizer prices rather than liberalize fertilizer imports, a cheaper alternative that might have threatened Japanese producers. He was also a vocal opponent of plans to stabilize rice prices by reducing planted acreage, favoring instead a limited reduction in production of late-season rice.[97] However, neither Araki nor anyone else in the military community presented the public with an "army policy" for the countryside. Araki borrowed from ideas under discussion by the Ministry of Agriculture and Forestry but studiously avoided sounding as though he was trying to usurp its prerogatives in policy development. He could criticize or support specific policies on the basis of their relationship to national security, but he did not try to put the army in the farm policy business. Perhaps he feared that the more he intruded into the affairs of other ministries, the easier it would be for them to interfere in the running of the army. Hayashi Senjūrō, Araki's successor as army minister, was very reluctant to involve himself in domestic policy for just that reason, pointing out that should he do so, what was to stop the agriculture minister from developing a plan for national defense?[98]

Army and navy leaders were quick to understand the liabilities of their new relationships with bureaucrats like Gotō, not to mention the potential cost to their images of their own budget successes. Araki's discussions with Gotō and others about the countryside signaled the army's public involvement in an area that until late 1933 it had seen fit to neglect. The timing was certainly right for Araki to say something, and it was easy enough to make a case for the links between a strong, healthy countryside and a viable national defense. The unique combination of perceived foreign threats and domestic problems made military involvement possible if not necessary.

Yet Araki's choice of time and content could be interpreted as in the best interests of the army for other reasons as well. The ministers' conferences had made it clear that the upcoming battle over the budget would be a fierce one, and it seemed increasingly likely that were the military to come out ahead, domestic spending would have to suffer. It is hard to resist the conclusion that Araki's leap to the defense of the farms came when it did as part of a strategy to blunt public criticism that the villages had been sacrificed to pay for the military's budget. What better way to show one's support for the villages than to side with the Ministry of Agriculture and appear in the national press calling for help for the countryside?

Both military services were quick to take action to support their public statements. During the Sixty-fifth Diet, the army tried to impress on politicians the role that military spending would play in providing relief. The army estimated that 120 million yen of its 160 million budget would eventually make its way into civilian hands, providing more than 19 million days of employment. Some of those jobs would go to people from Japan's northeast, spokesmen went out of their way to emphasize, for the army planned to send recruiters to the Tōhoku region in search of able-bodied men to work in the production of military materials.[99]

After the Diet, both services took steps to increase their purchases of agricultural and other commodities directly from villages. This is not to say that they had never bought farm goods before, only that most purchases had been from merchants and wholesalers. The new strategy was to try to bypass the middleman and go directly to the producer or to producers' organizations.[100] (The Economic Revitalization Campaign would expand the ability of the industrial cooperatives to act as local intermediaries.) In April 1934, naval bases in Yokosuka, Kure, and Sasebo were ordered to buy as much farm produce as possible directly from villages. Bases were urged to pay special attention to local specialties—cabbage from Miyagi or tofu from Nagano, for instance—and to concentrate their purchases in prefectures where the economic situation was poor. The navy publicized plans to hire two thousand Tōhoku residents for employment in naval arsenals, and supply officers started touring communities to identify local products for purchase. Eventually the navy sponsored exhibitions to attract the best possible materials; on May 27 (Navy Anniversary Day), one such exhibition helped the navy explore possible uses for domestic silk.[101]

The army took similar steps to ensure that, whenever possible, purchases be made from the agricultural associations and industrial cooperatives, avoiding commercial middlemen. Planners ordered that provisions for the troops in Manchuria be bought from the Tōhoku and Nagano regions, for example. Items recommended for direct purchase included rice, horses, wool, furs, beef, and fish. In some areas the army's interest in wool led to an increased interest in sheep raising; rabbit production was also up, their fur useful in winter clothing.[102] In some cases the military's needs dovetailed nicely with the crop diversification and rural manufacturing processes advocated by the Economic Revitalization Campaign.

Even as direct rural relief was winding down, the military seems to have emerged from the budgeting debates relatively unscathed. Araki's public defense of Gotō and of the countryside offset any damage that the military's voracious appetite for money might have caused and left the services looking both worried about rural communities and able to do something about those concerns. Since these debates played out in the press and in the Diet at the same time as the trials of the army, navy, and civilian defendants charged in the May 15 Incident, the atmosphere was one rich in sympathy for the military.

Moreover, since the choices between rural relief and military spending were never again as clear-cut, there is little to suggest that the services ever faced the same degree of criticism from their rural constituency as they did in late 1933. The military's allegiance to the countryside—and vice versa—seemed quite secure in the aftermath of the budget debates. In the meantime, the Diet and the parties had demonstrated again that they were unable or unwilling to protect rural voters. Even groups like the Imperial Agricultural Association were bypassing the parties in favor of direct connections to the bureaucracy. It is possible to make too much of these changes, but they lend additional credence to the idea that as the decade wore on the parties were increasingly marginalized as ineffective and unresponsive in areas that mattered. The initiative had passed into the hands of the bureaucrats and the military.[103]

## Conclusions

The Sixty-fifth Diet eventually restored to the budget some of the items Takahashi had trimmed, but there was nevertheless little to show for Gotō's efforts in the Domestic Policy Conferences.[104] The overall results of the budget process dealt emergency relief funding a substantial blow. The government had agreed to spend some 366 million yen on relief in 1933, but the following year offered only 235 million yen, a reduction of more than a third. The Ministry of Agriculture's share of new funding for emergency relief spending was just under 35 million yen, or about 35 percent of all new funding for relief. Even with low-interest loans added in, the amount that would be paid out in wages for rural public works projects in 1934 was almost half of what it had been the year before. Assuming that wage levels were kept constant at 0.7 yen a day, the state could pay for 48.6 million days of work in 1934, considerably less than the 90.9 million days of work it funded in 1933, or the 74.3 million in 1932.[105] Overall, the Ministry of Agriculture suffered a 13 percent (14.3 million yen) loss in funding from 1933 to 1934. Only the Foreign Ministry fared worse.[106]

The timing of the spending cuts was particularly poor. After a year of record harvests in 1933, the summer of 1934 was rainy, cold, and overcast in much of the northeast, resulting in one of the worst crops in modern memory and plunging that part of the country into famine or near-famine conditions. Although the state eventually responded to the crisis, it was clear that the 1933 decisions to cut back on relief spending represented an end to any long-term, direct financial support for public-works wages and credit. Whatever might come out of the state's coffers from that point on would be on a strictly ad hoc basis, given only in cases of demonstrated hardship and not as part of a sustained program of assistance.

Yet it was also clear that as of 1934 the rural depression was still very much with farmers and their families. Takahashi's spending programs had indeed had an effect on the economy, for the industrial and manufacturing sectors began a quick return to prosperity. Some of that largesse was making its way to the countryside; in Sekishiba, as elsewhere, the combination of public works and more funding for the military was having an impact on local incomes. Rural communities in general, however, were much slower to recover from the depression than the cities, and few observers of the countryside believed that it had overcome the challenges of the depression by 1934.

Revitalization was thus the farmer's last and best hope for recovery from the depression. The rhetoric of relief deployed by Takahashi, the prime minister, and others left little doubt that the administration placed great stock in the effectiveness and appropriateness of self-revitalization. Of all the components of rural relief, economic revitalization had by 1934 emerged as the dominant paradigm of the process of recovery. Its tenets of community-based reform, social harmony, and a more robust rural economy increasingly informed the popular vision of the countryside's future.

# 6   Revitalization

UNLIKE OTHER RURAL RALLIES OR the petition movements that were gaining strength in the spring of 1932, the Farmers' Self-Revitalization Festivals (Nōjin jiriki kōsei matsuri) in Hyōgo were not about to demand help from the state. Quite the contrary; the festivals spread a different gospel, one not of salvation from without but of restoration from within. There were six festivals in all, held on different days and at locations throughout the prefecture. Invitations went out to local farmers, school principals, leaders of local civic groups, and to a handful of reporters. The festival sites were always full; as busy as farmers were, many took a day off that May to participate. Using motivational speeches, testimonial accounts, and leaflets, the festivals presented attendees with a program of reforms developed by the Hyōgo Prefecture Agricultural Association, one that association leaders hoped to introduce to a wider audience than the handful of communities already participating in it.

They succeeded beyond their expectations. Within a few months of the first festival, the basic tenets of the Hyōgo Association's approach to rural reform and recovery had been adopted by the state as the central component of its national effort to help rural communities recover from the depression. What in Hyōgo had been called "self-revitalization" (*jiriki kōsei*) became on the national stage the Economic Revitalization Campaign. By 1941, the campaign's final year, close to four-fifths of the nation's rural communities were campaign participants.

The Economic Revitalization Campaign's wedding of sweeping reforms of rural life to the more narrowly conceived policies of debt arrangement and public works reshaped the countryside of the 1930s. The campaign introduced economic and social practices designed not only to help communities recover from the depression but also to construct a countryside that was at heart healthier, vibrant, prosperous, and more than an equal to the nation's growing cities. Although it fell far short of the changes necessary for sustained stability and prosperity, the campaign nevertheless was responsible for a series of significant changes in rural life. Over time, this emphasis on rural prosperity and rebirth was itself transformed by the war in China and its demands on the nation's economy and polity. The techniques and enthusiasms of revitalization were easily adapted to mobilization's needs. Later chapters document these developments; this chapter focuses on the circumstances surrounding the emergence of revitalization as a key relief policy.

The rise of revitalization as the dominant force in the countryside's recovery was guided by three complementary impulses. The first consisted of local initiatives aimed at reform; by 1932, a number of groups were experimenting with programs of economic planning and restructuring, in some cases building on years of trial and error at the village level. The Hyōgo Agricultural Association was one such group; it had developed what its members believed to be a successful program, one that by 1932 they were eager to promote as part of a national solution to the rural crisis. The association's blueprint for local revitalization played an important role in shaping the state's policies.

Second, key policymakers, the prime minister and Takahashi among them, were receptive to the premises of revitalization and became early and enthusiastic supporters of it. After being inundated with requests for assistance and with pleading citizens, both men were openly critical of what they felt was a lack of initiative on the part of farmers and their growing dependency on the state. Revitalization offered a way out, one that put the ball back in the farmers' court by making recovery contingent on their hard work. Better yet, even though revitalization looked like a massive undertaking for the state, it was in fact far cheaper than public works.

Finally, and this is the third factor, the appeal of revitalization extended to the countryside and to communities already interested in the ideas and practices associated with reform. An audience already existed for the messages that the Economic Revitalization Campaign seemed to embody—an audience shaped by the coming of age of a well-educated cohort of young men and women, by the rapid expansion in the 1920s of media directed at rural consumers, and by the sense of a widening cultural and economic gap between city and country. The rural social landscape of the early 1930s was quite different from what it had been even a decade before. Revitalization fit well with the vision that many farmers and their families were even then constructing of their futures.

## Local Reform

Local efforts at reform were plentiful and varied. A survey commissioned by the Ministry of Agriculture and Forestry and conducted by the Imperial Agricultural Association in 1932 found that 862 villages and five cities had drafted some sort of community-wide plan aimed at economic recovery. The majority of these blueprints were drawn up on the village level and were the responsibility of that community's agricultural association. Village offices, local unions, combinations of industrial cooperatives and farmers and the local agricultural association designed the rest. Three-quarters of the plans had been drawn up in the past three years, probably in response to growing economic hardship.[1]

It was not uncommon for local officials to be involved in the planning process. In Nagano, bureaucrats established a Prefectural Farm Village Economic-Reform Committee in April 1932, which helped oversee local industrial cooperative surveys and planning efforts. Village-level planning started in Shizuoka in 1930, with model communities designated the following year. In Kyushu, a program led by the local agricultural association got under way in Fukuoka in 1930, while a cooperative effort between the prefectural government and the prefectural agricultural association started in Kumamoto that same year.[2]

These efforts had little in common with one another. Despite the involvement of the local branches of national organizations, there had been, as of 1932, no serious attempt by either the Imperial Agricultural Association, the industrial cooperatives, or the central government to provide guidelines to towns and villages on the uses of community planning and reform. Planners were left to their own devices—and to their own concerns. The scale of the local plans thus varied widely, since some were written with a single village in mind and others for only a single hamlet. Most plans promised to improve the economic conditions in the community, but not all shared even this goal. According to Imperial Agricultural Association Secretary Okada

Atsushi, his feeling after looking over a description of plans in late 1931 was that "there are far more plans to improve farm management than there are Village Plans."[3] In other words, those plans for reform emphasized the short-term advantages of improved management styles and not the long-term vision of rural improvement that Okada had hoped to find.

There is little to suggest that the Ministry of Agriculture and Forestry or other parts of the government were developing a policy for village planning and reform before the summer of 1932. An Agriculture and Forestry Deliberative Council (Nōrin shingikai) report issued in February of that year recommended further study of village planning as one element of a debt arrangement policy but stopped short of more specific recommendations.[4] Matsumoto Gaku, an associate of Gotō Fumio and, at the time, director of the Home Ministry's Social Bureau, wrote an article in praise of the Fukuoka recovery project in late 1931. (Matsumoto had been governor of that prefecture until assuming his post in the Social Bureau.) That local attempt at *keizai kaizen* (economic improvement) focused on debt management, homemade fertilizer, and coordination of sales and purchases. Plans for recovery were based on careful surveys of local conditions and were implemented at the hamlet level by farming associations.

According to Matsumoto, the results after a year and a half were promising. Consumption of cash fertilizer was down, and crop yields had remained stable. They were even making progress on farm debt, he noted. But Matsumoto stopped short of advocating the development of a similar approach for the whole country, or even the expansion of Fukuoka's model beyond its borders. His article was thus less a blueprint for action than a bit of "reference material" for people in other parts of the country.[5] No one would stop farmers from adapting plans like the ones in Fukuoka to their own needs, but no one in the government seemed interested in helping them do so, either.

The impetus for the development of a national effort at rural reform came from outside the state. As we have seen in earlier discussions, nongovernment activists and their organizations were able to raise specific issues, offer model solutions, and demand help from the state for a variety of farm problems. Something similar happened with the idea of village planning and economic revitalization. In the period between the start of the Sixty-second Diet session and the end of the Sixty-third, it became more and more common for petitioners, especially those with links to the Imperial

Agricultural Association, to call for the pursuit of self-revitalization in their appeals to the state. Over these same few months, a parallel development occurred within the cabinet and within the Ministry of Agriculture and Forestry as self-revitalization became the catchphrase for the state's newest and most substantive response yet to the depression. The story of how and why that happened begins with the Hyōgo Prefecture Agricultural Association.[6]

Late in 1931, Nagashima Sadashi, secretary of the Hyōgo Prefecture Agricultural Association and a leading light in local self-revitalization, watched in wonder at the scene in Kobe's Youth Hall. In an ingenious marketing technique, the city's hat makers had hired out the hall to stage a mock memorial service in honor of the summer season's straw hats. Passersby and invited guests were urged to bid farewell to their old straw hats (which were donated to a clinic in Okayama prefecture for Hansen's disease) while being treated to speeches that described in glowing terms the hats' past services and offered not-so-subtle enticements to invest then and there in a nice new winter hat.[7]

Inspired by the techniques if not the product, Nagashima resolved to somehow bring a similar level of enthusiasm, organization, and excitement to his campaign for rural reform. This he did, locally at first through a series of Farmers' Self-Revitalization Festivals that began touring Hyōgo in May 1932. Part exhortation and part exposition, the festivals offered testimonial tales of farmers rescued by their own hard work and skill from the depression's grasp, self-help lectures, and spontaneous acclaim from audience members overcome by the promise of the moment. Nagashima and his colleagues soon took the messages of self-help that they had honed in rural Hyōgo to Tokyo, where audiences were no less receptive.

The Hyōgo Prefecture Agricultural Association was a pioneer in the use of village-level economic planning. Three men—Association President Yamawaki Nobukichi, the above-mentioned Secretary Nagashima Sadashi (who was reportedly the originator of the phrase "self-revitalization," or *jiriki kōsei*), and Agricultural Engineer Ishiwara Jirō—started working with communities and farmers within the prefecture as early as 1927.[8] According to Shōji Shunsaku, the leading scholar of the self-revitalization movement in Hyōgo, their approach was built on two complementary techniques. Part of what they did was teach individuals how to better manage their farms and make better use of the resources available to them. Nagashima called this aspect of the agricultural association's activities "Reform Leadership Projects." In addition to those efforts on the household level, the association was involved in efforts to develop community-wide plans for economic rejuvenation, or "Farm Village Production Plans."[9]

In both the private and the communal spheres, prefectural planners emphasized *kinrō shugi* (diligence). Nagashima described hard work and family manpower as "more important than anything" in the struggle to get past the point where all income went to pay back debt and into a position where assets could begin to accumulate.[10] Agricultural association surveys had shown that the average farm household made full use of the manpower available to it only a few times a year, and the rest of the time let that precious labor go to waste. If farmers and communities learned to put that labor to work on side-projects, new crops, or land development, their income would rise accordingly, leaders of the Hyōgo Agricultural Association argued. Spending would either drop (if families managed to provide for themselves items they used to buy), or it would at least rise no more quickly than income.

Although Nagashima and the others stressed how a rational, almost scientific approach to farming could balance budgets, they did not ignore the broader implications of self-revitalization. "There are no definite opinions about how to get out of our present predicament," wrote Nagashima, "or about how we ought to reform farm management, or about where we should go from here." Persistent temporizing had left the countryside severely weakened, so that falling incomes and heavy debt were little more than symptoms of a much deeper malaise. The only way out of the "abyss" into which the countryside had fallen was for communities and farm households alike to rely on self-revitalization to guide the way.

The agricultural association's program worked by using methods like "reform leadership" and "production plans" to instill a new sense of hope and empowerment in communities and households alike. And since those two methods were "deeply rooted in the private economies of the village and farm household, and firmly based on a position of comprehensive farm family management," it was a relatively simple task to build any number of additional rehabilitative policies on that foundation. The key was to make self-revitalization accessible and understandable; once that happened, the road to recovery would be clear. Local planners expected to create "villages and farms resurrected with an overflowing of energy, embracing brilliant hopes."[11]

Okada Atsushi, the well-known secretary of the Imperial Agricultural Association, had long been an advocate of a similar approach to the village problem and had a strong influence on the planners in Hyōgo. In a speech to supporters of the movement, Okada said:

The first condition of self-sufficiency is to make use of manpower, capital, and land that aren't being used now and to produce goods for your own support. There is plenty of room to pursue this, [but] in this situation, rather than making a calculation based on a regular economic outlook, you must think about it differently, as having gone from having nothing to having something. The thinking in this situation is that just 10 *sen* a day is ample pay for one's work. An outlook that says that it is better to sleep than to earn 10 *sen* or 30 *sen* is the opposite of diligence.[12]

Okada's emphasis on hard work was one part of the picture; his insistence that farmers not become dependent on the state was another. (This, of course, was despite the fact that the Imperial Agriculture Association was hardly innocent of making demands on the state.) Both beliefs were evident in the way the Hyōgo program was put together and in how its leaders presented their accomplishment to the public.

When the prefectural agricultural association first drafted its plans, its leaders hoped to select five villages a year, beginning in 1927, and to have one community pursuing self-revitalization in each of Hyōgo's twenty-five counties by the end of 1932. They underestimated the program's popularity, however, and this early plan could not keep pace with demand. After 1929, the prefectural organization expanded the role that local (village and county) agricultural associations could play, thus permitting a more rapid growth in the number of communities approved for participation. Almost 110 villages were chosen in 1930 and 1931 alone.[13]

The Hyōgo Association placed a great deal of emphasis on village planning, marketing, and other aspects of commercial farming during the latter half of the 1920s. The organization's ability to provide participating villages with guidance, and with grants to support those goals, was certainly an important reason for the popularity of the agricultural association's program. Hyōgo had other advantages, one of them the strength of the overall agricultural association organization. People like Nagashima and Yamawaki provided leadership at the prefectural level, but without a solid local base, their ideas would have gone nowhere. The prefecture's hamlet-level agricultural associations experienced rapid growth in the 1920s and were much more active than was the case in other prefectures. Their existence made it that much easier for the prefectural association to mobilize local energies.[14]

The self-revitalization program had elements in common with planning efforts of the past. It was designed first to survey the resources available to a community and then to help that community apply those resources more efficiently and profitably. Committees of local agricultural association members conducted the surveys, elicited not only information but also suggestions, and provided the guidelines (and the paperwork) that each household needed to create its own plan. Side-projects, crop diversification, and the increased use of farm animals as sources of income, fertilizer, and food were a few of the techniques that were encouraged.

In its publications, the Hyōgo Agricultural Association offered Kamitaka village as an example of a community that had benefited from the program of self-revitalization and planning. Designated as a program participant in 1929, the community that year had an average household income from farming of 434 yen. Despite the collapse of commodity prices in 1930, income from farming had risen to an average of 494 yen by 1931 and was higher still in 1932, at 569 yen per household. Farmers diversified their crops, used less chemical fertilizer than they had prior to participation in the prefectural agricultural association's program, doubled the amount of income derived from side-projects, and by 1932 made five times as much on the sale of chickens and vegetables as they had three years before.[15]

Another factor cited in the success of the self-help approach was its use of local competitions to stimulate interest in planning and to help motivate those already participating. Kamitaka's version of this was a village-wide contest to find the best farmer. Points were allocated in a number of categories, but the emphasis was clearly on the fruits of hard labor:[16]

| | |
|---|---|
| Pure income | 30% |
| Grain income | 10 |
| Side-projects | 17 |
| Area under cultivation | 8 |
| Farm labor days | 20 |
| Yield per *tan* | 8 |
| Percentage of self-produced fertilizer | 7 |
| TOTAL | 100% |

Shōji Shunsaku has described this system as one that linked diligence with commercial success. If the contest is any measure of what farmers thought was important in what they did, then hard work and its by-products are clearly paramount. Technical skill, landholding, and the like are not ignored but do not weigh heavily in comparison to income and days worked. The superior farmer made the best possible use of the resources available to him and made the most money doing so.

Competitions were not a new part of village life, but those before self-revitalization had as a rule focused primarily on technological advancement. Winners were those with a better strain of rice, a new breed of silkworm, a better irrigation system. These achievements were important but not accessible to the average farmer. Participation had been limited to the wealthier members of rural communities and took place across community boundaries. Thus, in previous competitions, the best farmer from Village A would be more interested in what his counterparts in Village B and C were up to than he would be in what happened within his own community. He might not even have a counterpart in his own village with whom to compete.

The Hyōgo Agricultural Association's approach as it worked in Kamitaka was far more limited geographically and had a much broader social base. The organizational and competitive building blocks were the hamlet and the village; if inter-village competition took place, it was of minor importance. Initial contests among all producers within a hamlet led to the selection of its representative, who went on to participate in the village-wide competition. Based on the results of competition in at least one community, it would appear that middle-level farmers did at least as well in the contests as others with considerably more land and resources.[17] These competitions helped both to encourage stronger efforts from farmers and to reinforce the messages about hard work and productivity that agricultural association planners wanted to send. Although there was little new or radical in their advocacy of self-revitalization and hard work, the Hyōgo Agricultural Association seems to have touched a chord both at home and with national leaders.[18] The Farmers' Self-Revitalization Festivals offer additional insight into the program's appeal.

In May 1932, the Hyōgo Agricultural Association leadership took their program on a tour of the prefecture. Local leaders, union presidents, school principals, reporters, and presidents of youth organizations invited to the Farmers' Self-Revitalization Festivals responded with enthusiasm. The festivals themselves were simple affairs: their goals were to inform, inspire, and proselytize. As Ishiwara described them, the meetings began with the presentation of data on the state of the economy, and with speeches on village conditions and the farm family. Yamawaki spoke of the need for self-revitalization in the face of the unprecedented agricultural depression; he was followed by Nagashima, who explained in detail the specific steps that villages and farmers could take to participate in the planning program. People from the audience were then invited to the rostrum to describe their own experiences and their own problems.

To help attendees better understand the points that Nagashima and the others were making, festival participants received a collection of "Materials Explaining Farm Village Self-Revitalization." The first thing participants in the festivals saw when they opened their copy was a chart outlining the major sources of farm poverty and distress (Fig. 1). This chart lays out the origins of rural poverty—namely, an imbalance of income and expenses and the assumption of too much debt at too high an interest rate. One constant refrain in these documents was that the causes of rural poverty were known, uniform, and could ultimately be overcome. Readers of the pamphlet from which this illustration came had only to turn the page for an equally detailed diagram of how self-revitalization would address the causes of farmers' distress point by point. Readers were told to abandon their "one-day-at-a-time approach" and to adopt instead "planned initiatives," to throw out "arbitrary, uniform proposals from on high" in favor of "proposals based on what the people know, and developed by them."[19]

The latter description showed self-revitalization in concrete terms and laid out the recovery process from start to finish. The first step on the road to recovery was a survey of "actual conditions" at both the family (for farm management reform) and the village (for production planning) levels. It was followed by "critical research," or an honest reflection on the economic health of the family and the community. Once everyone had solid, reliable information in hand, it was time for the third step, or the framing of a plan. The plans would vary according to circumstances and each household and community's resources and needs, but the broad patterns would be the same throughout. They would feature aggressive efforts to boost production (and thus income) in a variety of areas. In addition to increasing yields, planners were expected to look carefully at improvements in sericulture, livestock, and forestry, and at the possibility of processing some of what the community raised for sale.

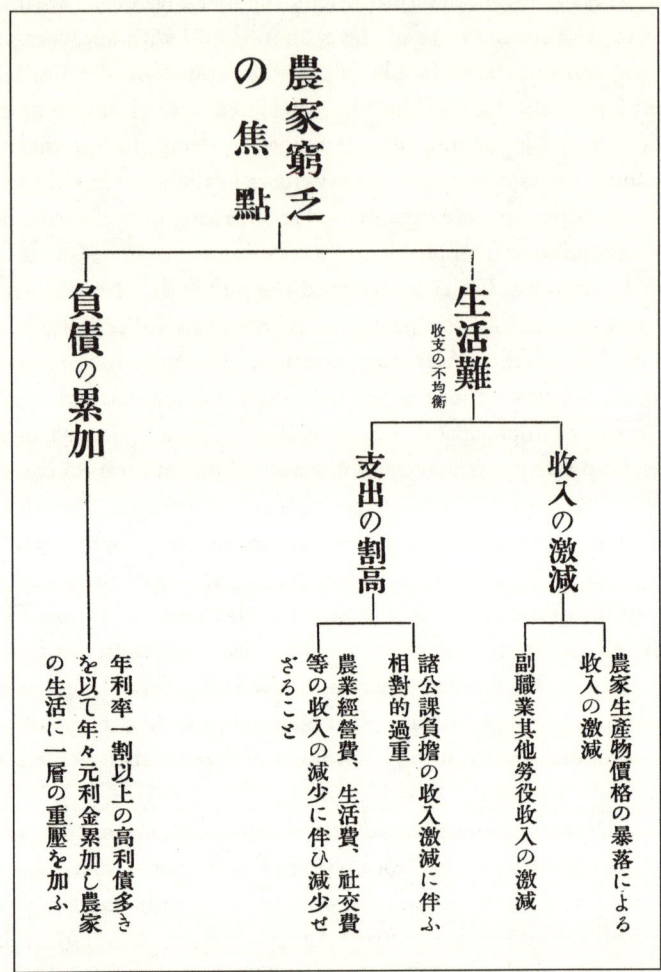

Fig. 1  The major sources of farm poverty and distress. This diagram was included with materials distributed to attendees of Hyōgo Prefecture Agricultural Association Farmers' Self-Revitalization Festivals, 1932 (SOURCE: Hyōgo-ken nōkai, *Nōson jiriki kōsei setsumei shiryō, 1932*, reprinted in Takeda Tsutomu and Kusumoto Masahiro, eds., *Nōsangyoson keizai kōsei undō shiryō shūsei*, pt. 1, vol. 1, p. 422).

Incomes would rise if all went well with that part of the plan. To make sure that the surplus wasn't eaten up by new spending, farmers were also expected to lower household and management expenditures and to spend less on "luxuries." To further reduce cash outlays, participants would become more self-sufficient. This might mean making one's own soy sauce or miso instead of buying it, or relying more on homemade fertilizer instead of the much more expensive, commercially available varieties. No matter what the final decisions were, households and communities had to give careful and reasoned thought to the possibilities available to them and take every advantage they could find.

Once the plans had been drawn up, the fourth stage was to get the message out to the village. General meetings and family conferences helped make everyone aware of what the community was trying to accomplish and would also ensure that non-participants and those who needed extra help would be identified early on. Once the community had been through that process of group affirmation, all that remained was to "put cooperation into effect." Farmers would do their work; the plans would take care of the rest.[20]

That these were not simply pie-in-the-sky proposals was evident in other documents made available to festival attendees, which described how several families and one community had begun to use the suggested planning methods to improve their economic situations. The association compared two sets of farmers—one a pair of anonymous "regular" farm families, the other the Morikawa and the Takada households, both practitioners of the association's revitalization program. Charts compared the percentage of days actually worked by each household with the total number of days they could have worked (see Fig. 2). The seasonal cycle of labor is obvious in the charts describing the "regular" farm families. Both approached 100 percent in the spring and again at harvest time, but the rest of the year they worked only a fraction of the days they could have in any given month.[21] The Morikawa and Takada households, in contrast, rarely fell below the 90 percent level and often exceeded the 100 percent mark, a feat accomplished by working longer hours per day than the average farmer.

As materials that accompanied the charts made clear, the "hardworking" families put their extra labor to use by diversifying production. Whereas the regular families stuck to just a few crops, the Takada family grew five. The Morikawa family pursued a similarly diverse approach, growing eight

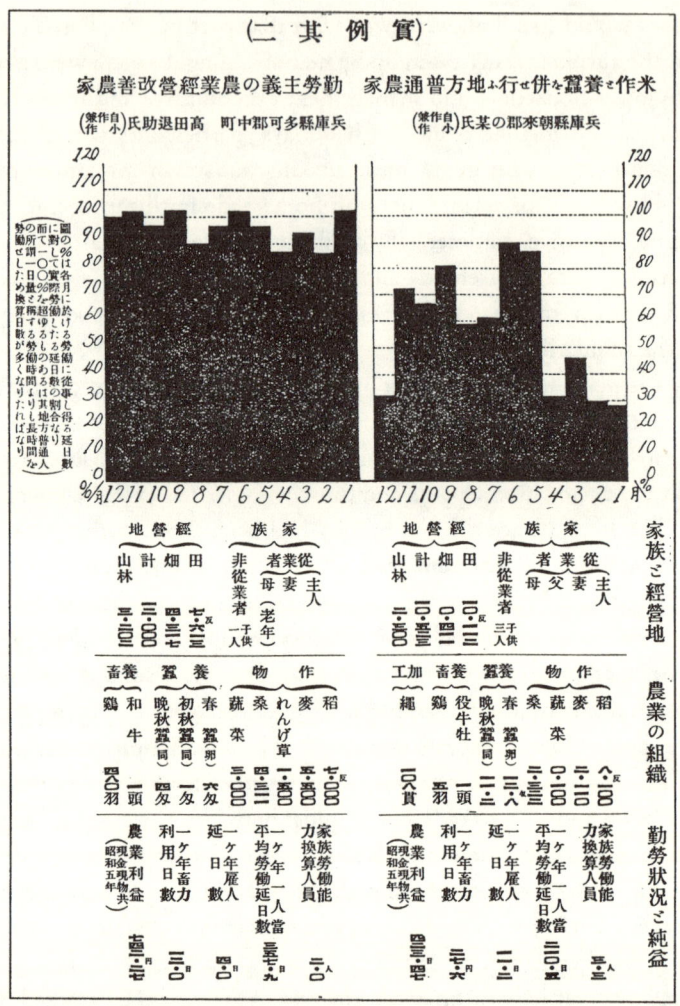

Fig. 2 The effects of diligence on the family farm. This diagram was included among materials distributed to attendees of Hyōgo Prefecture Agricultural Association Farmers' Self-Revitalization Festivals, 1932 (SOURCE: Hyōgo-ken nōkai, *Nōson jiriki kōsei setsumei shiryō, 1932*, reprinted in Takeda Tsutomu and Kusumoto Masahiro, eds., *Nōsangyoson keizai kōsei undō shiryō shūsei*, pt. 1, vol. 1, p. 426).

different crops and raising both chickens and a cow. Their "regular" counterparts, with more land, did less.[22] According to the material handed out at the festivals, the Morikawa and Takada families were well rewarded for their hard work and took in considerably more profit than their less committed counterparts. Based on this evidence, it would be hard to avoid the conclusion that hard work coupled with a diversified approach to farming was a sensible and profitable approach to the economic crisis. Those two qualities alone were evidently responsible for the success of the Takada and the Morikawa families. The reader is given no information about other issues that might affect productivity, such as rent, land quality, or the health of the family, which are presumably irrelevant to the broader message.

One final example of the association's proposals focused not on a single family's course of recovery but on an entire community's, in this case Yamada village of Kanzaki county in Hyōgo (see Fig. 3). These plans are laid out in a visually interesting manner. Income and expenditure categories appear as objects on opposite ends of a balance beam, with each tray filled with weights labeled "farm income" or "living expenses," so that in the 1930 plan (at the bottom of the page), the beam is tipped deep into the part of the scale marked "poverty." At the end of ten years, the income weights are much bigger, spending is smaller, and the "debt" weight has fallen off altogether. The result is that the scale (now at the top of the page) is tilted sharply in the opposite direction, well away from want and over into "wealth."

This fairly simple description painted a realistic picture of a village in economic difficulty and at the same time helped make the recovery process seem both concrete and straightforward. The materials noted that an average family in the village in question spent 809 yen in 1930 but had only 709 yen in income. According to the village's plan, households would allow spending to rise in 2- or 3-yen increments over the next ten years, which they could do because income was expected to rise in 35-yen increments over the same period. Using the principles laid out by the association, hard work, planning, and diligence would transform the community. The average household budget would be balanced after the first four years and would show a surplus of 229 yen per family after a decade.[23]

By emphasizing the importance of hard work, frugality, diligence, and community solidarity in the pursuit of recovery, the Hyōgo Agricultural Association clearly drew on past practices and rhetoric. Ninomiya Sontoku

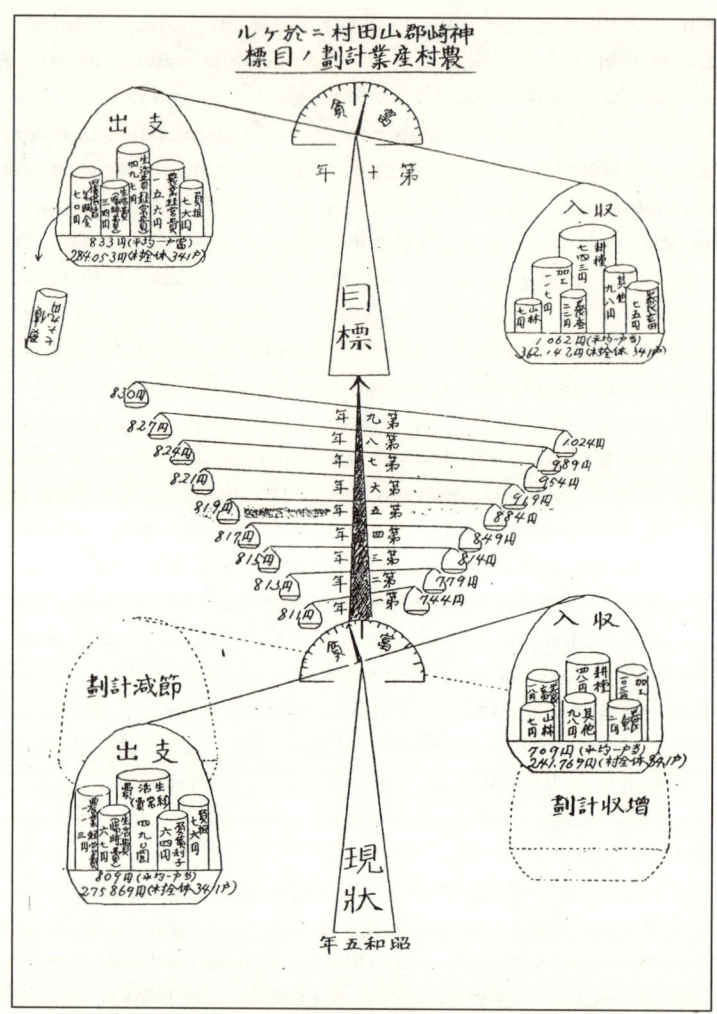

Fig. 3 Village-level revitalization materials illustrating the effects of ten years of planning. This diagram was included among materials distributed to attendees of Hyōgo Prefecture Agricultural Association Farmers' Self-Revitalization Festivals, 1932 (SOURCE: Hyōgo-ken nōkai, *Nōson jiriki kōsei setsumei shiryō, 1932*, reprinted in Takeda Tsutomu and Kusumoto Masahiro, eds., *Nōsangyoson keizai kōsei undō shiryō shūsei*, pt. 1, vol. 1, p. 424).

would likely have been comfortable with many of the precepts laid out at the festivals, and this vintage language no doubt was part of revitalization's appeal to Takahashi and Prime Minister Saitō. Still, not all the wine in self-revitalization's new bottles was past its prime. Clearly emphasized in each document and in each speech was the rational application of resources toward a known outcome. The future might not be one of tremendous wealth since, as the examples suggest, gains would be modest even after a decade, but the progression from poverty to solvency was orderly, predictable, and, as the materials seemed to prove, possible for almost anyone to achieve. The application of the vocabularies and principles of economics and of science marked this approach to recovery as a modern one and not simply a holdover from the nineteenth century. Recovery wasn't just about doing more with less; though there were elements of self-denial woven into the association's propaganda, the proactive features are equally striking. The association promised change for the better, not more of the same.

That these vocabularies and principles were meant to be accessible to the widest possible audience of farmers suggests that something else had changed as well. The message of self-revitalization was not directed solely to landlords and local elites, as that of many past reform movements had been, but to the entire community. The village was the audience, and the association seemed to assume not only that most farmers could participate in the re-creation of their communities but that they should do so. Revitalization clearly promoted community solidarity and social harmony—neither one of which was a new idea. Yet the suggestion that the village be understood as something like an economic enterprise in which everyone had a stake was a step in a new direction. At no point did the planning or recovery process separate individual achievement from the broader needs and goals of the village. Individual success was transformed by diagrams like Figure 3 into a village-wide equation of profit and loss. These messages of broad participation, modern methods, and change for the better were seldom far from the surface in the Economic Revitalization Campaign.

The festivals closed with a pledge for all those in attendance. "We will promote the self-revitalization movement of the farms and the farmers," they repeated. "Let each of us move ahead and make something of self-revitalization." Thanks to another idea of Nagashima's, festival participants left with more than memories of their commitment. Each took home a "self-revitalization doll"—a small wooden figure of a farmer holding a hoe in his right hand.²⁴ This time Nagashima said he had been inspired not by Kobe's hat makers but by history. The idea for the statues came to him, he said, in Mito city, during a visit to the former domain of Tokugawa Mitsukuni, himself an early advocate of agricultural reforms. Tokugawa was said to have kept a small figure of a farmer with him to remind him to be grateful to the hardworking rural population for every meal he ate, and it was from this example that Nagashima borrowed.²⁵

## Self-revitalization on the National Stage

With their successes at home to give them confidence, the leaders of the Hyōgo Agricultural Association began to look beyond the borders of their prefecture. Although their program had initially been confined to Hyōgo, the problems facing farmers were clearly national in scope. Local policies and local planning were no longer sufficient to maintain the status quo, much less to improve conditions for the majority of rural communities. There was little if any indication that the state had policies of its own waiting in the wings, and the alternatives to the government (the Imperial Agricultural Association, for instance) had not risen to the challenges of the depression. By the early spring of 1932, the Hyōgo Agricultural Association was ready to take its case to the rest of the country.

Nagashima Sadashi's slogan of "self-revitalization" and a mass mailing campaign brought the association's accomplishments to the attention of national leaders. The association printed twenty-six thousand copies of a "manifesto" that it sent to agricultural groups within the prefecture, to prefectural assembly members, and to local newspapers. Saitō's cabinet received copies, as did Diet members with links to farming communities, national newspapers, and other national agricultural groups.²⁶ The manifesto was clearly designed to catch the eye of the recipient. The headlines on one page read, "The Coming of the Depression in Agriculture!" and "Farm Economics on the Brink of Catastrophe!" On the next page, the text read:

Get going with serious efforts in Self-Revitalization!

People of the villages and the farms, promote the spirit of Self-Revitalization, take a stand against these difficulties: one by one and all together, put all our energy into the reform of agricultural management! Let us farmers take care of our stability ourselves. Let us start with the Agricultural Association, and other village and farm leadership organizations standing at the head of the farmers, and light the flame of Village and Farm Self-Revitalization!²⁷

In addition, the Hyōgo Agricultural Association printed and mailed an additional several thousand copies of a large, two-color graph showing how farm incomes had plunged over the past few years. The accompanying text explained that market prices for the crops grown by farmers had fallen whereas taxes had not, which put the average farm household in a very unpleasant position. Self-revitalization, argued the mailing, was the only solution to those caught in this bind.[28]

The mailings were effective. Yamawaki was invited to meet with the home minister, who praised the group for the quality of the materials and noted that if things in Hyōgo were as grim as the association suggested, then the rest of the country must be in even worse shape.[29] The state's growing interest in the value of the Hyōgo experience to the rest of the country was evident in the telegram that Kodaira Gonichi sent to the festivals' organizers. He wrote: "The fundamental solution to the agricultural depression is the self-reliance of the farmers, the development of the way of revitalization, and putting cooperation into action. I have high hopes for your vigorous efforts."[30]

Kodaira had for some time been concerned about the direction the villages were taking and found the approach advocated in Hyōgo well suited to his own thinking. Although Kodaira felt that rising debt and falling prices were an important part of the problems crippling the countryside, an even graver problem was farmers' inability to rally to their own cause. "I have a feeling that the spirit of self-assistance has grown weaker and weaker in the villages," Kodaira wrote in 1930, "and that they have moved ever closer to relying on others." The essence of the village community, of village self-government, was *"jiriki shugi* (reliance on oneself, self-empowerment), not *tariki shugi* (reliance on others)."[31] As an example of what he meant, Kodaira pointed to what had happened when the record rice crop of 1930 flooded the market, sending prices plunging. There was little the state could do to control prices under those conditions, he argued, but if farmers worked together and agreed to store some of that rice, they themselves could see to it that prices were stable. That they had not done so was a strong indication of just how reliant on others farmers had become.

Kodaira noted that there were several obstacles to coordinated action by the farmers. There were many agricultural organizations within any given village, but coordination among them was so poor that it was almost impossible to decide on and implement a common policy, with or without the help of the state. Farmers needed not another organization but better use of what they had, plus a way to coordinate and direct farm production and marketing.[32] "One for all and all for one" was the slogan Kodaira used to describe his prescription for the rural community in 1930. The success of the organizational changes he advocated depended on changes in the farmers' attitudes. As long as farmers continued to look to the state for answers, they would likely get nowhere, wrote Kodaira. The more they relied on themselves and the more they looked to the farming community, the better off they would be.

By 1932, Kodaira's arguments were even more relevant. Nothing the state had done since 1930 had been able to prop up the prices of important farm commodities. "Each farmer for all and all for each" was not often on the lips of those who petitioned the state. The Hyōgo program's approach was one of the few that placed responsibility for recovery primarily within the farming community. The steps it advocated were similar to those proposed by Kodaira several years before: better coordination within the community, attention to the market, coordination with national organizations, and so on.

Nagashima Sadashi also made it clear that he shared the fears expressed by Kodaira about the farmers' failure to find their own solutions. In an article from early 1932, he suggested that long years of servitude had left the Japanese farmer without an independent will and all too prone to rely on others. To the extent that this passivity was one cause of the current crisis, there would be no escape from the depression as long as farmers continued to rely solely on the state for help. Their passivity and dependence had to be replaced with self-reliance and self-empowerment as a first step in any recovery effort. To make water pure, he wrote, one has to start at the source.[33] The appeal of this approach to Kodaira, and thus to the Ministry of Agriculture and Forestry, is easy to understand. Its appeal to other, considerably more influential members of the government was based at least in part on a similar set of shared worries about the condition of the farmer.

The new prime minister, whose knowledge of agricultural issues was limited, was aware that the countryside was experiencing difficulty and listened to the petitioners who were permitted to see him. Their tidings were grim, but Saitō was more worried about what they wanted than about what they said. The prime minister expressed his concerns to Furuya Keiji, executive secretary of the Central Federation of Moral Suasion Groups (Chūō kyōka dantai rengōkai), in the middle of June 1932.[34] (Saitō had become president of the Central Federation in August 1931 and kept his post after assuming the prime ministership.) Saitō summoned Furuya to the prime minister's residence and spoke with him about all the petitioners he had met. As prime minister, he was inclined to agree with them about the need for the state to do something to provide relief to the countryside. What bothered him most, he told Furuya, was what people were telling him would happen if the state did nothing. Furuya remembers Saitō saying, "They all say the same thing, even though the speakers are different. To help people out of their difficulties, there is no other approach but for the state to provide a tremendous amount of assistance." Without it, they told Saitō, the people and their communities would never recover.[35]

The prime minister thought their attitude almost sacrilegious. "Doesn't someone with a little intelligence," wondered Saitō, "understand the perfectly obvious—that the state's burden is eventually the burden of its citizens?"[36] In his opinion, it was clearly unwise for the government to fulfill all the demands for help, or even try to do so. The financial cost would be enormous, as would the spiritual cost to the country. Too much aid would create excessive reliance on the state, and the end result would almost certainly be a people unable to fend for themselves and a much weakened nation.

According to Furuya's account, Saitō announced that he wanted to turn the situation around by calling on each individual and each community to pull itself up and out of the depression. Saitō argued that self-reliance, coupled with a spirit of mutual assistance and cooperation, would solve the nation's problems, and he wanted the Central Federation of Moral Suasion Groups to take the lead in getting this message to the people. Furuya said it sounded like the type of project that the Central Federation ought to undertake and mentioned to the prime minister that he had heard of a similar program under way in Hyōgo prefecture, where they called it "self-revitalization." Saitō supposedly laughed, clapped his hands in decision, and said, "That's it; let's use that."[37] Self-revitalization entered the official lexicon of rural relief soon thereafter.[38]

Nagashima and his colleagues had reason to be proud of their accomplishments. Within a few months of the start of their national publicity drive, the Hyōgo program of self-revitalization had attracted considerable attention. Not only had the Imperial Agricultural Association shown signs that it would support plans like those developed in Hyōgo, but bureaucrats and politicians alike had been attracted to the self-revitalization approach. Kodaira valued the ways self-revitalization addressed his concerns about the demise of the farm community and self-initiative. Prime Minister Saitō shared those worries about a dependent populace and was quite pleased to have found a way to deal with the problems of the countryside that did not involve further draining of the state's coffers. Others within the government shared their sentiments. It was hard to find a good reason to be against the self-revitalization approach.

## Development of a National Self-revitalization Program

The process of adapting the ideas developed in Hyōgo to a national scale was under way by the end of June 1932 and lasted for several months. It consisted at first of a series of draft proposals drawn up within the Ministry of Agriculture and Forestry and submitted for cabinet-level discussions. The key questions for the bureaucrats were ones of money and scale. How much funding could they expect from the Ministry of Finance, and how many villages could they reasonably expect to involve in the program? By the time the final budget was submitted to the legislature, the Ministry of Agriculture had considerably less money to work with than its officials had originally hoped for. The possible goals of the program were adjusted in accordance with each shift in the fiscal tides.

There was also a public side to the development of a national self-revitalization program. The prime minister had to introduce the public to self-revitalization and win support for his administration's plans to make it a key element in the government's rural relief package. Similarly, the cabinet and key bureaucrats played a role in selling this approach to relief to the Sixty-third Diet. The parties had not been involved in the development of the program and showed little interest in it once they became aware of it, but it was important to have their support nevertheless.

The combination of public speeches, radio talks, and Diet testimony offers many useful insights into official views of the countryside and of the nature of rural reform. One of the earliest public indications of the state's decision to promote self-revitalization came during Saitō's July 6, 1932, radio address to the nation, discussed in Chapter 5. A few weeks later, the prime minister again took the opportunity to publicize the importance of self-revitalization. He did so during the annual Governors' Conference, where he was joined in speechmaking by Finance Minister Takahashi and Home Minister Yamamoto. All spoke in glowing terms about the benefits of self-revitalization. Saitō pointed out that modern recessions were far from temporary events and that reliance on public facilities alone would not pull the nation out of the current depression. "The people well understand the international situation and the reality of the country's present difficulty," said Saitō. In his opinion, it was crucial that the citizens "not rely on relief from others but pursue self-reliance (*jifun jirei*) together, [in order] to work as hard as we can, each man attending to his affairs, to have the courage to break out of one's difficulties, to have the determination of self-revitalization to resolve the crisis, and to move ahead in the manifestation of public spirit, not shirking from necessary sacrifices."[39]

If Saitō's message wasn't clear enough, Takahashi drove the point home:

Especially of late, the idea of seeking help for various groups or for oneself by placing the burden on the national treasury has taken root in many areas. For the government, which must consider the advantages and disadvantages for the entire nation, it goes without saying that these types of demands cannot be met. Moreover, the country will surely collapse if thinking that consists of not paying attention to damage to society or to sacrifice, but only to helping oneself, spreads throughout society.

As for requests for aid from groups, if the central government or local officials consent randomly to these, without paying any attention as to whether or not they have the spirit of self-revitalization, then not only will revitalization never get under way but people's morale will be damaged by these facilities and it will be impossible to prevent regrettable results for the country's future.[40]

The state's emphasis on self-revitalization was not lost on the participants in the conference, who were keen to get something a bit more concrete out of the government than exhortations to work hard. As we saw in Chapter 5, the governors were not necessarily unhappy with the prospect of a self-help program, but they were far more concerned about whether there would be enough public works projects to go around. They pressed hard for some sort of assurance that the regions that needed relief projects would be given the wherewithal to run them. As long as the cabinet was willing to do that, whatever it wanted to do about self-help was fine with the governors.[41]

Although the governors may have been a bit skeptical, the prime minister did manage to pick up one very important endorsement. The emperor's presence had been arranged by the cabinet to reassure those attending the conference and to lend an air of stability at a time when other sources were absent. On July 20, 1932, the governors dined in the Imperial Palace, with the emperor, of course, attending. When he met the governor of Hyōgo, the emperor reportedly commented favorably on the agricultural association's programs in that prefecture and urged them to stay the course. The governor was so moved by the occasion that he sent telegrams home describing the experience, including one to Yamawaki.[42]

Meanwhile, planning within the government had begun. One of the earliest indications of what a national self-revitalization program might look like came in August. In an article published in the journal *Shimin*, Kodaira outlined the direction of Ministry of Agriculture and Forestry policy and made clear the ministry's commitment to self-revitalization. In an argument very similar to the one he had used in 1930 (indeed, the phrasing is often identical), Kodaira expressed concern over the increasing reliance of villages and farmers on others and argued that communities had to rely on their own strengths in order to recover from the economic crisis.[43] Granting that conditions were now too poor to expect farmers to be able to do everything on their own, Kodaira outlined two or three steps that the state and local governments could take to help farmers help themselves.

One step that Kodaira called for was the establishment by villages of something like self-revitalization committees, which would in turn help develop recovery plans for the community. Implementation of the plans would be the job of an expanded industrial cooperative. The membership of the bigger and better industrial cooperatives would include at least one person from every farming household in a given community, which would assure village-wide participation in any recovery effort. The unions would help members pursue debt arrangement and would also have a role to play in controlling production at the local level—Kodaira imagined how beneficial it would be if everyone agreed to cut back on rice production. They would also pursue self-sufficiency drives in fertilizer, soy sauce, and other items.

As in 1930, Kodaira rested his argument and his policies on the "power and cooperation" of the village community. The state could take limited steps to help the countryside, but nothing would come of it without real commitment by farmers to the ideas of self-empowerment and self-assistance. Unlike the situation in 1930, when Kodaira could advocate only that communities take greater steps to cooperate or that they try to rationalize farm organizations, by the late summer of 1932 bureaucrats had a clearer idea of what they wanted farmers to do to help themselves.

The development of those ideas is sketched out in a three-part series of Ministry of Agriculture and Forestry drafts on rural relief policies. The first, which probably dates from late June 1932, gives little mention to self-revitalization.[44] The second, completed on July 10, introduces specific proposals for village revitalization,[45] including the development of revitalization plans in ten thousand villages (just about every village in the country) within six months and the creation of state and local administrative facilities to assist in the planning process. The industrial cooperatives would play a vital role in the program and be helped to expand their membership through a revision in the laws governing union membership.[46] Both aspects of the program—the establishment of revitalization plans and the expansion of the industrial cooperatives—were well funded under the plan. In 1932, planning efforts would receive 7.15 million yen and industrial cooperative expansion 1.9 million. The next budget year, planners called for funding of 13.2 and 2.9 million yen, respectively. By 1935, the ministry proposed spending a total of 55 million yen on the two main elements of their Village Revitalization Plan.[47]

By the end of July, the government's plans for village revitalization had been downsized considerably. The third draft, or the Ministry of Agriculture and Forestry's "Village Revitalization Planning Facilities Outline," reflected some of the points covered by Saitō and Takahashi during the Governors' Conference. The emphasis shifted away from hefty administrative and financial support by the state for the pursuit of local economic revitalization and toward an approach that put more of the burden on the communities themselves. The new outline said that "villages should rise up on their own" and not rely solely on the government's policies to solve the problems confronting them.[48] The scale of the program was also reduced. Where the July 10 proposal had aimed to have revitalization plans established in ten thousand villages in half a year, under the new guidelines the ministry hoped to establish plans in only a thousand villages a year over the next five years.

These developments were not especially well funded. The more than 7 million yen that the ministry had originally asked for was cut significantly. The budget associated with the third iteration of the Ministry's revitalization program was for only 431,000 yen in 1932. In 1932, 50,000 yen was to go toward developing plans at the village level, and another 50,000 for assistance in placing agricultural technicians in the community. The rest of the funding would be used to cover administrative costs and for industrial cooperative programs.[49]

Another indication that the activist side of the program was being scaled back was the proposed creation of separate organizations to oversee the spiritual aspects of village revitalization. Central and local organizations would handle the spread of *kōsei seishin* (the spirit of revitalization), for which the budget allowed them almost 100,000 yen the first year and about twice as much in 1933. Although that part of the budget was still much smaller than the amounts allotted to the development of economic plans, the splitting of the originally unified program into two separate parts placed new emphasis on the spiritual aspects of revitalization.[50] And even though Ministry of Agriculture and Forestry bureaucrats did eventually manage to wrest a larger share of the budget for the strictly economic aspects of the revitalization program, the morale-building efforts remained.

## Self-revitalization, the Ministries, and the Sixty-third Diet

At the same time that the size of the program seemed to have been scaled back, the government intensified its efforts to promote the utility of self-revitalization. During the Sixty-third Diet, called specifically to deal with the rural crisis, it was clear that the state was putting more and more of its hopes on self-revitalization as a solution to the countryside's problems. In their opening speeches to the Extraordinary Session of the Diet, both the prime minister and Finance Minister Takahashi spoke hopefully about self-revitalization. Prime Minister Saitō was first to address the legislators:

It is a truly wonderful thing that the people have begun self-revitalization on their own to get themselves out of the depression. The government also intends to encourage this spirit of perseverance. Appropriate aid will be given toward the establishment of revitalization plans under this spirit, and the facilities of the state and the self-revitalization of the people will work together, in perfect harmony, to find our way out of these difficulties.[51]

Takahashi made similar points:

Every nation is in serious difficulty, but no proposal has yet been discovered that produces results at once. Eventually every type of measure is tried in every area, and through this depressions are eliminated. The government will propose various types of facilities, ones that are believed to be the most efficacious as emergency policies, given the resolution and opinions in the previous Diet session. Still, in dealing with the present crisis, the expected results will not be obtainable should the people simply rely on steps taken by the government. The people themselves must be prepared to believe in self-revitalization and use it to get out of the crisis. I cannot stop hoping, at this time of crisis in the accumulation of domestic and foreign difficulties, that our citizens will demonstrate that special spirit of fortitude and overcome this worldwide ordeal.[52]

As both statements make clear, the government was working hard to lower expectations for proposals other than self-revitalization. The emphasis was on the importance of keeping a balance between what the state could do and what the people ought to do to help themselves. It was this combination of efforts that Saitō and Takahashi held up as the best approach to emerging from the depression.

The content of the state's Economic Revitalization program (how many villages would participate, what participation would entail, and so on) was not subject to Diet approval, but the tools that the program would need were. In an "Outline of Village Economic Revitalization Facilities," produced on the day the Sixty-third Diet session opened, the Ministry of Agriculture and Forestry sketched in broad strokes the planning process, the role of the debt management unions, and what the government would have to do to ensure the program's success. The new outline spoke of "the establishment of controlled, organized facilities for economic revitalization through the cooperation of the people and the state." Basic to the revitalization process were surveys of local economic conditions and crafting of the actual economic revitalization plan for the community and its members. That plan would cover fourteen topics, ranging from "the distribution of land use" to "the control of agricultural production," debt liquidation, and health, education, and financial reform.[53] How the economic plans would be set up was also explained: Each village would establish a committee with the appropriate people, draft a plan, and submit it to the prefecture for approval. All the local organizations in the village—the agricultural association, the industrial cooperative, and, of course, the hamlet-level farming associations—were expected to work together to see the plan through to fruition.

The ministry had also managed to win stronger support from the Finance Ministry than earlier drafts had suggested. The budget proposal submitted to the Diet gave more than 3.3 million yen to the program.[54] This was less than the 7 million that planners had originally hoped for, but much more than the paltry sums mentioned in the ministry's proposal from late July.

Minister of Agriculture and Forestry Gotō no doubt drew on the newest outline for his comments in the Diet. In response to a legislator's inquiry concerning the government's budget proposals for village relief, Gotō said:

> I have spoken about the need for planned economics and village planning for the revitalization of the villages, but what does this mean? I expect that you are aware of the connection between this and the Village Economic Revitalization section in the budget, but I think that today there remain many fundamental problems in the villages, one of which is that there is still plenty of room for the villages to plan their economies and that this is something that they must do. Whether a farm family or a farm village, and whether in the area of industry, production, consumption, sales, or in other areas, they must go forward with a plan and with an organized structure. We must start with this permanent policy from today.[55]

As in Hyōgo, planning was a vital part of the state's recovery program. In Hyōgo, the prefectural agricultural association had been able to rely on local village and hamlet-level branches, which made it relatively easy to reach individual households. The unique organizational strengths of Hyōgo were not shared by other prefectures. To implement a program like the one in Hyōgo throughout the country, the Ministry of Agriculture and Forestry faced a daunting administrative challenge. No matter how effective the plan, little would come of the attempt at reform if its basic building blocks—namely, the hamlet and village organizations—could not be counted on to cooperate with each other and with the state. The ministry proposed a series of bills that would give it the organizational strength it needed.

The bills addressed two areas of concern for the Ministry of Agriculture: how to have an organization that was powerful enough to do the things that the movement would demand but flexible enough to reach the hamlet effectively was one issue; the other revolved around how best to address the problem of village debt. The debt problem was long term and had a life that was at first entirely separate from the Economic Revitalization Campaign. But since there could be no economic progress unless debt was dealt with, and since debt was best handled at the hamlet level, debt arrangement and the Debt Arrangement Union bill were closely knit to the campaign. The failure of those initiatives in the Diet (described in Chapter 3 above) delayed implementation of the complete Economic Revitalization program until passage of a revised version of the union law early in 1933.

The targets of the other legislation were the industrial cooperatives and Farm Practice Associations (Nōji jikkō kumiai). Three bills, all of which passed, improved the financial standing of the industrial cooperatives while making membership in local cooperatives open to members of practice associations.[56] Linking the practice associations (traditionally under the control of the agricultural associations) to the industrial cooperatives gave the Ministry of Agriculture and Forestry the organization it required. The industrial cooperatives provided the village-level economic power and links to the markets that farmers needed to pursue crop diversification.

Most farming associations were made up of members from a single hamlet and lacked the economic clout of the industrial cooperatives, which could offer access to low-interest loans, marketing networks, and so on. (The local agricultural association could also act as a middleman of sorts for farmers hoping to sell their produce, but that role was limited.) From the point of view of the ministry's bureaucrats, however, the farming associations could be very effective links to the individual farm household. The industrial cooperative had tended not to reach into the hamlet, and in practice many small and medium farmers were excluded from membership in that organization. But any planning effort involving the farming associations and their broader-based membership would be sure to include the majority of farm households in the hamlet.[57]

The government's enthusiasm for revitalization did not pass unnoticed within the Diet. During discussions of the bills associated with the campaign, politicians were openly skeptical of any program that sought to rebuild the villages on a bargain-basement budget. Yet it was hard to disagree with the tenets of the campaign as it was being described by the cabinet and by people like Kodaira. Legislators tempered their criticism accordingly, for none was willing to argue that hard work and self-reliance were not important qualities and ones that the state should promote. Skepticism was more likely to creep into discussions that focused on whether or not the campaign alone could contend with the crisis in rural Japan. Most of the politicians and commentators who considered that question concluded that it could not. Shimizu Ginzō (Seiyūkai, Shiga) put it this way:

I believe that the state's calls for self-revitalization are truly well timed, but under the current situation and under the current system, and with the burdens on the people as heavy as they are, will the people be able to rehabilitate themselves? If the government is going to call for self-revitalization now, then it ought first to lighten burdens, or do something about the root cause of the current sickness, so that self-revitalization is possible.[58]

Saitō's response was to avoid Shimizu's point about the need to reduce the burden on the countryside and talk instead about the spiritual importance of self-revitalization. The government did not, insisted Saitō, plan to provide any direct assistance in the form of funding in order to implement self-revitalization. Emergency relief efforts would be undertaken in many areas, but he was pleased to note that self-revitalization was being pursued already without the crutch of state assistance. Shimizu replied:

When you are sick, an injection provides temporary relief, but the more shots you get, the less the effect. The emergency policies the state is advocating will, I think, have an effect that is the opposite of self-revitalization. Unless some fundamental steps are taken alongside emergency policies, the current crisis will get deeper and deeper, the government's finances will get worse and worse, and the burden on the people will become heavier and heavier if self-revitalization is going to be used to solve the crisis. I'm afraid that this will make the citizens more and more dependent, which is the opposite of self-revitalization.[59]

Saitō simply responded that the spirit of self-revitalization would not lead people into dependency. He declined to discuss the issue of burden reduction, deferring it to some later date.

The exchange between Shimizu and Saitō can hardly be called a debate about the merits of self-revitalization. Shimizu wasn't really critical of revitalization, only of what he thought was the cabinet's attempt to avoid dealing with the fundamental problems of the countryside. Self-help was fine, argued Shimizu, but it wouldn't come to much unless it was pursued side by side with other policies. Burden reduction, one of the Seiyūkai's favorite rural policies, was the "other" policy that Shimizu happened to raise with Saitō, but other politicians could have mentioned farm debt or commodity pricing policies just as easily.[60] In the form that Saitō and Takahashi (and to a lesser extent Gotō) presented self-revitalization to the Diet, there was little to disagree with, other than how much importance self-help would be given relative to the more expensive policies that the parties sought.

When politicians from the established parties did begin to look more closely at the Revitalization Campaign, they found that there was ample room for improvement. The Seiyūkai's Tago Ichimin (Iwate) did so in an article published soon after the end of the sixty-third session. While he may not have spoken for the entire party, as a former Home Ministry bureaucrat (he was head of the Social Bureau under Hara) turned politician, his opinions must have carried some weight. And his opinion was that the state needed to do far more than just provide lectures and speeches if it expected the countryside to recover.[61]

Tago began by contradicting the government's claim that the farmers were calling out for self-revitalization. "The calls for village revitalization, and for the self-revitalization of the village," wrote Tago, "have come less from the farmers themselves than they have from village institutions." The farmers, Tago contended, were more concerned about the destitution of their communities and the fact that that destitution was caused by forces beyond their control. The gradual exclusion of the countryside from the governing process, the incursion of industry into an unprepared agricultural economy, and the urbanization of education were all factors that Tago pointed to as sources of the countryside's distress.[62] He likened what the state had proposed thus far in terms of self-revitalization to "explaining hygiene to a man on his deathbed"—in other words, too little, too late—and argued that it would be better to provide laws that would enable people to stand on their own and create an environment in which they would have the energy and strength to do so.

Azuma Takeshi, another Seiyūkai veteran and one of the party's leading rural representatives, made similar points in his comments in the early days of the Sixty-fourth Diet session. He agreed that economic revitalization was a good idea for the villages and applauded the cabinet for its efforts in popularizing self-revitalization. But, he wondered, "even if the plans are established [by local self-revitalization committees], who is going to implement them?" Unless the cabinet was willing to provide significant funds to help pay the salaries of the local agricultural association technicians, "any number of plans can be created, but I think that in fact revitalization will be completely impossible."[63]

Azuma went on to make a case for the indispensability of the technicians to the success of the revitalization program and thus for increased state support for the hard-pressed technicians. Leaders were rare in the village ("There isn't a Ninomiya Sontoku . . . in every village," he noted), but the cabinet could help provide the necessary leaders by coming up with the 5 to 8 million yen he estimated the technicians would need. Only then could the cabinet hope to accomplish its goals for the self-revitalization programs in villages where at the moment "in thought and in spirit there is no conscience, there is no freedom, no security, no bravery, no light whatsoever ahead. [The villages] are in darkness, without hope."[64] Azuma's endorsement of the revitalization program was qualified, but he does not seem to have doubted that if the agricultural association technicians received the support they needed, economic revitalization planning would work.

The Minseitō brought its own concerns to the revitalization programs, but in general the party was more likely to support unconditionally the Saitō cabinet's proposals than their colleagues across the aisle. In a roundtable session on farm policies that appeared in the July 1932 issue of the party magazine *Minsei*, legislators mixed lukewarm demands for better debt and relief policies with suggestions that the farmers learn to stop relying on others for help. Before the Sixty-third Diet, the party's Special Committee on Village Policies (Nōson taisaku tokubetsu iinkai) expressed support for self-revitalization and for the establishment of village planning.[65]

Wakatsuki Reijirō reiterated his party's support in a Diet speech in late August, saying that revitalization was "essential for the future of the nation and the continued prosperity of the people."[66] Once the outlines of the Economic Revitalization program had been drawn by the Ministry of Agriculture and Forestry, Minseitō spokesmen offered their continued support. Arakawa Gorō (Hiroshima) wrote in October 1932 of the importance of self-revitalization planning, which he said included such steps as improved self-sufficiency, reductions in unnecessary spending, and improved cooperation among and within communities.[67] Except in special cases, state welfare policies were to be eliminated in favor of self-reliance. One must realize, wrote Arakawa, that the nation made progress and people became prosperous by relying on the strength of its citizens, not when people relied on the state for help.[68] Arakawa wanted the state to make an unspecified amount of funding available to the Economic Revitalization programs and argued that state schools should cover more of their own costs, but on the whole he seemed content that the government's proposals would be enough. Minseitō support for the Saitō cabinet's emphasis on self-revitalization continued well into 1933, faltering only with the various controversies surrounding the 1934 budget.[69]

The upper house also found reasons to support the campaign. Baba Eiichi, who in early 1933 was both a member of the upper house of the Diet and director of the Nihon Kangyō Bank (Hypothec Bank of Japan), had a clear idea of what the Self-Revitalization Campaign should mean for the countryside. Since the Meiji Restoration, the rural self-supporting economy had been drawn into the orbit of the urban exchange economy, a process Baba thought had led to the current farm crisis. Farmers had to spend too much to buy goods produced in the city and received too little for the produce they sold there, he pointed out.

Stealing a page from the economic revitalization book, Baba argued that the best way to deal with this was to organize the countryside so that it could meet the exchange economy on an equal footing. For Baba, this meant encouraging diversification and creating stronger cooperative unions for production, purchases, and sales—steps that would require not only a fair number of years but also the commitment and effort of the farmers themselves. In the meantime, Baba's solution was to pursue a return to the traditions of self-sufficiency, by which he seems to have meant returning to a time when the countryside was able to supply most if not all of its own needs.

Although this suggestion that farmers remove themselves from the modern economy until they were strong enough to face it on their own terms was not what the Ministry of Agriculture and Forestry intended for practitioners of economic revitalization, Baba's ready employment of at least part of the self-revitalization argument is evidence of its attractiveness to those outside the bureaucracy. "Heaven helps those who help themselves," wrote Baba, and "I must hope that our farmers will follow the path of self-revitalization with a tenacious spirit, and through their own strength call forth the fundamental prosperity of the villages."[70]

Kōsei (revitalization) and words like it (kōshin, for instance) were so attractive to public figures that in the months following the Sixty-third Diet ministers, politicians, and bureaucrats employed the terms frequently. For the most part, the revitalization they talked about had little to do with farming and planning and a great deal to do with the state of mind of the Japanese citizenry. Prime Minister Saitō's July radio address to the nation has been mentioned previously; it is an early example of the way that economic and spiritual revitalization were held up as complementary parts of a greater whole. In early September 1932, Home Minister Yamamato followed suit with a radio broadcast on the topic of "Hopes for Awakening the People in the Face of the Crisis."[71] In his address he spoke of the need for the government to limit spending to reasonable levels to avoid placing a heavy burden on citizens at some later date. In rhetoric very similar to that employed by Saitō, Yamamoto continued:

Happily, of late not only have I heard calls for what is known as self-revitalization along with the demands for emergency relief, but there are also communities in which this has been put into effect. In their heart of hearts, citizens have been inspired by their difficulties and have aroused a spirit that even in the depths of poverty and despair will not rely solely on state aid, but through self-action and one's own power will win out over this depression.[72]

The Home Ministry's role in the campaign to bring the country and the countryside back from the brink was embodied in the so-called Citizens' Revitalization Campaign. Yamamoto described this campaign as one that would help support the development and implementation of revitalization plans through financial assistance and through a broader drive to publicize the self-revitalization message. The first goal of this campaign, said Yamamoto, was to unite the country to overcome the current crisis, to help everyone "cooperate as one big family." The second goal was to promote the idea of self-revitalization. If people remained passive and relied only on the state's help, Yamamoto argued, then "even if a tremendous amount of relief money is spent, it will end with a temporary, empty recovery, and will lead cities and villages alike down the road to decline."

The campaign to which Yamamoto referred was the product of quick planning on the part of the Home Ministry. In August the ministry issued an "Outline of Plans for the Citizens' Revitalization Campaign" (Kokumin kōsei undō keikaku yōkō) to governors. The ministry received 100,000 yen in its supplementary budget for use in the Citizens' Campaign, and bureaucrats used the "Outline" to describe how their ministry hoped to make use of the revitalization boom.[73] Home Ministry officials were told to work closely with reform groups, the local agricultural association, and other organizations to bring the revitalization message to the people. The ministry would seek the cooperation of newspapers and magazines and issue pamphlets and other informational materials to supplement a series of lectures, movies, and informative gatherings that would be held throughout the country.[74]

For the Home Ministry, "revitalization" was about morale and about spirit. More clearly, it was about regaining an outlook that citizens had lost over the years. Yamamoto concluded his radio address with these remarks:

From the first, whenever the people of this nation have encountered a difficulty, they have manifested the spiritual power of a great race and have overcome it. Based on my deep faith in the traditional power of the spirit of the citizens, even with our current problems I have bright hopes for the road ahead. It is my earnest hope that, through the power of national unity, the crisis will be overcome as soon as possible, and that a splendid rebirth will occur in the lives of the people.[75]

The Ministry of Education was also moving to involve itself with rural recovery, although in a peripheral way. Ministry bureaucrats wanted to make the education system more suited to the needs of rural students and in doing so train the future leaders of the community. The specific steps involved in this were unclear when the Economic Revitalization program was getting under way, and there was no money in the ministry's supplemental budget for revitalization-related spending.[76] Ministry bureaucrats nevertheless discussed plans to mobilize youth and women's groups in support of rural reform, plus long-term plans to "rationalize lives in the midst of a consumer economy" and "revive manners and customs."[77]

Both the Home Ministry and the Ministry of Education continued to pursue a broadly "spiritual" approach to rural reconstruction. They made no attempt to usurp the Ministry of Agriculture's claim to the economic aspects of recovery in the villages, and at least the Home Ministry initially went along with the Ministry of Agriculture's organizational efforts in the hamlet. Friction between the ministries did surface from time to time, as when Education Minister Hatoyama refused to attend the cabinet conferences on the 1934 budget, supposedly because of a dispute over control of leadership training centers. As education facilities, the centers would normally have been under the jurisdiction of the Ministry of Education, not the Ministry of Agriculture and Forestry.[78] Hatoyama made his point, but the centers stayed where they were.

Friction with the Home Ministry was more deeply rooted. The Economic Revitalization program's emphasis on the hamlet as the most important place to organize the community's economic and social activities was different from the Home Ministry's focus on the village as the single most important administrative unit. (Remember that the Home Ministry's Local Improvement movement had tried to replace the hamlet with the village in the hearts and minds of farmers.) Until a 1941 decision resolving the problem, the two ministries remained at odds over the "Home Ministry route" and the "Ministry of Agriculture and Forestry route" into the village. This may overstate the case somewhat, as it seems unlikely that villagers were particularly inconvenienced by, or even aware of, the problem.[79] The battles about "routes" and jurisdiction over schools were fought behind the scenes in Tokyo.

The importance of the Home and the Education ministries' revitalization policies is hard to assess. Their emphasis on "spiritual development" is one problem: how much difference did morale make? Was education in 1936 more in tune with the needs of the rural youth than it had been, say, in 1931? Were the Home Ministry's pamphlets and lectures helpful in convincing people to participate in the campaign? A second issue is the fact that, unlike the case with the Ministry of Agriculture and Forestry, revitalization was not a prominent institutional goal for either the Home Ministry or the Ministry of Education. Both had other programs that were far more important. A third consideration that makes assessment difficult is that as the decade wore on, the problems of spiritual and general mobilization overshadowed concerns about the recovery of the countryside. The revitalization idea was flexible enough so that it is hard to tell where it ends and something else begins. Calls from the Ministry of Agriculture for better cooperation within the hamlet are, fairly clearly, the result of concerns about production and about the well-being of that community. A similar exclamation by a Home Ministry bureaucrat or a Ministry of Education official might mean something very different.

## The Framework of Revitalization

The Sixty-third Diet gave Ministry of Agriculture bureaucrats most of what they had sought for the revitalization program. New laws eased requirements for participation in village industrial cooperatives, lowered other barriers to the smooth operation of economic planning, and provided enough money to get the Economic Revitalization Campaign off the ground. The only key item missing was the Debt Arrangement Union Law, which, as expected, eventually passed in the next Diet session. Once past the initial hurdle of the Diet, the campaign was seldom again the subject of Diet discussions.

Kodaira Gonichi assumed his new post as director of the Ministry of Agriculture and Forestry's Revitalization Section (Kōseibu) in late September 1932. He kept that job for almost six years before being promoted to a new post in early September 1938.[80] If nothing else, Kodaira's presence gave the section a consistency of purpose; his connections both within the ministry and outside the government served the campaign well, sheltering it at times from competing factions. Kodaira, for example, developed a unique approach to the budgeting process, one that allowed him to avoid the usual committees and negotiations in favor of direct appeals to his superiors and, when necessary, to Finance Minister Takahashi.[81]

Decisions about the course of the campaign were made by Kodaira in consultation with the members of the Central Committee for Farm Village Economic Revitalization.[82] The fifty or so members of the committee were drawn from the bureaucracy (including representatives of the Home, Finance, Commerce, and Education ministries), academia, elected officialdom, and the larger farm organizations. The roster included some of the best-known names in farm policy, such as Ishiguro Tadaatsu and Kodaira's friend Nasu Hiroshi.[83] In addition, all the major rural organizations are listed as cooperating institutions in the section's organizational charts, including the National Association of Mayors of Towns and Villages, the Imperial Agricultural Association, the Central Association of Industrial Cooperatives, and the Greater Japan Federation of Young Men's Associations (Dai Nihon rengō seinendan), to name but a few.[84]

From Tokyo, the Revitalization Section issued directives and guidelines to newly created counterpart offices at the prefectural level; villages dealt directly with the latter, but ministry bureaucrats kept close tabs on local developments through regular conferences, surveys, and field work. The earliest directive went out in October 1932; in it, bureaucrats sketched the basic tenets of the Economic Revitalization Campaign and ordered prefectural officials to lay the groundwork for the concrete plans to follow. Gotō's language hinted at what was to come: "Making practical use of the unique and fine custom of the spirit of mutual assistance in the hamlets of the villages and applying it to economic life, we must take steps for the planned and organized reform of production and economics in farm, fishing, and mountain villages."[85]

Two months later, the ministry released the promised detailed directives. The seventy pages of the "Policy for the Establishment of Village Economic Revitalization Plans" incorporated the results of meetings between Ministry of Agriculture and Forestry bureaucrats and the members of the Central Committee for Farm Village Economic Revitalization and laid out how villages were to go about re-creating themselves.[86] The details of that process are dealt with in the next several chapters, which explore Sekishiba's experiences as a campaign village. The remainder of this section sketches the broad outlines of the campaign as it took shape in late 1932.

Planners made it clear from the start that the campaign was not for everyone. Participation was a privilege, not a right; candidate villages would first be screened at the prefectural level and eventually vetted by the ministry itself before being allowed to join the campaign. Applicant villages had to demonstrate the administrative acumen necessary to complete the complex paperwork associated with the campaign—and, obviously, a willingness to embrace the campaign's goals. Grounds for disqualification were plentiful; communities in which political or social unrest were evident, for example, would not be allowed to participate. Ongoing tenancy disputes, bitter party factionalism, and the like were all enough to keep a village out of the campaign. The ministry wanted clear signs of commitment to the process.[87] Despite these barriers, applications to participate in the campaign poured in. Close to 1,500 communities were admitted to the campaign in the few remaining months of 1932, and 1,769 joined the following year. Just over half of all the towns and villages that would ever participate in the campaign began doing so between 1932 and 1934.[88]

For communities selected, or designated, to join the campaign, revitalization was at its simplest a three-part process. The first step was structural. Because existing village institutions had been unable to overcome the depression, the campaign proposed a reorganization of local leadership into an Economic Revitalization Committee (Keizai kōsei iinkai). No one was explicitly excluded from membership, but the preferred list of candidates included village officials, teachers, leaders of local agricultural organizations, experienced farmers, and those with contributions to make in other fields. No formal structures were in place at the village level to allow the sort of cooperation and sharing of ideas that the campaign required; the committees were supposed to fill that gap and to oversee the administrative burdens of revitalization. One telling feature of the Revitalization Committee was that it was not necessarily dominated by landlords, as it might have been had the ministry given local leaders complete leeway over membership. As it was, the guidelines strongly suggested that skill, not status, be a prerequisite for a position on the committee. By bringing together the leaders of a variety of village bodies, the ministry appears to have deliberately set out to reach producers at every level of the community.

Planning was the second step. In a process very much like the one developed in Hyōgo, communities were instructed to conduct detailed surveys of each household. Those surveys touched on productivity, the family's financial situation, and a host of other categories designed to yield the clearest possible picture of the state of the farm, the hamlet, and the village. The depression caught the countryside uninformed about the state of the local economy, and thus unaware of the true extent of damage to individual households or to the village as a whole. Surveys were a first step toward a clearer picture of where they stood and at the same time would establish a baseline against which future development could be judged.

From the surveys sprang the revitalization plans. Each household would have one, and each village; the latter was a published and public document subject to review by the prefectural authorities. The ministry's guidelines made provisions for as many as a dozen components to any given revitalization plan, laid out in annual divisions over a five-year period. There were no quotas, no targets to be met. This meant that whereas no two communities (or households, or hamlets) would have exactly the same plan or the same goals, they would all share common categories of activity. Of obvious administrative benefit to the Ministry of Agriculture and Forestry and the prefectural offices that would have to collate and assess plans, the twelve categories also defined those areas that central planners felt were most in need of local effort:

1. Land distribution and rationalization of land use
2. Village financial reform
3. Rationalization of labor use
4. Reform of the organization of farm management
5. Reduction of production costs and other management expenses
6. Reform of production methods and the control of production
7. Control of commodity sales
8. Controls on the distribution of materials for farm production
9. Reform of farm household economics
10. Establishment of disaster prevention facilities, a relief fund, and other efforts to encourage savings
11. Promotion of cooperative efforts among the various organizations in the village
12. Reform of village education, hygiene, lifestyles, and other village facilities[89]

As even this short list illustrates, the range of potential reforms within the village was large and clearly focused on the economic health of the community. Eleven of the twelve planning categories deal with potential improvements in farming methods, interaction with the market, and cooperation within the village. Even the twelfth category, which focuses on social change, is very much a part of the items that precede it. The proposed educational reforms focus on the role that a more practical, farming-oriented education would play in the economic recovery of the community. Planners hoped to "develop practical knowledge" in primary school, to train young people in techniques that would help them "provide leadership truly appropriate to the village economy," and to educate women in skills that would give them insight into the economic situation in the village.[90]

There are at least four broad (and overlapping) categories of reform: (1) resource management, (2) production and marketing, (3) organization, and (4) management. Resource management begins with land, the most basic necessity for any farmer. The guidelines feature a long list of how communities could make better use of available acreage. In addition to double cropping, crop rotation, and land improvement projects, planners were expected to consider such issues as the balance between owner- and tenant-cultivated land and measures that might be taken to prevent any shift from the former into the latter category. Land that was given over to residential use or that wasn't being used at all could be returned to agricultural use; ponds and swamps could do double duty as fish farms. New roads and irrigation facilities, it was noted, might also allow farmers to get more out of existing acreage. (At the same time, the guidelines urged local planners to pay close attention to the costs of infrastructural projects such as road work. It wouldn't do, the ministry maintained, to saddle farm households with additional debt.)

There were other resources to consider besides land. One of these was capital, and planners designed a series of financial reforms to make better use of it. The emphasis of the proposed reforms was quite simple: to place as much control over local finances as possible into the hands of the industrial cooperatives. That meant relying on the industrial cooperative as the primary lender within the village, and as the place where households and organizations would deposit their savings. Private lenders, banks, and even traditional savings clubs were to be avoided. Lending would be conducted fairly but with careful consideration given to the potential borrower's creditworthiness. No one would be able to borrow more than he or she could reasonably repay from the proceeds of farming. For those who were already in debt, debt arrangement was, of course, an important element in the recovery process.[91]

Labor was the other resource that farmers had to take special measures to address. As the Hyōgo Prefecture Agricultural Association had gone to such pains to make clear, many farm households were not using the labor available to them in the most productive way, so ministry planners set out to correct that. They urged communities to put plans in place that would bring sharp reductions in the use of hired labor, for which family labor would be substituted, encouraged cooperative efforts in the fields throughout the growing cycle and the introduction of both more draft animals and farm machinery. During the off-season, farmers were urged to make the most of household labor through public works employment, cottage industries, and cooperative side-production. Cottage industries were an especially good idea, planners agreed, but only as long as they met a number of conditions: they had to be projects that could be begun and maintained with a minimum of capital, that used readily available local supplies, and that had a guaranteed demand. There was no sense in wasting money and time on something that couldn't be sold.

On a closely related point, planners set out to improve how farmers grew their crops, sent them to market, and purchased their supplies. One aspect of this was a broad-based effort to cut the costs of production, which relied in part on having farmers make more of what they needed at home and buy less on the open market. Fertilizer, feed, agricultural chemicals, and tools could all be either supplemented by local production or purchased at lower prices via the industrial cooperative. Cooperative purchases could put useful but expensive items like rice hulling and polishing machines within the reach of many communities and would free farmers from their dependence on the fertilizer merchants' credit. The same industrial cooperative that could be used to make purchases could also be used to sell what farmers grew. By putting their goods in the hands of the industrial cooperative, farmers would be certain of getting a fair price for what they sold. Access to the union's storage facilities and financial facilities gave them the freedom to sell when prices were best.

Improving production involved both choosing the appropriate crops or livestock for local conditions and deciding how best to raise and harvest them. Technical reforms could be included in the plans, such as the spread of better information about crop strains, fertilizers, and pesticides. Properly implemented, these measures would lead to higher yields for the average producer. Farmers would also benefit from better understanding of the markets in which they sold. Information provided by the industrial cooperative about consumer demands, price levels, and competition would help farmers decide what to grow and when to grow it. If communities set up an inspection system for their crops, noted the ministry's guidelines, they could prevent the shipment of imperfect goods to market and, in so doing, boost consumer confidence and ensure that prices stayed high.

Organizational reforms were linked with the areas mentioned above, especially where the industrial cooperative was involved. For instance, the industrial cooperative's role rested on the community's ability to expand membership and to ensure close cooperation among other village-level organizations. Farming associations, the local agricultural association, the various sericulture and livestock unions, and so on would all have to strengthen their ties to the industrial cooperative to make planning efforts work.[92] The Economic Revitalization Committee within each village would coordinate planning efforts and, in so doing, would bring together the leaders of the various farm organizations. That development alone marked a significant departure from earlier efforts at organizing the village economy.

Management reforms encompassed both general suggestions about attempts to concentrate capital and labor to compensate for the small size of Japanese farms and specific ones calling for the spread of bookkeeping methods at the household level. Planners were anxious to have households produce more of the items they used every day: items such as soy sauce, miso paste, and clothing could all be made at home or together with other households at a fraction of what it cost to buy them commercially. Households would also have to take a much closer look at spending and income; although changes in income were closely linked to the success of the other reforms, it was a given that farm families should try to "average out" their sources of income. This meant not relying solely on any one crop or type of crop but ensuring that there was money coming in from side-projects, forestry, and other areas. At the very least, households would be more likely to have a steady income throughout the year and would thus have better luck reducing their debts, managing a budget, and setting aside money in savings.

Implementing the plans was the third and final stage of the revitalization process. Here the national campaign diverged from the Hyōgo model somewhat, in that it divided responsibility among the various village institutions rather than relying solely on the local agricultural association to make things work. Industrial cooperatives, the schools, and a long list of other bodies were brought into the campaign and expected to do their part. From the point of view of the ministry planners, however, neither the agricultural association nor the industrial cooperative could be counted on to provide the hamlet-level organization necessary to the campaign's success. For that, the bureaucrats turned to the farm practice associations (*jikkō kumiai*) and invested them with responsibility for the day-to-day workings of the revitalization plans.

Revisions in the laws governing the industrial cooperatives made it a relatively simple matter to enroll members of a practice association in a village's industrial cooperative. This gave each and every hamlet access to the industrial cooperative while ensuring the cooperative much closer links with almost every household in the community.[93] The fact that the heads of all the major organizations in the village were likely to also be members of the Economic Revitalization Committee made coordination and cooperation that much more possible (at least on paper).

Participating villages were required to submit progress reports and undergo a more detailed self-assessment at the end of the first five-year planning period. There was simply no way, however, that the ministry or even the prefectures could accurately measure the campaign's progress. There were too many variables, too much local knowledge necessary, before a fair assessment could be made. Yet as the guidelines suggested, and as practice would eventually prove, it didn't much matter which goals were set and which met. A successful plan was its own reward, and there were no penalties for those that went awry.

That ministry planners were willing to rely on local enthusiasms to sustain the campaign says a great deal about the state of the countryside in late 1932. That other institutions appropriated the terminology if not the goals of the Ministry of Agriculture and Forestry's programs speaks to their recognition of revitalization's potential appeal to the rural population. The agrarianists had already demonstrated, through their successful petition appeals, how powerful the desire for change was; one could certainly argue that the tenancy movement had tapped into the same current. It should come as no surprise that the state, too, would seek to associate itself with the impetus for change in the countryside. The section that follows outlines the developments in rural society that had by the early 1930s created an environment amenable to revitalization—and, eventually, to the sorts of changes advocated by the Economic Revitalization Campaign.

## The Popular Culture of Reform and Revitalization

Nishiyama Kōichi, a Niigata tenant farmer, began keeping a diary in 1925, at the age of seventeen; he continued to record details from his daily life until shortly before his death in 1995.[94] One quality abundantly displayed in the diary is Nishiyama's lifelong interest in learning; although his formal education ended relatively early in life, Nishiyama and his friends continued to meet informally in reading and study sessions. Together they sustained an ongoing engagement with texts and ideas that was distinct from their equally enthusiastic search for new and better farming practices.

Indications are strong that this sort of interest in self-improvement and the betterment of rural society was commonplace in the countryside of the 1920s and 1930s and that it influenced the choices that farmers and their communities made about how to respond to the depression. The local initiatives of groups like the Hyōgo Prefecture Agricultural Association and the considerations of politicians and policymakers tell part of the story of the Economic Revitalization Campaign's construction; what might be thought of as a popular culture of revitalization is another key element in that narrative.

For a generation of young people educated and coming of age in the early Meiji era, the principles of self-improvement and self-betterment defined their career and educational goals.[95] Samuel Smiles's *Self Help* and an array of journals guided their ambitions, as did an increasingly accessible and uniform school system. Japan achieved very high rates of attendance at the elementary school level by the turn of the century—and all the changes that schooling brought. For young men at least, the experiences associated with conscription and military training were also a part of growing up, so that both the schoolroom and the barracks were familiar in ways that their parents could only wonder at.

Though many of the promises of the Meiji education system proved false, and large numbers of young people found themselves shut out of higher education and the careers they longed for, it is clear that the same system continued to produce well-trained, ambitious, and inquisitive men and women. As Earl Kinmonth and others have noted, what it meant to "rise in the world" and serve the nation was transformed by changes in the economy and by the state's ability to absorb new college graduates, but was never abandoned.[96] By the time of the depression, the number of leaders of rural communities and farmers' organizations who were not products of the Meiji education system was dwindling; the generation that was preparing to take on positions of responsibility in their families and communities in the late 1920s and early 1930s knew nothing else. They were the product of a mature educational and socializing process, one that sought to instill both the factual and the ideological foundations suited to the modern nation.

The well-educated countryside proved fertile ground for local experimentation with self-improvement and often for efforts to engage in a broader social activism as well. Nishiyama Kōichi's diary is a case in point and an example of a wider phenomenon associated with his generation. Of the ten prewar rural diarists known to Japanese scholars, seven were men born around the time of the Russo-Japanese and Sino-Japanese Wars, in a span that extends from 1898 to 1908, the year Nishiyama was born. Those who were farmers rented all or most of the between 2 and 3 *chō* of land they worked. All had roughly the same level of education and shared a hunger for knowledge, for more schooling, for reading.[97] They reached adulthood at a time when those appetites could be easily fed.

The mid-1920s saw an explosion in the number and variety of magazines and other publications directed at a mass audience. Thus in rural homes Samuel Smiles could well have shared bookshelf space with journals like *Kaizō*, one of a group of leftist magazines that helped introduce readers to a body of social and political criticism (within the limits imposed by censorship, of course; the emperor was one among many topics almost entirely off-limits). Local and eventually national publications invited participation in the form of letters to the editor, articles, and even works of fiction, offering platforms for the ideas and complaints of average readers. In the countryside, newspapers put out by young men's associations in the 1920s and early 1930s gave voice to a generation of farmers who often spoke critically and clearly of the state of the countryside.

No such medium had existed in any meaningful way prior to the 1920s; one could argue that it wasn't until then that rural citizens emerged as a distinct audience worthy of being written about and for.[98] Though no single understanding of how to solve the rural crises emerges from the pages of these local papers, they demonstrate a deep commitment on the part of rural youth to the pursuit of improvement, for themselves and for their communities.[99] In a mid-1932 national survey of Young Men's Association members, one commentator, who had spent ten days observing conditions in Niigata and northern Nagano prefectures, came to this conclusion, which mirrored the sentiments of many:

If our country's villages are *jinriksha*, then big cities are automobiles, automobiles that run on a lot of the gasoline of capitalist economic organization. It is meaningless to help the *jinriksha* just because it lost the battle with the automobile. I really have to wonder about the mental health of those who think that doing more to help the *jinriksha* will deal some sort of blow to the automobile. And aren't there enough agricultural commentators on their way to mental institutions already?

I am quite convinced that right now the only way to save the *jinriksha* villages is to transform them into motorcycle villages to compete with the [automobile] cities. Of course, rebuilding the villages is a very hard job. In the process of this reconstruction, because of rationalization, a number of stragglers may appear in the villages. Maybe the leadership class will change. However, helping those who have fallen down, and ought to have fallen down, is the responsibility of social work and not within the bounds of policies for rural revitalization. Before such a major undertaking, we have to eliminate tearful sentimentalism.

Open the window! Don't you want to let the new air in?[100]

Far better known and much more widely read than local journals, no magazine promoted the ideas of rural self-improvement and reform more assiduously than *Ie no hikari*. Publication began in 1925, and *Ie no hikari* was by the mid-1930s the countryside's most widely read publication, reaching close to one in every three rural homes. Unlike other popular magazines of the day, *Ie no hikari* never saw the inside of a bookstore; it was available only through prepaid purchases and distributed solely within the national network of industrial cooperatives directly to rural homes. This makes its reach all the more impressive; the magazine's circulation exceeded two hundred thousand in July 1932, and by July 1935 a million copies were sent out each month. Circulation approached 1.5 million in 1937, a prewar record.[101] The magazine's appeal rested in part on the membership base of the industrial cooperatives, which grew rapidly alongside the Economic Revitalization Campaign, but equally important were the careful efforts of the editorial staff to construct a journal that reflected the needs of its rural audience.

A series of changes in the tone and structure of the magazine was already under way when the rural depression began. A new editor, Umeyama Ichirō, took deliberate steps to boost *Ie no hikari*'s appeal among farm readers. After 1930, the editorial and exhortatory portions of the magazine were limited to less than a third of the total content, while the remaining pages were devoted to entertainment, readers' submissions, and a separate children's magazine at the back of each issue.[102] Articles encouraging self-sufficiency and love of the land—themes that Yamazaki Naokichi had raised again and again in his long-running pieces in the magazine's early years—were joined after 1930 by more practical and more aggressive advice.

*Ie no hikari*'s readers were increasingly urged to take positive steps to improve their lives and their communities. At one level the focus was on the nuts and bolts of better farm management and the services that the industrial cooperatives could provide, but the magazine didn't stop there. It also devoted considerable space to discussions of rural culture, the arts, and social reforms, a broad approach that the Economic Revitalization Campaign would soon mimic. Three strategies were employed. One was to copy the approach of other popular magazines and feature literature, plays, film synopses, humor, and cartoons, in effect bringing a shared national culture into the countryside. For example, serialized novels by Yoshikawa Eiji, Kagawa Toyohiko, and others began appearing in mid-1932 and were well received by readers.

The second strategy was to draw readers' attention to the qualities of rural village culture that were distinct from its urban alternative, and to encourage the preservation and development of those qualities. Part of laying out for readers what was good about village life naturally involved detailing what was wrong with urban living, and *Ie no hikari* made frequent references to the dangers of moving to the city, to the venality of capitalism, and to the decadence of urban culture.[103] The magazine's editors pointed to the cooperation, harmony, and stability long associated with farm communities as evidence that a separate rural culture existed and ought to be preserved. Toward this end, the magazine encouraged the formation of local acting groups (short plays with rural themes were featured in several issues) and called for the submission of both documentary and fictional works dealing with local life and rural families.[104] *Ie no hikari*'s suggestion that there was plenty to be proud of in the hard work and values of the countryside was meant to offset the siren's lure of the cities and to offer an alternative to those in search of a brighter future.

A third strategy was to draw the connection between a prosperous and vibrant countryside and specific but plausible changes in one's lifestyle, farm management practices, and daily activities. Post-1929 columns increasingly touched on the everyday issues confronting farm families and offered detailed real-life examples of strategies that families had used to overcome their problems.[105] Household budgets, crop diversification schemes, and plans for more rational uses of family labor and time made frequent appearances, as did a series of roundtable discussions about the best local policies for addressing the deepening depression.

The magazine clearly drew on the so-called Campaign to Improve Daily Life (Seikatsu kaizen undō) for at least some of its inspiration in this area. The Campaign to Improve Daily Life had started out in the early 1920s under the Ministry of Education as an effort to improve household hygiene and nutrition and to promote a more rational, scientific approach to the everyday activities of the modern household and family.[106] Originally focused on urban families, the concept was malleable enough to find quick application to rural households as well. From the late 1920s on, Ie no hikari made regular references to the importance of these reforms and to their role in the construction of a rural society that was not only economically prosperous but culturally rich as well. Better time management, for example, held out the possibility of leisure, and of finding time in one's hectic schedule to pursue hobbies and interests in the arts, or simply to play. Here one catches glimpses of the countryside as a competitor to the city, in that the assumption behind many of these reforms—and the articles that promoted them—was that young people would continue to flow out of their villages and into urban centers if all that remained for them at home was the prospect of dull, backbreaking work, miserable health, and a monotonous diet for the rest of their lives.

The reform of daily life in its many guises offered something better. When Ie no hikari's contributors painted a picture of the countryside's future, it wasn't of communities merely mimicking the bright lights and cafés of Tokyo, nor did they envision a return to some imagined idyllic past. Instead, readers of Ie no hikari and a wide range of other journals directed at a rural audience were encouraged to think of a modern countryside, but one in which the modernity was of the countryside's own making.[107] These ideas, and proposals to make them real, were part of a public discourse of rural reform that was in place well before the start of the Economic Revitalization Campaign.

The appeal of the broad approach to rural recovery, one that brought together economic and social reforms, is also evident in the surge in popularity of the teachings of Ninomiya Sontoku (1787–1856) in the early 1930s. His advice to farmers to "Work much, earn much, and spend little!" retained much of its appeal in the aftermath of the depression, as advocates of Ninomiya's Hōtoku approach to social and economic reform quickly made clear.[108] In alliances with state bureaucrats and in private efforts at the national and local levels, Hōtoku activists helped influence both how many rural Japanese thought about the problems they faced and how they went about responding to them.

Ninomiya's teachings had long been popular in the countryside and in some government offices. State support for organized attempts to spread the Hōtoku messages of planning, frugality, and the value of farming peaked during the Local Improvement Campaign, but bureaucratic interest remained high even afterward. The two national Hōtoku organizations, the Chūō Hōtokukai and the Dai Nihon Hōtokusha, were still going strong at the beginning of the 1930s. The former was responsible for publishing the journal *Shimin*, in which people like Gotō Fumio and Ministry of Agriculture and Forestry bureaucrat Kodaira Gonichi expressed their support for Hōtoku-ism and sought readers' support for economic revitalization.

The depression also gave the Dai Nihon Hōtokusha ample opportunity to put its tenets to the test more directly. As early as 1931, members of the association began using Hōtoku methods to help "rebuild" and reform several villages in Shizuoka as part of the prefecture's own rural recovery program. Sasai Shintarō, vice president of the Dai Nihon Hōtokusha and one of the country's foremost interpreters of the teachings of Ninomiya, helped lead the effort in Hijikata village, where he used surveys, planning, debt repayment, and spiritual exhortation to put the village back on the right track.[109] The similarities between this approach and the one eventually used by the Ministry of Agriculture and Forestry are obvious, a link made even clearer by Hijikata's later award-winning performance as an Economic Revitalization village.[110]

Sasai often referred back to what he had accomplished in Hijikata in the lectures and training sessions that became the second part of Dai Nihon Hōtokusha's contribution to depression-era policy. Sasai and Hōtoku activists like him ran a series of fifteen "Leadership Lectures for Rebuilding the Lives of the Citizens" (Kokumin seikatsu tatenaoshi shidōsha kōshūkai) from 1933 until 1938. Closer in content to a seminar or workshop than to a simple lecture series, sessions often lasted as long as forty-five days, although about half ran only two weeks from start to finish. Attendees received intensive instruction in Hōtoku principles and leadership skills, as well as one-on-one counseling on their personal situations and problems in their communities. More than twelve hundred people attended the sessions.

Like any Hōtoku enthusiast, Sasai was an outspoken advocate of the basic tenets of Ninomiya's teachings. In one discussion he used the difficulties that Ninomiya faced in his time to put some perspective on the crises of the early 1930s, concluding as he did so that what had worked for Ninomiya then would work just as well in the present.[111] The problems facing the villages in the 1930s had been with them for some time, he argued, and quick fixes would accomplish little. Thrift, diligence, and service for the community were themes that cropped up again and again in his work. Sasai tempered these abstract concepts with his own personal knowledge of village-level reform, incorporating both the more abstract qualities of Hōtoku tenets and down-to-earth advice on how to turn around a struggling community. "Today there are any number of groups in the village—the young men's association, the women's group, the agricultural association, and the industrial cooperative—but all are nothing more than cliques," Sasai pointed out, adding that "the cliques lead to struggles in the village, so there are not a few examples in which the communities have been plunged into chaos." Ineffective institutions, coupled with the misapplication of low-interest loans and other relief measures, he argued, were keeping the villages from recovery.[112]

Sasai advised his listeners to make themselves aware of the power of self-revitalization. Freedom from reliance on others was a key part of the recovery process, but at the same time Sasai made a strong argument in favor of an approach to recovery that emphasized community-wide solutions, one that he labeled, not very originally, *kyōka* (often translated as "moral suasion").[113] Although it was hard to pin Sasai down to any single description of the *kyōka* method, at least two ideas were consistently important to him in discussions of it. One was the need to replace a Western, individualistic, and competitive approach to life with a more holistic, Hōtoku-inspired worldview. The second was to create organizations at the village level that would allow people to put these new values into practice.

According to Sasai, *kyōka* at the village level began with the establishment of regularly held hamlet- and village-level assemblies. Once a month, each of the hamlet's households would send at least two people to participate in an assembly. Village-wide meetings would also be held, but less often. Once at the assembly, villagers would enjoy a series of talks by local leaders, talks meant to inform and inspire. Recovery plans would be laid out in detail, questions answered, and goals clearly defined. Sasai believed that the assemblies would get community members working toward the same goal, for the same reasons, and with a good understanding of the tools available to them. Most village institutions met too infrequently and involved too small a percentage of the population to bring about real change. Without the community-wide effort involved in kyōka, argued Sasai, they would never be able to serve the community well.[114]

One of the goals of the assemblies would be to challenge existing approaches to the crisis and to introduce local people to different ways of thinking about their problems. Sasai wanted to pay particular attention to the damage that Western ideas had done and to repair that harm by providing people with new ideas better suited to Japan. The Western influences that Sasai rejected were numerous, but conflict, competition, and individual gain are recurring themes (all values that, in other contexts, rural Japanese might have associated just as much with cities).[115] He pointed to Darwinian theory as one example of the extent to which these three factors were built into the Western understanding of the world. Darwinian theory, Sasai pointed out, emphasized the success of one species at the expense of another. If Darwin was to be believed, progress was built on a foundation of conflict and destruction. The message was clear: The only way to get ahead was to vanquish someone else.[116]

Sasai tried to set out an alternative view of how the world works. He argued that Hōtoku-ism taught one to view the environment and the community as a whole. The gains and losses of individual members, which the West found so important, were irrelevant. As an example of what he meant, Sasai described two different ways of thinking about what a bank was supposed to do. The Western concept of a bank began with the officers, the shareholders, the depositors, and the borrowers, all of whom had slightly different interests in the bank. Shareholders wanted high dividends; depositors, high interest rates; borrowers, low ones. Any attempt to satisfy all these needs at once would bring the bank down, so the different concerns were in a constant struggle to gain the upper hand. Ninomiya's approach said that the people who ran the bank should be happy to receive deposits and just as happy to loan money, since it was their job to provide money where there was none. Shareholders would also be at the center of those projects; depositors would know that their money was being put to good use. In other words, it was vital to think of the participants in the bank as different aspects of a single enterprise, working in harmony toward a common goal. Once that approach to banking was adopted, issues of conflicting interest and competition would no longer be relevant. "It is because people are all in different, separate positions that the struggle over profits occurs," he concluded.[117]

Sasai's advice on how to overcome these problems was straightforward. It was clear that the institutions of village life (no less caught up in conflict than the bank of Sasai's example) were themselves unable to reform society. To make *kyōka* possible, villagers would have reorganize themselves in ways that stressed harmony over conflict and unity over disparate interests. "That organization will not be successful," Sasai wrote, "unless it unites each hamlet, village, and region, and undertakes organized reform." It would not be enough to appoint a few people to a committee and expect them to lead everyone else; the whole community had to be together or it would be impossible to revive the village, the town, and the nation.[118] Since it was essential that the hearts and minds of the people be settled before any actual reforms were started, Sasai leaned toward hamlet assemblies and village Hōtoku societies as especially well suited to these purposes.

The concept of revitalization was malleable enough that it could be embraced by many spokesmen at once and thus reach the countryside through a variety of channels. The rhetoric and practice of revitalization would have been hard to escape, in what I suspect was a new set of circumstances for rural communities. By the mid-1930s it was possible to reach into villages and into the lives of farm families in ways that would not have been attempted even a decade before. Magazines like *Ie no hikari* and other popular journals had an extensive rural readership by then, an expansion that went hand in hand with the growth of other forms of mass media. The growth of the industrial cooperatives marks another watershed. Whether in the form of cooperatives, young men's associations, women's groups, or even the agrarianist societies that helped spark the drive to rural reform, farmers were increasingly well organized in the 1920s and 1930s.

Perhaps more important, the post-depression era marks a transformation not only in the means of reaching into rural communities but in the reasons to do so. The Economic Revitalization Campaign, the Industrial Cooperative movement, and even Ninomiya's activists implicated the entire community in reform. No one was left out. Not only could everyone be involved in reconstructing the village, but bureaucrats, activists, and, increasingly, rural Japanese themselves believed that they should be. How this rhetoric of reform was reflected in practice is the next subject of this study.

# 7   Revitalization in a Famine Year: Sekishiba, 1934–1935

AS THE ECONOMIC REVITALIZATION campaign moved toward its third year, the countryside already seemed to be changing for the better. Some three thousand communities had been chosen to participate in the campaign, well above the number the Ministry of Agriculture and Forestry had expected to apply. The campaign was popular beyond all expectations. "In the villages, belief in economic reform is evident," Kodaira Gonichi reported to the committee overseeing the campaign's progress, "and there are many designated villages that can see the light ahead of them."[1] Savings rates were up, villages were spending less on weddings and funerals, and many local leaders were making positive comments about a new spirit of coordination and cooperation among their communities' farming organizations.

Other improvements had nothing to do directly with the campaign but were nevertheless welcome. Prices for most farm products had stopped their downward spiral, and there were signs that Finance Minister Takahashi's spending programs were having a beneficial effect. Exports and heavy industry were starting a comeback, and as these sectors turned around, it seemed certain that the rest of the economy would soon see brighter days ahead.

That the countryside was not recovering quite as quickly as planners had hoped was troubling, though Kodaira tried in early 1934 to put a positive face on the persistent rural depression. The downturn had been so severe and had lasted so long, he argued, that all the flaws of rural society were fully exposed. Anything that could go wrong had already done so; years of hard times had made it easy to decide what needed to be fixed and what could be safely left alone. The campaign would address these failings. Kodaira found another bright point in the drawn-out rural recession: plans that were developed during such a difficult period in the nation's history would endure anything else the economy might throw at the countryside.[2] Kodaira assured farmers and local leaders that even though they were not yet out of the woods, the road ahead was certain to be easier.

He was mistaken. Bad weather in 1934 led to one of the worst famines in Japan's modern history. Huge crop losses devastated rural communities, hitting hardest in the northeast, where tens of thousands of children and adults were eventually reported to be on the verge of starvation. Coming as it did while the effects of the depression still lingered, the famine added insult to the injuries that farmers already bore. Coming as it did when the industrial sector and factory workers were beginning to enjoy the fruits of recovery, the famine reminded farmers of how far their countryside was from the bright lights of the city.

This chapter explores the campaign's reception in the countryside, and initial grassroots efforts at reform, through Sekishiba's experiences in 1934 and 1935. Sekishiba was an early and eager participant in the Revitalization Campaign, winning official designation as a campaign village in 1934.[3] Planning and restructuring efforts were thus already under way when the famine began; the new crisis delayed implementation of local reforms and modified them in some ways, but the community never wavered in its commitment to them. If anything, the famine seems to have focused attention even more closely on the need to protect the village against future calamities. The depression had demonstrated how vulnerable and backward the countryside had become; the famine, at least for Sekishiba, brought these points home even more clearly. The campaign offered tools and techniques that might finally bring the village to the point where it could flourish as a key part of a modern nation and not lag behind as an object of pity, charity, and, ultimately, contempt. Sekishiba embraced the possibilities of revitalization.

## Embracing Revitalization

The bundles of forms, filled with sheet after sheet of a finely drawn template of lines and ample blank space, first reached Sekishiba's households in the early fall of 1934. In what was for most families their first direct encounter with the campaign, the arrival of the Basic Surveys and revitalization planning forms was a tangible sign of the role they were expected to play in the village's campaign. At meetings held within each hamlet after distribution of the paperwork, the mayor and other members of Sekishiba's newly constituted Economic Revitalization Committee (Keizai kōsei iinkai) explained how to complete the surveys and plans, responded to questions, and reminded listeners of the importance of these first steps to the rest of the campaign.

Villagers were asked to complete two distinct but related tasks. The lengthy Basic Survey raised detailed questions about the household, farming practices, income and expenses, family and business finances, and so on—questions that had not been asked of these families before in any systematic way. Households were asked to estimate both their living expenses and how much it cost to produce their crops. How much did they spend on weddings? On funerals, on taxes? How much did they owe, and to whom? Respondents were told to answer the questions based on the state of the household in the year immediately prior to the survey, which in Sekishiba's case was 1933.

The second part of the process was even more important. Once the Basic Survey was complete, villagers turned next to planning. Where the survey had asked about conditions in 1933, each revitalization plan required the family to indicate how it would transform the household's economic circumstances in each of the next five years. The plan mirrored the survey in many respects. For every category of answer the family had given about its status in 1933, for example, villagers provided estimates as well of where it hoped to be at the end of every year from 1935 to 1939. Household spending, income, taxes, even family size and wedding expenses were included in the plans. But so too were a number of categories that had not been part of the survey. The planning forms encouraged respondents to add additional crops to the list of what they already grew, to identify new sources of income, or by breaking down expenses into ever more minute detail, find room for frugality where none had been visible before. This is where the rhetoric of revitalization was most important. At the hamlet meetings that coincided with the planning process, the mayor and others had to speak clearly and realistically of what planning could do and of how the village could change for the better.

Both sets of data, one each households' Basic Survey and the other each household's description of how it planned to pursue revitalization, were eventually collected within each hamlet and sent from there to Sekishiba's Economic Revitalization Committee. The Committee collated the results and produced a version of the survey and of the planning documents that encompassed results from the entire village. The final draft of Sekishiba's Basic Survey and Economic Revitalization Plan was almost fifty handwritten pages long. It had at least two reading audiences. One was local, where villagers and administrators referred to the survey and planning results to gauge the Campaign's progress. The other was much wider. Bureaucrats in the prefectural offices of the Economic Revitalization Campaign reviewed village plans before publishing abridged versions of them in annual reports and before passing them along to the Ministry of Agriculture and Forestry. As befit this more distant readership, the village's Basic Survey included background on Sekishiba's history, geography, the number and type of shrines and temples within its boundaries, and village traditions surrounding weddings, births, deaths, and other rites of passage.[4] The campaign was thus understood to bear on every aspect of village life, and not just on production and spending.

In its later reports to the prefecture, and in almost all the records that have to do with the campaign in Sekishiba, the village as a whole is the primary focus. Administratively, that makes a great deal of sense, but it leaves a large blank at the heart of the recovery program. After all, it was what happened at the household and hamlet levels that was central to the success of revitalization. Knowing what the revitalization process was supposed to accomplish for a typical family reveals a great deal about the reach of reform and its potential significance in the lives of a farm household. Such records exist for one of the village's hamlets, Komatsu. This small hamlet at the village's northern end was home in the 1930s to fewer than twenty families, among them that of the mayor, Satō Sakichi.

The economic status of Komatsu's households was not so different from that of the village as a whole. In 1923, the last year for which landholdings can be reasonably determined, the hamlet had a slightly larger share of farmers who worked only their own land (about half of Komatsu's families, compared to about a third for the village as a whole), while the proportions were reversed when it came to households that both owned farm land and rented some (roughly a third of Komatsu's households fell into this category, while slightly more than half of all Sekishiba's farmers did). The percentage of tenant households was thus roughly equivalent in both Komatsu and in the greater village. None of the village's largest landlords lived in Komatsu, although five Komatsu residents did rent at least some farmland to others.[5]

In October 1934, each of the hamlet's eighteen households submitted a recovery plan to Watanabe Shinta, who was a farmer, landlord on a very small scale, village council member, and member of the Economic Revitalization Committee. Watanabe collected the plans, collated the answers they contained, and drafted a revitalization plan for the entire hamlet.[6] Although these plans were developed in 1934, 1933 was used as the baseline against which future developments were measured. (The same would be true of the village plan.) Each plan was in four sections. The first listed the number of people in the household in 1933 by gender and status (farmer or non-farmer), and asked for estimates of changes over the next five years. Households were then asked to provide information about their land use and landholdings. How much paddy, upland, forest, or residential land they owned or rented was recorded, as were the changes that families planned to make in each of those categories over the five-year span of the plan (i.e., through 1938).

The second part of the plan covered household income, which was broken down into farm products (rice, potatoes, barley, and wheat, for instance), fruit, sericulture, crafts (bamboo goods were the most important), livestock, fish, lumber, and "other." The divisions within "Expenses," the third section, were even more specific. Households were asked to estimate how much they spent in nineteen different categories of farming-related costs, twenty-five separate types of household expense, and six varieties of taxes and fees. Trends in both income and expenses were projected over the next five years.

The fourth and final part of the plan dealt with household self-sufficiency. Planning documents asked farmers to report the value of the homemade fertilizer and homemade clothes they had produced in 1933 (to give just two examples) and then to lay out estimates for each over the next half decade. The idea, of course, was to help farmers get a clear idea of what they spent on different consumables, thus encouraging them to produce as much as possible of what they needed themselves. The more they relied on "homegrown" alternatives, the less cash they would spend and the less money they would need to borrow. Komatsu's plans provided seventeen different categories for self-production, including not only fertilizer and clothes but also grains, other foodstuffs, livestock, feed, fish, and firewood.

Komatsu's recovery plan did not involve significant shifts in the size of its population or in its land use. Families predicted that the total number of people in the hamlet would likely remain almost unchanged, at just over 140, although there would be more people working as farmers after five years than was the case when the plan was drafted (65 versus 54). Residents reported using 21.7 *chō* of paddy land and almost 11 *chō* of upland fields in 1933, and planned to use 2 *chō* more of paddy by 1938 while keeping upland use constant. Farmers expected that they would farm less of their own land in each category and rent slightly more. In Komatsu, this meant that the share of paddy land that was owner-cultivated would fall from 75 to just under 70 percent; for upland fields, the decline would be from 90 to 86 percent. How this worked will become clearer when we examine a few individual cases below.

Asked to develop plans that took into account the various sources of income available to them, Komatsu's residents responded with vigor.[7] They predicted that the value of their rice crops would increase by 25 percent over the next five years and that income from all farm products would be 28 percent higher in 1938 than it was in 1933. The increase would come not just from the rice crop but from barley (which would fetch twice as much), soybeans (an 80 percent increase), and vegetables (farmers hoped to make more than four times as much on this crop in 1938 than they had in 1933). The persimmon crop was expected to grow in value by more than 50 percent; while other varieties of fruit were worth only 17 yen at the start of the plan, they were expected to be worth more than ten times as much by 1938.

More modest gains were predicted in silk production, but like rice it would remain one of the most important contributors to local income. Planners expected the value of the hamlet's silk-cocoon crop to rise from just over 2,000 yen to just under 3,000 yen. There were also signs that farmers were at least thinking about diversification: over the next five years, they expected to sell more chickens, more eggs, and more rabbits. There were plans to raise goats and fish, both new additions to Komatsu's farms. By boosting their production of these extra crops, Komatsu's farmers indicated a commitment to the diversification that economic revitalization planners advocated. Rice remained the hamlet's foremost crop, however, despite the added emphasis on other products. Rice alone accounted for 95 percent of the income from farming in 1933 and would provide for more than 92 percent five years hence, if all went as residents expected.[8]

By growing and selling more of their standard crops and adding to them a few new products, the hamlet expected to boost the value of its production by about a third in only five years.[9] The other side of the planning coin, of course, was how much people expected to have to spend each year. How much would it cost them to make the improvements in crop yields and to raise more livestock? The money for these animals and these improvements would have to come from somewhere, and farmers had to reckon with the possibility that both might cost more than they were worth. Planning was supposed to help them consider this possibility with care. In the planning documents, spending was divided into the two categories of farm and family outlays. For the former, households were asked to measure everything from the cost of seeds and fertilizer to how much they paid for labor and farm tools.

The result was a plan in which hamlet households would spend about 10 percent less on farming-related expenses in 1938 than they had in 1933. Spending was projected to decline in eleven of the nineteen planning categories. In 1933, the three largest expenses for local farmers were fertilizer, rent, and labor, in that order. Fertilizer alone accounted for almost two-fifths of all farm spending when the plan went into effect, and rent accounted for another fifth. Komatsu's farmers proposed cutting their spending on fertilizer by 16 percent, and that on labor by more than a third. This was in keeping with the Economic Revitalization program's emphasis on homegrown fertilizer, and it also reflects the campaign's push to make better use of the labor in each household. If Komatsu's farmers were able to cut back as much as they planned, by the end of the fifth year fertilizer would still account for roughly the same share of all spending, but labor costs would have dropped from 14 percent to only 10 percent of the total.

Not every type of spending was reduced. Total spending on rent—a subject on which the Economic Revitalization program had almost nothing to say—was expected to rise very slightly. This is not surprising, given the plans by some families to borrow more land. The cost of animal feed was also expected to increase substantially, from 115 to 381 yen, while building maintenance would become only slightly more expensive. Residents also anticipated minor increases in items such as land improvement costs and spending on silkworm cards, but these were seldom more than a few yen a year. In general, Komatsu's farmers seem to have done a very good job of either maintaining or reducing the costs associated with running a farm.

Komatsu's residents were just as enthusiastic about cutting costs at home. Although it was almost impossible to reduce taxes and fees, there was plenty of room for flexibility in household budgets. The hamlet reported spending 8,300 yen on household and family expenses at the start of the planning period and planned to cut back by almost 1,300 yen over the next five years. Reductions were proposed in fifteen of twenty-five spending categories, with the largest ones in areas such as clothing (a 20 percent cut), medical expenses (from 650 yen to 228, a cut of almost two-thirds), and alcohol.

The latter category merits some further discussion. When the plans were drawn up, alcohol was the third largest spending category in the hamlet, ranking after clothing and "other." Despite the fact that residents planned to spend 15 percent less on drink by the end of the planning period, sharper cuts in other areas meant that alcohol would be the second largest single outlay in the hamlet by 1938 if all its residents behaved as they said they would. At 834 yen per year, it would run a very close second to the 840 yen that residents expected to spend on clothing in 1938. It is also worth pointing out that alcohol was one of the few areas in which self-sufficiency was not encouraged by the government.

The Economic Revitalization program did encourage self-sufficiency in other areas, however, and the final section of the plan dealt specifically with the homemade and homegrown. As might be expected of a farming community, residents of the hamlet did very well at supplying themselves with grain, made some of their own fertilizer, and did fairly well at providing their own firewood. Yet they do not appear to have harbored any illusions about their ability to do much better in the five years after 1933. They expected to boost the value of the grains they produced for their own use by about 5 percent, fertilizer by about 10 percent, and seedlings by about 25 percent. Fertilizer was probably the most pressing concern, given that it accounted for such a large chunk of what farmers spent to raise their crops. Any increase in what farmers raised on their own would decrease the amount they had to buy, freeing up that money for other uses.

Komatsu's Economic Revitalization Plan was no better and no worse than the sum of its parts. This brief review of the hamlet's plan offers some clues about how residents reacted to the Economic Revitalization program, but the best insights are to be found in the individual plans themselves. For the average Sekishiba farmer, the most concrete aspect of revitalization was, surely, the development and implementation of plans for economic recovery. Sixteen of Komatsu's eighteen families submitted complete revitalization plans that are remarkable in their attention to detail and in their insistence that farmers apply the same kind of painstaking care to managing their crops and households. Summaries of the main points of these plans appear in Table 7.

Table 7
Projected Results for 1939 of Economic Revitalization for Sixteen Households in Komatsu Hamlet, Sekishiba
(1933 = 100)

| Name | Rice | Other foods | Silk cocoons | All income | Farm expenses | Family expenses | All expenses |
|---|---|---|---|---|---|---|---|
| Hara Haruji | 125 | 197 | 44 | 99 | 70 | 95 | 87 |
| Watanabe Masaichi | 94 | 109 | 89 | 94 | 89 | 79 | 85 |
| Watanabe Kyuichi | 178 | 198 | 900 | 169 | 163 | 89 | 137 |
| Utsumi Haruki | 141 | 572 | 59 | 50 | 50 | 34 | 40 |
| Watanabe Hikoe | 103 | 98 | 32 | 89 | 91 | 83 | 87 |
| Watanabe Shinta | 100 | 100 | 100 | 101 | 100 | 100 | 99 |
| Hara Yoshitomi | 110 | 136 | 86 | 82 | 101 | 96 | 78 |
| Kobiyama Zenhachi | 220 | 84 | 170 | 303 | 391 | 112 | 170 |
| Satō Chōta | 125 | 138 | 74 | 151 | 90 | 98 | 92 |
| Watanabe Taichi | 76 | 781 | 333 | 151 | 98 | 55 | 73 |
| Satō Sakichi | 120 | 136 | 400 | 201 | 85 | 91 | 85 |
| Kobiyama Kichiji | 100 | 100 | 100 | 113 | 100 | 100 | 86 |
| Hara Masaru | 123 | 596 | 98 | 88 | 115 | 76 | 88 |

|  |  |  |  |  |  |  |
|---|---|---|---|---|---|---|
| Satō Kichishirō | 100 | 100 | 100 | 100 | 100 | 100 | 96 |
| Kobiyama Sutekichi | 100 | 100 | 47 | 91 | 94 | 100 | 43 |
| Kobiyama Gosuke | 94 | 110 | 58 | 91 | 65 |  | 57 |
| *Hamlet Average* | *125* | *196* | *85* | *102* | *90* | *85* | *77* |

NOTE: The figures above represent projected crop production, income, and expenses for 1939, the fifth and final year of Sekishiba's first economic revitalization plan, with results in 1933 equal to 100 in each category and for each household. The estimates were produced in 1934. Mathematical mistakes in the original documents were corrected where found. Two reports were omitted; neither Endō Kōzaburō nor Uda Riki completed survey forms, so results from those households have not been included in this discussion. The remaining reports are listed in the order in which they originally appeared.

SOURCE: Compiled from SMY, *Komatsu buraku kakuko keizai chōsa bo*, October 1934, KST.

As noted previously, figures for the hamlet of Komatsu as a whole suggest that families planned to boost their income from farming while simultaneously cutting back on spending. However, a look at the goals drawn up by individual households reveals that no two were exactly alike in how they approached economic revitalization. Families pursued a wide variety of revitalization "strategies." In more than 120 different categories, respondents recorded their income, expenses, crops, family size, landholdings, and land use as they stood at the time of the plan's inception (in Sekishiba's case, 1933), and then again for each of the next five years.[10] The broader implications of this sort of discipline are interesting, but at their simplest, the plans and the explanations that accompanied them encouraged families to exploit new sources of income, diversify their crops, and cut back on expenses where possible. Let me provide examples of how three farm families approached this challenge.

## THE MAYOR

Satō Sakichi's enthusiasm for the Economic Revitalization Campaign was no secret. He expected great things from it and was an early and outspoken proponent of the campaign's value to the village. Chapter 9 below describes Satō's engagement with the campaign in his capacity as a local leader. Here the focus is a little different. The mayor's situation presents a double opportunity, for he was at once a public figure active in the revitalization of the community and knowledgeable in the workings of the campaign and also the head of a relatively prosperous farming family. This section explores how he hoped to apply the principles he preached publicly to the private sphere of his own household.

Satō's eleven-member household was the top taxpayer in the hamlet of Komatsu, a consequence less of large assets than of the mayor's salaried income and pensions. Within Komatsu, the Satō family was only slightly above average in terms of production and landholdings. It owned 1.4 *chō* of paddy land, 1 *chō* of upland fields, and more than 5 *chō* of woodland. Much of the land family members worked themselves; in 1934, five classified themselves as full-time farmers. What the family didn't farm, it rented to local tenants; in the early 1920s, about half the upland fields and a little over half of the paddy land had been rented out. Records suggest that family members brought more paddy land back under their own cultivation by 1933, but likely continued to rent out small plots to others.

Like other farmers with ample landholdings and labor, the Satō family produced many different crops and generated income from a variety of sources. Rice was the single most important product, but the family also grew potatoes, a variety of grains and vegetables, and persimmons and other fruits. Chickens, rabbits, and a small sericulture operation rounded out their farming endeavors, while lumber was an important source of extra income. Their forest land gave them access to consistent supplies of lumber for general use as well as wood from the *kiri* (paulownia) tree, which was highly prized for use in furniture and musical instruments. In addition, the family could count on the mayor's salary and pensions; though not huge amounts of money, these were at least consistent in ways that income from farming often was not.

By local standards, the Satō family was successful. It wasn't immediately obvious how economic revitalization planning might make an already good situation better. The family had already diversified its farming practices, so there was relatively little leeway there for major changes. Instead—and here the Satō family reflects the commonest approach to planning among the better-off families in the hamlet—the mayor proposed incremental changes in production and slight adjustments in spending to move the household toward a slightly more efficient, more profitable position. He planned, for example, to increase rice production by about 20 percent by the end of five years, with all the increase coming in the final two years of the planning period. The mayor also expected his family to be able to eke out a little more barley and wheat, to triple the persimmon harvest, and to quadruple the value of the family's silk production.

Even with these changes, however, the relative importance of the various crops would not shift significantly; rice would still account for the lion's share of income from farming. Only the family's plans for the use of its lumber reflect a change in this balance; in the fifth and final year of the plan, they expected to generate 500 yen in income from the sale of paulownia wood (much more than the 2 yen in annual income up to that point); at that level, the trees would be worth more to the family than its rice crop. In any case, the lumber represents an expansion of the family's use of existing resources, for they don't appear to have planned to move resources or labor out of any other area in order to chop down more *kiri* trees.

On the expenses side of the equation, the Satō family again pursued an incremental approach, shaving off spending here and there without making large cuts anywhere. They hoped to be able to reduce the costs of managing their farm by about 15 percent over five years, almost all as a result of using more homemade fertilizer and spending less on the store-bought variety. Other farming outputs would remain more or less unchanged, although, as already mentioned, farm production itself was expected to rise over time. These cuts in management outlays were not quite matched by reductions in other areas. In 1933 the family spent more than any other household in the hamlet on so-called family expenses (education, entertainment, food, and the like). By 1938 they hoped to be spending only about 10 percent less. The mayor promised to cut back on the budgets for fish, candy, and entertainment by 5 yen each, and to allocate 50 yen less to education at the end of the first planning period.

## UTSUMI HARUKI

There were four families in the hamlet's uppermost tax bracket. Utsumi Haruki (b. June 21, 1884) was the head of one of them. His efforts at revitalization extended beyond his household, however, for once the campaign was under way, he often joined Mayor Satō in efforts to promote economic revitalization. His particular interest was in the teachings of Ninomiya Sontoku and their application to rural recovery. Utsumi later took the lead in the drive to form a Hōtoku society in Komatsu, and he was one of several local farmers who received intensive instruction in Hōtoku methods.

The eleven-member family embraced diversification. In 1933, 640 of the 658 yen the family made on farm production came from rice. (The family owned 1.4 *chō* of paddy land, rented a small plot, and could also farm just under 1 *chō* of upland fields.) By the end of five years, Utsumi planned to have increased rice production and the income from it by about two-fifths, while adding barley, vegetables, *azuki* beans, and potatoes to the list of crops the family already grew. These new crops, together with larger yields on existing ones, were expected to raise farm income by more than half and to lower the share of rice to less than 90 percent. The persimmon crop would triple, although silk-cocoon production would fall. The family raised cocoons worth 435 yen in 1933 but planned to take in only 250 yen from this source at the end of 1938, a drop of more than two-fifths.[11]

Another sign of Utsumi's commitment to planning was his scheme to add livestock to his family's repertoire. Although he was starting from scratch, he wrote of his desire to raise rabbits, chickens, and chicken eggs for market. At the end of the planning period, these products would net the family 40 yen a year, he hoped. He was also able to predict where income was likely to be cut. His family had made 550 yen in 1933 by selling lumber and firewood, no doubt from the family's fairly large holdings of wooded land. Although family members would continue to make use of these resources, they would not use as much as they had, and income from this source was also expected to fall to about 150 yen. This meant that—despite diversification, larger crop yields, and increased income from farming—the family's total income would actually be about 10 percent lower in 1938 than in 1933.

By cutting farm expenses by two-fifths (both fertilizer and labor costs were sharply reduced in the family's plan), Utsumi hoped to compensate for the decline in income. Some costs were fixed, however. He would have to pay 56 yen per year for the land he rented, plan or no plan. At the start of the planning period, rent accounted for only 10 percent of all farming expenses, but as the family made cuts in other areas, that 56 yen would eventually take up two-fifths of the farming budget, making it the second most expensive item after fertilizer.

According to Utsumi's detailed description of family expenses, 1933 had been a very expensive year for the household. He recorded outlays of 500 yen in wedding costs, 200 yen for a graduation, 360 yen for the cost of renting another home, 300 yen in "job search costs," and 200 yen for clothing. These expenses were probably faced by many families in the community at some point, although by village standards Utsumi's budget is close to extravagant. (Remember that the Basic Survey reported that families in the "upper" tax bracket, or those paying more than 25 yen in Special Household taxes each year, spent less than 400 yen on average per wedding in 1933.)

Even though Utsumi was relatively well off, he had been forced to borrow some 1,400 yen to cover his additional expenses. Not only that, but he also planned to pay for at least one more wedding in the near future. These extra costs could end up totaling much more than his family's entire budget for regular expenses. In 1933, for instance, Utsumi recorded spending almost 1,000 yen on normal family costs, while outlays in the "other" category (some of which are described above) ran to 1,700 yen. At the end of the planning period he hoped to have reduced his normal budget by more than 30 percent, but still expected to pay much more than that in extraordinary costs. In

Utsumi's case, it is easy to see how family events and responsibilities could overwhelm any attempts at economic planning.

## THE KOBIYAMA FAMILY

Kobiyama Zenhachi (b. November 17, 1892) was head of a nine-member household that owned only 3.5 *tan* of upland fields, rented another 2 *tan* of paddy land, and paid the least household tax of any family in the hamlet. When they drew up their plan, they were using their land to grow very small amounts of rice, wheat, barley, and a few other items. Altogether these crops provided a farm income of only 29 yen in 1933, of which rice accounted for only 8.2 yen. For the Kobiyama family, the best course seemed to be to move away from crop diversity—since they already had that—and toward boosting their production of rice and barley. By the end of five years, they planned to have eliminated some crops entirely, to have cut back on wheat, and to have almost doubled the value of their barley and rice crops. He also planned to more than double silk-cocoon production, and thus income from that source, from 35 to 77 yen. The family was raising four rabbits in 1933, and Kobiyama predicted that they would have fifty by 1938. Chickens, their eggs, and carp would help round out the family's new enterprises. Altogether these new projects were expected to bring a substantial jump in income, up from only 2 yen for fish and livestock in 1933 to the 205 yen he hoped to bring in at the end of the planning period.

According to Kobiyama's plan, these attempts to increase yields and the addition of the new products would bring a 70 percent increase in the family's total income during the first year the plan was in effect. After five years, income would be triple the 1933 figure. Put another way, the family would go from having a 1933 income of 13.3 yen per member from all sources to 40.3 yen after five years. Because of increased output, Kobiyama anticipated spending much more on farming than he was used to. In 1933 he reported spending only about 33 yen toward farm management, but he expected expenses to have risen by 100 yen at the end of 1938. The biggest increases would come in fertilizer (almost triple what it had been), feed for livestock (from nothing to 50 yen), and rent. The family hoped to defray some of the fertilizer expense by producing more of their own but would likely still have to purchase more than they had in the past. In 1933 they were paying only 16 yen a year in rent but expected to pay 45 yen the following year.[12]

Kobiyama also planned for slight increases in the cost of supporting his family. By spending more in categories such as education, salt, and a number of lesser items, the overall family budget was predicted to increase by about 3 percent the first year, climbing to 12 percent above 1933 levels after five years. The household's entertainment costs were expected to rise from 50 sen to 80 sen, while alcohol (in 1933, at 8.5 yen, the fourth largest budget item, after gifts, education, and lighting) would rise to 10 yen. The family apparently bought no meat but did plan to spend an additional 20 sen on fish, which brought the total for that item up to 1.5 yen per year.

For the Kobiyama family, the economic plan and the Economic Revitalization movement do not seem to have meant simply cutting back and cutting corners. Their plan seems to be a carefully thought-out attempt to improve their situation through doing more with what they had, which suggests that the campaign and its tenets found at least some support outside of the wealthier, landed farmers in the community. Raising more cocoons and adding the planned livestock and fish meant a great deal of extra work for the Kobiyamas, for example, since there are no indications that the family was willing to hire outside help.

This is exactly the sort of approach that the Economic Revitalization Campaign advocated: diversification, increased production when possible, and avoiding waste of labor. Kobiyama might have pursued these changes without the economic plan or the campaign; still, it would be foolish to discount how important these two elements were when Kobiyama considered his future. As a sign of how seriously he took the planning process, it is interesting to note that, of all the plans submitted in the hamlet, Kobiyama's was the only one to include price tables. Kobiyama wrote out an estimate of what he thought would happen to commodity prices in the near future and included a list of post-1934 prices for almost everything he produced. He used that list when calculating his production income; no one else seems to have been as systematic in his approach to planning.

## Revitalization Strategies

The differences among families may mask underlying patterns. Although it would be a mistake to draw conclusions about the village as a whole from a sample as small as Komatsu hamlet, a few observations tell us something about general trends. One is that the number of households in which total income would exceed total spending was expected to rise as a result of planning. In 1933, only four of the sixteen Komatsu families discussed above had budgets that were in the black; by the end of the planning period, that number had risen to ten.[13] Although this may not be a particularly fair way to measure the impact of planning (since it is not clear that households were ever told that they ought to think about whether or not their budget was balanced), it does suggest that the process held out some hope of an improvement in one's situation. For some of the households in the hamlet, economic revitalization promised something besides just more of the same.

Another interesting point can be made about the different approaches to revitalization evident in Komatsu. There is some correlation between a family's relative economic status within the hamlet, the way households hoped to use the planning process, and the results they sought. Families with relatively little land to farm planned to increase their incomes more than did families with larger amounts of land. A corollary is that families with little land also expected to do less well at reducing the costs associated with their families and with farming. The eight families who owned less than 1 *chō* of paddy land planned, on average, to increase their total income by about 36 percent; those with more than 1 *chō*, by only about 10 percent. The difference is also evident when other types of relationship to the land are considered. When the families in the hamlet are divided into those that owned or rented 2 *chō* or less (of paddy and upland fields) and those with more than that amount, the results are even more striking. The six families with less than 2 *chō* of land at their disposal hoped to boost their incomes by an average of almost 53 percent; those with more than that, by only about 5 percent.[14]

The spending patterns that families drew up worked a little differently. When expenses were considered, the less land one owned, the less likely one's household was to make sharp cuts in either the family or the farm budget. Using the same criteria as those for income predictions, planned spending by families with less than 1 *chō* of paddy land was expected to increase by about 4 percent by the end of 1938, whereas the rest of the hamlet, on average, hoped to cut spending by roughly 20 percent. Similarly, when rented and owned land together added up to less than 2 *chō*, households expected to have to spend almost a third more for family and farming expenses in 1938 than they had in 1933, whereas those with access to more than 2 *chō* of land thought that they could cut their budgets by about a fifth.[15]

I mention these points to help make another. These disparate strategies suggest that there was enough leeway within the planning process to accommodate families from a wide variety of economic backgrounds. Revitalization cast a wide net. For households at the lower end of the economic scale, its utility seemed to lie in the possibility of growth. Those families planned to boost their incomes at much higher rates than was common among the wealthier households. Those starting with more land and larger incomes used their plans to identify areas in which to reduce spending or weed out less profitable enterprises, such as sericulture. If Komatsu's proposals are any indication of ones drawn up elsewhere, then it is a little easier to understand how participation in a community-wide effort at economic planning might seem reasonable and beneficial to a fair number of people.

No one promised farmers that economic revitalization would make them rich or turn them into landlords overnight. There is little reason to think that families drew up their plans with those goals in mind. What the campaign did offer was the hope that the situation might improve—and the likelihood that it would get no worse. Both prospects were welcomed by farm families tired of uncertainty and afraid of what might lie ahead. As October 1934 drew to a close, the contrast between the future that their plans promised and the reality of their situation was striking. All around them in the fields, as far as anyone could see, were the remnants of the worst harvest in a generation.

## The 1934 Famine

As in most villages in northeastern Japan in 1934, the summer months in Sekishiba had been unseasonably cold, wet, and cloudy. The temperature in July and August was well below normal and the number of sunny days far fewer than farmers had come to expect of Fukushima weather. During a normal summer, high pressure systems from the south brought warm air to the Tōhoku prefectures. The arrival in July of an unusually strong Siberian cold front disrupted that pattern, preventing the warmer weather from reaching the north.[16] The two systems, warm and cold, met in an irregular front that extended over the Hokuriku region and southern Fukushima. Northern Aomori and Hokkaido, under the cold weather system, were thus cooler than normal but had an almost normal number of sunny days. Further south the weather was cold and cloudy, and close to where the warm and cold air met over Fukushima, Yamagata, and Miyagi, it was cold and rainy.[17] The wet, overcast cold weather continued for weeks.

Unwelcome under any circumstances, such conditions were especially damaging in the northeast. Most strains of Japanese rice require "sustained high temperatures, both night and day, with a summer (July to August) mean of not less than 20° C" to do well.[18] Even under the best conditions, farmers in the northeast had pushed the limits of rice's adaptability, planting in an environment that even in good seasons provided a narrow window of opportunity for a successful crop. In 1934, that window slammed shut. Average temperatures in July and August were one to two degrees below normal, sending many rice-growing districts either below or perilously close to the 20° C limit.

Rice plants normally reached full size from late June through July, while flowering and development of the grain took place during August. In 1934 the lack of sunshine and lower temperatures kept crops in most of the northeast from maturing normally, so that by August crops in the low-lying plains were one to two weeks late, while those at higher elevations were delayed even more. Rice blight, a disease exacerbated by the cold and by overuse of fertilizer, began to take a toll. Severe storms at the end of September made matters worse, and continued cold weather in October further reduced the quality of those crops that remained to be harvested. More than one journalist wrote of farmers going into the fields only to throw down their tools in despair after collecting just a few bundles of grain, the crop a near-total loss.[19]

Central and prefectural authorities did what they could to limit the impact of the weather. By August, both had begun issuing guidelines to towns and villages on steps that farmers could take to protect their crops from the cold. It is unclear how effective these measures were or whether they were widely followed. As the Imperial Agriculture Association noted in one of its reports, it had been so long since the last major famine that few farmers had direct experience of just how serious the situation could become, so they were unlikely to pay much heed to recommendations that they take extraordinary steps.

The communities that might have benefited most from preemptive steps were also the ones least likely to be able to pursue them. Procedures for protecting rice plants from the effects of the weather involved flooding the fields to a deeper than normal depth, keeping them flooded for a longer than normal period, and constructing holding ponds to allow irrigation water to warm up before it was used. These were relatively complex tasks. Villages with a full-time agricultural technician on hand were in a much better position to make them work, but even then success wasn't guaranteed.[20] Sekishiba seems not to have had any luck with preventive measures.

The effects of the weather were understood and to some extent predictable, but few of the early estimates came close to an accurate measure of just how much damage had been done. The government's first rice-crop estimates of the season were released in late September. Not surprisingly, they predicted very poor harvests in each of the northeastern prefectures. The rice crop in Fukushima was estimated to be only about three-quarters the size of a normal harvest, while farmers in Iwate were expected to bring in only about half as much rice as they had (on average) over the previous five years. Estimates released a month later showed that losses were actually much greater. The average reduction across all six Tōhoku prefectures was approximately 40 percent, with considerable variation among them. Akita's farmers escaped with the least harm, since their rice crop was still about three-quarters of its normal size.[21] The most serious crop reductions were reported in Iwate, where farmers were estimated to have harvested only about 45 percent as much rice as in a normal season. The most successful of all the counties in the prefecture ended up with a crop that was only 60 percent as large as in a normal year, and several areas reported harvests that were less than a tenth their normal size. Table 8 provides a more complete picture of the problem.[22]

Conditions in Fukushima bear closer scrutiny. As Table 8 suggests, the prefecture as a whole escaped relatively lightly compared to Iwate, Yamagata, Aomori, and its northern neighbor Miyagi. Fukushima's average, however, masks important regional differences within the prefecture. The areas nearest the Pacific and those in the central part of the prefecture were not especially hard hit; they reported harvests only about a quarter to a third below normal levels. Counties further inland and those at higher elevations suffered more from the cold and rain; the Minami Aizu and Yama districts did very poorly. The rice harvest in Minami Aizu was only about a quarter its normal size, and that in Yama county was less than half as large as it had been, on average, over the previous five years. Losses in these districts were at least as severe as those in the hardest-hit northeastern prefectures.[23] Local teachers in at least one Aizu community asked farmers to stop feeding their livestock at times when students were likely to pass by on their way to and from the school. Having to watch the animals eat while they themselves went hungry was more than the children could bear.[24]

Table 8
Rice Farming in a Famine Year in the Six Tōhoku Prefectures, 1934

| Prefecture | 1929–1933 Average rice production (koku) (A) | 1934 Rice production (koku) (B) | 1929–1933 Average rice value (yen) (C) | 1934 Rice value (yen) (D) | B/A (%) | D/C (%) |
|---|---|---|---|---|---|---|
| Aomori | 1,116,356 | 598,413 | ¥19,087,315 | ¥14,691,665 | 54% | 77% |
| Iwate | 1,131,908 | 514,856 | 21,564,004 | 13,614,017 | 45 | 63 |
| Miyagi | 1,851,297 | 1,142,922 | 35,920,098 | 28,703,372 | 62 | 80 |
| Akita | 2,045,671 | 1,522,832 | 40,257,945 | 39,329,106 | 74 | 98 |
| Yamagata | 2,088,355 | 1,129,240 | 41,126,658 | 29,588,645 | 54 | 72 |
| Fukushima | 1,894,285 | 1,261,386 | 35,307,033 | 30,601,360 | 67 | 87 |
| Tōhoku total | 10,127,872 | 6,169,649 | 193,263,052 | 156,528,165 | 61 | 81 |
| National total | 62,673,541 | 51,840,182 | ¥1,359,906,890 | ¥1,384,621,928 | 83% | 102% |

SOURCES: See Nōrin daijin kanbō tōkeika, *Nōji tōkeihyō*, vols. 6–8 (1930–1932), pp. 18–19; vols. 9–11 (1933–1935), pp. 12–13.

The extent of the damage to Sekishiba's rice crop can be inferred in part from Tables 2 (p. 55) and 3 (p. 59). The 1934 rice harvest was only two-fifths as large as the one the year before, or about 44 percent of the average size of the previous four harvests. (The yield on a per-hectare basis fell just as far.) Because rice prices had gone up slightly, the drop in yen value was not quite as sharp; the rice crop in 1934 was worth roughly two-thirds as much as those in the previous four years, or about half as much as the one in 1933 (bearing in mind that the previous four years had not been good ones for farmers, either). On a per-household basis, the value of farm production fell by almost half between 1933 and 1934 and was only two-thirds as much as it had been, on average, between 1930 and 1933. Much of the drop in income can be attributed to the size of the rice harvest, but most other crops were similarly affected by the weather. Farmers took in considerably less barley and soybeans and far fewer persimmons than normal; the persimmon crop was down almost 60 percent from 1933 levels.[25] The exception to these sharp drops in yields may be cocoon production, which, as Table 1 (p. 54) suggests, was lower than normal but not tremendously so. Unfortunately for sericulturalists, however, 1934 prices for cocoons were less than half what they had been the year before (and were in fact the lowest they had been in several decades).

Variations in land quality, skill, and luck meant that some farmers would cope with the famine better than others. Mayor Satō and his neighbors in Komatsu hamlet were among the hardest hit by the inclement weather, so he was no doubt a willing spokesman for the village's plight. In a normal year the mayor could expect to harvest just under 33 *koku* of rice; together with the family's other crops, a year of labor on the farm brought in a harvest worth close to 778 yen. In 1934, however, they managed to bring in only 2 *koku* of rice. The combined value of everything they raised on the farm that year came to only 76 yen, less than a tenth the amount generated in a normal growing season.

Others in the hamlet and elsewhere in the village were in a similar situation. Of the roughly 400 farming households in the community, 357 reported that their 1934 rice harvest was at least 50 percent smaller than that of a normal year (meaning the average of the previous five harvests). The same December 1934 survey that provided that information also established that 303 of those families ended the season with somewhere between half and a

Table 9
Rice Crop Losses and Farmland in Sekishiba, 1934

| Cultivated land (chō) | Surveyed households | Losses of between 50 and 75% | Losses of between 75 and 99% | Losses of 100% |
| --- | --- | --- | --- | --- |
| Greater than 3 | 15 | 11 | 4 | 0 |
| Between 2 and 3 | 62 | 60 | 1 | 0 |
| Between 1 and 2 | 127 | 120 | 6 | 0 |
| Between 0.5 and 1 | 88 | 64 | 20 | 4 |
| Less than 0.5 | 81 | 49 | 9 | 9 |
| TOTAL | 373 | 304 | 40 | 13 |

NOTES: Two households (one in the 2–3 chō category, one in the 1–2 chō category) reported reductions in their rice crops that were not consistent with their reported income from the crop; both were omitted. Fourteen households in the "less than 0.5 chō" category were not rice producers, although they did raise small amounts of other crops. Their absence accounts for the gap between the 81 surveyed households and the 67 reporting a reduced rice harvest in that category.

SOURCE: Based on "Beisaku sono hoka ni yoru genshū sha chū," which are part of the "Survey of Famine Conditions" ("Kyōsaku jōkyō chōsa") conducted in December 1934. These records may be found in SMY, *Kyōsaku kankei shorui tsuzuri, 1934*, KST.

quarter as much rice as normal. Forty-one households (the mayor's among them) reported yields that were more than 75 percent below regular levels, while the rice crop was a complete loss for more than a dozen families.[26]

As Tables 9 and 10 help illustrate, the weather took its toll on just about every farming family in the village. Crop damage cut across boundaries of landholding and status, so that households with relatively large areas of land under cultivation were no better protected from the cold and rain than those with small plots. Although none of the fifteen farmers with more than 3 chō of paddy land experienced total losses, four of them experienced reductions in the rice crop of more than 75 percent (see Table 9). Households in the 1 to 3 chō range (about half of all farming households), while less likely to suffer very large cuts, did have to cope with what were still significant reductions. Those at the lowest end of the scale in terms of acreage were clearly the most vulnerable to total or near-total crop losses. Among the families raising rice on very small plots, close to one in four either lost the crop completely or had to make do with yields that were less than a quarter their normal size. Common sense suggests that those farmers with more land had a larger potential rice crop from which to salvage the final harvest, which may explain why no one with 1 chō or more of land ended up empty-handed.[27]

At the same time that households with different patterns of landholding and crop production faced more or less the same level of damage to their crops, the implications of that damage for individual families varied widely. It is easy to see why this was so. For families with access to mid- and large-sized plots of land, who could normally rely on relatively large harvests, damage to those crops meant less rice to eat and less rice to sell but only a small risk of actually running out of the staple. Even with a sharply reduced crop, an average household working more than 3 chō of land ended the 1934 season with almost as much rice as a household in the 1 to 2 chō category could expect to harvest in a normal year (see Table 10). In the meantime, an average family in the latter category harvested just over 15 koku of rice in 1934—about 5 koku less than a typical household with half as much land produced in the years leading up to the 1934 harvest.

Since there are no indications that family size increased greatly with one's landholdings, it is reasonable to think that most households in the village could at least make do with a harvest as large as the ones normally enjoyed by farms with medium-sized landholdings. Even relatively better-off families would face a considerable reduction in the amount of rice they could sell and still expect to have enough left over to eat. Households used to generating considerable income from the sale of rice no doubt had financial problems, given the difficulties involved in cutting back on expenses and paying off fixed costs. Still, the size of their rice harvests, even during a famine year, provided them with a buffer that many in the village did not enjoy.

The 1934 harvest was bound to raise at least two major, immediate problems for local farmers. The first and most obvious was the lack of food. For some families, loss of even a small portion of the harvest could mean the difference between having rice on hand come the following spring and having to buy it then, when prices were highest. Households that rented some or all of their land had to meet their obligations to the landlord, which meant that they couldn't simply hold on to all the rice they produced. Unless rates were renegotiated, just paying the rent could easily take a significant

Table 10
Famine Effects and Farmland in Sekishiba, 1934

| Cultivated land (chō) | Households | Average household tax | Average rice yield, normal year (koku) (A) | Average rice yield, 1934 (koku) (B) | B/A (%) | Value of all farm production, normal year (C) | Value of all farm production, 1934 (D) | D/C (%) |
|---|---|---|---|---|---|---|---|---|
| Greater than 3 | 15 | ¥39.89 | 109.77 | 34.95 | 31.84% | ¥2424.93 | ¥1004.07 | 41.41% |
| Between 2 and 3 | 62 | 14.98 | 66.56 | 24.62 | 36.99 | 1536.32 | 661.90 | 43.08 |
| Between 1 and 2 | 127 | 13.85 | 42.46 | 15.22 | 35.85 | 1007.35 | 420.00 | 41.69 |
| Between 0.5 and 1 | 88 | 6.93 | 19.90 | 5.94 | 29.85 | 483.72 | 172.83 | 35.73 |
| Less than 0.5 | 81 | 3.88 | 6.02 | 1.81 | 30.06 | 160.33 | 56.00 | 34.93 |
| Total | 373 | ¥11.29 | 37.07 | 12.47 | 33.64% | ¥844.81 | ¥346.34 | 41.00% |

SOURCES: Based on records of *kosūwari* (Special Household Tax) assessments that appear in the *Sonkai giroku, 1934* and a series of survey records contained in SMY, *Kyōsaku kankei shorui tsuzuri, 1934*, KST.

portion of a tenant's or owner-tenant's crop. The implications of this are discussed in more detail below.

The second problem, and one closely related to the first, was that of income. Since so much of the value of an average farm's production came from rice, halving the size of the rice crop was almost the same thing as halving the household's income for a year. (Price fluctuations and income from other sources kept the two from being exactly equal.) Bear in mind as well that most of the costs associated with raising a rice crop were unlikely to change much just because the weather took a turn for the worse. Farmers paid for (or borrowed on the expectation of paying for) enough seed to raise a full crop and likely used just as much fertilizer and labor as they would have in a normal year. Households that lost a good portion of what they had planted quite early may have saved on labor and on some other costs by abandoning work on those crops, but there is no indication that farmers were willing or able to do so in most cases.

In a process repeated in villages throughout the northeast, Sekishiba's officials tried to measure the famine's human cost as best they could. Quantifying the damage was important because the prefectural government required clear answers to its questions before it would provide any assistance. At their most straightforward, famine surveys asked the village to predict how many families would run out of food between late 1934 and summer 1935, and of those, how many would be completely unable to make up for the shortfall through other means. Eligibility for inclusion in the survey, and thus for state assistance, confirmed that all other avenues of help had been exhausted. Hence families who were already receiving some other form of state aid, such as those covered by the provisions of the Relief Law, were kept out of the survey. The state's stringent definitions of need almost certainly excluded some households that a more reasonable set of standards would have included.[28]

Even with these limitations, Sekishiba reported that almost a fifth of the village's households and roughly the same share of its population (77 families and 539 individuals) would fall into the category of the "truly needy" by the end of December 1934. Those figures were expected to increase from one month to the next. By the end of March, 123 families and 846 residents would be without rice; by the end of May, two-fifths of the local population was expected to have run out of rice to eat and to be unable to buy, beg, or borrow what they needed to make it through the month. Providing those families with a minimum amount of rice would mean making more than 550 *koku* (or just under 100,000 liters) of rice available to them.[29]

Surveys like the one in Sekishiba provided one set of insights into the impact of the famine; others came from local governments, farmers' organizations (the Imperial Agriculture Association published extensive and detailed accounts of the famine's causes and effects),[30] and the press. The situation in the northeast received ample and often dramatic coverage in national newspapers and journals. Crop and weather conditions were carefully tracked, the articles filled with data on the latest estimates of lost income, food shortfalls, and hungry children. It was the human interest stories that seemed to capture the crisis most vividly for the reading public, however. The nation's newspapers began printing articles describing the plight of the northeast's farmers by early October, and they quickly made the famine of 1934 a topic of widespread concern. The *Tōkyō asahi shinbun* was especially good at this type of coverage, running a series of articles about the famine's effects that began in October and ran well into the next year.

Although later columns were limited to photographs and a list of donations from the public, early pieces were full-length and often poignant essays about the extent of the poverty that reporters found in the Tōhoku villages they visited. Graphic descriptions of hungry children, of daughters being sold into prostitution for piddling sums of money, of suicides, and of families forced to eat roots and other primitive foodstuffs were common elements in these articles. One report reprinted part of a letter by an elementary schoolteacher in Iwate prefecture, in which she wrote that she had assigned her students an essay in which they were to talk about the things that concerned them most. "Most of [the essays] were about nothing but their worries over food," she explained. "I cried so hard that I couldn't finish reading them."[31] Press reports and statements by local officials commonly referred to children as being at risk of outright starvation or at least serious malnutrition. One Bank of Japan survey suggested that as many as 4 percent (or more than 10,000) of the children in Fukushima were not getting enough food, and that in Yamagata the figure might be as high as 7 percent. Another estimate had the figure for all six Tōhoku prefectures at close to a million children.[32]

Anecdotal evidence supported the conclusion that this was more than just a bad year. In the first of its series of articles on conditions in the northeast, the *Tōkyō asahi* reported an exchange between a member of the Diet come to express his sympathies and the mayor of the northeastern village he was visiting. To the legislator's remark that he had come to "inquire about the damage from the cold," the mayor mockingly replied, "Cold damage! What we have here isn't anything as mild as damage from the cold. What we have here is a famine!"[33] When the governor of Fukushima visited Kitakata in November 1934, as part of a similar inspection tour of the communities hardest hit by the weather, reporters described with particular candor his encounter with the hundred or so local leaders who had gathered to meet him. One mayor broke down in tears as he struggled to describe the conditions in his village, while others wept silently alongside him; many had brought with them samples of the barely edible foodstuffs that had replaced a normal diet in nearby farmhouses.[34]

Photos of villages in the northeast that fall and winter almost invariably depicted either the very young or very old preparing to eat something so far beyond the pale that readers had to have it described to them in detail.[35] Others documented local efforts to prevent the sale of young women to ubiquitous recruiters and reported with considerable sympathy the plight of those families who felt they had no choice but to send a daughter into prostitution. Official and unofficial descriptions of the northeastern countryside were uniformly bleak.[36]

## Surviving the Famine

That the 1934 famine was a watershed event for many communities and for the nation ultimately has little to do with how it compared to past disasters.[37] By all accounts, conditions in the northeast in 1934 were desperate but never came close to approximating the human toll associated with earlier, infamous episodes of crop failure. The Kyōhō famine of 1732–1733, the Tenmei famine of 1783–1784, and the Tenpō famine of the 1830s together killed tens of thousands, laying waste to farming communities and depopulating entire regions.[38] The social dislocation in their wake took years to repair. More recently, on several occasions since the turn of the century, bad weather had sent rice yields even lower than those experienced in 1934—once in 1913, and repeatedly before that, in 1902 and 1905.[39] Both historical memory and the remembered experiences of older farmers offered assurances that what was happening in 1934 was neither unprecedented nor as bad as it might have been. Whether that knowledge was comforting to farmers about to enjoy their first meal of bark and bulbs is not known, but it strikes me as unlikely.

What is clear is that the famine did play an important though sometimes indirect role in reshaping depression-era rural society. At the most general level, the famine refocused the public's attention on rural poverty and backwardness, and generated a widespread campaign of public and private donations and charity for northeastern farmers. This was Japan's first modern famine; media coverage, photographs, and travel brought the farmers' plight to newsstands and homes across the country and made local tragedies national news.

Coming as it did as the urban, industrial economy had begun to rebound from the depression, the famine was in many ways a reminder of just how wide the gap had become between the modern, developed sector and the countryside. The Economic Revitalization Campaign was supposed to bridge that chasm, and though it was clearly powerless in the short term against the forces of nature, one consequence of the crop failure of 1934 was to reinforce the campaign's message of rational planning, community solidarity, and social reform for the countryside.[40] Famine relief was quickly linked to ongoing efforts to recover from the depression, even as the campaign itself took on a new shape and new goals in the famine's wake.

Only two years after the petition movements of 1932 and the Village Rescue Diet session, a new round of appeals and petitions made its way from the northeast to Tokyo from late 1934 on.[41] These appeals led first to funding for short-term emergency public-works projects and to a series of transfers of government-surplus rice to needy families. Both were welcomed by Sekishiba's farmers, who, as the village's surveys had demonstrated, were in desperate need of both cash and food. Though the budget for most public works projects had been cut in the aftermath of the 1934 budget talks, emergency funding (the Diet met again in special session in early 1935 to vote for aid for the northeast) kept some money flowing into the hardest-hit villages, Sekishiba among them.

Low-interest loans were another tool in the fight against starvation, as was the transfer of rice to hard-hit communities. The authorities also provided local farmers with seeds, tax exemptions, and reductions in some shipping fees (all approaches to handling famine with long antecedents in the Japanese countryside). Sekishiba didn't get nearly as much rice as administrators had hoped for, but the village did conduct two sales of government grain, the first in June 1935 and the other in September, to more than 700 individuals in 118 families.[42] Villages throughout the northeast received similar benefits of rice and public works funding; the combination of the two, and the relatively speedy response of the government to local need, seems to have kept most families from running out of food altogether.

Donations from private sources were also important, and an indication of a substantive public awareness of the countryside's difficulties. The Mitsui, Mitsubishi, and Sumitomo corporations gave a total of 551,000 yen for use in Fukushima prefecture, specifically to improve the physical and moral well-being of villages through the development of cooperative work facilities.[43] Food supplies and monetary contributions poured in via collection efforts organized by the *Tōkyō asahi shinbun*, the *Tōkyō nichi nichi shinbun*, and others. Even the imperial family joined in, making a very public contribution of 50,000 yen toward the building of community storehouses; that funding was combined with state assistance in an attempt to reduce the cost of construction for individual communities.

Sekishiba was one of the villages to benefit from the imperial gift and completed its first storehouses in 1935.[44] Under the provisions of the relief funding it had received from the prefecture, the village also agreed to make every effort to keep those storehouses full of grain in the future or face having to repay the cost of the rice it had been given. Such programs sought to protect the community from future food shortages, but there was more to it than that. The expansion of storage facilities, the road work, and the construction of cooperative work areas very quickly became part of the Economic Revitalization Campaign's efforts in Sekishiba, in tandem with an expansion of the campaign itself. In the aftermath of the famine, the campaign's boundaries were renegotiated to encompass a broader role for the state and to rule out alternatives to revitalization's definition of the ideal village.

During the campaign's first few years, little had been done to modify the campaign itself. What changes there were focused on relatively minor organizational issues and improvements that could be accomplished at little expense. Ongoing budget conflicts between advocates of increased spending on the countryside (Gotō and others) and their opponents (Takahashi especially) had usually been resolved in favor of the latter camp. As a result, designated villages received plenty of advice about how to proceed with their plans but very little material assistance. Innovations and improvements that had been out of reach before the campaign were for the most part still out of reach.[45]

Plans to expand the scope of revitalization aid began to take shape in the aftermath of the famine. By then the basic administrative structure was working more or less as bureaucrats had hoped it would, and the campaign had proved to be quite popular; there was no lack of communities anxious to participate. "However," Kodaira would later write, "among the communities [that had been designated, had established plans, and had tried to put them into effect], even though the people are enthusiastic, there have been instances in which the plans could not be implemented because of poverty. That is, there are not a few communities in which it is feared that the plans will end in failure due to lack of funds."[46]

The Special Assistance (Tokubetsu josei) program was the Economic Revitalization Section's solution to the situation described by Kodaira. Bureaucrats grafted this addendum to the existing recovery campaign as a way of getting money to the more promising and more needy of the already designated Economic Revitalization villages. Through a combination of low-interest loans, cash from the communities themselves, and outright grants from the government, planners expected to be able to help some villages fully implement plans stalled by a lack of funds. Although much of what economic revitalization advocated at the local level consisted of inexpensive reforms, there were some projects that were both important to the community's recovery and well beyond its reach. Road and irrigation works, production facilities, and the purchase of farm animals were expensive but necessary counterparts to the organizational, "spiritual," and other less costly aspects of recovery planning. The famine had highlighted the continued vulnerability of the countryside, and it was clear that neither the campaign as it was originally conceived nor any other state program could provide the assistance that many communities required.

There was also an element of preventive medicine involved in the Special Assistance program. The longer villages were allowed to languish with plans in hand but no way to implement them, the harder it would be for economic revitalization as a whole to achieve concrete results. The program would clearly suffer if it was believed that the government had reneged on its commitment to rural recovery. Certain members of the Diet could be expected to voice their displeasure as well. Commentary on the recovery program during the Sixty-third Diet had often been skeptical of how economic revitalization could accomplish so much with so little. It is also worth noting that after several years, the campaign had done little to stem a rising tide of rural unrest. In one of the largest year-to-year increases ever, the number of tenancy disputes jumped from 4,000 in 1933 to 5,828 the following year, and then to 6,824 in 1935. The latter record number of tenant-landlord conflicts was never surpassed.

However, as the results of the 1934 budget conferences had made very clear, Takahashi and the Finance Ministry were loath to spend additional money on the countryside. It was also true that if any money could be had, it would be hotly contested within the Ministry of Agriculture and Forestry. Road work, irrigation-related projects, land development, and other infrastructure-related projects were normally within the jurisdiction of other departments within the ministry. By seeking to make the funding, and thus the control over these projects, flow not from those departments but from the Economic Revitalization Section, Kodaira and the other planners of the Special Assistance program faced a major jurisdictional as well as a fiscal challenge.[47]

The battle for funding for the Special Assistance program began in the summer of 1935. The first step for bureaucrats in the Economic Revitalization Section involved compiling and printing the funding requests for each of the one thousand villages initially picked for special designation. Working well into the night for several days in a row, Kodaira's assistant produced a collection of plans so large that a single set stood as tall as a man.[48] Next, rather than use these materials to make a case for support within the ministry, which would have involved negotiations with other departments, Kodaira took the unusual step of presenting the plans directly to Agriculture and Forestry Minister Yamazaki, thus bypassing risky interdepartmental discussions. Yamazaki agreed to back the special funding proposal in meetings with the finance minister.[49]

What followed was a vigorous effort to win Takahashi's support. In a move that showed Kodaira's bureaucratic skills at their best, he had copies of Maeda Masana's *Kōgyō iken* printed up and distributed within the office, making sure that Takahashi also received a copy. By making it clear that the economic revitalization bureaucrats valued the lessons of Maeda's work (careful attention to detail, consideration of local conditions, and a desire to spend money wisely), Kodaira drew on a tradition he knew Takahashi shared. As a young bureaucrat, Takahashi had worked under Maeda and was involved from early on in the production of the *Kōgyō iken*.⁵⁰ The gift of a new copy of the book was thus a subtler strategy than it might appear to be at first glance because it allowed Kodaira to build a bridge between Takahashi's past and the Economic Revitalization Campaign. The finance minister was reportedly quite pleased with the present.⁵¹

When Yamazaki and Takahashi actually met to decide the fate of the special funding, Takahashi reportedly didn't even look at the huge report compiled by the Economic Revitalization Section. When Yamazaki had finished his explanations, the finance minister is said to have asked, "What exactly is it supposed to assist?" Yamazaki replied, "It will assist the mainstays of the village"—a reference to those local farmers who shared a commitment to revitalization and a willingness to lead. Takahashi approved of this human touch. He told Yamazaki, "If it had been 'things' you were going to spend money on, I was going to refuse, but it's interesting that it's people you are helping."⁵² The only condition he put on approval was that he wanted to see a list of the thousand village "mainstays," a request that forced Kodaira's assistant to rush out and send telegrams to each of the villages asking each one to send the names and personal histories of its candidate. The lists were compiled as information came in, with special care to keep errors to a minimum. "If even one item in the name or personal history of someone Takahashi knew was wrong," an official remembered, "then no matter how big a list we made, we would have failed."⁵³ That the finance minister eventually gave his backing to the program tells us that they did not.

By late autumn 1935, the Special Assistance program had been more clearly defined by Economic Revitalization Section planners.⁵⁴ One concern was making sure that the right communities were selected. While preference would be given to the regions in greatest need, neediness alone wasn't enough. Villages lacking the right attitude toward self-revitalization, or toward cooperation with one another, would never get funding "no matter how impoverished they were."⁵⁵

Similarly, communities had to pursue projects that promised to spread benefits more or less equally among their inhabitants. Every attempt would be made to ensure that the benefits that accrued from special funding went to the people who needed it most, not to "a few landlords" or to "households that have rice to sell."⁵⁶ In the end, the section settled on four conditions that villages had to meet to be eligible for selection:

1. The village must have had an Economic Revitalization Plan in place for at least one year.
2. Villagers must be in harmony, various organizations must be in place, and every effort must be made to implement the plan.
3. It must be impossible, due to poverty, for the community to implement important parts of the plan using its own resources alone.
4. There must be *chūshin jinbutsu* (mainstays) within the community.[57]

If it worked as planners hoped, the Special Assistance program would permit villages that had proved themselves willing to pursue economic revitalization to do so. The four conditions restated some of the campaign's original tenets, but in the context of the post-famine Special Designation program, they took on new significance. Two issues in particular stand out. One is the importance attributed to mainstays—that is, to the presence of local producers who were willing and able to lead. This focus on individuals reflected a growing interest on the part of the ministry and some farmers' organizations in identifying and training qualified producers to guide their communities.

Second, the campaign had not in the past differentiated much between prosperous and less well-off communities, whereas special designation did so. In 1937 the selection process was altered again, to give precedence to communities in impoverished regions, which further shifted the balance in favor of the less well-to-do. However, planners also made it clear that special funding was not just another form of public relief project. Kodaira, writing in mid-1936, expressed the view that what his ministry had in mind was not just another attempt to put cash into the hands of strapped farmers. The special funding program "completely rejects the thought behind the so-called unemployment relief projects to employ people and to supply wages." Villagers were expected to work on the projects out of a spirit of service, for their own recovery, and for the rebuilding of their community. The program "will not cause a feeling of dependence to arise but rather will instill more and more the desire for revitalization, and I am certain that it will lead to the rapid implementation and completion of the plans."[58]

The focus remained on the revitalization plans and what they had been supposed to accomplish: debt arrangement, a balance between income and expenditure, and the stabilization of life in the community. At the same time, special designation implied a limited admission that, even if willing, not all communities were able to take the steps necessary to revitalize themselves. More help was needed, and extra funding was the answer. In expanding the campaign in this way, the Ministry of Agriculture dangled a carrot in front of villages willing to remain committed to the ideals and practices of revitalization. Special designation upped the ante at a time when interest might otherwise have flagged.

The original plan was for a total of 7,700 communities to be designated for special assistance over a five-year period, with each community receiving an average of 15,000 yen in grants and an additional 20,000 yen (on average) in low-interest funds.[59] The Ministry of Agriculture and Forestry revised these figures downward to 1,000 villages and only 10,000 yen in grants and 10,000 yen in low-interest funds, but the Finance Ministry further reduced the program to only 500 villages a year, with an average funding level of 10,000 yen per village in grants. In practice, the number of communities actually selected each year fell well below 500. During its best year, the ministry selected only 407; by 1941, the figure had fallen to only 69. After six years in operation, a total of 1,595 communities had been chosen to receive special assistance—far fewer than originally hoped.[60] Kodaira has estimated that the grants ranged from a minimum of 8,000 yen to a maximum of 30,000 per community. This range is not unreasonable; the total grant budget would have allowed an average of 14,000 yen in grants to each of the 350 designated villages in 1936. Recipients in coming years could expect less than that, though more than the ministry's original "10,000 yen per village" estimate.[61]

That the Special Designation program didn't meet its institutional goals shouldn't blind us to its importance to those communities that were chosen. Between 1936 and 1941, a total of thirty-six towns and villages in Fukushima were selected as "specially designated" communities. Of the thirty-six, only four were in Yama county, three of which were Kitakata's neighbors: Keitoku, to the southwest (1938); Kamisanmiya, to the northwest (1938); and Sekishiba, which was selected as a specially designated community in 1937.[62] With so few villages chosen, Sekishiba's designation was treated by the village and the local press as an important event.[63] Special designation was in many ways a recognition of the hard work that the village had done since the famine, and a sign that its goals were ones that the state and the nation valued. Sekishiba's goals as they took shape in 1934 and 1935 are discussed below; how they expanded to accommodate changes in the campaign (special designation among them) is explored in Chapters 8 and 10.

## A Village Plans

In the spring of 1935, Sekishiba's Economic Revitalization Committee laid out the village's future in forty-five handwritten pages. The village's revitalization plan drew on the proposals drawn up by individual households and hamlets and supplemented them with descriptions of reforms that could only be pursued community-wide. The components of the resulting plan are evident in its table of contents:

1. Boosting production
2. Reducing the money spent on cash fertilizer
3. Plans related to lumber
4. Reform of farm management
5. Expansion and improvement of cultivated land
6. Sales and purchasing
7. Financial matters
8. Development of the industrial cooperative
9. Debt arrangement methods
10. Reform of daily life
11. Improvement of hygiene facilities
12. Improvement of social facilities
13. Improvement of educational facilities
14. Matters connected with the moral suasion of village residents

The village had little control over the scope of the plan. The subjects discussed in Sekishiba's plan were similar if not identical to the ones discussed by the forty or so other communities that drafted plans in Fukushima in 1934.[64] The categories for planning had already been established by the authorities, so local planners had only to decide what they wanted to do about financial reform or the rice crop, not whether those topics ought to be involved in planning at all. This arrangement left communities with plenty of leeway to omit minor areas while ensuring that they would deal with the bigger issues. There was no way to avoid making plans for improvements in farm management, in spending on fertilizer, and in household finances. Those topics, and ones like them, were areas in which it was commonly understood that reforms were necessary and that economic revitalization planning was the way to bring them about. The sections that follow summarize the key elements of Sekishiba's proposals.

## PRODUCING

Not surprisingly, many of the trends that were evident in Komatsu's planning efforts are reflected in Sekishiba's. As in the hamlet, the village's farmers as a whole proposed to raise more and better crops, and to do so without expanding the amount of land under cultivation. Of the seven major cash crops covered by the plan, only wheat would be grown on more land at the end of the plan than at the beginning of it.[65]

The importance of the status quo in land use is apparent when one considers that the village hoped to boost its rice and barley yields by close to 20 percent over the five years of the plan, potatoes by 37 percent, the wheat crop by 60 percent, soybeans by more than 70 percent, and persimmons by more than 75 percent, all while almost doubling the vegetable crop. It would be one thing for farmers to raise more of a product simply by growing more of it on more land; one could double the size of the crop by doubling the size of the field, planting the new land as densely as the old. Farmers in Sekishiba could hardly do that, which meant that they were proposing to do more with the same fields. In other words, instead of producing 2.7 *koku* of rice per tenth of a hectare, which was the village average in 1933, they planned to get 3.3 *koku* out of the same area by the time the first plan was complete. Much the same would have to happen for the other crops as well, the exceptions being wheat (the area devoted to wheat would be expanded, though the yield per hectare was also expected to rise) and persimmons. Getting more persimmons involved planting more trees, probably on land that would not normally be used for crops.[66]

The plan didn't stop at providing a list of targets but went on to provide a brief list of the ways farmers could accomplish their goals. In addition to using better strains of seed or seedlings, the plan called for guidance from the local agricultural association and farming associations on better farming methods, the use of cooperative seed beds, and the development of practices like "the rational application of fertilizer." The village's farming organizations, stated the plan, would hold lectures on new and improved techniques for farming; through the agricultural association's technician, they would also see to it that these reforms were implemented.

Other sources of improvements in crop yields were actually covered later in the recovery plan, under "Improvements in Farm Management," but are relevant here. Adding more land to the amount already double-cropped would help the community grow more barley and tea. Households would also be urged to plant new trees (one cherry, two persimmons, and two grapevines per household was the suggested ideal) around their homes. Farmers, said the plan, could grow vegetables alongside mulberry bushes and thus make better use of that land as well. Finally, the village had plans to undertake irrigation and drainage construction that would affect some farmland and presumably improve it in the process.[67]

Similar proposals were put forth for the other major areas of production in the village: livestock, sericulture, side-projects, and forestry. The agricultural association, industrial cooperative, and farm practice associations, for instance, were to help the village increase the number of chickens it raised from 2,300 in 1933 to an estimated 12,000 five years later. They also hoped to add 200 goats (there were none in the village in 1933), more than 3,000 rabbits, and a few dozen pigs to the local population by helping households who already had some raise more and by helping other families get a start in the livestock business.[68] Planners also advocated cooperative purchases of feed for the animals and of the animals themselves when necessary, and the cooperative sale of the end product. This would be the job of the industrial cooperative.

Families would expand their efforts in other potentially lucrative fields as well. Under "Side-Projects," the Economic Revitalization Committee outlined plans for substantial increases in the production of straw bags, rope, bamboo handicrafts, tofu, and homespun cloth, to name but a few items. In 1933, total income from this sort of production had been less than 3,000 yen for the entire village, but under revitalization, revenues were expected to grow to more than 14,000 yen, roughly a third of which would come from the sale of straw bags. Planners expected to make that much by adding fifty households to the two hundred that already made the items and boosting total production from about fourteen thousand bags a year to fifty thousand. As with livestock, individual initiative in side-projects would be supplemented with lectures, support from the agricultural and farming associations, and cooperative sales and purchases where appropriate. Interested parties would thus have access to the information they needed to succeed, relatively inexpensive materials, and a means of selling what they produced.[69]

Sericulture was the only facet of local production that the Economic Revitalization Plan did not expect would increase. When planners considered what would happen over the course of the next five years, they concluded that the village as a whole would raise slightly fewer cocoons, take in less money as a result, and reduce the amount of land used to raise mulberry. However, these changes are less drastic than they appear at first glance. The 13 *chō* reduction in mulberry acreage would take place alongside improvements in the remaining land and crops that would more than make up for lost space. In fact, farmers were expected to produce more mulberry, not less, as a result of the changes. Land that had been used to grow mulberry could be used for other crops; the increase in wheat fields would likely come from this acreage, for instance. Meanwhile, farmers planned to shift some of their silkworm production out of the spring season and into the summer and fall. The net result would yield a slight (2 to 3 percent) decline in income from sericulture, which was probably not regarded as significant. As with other crops, the changes in silkworm production were to be accompanied by full technical support from the local farming organizations and by cooperative buying and selling wherever possible.

## CUTTING COSTS, INCREASING MARGINS

There was more to cutting costs than simply spending less. While the Economic Revitalization program urged farmers to cut back on luxuries and wasteful spending in general, it also called on households to produce more of what they consumed. This might mean making clothes instead of buying them or growing more of the food that the family ate. Local plans to raise fish, for instance, stemmed at least in part from this principle of self-supply. Fertilizer was the single most important item when it came to substituting the homemade for the store-bought, however, as was evident in Komatsu's case.

Sekishiba's revitalization plan called on the village to reduce its consumption of "cash fertilizer" by 40 percent over five years. In 1933, local farmers used an average of 25 *kan* of store-bought fertilizer per tenth of a hectare of farmland, but would have to cut back to only 15 *kan* under the plan. To help make up for the lost nutrients in the soil, farmers planned to increase their production of compost and to match the 40 percent reduction in cash fertilizer use by spreading that much more of the homemade alternative on their fields. They would also start growing more of what might be called "green manure crops"—plants that could be used to supplement standard fertilizers. All this would take place under the watchful eye of the local agricultural association, the industrial cooperative, and the farm practice associations. Together these organizations would encourage farmers to buy their cash fertilizer through the industrial cooperative, which would at least help cut costs, and to attend lectures on compost production, rational fertilizer use, and other relevant topics. The village would also sponsor a series of competitions to see who could make the most compost and raise the largest crop of green fertilizer.[70] Given that the farmers were already committed to growing more crops on the same amount of land, it was essential that that land be as fertile as possible. Achieving that goal—alongside the ones calling for farmers to use less of the product that had brought them to their current level of productivity—was clearly going to be tricky.

## SAVINGS AND DEBT

The Basic Survey had helped the community learn where its money was, or at least where it had gone. Sekishiba found out, for instance, how indebted it was and to whom. Residents learned how much was being saved and where it had been deposited. The role of the Economic Revitalization Campaign in all this was to suggest how best to deal with existing debt, what to do about borrowing in the future, and where people should deposit their money to bring the most good to the community.

At the center of Sekishiba's plans for a stronger financial future was a bigger role for the industrial cooperative as a source of credit and as the destination for deposits. The cooperative was ideal as a low-interest lender, both because it could tap into government sources of funding that targeted rural projects and because it was far more likely than other sources of funding to offer loans to individual farmers. The cooperative was also preferred to local banks and other institutions as the place for residents to save their money. Deposits with the cooperative made their way back to the community in ways that money in the bank never would; thus the revitalization plan proposed several strategies (savings campaigns and the like) to get people to put more of their hard-earned cash into the industrial cooperative.

Debt remained a sticky issue in 1935. The village had estimated in 1933 that residents were 800,000 yen in debt; the plan outlined steps to start paying back a fraction of that via the industrial cooperative but stopped short of advocating anything more concrete.[71] Sekishiba had been very slow to embrace debt arrangement, although it had been available as a potential tool for several years. There were no debt arrangement unions in the village, nor did the plan call for their creation in the near future. In this area the Economic Revitalization Committee chose not to make any bold moves.

## COOPERATIVE ENTERPRISE

"It is regrettable," noted the authors of the recovery plan, "that the present condition of the Industrial Cooperative in the village is that in both organization and activity there are a number of flaws and that in general there are few areas in which it has improved the economy of village residents." So began the section that pledged the village to expand and reform the industrial cooperative. Sekishiba's cooperative had been plagued with participation rates considerably lower than planners had hoped for. In 1933, about 299 people were fully qualified members—only about three-quarters of all those eligible. Members tended to be from the "moneyed" class in the community and to live in either Hirabayashi, Sekishiba, or Shimoshiba. People outside those parts of the village, and especially the less well-off residents of the other areas, were less likely to participate. Planners promised to increase membership by pursuing more aggressive activities in the rest of the community. At the end of five years, the cooperative expected to have enrolled every member of the other farming cooperatives in Sekishiba. Since every farming household was supposed to be a member of its hamlet's farming association, bringing these smaller unions into the industrial cooperative would ensure village-wide participation. At the end of the period there would be at least one member from each of the village's 396 farm households in the cooperative.

The cooperative's role in the community was expected to expand with its membership. It would continue to serve as a local financial institution, providing more loans and expanding deposits, but it would also take on a larger role as an intermediary between local families and outside markets. In 1933, only 2,160 *koku* of the 10,000 *koku* of rice sold by Sekishiba farmers was sold through the cooperative, but under the Economic Revitalization Plan, a total of 9,000 *koku* was to be sold by the end of five years. Similar progress was outlined for other major crops. When it came to purchases, the union hoped to convince farmers to use it to buy most of their fertilizer and animal feed, as well as at least some of their rubber shoes, sake, and tea.

There were also plans under way to establish cooperative production facilities in four different parts of the village. Under the plan, four rope-making machines and four rice-hulling machines would be bought and made available for use by the community. These concrete signs of a bigger and better union would be supplemented by the union's pledge to take on a new role as a coordinator among the agricultural association, the youth groups, and the other "powerful organizations" within the village—all as part of the drive to bring revitalization to the community. Through lectures at the village and hamlet levels, the distribution to every household of published information (including *Ie no hikari*, the national magazine of the Industrial Cooperative), and the establishment of a model Sales Union in the elementary school, the cooperative planned to have a higher profile in the village's educational life as well.

## REFORMS IN DAILY LIFE

With farming, finance, and the reorganization of the local economy out of the way, the final few sections of Sekishiba's Economic Revitalization Plan were free to focus on other aspects of village life. In many ways these parts of the plan are different in tone and purpose from the sections that precede them. There is certainly less emphasis on economic reform and more on trying to change some of the most basic elements of daily life in the community. Problems are framed differently as well, in that it was much harder to describe where the village stood on "the thought problem" or "public spiritedness" than it was to report on industrial cooperative membership or how much rice farmers grew.

Much the same was true when it came to suggesting solutions: The way to make the industrial cooperative stronger was to add more members and expand its activities, and at the end of five years it would be easy enough to look back and measure the village's progress. But how did one go about improving the "public spirit" of Sekishiba's farmers, and how could people be expected to know when or if it had improved?

Local planners must have felt that they had the answers to these questions, because Sekishiba's plans for improvements in everyday life listed a half-dozen areas where progress was needed and thought possible. Punctuality was singled out for attention; "Although the meetings of the heads of the wards and of the Village Council are always prompt," explained the comments accompanying the plan, "in general that is not the case."[72] Village leaders hoped to promote more clock-watching among residents. Wasteful spending in the home was also identified as a problem, and as an extravagance attributed to "old customs." The remedy for this particular sin was to use lectures, the distribution of printed material, and meetings within the hamlet to encourage households to become more self-sufficient in a number of items of daily use. Plans were drawn up to help people make more of their own pickles, soy sauce, and other supplies. The more farmers could produce at home, the less they would have to spend at the local store. Frugality was a skill to be taught and treasured like any other.

In keeping with the concerns central to the improvement of daily life, Sekishiba also outlined its plans to improve nutrition (through seminars on cooking) and family hygiene (through the improvement of local kitchens and sanitary facilities).[73] The village needed new and better toilets, wells for drinking water (most people still relied on rivers and streams), and a more widespread attempt to deal with intestinal parasites. These projects would involve the hamlet assembly in a variety of public education efforts; village-wide projects to promote a love of rural culture were also high on the committee's agenda. In the end, revitalization held out the promise that the community was limited only by its own imagination in what it might achieve.

## The Best-Laid Plans

This chapter has explored Sekishiba's early efforts to chart a course out of the depression. With the Economic Revitalization Campaign as its guide, and the revitalization plan a map, the village proposed a fundamental reshaping of community and economic life. From the promise of an improved standard of living through spending less and earning more to the prospect of an approach to managing one's farm and money that was in accord with the greater good, the plan had it all. The campaign's appeal—especially in light of the mayor's zeal for reform and the support of businessman and local large landowner Yabe Zenbei (both topics pursued in greater depth in Chapter 9)—is easy to understand. It offered much and seemed to require little that the village didn't already have in abundance: diligence, hard work, frugality, imagination. Alternatives to revitalization were scarce. The campaign provided the only safe destination for communities desperately in search of a way out of their present circumstances. The state offered no other options, at least not yet.

The appeal of a planned and more efficient farm and future was hardly new. Farm manuals such as Ōkura Nagatsune's popular 1822 *Nōgu benriron* (On the Efficacy of Farm Implements) were replete with admonitions to develop one's technical skills, make the best use of one's time and labor, and manage one's resources with care.[74] Long before the 1930s, farmers were conscious of frugality's value, of time's worth, and of the importance of both. The rhetoric of planning went back many years, and at some level the campaign happily recycled a treasure trove of hoary sayings, elusive goals, and false promises.

Yet the 1930s offered a fundamentally different context for the pursuit of planning than any the countryside had seen, and a new approach to its role. Where past efforts at planning had focused, more often than not, on the achievements of a single farmer, revitalization took the village and, ultimately, the nation as its template. By the 1930s, administrative and educational improvements had made it possible to enlist the entire community in a shared endeavor of careful planning, something that Tokugawa-era reformers didn't have the luxury to pursue. Where past planning had been the domain of the well-to-do and the well educated, depression-era campaigns reached out to all farmers, rich and poor, landed and tenant. The campaign not only argued for the possibility of including all members of the community in the reconstruction it proposed, but argued that such inclusion was unavoidable and necessary.

From that belief grew new practices of communal, almost public record-keeping and planning, such as Komatsu witnessed when its residents prepared their revitalization documents. Every household in the community filled out the same forms for the same purpose, categorizing and regularizing the minutest aspects of their lives as farmers, as managers of community assets, and as family members. The implications of this collective documentation are certainly interesting; if the secrets of success were to be found somewhere in the pages of planning documents, in terms of inputs and measurable qualities, then who is to blame for any one farmer's failure? Certainly not outside forces or even the government, as long as the definitions of what it took to prosper remained intact. Planning located responsibility for recovery squarely within the village; individual effort and skill were part of the equation, but so, too, were reforms of village institutions. Both were necessary for revitalization to succeed.

Revitalization planning encompassed more than Tokugawa-era farmers' manuals (or later but similarly inspired efforts) had ever thought to. The scope was broader; no longer limited to planning for a slightly bigger crop, committee members and families in Komatsu embraced a wide range of reforms in which making more money was one of several components. Social transformation on a wide scale was openly endorsed, provided it was in a direction the state sanctioned. And here is another part of the context of the 1930s: although local initiative remained the premise on which self-revitalization rested, the state was never far from the hearts or minds of the reformers. The campaign was a government-sponsored endeavor from start to finish. Even as revitalization contained local enthusiasms within the community, it promised a nationwide commitment to the process. Everyone did his part, each understanding what was expected of him.

If, after a year of famine, residents of the village harbored any doubts about the need to pursue economic revitalization, the mayor did his best to overcome them. His September 1935 message to hamlet chiefs outlining how the recovery plan would be implemented began by thanking those local leaders for their help in drafting it. He continued:

The causes of the present impoverishment of the villages are not just the result of the recent extraordinary recessions in the domestic and foreign economies. It is clear that there is a strong link to the management and organization of the village economy. To ensure that farm households awaken and that the causes of the trouble are swept away, the first step is to undertake the promotion of the old-fashioned, beautiful traditions of mutual assistance in each hamlet. For this to have a full effect in economic life, we are aware that we must pursue innovations in organization, and in planned production and a planned economy.[75]

With the famine behind them, the mayor was ready to pursue the village's revitalization plan in earnest. Chapters 8, 9, and 10 describe those efforts, and their implications for the community.

# 8 The Village Economy, 1935–1939

BY THE TIME SEKISHIBA'S RESIDENTS had recovered from the worst effects of the famine and were ready to start work on revitalization, there were signs that some sectors of the Japanese economy were on the rebound. The nation's GNP had returned to pre-depression levels as of the end of 1934. Exports and manufacturing had also returned to where they had been prior to the start of the economic crisis. The total value of manufacturing in 1934 was, in fact, more than a fifth higher than it had been in 1929. Growth in the industrial sector was evident even within Fukushima. The number of those employed in heavy industry in the prefecture grew more than tenfold between 1931 and 1936, and the value of what they produced increased by a factor of fifteen.[1]

For the countryside, however, and certainly in Sekishiba, the economic crisis was still very much a concern. As of 1935, most farm products still sold for less than they had in 1929. Only rice had returned to pre-depression levels, and it took until 1937 for other farm prices, on average, to recover.[2] Even when prices began rising, farmers had no way of knowing how long the upturn might persist. The last plunge had been so sharp and so rapid that anything seemed possible. There were no guarantees that the market would remain stable. In 1935, Mayor Satō could still talk about the need to "overcome the depression" and know that he would be understood.[3]

Sekishiba's transformation along the lines laid out in household, hamlet, and its own village revitalization plans began in 1935 and was still under way in 1941, when the Economic Revitalization Campaign drew to a close. This chapter and Chapter 9 examine the community's efforts to re-create itself in the wake of the depression. The first and perhaps most fundamental step in this process was the economic restructuring of the village, the topic of this chapter. New business practices, better coordination among farm organizations, and simpler steps like crop diversification were key elements in the post-depression village economy. So, too, over time, were the demands of an increasingly mobilized national economy.

Even as the mayor and others actively pursued the ideas laid out in their Economic Revitalization Plans, they found themselves adjusting their goals and practices to accommodate wartime realities. The state's demands that farmers produce more with less were close enough to the campaign's original ethos that the two sets of goals—re-creating the community through planning and reform, and providing a stable and productive home front to support the war in China—became, over time, almost one and the same. Thus the period from 1935 through 1939 both covers the first five years of the campaign in Sekishiba and bridges the transition from peacetime to the early stages of the mobilized economy.

Revitalization and mobilization together also altered the nature and scope of local leadership; this is a second axis of the village's transformation and one of the subjects of the next chapter. By creating new structures through which economic and social leadership were projected, the Economic Revitalization Campaign supplemented and sometimes supplanted existing village institutions in decisionmaking about the local economy. Sekishiba's Economic Revitalization Committee, for example, brought together many of those who were already in positions of power as well as some new faces to fill important roles in coordinating the village's recovery. The committee was one of several new platforms from which local reformers could reach out to residents and urge them to pursue a particular vision of change. The mayor and his allies in revitalization, local businessman Yabe Zenbei among them, made ample use of these platforms and pulpits to speak out, to organize, and to lead. The campaign and the mobilization that followed it were thus also responsible for a very subtle shift in power in the countryside, one that favored producers and village "mainstays" over long-entrenched landed elites.

Social reforms constitute the third element of Sekishiba's post-depression recovery. Here the potential for change was thought to be considerable, as the mayor and Yabe tried hard to instill in villagers a sense of the importance of moral reform, improvements in daily life, and commitment to the community and the nation. And here, as in the case of the economic and institutional reforms, the lines between revitalization and mobilization were increasingly blurred. What began as an optimistic vision of a more prosperous and vibrant countryside was transformed into something that incorporated both the rhetoric of modernity and a propaganda of sacrifice and service to the nation.

## Organizing for Recovery

Sekishiba was home to three varieties of farming organization in the 1930s. Both the agricultural association and the industrial cooperative operated throughout the village; the farm practice associations were strictly hamlet affairs. As noted in Chapter 3 above, all were long-standing institutions but, by the time of the depression, largely ineffectual. The campaign set out to revamp these bodies. Over the village's years in the Economic Revitalization Campaign, all three organizations changed the way they worked and expanded the scope of their activities. The agricultural association and the industrial cooperative both strengthened their ties with the hamlet unions and through them interacted with more of the farming community than had been possible before. The hamlet associations, for their part, were responsible for bringing the innovations and techniques promoted by the two village-wide organizations directly to local farmers.

Of the three, the hamlet unions were the most involved with the daily practice of farming and with the actual work of economic revitalization on the farm. Unfortunately, their activities are also the least well documented. What we do know is that each of the village's hamlets had a farm practice association and that practically all the village's farming households belonged to them. The farm practice association helped coordinate farming practices within the hamlet (or among them, when that was necessary), introduced new techniques and crop varieties, and in general implemented the reforms in farm management advocated by either the agricultural association or the industrial cooperative.[4] Without the practice associations, the Economic Revitalization Campaign ran the risk of reaching only the top layers of village society; with the practice associations on board, local planners were more confident of their ability to involve the entire community in the revitalization process.

Legislation earlier in the decade had made it easier for a practice association to incorporate as a legal body for the purpose of then joining, as a legal entity, the local industrial cooperative. There were several advantages to this approach. Bringing the incorporated practice associations into the cooperative was cost effective for members of the practice associations because it provided access to cooperative resources without the added expense of individual membership. For the industrial cooperative, allowing the associations in boosted participation rates considerably, since for most farmers membership in their hamlet's farm practice association was a given.

In Sekishiba, every farm household in the village was represented in the industrial cooperative by 1938. This was a welcome development, but the village hoped to do even better. The agricultural association and village officials promised to commit 70 yen to the practice unions to pay for the legal transformation from private body to public entity.[5] By 1940, all Sekishiba's farming associations had incorporated. Though the process was more drawn out than local planners had hoped, the village eventually achieved the top-to-bottom coverage it had set out to achieve in 1935.

Such coverage mattered because it provided the foundation on which the resurgent agricultural association and industrial cooperative could act. Though of quite different characters, the two bodies were both essential to the campaign. The agricultural association's constituency, for example, was generally at the upper end of the local economic scale. The issues it concerned itself with and the policies it pursued were of more interest to the landowning farmer than to his tenant neighbor. Though the campaign didn't do much to transform the general goals of the association, in which the improvement of farming through better technology and skills figured prominently, it did try to ensure that those goals were shared by a wider percentage of the village population. Under this new mandate, the association sought out the landed farmer, as well as his tenant neighbor, as a likely audience for its instruction.

The agricultural association reached out to farmers through a variety of mechanisms. From 1933 on, it employed a full-time technician to help improve the quality and quantity of the crops produced locally. His regular appearances in the hamlet assemblies (discussed in Chapter 10 below) made what had been essentially private knowledge a public commodity. The technician thus became a community resource, not solely an association asset. Throughout the 1930s, the association also sponsored more events designed to increase farmers' interest in particular crops and farming techniques. Local fairs and exhibitions featured different varieties of compost, seedlings, and farm products, allowing farmers a chance to examine their options at close range.

The idea for the exhibitions was not new, and the agricultural association had been running exhibits of compost and fertilizer well before the start of the Economic Revitalization program. The difference is that after 1934 they were part of a much broader offensive, one that combined lectures, the presence of an agricultural technician, events like the product exhibitions to bring home to local farmers the potential of farm reforms, and loans from the industrial cooperatives for those interested in making the changes suggested by the exhibitions.[6] The campaign gave new direction to the association's traditional role in the village as a source of technical instruction and as a channel for farm policies from the state.

The industrial cooperative's responsibilities were more complicated. Sekishiba's cooperative, although vital to the success of economic revitalization, had not performed well in the past. The collapse early in the decade of the bank that held much of the cooperative's assets had left the body almost dead in the water, and participation in the cooperative had in the past been skewed toward the better-off farmers in the village. The cooperative had to be revived and its membership broadened for the campaign to reach its full potential. No other institution in the community could provide the cooperative's financial support or replace it as a mediator between the local and national markets. The cooperative's importance to the campaign had been clear from early on, and in 1932 the Ministry of Agriculture had lent its support to a five-year plan to expand the cooperative's reach and activities. The plan proposed steps that would eventually bring almost all farmers into the cooperative and ensure that each cooperative provided four key services to the community: credit, sales of farm products, purchases of supplies, and the cooperative use of farm equipment.[7]

The plan was largely a success. From a membership base of just under 5 million in 1932, the cooperatives grew to more than 6.2 million by 1937, and to more than 7.1 million by the end of 1940.[8] Nationally, membership rose from 61.1 percent of farm households in 1931 to 76.6 percent in 1936.[9] The circulation of *Ie no hikari*, the industrial cooperative journal, skyrocketed from two hundred thousand issues in 1932 to a million in 1935, and the cooperatives' scope of services quickly expanded to address local needs. In 1932, fewer than a third of all cooperatives provided all four possible services available to members (see above); by 1937, 71 percent did.[10]

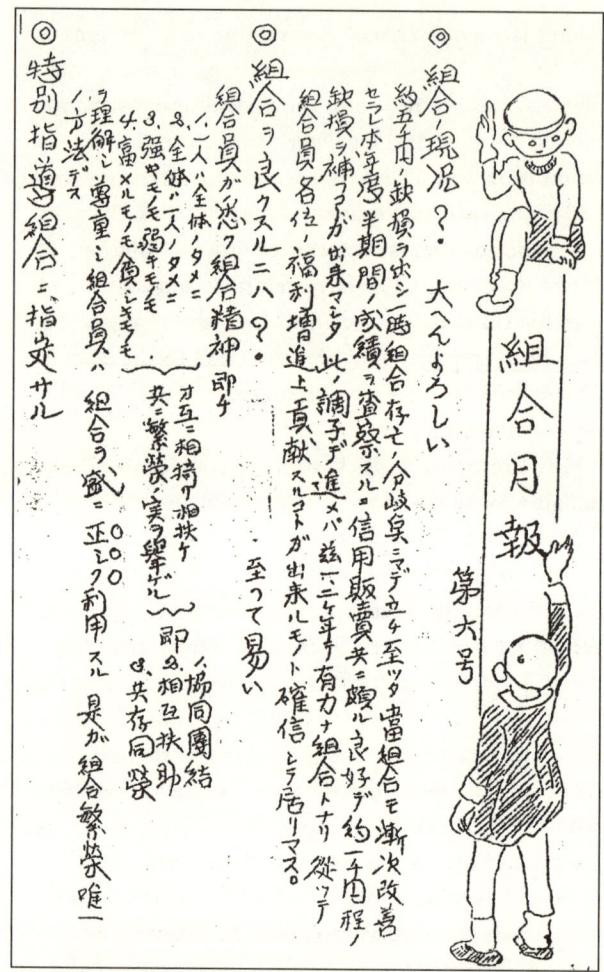

Fig. 4 *Sekishiba Industrial Cooperative Newsletter*, 1936 (SOURCE: Sekishiba village documents, Office for the Compilation of Municipal History, Kitakata City).

When Sekishiba first drafted its revitalization plans, expanding the reach and services of the local cooperative was a priority. Membership was spotty, and the cooperative's role in the village was similarly haphazard. Under the auspices of the Economic Revitalization Campaign, that began to change. The cooperative's new monthly newsletter (see Fig. 4), which first reached readers in early 1936, points to the organization's growing confidence and vitality. The newsletter included reminders to members of the cooperative's local activities and the services it provided and exhorted readers to make better use of the cooperative's resources.[11] Thus it supplemented the similar messages appearing in *Ie no hikari* and provided specific, up-to-date information about local conditions and campaign goals.

In 1937, the village began allocating some of its Economic Revitalization Campaign Special Assistance funding to the cooperative, providing a welcome infusion of cash. Representatives of the cooperative appeared regularly at hamlet assemblies, explaining how the cooperative could be of use and urging those farmers who were not yet members to join. Many did; by 1938, every farm household in the village was represented in the cooperative, and hamlet-level farm practice associations were making themselves eligible for membership as well. A much larger part of the community had access to the cooperative under the campaign than had been the case before.

The cooperative's role as an advocate and agent of economic revitalization was similarly enhanced in several key areas. Fertilizer was an indispensable part of modern farming, and a good indicator of the cooperative's importance in the local economy was its role in the village fertilizer market. One of the goals of the campaign had been to get farmers to make more of their own fertilizer and thus reduce both their cash outlays and their reliance on fertilizer salesmen. Local farmers pursued this strategy but at the same time couldn't do away with the store-bought variety entirely. The targets that the campaign set for larger yields on a more diverse collection of crops could only be met with the help of quality fertilizer, not all of which could be produced locally.

National fertilizer use reflects the reality of post-depression diversification and efforts to boost crop yields. Use of nitrogenous varieties grew in volume by a third between 1925–1929 and 1934–1939, phosphates by 27 percent, and potash by 42 percent. The balance between store-bought and self-manufactured fertilizers in each of these categories shifted slightly in favor of the latter. At the same time, however, farmers were moving away from the fish- and soybean-based products that had been the staples of store-bought fertilizers for many years in favor of more sophisticated, expensive, and effective manmade alternatives.[12] Even as they were able to increase their self-sufficiency in some respects, farmers thus remained tied to supplies of manufactured fertilizers. As important a part of the campaign's equation of higher yields and diversified crops as homemade compost and fertilizer were, there was never any doubt that farmers would have to continue to turn to the market to keep their fields fertile.

The question, then, was one of where and on what terms those purchases would be made. Many farmers purchased fertilizer on credit, repaying the debt with interest once the harvest was in. Though lucrative for local merchants (nationally, many of these businesses were landlord-owned), farmers were caught in a risky cycle of indebtedness. In Sekishiba, one of the campaign's premises was that the local cooperative would, where possible, replace merchants as the intermediary between farmers and the producers of chemical fertilizers. The cooperative had some advantages: it could use its purchasing power to negotiate better prices with sellers than individual farmers could hope for, and it could also offer far more favorable terms on credit than local sellers would abide. Yet the weight of past practice and established relationships was clearly on the side of the fertilizer merchants.

Over time, the different factors found a balance in Sekishiba. The cooperative handled the sale of almost 147,000 pounds of fertilizer in 1933. This was only about 10 percent of the total fertilizer market in the village, and only about half of the cooperative's average 19 percent share nationally.[13] With its publicity and membership campaigns in full swing, the village cooperative worked hard to win new customers, with good results. By 1937, the cooperative was selling almost four times as much fertilizer as it had in 1933, with one report stating that the cooperative's share of the market in 1937 was about 55 percent. By 1939, the cooperative's sale of fertilizer had reached five times the 1933 level.[14] At those rates Sekishiba's cooperative was doing substantially better than the national average, which by 1937 was 39 percent.[15]

The cooperative also tried to expand its role as a middleman for other goods. The amount that residents spent on materials purchased through the village's cooperative more than doubled during the first five years of the revitalization plan. In 1933, cooperative organizations handled just under a fifth of the money spent on village purchases; by 1938, their share was close to a third. The cooperative was far from having a strong grip on the local economy, but it was clearly making inroads.[16]

Similar developments were under way in the cooperative's role as an intermediary marketer of local produce. Planners had hoped farmers would sell more of their produce through the cooperative; local merchants and other businessmen provided the regular routes to market, but the cooperative promised to perform the same services at lower cost to the farmer. In Sekishiba the cooperative went after local rice first—an obvious candidate, in part because there was clearly room for improvement in how farmers managed the sale of their most important crop. At the start of the planning process, the cooperative handled less than a fifth (by volume) of all the rice sold by the villagers. By 1939, planners predicted that 90 percent of all marketed rice would pass through the cooperative's hands. Figures from 1937 suggest that the cooperative was by then managing close to 60 percent of all rice sales, a sharp rise over earlier levels. Problems with recordkeeping make comparisons after 1937 difficult, but there is no reason to think that the cooperative did any worse after that year.[17] In yen terms, about 30 percent of the village's sales were handled cooperatively when the plan went into effect, or roughly 78,000 yen worth of goods. By 1938 the industrial cooperative and the hamlet organizations together handled sales of more than 120,000 yen for the community, which represented 36 percent of all sales that year.[18]

Given that the industrial cooperative had been more or less defunct when the village first began work on economic revitalization, its resurgence is one measure of the recovery program's efficacy. Residents were unwilling to abandon the wonders of the private economy completely, but they were willing to give the cooperative a significant share of what they did spend and to entrust it with the sale of a good share of what they produced. Both developments were signs that reforms were taking hold, and both pointed to the growing importance of the cooperative and other village organizations to local farmers.

## Community Infrastructure

By the end of the first five-year revitalization plan, the physical face of the community had changed in some important ways. Construction on cooperative work sites and crop storage facilities began in 1935 and lasted for several years. The storage facilities were funded in part by a gift of money from the imperial family, donated in the aftermath of the 1934 famine. The first were built in Shimoshiba, Hirabayashi, Kyōde, Kamitakahitai, and Nakazato; by 1940, eleven of the village's fourteen hamlets had at least one. The structures served several needs, the most obvious being a secure site at which to warehouse rice after the harvest. Before 1935, no such local storage facilities were in regular use, so that most farmers were forced to sell their crop soon after bringing it in from the fields and were thus unable to hold back even part of their harvest until prices improved. The storehouses also enabled families in need to borrow rice from the community between harvests, rather than buy it on the open market at inflated prices, and served as a primitive sort of famine-prevention device. When the government made its rice available to the village after the 1934 famine, it did so with the stipulation that the village put an equal amount into storage as a hedge against future disasters. The storehouses made such a policy possible.[19]

The cooperative work sites (*kyōdō sagyōba*) were built with help from the Mitsui and Mitsubishi corporations, which, like the imperial household, gave money to villages throughout the country to help with famine relief. Eight buildings were constructed between 1935 and 1940; this sort of communal space had been in short supply before the campaign, and the new spaces were quickly adopted to multiple uses. In Komatsu, for example, the first floor of that hamlet's building was given over to work space, while the second floor was used regularly for hamlet assemblies. Local farmers relied on the workshop space to pursue side-projects and other types of indoor work, a typical product of the campaign's emphasis on generating cash from all possible sources. A community work space saved money by lowering heating and lighting costs and presumably provided a more convivial atmosphere in which to work. In addition, several of the sites featured cooperative-owned farm and crop-processing machinery and other tools that were available for community use.[20]

These new machines and, to some extent, the buildings that housed them were part of a wave of improvements in technology and infrastructure that swept the countryside in the depression's wake. Some small-scale land- and irrigation-improvement projects continued to receive funding after money for emergency relief dried up, but rural communities nevertheless struggled to find ways to keep up with the rising urban demand for farm goods. Those communities lucky enough to be designated a Special Assistance recipient, as Sekishiba was in 1937, could do better. Sekishiba laid out a detailed program of road improvements, repairs and additions to the irrigation system, and a series of other projects that promised to boost local efficiency and productivity.[21]

Though each project on its own was quite small and narrowly focused, taken together they represent a significant if not unprecedented redrawing of the local infrastructure. As Figure 5 suggests, the scope of the Special Assistance projects was substantial. Few areas of the village remained untouched by at least one if not several improvements. That planners chose to represent

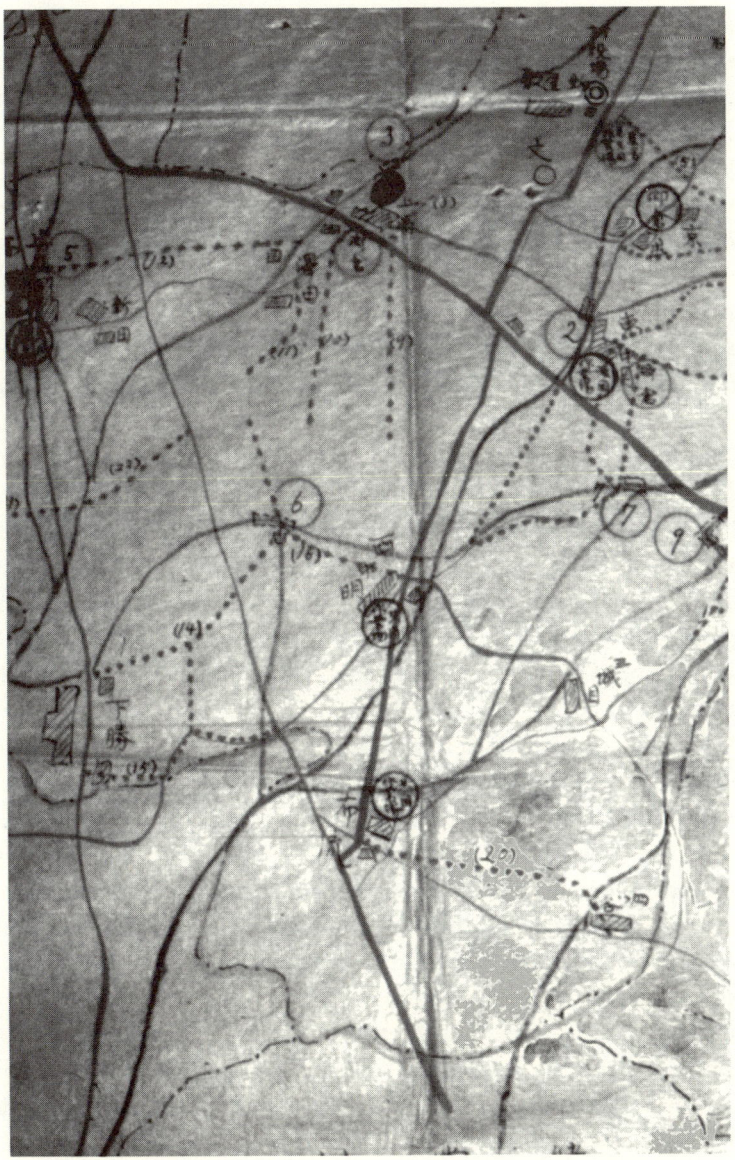

Fig. 5 Map of special assistance revitalization projects in Sekishiba, 1937–1938 (SOURCE: Sekishiba village documents, Office for the Compilation of Municipal History, Kitakata City).

the impact of special designation graphically, via a village-wide map, is telling in itself. It suggests the degree to which the 1937–1938 changes in the village were conceived of as part of a coherent process involving the entire community. The various layers of projects, ranging from road work to the construction of new buildings, mapped reform to the local landscape.

Other improvements aren't represented on the map shown in Figure 5 but were important nonetheless. Inside several of the new cooperative work buildings, the village installed motorized farm tools, including a Noda-style hulling machine, rope-makers, flour mills, and a series of other devices well beyond the reach of the average farmer.[22] Sekishiba could afford them because it could tap into Economic Revitalization Campaign Special Assistance funding and low-interest loans; together with some direct contributions by the village and the industrial cooperative, the costs were within reach.

The introduction of new and better machinery in Sekishiba brought the village in line with national trends. A gradual mechanization of the countryside had been under way for many years, but its pace increased dramatically in the late 1930s. There were only 537 tractors in use nationwide in 1937, for example, but by 1941 there were 7,968, an increase of more than fifteenfold.[23] Some 90,000 mechanized threshers were in operation in 1935; seven years later, the number had climbed to 360,000.[24] To some extent mechanization was a response to growing shortages of able-bodied males caused by the start of the war with China, as farmers sought to substitute horsepower for manpower in the fields and at the farm. In Sekishiba, however, the impetus clearly predates mobilization and owes something to the Economic Revitalization Campaign's hopes for the village.[25] Making these machines accessible at low cost to local farmers saved time and money, both of which could then be profitably turned to other uses.[26]

Although Sekishiba's new buildings did not differ in appearance from the ones around them, the storehouses and the work buildings were tangible signs of the community's commitment to reform. Subsidized or not, buildings were not cheap; their construction was not a decision that could be made lightly. Hamlet residents had to weigh the potential benefits against the known cost of construction. Many villagers were convinced that the advantages of the buildings outweighed their expense. They may have been aided in their decision by the fact that the facilities were ultimately of the hamlet, not of the village. By giving many hamlets a place to call their own, the buildings provided a profoundly local focus to the business of farming and made it that much easier for residents to work toward common goals. In function and in form, they may have epitomized the ideals of the Economic Revitalization Campaign.

## Farm Production

Sekishiba's 1935 goals for farm production remained more or less unchanged for the next five years. They also remained largely out of reach. Try as they might, Sekishiba's farmers were in most categories unable to boost crop yields as high as they had hoped. The village assigned production goals to almost fifty different types of crop, livestock, and farm products when the plan was drawn up. As of 1939, farmers had met those goals for only a dozen items. Table 11 looks at a few of the crops covered by the Economic Revitalization Plan.

The 1935 plan turned out to have been far too optimistic. As Table 11 helps make clear, revitalization planning was only a partial success by the standards established in 1934. When farmers added up their tallies at the end of the harvest in 1939, they were nowhere near their targets for most crops. Rice production, for example, had fallen well below the intended 17,351 *koku* mark. The wheat, barley, and soybean crops had also been a bit of a disappointment to planners because they, too, were below the levels envisioned for them (and were generally smaller than they had been in 1933, or even in 1935).

There were some high points. The village could boast increases in production for onions, mulberry leaves, cattle, sheep, and lumber above and beyond its stated goals. The 55 head of cattle in the village were 20 more than the plan called for and 32 more than there had been at the start of the recovery effort. There were no sheep in the village in 1933, but by 1939 farmers owned 266, a figure that was also much higher than originally planned. Rope, straw, and silkworm-egg cards were also successful side-products for the community, since each brought in slightly more money than planners had predicted.[27]

The village had hoped to accomplish much in five years and perhaps should not be criticized for having set such high standards. The failure of local farmers to meet or exceed the goals they set does not mean that the steps taken to improve farm management and production techniques had not

Table 11
Harvests Under Sekishiba's Economic Revitalization Plan,
Selected Crops, 1935–1940

| Crop | 1935 | 1936 | 1937 | 1938 | 1939 | 1940 |
|---|---|---|---|---|---|---|
| *Rice (koku)* | | | | | | |
| Annual goal | 14,828 | 15,459 | 16,089 | 16,720 | 17,351 | 13,271 |
| Annual production | 12,698 | 13,769 | 13,918 | 12,557 | 14,383 | 14,760 |
| Percentage of goal | 86% | 89% | 87% | 75% | 83% | 111% |
| *Onions (kan)* | | | | | | |
| Annual goal | 3,600 | 4,200 | 4,800 | 5,400 | 6,000 | 6,000 |
| Annual production | 4,250 | 5,250 | 5,500 | 5,700 | 6,000 | 6,200 |
| Percentage of goal | 118% | 125% | 115% | 106% | 100% | 103% |
| *Plum trees (trees)* | | | | | | |
| Annual goal | 560 | 600 | na | 1,100 | 2,000 | 2,000 |
| Annual production | 417 | 433 | na | 1,400 | 1,800 | 1,850 |
| Percentage of goal | 74% | 72% | na | 127% | 90% | 93% |
| *Sheep (head)* | | | | | | |
| Annual goal | 40 | 80 | 120 | 170 | 200 | 250 |
| Annual production | 6 | 68 | 152 | 169 | 269 | 253 |
| Percentage of goal | 15% | 85% | 127% | 99% | 135% | 101% |
| *Silk cocoons (kan)* | | | | | | |
| Annual goal | 6,596 | 6,696 | 6,671 | 6,680 | 6,545 | 6,545 |
| Annual production | 5,082 | 5,082 | 5,588 | 4,701 | 5,424 | 5,080 |
| Percentage of goal | 77% | 76% | 84% | 70% | 83% | 78% |
| *Rope (yen)* | | | | | | |
| Annual goal | 1,142 | 1,462 | 1,782 | 1,810 | 2,422 | 2,000 |
| Annual production | 1,400 | 1,600 | 1,623 | 1,650 | 2,560 | 1,378 |
| Percentage of goal | 123% | 109% | 91% | 91% | 106% | 69% |

NOTE: Not a complete list of crops (1 *koku* = 180 liters; 1 *kan* = 3.75 kilograms).
SOURCE: Based on SMY, "Keizai kōsei keikaku jikkō hōkoku," 1936–1941, KST.

been effective. As we saw in Chapter 7, Sekishiba's Economic Revitalization Plan was based on data from the extraordinarily bountiful 1933 harvest. What that meant in practical terms was that farmers were at a serious disadvantage when it came even to repeating what they had accomplished in 1933, much less improving on it. It took until 1940 for the village to harvest a rice crop larger than the 1933 yield, and even then the increase over 1933 was small.[28]

Measured against past performance and not against the goals laid out in the Economic Revitalization Plan, a more positive assessment of the village's accomplishments emerges. Although yields on some crops remained far from the targets established in the plan, they were still larger than they had been at the start of the planning process. There were only 400 plum trees in the village in 1933, but an additional 1,400 were growing by 1939. The size of the persimmon crop doubled while the plan was in effect, and the cucumber crop came close to doing so. Significant increases in the size of the burdock, eggplant, squash, and other vegetable yields can also be attributed at least in part to the recovery program, as can the 15 new pigs in the village, the more than 1,500 new chickens, and the 1,500 new rabbits (although the rabbits certainly deserve some credit).

It is also worth pointing out that village farmers succeeded in improving a key measure of their technical skills. The average amount of rice that the village harvested from a single *tan* of paddy land grew significantly after the start of the Economic Revitalization program. Yields improved by about 4 percent between 1926 and 1932 and by slightly less than that between 1932 and 1935. Over the next several years, however, the yields per *tan* jumped. In 1936, farmers harvested about 8 percent more rice per unit of land than they had in 1935; by 1939, they brought in 12 percent more, and by 1940, 15 percent.[29]

These improvements occurred at the same time that the village was cutting spending on store-bought fertilizer. The agricultural association and its technician were quite active in this area. Their efforts helped the village make noticeably more use of noncommercial fertilizers. Compost production grew almost 20 percent between 1933 and 1939, and farmers reported using more of it on their crops. Farmers also set aside more land to raise crops that could be used as "green manure."[30] One result was decreased village spending on store-bought varieties of fertilizer. Exactly how much less is not clear, although the village administration was quite positive on the issue. "Although fertilizer prices have been rising year on year," officials wrote in 1937, "the difference [between now] and 1934 is large, or approximately several thousand yen a year in reduced costs for cash fertilizer."[31] In other words, farmers had been able to find ways to use less store-bought fertilizer and at the same time boost crop yields. This was no easy feat.

Both the diversification of local crops and the increased yields mirror national trends. From 1935 to 1939, farmers throughout Japan were pursuing goals similar to Sekishiba's. Farmers raised larger and more diverse crops in the late 1930s than ever before. Though rice still reigned supreme as the single most important crop, sericulture began to lose ground to upstarts like apples, wheat, and livestock. The popularity of these new crops reflected ongoing shifts in the Japanese diet, as the rising urban population began to enjoy the fruits of its labors.[32] Farmers were eager to respond to the opportunities represented by these new markets, and cash crops flowed to the cities. Sekishiba's farmers were well positioned to respond to the new opportunities, and over time most families began to reap some of the benefits of their efforts.

## Family and Village Finances

Farm families began to see some improvement in their situations by the mid-1930s; by the end of the decade, the signs were unmistakable. As Table 2 (p. 55) helps illustrate, by 1937 (and possibly earlier; data for 1935 and 1936 are not available), the average per-household value of farm production in the village had risen to more than 1,000 yen, which is as high as it had been in Sekishiba at any time since 1924. By 1939, the last year for which figures are available, income from farming had reached more than 1,700 yen per household. In other words, at the end of the decade (and the end of five years of revitalization planning), an average Sekishiba household was producing goods that were worth almost three times as much as the value of production in 1931. The increase between 1937 and 1939 alone was 56 percent.

Inflation accounts for some but by no means all of these gains. Rice prices rose slightly more rapidly between 1931 and 1937 than the value of production did. According to the village's calculations, local rice prices came close to doubling over that period, while per-household value of production increased by only about 85 percent.[33] After 1937, however, the value of per-household production outpaced rice prices. In 1939, rice sold for about 2.7 times the 1931 price, while household production had grown 2.9 times. Prices in 1939 were 41 percent higher than in 1937, while the value of production per household was up 56 percent. The gap is even more pronounced if we look at indicators other than rice. Prices for consumer goods in general were 27 percent higher in 1937 than in 1931, and 50 percent more by 1939, having risen by about a fifth between 1937 and 1939. Fertilizer costs, which might well have eaten into farmers' earnings, did indeed increase but did not outpace the growth in value of farm production in Sekishiba.[34]

That conditions in the village had improved is borne out by other evidence as well. Between 1938 and 1940, local administrators drew up their own annual estimates of total income and total spending in Sekishiba. What they discovered was that the village brought in considerably more than it paid out; the community as a whole had a surplus of more than 34,000 yen in 1938, was 94,700 yen ahead the following year, and had more than 100,000 yen to spare in 1940. Given that the village had reported a deficit of close to 96,000 yen in 1935, it is clear that the effects of the depression were waning.[35] Sekishiba's results are similar to those reported nationally. Surveys suggest that, on average, farmers were back in the black by 1936 and that they remained there even during the hardest years of the war.[36]

At least some of this good fortune made its way into local pockets, for savings increased while household debt decreased. Estimates varied as to how much villagers owed each other and creditors from outside the community. Reports submitted by the village to the prefecture in the early 1940s stated that residents owed close to 313,000 yen (or about 780 yen per farm household) in 1933. Although the reports give no indication of how precisely families were doing it, their authors do make it clear that household debt was gradually being retired. In 1938, total village debt had fallen only 28,000 yen from its level in the mid-1930s, but within a year residents had managed to pay back another 83,000 yen. They followed that with another 8,700 yen in payments by 1940, so that at the start of the decade it was estimated that the average farm household was only 480 yen or so in debt.[37]

Organized attempts to do something about local debt had been discussed in the recovery plan and advocated in a general way, but there is little evidence to suggest that much came of them. It took until 1937 for the village to set up an official Debt Arrangement Committee, although it had selected nominees for one as early as 1932. By the end of the decade, only one hamlet in the whole village (Furu) had gone so far as to set up a Debt Arrangement Union. It seems unlikely that local farmers devoted much time or energy to the negotiations and additional borrowing that debt arrangement entailed. Inflation should probably get most of the credit for whittling away at Sekishiba's debt; as prices rose, back debts became that much easier to pay off.

Villagers had better luck with their savings than with their debts, but then there was plenty of room for improvement. In 1933, only 25,000 yen or so were deposited with the local credit union, and another 15,000 yen of local savings were in the hands of banks and postal saving accounts. Together they accounted for just over a quarter of all "deposits" in Sekishiba, where the bulk of local money still went to moneylenders and savings clubs. The recovery plan called on residents to increase their deposits in the more legitimate institutions by 1,000 yen per year, or 200,000 over twenty years. (The industrial cooperative alone hoped to double its deposits to 50,000 yen within five years.) Savings grew in Sekishiba by only 16 percent between 1933 and 1938, or from about 360 yen per household to just over 400 yen. This meant that the village had added, on average, 5,000 yen each year to savings. Although any improvement at all is worth noting, this slight increase in savings levels was outpaced by rising price levels and much higher values for what farmers were producing.

Savings deposits begin to reflect the improving farm economy only in 1939, when the village reported deposits worth almost 330,000 yen—an increase of 176,487 over the previous year and more than double what had been saved in 1933. The deposits for 1940 were even bigger. The shifts may reflect a recovering economy but are more likely the direct consequence of the state's new policies encouraging (and ultimately mandating) citizens to put more and more of their money into publicly held accounts, where the government could draw on it for its wartime needs.

## From Recovery to War: The Village Economy at the End of the Decade

While it seems clear that by the end of the first five-year planning period Sekishiba was in better financial shape than at any point in the previous decade, what this newfound prosperity meant for the village is harder to determine. In their reports and public statements, the mayor and others referred regularly to the great strides Sekishiba had made, yet the extent to which these changes had translated into tangible benefits for local farmers is difficult to gauge. On the one hand, the village was once again generating a surplus: yields were up, farmers had made a successful transition to a more diversified set of crops, and the crushing burden of debt was almost a memory. Local institutions were once again active and influential after years of dormancy. By all these standards, Sekishiba was at the end of the decade well on its way to becoming the revitalized community local planners had described in 1934. On the other hand, the same local commentaries that praised Sekishiba's progress spoke of the need to continue to pursue reform. That the village might have exhausted revitalization's potential seems not to have been taken very seriously by local leaders, for at least two reasons.

First, despite the beneficial effects of inflation and higher prices for farm products, there was ample evidence that the countryside faced continued economic hardship. Sekishiba's example notwithstanding, government surveys of rural conditions late in the decade revealed persistent pockets of poverty and poor health. As part of an effort to better understand the effects of the burgeoning China War on rural communities, the Ministry of Agriculture late in 1938 dispatched two dozen observers into the countryside to conduct careful assessments of conditions at the village level. In the confidential report the observers produced in March 1939, the frequent notes of alarm and surprise are striking. Not only were long-standing concerns about infant mortality, poor hygiene, and inadequate nutrition still pressing, but the demands of the mobilizing economy seemed to be making matters worse.[38] Clearly, it was worrisome that many communities had been unable to address their fundamental problems of making adequate food, clothing, and shelter available to all, despite their access to the reform programs of the early 1930s and the effects of economic recovery itself. Sekishiba was doing better than many communities at dealing with these problems, as the recognition and awards that flowed its way suggest, but less successful villages served as constant reminders of where the village had been and of whence it might return.

Mobilization was the other issue confronting Sekishiba at the end of the decade. As more and more troops and resources were committed to the fighting in China, the national economy and the local economy were both slowly drawn into the military's folly. The implications for rural communities of this latest transformation of the economy were far-reaching. By 1939, Sekishiba had begun redefining the structure and purpose of the Revitalization Campaign to reflect the new realities of mobilization, in effect putting the skills and methods developed to free the community from the depression's grasp to use in the service of the state and the war.

9   *Reconstructing Community:*
*Sekishiba, 1935–1937*

AS IMPORTANT AS ECONOMIC recovery was, there was more at stake in Sekishiba than the bottom line. The sense of crisis that helped foster revitalization had been triggered by the collapse of the rural economy but was also driven by the belief that the fabric of rural society was itself in need of repair. Petitioners and local activists alike had spoken of their desire to create not just a more profitable countryside but one whose prosperity was measured in the satisfaction and well-being of the people who lived there. That economic and social reforms went hand in hand at the village level was an idea at least as old as Ninomiya Sontoku's teachings. In the 1930s, however, the belief that one could not proceed without the other had a particular appeal. The agrarianists had focused to good effect on the growing gap between city and country, factory worker and farmer, by arguing in part that the benefits of modernity and development were accruing more to the former and seldom to the latter. Money was only one element of those benefits; the countryside seemed to be losing its sense of values, of why it was worth working as hard as farmers did. This chapter examines the efforts of revitalization's proponents in Sekishiba to imagine what a prosperous, stable community might look like and how they went about constructing it.

In this they had the support of the state, which actively promoted the reconstruction of rural society along several axes. Kodaira Gonichi had spoken out in early 1934 about a renewal of the spirit of villagers and of a "rise of the spirit of the farmer" as part of a broader discussion of what revitalization could do to help farmers feel pride in their own community and to encourage them to act on behalf of the village. The spirit of mutual assistance, he argued, both instilled in farmers the desire to help each other and reflected the best of the traditions of the rural community.

Kodaira wrote that "the villages are the true cradle of the spirit of the Yamato race" and described "farmers' spirit" (nōmin seishin) as love of one's home place, the spirit of hard work, love of country, and love of the land.[1] At roughly the same time, other Ministry of Agriculture officials and those involved in overseeing the Economic Revitalization Campaign began to move in a similar direction. Earlier statements about farmers' spirit had invoked the traditions of the farming community and the hamlet in support of the planning process but had not generally treated the problems of rural culture or the farm spirit as issues that ought to be dealt with specifically by the campaign. By mid-1934, the campaign had begun to address more directly how it might promote social reforms alongside economic recovery.

Two themes stand out in both the emerging national discourse of social revitalization and its local practice in Sekishiba. One is the creation of stronger communities through new civic structures; the Economic Revitalization Committee was one example, while local Hōtoku societies and hamlet assemblies were two others. By bringing village residents together in new forums, the campaign tried to replace deep-seated conflicts and class tensions with a cooperative approach to rural life. As part of that process, the campaign also began a gradual transformation not just of how the village organized itself but of who did so.

The search for "village mainstays" (chūken jinbutsu) got its start in the mid-1930s and took on added importance after 1937, as Chapter 10 below demonstrates. Even before the start of the war with China, however, it was clear that the campaign was helping bring new people into positions of authority in the community. In many villages the existing patterns of leadership and institutional control favored landowners and other local notables; the Revitalization Campaign's efforts to identify members of an emerging well-educated and well-trained younger generation of middling farmers were in some ways a tacit recognition of the failure of that older cohort to hold the village together. By providing qualified young men with additional training and easing their access to positions of authority in the community, the campaign promised a gradual transformation of the face of leadership in the countryside.[2]

Helping communities develop and preserve the qualities of farmers' spirit and "village culture" (nōson bunka) was another theme increasingly prominent in national and local discussions of revitalization. According to Kodaira, farmers' spirit could encompass a broad range of attitudes, including "devotion to farming," the pursuit of mutual assistance, and a willingness to get things done no matter what.[3] Village culture was offered in contrast to its antithesis, "urban culture," where the former represented the values of diligence and mutual aid and the latter represented greed and rampant individuality. The village in this sense was less a particular place than that part of the nation as yet uncontaminated by city culture.

The concerns expressed about these issues during 1934 meetings of the Economic Revitalization Campaign Central Committee are revealing. During subcommittee discussions, members grappled with the questions of how to define "farmers' spirit" and what exactly they wanted to encourage when they called on villages and village organizations to "promote culture." As mentioned above, Kodaira took one stab at it. When asked what the relationship was between implementation of Economic Revitalization Plans and the promotion of village culture, he replied: "It means that even though they pursue economic recovery, they ought not to read 'rubbishy' magazines or be influenced by the bad parts of urban culture. That is, to allow in the good things about urban culture and not be influenced by the bad parts."[4]

Later, the committee decided to alter the original text of one of its directives that had called for "the promotion of culture" to read "the promotion of village culture," because, explained one participant, "just 'culture' doesn't feel right."[5] As the discussion turned to a third and final clause, the line between urban and rural was drawn even more plainly. The text under discussion read:

Given that the village is the source of our country's citizens' steady thought, village Economic Revitalization Plans will maintain the traditional culture of the villages and move toward the creation of a new village culture. In addition, efforts will be made to prevent the calamity of the imitation of modern urban culture.[6]

The specific steps that would be taken to achieve these aims included the cooperative purchase of "worthwhile" reading materials, the spread and increased use of local museums and libraries, and cooperation between youth and women's groups (*kyōka dantai*) and production-oriented organizations to prevent the introduction of "unsound" (*fukenzen*) thought and culture.[7] In response to one person's suggestion that it might make sense for people to have a full understanding of both the good and bad aspects of urban culture so as to recognize the value of rural culture, Committee Chairman Count Arima replied:

> People come all the time from the countryside to Tokyo, but I think that is a problem. The Imperial Palace and Meiji Shrine are fine, but [if] they walk here and there around Ginza, they will see only the bright side of Tokyo. Recently, I heard that a teacher from the countryside [took his students] walking around Honjo and the poor people's neighborhood in Fukagawa, and this is something to think about. I think that informing people that urban culture has an extremely bad side is a way of approaching it from the opposite direction.[8]

Count Arima and others on the committee were obviously worried about the potential dangers of urban culture to impressionable country youth. But if the dangers of the city were very clear, the attractions of the countryside were left undefined. What it was that the Economic Revitalization Campaign was supposed to protect from the various bad influences was never made entirely clear and exactly how it should pursue that defense was left open to interpretation.[9] In Sekishiba, as in many other communities, there was no lack of ideas about how to proceed.

## The Mayor, the Businessman, and the Committee

Two men and a committee gave Sekishiba's revitalization its personality and particular vision for the community. Satō Sakichi, its mayor, and Yabe Zenbei, a young businessman from the neighboring town of Kitakata, shared an interest in the teachings of Ninomiya Sontoku. Yabe's concern with the village stemmed in part from the land he owned there; his family had long been local landlords, and he continued the tradition of maintaining close relations with his tenants. Both he and the mayor benefited as well from the possibilities for change implied by the Economic Revitalization Campaign, possibilities that they exploited to the fullest in their efforts to reform Sekishiba. The village's Economic Revitalization Committee, of which the mayor was a member, brought together thirty of Sekishiba's farmers, administrators, and local leaders as the agents and coordinators of revitalization. Together with Satō and Yabe, the newly formed committee pointed the way toward the village's future.

Sekishiba was administered by a mayor, an assistant mayor, a treasurer,

Fig. 6   Sekishiba village leaders with Mayor Satō Sakichi (front row, seated, fourth from right), at the dedication of the new village office on September 11, 1932. Also included in the photograph are future Economic Revitalization Committee members Igarashi Shoki and Yanatori Hachigoro (front row, third and fourth from left, respectively), Tabe Seiji (front row, first on right), Fukushima Takamitsu and Anazawa Masayasu (standing, first and second on right, respectively), Endō Dentarō, Teishirogi Chiyoichi, and Suganuma Eihachi (standing, first, second, and third on left, respectively). (Photograph courtesy of the Office for the Compilation of Municipal History, Kitakata City.)

several clerks, and a twelve-member village council (one of the duties of which was choosing the mayor).[10] Mayors served terms of varying length, but in Sekishiba they seem to have had more staying power than was the case in most villages. From 1889 until the end of the Second World War, Sekishiba had only five, considerably fewer than most of the other nearby communities. This low rate of turnover is explained by the long and presumably successful tenures of two mayors. Uda Seiichi, a veteran of the Freedom and People's Rights movement, held the post from 1905 to 1917. Uda's immediate successor held office for only a few years and was followed by Satō Sakichi. Satō's hold on the position was well nigh unshakable. He served as mayor from January 1924 until November 1946.[11]

Born in 1880, Satō Sakichi (Fig. 6) was a Sekishiba native from the hamlet of Komatsu, one of the village's smallest. He graduated from the Fukushima Prefecture Normal School in 1902 and went on to teaching positions in schools in Iwase and Shinobu counties before returning to the Kitakata area in 1909. A series of promotions and transfers followed, so that by the time he quit teaching in 1920, he had served as an instructor and principal in schools throughout Yama county, garnering several awards in the process. Although Satō never taught in Sekishiba, he seems to have had no trouble making the transition from teacher to politician in his home village. He was elected to the village council for the first and last time in 1921 and went directly from there to his position as mayor of the village. He was relatively young when chosen. At forty-four, he was more than ten years younger than Uda had been in his first year in office. Satō's economic standing in the community was neither remarkably high nor low, as the discussion in Chapter 7 suggests. By the mid-1930s, he was supporting a family of eleven on his salary as mayor and on income from farming. Though the mayor was also a landlord in a small way, his total holdings were enough to make him only the fifth largest farmer in Komatsu hamlet.[12]

Satō brought a reformer's zeal to the village and to village administration. Far from being a mere symbol of authority, Satō's energy and drive kept him involved in almost every aspect of community life. Descriptions of Satō's role in the community referred to his dedication to the job and his success in getting everyone to work together. As a sign of the seriousness with which he took his work, one observer noted that Mayor Satō was in the habit of coming into the office an hour before the start of the normal work day and staying an extra two or three hours past quitting time. Since he often worked on Sundays and seldom took holidays, Satō reportedly put in 336 full days of work for the village in 1932. He is credited with improving the efficiency of the village office and relations within the community itself (an accomplishment that included but was not limited to the elimination of all traces of political strife from Sekishiba). Satō's political affiliation remains unclear.

There were more concrete benefits to the community as well. One of the first tasks that Satō tackled on taking office was to cajole villagers who had not been paying their village taxes. Since that list reportedly included a number of the community's most influential residents, it may have been harder than it sounds to persuade everyone to pay up. The village reached the point in the 1920s where it was relying on short-term loans to pay teachers' salaries. Satō's approach was to pay early morning visits to the homes of those who had not paid to catch them before they went out or to wait for them to come back late in the evening and persuade them to make good on what they owed. He kept this up as long as it took, with much success. The tax payment unions that he helped organize kept residents up to date from that point on and made Sekishiba's tax collection a model for the rest of the prefecture.

Satō is also credited with keeping village budgets in line while simultaneously ensuring that the community committed itself to important projects. In Sekishiba, that included building new facilities for the school in 1927 and making major road repairs from 1929 on.[13] All this was before he got involved in what would become his greatest project: the reshaping of the village through economic revitalization planning and Ninomiya's teachings.[14] In this he was joined by Yabe Zenbei.

When Yabe Zenbei (Fig. 7) returned to Kitakata in the spring of 1930 after several years in Tokyo, he knew he had at least two serious problems on his hands. The first and most pressing was that the family fortunes had gone into decline since his father's death a few years before. Although the family was a large shareholder in Aizu Denryoku (Aizu Electric Power), the Aizu Bank, and many of the region's other large enterprises, the financial collapse of the late 1920s and the subsequent poor performance of those stocks meant that things were not as rosy as they had once been. Disputes broke out within the family over control of its assets, which Yabe would have to resolve, and there was also the family dry goods store to think about; it had to be watched over every day. Yabe had managed to postpone dealing with those issues for at least a short time by staying in Tokyo to finish his degree at Tokyo Shōka Daigaku (Tokyo Commercial College, the present Hitotsubashi University). His mother did her best on her own until his graduation, but Yabe knew that it was his responsibility to put the house and the business in order. He was twenty-two when he returned.

The family also owned a considerable amount of farmland in Sekishiba, which meant that Yabe would be drawn into the rural crisis as well. When he took over his father's business, he also took over as proprietor of the family's landholdings. Like it or not, Yabe became one of Sekishiba's larger landlords overnight. In 1933 his family owned almost 25 *chō* of paddy land and some upland plots in the village, almost all in the hamlet of Kamitakahitai.[15] There were few people outside the village with more of Sekishiba's

Fig. 7 Zenbei and Tsuneko Yabe, 1933 (SOURCE: Watanabe Eiichi and Tsuneko Yabe, eds., *Yabe Zenbei den*, p. v).

land.[16] Yabe was well known to the people there, and he and his family had long-standing relationships with a number of families in the hamlet.[17]

Yet his family concerns were only part of what troubled Yabe. Even before he had gone off to school, Yabe realized that he faced an even more fundamental problem. Like his father before him, he was destined to become a businessman, but unlike his father, he harbored an intense distaste for business. "Ever since I was a little boy," he later recalled, "I disliked my family's business. My father instilled in me a strong sense of patriotism, but business doesn't mix with patriotism."[18] The apparent contradiction between the needs of a businessman and the needs of society as a whole troubled him greatly. It didn't seem right, he later claimed, that the only way for a business to flourish was for its owner to somehow get the upper hand on the customer, to manipulate others for profit. That "it was okay to lie as long as you won" was anathema to Yabe. "I couldn't bear the idea of spending my life doing such meaningless and vulgar work," he recalled. Yabe went in search of some way to add value to his life.

He didn't have much luck in that pursuit as a student in Tokyo. Yabe found neither student life—dominated, in his memory of that time, either by left-wing activists or do-nothing slackers—nor the intellectual life of the classroom satisfying.[19] He had better luck outside the school. His interests drifted first to the works of well-known ideologues like Kakei Katsuhiko and Kihira Masami, as well as to that of the less well-known but no less influential figure of his *kendō* instructor. All three men were staunch advocates of "national studies."[20] Yabe took strength from their views and the closeness of their vision of patriotism and the "imperial spirit" to his own, but he still found the overall atmosphere of the campus almost too much to bear. He wrote, "I was so caught up in anger, impatience, and uncertainty that I couldn't sleep at night."[21]

Ninomiya Sontoku's teachings provided Yabe with a worldview to call his own. "What flashed through my soul from the depths of that distress," Yabe later wrote, "was what my father had taught me about Ninomiya Sontoku." Yabe apparently first began his research into Ninomiya's Hōtoku methods while he was still in college, but it wasn't until after graduation and several months of trying to straighten out his family's affairs that he turned in earnest to Ninomiya's teachings—and to Sasai Shintarō, vice president of Dai Nihon Hōtokusha.

The first in a series of meetings with Sasai took place in January 1931, at which point Yabe sought guidance on how best to solve his family's problems. Sasai apparently gave freely of his time and his advice, and the more time the two spent together, the more interested Yabe became in the implications of the Hōtoku methods for his business and, ultimately, for Sekishiba. In February 1933 he attended the first of the Dai Nihon Hōtokusha's "Leadership Lectures for Rebuilding the Lives of the Citizens." Sasai was the principal speaker, and that six-week session made a deep impression on Yabe.[22] Over the next several years, he became increasingly involved not only in revamping the way his shop operated but in reform in Sekishiba as well. There he and Mayor Satō joined forces with the Economic Revitalization Committee to pursue their version of revitalization.

The Economic Revitalization Committee (Fig. 8) led the fight against the "village problem" from within the village itself. The Ministry of Agriculture and Forestry's bureaucrats placed the committee at the center of each designated community's efforts at recovery and made it responsible for conducting the Basic Survey, for overseeing hamlet-level planning efforts, and for drafting the village's Economic Revitalization Plan. Once those steps were complete, the committee served as a coordinating body for any and all revitalization efforts within the village. The committee's organization and membership shed light on the mechanics of reform and on the people who were supposed to provide solutions to Sekishiba's problems.

Committee membership embraced representatives from many areas of village life. In practice, this meant recruiting the leaders of all the local farming bodies and unions, teachers, the head of the fire brigade, and others with experience and status within the community. By bringing these individuals together into a single organization, Ministry of Agriculture bureaucrats hoped that the committee would be able to achieve what local governments and existing leaders had been unable or unwilling to—namely, improved coordination among the various farming organizations and village-wide involvement in the recovery process. At the same time, the committee would serve as a conduit of information, ideas, and exhortation into each hamlet and each household.[23]

The committee's structure reflected the broad sweep of the revitalization effort. As Figure 8 illustrates, members were divided into what amounted to four subcommittees, each with a different area of expertise and responsibility.[24] General Affairs was to research the expansion of self-sufficient production and to handle anything to do with the public economy, public works, personnel and employment, and the management of the other three sections of the committee.

The Production section had an even more specific mandate: it oversaw improvements in farming, especially those related to crop yields, and encouraged farmers to replace cash fertilizer with homemade alternatives. In addition, the Production section was in charge of general improvements in farm management, public works on the farm, and anything having to do with the agricultural association and farm practice associations.

Meanwhile, the Economics section dealt with the management of sales and purchases and with cooperative production efforts, for the industrial

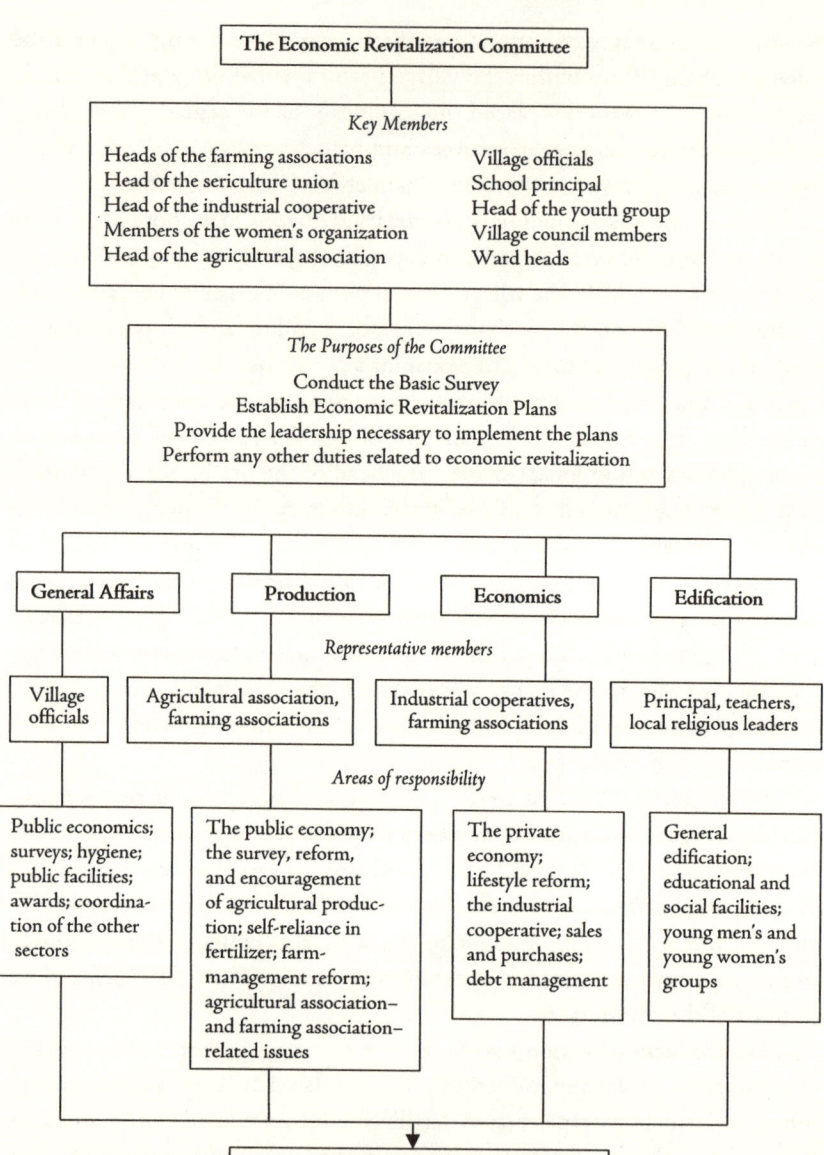

Fig. 8  Structure of the Sekishiba Economic Revitalization Committee, 1934–1935 (SOURCES: Satō Sakichi to ku chō, "Keizai kōsei keikaku jisshi ni kansuru ken," September 9, 1935, *Keizai kōsei* materials, KST. See also the diagram "Keizai kōsei iinkai kikō," in Kamisanmiya village's *Keizai kōsei keikaku sho*, April 1936, KST).

cooperative fell under its jurisdiction. The Economic section's mandate included anything related to "the private economy"; thus debt surveys, poverty prevention, relief of the poor, the encouragement of savings, the distribution of bookkeeping materials, and the overall improvement of daily life were all the responsibility of members posted to this part of the committee.

The fourth and final subdivision was the Kyōkabu, or Edification section. As the name suggests, its mandate was the moral and spiritual recovery of the community. Local education, social facilities, and the dissemination of information became the responsibility of committee members in the Edification section. Coordination with the village's Hōtoku societies, youth groups, and reservist organizations was another duty that Kyōkabu members pursued.

As head of the village, Satō Sakichi was chairman of the Economic Revitalization Committee and in charge of selecting the thirty or so other members. According to committee guidelines, the mayor was to make his choices from among several categories of potential members. Elected and appointed officials were one group of candidates; another included participants in the various economic organizations in the village (the industrial cooperative, farm practice associations, agricultural association, and so on). Youth groups, women's groups, military reservists, fire brigade members, schoolteachers and principals, and those with extensive farming experience were also eligible for membership.[25]

Satō filled the committee largely from the ranks of those already active in running Sekishiba. The village administration was represented by the mayor; by Abe Tadashi, the assistant mayor of the village and a director of the industrial cooperative; and by the village treasurer. Village clerks performed similar roles within the committee. The local primary school made its presence felt through Watanabe Kyūgo, who was principal, head of the Young Men's Association, and an instructor in the school. Three other teachers served, including the committee's only two female members. The heads of both the industrial cooperative and the local reservist organization were selected, while the agricultural association was represented by Sonobe Shukei, the village's agricultural technician. Each of the hamlets had at least one representative on the committee, and some more than one. Seven of those were village council members in 1934; two others had been elected to the council at least once before.

As the Ministry of Agriculture and Forestry's planners had hoped, the committee in Sekishiba had enough expertise in its ranks to make informed decisions about the issues within its jurisdiction. Each of the village's economic organizations was represented, as were many if not all of the social ones. (An important exception was the exclusion of women and women's groups, despite their importance to "reforms of daily life." A later section of this chapter returns to this issue.) The presence of representatives of those organizations also meant that decisions made within the committee could then be implemented by groups like the agricultural association or the industrial cooperative. Ward chiefs—Komatsu's Watanabe Shinta, for example—could be expected to keep hamlet residents up to date about their role in the revitalization process. The committee thus provided a structure that made it possible both to develop a single set of goals for the community and to involve the better part of the village in their pursuit.

With a few exceptions, committee members were among the most heavily taxed households in their hamlet. Since the Special Household Tax is based both on an estimate of a family's assets and on an estimate of (some types of) income, higher payments generally correlate with a higher relative economic position within the hamlet. Committee members also did well when compared to the rest of the village, not just their neighbors. The average 1934 tax payment for the twenty-three committee members whose records could be found was 42.5 yen; the village average was just over 11 yen.[26]

Their higher than average tax payments may reflect the fact that many committee members came from households that farmed more than average amounts of land. Members generally used more land and raised more rice than was typical in their hamlet or in Sekishiba as a whole. (See the Appendix for land-use rankings in 1934.) At 1.73 *chō*, the size of the average committee member's plot of paddy land was almost 0.5 *chō* greater than the village norm.[27] A typical member harvested close to 50 *koku* of rice in a normal year, significantly more than the village average of 36 *koku*. Moreover (although this is not included in the Appendix), records reveal that members farmed larger than average upland fields and that many were involved in sericulture as well. Their own reports show them to have brought in about 40 percent more income from farming in a typical year than the village average.[28] Committee members were obviously deeply involved in the business of farming.

Questions about landownership (as opposed to land use, the subject of the previous paragraph) are also worth asking, although village records do not allow for much precision where these points are concerned. Committee members who were farmers were more likely to be mid- to large-scale landowners and small-scale landlords than tenant farmers. Some but not all of the village's largest landholders were members. Of the seven families that Mayor Satō identified in 1936 as having more than 10 *chō* of paddy land, three were on the committee.[29] Endō Gengō, the largest landholder in Sekishiba, was one of them. At the other end of the spectrum, members like Endō Dentarō, Igarashi Shoki, and Anazawa Masayasu had very tiny plots. Igarashi, in fact, may not have owned any land at all.[30]

The information we have about the economic status of the committee members in 1934 suggests that "the faces of revitalization" in Sekishiba were those of the village's middle- and upper-class farmers. These were people who were closely tied to the local farm economy and to the existing organizations it supported. Someone expecting the committee to replace the existing leadership of the village completely would have been sorely disappointed. As we have seen, the members chosen by Satō were a cross-section of the people who ran Sekishiba when the campaign got under way. They brought with them their experience as union leaders, ward chiefs, and the like, and their ties to the parts of the community they represented. Their participation in the committee—and their identification on official documents as leaders of local economic and social organizations—linked the local school, the unions, and the agricultural association to the Economic Revitalization Campaign in a public and formal way. Given their economic status in the village, committee members could also be counted on to speak to the issues of concern to middle- and upper-level farming families.[31]

The mayor, Yabe, and the committee thus brought to Sekishiba's campaign an interesting mix of perspectives. On the one hand, Yabe's participation in rural reform could easily be understood as a classic example of a paternalistic landlord's concern for his tenants (a concern that was well within the traditions of such behavior in the northeast). The only new facet to Yabe's actions was the wide access that the campaign and Yabe's own interest in the Hōtoku movement afforded him to other hamlets and to farmers other than his tenants. Without the campaign, it is hard to imagine a scenario in which Yabe could have influenced village affairs as much as he did for as long as he did.

The mayor's position, though more complicated, has some of the same flavor to it. A well-educated landlord and farmer with plenty of experiences and contacts outside the village, Satō was at ease in his role as mediator between the state and the community—and was a perfect foil in many respects for the ideals both of the Hōtoku movement and of the Economic Revitalization Campaign.

Yet where both men are concerned, and in light of the membership of the committee, Sekishiba after the depression was not simply re-creating past patterns of economic and social control by landed elites. There is a tension in the backgrounds and goals that the campaign's leaders and committee members brought to the village. Although many of them hailed from positions long associated with landlord authority (again, especially in the northeast), in most cases it was their positions as farmers and producers that the campaign claimed to value. The committee was large, and though it included many of the existing village leaders, it also included many who had not acted as leaders before and whose claim to membership rested on qualities other than the amount of land they owned. The campaign as it was conceived in Tokyo, and perhaps even as it was practiced in Sekishiba, sought to bring together a group of leaders based not on their landholding status but on their status as farmers; this emphasis would become even more pronounced after 1937, for reasons that will be clear presently.

Yabe is in some ways the wild card in this equation. Although he had no official status within Sekishiba's campaign infrastructure, he was clearly influential as a purveyor of ideas and of a particular vision of rural life. Mayor Satō and other Hōtoku enthusiasts endorsed essentially the same ideas and the same vision as Yabe. In other respects, though, Yabe was not of the village and not of the farm. He really wasn't even quite the absentee landlord, for he remained in close physical and social proximity to his land and his tenants. His participation in the campaign thus marks it in many ways, not least as a process that was in and of itself not terribly threatening to a landlord such as himself. Yabe would hardly have supported a set of reforms that put his family's assets at risk or directly challenged his own status in the community. He clearly was not worried by what he understood as the campaign's goals and likely effects. On the contrary, Yabe found in the idea of rural reform a set of solutions to Japan's problems that he could stand behind a hundred percent. Knowing what we do about Yabe's disgust with the Left and his affection for national studies, it is obvious that, to him, rural reform also didn't stray far from the qualities of Japaneseness he valued.

The campaign's character and its contradictions are not easily disentangled from its leaders. In Sekishiba's case, as the next several sections suggest, the parts of the campaign that built on age-old traditions stood alongside ideas that promised a very different future—different even, perhaps, than the future as Yabe envisioned it.

## Harmony, Culture, and Discipline

Sekishiba's revitalization plan alluded to the importance of changing not only the practices of farming but the practices of everyday life. As the campaign got under way, the mayor, Yabe, and the Economic Revitalization Committee pursued a series of efforts to transform the private lives of villagers. These changes moved the village toward what initially appear to be two different goals at once. One was the development of community solidarity and social harmony. Accomplished in part through local Hōtoku societies and hamlet assemblies, which brought villagers together in new ways, this aspect of the campaign was a conscious attempt to overlook the many fault lines within the village in favor of a stance that emphasized a shared identity as farmers. The Hōtoku societies and other new mediums discussed below became the platforms from which the mayor, Yabe, and others reached out to villagers with appeals for an end to divisiveness and harmful individuality. "Village culture" was clearly a component of these appeals, as local leaders sought to instill a sense of the value of rural life and, perhaps, to justify the hardships associated with it.

The other axis along which the village was supposed to change measured Sekishiba's progress along a continuum of reforms of daily life and personal discipline. Issues such as household nutrition, kitchen improvements and family health, day care for children, and education appropriate for the countryside fell within the boundaries of the campaign. Many of these projects and others associated with the long-standing if seldom realized goal of the reform of daily life (*seikatsu kaizen*) were actively pursued from 1935 on.

Closely related to these public improvements were private practices of personal discipline. These encompassed a range of behaviors and beliefs that revitalization sought to instill in villagers. That frugality and diligence were keystones of the campaign should come as no surprise given its antecedents, and at first glance the village's efforts to convince farmers to spend less and work harder bear a strong resemblance to edicts directed at eighteenth-century peasants. A closer look reveals, however, that there was more on the table than exhortations to live frugally. In Sekishiba and certainly in the popular culture of revitalization, the pursuit of personal discipline had a decidedly modern ring to it. These changes were not about stepping back toward the practices of one's ancestors but about moving ahead toward a more rational lifestyle, one that brought the full benefits of modernity to its practitioners.

Sekishiba's campaign took the reform of daily life and the strengthening of the community seriously. In trying to pursue both at once, residents had their work cut out for them. The campaign's emphasis on harmony and the elimination of conflict required that villagers largely ignore tenancy and its implications for the community, to say nothing of the other differences that also seemed to be actively denied by the campaign. The argument in favor of mutual assistance and cooperation thus looked toward an imagined past, one in which Ninomiya's ideas worked and the village was insulated from outside influences. At the same time, the very men who in one breath invoked the timeless essence of the village to aid in their community-building in the next breath urged farmers and their families to move into the modern world of bookkeeping, economic planning, and a vibrant rural culture. Sekishiba would have to find some way to reconcile these alternative interpretations of its past, present, and future.

## Yabe and the Hōtoku Societies

Yabe Zenbei's views on the problems facing his business and his community are reflected in articles he wrote in the late 1930s, several years after he was most active in Sekishiba. A biography and a small book he published privately in 1940 in honor of his mother are additional sources. His first and longest original piece appeared in two parts, in the January and February 1938 issues of *Shimin*. Originally a presentation that Yabe made for a group called the Hōtoku Economics Society (Hōtoku keizai gaku kenkyūkai), the article deals with Yabe's own experiences with Hōtoku methods and outlines his opinions on the state of Japanese society. It was followed by a slightly shorter work about a year later, also in *Shimin*, in which Yabe responds to the commentary that his earlier article had elicited. Yabe also appeared in published dialogues with Sasai Shintarō and other Hōtoku leaders.[32]

Yabe's reflections and his interpretations were, of course, colored by the climate of the late 1930s and by several years of contact with Sasai Shintarō and the Hōtoku movement. It would be a mistake to assume that the Yabe we hear speaking through the articles was the same person whom villagers in Sekishiba heard in 1933 or even in 1935. That said, much of what Yabe recounts in his written work consists of reflections on what he tried to accomplish in Kitakata and the villages nearby. And although it is important to bear in mind the gap in time between Yabe the national figure and Yabe the speaker at meetings in Sekishiba, there is little evidence that he underwent any major change of heart during that transition. In fact, much of what Yabe describes in 1938 as his own beliefs bears a strong resemblance to what Sasai was writing and saying in the early 1930s. Yabe likely adopted Sasai's teachings as gospel early on in his studies and added to them his own experiences as a local leader. His articles, therefore, offer a very close approximation of the messages that Yabe tried to get across first to his local audience and then, by the end of the decade, to a much larger one.

The points that Yabe stressed in his *Shimin* articles can be quickly summarized. According to Yabe, conflict and the struggle for personal gain lay at the heart of the problems facing Japan. Moreover, those tendencies were not native to Japan but had arrived with Western notions of progress and economic growth. For the nation to free itself from the burdens imposed by the Western approach to economic life, it had to respond with economic theories and methods that conformed to the Japanese national spirit. This meant the development of what Yabe termed "Hōtoku economics," in which the teachings of Ninomiya were used as guidelines for proper economic conduct at home and in business. Self-sacrifice (*suijō*), sound finance (*bundo*), and harmony would replace existing ideas about personal gain, selfishness, and the necessity of conflict. The West's separation of morality and economics, meanwhile, would give way to a Hōtoku-inspired unity of the two concepts.[33]

The exact nature of the problems the nation faced in the late 1930s was left to his readers' imagination. Yabe shied away from mentioning specifics, preferring to contrast in a general way the benefits of a worldview inspired by Ninomiya's teachings and the harm that a Western approach inevitably caused. He used the example of a farmer to illustrate the differences. The farmer who thinks of the rice he raises as a commodity to be sold to earn money, argued Yabe, is someone in pursuit of "the private good." His counterpart, who grows rice in the knowledge that he is making it possible for another person to have enough food to eat, is an example of someone "living a life for the public good, for the world and for others." The former is an example of a life filled with struggle and conflict, the latter, one of harmony. Yabe left little doubt as to which was preferable.[34]

Yabe was willing to give credit where credit was due, noting that science, technology, and management skills had all been introduced by the West with good results. "Since the Restoration, Japan has quickly brought in Western culture," wrote Yabe, "and through the economic life of the West, has made considerable economic progress." But, he continued, "Struggle and conflict have led to a complete standstill on several fronts, not only in economics but also in thought and politics, where there is a great deal of excitement and unrest, to the point where there is a potential for collapse. On the surface everything looks fine, but there is no real happiness."[35]

By not pinning specific shortcomings on the failures of Western economic theory, Yabe ended up blaming it for everything that was wrong with the country. The "complete standstill" confronting the country was clearly not something that could be addressed by a few well-focused policies.[36] The problem was systemic, and only a complete change in the way people felt about and participated in their communities would be effective in solving such a crisis.

Whereas the Western premise was one in which the basis of economic life was a constant attempt to satisfy one's desires, Hōtoku economics began with the same spirit in which Amaterasu Omikami had founded the Japanese islands—namely, that of making something where there had been nothing, thus creating the "virtue" of those things, and of taking pleasure in the making. In Yabe's words,

Western-style budgets begin with spending and end with income. That is, one's desires and hopes are put first, and hard work comes later. The sound finance (*bundo*) of Hōtoku begins with a measurement of one's nature and looks carefully at income. Later, how it will be put to use and spent is decided. Effort is put into creation (*kaibyaku*) before anything is done about using a thing.[37]

In Japan, Yabe suggested, farmers had forgotten how to take pleasure in the effort that went into making and maintaining the land they worked. All they cared about was the income that came out of the land. Their ancestors, Yabe claimed, had been content first to develop the land and, when that was done, to keep it fertile enough to support crops. Nowadays, not only had work become distasteful but whatever people gained from their work went immediately toward entertainment and the fulfillment of desires. Yabe located this transition from the old to the new attitude near the end of the Russo-Japanese War. Before then people had been happy to work to make the nation stronger, but after the victory the focus had somehow shifted to the individual and the satisfaction of his or her needs.[38]

Something had to be done to counteract these unfortunate trends, argued Yabe, and he was ready with suggestions. Like his teacher before him, Yabe had in mind the replacement of Western ideas about economics with ones inspired by Hōtoku teachings. He used his first *Shimin* article to give concrete examples of what he had done thus far to bring that about and to outline the steps that he thought should be taken next.

Part of what Yabe had already accomplished involved changes in the family's business practices. These reforms were implemented not long after Yabe returned to Kitakata from school and were based both on Sasai's guidance and on Yabe's own feeling that it was important to demonstrate personal initiative and success before trying to lead others. Yabe described what he had done to transform Daizen, his family's two-hundred-year-old dry goods business, into a laboratory in which to test the Hōtoku method. His "experiments" took many forms, but from Yabe's point of view the most important ones dealt with the relationship between the management and employees of the shop and their customers. Remember that Yabe had long been dissatisfied with his family's chosen profession, on the grounds that being a merchant meant always having to try to get the better of the customer. Not surprisingly, Yabe's first move was to try to alter the nature of the merchant-customer relationship.

This he did by first changing the way the shop priced its goods. Most stores, he said, affixed price tags to what they sold, but customers still expected to haggle over the actual price. This meant that every encounter between customer and merchant was a struggle in which each tried to get the better of the other. Yabe's solution was to put the fixed, final price on a product and not allow any bargaining between his staff and the customers. Second, he abolished all sales on credit and demanded cash up front for everything. This prevented what he called "high-pressure sales techniques" in which customers were encouraged to buy more than was actually good for them; although such techniques worked to the merchant's advantage in the short run, they eventually worked against both buyer and seller. Yabe also hoped to be able to lower prices on what he sold, reflecting a new sense of what was an acceptable level of profit. He instituted reforms in bookkeeping and held regular meetings with his employees, who were initially quite reluctant to try things his way.[39]

At first it didn't look good for the reforms. In addition to opposition from within the store, Yabe's changes drove customers away. Potential customers apparently associated the new policies of no bargaining and no buying on credit with higher prices, and neither the store's handbills nor word of mouth succeeded in convincing them otherwise. Sales remained poor for many months, but Yabe was consoled by the gradual conversion of his employees to the Hōtoku approach. They eventually came to share his conviction that the store was there to serve not just the owner but the customers as well. They redoubled their efforts to explain the new policies to customers, and Yabe remembers having to warn his employees not to work themselves too hard.

Their conversion to the Hōtoku method was followed by a gradual return of the customers they had lost. Yabe reported a 20 percent annual increase in sales after 1931, so that in 1936 the shop's sales were almost triple the 1930 level. According to Yabe, "The 'correct pricing' and cash sales of the Hōtoku management method were responsible for some temporary customer dissatisfaction, but the explanations provided by all the employees and their attitude reassured and satisfied the customers." The Hōtoku method was a singular success for Yabe. Not only did he improve the family business, but he also proved to himself, his employees, and his customers that the Hōtoku method worked. The next step was to take the message out of the store and into the community.[40]

Putting a family business back on its feet and doing the same for a farming community were two very different things, as Yabe was well aware. He had no experience in farming, he was young, and he had a growing number of responsibilities at home. But the Hōtoku method had been designed to help rural communities, and Yabe's careful study of Ninomiya's teachings gave him ample ideas about how it should work. There were also Sasai's experiences in Hijikata to draw on and the teacher's ongoing instruction to help guide Yabe when he needed it. Most of all, Yabe had his own personal convictions about the importance of what he was trying to do for his community. He seems to have had little doubt that the Hōtoku approach would bring better times.

The Hōtoku method, as Yabe understood it, was fairly straightforward.

The first step was to teach residents about Ninomiya and the Hōtoku doctrine and to gain their full understanding of the basic tenets. The formation of Hōtoku societies would follow; the real work of economic and spiritual recovery could then begin. The societies would implement savings programs, debt arrangement, and interest-free loans. Regular monthly meetings would bring participants together for continuing instruction in the Hōtoku way and would also provide a forum for discussions of specific farm-related issues. The meetings themselves would form the basis for the creation of a harmonious, conflict-free hamlet in which economics and morality would go hand in hand.

Yabe was careful to emphasize the importance of having both a sound practical program and a solid spiritual foundation in any attempt at recovery. This is quite clear when he discusses how Hōtoku methods complemented what the state was trying to do through economic revitalization. Like Sasai, Yabe approved of the idea of the Economic Revitalization Campaign but was convinced that its potential was almost never realized. It took good leadership and an enthusiastic Hōtoku movement to give Economic Revitalization Plans the added dimension they needed to be truly effective, he asserted. For most communities, economic revitalization meant that "a plan is developed and various types of facilities are discussed, but thorough leadership of the villagers is forgotten. Moral suasion (kyōka) is left out."

The plans themselves were often little more than efforts in theory. Even when they managed to improve yields or self-sufficiency, Yabe complained that "there is very little done about the establishment of a sound financial lifestyle and surprisingly little success in returning loans through depression and boom, good and bad harvests. Nor is there much in the way of moral improvement, as in the elimination of strife, the struggle over wealth and honor, and dependency."[41]

There were exceptions, of course, and Yabe was full of praise for those communities in which the Hōtoku method had brought the village back from the brink of disaster. He cited the example of Ōta village in Fukushima's Sōma county, which was one of five Fukushima villages singled out for praise by the prefecture in 1933. Ōta's leaders had attended a long-term Hōtoku lecture series, established a Hōtoku society, and fully unified the leadership of the various other organizations in the village. The result, according to Yabe, was an improvement in economic indicators across the board and similarly impressive results in the social sphere. People were paying their taxes, donations at the hamlet level were up, and there were plenty of examples of "commendable acts of self-sacrifice" (suijō).[42] Yabe went on to cite several more cases across the country where Hōtoku leadership and organization had produced excellent results.

Although Yabe never ruled out the possibility of a successful recovery without Hōtoku-inspired leadership, he made it clear that the odds were against it. He recalled a meeting in 1936 sponsored by the Fukushima prefectural government's Economic Section. The meeting brought together representatives of the fifteen top Economic Revitalization villages in the prefecture for an "economic revitalization roundtable discussion." Once they were all there, wrote Yabe, "both the prefectural officials and the heads of the villages were surprised to discover that most of the villages had done as well as they had by putting a Hōtoku plan into effect."[43] The combination of hamlet societies, the meetings that went with them, and the Hōtoku vision of how society ought to work was Yabe's formula for success, and one he was eager to try in Sekishiba.

Yabe was involved in organizing Hōtoku societies both within Kitakata and in nearby farming communities. The Kitakata Minami-chō Hōtoku Society didn't get under way until 1937 because, as Yabe wrote, it took that long for the townspeople to make up their minds about whether Hōtoku was of any use to them. What had happened in the local villages and in Yabe's shop was apparently enough to convince at least some of Kitakata's residents to go ahead. Under Yabe's guidance, an urban Hōtoku society took shape in the neighborhood near his store, a part of the town that had become less and less popular as a shopping district. A total of thirty-four people in his neighborhood signed up as members, and Yabe quickly involved them in local meetings, campaigning for extra streetlights and holding cooperative sales among the various local merchants. Although the group hadn't existed for long when Yabe wrote his first piece for *Shimin*, he had high hopes that the rest of the town would take steps to pursue similar goals. Moreover, "it made me very happy," wrote Yabe, "to go from the Hōtoku way of running things in one store to the experience of using Hōtoku methods to restore the community itself."[44]

As already noted, however, the society in Kitakata came together several years after Yabe's first organizational efforts. The area's first Hōtoku society in modern memory was established by Yabe in Sekishiba's Kamitakahitai hamlet in 1933. Yabe chose that hamlet for several reasons. First, both the village and the hamlet were in poor shape compared to their neighbors. Yabe also believed that he had a better chance of accomplishing something at the village level than he did among his own neighbors in town. He wrote:

> Since it was beyond my powers to do anything with the townspeople, and as it was a time when the need for village relief was great, I organized a Hōtoku society in the neighboring village of Sekishiba's Kamitakahitai hamlet. I also made some progress with farm village revitalization (*nōson kōsei*), and we saw the first signs of that revitalization in Sekishiba, which was much worse off than the villages around it. Sekishiba's chief set up an administrative plan for the whole village based on Hōtoku methods, and within three years that community was one of the most prominent and excellent in the prefecture.[45]

Both Yabe's mother and his new bride were opposed to Yabe's plan when he first proposed it. To make matters worse, many of the residents of Kamitakahitai were even more skeptical than his family, and Yabe soon discovered how little he understood about rural life. He went to the village every day, rain or shine, but still found it hard to win people over to his side. "I couldn't get them to understand," he recalled. "They were opposed, they laughed at me, and they were obstructive, or they just wanted to leave it be." In a way, it is easy to see why villagers had a tough time taking the young, inexperienced Yabe and his ideas seriously, landlord or not. He was not a farmer, not even a real member of their community. The only thing that Yabe could do to overcome their skepticism was to be as persistent and sincere as he could.

Yabe had both qualities in abundance, and he did his best to swing opinion in his favor. He was often out past midnight trying to convince the farmers to go along with his ideas. (His widow's memories of her husband coming home from the hamlet well after dark, paper lantern in hand, were still vivid in the 1990s.)[46] After months of effort on his own, Yabe enlisted outside help. He asked Sasai Shintarō to come to the hamlet in early July 1933 for three days of lectures on the Hōtoku method. Sasai agreed, and his presence seems to have done the trick: Within a month, the residents of the hamlet formed a Hōtoku society.

The creation of the Kamitakahitai society marked the beginning of an upswing in popularity for the Hōtoku method in the Aizu area. Yabe helped organize a series of lectures and seminars in the region; both he and Sasai were frequent speakers at these events. A three-day "Hōtoku Leadership Seminar for the Revitalization of the Lives of the People" held in September 1934 drew five hundred attendees from throughout the prefecture to the Kitakata Middle School; the same forum a year later attracted some eight hundred people.

Umbrella organizations were created to oversee the spread of Ninomiya's teachings in the region. The Aizu Hōtoku Development Society was formed in 1935, for example, and headed by none other than Yabe himself.[47] The heightened publicity helped lead other communities to form their own Hōtoku societies. Between 1933 and the end of 1939, fifteen societies were formed in six communities in the Aizu area. Five of those societies were in Sekishiba. After Kamitakahitai in 1933, the Furu Hōtoku Society was created in October 1936. Early in 1937, Tōjō Genbei helped found the Shimosugure Hōtoku Society, and the next spring Nakazato followed suit with its own association. The residents of Komatsu hamlet also set up a society, probably sometime in 1939.[48]

Hamlets with Hōtoku societies differed from those without, not least because of their more public commitment to Ninomiya's teachings. Members participated in more complicated savings promotions than did residents of other hamlets and almost certainly received more detailed guidance on household planning efforts. Their hamlet meetings were more likely to feature discussions with Hōtoku-related messages, and their local leaders were more likely to attend one or more of the Dai Nihon Hōtokusha lecture series. Whether this had a recognizable effect on the economic recovery of hamlet residents is open to debate, since there is scant evidence that differentiates the recovery of one hamlet from that of another. It is probably more helpful to think of the spread of the societies in Sekishiba as an endorsement of the ideas that Mayor Satō and Yabe Zenbei brought to the community. They are good evidence that many in the village were not content to remain passive in the attempt to reshape their community. Participation in the Hōtoku societies was one way residents could feel that they were playing a bigger role in the revitalization not only of their own household or hamlet but also of the whole village.

## The Hamlet Assemblies

Sekishiba's first hamlet assemblies (*buraku jōkai*) were held in the early autumn of 1934. The monthly meetings continued throughout the life of the Economic Revitalization Campaign. Over the two-and-a-half-year period from September 1934 through February 1937, each hamlet averaged one meeting a month, or thirty sessions in all. (Records are not complete after February 1937, but there is nothing to suggest that the village lost interest in the meetings after 1937.) The assemblies usually lasted for two hours and were held at a variety of locations within the hamlet. Private homes, local temples or shrines, the elementary school, and, in Kamitakahitai, the building that housed the Hōtoku society were common sites. Attendance rates ran high; Sekishiba came in at the low end with a 69 percent showing, whereas the village as a whole averaged participation rates of close to 98 percent.[49]

These meetings served a number of purposes. They allowed village officials to reach households with information about the Economic Revitalization program and other aspects of village administration and to gain the understanding of residents on issues of concern. In this sense the meetings were a practical solution to the problem of keeping people both informed about and involved in a long-term effort like the Economic Revitalization Campaign. It was impractical to bring the entire village together on a regular basis, but it proved easy enough to bring village officials to the hamlet.

The assemblies were also forums at which visiting lecturers spoke to the gathered household members about issues related to revitalization, thus serving as yet another reminder of the ties between economic recovery, hamlet life, and social reforms. "These assemblies have been established to shape popular sentiment," began the assembly bylaws, "to plan for stability in life, for people to help each other, and to advance the revitalization of this hamlet."[50] The Ministry of Agriculture and Forestry certainly put great stock in the meetings, as did the village administration in Sekishiba. Detailed records were kept of what was discussed, who lectured, how many people attended, and so on.

In Sekishiba, the message that local leaders sent via the meetings was strongly influenced by Hōtoku teachings. The intermingling of the "official" economic revitalization approach and the unofficial Hōtoku element began with the basics. Satō instructed the heads of the hamlets to be sure that a portrait of Ninomiya Sontoku and a copy of the Hōtoku Creed (as well as a symbol of the imperial family) were displayed, visible to everyone, at the front of the room in which the meetings were held. Meetings began and ended with attendees bowing in respect toward the front of the room. Opening ceremonies were followed by the reading of an imperial edict; reports and resolutions were read when necessary. Once a year, most often in

April, the assemblies were required to include a detailed report on a number of administrative issues. They covered the village budget, for instance, and heard reports on the status of the various community organizations; representatives of the agricultural association, the reservists, and the industrial cooperative all described their activities during the previous year. April was also when the hamlet had to publicly assess its progress in implementing its Economic Revitalization Plan. Since these reviews took place only once a year, however, the rest of the meetings could touch on any number of topics.[51]

A typical hamlet assembly featured at least one lecture and sometimes as many as three or four. Mayor Satō was almost always present and commonly gave one of the talks. Assistant Mayor Abe (a director of the local industrial cooperative), the agricultural association technician, and the principal from the local elementary school were frequent lecturers, and Yabe Zenbei also made regular appearances.[52]

Lecture topics fell into several, sometimes overlapping categories. Table 12 provides a sample of some of the topics covered during early meetings. Talks about the Economic Revitalization Campaign or planning were given regularly. Discussions of farm technology and farm management reform as well were a regular part of the assembly program. These talks were usually the responsibility of the agricultural association technician, although outside speakers also appeared from time to time. It was rare for a hamlet assembly to take place without some sort of expert commentary in this area. A common approach was to discuss what farmers in the hamlet ought to be doing over the course of a particular month. Topics included lectures on fertilizer use; the raising, processing, and sale of rabbits; charcoal making; and pumpkin farming. Through these talks, the agricultural association technician and other speakers brought farmers up-to-date information on farm practices for the crops they already grew and helped them make decisions about branching out into other areas.

Speakers from the industrial cooperative supplemented what the technician had said. Listeners were told about the various things that the cooperative did in the village, what it wanted to do, and how they, as farmers, might benefit. Detailed presentations explained how to become a member and how to make use of the cooperative's credit program. Residents were urged to rely on the cooperative to handle the sales of their farm products and to let it handle purchases of staple goods. Speakers outlined debt arrangement practices and gave "how-to" lectures on the establishment of debt arrangement unions. Lectures in this category furthered the goals of economic revitalization by helping residents participate more fully in the campaign. At the same time, they encouraged better efficiency through reliance on organized economic activity.

Not all the lectures dealt directly with economic issues. In fact, as Table 12 helps illustrate, Mayor Satō and other local leaders regaled local audiences with their ideas about reform, Hōtoku methods, and community life. Although we can only guess about the exact content, it is reasonable to assume that Yabe's speeches dealt with many of the same issues discussed in his writing. Satō, Principal Watanabe, and people like Utsumi Haruki received most if not all of their training in the Hōtoku method either from Yabe himself or at one of the Dai Nihon Hōtokusha lecture series. Thus the arguments that they presented to their audiences were likely to reflect the ideas that Sasai Shintarō and Yabe were helping to promote.

Notes taken by a secretary at a Kamitakahitai hamlet assembly in early 1936 (the assemblies were also the regular meetings of that hamlet's Hōtoku society) suggest that Yabe's talks touched on what was, for him, the familiar theme of Japanese versus Western economics. After discussing the international situation, Yabe pointed out that conditions in Europe and the United States were unstable. For contrast, he then turned to a discussion of the "ancient customs of the civilizations of the East [in which Japan is the leader]," and followed that with "the development of Japan, the Japanese spirit, and Hōtoku." By the time he was ready to talk about conditions in Kamitakahitai, the superiority of the Japanese-Hōtoku approach was no doubt obvious. To incorporate this approach into their own lives, he called on family members to hold regular meetings to reflect on what had happened over the past year and to prepare for the year to come.[53] Planning—and a life lived according to the principles set out by Ninomiya Sontoku—would keep the family and the community secure and prosperous.

One should not overlook the significance of the messenger as well as the message. Yabe was not the only one calling for reform. Key members of the village administration, from the mayor on down, demonstrated support not only for economic revitalization in general but for Hōtoku-inspired reforms in particular. They included Assistant Mayor Abe, elementary school

Table 12
Sample Lectures from Sekishiba's First Year of
Hamlet Assemblies, 1934–1935

| Speaker | Topic |
| --- | --- |
| Mayor Satō | Procedures for a Hōtoku-style hamlet assembly in Sugiyama hamlet in Shizuoka prefecture |
| | The true story of Hijikata village in Shizuoka prefecture |
| | How to establish a hamlet assembly |
| | How should we resolve the difficult situation of the village? |
| | Economic Revitalization Planning and the hamlet assembly |
| | On Hōtoku and tax payments |
| | On "sound finances" |
| | The revitalization of a village via the Hōtoku society |
| | Impressions on my inspection trip to Shizuoka |
| | The purpose of the hamlet assembly |
| | The life of Ninomiya Sontoku |
| | This is how we should save money |
| | An explanation of the 1936 village budget |
| | On the export of Japanese light industrial goods |
| Yabe Zenbei | The need for Hōtoku |
| | On the Shizuoka Prefecture Yamaguchi Hōtoku Society |
| | An explanation of Hōtoku |
| | The shape of the Hōtoku movement |
| School Principal Watanabe | On the reform of daily life |
| | On farm household economics |
| | Young People's Schools and "farmers' spirit" |
| Agricultural Association Technician Sonobe | What farm households should do this month |
| | Guidance for living with bookkeeping |
| | Issues relating to seedling beds |
| Assistant Mayor Abe | Economic Revitalization and the need for hamlet assemblies |
| | The reconstruction of economics |
| | The development of links between organizations |
| | Cooperation and unity |
| | An explanation of Economic Rehabilitation planning |

Table 12, CONT.

| Speaker | Topic |
| --- | --- |
| Utsumi Haruki | On the Hōtoku method |
| | On the patterns of a Hōtoku life |
| | How to establish a Hōtoku society |
| Endō Gengō | The state of the Kamitakahitai Hōtoku Society |

NOTE: Many lectures were given more than once to different hamlets, although Mayor Satō rarely repeated himself.
SOURCE: SMY, *Buraku jōkai nisshi*, vol. 1, September 18, 1934–August 15, 1936, KST. See Kitakata-shi shi hensan iinkai, *Kitakata-shi shi*, pp. 653–654 for a list of close to seventy topics covered by the hamlet assemblies from 1934 on into wartime.

principal Watanabe, village clerk Anazawa, village council members Endō Gengō and Teishirogi Chiyoichi, and Komatsu hamlet's Utsumi Haruki. This list, though far from complete, shows that there was a sustained and fairly broad interest in bringing change to the community among local leaders. At hundreds of meetings across more than seven years, they touted revitalization and reform,[54] calling on villagers to take steps to make their lives and their communities better.

According to the mayor, the benefits to the community from the hamlet meetings were quickly evident. Satō explained in a report to the prefecture that every one of the village's hamlets was more harmonious and unified than before the start of the meetings. About Komatsu, he wrote: "Although this hamlet had long been one in which harmony and cooperation were widespread, since the start of the meetings relations have gained in intimacy."[55] Similar benefits were described for the other hamlets. The meetings were credited with improving relations between the two parts of Sosogi, which had not had much contact in the past. Sekishiba, explained the report, covered a wide area, which meant that clusters of homes were often far apart from each other. As a result "there were places," officials said, "in which a spirit of cooperation and unity was lacking." Since the start of regular hamlet meetings, however, Sekishiba was happy to report that "these bad habits have been swept away, and friendship prevails."

Other benefits as well were attributed to the meetings. Tax payments were up. In 1933, about 72 percent of taxes were paid by the due dates; that figure had risen gradually, so that by 1937, roughly 97 percent of all taxes were paid on time. People were more punctual; lateness was much less of a problem since the start of the hamlet assemblies. Perhaps most important, the village as a whole was filled with a sense of unity. Residents had a much better understanding of how the village was being run, and why. Opposition to the steps taken by the village office had vanished as a result, and the community had reached the point where it was truly harmonious. The mayor had no qualms about attributing all these improvements and more to the effects of the hamlet assemblies. He wrote:

Since the village was designated as an Economic Revitalization community in 1934, there have been no instances of clashes within the village office, nor have there been any conflicts among the different hamlets. In general, conditions are exceptionally peaceful, with the village office at the center of a sort of folkish simplicity. Village and hamlet meetings are being held in the spirit of progress, informed by a faith in the principles of Hōtoku.[56]

Unity and cooperation are themes that surfaced again and again when Sekishiba's leaders reflected on their community. Not only had conflict between hamlets and individuals been eliminated, but it had been replaced, reports insisted, by an atmosphere of mutual support. The attitude that put the individual first had gradually given way to one in which neighborly assistance and cooperation prevailed.

The Election Purification Campaign of the mid-1930s is a case in point. Supported with enthusiasm by the national Hōtoku movement, this campaign sought to "cleanse" elections tainted by the nefarious practices of political parties. In part a straightforward effort to get out the vote, electoral purification was also a close cousin to revitalization and Hōtoku initiatives to lessen local strife. "Today it is finally the election," read one handbill. "Let's all be sure to vote. Throwing away one's vote is a disgrace to the nation. For the good of the country, and with the finest intentions, let us elect fine people."[57] For his part, Hōtoku spokesman Sasai made no secret of his mistrust of local political parties and frequently counseled villagers not to let the parties take precedence over the needs of the community. Strengthening the village could therefore also involve limiting the role that groups like the political parties played and replacing them with more community-friendly civic organizations. In Sekishiba the message found a ready audience.[58]

## The Reform of Daily Life

"The Sekishiba Village Agreement on Economic Retrenchment and Moral Reform" was probably Satō Sakichi's idea.[59] The six pages of the agreement supplemented the goals already outlined in the village's revitalization plan with a series of specific suggestions as to how individuals could pursue reform in their daily lives. "The reform of daily life" (*seikatsu kaizen*), a catchall category with a history that predated economic revitalization by many years, was readily adapted by the campaign.[60] In Sekishiba it encompassed both a wide range of tangible improvements to the village's social infrastructure and a less visible polishing of personal habits. Punctuality was one of the village's new goals ("Economic Revitalization begins with punctuality!" noted one report); others were the spread of bookkeeping methods, improved nutrition, kitchen remodeling, and better medical care and medical facilities.[61] A few more examples of specific proposals capture the scope and intent of what Sekishiba was after.

One way the campaign could transform daily life, according to the mayor, was by eliminating wasteful spending and irrational practices, which in the language of the agreement were often associated with major life events. As Sheldon Garon has noted, the state and many private bodies had long been enthusiastic promoters of frugality, so it is no wonder that it was an important part of rural reform as well.[62] Coupled with the campaign's hard sell of efforts to boost family savings (preferably with the industrial cooperative), frugality offered the potential of more money tomorrow as an incentive to deny oneself today. Thus the agreement proposed sharply curtailing spending on weddings, funerals, the birth of children, and even the departure of young men into military service.

No one demanded that all observance of these events stop, only that they be scaled back a great deal.[63] In the case of the death of a family member, for example, survivors were instructed to notify immediate relatives of the event by mail when possible and to make only sparing use of messengers and telegrams. (To save money, messengers were instructed to use bicycles to get from place to place.) Incense was allowed at the wake, but flower arrangements were not. Condolence gifts were out of the question unless the family specially asked for them, and the funeral itself, which might otherwise have been a grand affair, was to be simple and rather quickly conducted.

Similar cutbacks were proposed for the sendoffs of young conscripts and for the parties given in their honor when they returned to the village. The Basic Survey describes how these events used to involve family, neighbors, and friends, a number of farewell parties, and a great deal of sake. It was common as well for many people to turn out at the train station at either end of the conscript's journey. Under the agreement, these practices were to be replaced by a more solemn ceremony held at the local shrine, school, or site of the hamlet assemblies. Private farewell parties were prohibited, and well-wishers were simply asked to "line up on the route, see him off, and to the extent possible not leave the line." No alcohol would be provided to well-wishers.

Satō suggested that each hamlet form a committee to decide what constituted a reasonable amount to spend on weddings and other celebrations; he suggested as a guideline that they try to hold down the cost of weddings in particular to less than a third of annual income. It was the task of hamlet committees to visit local families who were about to hold a funeral or a wedding and seek their cooperation with the terms of the agreement. The hamlet head would copy out the relevant portions of the agreement onto a large sheet of paper that would be hung in plain view at the ceremony site, so as to help others comply with the guidelines.

The agreement drove home for residents the seriousness of the reform effort and reinforced the importance of the hamlet as the focus of daily life. The agreement put the power to decide the scale, timing, and details of many of the major events in one's life in the hands of the community. Although some sort of similar, informal mechanism of control may have existed before, these new rules gave the campaign a broad mandate to interfere in what had, until then, been private matters within the family.

To the pursuit of frugality and restraint, the village added education as an important component of the reform of daily life. Here Sekishiba's campaign sought improvement on several levels: education, planners insisted, should be inspirational and tied to public service.[64] It should instill in students a sense of patriotism and commitment to the nation. It should also be practical, more in tune with the needs of rural communities. This long-standing complaint was often directed at a curriculum that to many residents seemed better suited to training bureaucrats than farmers; no doubt the high cost of supporting schoolteachers played a role in the oft-voiced desire to change the focus of local education.

In Sekishiba, the campaign called on educators to help make both children and grown residents aware of the important role they played as farmers. Being a farmer in Japan had become so miserable an occupation, the common refrain went, that there was little incentive for young people to stay in the villages. One way the plan proposed to change this was to show farmers that they had reason to be proud of what they did and how they did it. Households would be helped to recognize the "position of farming in the nation" and "the relationship between the village and the nation," both of which were presumably more important than people had realized. Planners insisted that the schools do their part to instill "the spirit of the farmer" in students, through a combination of training in the habits of hard work, the school's own farming projects, and urging children to help out with the farming at home.[65]

The village reported generally positive results with its efforts to reform daily life. Residents made little progress toward building better kitchens, and local diets were similarly unchanged. By the end of the decade, however, spending on weddings and other ceremonial occasions was down. That frugality persisted even as the economy was on the rebound was a good sign. Residents were reportedly drinking less, and many more families were keeping budgets and household books than before, another sign that local life was indeed changing.[66] As with the hamlet assemblies, the local administration spoke in glowing terms of reform's effects on residents.

The steady stream of awards and accolades that the village began to accrue testifies to the fact that outsiders shared the village's opinion of itself. In 1937, Sekishiba qualified for Special Assistance funding from the Ministry of Agriculture and Forestry, something that only a fraction of campaign villages ever managed to do. That same year, the prefecture singled out Mayor Satō Sakichi for its "Economic Revitalization Award," noting that "his devotion to Economic Revitalization has led to a stunning reformation of the ways of the people (*minpū*)."[67] Though the village never became the equivalent of a poster community for the Revitalization Campaign, its embrace of the campaign's social reforms was convincing enough to win the praise of outsiders.

## Conclusions

The reforms in Sekishiba and the issues that sustained them were part of a national discourse about changing rural society in the 1930s. The state's commitment to stronger villages and a renewed rural culture was sustained long after 1935 in word and in deed. The Special Assistance component of the Economic Revitalization Campaign included funding directed specifically at the selection and training of village mainstays. Other components of the village's civic reorganization were similarly targeted for help by the government and by semi-private funding programs. Chapter 10 describes some of these efforts.

Perhaps more telling than the state's interest is the prominence that magazines like *Ie no hikari* gave to the reform of everyday life. In published roundtable discussions and a series of articles that appeared from the early 1930s well into the next decade, *Ie no hikari* gave readers a glimpse into a countryside deeply engaged in the pursuit of precisely those changes that Sekishiba sought for itself. Frugality, punctuality, "kitchen reform," bookkeeping, and family budgeting appear again and again in stories of local success and in exhortatory pieces pushing farmers to do more.[68]

Two aspects of these efforts to change personal behavior in Sekishiba and across the countryside strike me as particularly interesting, in part because of what they reveal more generally about changes in rural life in the 1930s. The first has to do with gender and families. Women clearly played a central role in facilitating not only social reform but all aspects of revitalization. Bookkeeping, part-time employment, cottage industry, and kitchen improvements—to say nothing of the extra work that women would have to do in the fields to support higher yields and crop diversification, or the time spent in the many meetings central to community-building—all made demands on the time and energy of rural women. In Sekishiba, the local Women's Association (Fujinkai) was given a new lease on life in 1936, after many years of inactivity, precisely so that it could bring women more completely into the Revitalization Campaign. The Fujinkai's bylaws describe the organization's purpose as "providing the best possible training for housewives through development of the knowledge necessary for everyday life and cultivation of womanly virtues, through which we will truly realize Economic Revitalization."[69]

By the end of the decade, the list of local women's activities in Sekishiba and many other communities had expanded to include a much wider variety of home-front support. In letters and commentary in *Ie no hikari*, these demands were acknowledged and sometimes deemed too much effort for too little return.[70] At the same time, there was considerable enthusiasm for reform and for the specific measures described here. Rural women, or at least the subset who participated in *Ie no hikari* forums or who bothered to write to the magazine, spoke of revitalization as the only way they could see of creating some space for themselves amidst the constant and overwhelming burdens of child care, farm work, and service to the family. For women, too, revitalization held out the possibility of a more modern lifestyle, one in which leisure played a part.

That revitalization made the promise of modernity and leisure while demanding even more of a commitment from women to the farm and to their families speaks clearly to the contradictions built into the vision of social change that it represented. Rural reform offered new roles for women by suggesting that they be trained to handle the household's books, to manage the home rationally, and to undertake a more scientific approach to nutrition. This differentiation between male and female roles in the household has been more evident in the urban middle class, but here we find signs of its pursuit in rural life as well.[71]

The problem, of course, is that rural women were in practice unable to free themselves from the other demands on their time and energy, for despite its promises, revitalization introduced no significant labor-saving techniques or devices into the rural economy. Farmers, women included, had to work longer and harder hours to achieve economic security in the post-depression countryside. Once mobilization and conscription began to take their toll, there was even less room for the construction of the new roles for women that revitalization seemed to offer. In the long run, it would take the postwar land reforms and improvements in the technology of farming to create a rural version of middle-class, urban domesticity, although it is worth noting its presence, however ephemeral, in the 1930s.[72]

A second aspect of revitalization's intersection with changing familial and individual identities lies in its pursuit of discipline, meaning both discipline as diligence and discipline as Foucault and others have described it. Revitalization clearly called for people to work harder and to work more rationally than they had in the past. At the same time, rural reform also deployed very "old-fashioned"-sounding language in discussions of Hōtoku and sometimes of economic revitalization as well. References to "beautiful practices of the past" crop up frequently both in local and national discussions of the campaign, but it is important not to conclude that such references implied a return to past practices.

In the context of the 1930s, this blending of a traditional rhetoric with reform coexisted quite readily with what many people interpreted to be steps that would modernize rural society. Commentary in *Ie no hikari* is clear in this regard.[73] Farmers in the journal consistently equated the social reforms described above—and revitalization more generally—with changes that would improve their efficiency, and thus possibly provide the time and resources that would permit rural life and rural culture to flourish. As it was, many complained of never being able to get ahead precisely because backward practices and wasteful activities kept them from doing so; *The Land of Milk and Honey*'s Tanaka Tōsuke, for example, was certainly bitter about being held back by the "traditions" of rural life. Diligence thus emerges as a means to an end, a tool that would permit rural communities to change for the better.

Discipline also surfaces in another way, and that is in the nature of the practices of revitalization. The emphasis on bookkeeping, on planning, and on recording and considering the minutiae of daily life reflects not only diligence as hard work but also a regularization of economic and personal activity, and the public character of the same. Although I don't want to equate farms in the 1930s with the schools, factories, and prisons of Foucault's France, there does seem to be some utility in his definition of discipline for thinking about rural life around the time of the depression. One consequence of revitalization's methods, for example, is that it linked the economic and personal behavior of each family to the village's own recovery, and thus, ultimately, to the nation's as well. Each step in the revitalization process was subject to observation or surveillance, whether through planning and reporting, participation in hamlet assemblies, or the conduct of the more mundane practices of everyday life. There are signs of these "panoptical" practices much earlier than the depression, but it strikes me that rural families were more deeply implicated in them after 1932 than before. These developments are in many ways signs of the arrival of modernity in the countryside—or at least of a more consistent application of modern ways of thinking about economic behavior, personal discipline, and the community than rural society had seen up to that point.

# 10   *Sekishiba in Wartime*

SEKISHIBA'S FIRST CASUALTIES of the war in China came within five days of each other in late October 1937. There were two dead: both men from the same hamlet, both with the family name Kobayashi, and both killed in Jiangsu, where the fighting was heavy as the army prepared to move on Nanking. They may not have been closely related, since there were many Kobayashi in Shimoshiba, but their deaths struck a hard blow to the village. They were young men, twenty-six and thirty when they died, but old enough to have families that would have to be cared for, children to look after. Though it would be more than two years before the village was told it had lost another son, by then the war had already begun to reshape the community and the nation.[1] This chapter explores the transition from recovery and revitalization to wartime in Sekishiba.

When fighting first broke out in China in July 1937, it seemed likely that this conflict, like other clashes between Japanese troops and forces loyal to the Nationalist (Kuomintang) government up to that point, would be resolved locally. Certainly many in the army, as well as civilian strategic planners, hoped so. Their sights were set on preparations for total war, but not necessarily one with China and not in 1937. Under their guidance the nation had already begun to prepare for a conflict that military strategists imagined would come later in the decade or early in the next. The imagined opponent was the Soviet Union, not China. Defeating the USSR was thought to be essential for Japan's continued role in Manchuria; that war might well set the stage for another, one with the United States and Great Britain, but that, too, was not expected for many years[2]—or so the military's best and brightest believed.

The problem for the strategists was that the fighting near the Marco Polo Bridge could not be contained. The local situation was complicated by Chiang Kai-shek's need to take a strong line against the Japanese and the refusal of Japanese army decisionmakers to back down in the face of a Chinese show of force. Calmer voices in Tokyo—including, ironically, those of the men who had helped orchestrate Japan's expansion into Manchuria and the preparations for war with the USSR—were drowned out by those who viewed the fighting in China as an opportunity high in glory and low in risk. As both sides sent more and more men into the fray, the balance in Tokyo tipped in favor of those who promised a speedy and efficient resolution to the conflict if only they were given the resources they needed. Troops and matériel poured into China, but there was no end to the fighting. Not in 1937, not after the destruction of Nanking, and not after years of bloody, ruthless campaigns. The military's commitment to China was as complete as it was foolish, and its intransigence in the face of Western demands for withdrawal set the stage for an expansion of the war into the Pacific in December 1941.[3]

By the time citizens gathered around their radios on August 15, 1945, to hear the emperor's voice announcing the end of that war, the nation's economy, polity, and social landscape had been profoundly altered. The war itself was responsible for some of the changes, as families and factory workers were forced to cope with bombings and constant shortages by making do with what was at hand or by picking up and moving on when there was nothing left. But other developments were more deliberate, part of a broader effort to mobilize the nation in support of the war. This effort had been quietly under way since early in the 1930s, as military and civilian planners laid the foundations for closer ties between the state and industry through legislation, regulation, and the promotion of companies friendly to the military's needs. The mobilization of the economy accelerated after 1937. Though it never reached the levels that the military hoped for and could be almost invisible at the local level, the state did achieve an impressive degree of control over resources, labor, and production. Some of these developments had important implications for the postwar economy as well.[4]

For residents of communities like Sekishiba, the economy was only one element in a much broader transition from peace to war that began in earnest in 1937 and left few aspects of their lives untouched. Villagers were expected to commit themselves completely to the service of the emperor, which meant supporting the war in both thought and deed. The average citizen was subjected to an almost overwhelming torrent of campaigns, slogans, and regulations to shore up morale and define proper attitudes. Political and personal freedoms, never broad to begin with, were ever more tightly constrained.

Beginning in 1940, the political parties and most civic organizations were dissolved and reorganized as components of the Imperial Rule Assistance Association (IRAA), the massive new body with which the state replaced or replicated those groups.[5] Local administrations were caught up in the web the IRAA wove, tying together citizens, political parties, block associations, and farmers' groups. As mayor of Sekishiba, Satō Sakichi became a functionary of the IRAA almost by default. Other choices were more personal; in 1941 Yabe Zenbei was appointed to a high office in the Fukushima branch of the IRAA. He reportedly fulfilled his duties with characteristic enthusiasm and energy, and eventually his efforts took him to Tokyo, where he served the Home Ministry briefly at the end of the war.[6]

Almost all potential sources of opposition to the state were co-opted. Once the parties, the unions, and many religious organizations publicly supported the state and the war effort, those that could not be silenced by the mere threat of punishment often became victims of a brutal police and military establishment bent on enforcing conformity and suppressing dissent. The boundaries between public and private, citizen and state, were first blurred and then redefined to create the appearance of the nation as family, willing and able to sacrifice itself in the name of the emperor.

Unlike Germany or Italy, two of her eventual allies in the war against the West, Japan possessed neither a mass movement nor leaders charismatic enough to act as the agents of this transformation. The absence of a coherent movement from below in support of a program of social and economic change has made it harder in Japan's case to explain how and why the country ended up so thoroughly mobilized, so stripped of the democratic practices that characterized the 1920s and, for a time, the 1930s. By way of explanation, it is clear that what Japan had instead of mass movements and charismatic leaders was a powerful state, a dexterous bureaucracy, and a military that was committed to winning at almost any cost. Instead of "fascism from below," Japan has thus often been described as a case of "fascism from above," which can be a useful way of thinking about developments in the late 1930s. Numerous studies describe the intellectual developments that accompanied these changes and the bureaucratic initiatives that gave them form.[7]

Part of what Sekishiba experienced in the late 1930s and early 1940s was simply a process of accommodation to demands and pronouncements from above. The Imperial Rule Assistance Association, conscription, rationing, and censorship required submission to—or, at best, cooperation with—directives from Tokyo. These and similar policies and practices clearly reflect the exercise of coercive power from the top down; Japanese scholars constantly and consistently refer to wartime "fascism" not because they've misunderstood the term all these years, but precisely because the state was able to achieve a degree of power and organizational reach that defies other labels. Although on one level Japan's political realities had relatively little directly in common with Nazi Germany or Mussolini's Italy, Japan in 1940 also did not much resemble the nation in 1920 or 1930. The changes in almost every aspect of the lives of Japan's citizens were substantive and directed toward goals that often look very much like fascism.[8]

At the same time that residents of villages like Sekishiba were accommodating themselves to the state's initiatives, however, they were also adapting many of the ideas and practices of revitalization to serve the needs of the wartime countryside. Not all the changes at the local level were the product of a passive acceptance of top-down directives. The rebuilding of the economy, the rejuvenation of village-level institutions and cooperative organizations, and the enthusiastic pursuit of social reforms were all features of the mobilized village, just as they had been of the "revitalized" community. Those continuities and others at the local level, between depression-era recovery efforts and the construction of a nation mobilized for total war, have important implications for our understanding of this period in Japan's modern history. To explore those continuities in Sekishiba, this part of the study deals primarily with the period 1937–1941, during which the countryside underwent a rapid mobilization of its economic, social, and political resources as the military pursued one war in China and prepared for another with the West.

There are two reasons for focusing on the early years of a war that continued until 1945. One is that the Economic Revitalization Campaign itself was brought to a close in early 1941; the local and national circumstances that had kept it going for so long no longer applied thereafter. The other reason is that many of the most important of the new policies affecting the rural economy and rural life were in place no later than the end of 1940. The exceptions are discussed below, but for the most part developments in the countryside after 1940 were built on foundations already in place and do not represent radical departures in either ideology or policy.[9]

The rest of this chapter examines Sekishiba's transition to mobilization from three perspectives. The first of these explores the connections between revitalization's attempts to restructure the local economy and the steps the village took to cope with war's demands on farmers and their families. Many of the methods associated with the village's recovery from the depression and the return of something like prosperity to the countryside were incorporated into the new wartime economy. The second perspective looks at the social mobilization of the village—namely, the adaptation of civic structures, local leaders, and some of the rhetoric of revitalization to the needs of the mobilized state. Emigration was another aspect of this process. Finally, a third perspective tries to place these developments within the broader context of the transformation of the countryside in modern Japan.

## Revitalization, the Rural Economy, and the Early Years of the War

The start of the war in China set in motion a slow unraveling of Japan's economy and polity. In hindsight the signs of collapse are unmistakable: the impossibly sanguine official estimates of how the conflict would progress in the field were matched only by equally overoptimistic assessments of the nation's ability to sustain a long and total war. Yet for many years both the domestic economy and the nation's social order seemed robust; the economy didn't come to a complete standstill until late 1944, and the social order remained, arguably, more or less intact at the time of surrender.

Until resources ran out, manufacturing and other areas of heavy industry grew to meet the military's apparently insatiable demand for more planes, ships, and munitions. Even agriculture reaped the rewards of the new economy, expanding and diversifying production to feed a growing and increasingly affluent consumer population. The state's efforts to maintain social order and assure domestic support for the war effort took shape early and met with little resistance. New campaigns sprang up to draw attention to heretofore neglected aspects of the moral and social lives of the average citizen and shape them to the needs of the state. Participation in these movements, as with the Economic Revitalization Campaign, was broad-based and often enthusiastic. It helped that many of the sentiments the campaigns in support of the war tapped into—including a mistrust of political parties at home and a belief in Japan's destiny abroad—reflected the values and attitudes of significant segments of the population. Sekishiba's farmers, for example, discovered that the mobilizing economy and their own local efforts at revitalization had a lot in common.

A third and final stage of the Economic Revitalization Campaign began at the end of 1938. The Central Committee for Farm Village Economic Revitalization was renamed the Agriculture and Forestry Planning Committee (Nōrin keikaku iinkai) in December 1938, a step that signaled a shift away from the promotion of general reforms and toward an almost exclusive focus on increasing the production of key crops.[10] Ministry directives issued in 1940 further strengthened the campaign's role as a manifestation of mobilization. These new guidelines described the modification of economic revitalization planning toward more production, tighter control over available resources (labor and fertilizer prominent among them), and a deepened commitment on the part of citizens to the war effort.[11]

At one level this was more of the same. The campaign had long advocated the rational application of labor and farm technology, and increased productivity was never far from local planners' minds. Precisely because of the groundwork laid by the campaign, the transition from economic recovery to economic mobilization in villages like Sekishiba was, at least initially, more one of degree than an abrupt change in direction. Productivity is a case in point. In Sekishiba, as in many other campaign communities, farmers had already demonstrated an ability to get more out of the land and their own labor than ever before. Mobilization demanded that they do even more with less, and for a while they did. The 1940 rice crop was the largest ever in Sekishiba and was achieved alongside a significant increase in yields of other crops as well. These results represent the culmination of several years of effort under the campaign and suggest the ease with which the campaign's methods and goals became mobilization's.

The mayor explicitly acknowledged the campaign's dual role early on, connecting the changes that the village was pursuing via the campaign to the benefits they brought to the war effort. Satō referred not only to improvements in harvest size but also to the important role that the community's restructured economic institutions were playing in helping mobilize all aspects of local society. He pointed to the industrial cooperative, the hamlet associations, and other groups as having made the village more efficient in its use of labor, fertilizer, and other resources.[12] The mayor harbored few doubts that the campaign would respond to the nation's new needs as effectively as it had to those created by the depression.[13]

One of the problems confronting villages—and thus the state—by the late 1930s was that, after several years of excess labor in the countryside (sustained in part by the large numbers of unemployed men and women who returned to their home villages in the early years of the depression), it had become more and more difficult to keep able-bodied workers on the farm. Factory employment was an increasingly popular alternative to farm work. In 1930, almost 1.9 million Japanese worked in factories of five or more employees, but by 1940 more than 4.4 million did—almost two and a half times as many.[14] Farmers represented 49 percent of the workforce in 1930, only 42 percent in 1940. While most of the new manufacturing jobs were the result of workers leaving other non-farm sectors, it was nevertheless obvious that the factories were a drain on rural villages. In absolute terms, there were more than 0.5 million fewer farmers in 1940 than there had been in 1935, as compared to almost 2 million new workers in the secondary manufacturing sector.[15]

Long-standing patterns of part-time factory employment for rural males were beginning to break down as the industrial economy heated up. In the past, *dekasegi* (work away from home) practices of seasonal factory labor had brought in needed cash during the off-season for farming. What was happening as the war in China dragged on was different. Male factory workers outnumbered female for the first time in 1935, and heavy industry's share of factory employment surpassed light industry's by the end of 1938.[16] More and more men were leaving the village and not coming back. For them the transition to factory labor and urban life was a permanent one, with obvious consequences for the countryside. In 1930, 43 percent of the agricultural workforce was male, but men made up only 36 percent of it by 1940, and less than 30 percent by 1944.[17] This loss of able-bodied males clearly threatened substantial reductions in farm productivity. As successful as the introduction of labor-saving machinery had been in the late 1930s, its pace slowed as the war drew more and more production to military use. Eventually, dwindling fuel and parts supplies put even existing machines out of commission.

Some of the steps that the state took to overcome these problems built on methods already in use by the Economic Revitalization Campaign. Cooperative, community-based solutions to shortages were strongly encouraged. From 1939 on, Sekishiba's Economic Revitalization Committee, for example, was charged with making sure that families facing labor shortages were supplied with extra help when they needed it most.[18] Better coordination among the local farming organizations—also a product of campaign reforms—made such adjustments feasible. Similarly, the careful record-keeping, economic planning, and resource management associated with the campaign allowed authorities to keep a close watch on the economy at the village, hamlet, and household levels. The ability of the state and of local communities to monitor and control economic practices was clearly enhanced by the Economic Revitalization Campaign.

Although the actual rationing of rice and other farm products didn't get under way nationally until 1942 (earlier in the major cities), steps were taken before then to tighten controls over the distribution of many items. Responsibility for many of the efforts to control key commodities in the countryside fell on those local institutions that had benefited most from campaign reforms. The industrial cooperatives, the agricultural associations, and hamlet-level farming unions all played key roles in facilitating local economic mobilization. The state turned to these better, bigger institutions to control the distribution of commodities like fertilizer and rice.

Many of the chemicals that went into store-bought fertilizer were imported, a practice that became harder to maintain as the international situation deteriorated. By the late 1930s, the state found it necessary to divert resources that would have gone into domestic fertilizer production to military use, which meant that overall fertilizer supplies were bound to decrease. Distribution controls on fertilizer were established on a temporary basis in 1937 and made permanent two years later.[19]

Concern over the size of the rice supply also led to greater involvement of the industrial cooperatives in farmers' lives. The 1939 drought in Korea sharply reduced rice imports from that source, and the 1940 domestic harvest was itself generally poor. In the autumn of that year, regulations went into effect putting the cooperatives in charge of collecting most of the available domestic rice, which they would then turn over to the state for distribution to consumers.[20] In 1941 the Agricultural Production Control Ordinance (Nōgyō seisan tōsei rei) established production levels, material allocations, and a variety of other controls on farm production, all administered locally by the agricultural association.[21]

As channels of goods and information, the local cooperatives, unions, and even the agricultural association were unsurpassed in their utility. As agents for the state, they enforced government regulations and quotas and saw to it that the right crops were produced at the right times and sent to the right destinations. Their efficiency at these tasks and to some extent the state's faith in their ability to carry them out were products of post-depression revitalization efforts. The cooperatives and agricultural associations, and the hamlet-level unions as well, had come into their own during recovery from the crises of the early 1930s and drew on that expertise during the crises later in the decade. Although one thread in Japanese scholarship has argued that the military and bureaucrats deliberately strengthened these groups precisely because of the important roles they would play in the new age of total war, a more useful observation might simply be that the economic imperatives of recovery from the depression and those associated with mobilization for war were never that different.[22]

Both sets of crises seemed to demand community-wide participation and coordination, total commitment, and a careful balancing of individual needs against the greater needs of the community. These qualities were, of course, much more sharply outlined and coercively applied during the war than at any time during recovery from the depression. Economic revitalization had been voluntary; nothing punitive happened to villages or to families that chose not to participate. Economic mobilization was different: by the early 1940s there was little that was voluntary about it. Mobilization eventually replaced revitalization's efforts to negotiate a better relationship with the burgeoning consumer economy with draconian measures to keep production on track.

By the time the state abandoned its reliance on existing, depression-era rural institutions in favor of a complete overhaul of the system, the war was all but over. The 1943 decision to create a single body, an Agricultural Organization (Nōgyōkai), out of all the major village-level farm associations effectively dismantled several decades of institution-building in the village. At the same time, however, the establishment of the Agricultural Organization can also be understood as the culmination of a process that began with the formation of Economic Revitalization Committees. Policymakers invoked some of the same language to describe the purpose of the newly unified Nōgyōkai as they had when revitalization was first discussed. The Nōgyōkai, they claimed, would provide leadership to the village's farmers, improve efficiency, facilitate communication, and bring stability to a potentially unstable countryside, all goals familiar to veterans of the campaign.[23] (Sekishiba's Nōgyōkai offered another type of continuity between depression-era reforms and wartime practices: many of its members were themselves veterans of the revitalization committees.)

Much like the revitalization committees, the Agricultural Organizations were designed to coordinate the efforts of local farmers and do away with institutional rivalries within the community. Unlike the revitalization committees, however, the Agricultural Organization could be much more coercive in its pursuit of the state's mandates.[24] Where the Revitalization Campaign encouraged diversification and the pursuit of cash crops, mobilization ordinances and the Nōgyōkai increasingly restricted farmers' ability to choose what they planted and what they did with their crops once harvested.[25]

The economic mobilization of the village for war—namely, the use of existing local institutions to enforce directives on rationing, production, and labor—didn't require any significant reworking of the methods of revitalization. The frameworks of planning, institutional coordination, and the community as the fundamental building block of prosperity, all of which were so important to revitalization, were readily adapted to the needs of the new wartime regime. What this meant in practice was that local farmers could be active participants in their community's revitalization, in its mobilization, and in the prosecution of the war at the same time. Revitalization had urged Sekishiba's residents to think of their labor and their production as part of a greater, community-wide and ultimately national effort in which rational action and hard work were prerequisites for prosperity. As one time of crisis gave way to another, farmers found themselves called upon to pursue similar goals.

Revitalization appealed to many local farmers because it promised a better future, one in which rural society was as modern and prosperous as the rest of the country. Nothing about mobilizing the village's productive capacity to support the war effort at first challenged these goals. As the mayor had insisted, revitalization meshed nicely with the needs of wartime; there was no sharp break between one set of practices and the other. Supporting mobilization didn't require that farmers turn back the clock and passively accept a reversal of fortune. Quite the contrary, the similarities between economic revitalization and the mobilization of the local economy were such that citizens could participate in the latter with the same enthusiasm they had shown for the former. The incentives for farmers to do so were not abstract; they and their families were considerably better off in 1939 than they had been at the start of the decade, and local administrations, at least, attributed their newfound good fortune to the practices and ideas associated with the Economic Revitalization Campaign. In the early years of the war, it was still possible to plan for a better future.

## Mobilizing the Village

The economy wasn't the only thing reshaped by the conflict in China and preparations for a broader war. From the mid-1930s on, village civic life was the target of a series of state and semi-private campaigns to remind citizens of their duties and of the consequences of not living up to their (growing) responsibilities as imperial subjects. The Election Purification Campaign is one example, the National Spiritual Mobilization Campaign (Kokumin seishin sōdōin undō), a product of the 1937 Konoe cabinet, another.[26] Under its auspices, propaganda about the war's goals and the glories of service to the nation flowed from the government, and promises to work harder, save more, and spend less were offered up by communities across the country in response.

Sekishiba's commitment to the movement bears a striking resemblance to its approach to the Economic Revitalization Campaign, and more specifically to its reforms of daily life. Sekishiba's guidelines for the National Spiritual Mobilization Campaign covered a wide range of social activities, including when to make neighborly visits and what to do at weddings, funerals, and other ceremonial occasions. Villagers were urged to recycle, to repair their clothes, and to cut down on drinking and smoking, all in support of the war effort. While little was proposed that the village hadn't already woven into its Economic Revitalization Plan three years before, the government no longer relied solely on local initiative and enthusiasm to carry the day. The option not to be enthusiastic was less and less available to citizens after 1937.[27]

The village's announcement in late 1938 that it would devote a week in December to a better understanding of "the nation's policies and the importance of economic warfare at this juncture" offers another example of how the state's messages reached a wide audience. The main goals of the week's program of lectures and instruction were to get residents to sharply restrict their end-of-the-year celebrating (and to send out fewer New Year's cards), to spend as little money as possible, and to save as much of their income as they could.[28] These were all noble goals, and again all very much in keeping with the tenets of the Economic Revitalization Campaign. There was little there that villagers were not already familiar with. However, the state's dictates and efforts at indoctrination, which were many even before 1937 and voluminous thereafter, reached Sekishiba's residents through new channels, ones that hadn't existed before the campaign created them.

Hamlet assemblies are a case in point. Sekishiba held the meetings once a month in each hamlet beginning in 1934; they were attended by at least one person from each household and often by several family members. Designed to support the Revitalization Campaign and promote cooperation within the hamlet, the assemblies also served as important routes for state-sponsored instruction and inspiration. Although records of what was talked about at the assemblies in Sekishiba are missing for the period from September 1936 to late December 1937, it is clear that their tone and subject matter after the start of the war in China differed in significant ways from what had come before. Until the late summer of 1936, meetings had commonly featured lectures by the mayor and others on a variety of subjects related to revitalization, economic planning, and Hōtoku teachings.

Although these topics did not disappear entirely after July 1937, they were joined by discussions that reflect the growing importance of mobilization. The new topics were both instructional and inspirational. Attendees heard lectures about the situation in China, discussed campaigns to promote savings to assist in the war effort, and reviewed air-raid drill procedures. By the end of the decade, it was common for assemblies to include lectures about the proper channels for the distribution of fertilizer, rice, and other controlled items. To these regulatory issues, Mayor Satō, the local elementary school principal, and others added discussions on topics ranging from "The Yamato Race and the Japanese Spirit" (June 1938) and "Spiritual Mobilization" (November 1938, August 1939) to "The Warriors of Aizu" (October 1941) and "Japan Surrounded" (January 1939).[29] Hōtoku-inspired lectures, some of them given by Yabe Zenbei, remained a regular feature of these meetings as well.[30]

We have no way of knowing whether these talks were quiet reflections or bellicose ranting, but it is clear that they reflect themes not present in the early years of the assemblies. It is interesting, too, that from 1937 onward, a local policeman was a regular attendee and frequent guest lecturer at the assemblies. In his earliest appearances he offered comments on clean elections, but in time he expanded his repertoire to include lectures on air-raid drills, crime prevention, and economic regulations.[31] His presence was new, and another sign of how the structures and methods associated with revitalization were being used to facilitate the war effort.[32]

Sekishiba developed another new channel between the state, the local administration, and village residents. The first issue of the new monthly village paper, the *Sekishiba sonpō* was released in January 1938 (see Fig. 9). Publication continued until at least April 1944.[33] A typical two-page issue featured a variety of local news items, official announcements, and the occasional human-interest column. (The latter usually consisted either of letters from local schoolchildren to village soldiers or edited letters from soldiers to correspondents back home. One of the newspaper's goals was to help bridge the distance between soldiers at the front and the hometown, so the village made every effort to send issues out to servicemen.) The newspaper replicated some of the information presented in the hamlet assemblies, in that it provided schedules of upcoming meetings, outlines and straightforward explanations of important agricultural policies, and results of the village administration's own surveys on a number of topics. By bringing together in one public document lists and explanations of all the policies and programs in which the village participated, the *Sonpō* provided a tangible expression of the many ways in which the community was seeking its own improvement, and the many ways in which the future might be a step up from the past. It is telling that as the war dragged on, the newspaper was increasingly dominated by long lists of new regulations, descriptions of proscribed behaviors, and exhortations to save more, work harder, and serve more conscientiously.[34]

Not unlike the hamlet assemblies, the paper thus provided another conduit between the government and farm households, one that acted through the mediating filter of a village-wide institution. The newspaper was devoted to Sekishiba; it offered no insights into what was happening in other villages, and much as the Economic Revitalization Campaign had tried to do, it

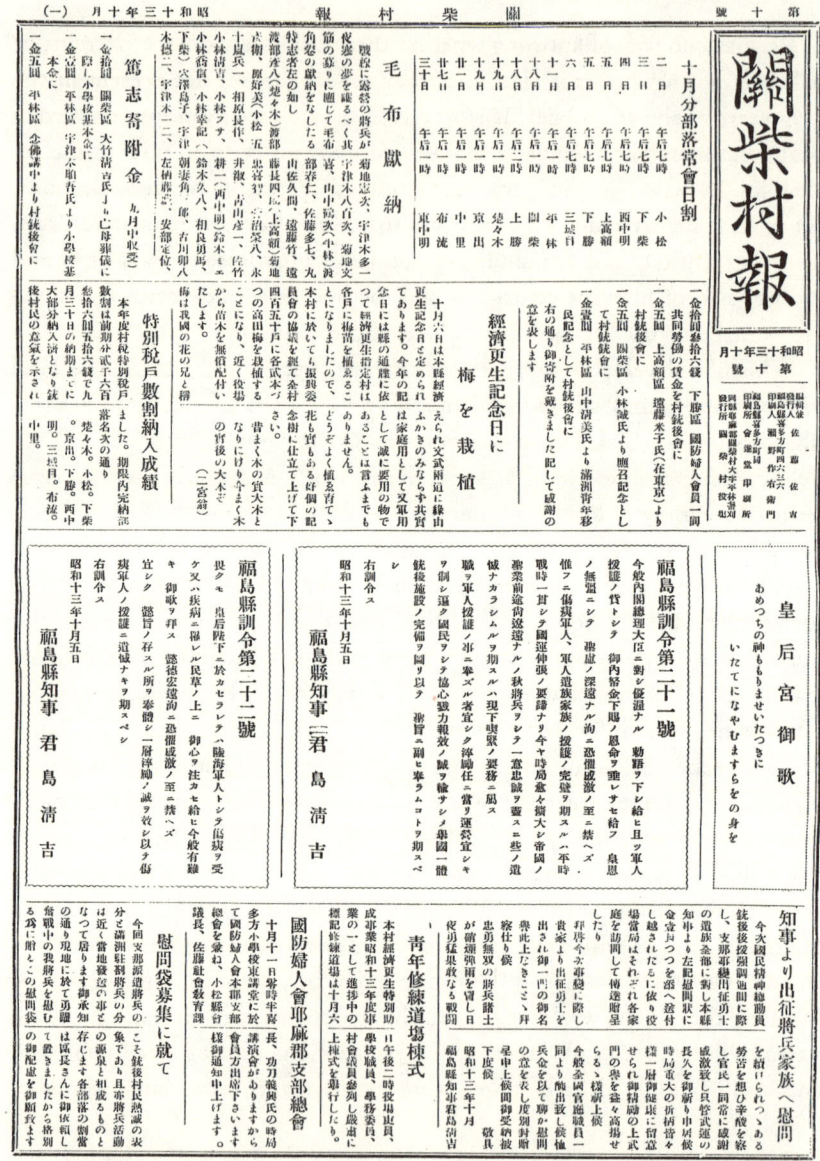

Fig. 9 Sekishiba's monthly village newspaper, the *Sekishiba sonpō*, October 1938 (SOURCE: Sekishiba village documents, Office for the Compilation of Municipal History, Kitakata City).

focused local activism and energy within the community. The *Sekishiba sonpō* reminded readers of their responsibilities to the village, of their village's importance to the nation, and, ultimately, of their dual role as citizens of the village and citizens of a nation at war.

## Village Mainstays

One of the campaign's effects on village life was to broaden the definition of who could and should participate in the village's revitalization; another was to provide opportunities to do so. These changes have some interesting implications. Unlike earlier efforts at reform (the Local Improvement movement, for example), the focus in the 1930s was clearly—and more successfully—on involving as many households as possible in the efforts at recovery. Where local landlords had once been the channels through which ideas and practices about reform and improvement had reached the countryside, the campaign modified this approach in favor of one that sought out a different constituency. Signs of this intent are evident in policies to strengthen the industrial cooperatives and other bodies led primarily by farmer-producers and are perhaps clearest in the state's program to find and train local "village mainstays" (*chūken jinbutsu*) in conjunction with the Economic Revitalization Campaign. That practice took on added importance after Special Assistance funding became available, and that continued until the campaign's end.[35]

The campaign encouraged villages to seek out potential leaders. Without local leadership, villages seemed doomed to just muddle along. With it, anything was possible, but it was no easy task to come up with knowledgeable, reliable individuals. Sekishiba addressed this concern by applying part of its Special Assistance funding toward identifying and training village mainstays.

The most important of these training efforts was Sekishiba's practice of sending local people to attend lecture courses sponsored by the Dai Nihon Hōtoku Society. Three people went in 1936, and local planners hoped that at least one person from each hamlet would eventually have the chance to go. By 1939, ten residents had attended the lectures.[36] Many more went to local seminars and lectures, and hamlet assemblies regularly featured attendees' reports on their experiences. The village also arranged for other types of instruction.

In their description of how the Special Assistance funding would be used, planners stated that they would send two young people each year to the Farmers' Training Centers (Nōmin dōjō) for training as village leaders. There were two centers in Fukushima that fit that description, and the village had plans to send students to both. The first was the Yabukigahara Training Farm (Yabukigahara shūren nōba) in Nishi-shirakawa county, and the other was the Aizu Mountain Village Hall (Aizu sanson dōjō) in Arakai village, Minami-Aizu county.[37] In 1937, the principal of the local high school and the agricultural association technician both attended "Economic Recovery Leader Training Lectures" at the Yabukigahara location. Over the next two years, the village sent others for training both there and possibly at the Aizu school as well.[38]

The campaign's emphasis on coordination and cooperation among a given village's economic and social institutions has been described by many scholars as an important stepping-stone into positions of power for many young farmers, precisely because it valued the skills and knowledge they brought to the effort to reform the community.[39] The growth of organizations like the industrial cooperative at the local level facilitated this process because it allowed younger, technically competent men to play a greater role in shaping their communities than had been possible in the past. This process was under way before 1937 and continued as the boundaries between revitalization and mobilization grew fainter and fainter. Training programs like those described above facilitated the rise of a new group of leaders as well. As Ōkado Masakatsu has argued, the people whom the Ministry of Agriculture tended to identify as "mainstays" were relatively young officeholders within the village and technically trained. Those qualities heretofore had not always been sufficient to gain access to local decisionmaking. In the context of the late 1930s, however, it was precisely those qualities that the village and the state sought to identify and nurture in its leaders.[40] The new faces that had begun to lead the community during one time of crisis—the depression—became the local faces of mobilization in another time of crisis—the war.

Sekishiba's Economic Revitalization Committee offers one example of the transition. In 1939, changes in the campaign gave the committee a wide variety of new tasks. "Under the present situation," the new rules governing its role in the village read, the committee would take jurisdiction "over matters related to general planning for increasing the production of significant foodstuffs, over the distribution of materials necessary for the production of those foodstuffs, and over the regulation of the supply of labor."[41] These were new responsibilities for the committee, which in its earlier incarnation had been charged only with "planning for the economic revitalization of farm households."

With the new responsibilities came a new organizational structure and new members. There had been four subdivisions in the original committee: General Affairs, Production, Economics, and Edification (see Chapter 9 above). None was part of the committee after 1939. Five new subdivisions took their place: The Economic Revitalization section was responsible for overseeing coordination between the other parts of the committee and for general planning; the Production Planning section was responsible for boosting the production of important food and farm products; and the Fertilizer Distribution Control and the Materials Distribution Control sections had obvious roles, as did the Labor Supply Regulation section of the revamped committee.

New rules dictated who would serve on the committee. The schoolteachers, the "honored farmers," the variety of choices that had characterized the older committee were missing. Their replacements were selected from the ranks of the hamlet heads and leaders of the farming associations—in other words, from those closest to the practice of farming and to hamlet residents. (The only exceptions to this rule were Mayor Satō, the assistant mayor, the school principal, and the head of the industrial cooperative.) Such qualities were becoming more and more important as the war effort robbed the village of people, farm animals, and access to necessities. By 1939, Sekishiba had lost a number of men to the military and to factory work away from the village. One of the roles of the new committee, in fact, was finding the labor needed to keep the farms going. (Mayor Satō reported that they were turning increasingly to the women's organizations in the village to provide the extra help.)[42] Appointing the heads of the hamlet and farm associations to coordinate these efforts made sense, given what they were being asked to do.[43]

Of the thirty-two people who served on the new version of the committee, fewer than half can be identified as having served on the original one. Of those who continued to serve, only a few held positions of power within the committee structure. Satō and his assistant were both veteran members, but only one of the five new section chiefs had also been on the committee when it was first formed. It may well be that the original members were replaced not as a matter of choice but of necessity. Some may have been conscripted, and others may have left to find industrial employment. Without ruling out a certain degree of randomness in the changing makeup of the committee, there are some interesting developments that suggest a more calculated process of selection, one that fostered the middling, mainstay farmers.

The original 1934 committee represented the middle and upper ranks of the village's farmers, bringing together a mix of landlord farmers, owner farmers, and a handful of members with very little land of their own. The committee in 1939 retained a similar cross-section of the village, in that it included at least one large landlord-farmer (Odagiri Yōgo) and others with smaller but still substantial holdings (such as the mayor). In looking at the new members, however (and within the limits imposed by complicated land records), it appears that committee membership was shifting slightly downward on the economic scale, toward the middle range of landholders.[44] In both the 1934 and 1939 committees, eleven members owned less than 1 *chō* of paddy land. In 1934, however, ten of the twenty-three members for whom landownership could be established owned 2 or more *chō* of paddy land, whereas in 1939 only seven did (and no one on that committee owned more than 10 *chō*, as one member had in 1934). There were six members of the 1939 committee with holdings between 1 and 2 *chō*, the proximate range of the middling farmer; in 1934 there had only been two. Among the twenty-two "new" members of the 1939 committee, I was able to estimate landholdings for fifteen; of the ten veteran members, I could do the same for eight. The average holding of the fifteen newcomers was 1.5 *chō*, compared to 2.3 *chō* for the veterans. Thus the average landholding of the 1939 committee was only 1.7 *chō*—half a *chō* less than the 1934 average of 2.2.[45]

The new committee had another quality that distinguished it from its predecessor: its members were younger. The average age of committee members in 1934 was forty-eight; five years later, despite the presence of twelve members from that original committee, the average age dropped to forty-five. The new committee members had an average age of forty-one, and thus were considerably more youthful than the veterans, who were on average fifty-three years old in 1939.[46] A useful comparison is with the village council, which was experiencing a similar though less pronounced change. The average age for council members fell from fifty-three in 1933 to fifty-two in 1937 and fifty in 1942, suggesting that some of the same factors were at work there as are evident in the Economic Revitalization Committee.

The trend toward more access by younger, middle-ranking farmers to positions of importance in the campaign, and in the village more generally, continued during mobilization in Sekishiba. There were limits to how far the transformation went; at no point was the existing local leadership threatened with complete replacement. Rather, the changes were gradual but substantive, reflecting the growing importance in several venues of one's status as a producer, one's training, and one's ability to function as a representative of hamlet farmers and their interests.

These developments in Sekishiba were more than matched by similar changes in villages throughout Japan. In a series of village case studies, Japanese scholars have demonstrated the rise to prominence of younger, middling farmers and have documented their impact on rural society. Young farmers took on new roles as leaders of local industrial cooperatives and other farmers' unions, as well as important positions within revitalization committees and even village councils. Mori Takemaro's study of Haga village in Gumma; Nishida Yoshiaki's extensive analysis of Nishi-shioda in Nagano; Nakamura Masanori's work on Urazato, also in Nagano; and Ōkado Masakatsu's work in Nagano and elsewhere—all point to the growing role that owner farmers, owner-tenant farmers, and others who fell within the "mainstay" category played locally.[47]

These developments were somewhat less pronounced in Sekishiba, and in the northeast more generally, than they were in Nagano.[48] Landlord authority, the lag in the commercialization of agriculture in the northeast, and the region's insulation from the social activism that was popular elsewhere help account for the comparatively mild changes in Sekishiba. In all these communities, however, the shifting pattern of power is one of the features that distinguishes the period after the depression from what came before. The agendas that the new local leaders helped promote in their new roles speak to their deep involvement in both revitalization and, eventually, the mobilization of rural society. And although the evidence of change is most pronounced in regions where sericulture's collapse produced some of the sharpest social and economic dislocations of the era, the broader trend is clearly national in scope.

The significance of the rise of the middling farmer in Sekishiba and elsewhere lies in several areas. First, it suggests that by the late 1930s it was the middling farmer who had become the focal point of many of the state's efforts to shape rural society. The Economic Revitalization Campaign's efforts to identify and train village mainstays are examples of how this manifested at the local level; as previous discussions have suggested, the campaign provided many others as well. After 1937, the state also began to intervene more directly in relationships between landowners, tenants, and the market for rice. These policies are another thread tying depression-era reforms to wartime mobilization, to the postwar countryside, and to middle-level farmers. At the same time that the campaign was opening doors for these farmers, new policies worked in other ways to encourage the formation of a secure, productive, landowning cultivator.

In 1926, the state began providing assistance for farmers who wanted to buy land of their own (or stay on land they owned but risked losing). The Ministry of Agriculture's "Regulations on Aid for the Establishment and Maintenance of Owner-Cultivators" inaugurated what was in essence a low-interest loan program for would-be buyers. Successful applicants to the program could borrow at a 3.5 percent interest rate, to be repaid over twenty-four years. The problem with the state's initiative, according to Nishida Yoshiaki, was that the formulas used to determine the purchase price of the land almost invariably placed it out of reach of the typical tenant. The price was set so as to guarantee a good return for the landlord, so it was seldom low enough to make purchase economical or even feasible for a tenant. And even though the number of participants in the program more than doubled between 1926 and 1932, neither the amount of land sold nor the number of families buying it was enough to make a significant dent in the tenancy problem.[49] Minor revisions to the plan in late 1937, shortly after the outbreak of the war in China, had little effect on its popularity.

It wasn't until the state took a series of steps after 1937 to ensure that farm production remained stable that the prospects for buyers improved. The Farmlands Adjustment Law (Nōchi chōsei hō) of 1938 was followed by regulations that reduced or capped rents.[50] In 1940 the state made it possible for tenants to send all their rice (except what they needed for their own use) directly to the government. The passage of the Food Control Act in 1942 made this mandatory. A dual pricing structure for rice also got its start here; in practice, this system paid landlords a much lower cash value for rent rice than its tenant-producers received.[51]

In conjunction with other limitations imposed on the transfer of land and on the unilateral termination of tenancy contracts, landlords were in an increasingly poor position as the war continued. As a recent work on the war and Occupation eras in Saitama prefecture has illustrated, by the end of the war rents had become a negligible expense for those families who rented land, while land had lost all but a fraction of its value for landlords. As a result, land reform was in some ways much less important to farmers than issues surrounding production quotas and food distribution. By 1946, those policies had the potential to affect a farm household's economic position to an extent that the transfer of land no longer possessed.[52] The state's desire to stabilize production at all costs had enabled bureaucrats to take steps that would have been politically unfeasible only a few years before.

In 1943 the policies to establish owner-cultivators were changed again, this time in a way that offered something new to potential buyers. The revisions included changes in how the purchase price of land was calculated, reflecting the controls that the state had placed on land prices. For the first time the program offered potential buyers the chance to purchase land at a reasonable price. Roughly 15,000 households had participated in the Owner-Cultivator Establishment program in 1943. The following year, under the new rules almost 80,000 did so. In the last year of the war, the final count was 155,122 households, and in 1946, before land reforms made the program irrelevant, the number exceeded 241,000.[53]

The direction of these policies was clear. Even if planners in the Ministry of Agriculture did not deliberately set out to undermine the economic position of landlords, the net effect was precisely that. In reaching out to middling farmers as a means of maintaining both farm production and rural stability, the state created numerous opportunities for them to reshape local society.[54] But that wasn't all. From 1937 on, revitalization, mobilization, and the middling farmer came together in one other effort to reconstruct the countryside: emigration.

## Emigration and Revitalization

Fukushima was the third largest source of emigrants to Manchuria in the 1930s and early 1940s among all of Japan's prefectures; Nagano was far and away the leader, and Yamagata a distant second.[55] By mid-1945, more than three hundred thousand Japanese were part of organized efforts to create emigrant communities in Manchuria. The earliest settlers began arriving not long after the Kwantung Army established the Manchukuo puppet state in 1932, but the movement of people in earnest didn't begin until after 1936.

That year, both the Kwantung Army and the Hirota cabinet announced ambitious, long-term plans to populate Manchuria with Japanese emigrants. The cabinet's policy proposal called for the recruitment and dispatch of a hundred thousand households between 1937 and 1942.[56] In 1938, the Economic Revitalization Campaign adopted emigration to Manchuria as an important new policy and began actively promoting it as part of its package of rural reforms. The state was still encouraging its citizens to begin a new life in Manchuria late in 1945.[57]

Emigration served many needs. It fed the nation's sense of its destiny in Asia and provided useful parallels with the colonial and emigrant practices of the other world powers. There were strategic benefits, though these proved more imagined than real. Kwantung Army planners favored placing groups of settlers in remote areas, often deliberately locating new communities in harm's way. In doing so, the army hoped to provide an extra layer of defense against local insurgents and possibly even Soviet troops in contested hinterlands and thus to supplement its own resources with civilian "soldiers." The young and able-bodied were highly favored, and special recruitment programs for the Young Volunteers for the Development of Manchuria and Mongolia (Manmō kaitaku seishōnen giyūgun) drew large numbers of candidates. Although in theory those chosen were between the ages of sixteen and nineteen, as Sandra Wilson points out, "many, perhaps most, were actually fifteen or sixteen."[58]

Emigration, and specifically emigration to Manchuria, was also held out as a solution to the countryside's problems of overpopulation and insufficient farmland. This argument had a powerful popular appeal and many articulate proponents. Tokyo University professor Nasu Hiroshi and professor emeritus Yahagi Eizō both tendered strong academic support for emigration as a tool to relieve overpopulation and free up farmland on the home islands; other scholars and officials eventually added their voices in favor of emigration.[59] Katō Kanji, the well-known agrarianist ideologue and educator, spoke out early and often on the virtues of creating ideal rural communities in Manchuria. Not only would the plentiful and fertile land (which Katō insisted was there for the taking) allow transplanted farmers in Manchuria to realize their dreams of self-sufficiency, landownership, and true communal harmony, but every farmer who left made it that much easier for those who stayed behind to achieve the same dreams.[60] Such arguments drove the decision to make emigration part of the Economic Revitalization Campaign's toolbox of reforms.

For campaign planners, emigration served many purposes. In advocating the relocation of many families at once, or the creation of "branch villages" in Manchuria, the campaign noted the benefits that would accrue to the original community. Because there would be less competition over scarce farmland, went the explanation, more farmers would have the opportunity to maintain themselves as landowning producers. Tenancy and the many problems associated with it would no longer weigh villages down; farmers would finally have access to plots of land large enough to be farmed efficiently and productively. Indeed, one key component of emigration's appeal to campaign planners was that it, too, supported revitalization's efforts to nurture "village mainstays"—namely, the middling farmers and local leaders who were increasingly the focus of the campaign.

Emigration was tied to the campaign's support of village mainstays in at least two ways. The first was that emigration furthered local prospects for the creation of independent landed farmers by encouraging marginal farmers to leave. Their departure would allow more efficient use of available local resources—land foremost among them. Productivity would rise as the average farm expanded to a size closer to the ideal for the region, and those farmers left on the land would reap the benefits, particularly the middling farmers who were favored to take control of the newly available acreage. The end result would be a stable, more prosperous community that was that much closer to revitalization's ideal village.

One could also argue that it was in the relocated branch villages that campaign planners, and presumably some farmers, saw the best opportunity to realize the ideals long held out by the campaign. A carefully planned economy, a higher degree of self-sufficiency, and a place for rationality, modern methods, and cooperative enterprise to flourish remained just out of reach in many villages, but who was to say that they wouldn't be easily realized in Manchuria? Among the key targets of recruitment for emigration were precisely those people who could make this happen. In Yamagata, for example, planners were quite explicit about this, identifying "those who in the future might become the mainstays of the relocated community" as their top choice for recruitment. Farmers with little or no land were third on the list, after those with special technical skills.[61]

The campaign's emigration initiative was oddly timed, coming as it did so soon after the start of the war on the mainland. Not only did the China conflict increase the already considerable risks facing settlers in Manchuria, but it drove the resurgent industrial sector to an even higher pitch of productivity. As suggested previously, the expansion of the domestic economy began to pull people out of the countryside and into cities and factories at a faster and faster pace after 1937. Manchuria's appeal—and its efficacy as a solution to the countryside's problems—declined accordingly, and few aspects of the emigration program met with success. The 69,822 households dispatched to Manchuria by May 1945 represented less than a quarter of the government's original goal and only 1.2 percent of the nation's farm households.[62] The situation in Manchuria for those who did go, as many settlers were no doubt shocked to discover, was far from what they had been led to expect. Conditions were often primitive and brutal, the prospects for productive farming always in doubt. Whatever revitalization's appeal might have been at home, there were few opportunities to create the ideal rural society that Katō and others had envisioned for Manchuria.

Some sense of both the early enthusiasm for emigration and its later decline can be had in Sekishiba's experiences and those of nearby communities. Fukushima announced its plans in support of emigration in July 1937, coincidentally within days of the outbreak of fighting in China. Over the next five years, prefectural officials promised, 55 villages would dispatch 2,502 households to Manchuria; 296 would leave in 1937 alone.[63] Sekishiba was one of the villages chosen to participate and offered to send 33 farm families by the end of 1942.[64] Yabe Zenbei was one of several local leaders to actively promote emigration. Hamlet assemblies featured talks on the subject on many occasions in 1938 and 1939; in July 1940, Yabe himself reported on his recent visit to Manchuria. Later, in his capacity as an official of the IRAA in Fukushima, Yabe worked on plans to promote emigration, in part to fulfill his vision of a model "Aizu village" in Manchuria.[65]

As of March 1941, however, it was clear that Manchuria's appeal had been overestimated and that no community had been able to meet its promised quota of eager emigrants, least of all those that had set their sights high. The prefecture had stated that it would send more than 2,500 households; the official count in 1941 was the misleadingly high figure of 2,891—misleading because it included 2,001 Young Volunteers for the Development of Manchuria and Mongolia, each of whom was counted as the equivalent of a single household.[66] These young people certainly represented a powerful embrace of Manchuria's potential (and some degree of encouragement, if not coercion, by teachers and other figures of authority). Sekishiba alone sent seventeen Young Volunteers, more than any other village in the county. Their enthusiasm was not catching, however, since they were joined in Manchuria by only three Sekishiba families. This meant that, in terms of the people whom the campaign and the prefecture had originally hoped to send—namely, intact farm families—neither Sekishiba nor any other community in the county met its original goals. Sekishiba managed to send less than a tenth of its quota. The prefecture as a whole did slightly better, but even so, only 890 Fukushima households made it to Manchuria, or 36 percent of the 2,502 originally promised.[67]

Those who went had their lives changed forever. Those who stayed behind found that whatever Manchuria might have meant in the nation's collective imagination, their lives remained largely unaffected by the realities of emigration.

## Mobilization and the Modern Countryside

In 1939, Sekishiba was designated by the prefecture as a *kyōka*, or "moral suasion," village.[68] Being chosen as a *kyōka* community brought limited material benefit to the village but considerable public recognition. As one of only seven villages so designated in the entire prefecture, Sekishiba's reputation as a model community was clearly on the rise. Yet this wasn't just another honor among the many the village collected in the late 1930s: designation as a "moral suasion" village was not unlike designation as a participant in the Economic Revitalization Campaign, in that it brought with it a public commitment to specific goals that were to be attained through particular methods. As one description put it, "moral suasion" meant planning "for the creation of the ideal village, in which production and education, morals and economics are bound together as one."[69]

Little in the five-year plan that Sekishiba's administrators duly drew up would have been unfamiliar to the village's veterans of the campaign. For the next half decade, the village monitored its progress in terms of how many village mainstays were trained, the frequency with which regular village and hamlet meetings were held, and a series of other gauges of the village's community-building. By its own accounts, Sekishiba continued to work toward a more harmonious, productive, and organized community well after the depression and the Economic Revitalization Campaign were all but forgotten.[70]

It is surprising how much of the public dialogue of the late 1930s and early 1940s is about the intersection of the economy and everyday life and thus about the issues that recovery from the depression had highlighted in many communities. Sekishiba offers one example of this continued engagement in rural reform and revitalization, but there is no lack of other examples. *Ie no hikari* was, for a time, full of articles and letters to the editor describing ongoing struggles between the backward practices of the past and the forward-looking habits of the future. As one woman lamented in 1940, she came home from a three-week stay at the local agricultural training center only to be overwhelmed by the contrast between the orderly, disciplined life she had been living there and the lackadaisical, undisciplined existence she returned to in her village. Such wasteful attitudes, she complained, were what drove young people away from the countryside. Only the introduction of a more rational approach to the use of one's time and effort would prevent even more people (herself included?) from seeking a better life in the city, she wrote.[71] One wonders what Tachibana Kōzaburō, released from prison that year, would have made of the ongoing efforts to bring modernity to the countryside.

After 1941, such complaints and the possibilities they implied were less frequently voiced.[72] By then, *Ie no hikari*'s emphasis on moving forward on several fronts (the economy, rural health, rural education) had given way to increasingly desperate attempts simply to keep from losing ground. In the countryside, too, the sheer difficulty of just bringing in the crops supplanted in most instances any sustained attempts at change. The magazine, like its readers, had fewer and fewer choices about what to hope for.

Wartime attrition accounts in part for these changes, as shortages of labor and resources made daily life harder and long-term planning another foregone luxury. Perhaps more important, however, there can be no mistaking the brutality and sheer irrationality of much of what passed for civic life in wartime Japan. While this chapter has pointed to some of the more rational if not modern aspects of rural reform efforts in the early years of the war (and suggests more below), it is essential that we never lose sight of the bigger picture. That picture is one of a society in which dissent in almost any form was punishable by incarceration or worse, in which the emperor's word was unquestioned and unquestionable, and in which a rhetoric of race, fear, and conquest dictated one's response to ideas and peoples from elsewhere. As paradoxical as it may sound, those realities cannot easily be separated from the other themes that crop up again and again in discussions of rural society in this period—namely, rationality, science, discipline, and harmony.

Some of this conflation reflects the fact that revitalization's emphasis on community and on the development of a moral economy clearly had elements in common with the state's efforts to impose absolute conformity on its citizens through slogans like "a hundred million hearts beating as one." Recovery from the depression, as revitalization imagined it, was built on the premise of a conflict-free, cooperative village, united as farmers. Though few communities achieved such ideal conditions in practice, it is significant that, even in theory, prosperity and stability demanded the absence of dissent. Designation as a revitalization community, and certainly as a recipient of the much sought-after Special Assistance funding, was refused to those villages in which tenancy disputes or other overt signs of conflict were allowed to boil over. The clear message, in the wake of the depression, was that conflict jeopardized recovery and reform. If prosperity necessitated a denial of difference, it was but a small leap from there to the even more absolute denials that war required.

Similarly, some of the institutional changes that revitalization brought to the countryside handily facilitated transmission of the rhetoric of mobilization and, eventually, enforcement of the state's dictates. The bigger and stronger industrial cooperatives and agricultural association, the hamlet assemblies and Economic Revitalization Committee were easily adapted to helping the local economy mobilize. Villages drew on many of their existing organizations (often improved by revitalization planning) to see them through the early years of the war; as noted above, it wasn't until relatively late in the war that the state abandoned these long-standing arrangements in favor of a more streamlined structure.

Similarly, many of the methods that villages recovering from the depression employed were equally powerful tools in the mobilization of the economy and of local society. Economic planning, the use of household accounts, the pursuit of self-sufficiency, and so on are just a few of the examples of an approach to farm economics and daily life that rural reformers had advocated with some success since the early 1930s. It was precisely these methods that farmers were called on to employ in the service of the state and the emperor when war broke out.

The village mainstays and the rural middle class that they represent are a final element in this balancing act between the rational, forward-looking elements of rural life and the forces tending to pull the countryside back into an imagined past. Mainstays and the middle class were clearly at the center of both the Revitalization Campaign and later efforts at mobilization. In Sekishiba, there were continuities in terms both of the actual personnel involved and the more general attributes of those participating. Several residents closely connected with Sekishiba's (successful) revitalization went on to play a key role in mobilization as well; the mayor falls into this category, but he is certainly not the only one.

Since it also seems to be the case that middling farmers were playing an ever-widening role in village reform, both revitalization and mobilization can be understood in part as a reflection of their goals and ideals for the community. The local notables and landed elites obviously didn't disappear overnight, but their power and their ability to speak for the community's course were increasingly compromised in the 1930s. In their place, mainstays and middling farmers were more and more often the nexus between the state and the village, and between the village's past and its possible futures.

Modernity in the form of more rational and efficient behavior—and economic practices that promised an ever-increasing standard of living—appealed powerfully to the rural middle class.[73] Woven into the policies crafted to lift the countryside out of the depression, these qualities clearly resonated with bureaucrats and social reformers in Tokyo as well. That these qualities remained an element of the mobilized countryside should perhaps come as no surprise, even though they are seldom associated with the regimented, authoritarian image of wartime Japan. The persistence of the promise of modernity in some areas of daily and community life at a time when other aspects of Japan's polity and social landscape seemed to be moving in a very different direction may help explain the depths of popular support for Japan's wartime authoritarianism. From one time of crisis to the next, farmers, their families, and the people who spoke for them struggled to cope with the challenges of increasingly complex relationships among the state, local leaders, the modern (international) economy, agriculture, and an almost wholly urbanized nation. This same promise of modernity clearly locates both the wartime era and the countryside itself within Japan's broader transformations from rural to urban, farm to factory, and imperial to popular rule.

# 11   The Elusive Revitalized Village

*The Land of Milk and Honey* appeared in print again in 1968, republished by *Ie no hikari* for a new generation of readers. One wonders what they made of it. Ōshio village, since 1954 part of the larger amalgamated community of Kitashiobara, is now a land of neither milk nor honey. It has, instead, negotiated a separate peace with the rest of the nation, finding in golf courses, a theme park, and hot springs new answers to its old dilemmas.

Sekishiba's choices have been little different. It, too, became part of a larger community in the mid-1950s, merging with the town next door and six nearby villages to create Kitakata city. In the years since, residents of the former village and the new city have continued to grapple with many of the same questions that confronted farmers in the wake of the depression: how can farming flourish in a modern, developed economy? What place is there for the village, and the rural community more generally, in a modern, urban nation? This final chapter explores the evolving answers to those questions.

## Occupation Reforms

As clearly as the Great Depression had illuminated the many contradictions of the rural economy, revitalization alone had not been enough to overcome them. In trying to solve agriculture's problems without dealing with the fundamental issues of landownership and the tenancy system, the Economic Revitalization Campaign and the other reform measures of the 1930s and early 1940s stopped short of providing a workable solution to the crises in the countryside. Rather, they encouraged farmers to change some aspects of rural life while keeping others off-limits. Sekishiba's residents embraced the pursuit of a better standard of living through more rational production. They sought space in their lives for leisure and for a modern but not necessarily urban culture, but did so without the freedom to do something about the basic inequities of rural society. With tenancy and the limits imposed by the scarcity of farmland outside the reach of reform, revitalization could do only so much.

Wartime intervention into the landlord-tenant relationship and into the marketing of rice itself foreshadowed the transformation of the post-surrender countryside. By the end of the Pacific War, the dual pricing system for rice—in which producers (including tenants) received one price for what they grew and landlords received another, much lower price for the rice owed to them as rent—had already made landowning a much less profitable enterprise. Restrictions on changes in the status of farmland and on rents severely limited landlords' ability to wrest more from what they owned, while producers were increasingly empowered economically. Political empowerment was also on the horizon for owner farmers and even for some tenants, although as discussed previously, those changes were leisurely and tentative at best.

In other words, at the end of the war there were signs that landownership and the issues that stemmed from it, off-limits for so long, were finally within reformers' reach. At the village level, tenants like Nishiyama Kōichi in Niigata, emboldened by these developments, took matters into their own hands. As the war drew to a close, they negotiated large-scale purchases of farmland from landlords on reasonable terms and with the support of the state.[1] Other tenants in other communities did the same.[2] The groundwork was thus laid for a slow shift in patterns of landownership, for a gradual transformation of the ways tenants and landlords interacted, and thus for a much-needed addition to the developments that revitalization had helped foster.

The American occupiers had little patience for gradual transformations. Though there was considerable variation in Occupation officials' familiarity with the realities of Japanese rural life, there was an almost unanimous belief in the connections between rural impoverishment, landlord power, and militarism. As part of the Occupation's broader mandate to democratize and demilitarize defeated Japan, the countryside thus came under considerable scrutiny. Americans viewed the social and economic practices of the villages as a foundation of the military's power and as impediments to democracy.

Such understandings were based in part on policymakers' readings of translated Japanese scholarly works and on the writings of the handful of Western scholars familiar with farming and rural life in Japan, many of which emphasized the early modern, feudal characteristics of the prewar countryside. Occupation policymakers were also influenced by the propaganda of the wartime Japanese state and military, which had emphasized the countryside's importance to the war effort and made explicit the connections between rural society and the military.[3] U.S. officials were thus convinced that nothing short of radical change would eliminate the underlying threat that poor, backward rural communities posed to Japan's stability.

Land reform was the tool of choice for dealing with the countryside's many flaws.[4] In conjunction with the other components of Occupation reforms—particularly the democratization of some parts of civic life—American planners had high hopes for the benefits that land reform might bring. In the short term, improving the terms of tenancy or reducing its prevalence would boost agricultural productivity, a serious concern since Japan's former colonies were no longer supplying any of its food. In the long term, land reforms promised a more equitable distribution of wealth and power in the countryside.[5] A more prosperous countryside, reformers reasoned, would be less likely to support a militaristic government or to bend so easily to the state's will.

Even if the occupiers oversimplified the complex relationships between rural citizens and the state—and exaggerated the depth and nature of support for the military—the land reforms they eventually proposed to correct the flaws that concerned them most clearly built on developments already evident in the countryside. As Japanese scholars have been quick to point out, it was the Japanese government, not the occupying forces, who first proposed a version of land reform. These early proposals were limited in what they sought to accomplish and were not favorable to tenants. American policymakers responded with a far more sweeping and inclusive set of reforms, but it is nevertheless significant that the Occupation was able, in effect, to hasten and modify a process already under way.[6] These continuities between the pre- and post-surrender era, perhaps as much as the logic of the policies themselves, help explain land reform's considerable success and longevity.

The land reform in question had three components. The first enforced reductions in tenant rents and their conversion to cash payments (as opposed to transfers in kind). The wartime pricing system had to some extent laid the groundwork for this, but Occupation policies expanded on it. The result was extremely low rent levels relative to the value of tenants' crops, so that by 1949 landlords received only about 1 percent of the cash value of a harvest—far less than the 30 to 50 percent they had commonly received before the war.[7] Other provisions sharply limited landlords' ability to raise rents and to displace tenants from land that they farmed.

The second element of the reform was the creation of owner farmers. This process, too, had a pre-surrender precedent in the Owner-Cultivator Establishment program, which dated from the 1920s. That program had helped facilitate purchases of tenanted lands by the people farming them through low-interest loans (see Chapter 10 above). The Occupation-era approach differed from past practices in several respects. For one thing, it was compulsory where the pre-surrender program had been voluntary. Moreover, by establishing limits on the maximum allowable acreage for owner-cultivators and resident landlords and by doing away entirely with parcels owned by absentee landlords, the reforms forced the sale by August 1950 of more than 1 million *chō* of paddy fields and almost 800,000 *chō* of upland fields—roughly four-fifths of all tenanted land. Almost three-quarters of all farm households (2,341,000 landlords and more than twice as many tenant families) were involved.[8] None of the sales involved direct negotiations between owners and tenants, another difference from the older methods. Instead, local committees handled the designation and, eventually, the transfer of farmlands, while the prefectural governor took responsibility for the actual purchase and resale of the land.

Democratized land committees were the third component of the reforms. Wartime versions of the committees had been created to oversee the movement of land in and out of cultivation and to regulate rents; they had, however, generally been dominated by landlords and had lacked the authority to enforce sweeping changes, regardless of who was in the majority. The much more powerful Occupation-era committees were consistently weighted in favor of tenants, who made up five of the ten members, to the landlords' three and owner farmers' two.[9] With considerable skill, they managed the complicated business of determining which parcels would be sold to whom and at what prices. Landlord resistance to the process, which was especially marked in the northeast, ultimately meant very little.

It is hard to overestimate the effects of the land reforms. In Sekishiba, 47 percent of the land in the village was rented by tenants at the end of the war; by 1950, less than 8 percent was. The number of tenant households underwent a rapid and permanent decline as they joined the swelling ranks of owner farmers. Similar patterns are evident in Fukushima, in the rest of the northeast, and nationally.[10] The transformation of the countryside was as complete as it was rapid, at least as far as landownership went.[11] Almost overnight, tenancy as a social problem all but vanished, as did the burden of high rents and uncertain access to land for those who did continue to rent.

There were some unforeseen consequences of the reform. One of the concerns voiced at the time, and occasionally since, was that the reforms didn't go far enough to undermine landlord authority, which it was feared might well persist in many communities.[12] The reforms as written did not dispossess landowners; they were paid what in 1946 was a reasonable price for their land. This raised the possibility that former landlords might lose their land but not their wealth, thus retaining their status and power in the village. Unfortunately for landlords, however, skyrocketing postwar inflation and the fact that the government paid them for the land in bonds—not up front, in a lump sum of cash—meant that within a short time it was almost as if they had given the land away.[13] Whatever the money from the sale of the land might have been worth in 1946, it had lost most of its real value by the time the land transfers were complete. Landlords could do very little to prevent this, and many families watched their assets vanish almost overnight. What began as an attempt to redistribute land, and thus opportunity, ended up leveling the playing field in a variety of other ways as well.

The democratization process had some other early consequences for Sekishiba. Sweeping changes in the Constitution changed politics and civic life profoundly; mayors were popularly elected for the first time (as were prefectural governors—another first), women gained the vote, and village councils claimed more autonomy and authority than had ever been the case in the prewar era. Add to this the rise of a unified farmers' organization, the Nōkyō (Association of Agricultural Cooperatives), and it is clear that there were relatively few institutional continuities between the pre- and post-surrender countrysides. There was also a fairly sharp break in the local face of leadership; in 1956, only 12 percent of the Nōkyō's officeholders nationally had held any public office before the surrender, and turnover in other positions was also high.[14] Local mayors and other officers had been among the first to leave power after the war. In their official capacities, many had served as the villages' highest-ranking representatives of the Imperial Rule Assistance Association (IRAA); purges of leaders in such positions were almost automatic.[15] Satō Sakichi served his last months as mayor in late 1946, having held the office since January 1924. He died in 1966.

Yabe Zenbei lost his official posts and more. Purged from public life because of his prominent role in the Fukushima IRAA, Yabe spent several years trying to get the family's dry goods store back on its feet. He had to: the land reforms had stripped him and his family of much of their land, thus severing his direct ties to Sekishiba, ending his days as a powerful local landlord, and undermining his family's economic position. The dry goods store, all but closed during the last years of the war, was almost all that remained. Yabe was still deeply committed to the Hōtoku movement, however, and once the purge directive against him was lifted in 1951, he returned to public life. For the next nineteen years, Yabe was a powerful and active advocate for Hōtoku's methods and its lessons for modern Japan, helping to rebuild a robust local movement in and around Aizu. He died in 1970.[16]

## Creating the Prosperous Countryside

As Ronald Dore was finishing his classic work on land reform in the mid-1950s, it was by no means clear that things would turn out well for farmers. In fact, there were indications that, as important as land reform had been, it might not have been enough to close the gap between city and country, farm and factory. The countryside had been on the brink of another rural depression in 1948, and although the harvest that year hadn't been as bad as people feared, there was no guarantee that the next year—or the year after—wouldn't bring something worse.[17] Resolving the tenancy issue had clearly not inoculated farmers against serious economic difficulty; problems, some of them serious, remained unresolved as the Occupation drew to a close.

Farm family incomes, for example, began to lag behind those earned by factory workers and continued to do so through much of the 1950s. Farmers were more productive than ever before, as landownership and better farm technologies took hold, but their gains were coming much more slowly than those for industrial workers. By the mid-1950s, it was also clear that rice farmers had reached a plateau of sorts and that crop yields were likely to rise only slowly from then on. Though tenancy was no longer an issue, farm size remained a constraint on productivity and efficiency. Even with all the land that had changed hands under the Occupation's reforms, the average farmer in the 1950s was still working a plot that was roughly the same size as farms had been before 1945. The average area under cultivation per farm has remained almost constant at 1.2 hectares (or 1.2 *chō*) in the postwar era.[18]

The reasons for the persistence of small farms are many and complex. There are substantial tax and financial benefits associated with owning farmland and growing rice, and these have limited whatever incentives marginal farmers might have had to sell or even rent land to someone else. The price of paddy land rose more than twentyfold between March 1947 and March 1954 alone; as Nishida Yoshiaki has suggested, farmland became a commodity whose value had relatively little to do with what could be grown on it.[19] Urbanization and the recovering economy sent land prices in general skyrocketing; farmland kept pace. To further complicate matters, with the memory of the land reform still relatively fresh, landowners were often reluctant to rent their land to others for fear of not being able to regain control over it at some later date.[20]

Because small and relatively inefficient farms remained the norm in the wake of the reforms, the gains that farmers had made during and immediately after the war in income, standards of living, and access to other markers of modernity seemed increasingly at risk.[21] As heavy industry and manufacturing began their resurgence, building on the trends of the prewar period and the possibilities offered in the postwar international marketplace, the countryside seemed destined to fall further and further behind the rest of the nation.

Farmers and, ultimately, policymakers sought a permanent set of solutions to the growing sense of crisis in the countryside. In 1959, the "Agriculture, Forestry, and Fishing Fundamental Problem Research Group" began deliberations as an advisory body to the Prime Minister's Office. Their policy recommendations were incorporated into the 1961 Agricultural Basic Law, which tried to resolve, once and for all, the growing disparities between agriculture and the rest of the economy. The Basic Law established a new baseline for how much farmers would be paid by the state for their rice.[22] Under these new guidelines, the state would buy rice from farmers at a price that took into account not only the actual cost of production (so that farmers would never again find themselves forced to sell rice for less than it cost them to grow it) but also changes in wage levels for industrial workers (so that, on average, a full-time, reasonably efficient farmer would earn a wage roughly equivalent to that of a full-time, reasonably efficient blue-collar worker). The state would then sell the rice back to the public at lower prices and absorb the cost of doing so. In other words, the new policy committed the state to something that it had never before been willing to undertake: it guaranteed that farmers would be paid at parity with factory workers. The price paid to producers for their rice doubled between 1960 and 1968, and the gap between per capita farm income and per capita factory-worker income narrowed. By the 1980s, if not before, farmers were actually ahead of factory workers.[23]

On balance, the combination of the land reforms and the Basic Law worked well for farmers, assuring them of a high measure of financial stability and prosperity. Some of the incredible wealth generated in Japan's postwar economic growth has made its way to the countryside, where it has certainly been welcomed, if not well deserved.[24] Few of the economic problems that farmers faced again and again in the 1930s are likely to resurface in the near term. Farm debt is no worse, apparently, than other forms of consumer indebtedness, and the paper wealth that farmers have accumulated as landholders is certainly unprecedented.

The state maintained this extremely costly system of subsidies and protection from international competition for several decades, in partial exchange for which the farmers' lobby remained a staunch supporter of a succession of conservative governments friendly to their interests. In recent years this relationship has been tested by external pressure to open Japan's lucrative markets to imported agricultural products, by an ongoing transformation of national politics, and by Japanese consumers less willing of late to shoulder the high costs of keeping farmers happy. In a process that began in the early 1980s, the state slowly but steadily modified the nature and extent of its support for agriculture, lowering barriers to imports and cutting back on other forms of assistance. The passage in July 1999 of the Food, Agriculture, and Rural Areas Basic Law marked a much sharper break with past practices and an almost complete reworking of the system in place since 1961. It remains unclear how the countryside will fare in this new environment, but it is highly unlikely that farmers will be allowed to wither on the vine.[25]

## City and Country

As the countryside's most pressing economic issues have been addressed in the years since the surrender, farmers and city dwellers alike have returned to a question that surfaced in the depression's wake: what place is there for the village, and the rural community more generally, in a modern, urban nation? The agrarianists and even, to some extent, the proponents of the Economic Revitalization Campaign insisted that the countryside was distinct from urban Japan, that it possessed unique qualities and values worth preserving against creeping urbanization. Even as reformers urged farmers to become more modern by learning to be more rational, more efficient, and thoroughly frugal, there was never any question about their becoming more "urban" or "Western" in the process. The modern countryside that the agrarianists and the proponents of revitalization were after was one in which the special qualities of Japanese community life were retained and honored.

Postwar answers to the same question took shape a little differently. Some sense of their direction can be found in the New Life and New Village campaigns of the mid-1950s. Minister of Agriculture Kōno Ichirō announced the New Village Development (Shin nōsangyoson kensetsu) Campaign at a news conference in late 1955. In his remarks and in later comments to the cabinet, Kōno pointedly referred to the declining fortunes of the countryside and to the need for a "new" set of solutions to the problems facing farm, fishing, and mountain villages. Rural communities were falling behind the rest of the nation in several key respects, he complained. Farmers were burdened with a lower level of income relative not only to the countries of the West, Kōno pointed out, but also to other types of employment available in Japan. Young people in the countryside were increasingly without hope as a result, as their communities floundered in the modern economy.[26] Something would have to be done to maintain the viability of farming and to shore up the still-important role that the countryside played in the nation's social order.

Kōno's proposed campaign mirrored economic revitalization in its emphasis both on the independence of each community and on shifting initiative for the policy into local hands. As part of his plan to "strengthen the core of the village," Kōno described the creation of local committees to coordinate planning at the village level; in a structure strikingly reminiscent of the economic revitalization committees, membership would consist of the mayor, representatives of each hamlet, and leaders of all the community civic and economic organizations. Along with the New Village Campaign's emphasis on the rationalization of daily life and economic activity, provisions for training a new generation of youth leaders, and plans to provide both a normal channel of financial assistance to participating communities and another reserved for those deserving of special assistance, Kōno expected to provide a comprehensive set of solutions to this new rural crisis.[27]

Whether he was aware of the clear similarities between what he was proposing and the long-defunct Economic Revitalization Campaign is not clear. As with many of the ministries, however, there was considerable continuity between pre- and postwar policy initiatives, and some continuity in personnel. Though Kodaira Gonichi himself was purged from public office in 1946 because of his role in the IRAA, he remained active in a number of private organizations and was a much sought-after advisor on farm issues.[28] (In 1951, the order purging him was lifted; he accepted the first of many official appointments to public advisory and administrative bodies eight days later.)[29] By then Kodaira and others had written extensively and positively about their experiences and goals while they administered the campaign, concluding that its approach was fundamentally sound. Kodaira had argued as early as 1948 that the goals of the Economic Revitalization Campaign had been to stabilize the farming community and ensure its economic strength, drawing a clear connection between past practice and the postwar needs of the countryside.[30] Pointing to the campaign's democratic attributes, Kodaira noted that revitalization plans had never simply been handed down by the state for implementation by the village. It was always the people, he stressed, not the state, who were responsible for their development and implementation. The plans themselves, and thus the Economic Revitalization Campaign in general, were "completely democratic."[31]

The state's pursuit of rural reform coincided with an official and popular resurgence of interest in the reform of daily life; hence the movement for a "new village" was paralleled by one for a "new life." The New Life Campaign (Shin seikatsu undō) "inherited the modernizing mission, and, indeed, the very language of the prewar campaigns" for the reform of daily life in much the same way that Kōno's proposals for the countryside had, calling on citizens to be frugal, rational, healthy, and mutually cooperative.[32] Instead of focusing on villages or farmers, however, the New Life Campaign paid particular attention to housewives, encouraging them to "professionalize" their activities in the home and to distinguish between their roles as women and their spouses' roles as men, among other things.

Support for the New Life Campaign, which also took shape in 1955, was broad and long-lasting. Its messages resonated with the public and with the corporations that supported it for several decades.[33] As Sheldon Garon suggests, "throughout most of the postwar era, the vast majority of the Japanese people—regardless of political orientation—remained convinced that they lived in a fundamentally poor nation in which the key to improving living standards lay in modernizing or rationalizing daily habits, rather than in substantially expanding consumption."[34] Moral suasion campaigns in the postwar period (of which there have been many) seem to have veered away from distinguishing between rural and urban constituencies and to have focused instead on common characteristics of class, gender, and, occasionally, national identity. The New Village Campaign was an exception, and not a very successful one.

The New Village Development Campaign was neither as well received nor as long-lived as the New Life Campaign. It had official backing for only seven years after its inauguration in 1956, during which time it made only minimal headway in the countryside. Compared to the much more enthusiastic popular and corporate response to the New Life movement, participation in the New Village Campaign was desultory at best.[35] Average citizens, rural residents among them, remained committed to rationality, frugality, and a more modern lifestyle but were unwilling to accept the New Village Campaign as the answer to agriculture's very real economic problems. Nationally, the Nōkyō refused to support it, and although local branches in some villages were reportedly going through the motions of participation, eager for the funding that came with the campaign, it was clear to most observers that its impact would be negligible. It generated neither the local support nor the tangible results that had characterized the earlier Economic Revitalization Campaign.

In some ways, the demise of the New Village Campaign marked the beginning of a new set of relationships between rural Japan and the rest of the country. The chaos and destruction of the final years of the war had temporarily leveled the playing field between city and country, farm and factory, without addressing the very significant differences that had developed between them. These gaps were part of what fueled the drive for reforms in the

1930s and were at the heart of what many farmers saw as their greatest concerns. Only land reform and the Basic Agricultural Law prevented the gaps from becoming a problem again in the postwar period. With the prosperous farmer the norm and not the exception, farm families have since the 1950s been able to participate fully in a shared national culture of (limited) consumption and modern lifestyles. William Kelly has suggested that the line between rural and urban was already starting to blur by the end of the 1950s, as the "enormous ordering power" of educational attainment, organizational life, and the nuclear family folded almost all Japanese into the middle class.[36] Prosperity reduced the distance between city and country by creating a shared middle-class culture to which farm families could aspire. That this culture is one in which frugality, seriousness of effort, and rational behavior are held in considerable respect speaks to continuities with the prewar efforts by middling farmers to instill these qualities in the entire farming population.[37]

The relationship between town and country has unfolded in another, somewhat ambiguous fashion. Villages have, in effect, become cities, and farmers are as likely to be found behind an office desk as in the field. Agriculture and small rural communities have become less and less a visible part of "modern" Japan. Although urbanization picked up speed throughout the interwar years, in 1930 some 70 percent of the population still lived in a town or a village, and two out of every five Japanese lived in a community of less than five thousand residents. This balance between the urban and the rural held fairly steady over the next two decades, so that in 1950 city dwellers were still in the minority, accounting for under 40 percent of the population.[38] People were moving into the cities (and back into cities destroyed during the war), but slowly.

This pattern of gradual migration into the city gave way to a much more rapid transfer of population and administrative control in the mid-1950s. Recommendations first by the Occupation's Shoup Commission and eventually by its Japanese counterparts argued that there would be substantial administrative and economic benefits to merging or amalgamating the nation's more than ten thousand towns and villages. After a period of several years in which prefectures were left largely to their own devices in encouraging towns and villages to come together, the state proposed and passed first a "Law for the Promotion of Amalgamation of Towns and Villages" in September 1953 and then a "Law for the Promotion of Construction of New Cities, Towns, and Villages" three years later.[39]

The effects of these efforts were impressive. Between September 1953 and October 1956, the number of villages in Japan dropped from 7,640 to fewer than 1,600. Those villages that were left were, on average, almost three times as large in terms of area and population as they had been before the amalgamations began.[40] In addition, by merging nearby towns and villages into neighboring cities, the state managed to transform Japan into an urban nation. By 1960, more than 60 percent of the population lived within a city's limits.[41] Sekishiba and Kitakata's other neighboring communities—Matsuyama, Iwatsuki, Kumagura, Toyokawa, Keitoku, and Kamisanmiya—were part of this transformation. The seven villages and one town were merged in 1954 to create the city of Kitakata.[42]

Agriculture slowly lost ground in other ways as well. Through the 1930s, 1940s, and much of the 1950s, farming, broadly defined, produced between a fifth and a quarter of Japan's GNP. In 1960 it accounted for only 15 percent of the total, and over the next ten years its share fell to less than half that. By 1990 agriculture made up only 2.6 percent of Japan's GNP—a "negligible" amount by at least one scholar's standards.[43]

Changes in the workforce reflect similar trends. Farmers accounted for about half of the workforce in the 1920s, made up 40 percent of it in 1940, and were holding on at 30 percent in 1960. That decline was a relative one, in that the number of people classified as farmers remained more or less constant from 1920 until 1960, at around 13 or 14 million. It wasn't until after 1960 that the farming population experienced a rapid and absolute decline, falling below 11 million by 1965, and to about half of 1960 levels by 1975. In 1990 there were only a third as many farmers in Japan as there had been three decades earlier; by then only one out of every fifteen men and women in the workforce was a farmer.

Even these figures can be deceiving, since agricultural subsidies, improvements in mechanization, and the introduction of other labor-saving devices have meant that farming is more and more a part-time endeavor for most families. Nationally, by 1989 agriculture accounted for only 18 percent of the average Japanese farmer's income.[44] In Kitakata the balance had tipped in favor of part-timers by the mid-1960s: in 1965, there were 1,061 full-time farm households within the city's borders; ten years later, there were only 366.[45]

A related phenomenon has been the "graying" of the farm workforce. One doesn't have to spend much time in the countryside to be struck by the predominance of elderly men and women tending the fields. Some are retirees back on the farm after career's end, while others have been farming all their lives and are the only ones left in the family whose labor is best spent farming, as opposed to earning wages at a local factory or retail establishment. The common lament of marriage-age males in the countryside—namely, that no one is willing to marry a farmer—reflects the other options available to young women and helps explain why so few young men are willing to enter farming as a career.

## The Elusive Revitalized Village

When recent administrators of Aizu-Wakamatsu (renamed in 1955 to reflect the amalgamation of the original municipality with several neighboring villages) described their community as "a city without smokestacks," they meant it in a positive way, not as a lament at having been passed over by heavy industry's largesse. Like Kitakata, its urban neighbor to the north, Aizu-Wakamatsu in the 1990s was doing its best to find ways to make the most productive use of its past. The fact that farming and so-called traditional products (miso, sake, and the like) continue to play a very visible role in the local economy (and in train-station souvenir shops) has been offered as a sign not of the region's backwardness but of the quality of life to be found in its communities. Attempts to attract "clean" high-tech factories to the area have met with some success, and the opening in 1993 of the University of Aizu, an institution focused on computer and software design, is seen as another step in the right direction. Tourism has emerged as a significant source of income and employment, driven in part by the ongoing desire of many Japanese to experience their own slice of rural native Japan—an opportunity that Aizu-Wakamatsu and the other communities of the Aizu basin are more than willing to provide. The irony of this new relationship between town and country can be a source of no small amusement to local residents.

Aizu-Wakamatsu and communities like it are offering one set of answers to persistent questions about where rural Japan "fits" in relation to the other components of modern Japanese society. The roles that local leaders have attempted to construct for their communities in the past thirty or forty years have interacted in complex ways with the public's image of the countryside and the qualities associated with it. Part marketing scheme and part social policy, a series of state and private efforts have focused popular attention on the importance of *furusato*, or "native place," to a citizenry all but divorced from direct contact with anything even remotely resembling rural life.[46]

*Furusato* invokes a wide range of meanings and implies an ancestral link to the rice-farming communities from which modern society supposedly developed, connecting urban families to a long-lost family back "home" in the countryside. Given that many city dwellers are removed from the rice fields by many generations, going "home" requires a certain suspension of disbelief. The search for "tradition" and the qualities that have come to be associated with rural life and farming—among them harmony with nature and with one's neighbors—is, of course, another part of the resurgence of interest in things rural;[47] so, too, is a desire to experience the exotic, to find places within Japan that challenge the sameness of everyday life yet reaffirm the essential unity of the nation. Travel agencies and rail lines have taken the lead in encouraging people to act on their impulses to seek out their rural roots and experience lost traditions, even if it means inventing them.[48]

Sekishiba and, now, Kitakata have come a long way from a time of crisis. It may be that their renegotiation of local identity—from rural backwater to something like an essentialized representation of an imagined past—marks a final chapter in the construction of the elusive revitalized village. In the wake of the Great Depression, residents desperately struggled to put the past behind them; in the 1990s, local leaders found themselves reaching back into the past to help preserve their community's future.[49]

Like Aizu-Wakamatsu, Kitakata has built up a thriving tourist industry around a theme of what might be called the "rural exotic." In Kitakata's case, two attractions are paramount. The first are the more than two thousand *kura*, or tile and mortar storehouses, scattered through the city and in nearby communities. Many Meiji-era towns and villages relied on *kura* as a protection against fire, vermin, and theft, but Kitakata is unusual in having preserved so many of them. Following a fire in 1880 that left little else but *kura* standing (or so the story goes), residents began building storehouses when and where they could. Possessing one's own *kura* became a mark of prosperity, which kept the style and the building methods alive. In recent years the city discovered that the structures, though no longer particularly useful or practical, were fascinating to people who had grown up surrounded by nothing but modern Japanese architecture. Existing *kura* have been restored and new ones built to accommodate the interest of visitors (one local entrepreneur even provides tours of the city in horse-drawn *kura* replicas), as local leaders and businessmen have worked hard to publicize the attractions of their "City of Storehouses, Kitakata."[50]

The city's other attraction is ramen, a ubiquitous noodle-soup dish of Chinese origin and Japanese antecedents. Kitakata has more than a hundred ramen shops, which specialize in a version that is clear-brothed, rich in sliced pork, and brimming with "curly" noodles; the combination is unusual enough that Kitakata ramen is counted among the handful of truly distinct regional variations. Prepackaged instant varieties of the local specialty have reached the shelves of supermarkets nationwide, a sure indication of its appeal. The busloads of tourists who line up outside favored local restaurants as part of their package tours are another sign that the city has found a formula that works. The combination of *kura* and ramen has placed Kitakata on the map in a small way, which is more than many rural communities in similar circumstances can claim. It says something about the city's sense of itself and of its place in Japan that its tourist brochures include directions not just from Tokyo but from Hokkaido and Kyushu as well.

The campaigns to promote Kitakata as a travel destination have been very successful. After the first television programs featuring the area were aired on NHK in the mid-1970s, the number of visiting tourists climbed past fifty thousand a year for the first time. Aggressive publicity efforts and frequent appearances on television travel shows since then have marked the region as one of the country's most popular "new" tourist destinations. The number of visitors broke the half-million mark in 1989, and from 1993 through 1998, the last year for which figures are available, the city welcomed more than a million tourists annually.[51]

This willingness to reach into the past to sustain and define the present manifests itself in at least one other way in Kitakata. The Office for the Compilation of Municipal History is housed on the top floor of a building that it shares with the municipal library and a small museum of artifacts of local life. From the inception of the office in 1978, its staff has been collecting and cataloging local records and other materials of historical value, assembling a group of local historians, teachers, and others to assist in the process. By the early 1990s, the office had begun publishing the first volumes of what will eventually be a twelve-part *History of Kitakata City*. The practice of publishing a local history is by no means unique to Kitakata, but neither is it something that every community attempts. Local interest is high and has ensured an audience for the books; the participation of local (and some professional) historians has helped produce high-quality work.

I mention the *History* here by way of a connection to the rest of this study, which has focused very closely on Sekishiba and its inhabitants. *The History of Kitakata City*, in contrast, brings together the pasts not of one community but of eight—namely, Kitakata and the seven villages that were once on its borders. The redrawing of administrative boundaries has produced a history that is made up of separate narratives; the first published volume is prefaced by a general history of the area but consists primarily of a collection of individual histories of each of the communities. These chapters share a common framework but offer ample evidence of how neighboring villages and the town differed, not only in their social and economic circumstances but in the nature of their responses to crises and change as well. No two villages are exactly alike, and none of the seven in question had that much in common with the town.

At the same time, however, the *History* creates a single meta-narrative in which the boundaries between communities are erased. The second published volume, a collection of documents, is organized chronologically and by subject matter: education, the economy, and administration are some of the categories within which materials from all seven villages and the town appear side by side. The tension between the experiences of one village and those of another, which is explicit in the chapters that deal with single community histories, is much less evident in this format. Here the differences are, at least in part, subverted in favor of the appearance of a common trajectory. Moreover, the shared narrative implied by such an arrangement is that of a transformation from rural to urban, from agriculture to service industry, from village to "City of Storehouses, Kitakata."

One could argue in any number of ways about what this approach to the construction of local history tells us about "imagined communities" in modern Japan, but what interests me more is what it might tell us about real ones. In looking at a single community apart from the others, which is what most of this book has done, it is easy to lose sight of how much a part of the surrounding social and economic landscape Sekishiba was. *The History of Kitakata* reminds us of just how often events in one place were mirrored in others, even though the communities themselves were quite different.

By drawing on Sekishiba's particular history, I hope not to have ignored these other communities but to have illuminated their experiences, and those of farming villages elsewhere in Japan as well. It also strikes me that *The History of Kitakata* reflects an ongoing negotiation between the countryside, urban Japan, and the state—a process that engages issues not only of local identity but of economic viability as well. In Kitakata, the villages became the city, but there is nothing to suggest that anyone views this as the final answer, or even as an especially good answer, to the problems that farmers and their families face within the modern industrial economy. That Kitakata has turned to tourism as enthusiastically as it has suggests that questions of rural identity and the place of rural communities in the greater nation are still unresolved, just as they were when local residents grappled with them in the 1930s.

The Office for the Compilation of Municipal History has a northern exposure, and its large glass doors open onto a small balcony. From there one can look out across a large section of Kitakata and, on clear days, watch the light move across the mountains that rim the basin. Or, as I often did, one can crane a little to the right and try to catch a glimpse of what lies on the other side of the bridge. Due east and across the river, Sekishiba once began.

*Appendix*

Appendix
Membership of Sekishiba's Economic Revitalization Committee, 1934

|  |  |  | Hamlet ranking | |
| --- | --- | --- | --- | --- |
| Name | Hamlet | Credentials | Land | *Kosūwari* |
| Satō Sakichi | Komatsu | Mayor, agricultural association president, sericulture practice union president | 10 (of 18) | 5 (of 18) |
| Abe Tadashi | Higashi-nakamei | Assistant mayor, production union director | 2 (of 16) | 2 (of 21) |
| Watanabe Kyūgo |  | Primary school principal, young men's association president | na | na |
| Watanabe Shinroku |  | Teacher | na | na |
| Sonobe Shukei |  | Agricultural association technician | na | na |
| Yanatori Hachigoro | Sekishiba | Village treasurer | 16 (of 69) | 5 (of 71) |
| Suzuki Midori |  | Teacher | na | na |
| Satō Mii |  | Teacher | na | na |
| Utsugi Taichi | Hirabayashi | Production union president, former schoolteacher | 36 (of 40) | 4 (of 50) |
| Teishirogi Takeshi |  | Army reserve association president, young men's association advisor | na | na |
| Watanabe Hatsuji | Sosogi | Agricultural association official | na | na |
| Tabe Seiji | Sekishiba | Village council, ward chief | 14 | 12 |
| Hasanuma Saichi | Sekishiba | Agricultural association official | 2 | 7 |

|  |  |  | Hamlet ranking | |
|---|---|---|---|---|
| Name | Hamlet | Credentials | Land | Kosūwari |
| Ōtake Seikichi | Sekishiba | Agricultural association official, ward chief | 6 | 3 |
| Watanabe Shinta | Komatsu | Village council, welfare council, ward chief, sericulture union official, former school principal | 6 | 10 |
| Kobayashi Tarōhachi | Shimoshiba | Ward chief, agricultural association official | 9 (of 22) | 6 (of 27) |
| Kikuchi Bunki | Hirabayashi | Sericulture union official, agricultural association | 5 | 8 |
| Kikuchi Sōsaburō | Hirabayashi | Village council, ward chief | 11 | 13 |
| Itō Bunpei | Kyōde | Head of a practice union | 4 (of 22) | 6 (of 25) |
| Kikuchi Isamu | Kamisugure | Agricultural association official | na | na |
| Endō Gengo | Kamitakahitai | Village council, agricultural association official, ward chief, Kamitakahitai Hōtoku Society vice president | 26 (of 56) | 1 (of 63) |
| Maruyama Sakuma | Kamitakahitai | Honored farmer | 15 | 3 |
| Igarashi Shoki | Kamitakahitai | Sericulture union director | na | 51 |
| Tōjō Genbei | Shimosugure | Head of a production union, fire brigade commander, agricultural association vice president, ward chief, village council, former teacher | 2 (of 15) | 2 (of 16) |
| Suganuma Eihachi | Nishi-nakamei | Ward chief, production union director, sericulture union director | 4 (of 23) | 3 (of 25) |

| | | | |
|---|---|---|---|
| Inomata Tadahiro | | Teacher | na | na |
| Anazawa Masayasu | Nishi-nakamei | Village clerk | 19 | 10 |
| Odagiri Yōgo | Higashi-nakamei | Ward chief, production union director, agricultural association official | 4 | 3 |
| Sagara Yuma | Nakazato | Statistical surveyor, honored farmer | na | na |
| Anazawa Kisohachi | Sanjōnome | Sericulture union director | 1 (of 7) | 1 (of 7) |
| Teishirogi Chiyoichi | Furu | Village council | 14 (of 29) | 16 (of 31) |
| Takahashi Shigehachi | Furu | Head of a practice union, statistical surveyor, agricultural association | 13 | 12 |
| Fukushima Takamitsu | | Village clerk | na | na |
| Endō Dentarō | Hirabayashi | Village clerk | 37 | 49 |

SOURCES: Here "na" means that the relevant data were not available. Membership and credential information appears in three slightly different versions; see SMY, "Keizai kōsei iinkai hi joseikin kōfu seigansho," July 20, 1934, *Keizai kōsei, 1934*, KST; SMY, "Sekishiba mura keizai kōsei iinkai kitei"; and "Keizai kōsei iin no ninmei," also in *Keizai kōsei 1934*, KST. The list that appears here is based on the July 20, 1934, document. Under "Hamlet Ranking," the "Land" category reflects the amount of paddy land reported under cultivation in 1934, and the *Kosūwari* (Special Household Tax) category reflects the total assessed tax in 1934. See SMY, "Yama-gun Sekishiba mura rokubetsu-zei kosūwari fukagaku kettei sho," in *Sonkai giroku, 1934*, KST.

*Reference Matter*

# Notes

For complete author names, titles, and publication data for works cited here in short form, see the Bibliography, pp. 451–467. For a list of the abbreviations used here, see p. xvii.

## Chapter 1

1. Advertisers and satirists were quick to exploit the term. "Hijōji" showed up in promotions for everything from medicines to record players, and in numerous commentaries on the sorry state of public culture. See Ōe Shinobu, ed., "Hijōji," in *Nihon, Shōwa no rekishi*, pp. 33–40. See also Sandra Wilson, "Bureaucrats and Villagers in Japan: *Shimin* and the Crisis of the Early 1930s," p. 125, for her reading of the vocabulary of crisis.

2. Gordon's *Labor and Imperial Democracy in Prewar Japan* is a good example of an attempt to broaden our understanding of non-elites in the 1920s and 1930s. Others include Downard, "Tokyo: The Depression Years, 1927–1933"; and Hastings, *Neighborhood and Nation in Tokyo, 1905–1937*.

3. A good example of the range of scholarly interest in the period can be found in Sumiya Mikio, ed., *Shōwa kyōkō*; Tokyo daigaku shakai kagaku kenkyūjo, ed., *Shōwa kyōkō, Fashizumu-ki no kokka to shakai*; Ōishi Kaichirō, "Sekai daikyōkō to Nihon shihon shugi"; and Nakamura Masanori, *Shōwa no kyōkō*, vol. 2 of *Shōwa no rekishi*.

4. Similar efforts were employed in the industrialized West as well. See Weir, Orloff, and Skocpol, eds., *The Politics of Social Policy in the United States*.

5. Peter Duus, "Introduction, Japan's Informal Empire in China, 1895–1937: An Overview," pp. xi–xxix, in Duus, Myers, and Peattie, eds., *The Japanese Informal Empire in China, 1895–1937*.

6. Berger, *Parties Out of Power in Japan, 1931–1941*.

7. Silverberg, "The Cafe Waitress Serving Modern Japan"; Martin, "Popular Music and Social Change in Prewar Japan"; and Yano, "Defining the Modern Nation in Japanese Popular Song, 1914–1932."

8. Iwasaki Akira, "Atarashii media no tenkai"; and Tasaki Nobuyoshi, "Toshi bunka to kokumin ishiki."

9. Kasza, *The State and the Mass Media in Japan, 1918–1945* details radio's growth.

10. The 1933 film *Japan in a Time of Crisis* is a case in point. Produced by the *Mainichi shinbun*, one of Japan's largest daily national newspapers, the lengthy "talkie" featured then Minister of the Army General Araki Sadao in a starring role. His narration laid out in no uncertain terms the many challenges Japan faced domestically and abroad. Though many of the film's images remind viewers of Japan's achievements in past wars (juxtaposing Russo-Japanese War hero Admiral Tōgō and scenes from Manchuria—an unmistakable reference to the Soviet threat), the message is clear that the nation faced new enemies, not all of them in uniform. The film presents a range of adversaries: men and women dressed in Western clothes, coming and going freely from their haunts in the Ginza, unmindful of the people or the nation around them. Communists, Western musicians, and other symbols of decadence fill out the list. The "heroes" are everyday people dressed in traditional clothing, hardworking men and women toiling in the fields (rural landscapes and rice paddies are recurring images), and, of course, soldiers. *Japan in a Time of Crisis* directed the viewing public to look both to the past and to an imagined future for solutions: from the past came simple traditions of the countryside; the future would yield technology and material strength. How these contradictory images might be wedded to practical policies was ultimately part of the crisis too. For more on the film, see Abé Mark Nornes, "Forest of Pressure: Japanese Documentary to 1946." For more on movies and popular culture, see Hanes, "Media Culture in Taishō Osaka"; and Silverberg, "Remembering Pearl Harbor."

11. Turner, *Dramas, Fields, and Metaphors*, pp. 38–39.

12. The urban experience was different. Although the depression did not pass the cities by, the changes it brought to urban Japan were not of the same quality as those evident in rural communities. Not only was the downturn in manufacturing short-lived compared to that in agriculture, but private and public attempts to cope with economic hardship in the cities were much more narrowly focused than those visited on the countryside. Unemployment relief projects underwent a sharp expansion in scale in the early 1930s, but not in kind. Attempts to win unemployment benefits or firing bonuses from employers were also part of the depression legacy, but these steps, too, were more evolutionary than revolutionary (although workers had to fight hard to get them). For a discussion of interwar unemployment relief policies, see Kase Kazutoshi, "Senzen Nihon ni okeru shitsugyō kyūsai jigyō no tenkai katei (1)," and idem, "Senzen Nihon ni okeru shitsugyō kyūsai jigyō no tenkai katei (2)."

Rural relief and reform efforts were full of references to the revitalization of the village and to the importance of sweeping reforms in almost every facet of farming and rural life. Such rhetoric was generally absent from discussions about the problems of the worker and the city.

13. Adachi Ikitsune, "Ie no hikari no rekishi," p. 71.

14. My reading of the novel is from Kagawa Toyohiko, *Chichi to mitsu no nagaruru sato*. An English version exists as Kagawa, *The Land of Milk and Honey*, trans. Marion Romer Draper (London: Hodder & Stoughton, 1937). *Ie no hikari* was the most widely read of any journal intended for a rural audience in the 1930s.

15. "Industrial cooperative" is a somewhat misleading but accurate translation of *sangyō kumiai*—misleading because it implies an industrial origin to what were, in effect, rural agricultural cooperatives for sales of farm goods, the purchase of needed supplies, easy credit, and technical help.

16. Kagawa did his homework, making sure that discussions of prices and farm management were accurate. Adachi Ikitsune, "Ie no hikari no rekishi," pp. 74–75.

17. Tōsuke was no Tom Joad; *The Grapes of Wrath* captures a rage and desperation entirely absent from Kagawa's fictional countryside. See Levine, "American Culture and the Great Depression," for an interesting discussion of depression-era popular culture in the United States.

18. The importance of this collection is discussed in the Acknowledgments.

19. Sekishiba mura yakuba (hereafter SMY), "Keizai kōsei iinkai hi joseikin kōfu seigansho," July 20, 1934. *Keizai kōsei, 1934*, Kitakata shiritsu toshokan shi-shi hensan shitsu (hereafter KST).

20. The castle at Aizu-Wakamatsu had been the scene of a particularly bloody encounter between troops representing the new Meiji government and those loyal to the old shogunal regime. Conflict resurfaced in the 1880s, during the nationwide Freedom and People's Rights movement. In 1882 local activists in the movement were arrested, sparking a clash in Kitakata between police and citizens in which many of the latter were killed, wounded, or jailed. See Bowen, *Rebellion and Democracy in Meiji Japan*, pp. 8–31. (Bowen refers to Chūzenji temple in the village of "Shibage"; the temple is in Sekishiba.) Vlastos, in his *Peasant Protest and Uprisings in Tokugawa Japan*, provides an illuminating analysis of world-renewal movements there and of the history of the region.

21. Some of these programs applied to only a limited part of the populace. From 1932 on, for example, the Relief Law provided aid to a small portion of the infirm, the elderly, minors, and other needy but unemployable members of society. In 1933, prompted by concerns about rural health, the government took the first steps toward creating a national health insurance system, which was eventually implemented in 1939. See Koji Taira, "Public Assistance in Japan"; and Hye Kyung Lee, "Development of Social Welfare Systems in the United States and Japan." The

central government also took over more and more of the burden of local expenditures, as towns and villages found their responsibilities mounting as their tax base shrank. See Ōishi Kaichirō, "Shōwa kyōkō to chihō zaisei, nōson zaisei o chūshin to shite," pp. 81–148; and Ōkurashō Shōwa zaisei shi henshūshitsu, ed. *Shōwa zaisei shi*, vol. 14, pp. 158–178.

22. Ōkurashō Shōwa zaisei shi henshūshitsu, ed. *Shōwa zaisei shi*, vol. 5, pp. 145–146, and vol. 3, pp. 5–7.

23. Nōrinshō keizai kōseibu ed., "Dai nikai nōson keizai kōsei chūō iinkai yōroku," July 1934, in *Nōsangyoson keizai kōsei undōshi shiryō shūsei* (hereafter NSS) 1:2, pp. 245–246.

24. Two overviews of German policy are Farquharson, *The Plough and the Swastika*; and Holt, *German Agricultural Policy, 1918–1934*; see also Case, "Farm Debt Adjustment During the Early 1930s."

25. Garon, "Rethinking Modernization and Modernity in Japanese History."

26. Garon, *Molding Japanese Minds*.

27. See Brinkley, *Voices of Protest*, for an excellent analysis of Long and Coughlin. See also Mertz, *New Deal Policy and Southern Rural Poverty*.

28. For useful insight into these issues and others, see Minichiello, ed., *Japan's Competing Modernities*; and Silberman and Harootunian, eds., *Japan in Crisis*.

29. The earliest scholarly assessments of the Economic Revitalization Campaign began appearing shortly after the end of the war, and include Kodaira Gonichi, "Nōson keizai kōsei undō o kentō shi, hyōjun nōson kakuritsu undō ni oyobu" (January 1948); Ishida Takeshi, *Kindai Nihon seiji kōzō no kenkyū* (1956), pp. 35–36; and Inoue Harumaru, *Nihon shihon shugi no hatten to nōgyō oyobi nōsei* (1957), pp. 355, 361. A second wave of more in-depth analyses began with Mori Yoshizō, "Shōwa shōki no nōson keizai kōsei undō ni tsuite, Yamagata-ken no baai" (1968), pp. 91–116; and Mori Takemaro, "Nihon fashizumu no keisei to nōson keizai kōsei undō" (1971), pp. 135–152. Scholars since have followed Mori Takemaro's lead in looking to the village for answers, even as they have moved beyond his initial arguments—as has Mori, who has suggested some revisions to his earlier work. See Mori Takemaro, "Nōson no kiki no shinko" (1985), pp. 135–166. For examples of excellent case studies that include discussions of the depression and relief, see Nishida Yoshiaki, ed., *Shōwa kyōkōka no nōson shakai undō*; Nakamura Masanori, "Keizai kōsei undō to nōson tōgo," pp. 197–262; Ōishi Kaichirō and Nishida Yoshiaki, eds., *Kindai Nihon no gyōseison*; and Unno Fukuju, "Nōson keizai kōsei undō to sonraku sangyō kumiai," pp. 109–133. The Nagano village of Urazato, described by Nakamura, became so well known as a model of recovery and reorganization that it was a regular destination for visiting bureaucrats, members of the imperial family, military men, and, in 1940, a group of touring Hitler Youth.

30. See, for example, Ōkado Masakatsu, *Kindai Nihon to nōson shakai*; and Mori Takemaro and Ōkado Masakatsu, *Chiiki ni okeru senji to sengo*.

31. Benjamin Schwartz, writing in 1962 not about modernity but about modernization, makes the same point more clearly when he described it as "ambivalent or rather 'multivalent' in its relationship to many possibilities in the spheres of culture, politics, social structure, etc. It has also served many purposes, some of them contradictory. What is required, I feel, is a sense of the ambivalence, the indeterminate relationship of modernization to many possibilities. There may be certain inevitable social and cultural concomitants of the modernization process everywhere, but much has been asserted in this area which has by no means been demonstrated by historical fact" (Hall, "Changing Conceptions of the Modernization of Japan," pp. 29–30). Many thanks to Andrew Gordon for pointing me toward Schwartz's comments in this chapter.

## Chapter 2

1. Takamura Kōtarō's poem "Two at the Foot of the Mountain" begins "The back mountain of Bandai that splits in two and leans, stares fiercely at the August sky above. Its skirts spread out, trail into the distance, and a profusion of pampas grass overwhelms." Takamura, *Chieko and Other Poems of Takamura Kōtarō*, p. 118. His wife Chieko was a native of Fukushima.

2. The Barrier is not so far from present-day Kōriyama.

3. Matsuo Bashō, *The Narrow Road to Oku*, trans. Donald Keene.

4. Twelve percent of northeasterners lived in a city in 1930; the national average was twice as high. Kyōchōkai; *Tōhoku chihō ni okeru shakai narabi ni keizai jō no tokuisei*, p. 11.

5. Thirteen percent in 1932, compared to almost 30 percent in the Kantō district; only Toyama and Hokkaido farmed less of their land. Kyōchōkai, *Tōhoku nōgyō no kenkyū*, p. 30.

6. The novelist Dazai Osamu, writing in 1944 about his home place of Tsugaru at the northern end of Honshū, noted that "Between the summer of 1615, when the forces of Toyotomi Hideyoshi were destroyed at the siege of Osaka Castle, and the present day, a time span of some 350 years, the harvest failed about sixty times. That means a harvest failure almost every five years." Dazai, *Return to Tsugaru*, trans. James Westerhoven, p. 63.

7. Kyōchōkai, *Tōhoku nōgyō no kenkyū*, p. 23.

8. Kyōchōkai, *Tōhoku chihō ni okeru shakai narabi ni keizai jō no tokuisei*, pp. 11–12.

9. In Fukushima men tended to drift down to Tokyo and to Kantō factory towns in search of work, while their counterparts further north tended to find work in forestry or fishing. Ibid., pp. 25–30.

10. Ibid., pp. 4–5.

11. Ibid., p. 53.

12. Land taxes generated more revenues than income taxes in the northeast, which was not true in any other district. Ibid., pp. 60–62, 64, 68.

13. In Fukushima alone there were 206 villages without doctors; 521,939 people resided in them. Ibid., pp. 62–64.

14. Ibid., p. 63.

15. Statistics calculated by the author from data included in *Dai Nihon teikoku tōkei nenkan*, 1920–1937; Naikaku tōkei kyoku, *Shōwa 10 nen kokusei chōsa hōkoku*, vol. 1, *Zenkoku hen*, pp. 124–125; *Fukushima-ken shi*, vol. 13, p. 1115.

16. See Gluck, *Japan's Modern Myths*, for a discussion of this process and its outcomes.

17. Vlastos, *Peasant Protests and Uprisings in Tokugawa Japan*, pp. 76–77. The uprisings that accompanied the collapse of the Tokugawa regime in Aizu are discussed with care in Vlastos's work.

18. See also Toyoda Takeshi, *Tōhoku no rekishi*, vol. 2, pp. 232–238; Kitakata no ayumi henshū iinkai, ed., *Aizu Kitakata no ayumi*, pp. 283–284; Aizu-Wakamatsu-shi shuppankai, ed., *Aizu no rekishi*, pp. 332–335.

19. Toyoda Takeshi, *Tōhoku no rekishi*, vol. 2, pp. 165–166.

20. By the early 1930s, the Tōhoku region in general was relatively well provided with rail lines, at least according to government estimates. The ratio of kilometers of rail to prefectural area was slightly above the national average in the northeast, and the ratio of track length to prefectural population was twice national levels. The northeast also had more than its share of the nation's roadways. Kyōchōkai, *Tōhoku chihō ni okeru shakai narabi ni keizai jō no tokuisei*, p. 30.

21. Ōishi Kaichirō, *Fukushima-ken no hyakunen*, pp. 107–110.

22. For a discussion of how Japan's experiences have differed from Europe's, see Nishida Yoshiaki, "From a Train Window."

23. Figures are for 1930. Kyōchōkai, *Tōhoku chihō ni okeru shakai narabi ni keizai jō no tokuisei*, p. 6.

24. In 1995, there were 337 people per square kilometer in Japan on average, but only 155 in Fukushima, and only 147 in the six northeastern prefectures; 1995 figures from Sōmuchō tōkei kyoku, ed., *Nihon tōkei nenkan*, pp. 34–35.

25. Kitakata-shi shi hensan iinkai, ed., *Kitakata-shi shi*, vol. 8, pp. 236–239.

26. Kitakata no ayumi henshū iinkai, ed., *Aizu Kitakata no ayumi*, pp. 320–324, 397–398.

27. Bowen, *Rebellion and Democracy in Meiji Japan*, pp. 8–31.

28. Ibid., pp. 28–31, 289–292.

29. Kitakata-shi shi hensan iinkai, ed., *Kitakata-shi shi*, vol. 8, pp. 247, 643.

30. In the 1930s, Fukushima sent nine representatives to the Diet; Yama county, of which Kitakata and its surrounding communities were part, elected five of them. Seisen kinenshi kankōkai, *Seisen no ato*, pp. 55, 56, 58. Shūgiin jimukyoku, *Shūgiin giin sōsenkyō ichiran* (1932); Dai 19 (1936); Dai 20 (1937); Dai 21 (1943), vols. 18–21, various pages.

31. See, for example, *Fukushima minpō*, May 18, 1930; August 12, 1931; August 26, 1931.

32. Seisen kinenshi kankōkai, *Seisen no ato*, pp. 55, 56, 58. Shūgiin jimukyoku, *Shūgiin giin sōsenkyō ichiran*.

33. Fukushima-ken, *Seishi kōba chō tsuzuri*, in Fukushima-ken, ed., *Fukushima-ken shi*, vol. 13, p. 435.

34. The pollution associated with the site has been a problem for many communities and effectively destroyed the local sericulture industry. Kitakata-shi shi hensan iinkai, ed., *Kitakata-shi shi*, vol. 8, pp. 890–892.

35. Ibid., pp. 351–354.

36. By 1950, only 5 percent of households described themselves as farmers, as compared to 37 percent involved in manufacturing and 27 percent in commerce. Ibid., pp. 343–344.

37. There were twelve physicians, six dentists, and nineteen midwives operating in the town in 1937. A small private hospital served local patients from 1923, but it wasn't until the 1943 construction of the Prefectural Kitakata Hospital that comprehensive medical care was available. Ibid., pp. 377–378.

38. Ibid., pp. 370–373.

39. Ibid., pp. 325–327.

40. Ibid., pp. 384–388; Kitakata-shi shi hensan iinkai, ed., *Kitakata-shi shi*, vol. 6, pp. 167–169; 628–629. See also Yama gunyakusho, ed., *Fukushima-ken Yama-gun shi*, for a detailed examination of the county and its administration.

41. Kitakata-shi shi hensan iinkai, ed., *Kitakata-shi shi*, vol. 6, pp. 824–827. The population of Wakamatsu city is from Fukushima-ken, *Fukushima-ken tōkei sho*, vol. 1, March 1931, p. 56.

42. Kitakata-shi shi hensan iinkai, ed., *Kitakata-shi shi*, vol. 8, pp. 247, 643.

43. The Sekishiba dam contains some of the flow of the Ubadō and Tatsuki rivers well upstream. Construction began in 1940 but wasn't completed until 1956. The original purpose of the dam was to create a reserve supply of water for irrigation; the village and nearby communities had suffered through several summers of drought-like conditions in the late 1930s. Kitakata-shi shi hensan iinkai, ed., *Kitakata-shi shi*, vol. 8, pp. 672–675; vol. 6, pp. 310–315.

44. Sekishiba was an average size community for the area. It was larger than Kitakata ($4.2 \text{ km}^2$) and Toyokawa ($8.7 \text{ km}^2$), slightly bigger than Kumagura ($21.5 \text{ km}^2$)

and Keitoku (20.1 km²), but considerably smaller than Iwatsuki (47.98 km²). Ibid., vol. 8, pp. 258, 549, 625–27, 703, 781, 859.

45. Ibid., pp. 629, 633–635.

46. Tadashi Fukutake, *Japanese Rural Society*, trans. Ronald P. Dore, p. 157.

47. Ibid., p. 156, describes this process, as does Steiner, *Local Government in Japan*, pp. 46–47.

48. Tadashi Fukutake, *Japanese Rural Society*, p. 157.

49. Gluck, *Japan's Modern Myths*, pp. 204–205; Pyle, "The Technology of Japanese Nationalism," p. 65.

50. The village of Sekishiba thus had a much smaller population than Kitakata, which during the decade in question had roughly 2,400 families in residence. Sekishiba had fewer households than villages like Iwatsuki (with around 600) or Kumagura (533 between 1925 and 1929), but had roughly the same number, or slightly more homes, than the communities of Toyokawa and Keitoku.

51. Kitakata-shi shi hensan iinkai, ed., *Kitakata-shi shi*, vol. 8, p. 666.

52. Ibid., vol. 6, pp. 638–639.

53. The village reported that there were 52 males and 107 female students in the school that year. Kitakata-shi shi hensan iinkai, ed., *Kitakata-shi shi*, vol. 8, p. 685.

54. Smethurst, *A Social Basis for Prewar Japanese Militarism*, pp. 41–43.

55. See ibid., pp. 41–43, for a discussion of the Youth Schools. As of April 1, 1937, there were 95 male and 65 female students attending Sekishiba's Youth School, which represented 100 percent of the eligible student population. Kitakata-shi shi hensan iinkai, ed., *Kitakata-shi shi*, vol. 8, p. 686.

56. Dore, *Shinohata*; R. J. Smith, *Kurusu*; and Kelly, "Finding A Place in Metropolitan Japan," pp. 189–216.

57. "Farmers" here includes both full- and part-time categories. Village statistics differentiate between the two only until 1933, when there were just over a hundred part-timers. SMY, *Tōkei hyō* files, 1927–1939, KST.

58. SMY, *Keizai kōsei keikaku kihon chōsa*, 1934, KST. There were also five households in public or "free" employment (teachers, for instance), and twelve full or part-time in some "other," unspecified category.

59. Kitakata-shi shi hensan iinkai, ed., *Kitakata-shi shi*, vol. 8, pp. 670–671.

## Chapter 3

1. Inomata Etsuzō, "Shūsen zengo no kiroku kara," p. 8. See also Kitakata-shi shi hensan iinkai, ed., *Kitakata-shi shi*, vol. 6, p. 760, for details on Yamazaki's death.

2. *Fukushima minpō*, November 29, 1931.

3. Tasaki Nobuyoshi, "Toshi bunka to kokumin ishiki," p. 179.

4. A quarter of urban households had a radio in 1932, while only 5 percent of rural homes did. See Kasza, *The State and the Mass Media in Japan, 1918–1945*, pp. 88, 94–97; and Iwasaki Akira, "Atarashii media no tenkai," pp. 240, 244.

5. Waswo, "The Transformation of Rural Society, 1900–1950," pp. 557–559.

6. Mariko Tamanoi, *Under the Shadow of Nationalism*.

7. E. Sydney Crawcour, "Industrialization and Technological Change, 1885–1920," pp. 53, 104.

8. Kozo Yamamura, "The Japanese Economy, 1911–1930," pp. 327–328.

9. Umemura et al., *Agriculture and Forestry*, vol. 9 of *Estimates of Long-Term Economic Statistics of Japan Since 1868*, pp. 160–161, 168–170. Prices for all farm commodities show similar patterns.

10. Kitakata-shi shi hensan iinkai, ed., *Kitakata-shi shi*, vol. 8, p. 646.

11. See Lewis, *Rioters and Citizens*.

12. Kitakata-shi shi hensan iinkai, ed., *Kitakata-shi shi*, vol. 6, p. 157. See also Ōishi Kaichirō, *Fukushima-ken no hyakunen*, pp. 156–163.

13. Umemura et al., *Agriculture and Forestry*, pp. 160–161.

14. Ohkawa et al., *Prices*, vol. 8 of *Estimates of Long-term Economic Statistics of Japan Since 1868*, pp. 135–136; Umemura et al., *Agriculture and Forestry*, pp. 160–161.

15. For English-language discussions of the interwar economy and agriculture, see Kozo Yamamura, "The Japanese Economy, 1911–1930," pp. 303–306; and Patrick, "The Economic Muddle of the 1920s," pp. 216–220.

16. Umemura et al., *Agriculture and Forestry*, pp. 160–161. This is based on indexes of prices received by farmers.

17. Lewis, *Rioters and Citizens*, pp. 14, 30, 244–246; Ōmameuda Minoru, "1920 nendai ni okeru shokuryō seisaku no tenkai."

18. Johnston, *Japanese Food Management in World War II*, pp. 47, 264. It goes almost without saying that these exports to Japan brought tremendous hardships to Taiwanese and Korean farmers and consumers.

19. Miyazaki Rikuji, "Taishō demokurashii ki no nōson to seitō," discusses the role of politics in the development of rural policy in the interwar years.

20. Ōmameuda Minoru, "1920 nendai ni okeru shokuryō seisaku no tenkai," pp. 52–53; Nōrin daijin kanbō sōmuka, ed., *Nōrin gyōsei shi*, vol. 4, pp. 174–175.

21. Nōrin daijin kanbō sōmuka, ed., *Nōrin gyōsei shi*, vol. 3, p. 955.

22. Ono Seiichirō, "Shōwa kyōkō to nōson kyūsai seisaku," p. 7.

23. Nōrin daijin kanbō sōmuka, ed., *Nōrin gyōsei shi*, vol. 3, p. 962.

24. Ibid., pp. 975 and 1089. Cocoon production rose by 50 percent between 1915–1919 and 1925–1929. Nōrin daijin kanbō tōkeika, *Nōrinshō tōkei hyō, 1925–1937*.

25. Nōrin daijin kanbō sōmuka, ed., *Nōrin gyōsei shi*, vol. 3, p. 960.

26. Teruoka Shūzō, *Nihon nōgyō mondai no tenkai*, vol. 2, p. 64.

27. Nihon ginkō Fukushima shiten, *Fukushima ken nōson jōkyō*, pp. 620–622.
28. Nōrin daijin kanbō sōmuka, ed., *Nōrin gyōsei shi*, vol. 3, pp. 1012–1015.
29. Ōishi Kaichirō, *Fukushima-ken no hyakunen*, pp. 182–183.
30. Ibid., p. 186.
31. Yasutomi Kunio, *Shōwa kyōkōki kyūnō seisaku shiron*, vol. 5.
32. Ono Seiichirō, "Shōwa kyōkō to nōson kyūsai seisaku," p. 34.
33. As Nakamura Masanori points out, the instability of the exchange rate was one reason that the government and some businesses supported a return to the gold standard and its fixed rate. The dollar-yen rate changed 68 times in 1927 and 91 times in 1928. See Nakamura Masanori, *Shōwa no kyōkō*, vol. 2, p. 228.
34. Practical considerations should not be overlooked. Returning to the gold standard at any ratio of yen to gold other than the one in effect in 1917 would have meant revising the 1897 law that had established that ratio. In 1929, the Minseitō was still the minority party in the Diet and would remain so until the election in February 1930. The Hamaguchi cabinet lacked the votes to set a new ratio had it wanted to do so. Returning to the old one was as simple as rescinding a 1917 Ministry of Finance directive. Ibid., pp. 220–221, 236–237.
35. For a good discussion of these indicators, see ibid., pp. 271–275. For an alternative view that emphasizes the strength of the economy, see Dick K. Nanto and Shinji Takagi, "Korekiyo Takahashi and Japan's Recovery from the Great Depression."
36. Mizunuma Tomokazu, "Shōwa kyōkō," p. 191.
37. Exporters compensated for falling prices by finding new markets for their goods, including new ones at home, but in 1934 they were still shipping two-thirds of domestic production abroad, and 80 percent of that to the U.S. This represents a decline of roughly 30 percent from 1929 in the volume of thread sent to America. The total volume of silk-thread exports for 1930–1932 was 13 percent higher than for 1925–1927. Shimizu Yōji, "Nōgyō to jinushi sei," pp. 262–264; Nakamura Masanori, *Shōwa no kyōkō*, vol. 2, pp. 271–275.
38. Ohkawa et al., *Prices*, p. 170.
39. The estimates were eventually revised slightly upward; 1930 didn't hold the record for long, however. The 1933 harvest came in at a tremendous 70.9 million koku. It took until 1955 for farmers to surpass it. See Umemura et al., *Agriculture and Forestry*, p. 168; *Nihon keizai nenpō*, no. 3 (1931): 202–204.
40. Comparisons are to the period 1925–1927. *Nihon keizai nenpō* 3 (1931): 204; Shimizu Yōji, "Nōgyō to jinushi sei," p. 256.
41. As a result, and as a reflection of widely varying circumstances with regard to tenancy, cash crops, and farming practices, Japanese scholars commonly describe not one agricultural economic crisis but three or more, depending on the region discussed. The commercialized districts of the Kinki region, the sericulture regions of

Nagano and surrounding prefectures, and the northeast are the most common archetypes. This chapter's discussion thus generalizes somewhat; for more specific analyses, see, for example, Teruoka Shūzō, Nihon nōgyō mondai no tenkai, vol. 2.

42. Shimizu Yōji, "Nōgyō to jinushi sei," p. 156; Nōrin daijin kanbō sōmuka, ed., Nōrin gyōsei shi, vol. 3, pp. 975, 1089; Ohkawa et al., Prices, p. 170; Nakamura Masanori, Shōwa no kyōkō, vol. 2, p. 307. Farm prices in general were at 52 percent of their 1925-1927 levels as of 1931.

43. Village records show gradual declines in the production of soybeans and chickens through the 1930s, while lumber and charcoal production were on the rise. See Kitakata-shi shi hensan iinkai, ed., Kitakata-shi shi, vol. 6, pp. 796-799.

44. Ohkawa et al., Prices, pp. 170, 183. For estimates of price changes in Fukushima, see Nihon ginkō Fukushima shiten, Fukushima ken nōson jōkyō, pp. 618-619.

45. Smethurst, Agricultural Development and Tenancy Disputes in Japan, 1870-1940, p. 101.

46. Kazushi Ōkawa, Miyohei Shinohara, and Larry Meissner, Patterns of Japanese Economic Development, p. 388; Nōrinshō nōmukyoku, Hiryō yōran 1939, p. 52.

47. Smethurst, Agricultural Development and Tenancy Disputes in Japan, 1870-1940, pp. 98-99.

48. Teruoka Shūzō, Nihon nōgyō mondai no tenkai, vol. 2, pp. 67-75; Smethurst, Agricultural Development and Tenancy Disputes in Japan, 1870-1940, pp. 94-95.

49. Smethurst, Agricultural Development and Tenancy Disputes in Japan, 1870-1940; see esp. chap. 5.

50. The critical response to Smethurst's work deals in part with this question as well; see Waswo, "Review of Agricultural Development and Tenancy Disputes in Japan"; Nishida Yoshiaki, "Growth of the Meiji Landlord System and Tenancy Disputes After World War I"; and Smethurst, "A Challenge to Orthodoxy and Its Orthodox Critics."

51. Ouchi Tsutomu, Nōka keizai, vol. 6, pp. 36, 49-54; Nishida Yoshiaki, Kindai Nihon nōmin undōshi kenkyū, pp. 73-75, 104-121; Teruoka Shūzō, Nihon nōgyō mondai no tenkai, vol. 2, pp. 67-75. For an example of official expression of mistrust of the results of a local survey of the depression's effects, see Nihon ginkō Fukushima shiten, Fukushima ken nōson jōkyō, p. 618.

52. The economic downturn caused considerable hardship for factory workers and urban residents. Unofficial estimates of the number of urban unemployed range from 1.5 to 3 million persons, or from 20 to 40 percent of the labor pool. Official estimates were of rates below 7 percent; they were not taken seriously. See Kazahara Yasoji, Nihon shakai seisaku shi, pp. 303-304, for a description of some of the flaws in the state's survey methods. He estimated that there were 3 million unemployed. For other unofficial estimates, see "Shitsugyō mondai no jissō to sono taisaku," Economisuto 8.14 (July 1930): 105; and Sumiya Mikio, "Kyōkō to kokumin shokaikyū,"

pp. 254–255. Nakamura Masanori's estimate for the same year is just under 2.4 million; see Nakamura, *Shōwa no kyōkō*, vol. 2, pp. 294–295, and also Hara Akira, "Keiki junkan," pp. 401–402.

53. Sumiya Mikio, "Kyōkō to kokumin shokaikyū," pp. 256–257.

54. SMY, *Keizai kōsei keikaku kihon chōsa*, 1934, KST.

55. I have calculated these figures by comparing total reported income from all sources (farming and "other"), and total reported spending (production, family, and "other" expenses) for those families reporting deficits. If income and spending for all families in the hamlet are included, then the total deficit is only 2,521 yen, and the average deficit drops to 143 yen per household.

56. For a discussion of the role of Special Household Taxes, see Ōishi Kaichirō, "Shōwa kyōkō to chihō zaisei," pp. 87–102.

57. The percentage figures are based on a survey population of 420 households. SMY, *Keizai kōsei keikaku kihon chōsa*, 1934, KST.

58. The average household tax in the hamlet that year was 12.8 yen, the median, 11.8. The reported village average was 11.1 yen, which puts Komatsu close to the norm for the community. *Komatsu buraku kakuko keizai kōsei chōsa bo*, October 1934, KST.

59. The relationship between landownership and the extent of a household's deficit in 1933 is harder to pin down, since only one household in Komatsu owned no land at all. That family reported an imbalance between spending and income of almost 430 yen, the second largest such deficit. Both the three smallest landholders and the three largest reported deficits.

60. Hara Masaru's family reported a deficit in 1933 of less than a single yen; it is included as among those in the black that year.

61. The Teikoku Nōkai (Imperial Agricultural Association) released a draft farm-debt arrangement plan that year. See also Kageyama Shikazō, "Fusai o seyo!"

62. Nōrinshō nōmukyoku, "Nōka fusai seiri jikkō jirei," October 1931, NSS 1:5, p. 128. Kodaira Gonichi, writing in 1931, was highly critical of the methodology employed in the Imperial Agricultural Association's survey but suggested that the lower end of their estimate was probably accurate as far as it went. See Kodaira, *Saikin ni okeru naigai nōgyō kinyū jijō no kōsatsu*, pp. 126–142, for a discussion of the survey, and idem, *Nōgyō kinyūron*, p. 876, for his conclusion that total farm debt was close to 4 billion yen.

63. Nōrin daijin kanbō sōmuka, ed., *Nōrin gyōsei shi*, vol. 2, pp. 195–197. See also Nishida Yoshiaki, "Nōmin keiei no tenkai," p. 965. See *Tōkyō nichi nichi shinbun*, June 4, 1932; and *Tōkyō asahi shinbun*, June 5, 1932.

64. Nōrin daijin kanbō sōmuka, ed., *Nōrin gyōsei shi*, vol. 2, pp. 197–198. The highest estimate, of 6 billion yen, comes from the *Nihon nōgyō nenpō*, and is cited by Teruoka Shūzō, *Nihon nōgyō mondai no tenkai*, vol. 2, p. 79.

65. Teruoka Shūzō, *Nihon nōgyō mondai no tenkai*, vol. 2, p. 80.

66. See ibid., pp. 79–80, for the comparisons to the value of farm production and farm income. The GNP in 1932 (at current prices) was 13.7 billion yen. See Ohkawa, Takamatsu, and Yamamoto, *National Income*, p. 200.

67. SMY, *Keizai kōsei keikaku kihon chōsa*, 1934, KST. The shift of deposits out of local institutions and into the national savings system was widespread, especially after the collapse of many banks in the late 1920s. See Fukushima-ken, "Nōson hihei jōkyō narabi sono taisaku," p. 593. Kase Kazutoshi, "Nōson fusai seiri seisaku no ritsuan katei Manshū jihenki nōgyō seisaku taikei no ichisokumen," provides the best available analysis of depression-era debt and debt reduction policies.

68. SMY, "Fukyō chōsa narabi ni taisaku ni kansuru ken kaihō," August 6, 1932, in *Shomu kankei shorui 1932*, KST. This figure is close to the prefecture's estimate of average household debt in 1931. Fukushima-ken, "Nōson hihei jōkyō narabi sono taisaku," p. 594.

69. SMY, *Keizai kōsei keikaku kihon chōsa*, 1934, KST. Unfortunately, this section does not provide a source-by-source breakdown of where Sekishiba's officials thought the 800,000 yen in debt had come from, or how they arrived at that figure.

70. In one part of the survey, banks and credit unions are shown to have loaned 113,599 yen to Sekishiba residents, but only 100,043 appears in the section of the survey that deals specifically with debt. The 11,000-yen figure was calculated using the smaller amount and an 11 percent annual interest rate.

71. Nihon ginkō Fukushima shiten, *Fukushima ken nōson jōkyō*, pp. 627–632.

72. Nishiyama Kōichi, Nishida Yoshiaki, and Kubo Yasuo, *Nishiyama Kōichi nikki, 1925–1950-nen*, pp. 1280–1282.

73. SMY, "Keizai kōsei iinkai hi joseikin kōfu seigansho," July 20, 1934. *Keizai kōsei, 1934*, KST.

74. Local spending in 1925 was more than four times what it had been in 1912; for a partial listing of the new burdens on local budgets, see Ōkurashō Shōwa zaiseishi henshūshitsu, ed., *Chihō zaisei, Shōwa zaisei shi*, vol. 14, pp. 3–7.

75. Kitakata-shi shi hensan iinkai, ed., *Kitakata-shi shi*, vol. 6, pp. 812–817.

76. Ōkurashō Shōwa zaiseishi henshūshitsu, ed., *Chihō zaisei, Shōwa zaisei shi*, vol. 14, p. 64.

77. Teruoka Shūzō, *Nihon nōgyō mondai no tenkai*, vol. 2, p. 82; officials in one Niigata village noted that unpaid taxes had, among other things, diminished their ability to provide education, hygiene, public works, recordkeeping, family records, youth training, and upkeep of temples and shrines for the community. Ōkado Masakatsu, *Kindai Nihon to nōson shakai*, pp. 249–251.

78. Ōkado Masakatsu, *Kindai Nihon to nōson shakai*, p. 255.

79. Nihon ginkō Fukushima shiten, *Fukushima ken nōson jōkyō*, pp. 604, 606; Ōishi Kaichirō, "Shōwa kyōkō to chihō zaisei," p. 107; *Fukushima minpō*, June 12, 1931.

80. Fukushima communities owed teachers more than 260,000 yen in October 1932 and more than 130,000 yen in August 1934. Nihon ginkō Fukushima shiten, *Fukushima ken nōson jōkyō*, pp. 660–662; *Fukushima minpō*, June 17, 1932.

81. Tamura Kō, "Aomori-ken no nōson kyōkō jijō taisaku fusai chōsa," p. 135; *Sennan nichi nichi shinbun*, June 4, 1932; *Fukuoka nichinichi shinbun*, January 12, 1932; *Chūgai shōgyō*, July 14, 1932.

82. Abe Tadashi, "Nōsangyoson kōsei kōrōsha hyōshō no ken," May 30, 1936, *Keizai kōsei, 1937*, vol. 1, KST. Sekishiba's payment rates were the subject of praise by the press; see *Fukushima minpō*, June 1, 1937, and April 17, 1938.

83. SMY, *Sonzei kankei shorui tsuzuri*, January 1929, 1932, 1935, 1937, 1939, KST.

84. *Osaka mainichi shinbun*, June 23, 1932, as quoted in Sumiya Yoshiharu, "Nōson kyōkyūsaku to shakai seisaku no genkai." Other accounts describe similar scenes in local pawnshops, where mothers had turned over their children's toys for enough cash to buy food or to seek medical care. See *Sennan nichinichi shinbun*, June 24, 1932.

85. For one official statement on this topic, see Nōrinshō sanshikyoku, *Kenshi-ka teiraku no yōsan nōmin ni oyoboshitaru eikyō*, pp. 6, 15–16.

86. *Tōkyō asahi shinbun*, July 28, 1932; Sumiya Yoshiharu, "Nōson kyōkyūsaku to shakai seisaku no genkai," p. 283; Tamura Kō, "Aomori-ken no nōson kyōkō jijō taisaku fusai chōsa," pp. 135–136; Kenmochi Seiichi, "Shōwa kyōkō ki to hoppō no kyōshi-tachi," p. 208; *Nihon keizai nenpō* 9 (1932): 124–136.

87. Hokushin fukyō taisaku kai daihyōsha, "Nōson kyūsai no chinjō o kiku," p. 25.

88. No allowance is made for differences in family size; in Komatsu the average family size for taxpayers in the highest bracket was over ten, just under eight for middle-level families, and seven exactly for those households in the lowest bracket. The variation, while worth noting, does not seem to be enough to account for the huge differences in spending reflected in the village-level survey.

89. Note that the "hygiene" category in the survey covers not only medical expenditures but also makeup, hairdressing, and barber's fees, and that at least some of the gap in spending between upper and lower categories may reflect those costs.

90. SMY, *Keizai kōsei keikaku kihon chōsa*, 1934, KST.

91. Waswo, "The Transformation of Rural Society, 1900–1950," p. 578.

92. In 1926. Nōchi seido shiryō shūsei hensan iinkai, *Nōchi seido shiryō shūsei*, vol. 2, pp. 50–51.

93. See Waswo, "The Transformation of Rural Society, 1900–1950," for a clear accounting of these developments. See also Dore, *Land Reform in Japan*, for his classic analysis of prewar tenancy.

94. Tenancy disputes also had a tendency to last much longer than strikes; as Nishida notes, more than half of all tenancy struggles in 1936 lasted more than a month, while less than 3 percent of labor disputes did. Nishida Yoshiaki, "Senzen Nihon ni okeru rōdō undō nōmin undō no seishitsu," pp. 288–289.

95. Waswo, *Japanese Landlords*, p. 96.
96. Kitakata-shi shi hensan iinkai, ed., *Kitakata-shi shi*, vol. 8, 1991, p. 648.
97. Ibid.; SMY, report from Satō Sakichi to the director of the Fukushima-ken keizai bu, "Kosakuchi kosakuryō chōsa no ken," August 24, 1936, *Jisakunō* documents 1935–1937, KST. Thirty percent of paddy land rents were due in November, 50 percent in December, and the remainder in January.
98. Waswo, *Japanese Landlords*, pp. 130–133.
99. Ibid., p. 97; Nōchi seido shiryō shūsei hensan iinkai, *Nōchi seido shiryō shūsei*, vol. 2, pp. 50–51.
100. Ōishi Kaichirō, *Fukushima-ken no hyakunen*, p. 215.
101. These tenancy dispute figures are from Nōrinshō nōseikyoku, *1930 nen kosaku nenpō*, September 1930, and *1939 nen kosaku nenpō*, December 1939, and Kitakata-shi shi hensan iinkai, ed., *Kitakata-shi shi*, vol. 6, p. 593. Note that Shōji Kichinosuke, in his study of tenancy disputes in Fukushima, provides different figures. See Shōji, "Chihō ni okeru Shōwa kyōkō to nōmin-rōdōsha no undō," pp. 223–228, 240. The only year the prefecture did not rank in the top ten was 1934. Nishida Yoshiaki, "Nōmin undō to nōgyō seisaku," pp. 296–297, 300–301; Fukushima-ken, ed., *Fukushima-ken shi*, vol. 15, p. 235; idem, ed., *Fukushima-ken shi*, vol. 16, pp. 182–189, 592, 609–610.
102. Teruoka Shūzō, *Nihon nōgyō mondai no tenkai*, vol. 2, p. 138. See pp. 140–143 for a discussion of disputes in Akita. See also Waswo, *Japanese Landlords*, pp. 130–133; Nihon ginkō Fukushima shiten, *Fukushima ken nōson jōkyō*, p. 665.
103. This is despite the slightly larger than average plots farmed by, and owned by, Sekishiba farmers. For comments by village officials on a perceived shortage of land in the village, see *Keizai kōsei keikaku kihon chōsa*, 1934; and SMY, Mayor Satō to Fukushima-ken gakumu buchō, "Nōsangyoson ni okeru dekasegi jōkyō chōsa no ken," December 20, 1934, *Kangyō* documents, 1934, KST.
104. Classification as an owner-cultivator implies that the household owned all the land it farmed; households farming both land they owned and rented land are categorized as owner-tenants, while those farming only rented land are categorized as tenants. Although it is possible and sometimes desirable to draw even finer distinctions within each category, for the purposes of this study the three main divisions offered here are sufficient. Twenty-seven percent of all farm households were tenants in 1930; that share remained more or less unchanged for the rest of the decade. Fukushima's average was the same in 1930, but increased to 31 percent by 1937. Kayo Nobufumi, ed., *Nihon nōgyō kiso tōkei*, 1977, p. 67; Fukushima-ken, ed., *Kindai shiryō 3, Fukushima-ken shi*, vol. 13, pp. 34–37.
105. Kitakata-shi shi hensan iinkai, ed., *Kitakata-shi shi*, vol. 8, p. 657. These figures are from 1947.
106. SMY, *Tahata jisaku kōsaku tanbetsu chō*, 1923, KST.

107. Most of these men lived in the southern part of the village. Three lived in Kamitakahitai, and one each lived in Sanjōnome, Shimosugure, and Nishinakamei. It is not clear where they owned the land. If it was all within the village boundaries, then together the seven account for about 28 percent of the paddy land (142.1 *chō*) and 20 percent of the upland fields (28 *chō*) in Sekishiba. See SMY, Mayor Satō to the Keizai buchō, "Jisakunō sōsetsu iji shikin kashitsuke ni kansuru ken," July 11, 1936, *Jisakunō* documents, 1935–1937, KST. Non-residents owned more than 131 *chō* of paddy land in Sekishiba in 1934. SMY, *Keizai kōsei keikaku kihon chōsa*, 1934, Chi moku betsu.

108. Waswo, *Japanese Landlords*, pp. 105–106.

109. See Kitakata-shi shi hensan iinkai, ed., *Kitakata-shi shi*, vol. 6, pp. 804–805. See Fukushima-ken, ed., *Fukushima-ken shi*, vol. 13, p. 94, for land-use figures in Yama county. The share of tenanted land was somewhat lower in the county as a whole than in Sekishiba.

110. Nishida Yoshiaki, "Nōmin undō to nōgyō seisaku," pp. 317–319; Nōrin daijin kanbō sōmuka, ed., *Nōrin gyōsei shi*, vol. 2, pp. 187–191. See also Haley, *Authority Without Power*, pp. 87–94, for a discussion of conciliation in landlord-tenant conflicts.

111. Waswo, "The Transformation of Rural Society, 1900–1950," pp. 564–566. Ōkado Masakatsu, *Kindai Nihon to nōson shakai*, offers an insightful analysis of these changes.

112. Vlastos, "Agrarianism Without Tradition," p. 94.

113. Iinuma Jirō, "Seitō seiji to Shōwa nōgyō kyōkō," pp. 165–168; Tasaki Nobuyoshi, "Toshi bunka to kokumin ishiki," p. 192; Hosaka Masayasu, *Go-ichigo jiken*, pp. 325–335, 348–354; Havens, *Farm and Nation in Modern Japan*, p. 247.

114. *Tōkyō nichinichi shinbun*, July 28, 1933. As the young officer went on to say, a peasant uprising would pit soldiers against their families, which could only harm the military. Clearly many of the officers worried about the countryside, but their motives were hardly altruistic. The military always came first.

115. Hosaka Masayasu, *Go-ichigo jiken*, p. 327.

116. Tasaki Nobuyoshi, "Toshi bunka to kokumin ishiki," p. 193.

117. See Waswo, "The Transformation of Rural Society, 1900–1950," pp. 589–597, for an overview of agrarianism in the interwar era, and, of course, Havens, *Farm and Nation in Modern Japan*.

118. Iinuma Jirō, "Seitō seiji to Shōwa nōgyō kyōkō," pp. 165–168; Dore and Ōuchi, "Rural Origins of Japanese Fascism," p. 197.

119. Hosaka Masayasu, *Go-ichigo jiken*, p. 333.

120. Ibid., pp. 331, 358.

121. Such sentencing practices were not unique to the May 15 Incident. Hamaguchi's assassin was sentenced to death in 1933 but pardoned soon after and released

from prison in 1940. Inoue's assassin received a life sentence and was also released in 1940. Dan Takuma's assassin, Hishinuma Gorō, received a life sentence, was pardoned, and was released in 1940. He went on to a successful political career with the Liberal Democratic Party after the war and was elected eight times to the Ibaraki Prefectural Assembly, eventually serving as its head before his death in 1990.

122. The *Tōkyō asahi shinbun* carried news of Tachibana's release in a brief page-two article. Hosaka Masayasu, *Go-ichigo jiken*, p. 373.

## Chapter 4

1. Little is known about Akutagawa. A search of local records revealed only that he was a Matsuyama resident, where his family owned a small amount of land. See *Matsuyama mura kaigiroku 1931* and *Matsuyama murayakuba chiso meikichō*, Book 7, 1938, KST.

2. *Fukushima minpō*, October 8, 1931; Ushiyama Kenji, "Shōwa nōgyō kyōkō," p. 179.

3. *Fukushima minpō*, October 8, 13, and 23, 1931.

4. Akutagawa was by then acting as spokesman for a renamed group of local farmers, the Yama County Residents' Volunteer Assembly (Yama gunmin yūshi taikai). SMY, "Chōson chōkai shikai reikai teishutsu jikō," July 16, 1932, *Chōson chōkai Yama-gun shikai kankei tsuzuri 1931–1934*, KST.

5. Ibid. See also *Fukushima minpō*, July 18, 1932. The newspaper article reports the association's plan to send the petition on to the ministers concerned.

6. The government kept an eye on the agrarianists but devoted most of its energy to suppressing the Left. Even after the events of 1932, the Home Ministry's *Shakai undō no jōkyō* gave only about 70 pages out of 1,600 to agrarianist groups and their activities. The Communist Party, all but defunct by then, received considerably more space. The Home Ministry did report on the agrarianist movement in somewhat more detail in Naimushō keihōkyoku, ed., *Shuppan mono o tsūjite mitaru Nihon kakushinron no genjō*, vol. 6, pp. 181–209.

7. Gluck, *Japan's Modern Myths*, pp. 189–204.

8. Havens, *Farm and Nation in Modern Japan*, pp. 64–72, 80.

9. More than 90 percent of villages, towns, and cities had at least one cooperative in place by 1914. Ibid., p. 83.

10. Ibid., pp. 73–74.

11. The four principles are *shisei*, *kinrō*, *bundō*, and *suijō*. Armstrong, *Just Before the Dawn*, pp. 232–234. See also Havens, "Religion and Agriculture in Nineteenth Century Japan," pp. 100–102.

12. Armstrong, *Just Before the Dawn*, pp. 232–234.

13. Ibid., p. 188.

14. Ibid., pp. 184, 187, 190–191.

15. This organization would be especially active in promoting rural reform in conjunction with the Economic Revitalization Campaign. Yagi Shigeki, *Hōtoku undō 100 nen no ayumi*, pp. 228–229, 231, 235. The year 1924 also marks the start of that group's participation in the Federation of Moral Suasion Groups (Kyōka dantai rengōkai).

16. Sakata Masatoshi, "Kaisetsu," p. 9. Hirata was agriculture and commerce secretary from 1901 to 1903 and home minister from 1908 to 1911. Ichiki served as both education minister and home minister between 1914 and 1916 and would later be head of the Privy Council and imperial household minister. He became head of the Dai Nihon Hōtokusha (Great Japan Hōtoku Society) in 1934. His younger brother Okuda Ryōhei was education minister in several administrations and involved in the spread of military training in schools. Sawayanagi was with the Education Ministry until 1908, before going on to a successful career as an educator. For the Local Improvement Campaign, see Pyle, "The Technology of Japanese Nationalism."

17. Pyle, "The Technology of Japanese Nationalism," pp. 52–53, 59–60, 65.

18. See Ōishi Kaichirō and Nishida Yoshiaki, eds., *Kindai Nihon no gyōseison*, pp. 325–338, for an example of how the Local Improvement Campaign worked at the village level.

19. Pyle acknowledges that many of the more concrete goals of the campaign were not achieved but suggests that it did succeed in "establishing systematic links with the leaders of local society and imbuing them with the nation's goals and ideology." See Pyle, "The Technology of Japanese Nationalism," p. 65.

20. The connection between the Home Ministry (led by Hirata Tōsuke) and Hōtoku-ism at the time was so strong that opponents of the Katsura cabinet used it as a political weapon, charging that the ministry's encouragement of Hōtoku teachings had led the country into a recession. Sakata Masatochi, "Kaisetsu," pp. 8–9. The Chūō Hōtokukai's (Central Hōtoku Organization's) journal *Shimin* became an important public arena for semi-official views not just on farm issues but on anything having to do with local reform and leadership. The magazine's message was well tailored to its audience of local leaders by the (mostly Home Ministry) bureaucrats, former bureaucrats, and Hōtoku officials who did much of the writing for *Shimin*. *Shimin* was issued between 1906 and 1944; average sales in 1921 were around ten thousand copies. For an informative and useful analysis of *Shimin*'s role in the early 1930s, see Wilson, "Bureaucrats and Villagers in Japan." I am indebted to Professor Wilson for her insights into the connections between the magazine and promotion of the Economic Revitalization Campaign.

21. In Sekishiba, the regulations allowed young men to remain members of their association until the age of twenty-five; in other communities, it was not uncommon to stretch membership out into one's thirties. See Nishida Yoshiaki, ed., *Shōwa kyōkōka no nōson shakai undō*, pp. 379–384.

22. Smethurst, *A Social Basis for Prewar Japanese Militarism*; Havens, *Farm and Nation in Modern Japan*, pp. 80–85; Gluck, *Japan's Modern Myths*, pp. 189–204.

23. Teikoku nōkai hensankai, ed., *Teikoku nōkai shikō*, pp. 521–523. The first set of items is from a resolution adopted by a meeting of the heads of the prefectural agricultural associations in late July 1930. The second comes from the response issued by the association's regular general meeting that met from October 28 to November 1, 1930. That response also urged households to cut back on wedding and funeral costs, to cut back on cash spending for everyday goods (substituting homemade items where possible), and to rely more on cooperative sales and purchases.

24. Vlastos, "Tradition: Past/Present Culture and Modern Japanese History." See Waswo, "The Transformation of Rural Society, 1900–1950," and Havens, *Farm and Nation in Modern Japan*, for useful analyses of agrarianism.

25. Vlastos, "Agrarianism Without Tradition."

26. Adachi Ikitsune, "Ie no hikari no rekishi"; idem, "Jiriki kōsei undōka no *Ie no hikari*"; Havens, *Farm and Nation in Modern Japan*, pp. 155–162.

27. Havens, *Farm and Nation in Modern Japan*, pp. 275–294; Young, *Japan's Total Empire*, pp. 318–325.

28. Yasuda Tsuneo, *Nihon fashizumu to minshū undō*, p. 414; Naimushō keihōkyoku, ed., *Shuppan mono o tsūjite mitaru Nihon kakushinron no genjō*, vol. 6, pp. 184–186.

29. Note that this assessment may have been written before the actions of some of Gondō's followers made him famous. Naimushō keihōkyoku, ed., *Shuppan mono o tsūjite mitaru Nihon kakushinron no genjō*, vol. 6, pp. 194–195.

30. Asahi shinbun sha, *Asahi jinbutsu jiten: gendai Nihon*, p. 1164; Havens, "Two Popular Views of Rural Self-Rule in Modern Japan," p. 251.

31. Nagano Akira, "Genjitsu ni sokuseru Nihon no kaizō," pp. 53–54. The six ministries are the Home, Foreign, Defense, Justice, Education, and Finance. As Thomas Havens has pointed out, Nagano was not interested in doing away with the central government completely, only with limiting its role as much as possible. See also Havens, "Two Popular Views of Rural Self-Rule in Modern Japan," and Naimushō keihōkyoku, ed., *Shuppan mono o tsūjite mitaru Nihon kakushinron no genjō*, vol. 6, p. 185.

32. Nagano's published works include *Nihon jichi shikan* (Historical View of Local Autonomy in Japan, 1932) and the five-volume *Jichigaku* (Studies of Local Autonomy, 1936). His articles include Nagano Akira, "Genjitsu ni sokuseru Nihon no kaizō" (July 1932; also appearing in that issue of *Keizai ōrai* were Kodaira Gonichi and Okada Atsushi, secretary of the Imperial Agriculture Association); "Nōson seigan undō no keika" (October 1932); "Hijōji haigo no hito—Gondō Seikyō shi to sono gakusetsu" (October 1933); "Nōson no jissō to sono kyūsai saku" (February 1934); and "Takahashi zaisei to nōmin mondai" (February 1935).

33. Naimushō keihōkyoku, ed., *Shuppan mono o tsūjite mitaru Nihon kakushinron no genjō*, vol. 6, pp. 181–183.

34. See ibid., p. 182, and Yasuda Tsuneo, *Nihon fashizumu to minshū undō*, pp. 389–394.

35. For a contemporary account of conditions in the prefecture, see Nagano-ken naimubu nōshōka, ed., *Nagano-ken no fukyō jitsujō* (August 1932), NSS 1:1, pp. 347–348. It estimates that roughly four-fifths of all farm households were involved in sericulture. Farm income in 1931 was thought to have been about half of what it had been in 1929.

36. Yasuda Tsuneo, *Nihon fashizumu to minshū undō*, pp. 191–210, 215, 229. They published over 1,700 issues a month. After October 1938, the magazine was called *Hinomoto*.

37. Nagahara Yutaka, "1932 nen 'Nōson kyūsai seigan undō' no tokushitsu, Jichi nōmin kyōgikai"; Yasuda Tsuneo, *Nihon fashizumu to minshū undō*, pp. 239–240.

38. Nagahara Yutaka, "1932 nen 'Nōson kyūsai seigan undō' no tokushitsu, Jichi nōmin kyōgikai," p. 2; Yasuda Tsuneo, *Nihon fashizumu to minshū undō*, pp. 219–220, 231. Wagō also promised to deal with the land and tenancy problems via a two-part policy. He would halve tenant rents and develop an owner-cultivator law that would use land taxes, not rents, as the basis for determining land purchase prices. As part of his plan to establish fair rent levels, Wagō made use of calculations developed by Tokyo University Professor Nasu Hiroshi. Later in the campaign, Wagō narrowed his platform to focus more on prefectural issues. Interestingly, one of the things he advocated was the establishment of a facility to help farmers pursue economic planning. Yasuda Tsuneo, *Nihon fashizumu to minshū undō*, p. 242.

39. Yasuda Tsuneo, *Nihon fashizumu to minshū undō*, pp. 243–244. The two successful non-mainstream candidates received 4,043 votes (for a right-wing nationalist) and 4,695 votes (for the Zenkoku rōnō taishūtō), respectively.

40. Wagō described Gondō's learning and spirit as "important national treasures for the creation of a new Japan." Yasuda Tsuneo, *Nihon fashizumu to minshū undō*, pp. 247, 395.

41. Ibid., pp. 399–400; Nagahara Yutaka, "1932 nen 'Nōson kyūsai seigan undō' no tokushitsu, Jichi nōmin kyōgikai," p. 3.

42. Takisawa Makoto, *Gondō Seikyō*, p. 172. Inamura graduated from Waseda in 1923 and was active in the farmers' movement soon afterward. His credentials as a rural activist were considerable even before the petition movement; he joined the Shakaitō (Socialist Party) after the war and was elected to the Diet in Niigata after the death of his brother Junzō in 1955. He left politics in 1969.

43. Ibid., p. 168. The comment was reported by Yamagishi Hiroshi, a naval officer. Inamura's account of the start of the petition movement puts Nagano, Wagō,

and to a lesser extent Tachibana at the center of things. See Inamura Ryūichi, *Inamura Ryūichi shi danwa (dai ni) sokkiroku*, pp. 108–109.

44. Yasuda Tsuneo, *Nihon fashizumu to minshū undō*, p. 414.

45. The fertilizer subsidy was to be paid at the ratio of 1 yen per *tan* of land farmed. A *tan* is a measure equivalent to 993 square meters. There are 10 *tan* in 1 *chō*.

46. The petition text is taken from *Tokkō geppō*, June 1932, p. 5. See Yasuda Tsuneo, *Nihon fashizumu to minshū undō*, pp. 30, 52–57, 404, for a discussion of earlier examples of petition movements in Nagano, including one following the 1927 mulberry crop failure.

47. See, for example, Scheiner, "Benevolent Lords and Honorable Peasants"; Kelly, *Deference and Defiance in Nineteenth-Century Japan*; and Walthall, *Social Protest and Popular Culture in Eighteenth Century Japan*.

48. See Walthall, ed., *Peasant Uprisings in Japan*, pp. 35–75, for a discussion of this incident.

49. Roberts, "The Petition Box in Eighteenth-Century Tosa."

50. Yasutomi Kunio, "Shōwa shoki kyūnō seisaku no keisei shōmetsu katei ni kansuru jakkan no kōsatsu," p. 150. See also Teikoku gikai shūgiin, *Dai 62 rinji teikoku gikai shūgiin hōkoku* (1932) and *Dai 63 rinji teikoku gikai shūgiin hōkoku* (1932). A total of 278 petitions concerned with village relief were presented to the Sixty-third Diet. Only 23 similar petitions were presented to the Sixty-fourth Diet, held in early 1933, and 52 to the Sixty-fifth Diet. *Dai 63 rinji teikoku gikai shūgiin hōkoku* (1932), pp. 100–101.

51. Yasuda Tsuneo, *Nihon fashizumu to minshū undō*, p. 415.

52. Nagano Akira, *Shōwa nōmin sōkekki roku*, p. 28.

53. Yasuda Tsuneo, *Nihon fashizumu to minshū undō*, p. 422; Nagano Akira, *Shōwa nōmin sōkekki roku*, p. 29.

54. Nagano Akira, *Shōwa nōmin sōkekki roku*, pp. 28–29.

55. *Tōkyō asahi shinbun*, June 3, 1932. The Home Ministry's estimate of just under 19,000 signatures on the three-clause petitions is considerably lower than this estimate, which is in line with Wagō's own figures. See *Shakai undō no jōkyō*, 1932, pp. 928–930. See also Teikoku gikai shūgiin, *Teikoku gikai shūgiin giji sokkiroku*, vol. 57, pp. 204–205, vol. 58, 221–225. Just recording the three-clause petitions in official Diet publications took up more than five pages of text, far more than any of the other petitions.

56. *Tōkyō asahi shinbun*, June 3, 1932.

57. The group's relatively high-status membership (which first came together in February 1932) has led Japanese scholars to use the statements made by its members to probe the opinions and attitudes of middle-class farmers at large. Yasuda Tsuneo, *Nihon fashizumu to minshū undō*, pp. 404, 407; Yasutomi Kunio, "Shōwa shoki kyūnō

seisaku no keisei shōmetsu katei ni kansuru jakkan no kōsatsu," pp. 146-147; *Tokkō geppō*. June 1932, p. 6.

58. *Tokkō geppō*, June 1932, pp. 6-7.

59. "Nōson kyūsai no chinjō o kiku," *Tōyō keizai shinpō*, June 18, 1932, p. 28.

60. Yasuda Tsuneo, *Nihon fashizumu to minshū undō*, pp. 404-405. See also *Tokkō geppō*, June 1932, pp. 6-7.

61. "Nōson kyūsai no chinjō o kiku," *Tōyō keizai shinpō*, June 18, 1932, pp. 19-20.

62. Ibid., p. 22, as argued by Uchikawa Yoshitoku, Kitamikami village, Kitasaku county. Uchikawa went on to note that in a nearby village the mayor had performed a debt survey in 1929. He found that the average household debt was about 800 yen, and instituted a policy of frugality which urged residents not to drink, not to use sugar, and not to eat sweets. "In 1932, after more than three years, what happened to the debt in that village?" asked Uchikawa. "The debt for each household is some 1500 yen. Under these conditions not only can we not pay back debts but we cannot even eat. Unless the state does something to solve the debt problem, we farmers will be unable to live."

63. "Nōson kyūsai no chinjō o kiku," *Tōyō keizai shinpō*, June 18, 1932, p. 25.

64. *Osaka mainichi shinbun*, June 7, 1932. Takeshita's speech is remarkably similar in parts to sections of a resolution on self-revitalization adopted on June 2 by a meeting of agriculture association officials in Osaka. See below, and Teikoku nōkai shikō hensankai, ed., *Teikoku nōkai shikō*, pp. 527-528.

65. *Osaka mainichi shinbun*, June 7, 1932. Both this article and one on the same day in the *Chūgai shōgyō* report the total number of signatures as between 45,000 and 46,000.

66. Yasuda Tsuneo, *Nihon fashizumu to minshū undō*, p. 424.

67. Teikoku gikai shūgiin, *Teikoku gikai shūgiin giji sokkiroku*, vol. 57, p. 140.

68. Ibid.

69. Soeda Keiichirō spoke for the Minseitō; Sugiyama Motojirō on behalf of the representatives from outside the two established parties; ibid., pp. 140-141, 144.

70. Yasuda Tsuneo, *Nihon fashizumu to minshū undō*, pp. 424-426.

71. Nagano and Takeshita spent the next several years trying to get a version of these amendments approved by the legislature.

72. *Jiriki kōsei* is discussed in detail below. See Nagano Akira, *Shōwa nōmin sōkekki roku*, p. 38, for his August 20, 1932, public statement announcing the amendments. The emphasis on food, shelter, land, clothing, and so on in the bill is quite close to the way Gondō described the basic elements of farm life. See, for instance, Havens, *Farm and Nation in Modern Japan*, p. 193.

73. Yasuda Tsuneo, *Nihon fashizumu to minshū undō*, p. 425.

74. Nagano Akira, "Nōson seigan undō no keika," pp. 91-92.

75. Yasuda Tsuneo, *Nihon fashizumu to minshū undō*, p. 431. According to figures in Naimushō keihōkyoku, *Shakai undō no jōkyō*, 1932, p. 932, the total number of signatures was 42,505. The smaller figure is Wagō's estimate.

76. In his first mention in the *Fukushima minpō*, Nagano is described as "the advance guard in the movement to build a new Japan"; in a later article, his movement is described as one "deeply colored by fascism," with a strong implication that the police were wise to keep a close watch on it. *Fukushima minpō*, July 2, 1932 and August 26, 1932. See also Naimushō keihōkyoku, *Shakai undō no jōkyō*, 1932, pp. 675, 930, 932.

77. Naimushō keihōkyoku, *Shakai undō no jōkyō*, 1932, p. 931. Also Yasuda Tsuneo, *Nihon fashizumu to minshū undō*, pp. 430–431.

78. Nagano Akira, *Shōwa nōmin sōkekki roku*, pp. 42–43.

79. See, for example, Nagano Akira, "Nōson seigan undō no keika."

80. Ibid., p. 91.

81. See also Wilson, "Bureaucrats and Villagers in Japan."

82. Nagano Akira, "Nōson seigan undō no keika," p. 91.

83. Ibid., pp. 90–91.

84. Ibid., p. 90.

85. Nagano Akira, *Shōwa nōmin sōkekki roku*, p. 25.

86. See *Tōkyō asahi shinbun*, June 2–5, June 7, June 9–11, June 14, 1932.

87. In attendance were people like Gotō Fumio, Katō Kanji, Soeda Keiichirō (Seiyūkai, Fukushima), Sugiyama Motojirō (National Labor–Farmer Masses Party, Osaka), Nasu Hiroshi, Fukuzawa Yasue (head of the National Association of Mayors of Towns and Villages), and others. Tōkyō nichi nichi shinbun keizaibu, ed., *Ikaga ni site nōson o sukūbeki ka*.

88. For example, the *Fukuoka nichi nichi* began its series on village life on June 18, 1932, at about the same time that the Sendai-based *Sennan nichi nichi* was running its collection of articles describing "the village crisis." *Fukushima minpō*, which I have looked at most closely, is from June through August 1932 full of descriptions of villages and farm families on the verge of collapse.

89. Kase Kazutoshi, "Nōson fusai seiri seisaku no ritsuan katei," p. 14. See also Nōrinshō nōmukyoku, "Nōka fusai seiri jikkō jirei," October 1931, in *NSS* 2:5, pp. 1–129, for a detailed description of prefectural policies.

90. Prefectural assistance was limited; Kase notes that in Fukuoka the prefecture spent only 8,250 yen. Kase Kazutoshi, "Nōson fusai seiri seisaku no ritsuan katei," p. 16, fn. 7.

91. Kodaira published his first *Shimin* article in 1915, and was a frequent contributor to that journal and others from then on. His books include a more than 900-page-long doctoral dissertation (also at Tokyo University) entitled *Nōgyō kinyū*

*ron* (1930), *Nōgyō kinyū to nōka fusai seiri* (Nihon hyōron sha, 1933), and many others. In addition to Kase Kazutoshi's excellent work on Kodaira and debt policy, see also Kusumoto Masahiro, ed., *Nōsangyoson keizai kōsei undō to Kodaira Gonichi*, and Kodaira Gonichi to kindai nōsei henshū shuppan iinkai, ed., *Kodaira Gonichi to kindai nōsei*, for discussions of Kodaira's role in the formation of agricultural policy.

92. Kodaira Gonichi to kindai nōsei henshū shuppan iinkai, ed., *Kodaira Gonichi to kindai nōsei*, pp. 14, 35–36, 138. The politician Arima Yoriyasu was another classmate at Tokyo University.

93. Kodaira's positions included chief of the Agricultural Policy Section, the Rice Section, and the Silk-Thread Bureau.

94. My description of Kodaira's views is based on Kase Kazutoshi, "Nōson fusai seiri seisaku no ritsuan katei," pp. 20–23. He in turn refers to Kodaira's *Nōgyō kinyū ron* (1930), *Saikin ni okeru naigai nōgyō kinyū jijō no kōsatsu* (1931), and *Nōgyō kinyū to nōka fusai seiri* (1933).

95. The 1933 Agricultural Chattel Credit Law addressed these concerns. See Kodaira Gonichi to kindai nōsei henshū shuppan iinkai, ed., *Kodaira Gonichi to kindai nōsei*, pp. 110–113, for a discussion of these points as they appear in Kodaira's *Nōgyō kinyū ron*.

96. Kodaira, *Nōgyō kinkinyū ron*, p. 877.

97. Kodaira Gonichi to kindai nōsei henshū shuppan iinkai, ed., *Kodaira Gonichi to kindai nōsei*, pp. 117–118.

98. *Ōsaka mainichi shinbun*, June 10, 1932; *Tōkyō nichi nichi shinbun*, June 9, 1932.

99. Teikoku gikai shūgiin, *Teikoku gikai shūgiin giji sokkiroku* 57, pp. 91–92.

100. Ibid., pp. 91–94. Washitani also suggested that the state run a lottery to pay for the costs of the program.

101. Ibid., pp. 177–178.

102. "Kengi narabi ketsugi jikō, Nōson kyōkyūsaku dankō ni kansuru kengi," *Teikoku nōkai hō* 22:9 (September 1932): 2–3. For more information on the agricultural association's position on debt arrangement unions, see Chapter 5 below and Kase Kazutoshi, "Nōson fusai seiri seisaku no ritsuan katei," p. 18.

103. The government's role in all this was to provide the low-interest loans necessary. Nōrinshō nōmukyoku, "Nōka fusai seiri jikkō jirei," October 1931, in *NSS* 2:5, pp. 125–129; Kase Kazutoshi, "Nōson fusai seiri seisaku no ritsuan katei," p. 19.

104. The plan proposed by the National Association of Mayors of Towns and Villages also relied on low-interest funds from the government for refinancing, but put control over it and debt arrangement in the hands of local officials. Nōrin daijin kanbō sōmuka, ed., *Nōrin gyōsei shi*, vol. 2, pp. 200–201; Kase Kazutoshi, "Nōson fusai seiri seisaku no ritsuan katei," p. 19; Nōrinshō keizai kōseibu, "Nōson fusai seiri ni kansuru shoan yōryō," August 1936, in *NSS* 2:5, p. 164.

105. The Seiyūkai had made at least one earlier attempt at passing a debt union bill, during the Fifty-ninth Diet in February 1931. For details on what was apparently little more than a political ploy, see Kase Kazutoshi, "Nōson fusai seiri seisaku no ritsuan katei," pp. 24-25.

106. One member from Nagano prefecture observed that "up until now, the attitude of the Agricultural Association has been one of calm, but now is not a time when these attitudes should be continued. Even in the Lower House of the Diet, representatives from the countryside have taken an unprecedented effort in emergency policies." For other examples of members' complaints, see "Kyōgikai keikai," *Teikoku nōkai hō* 22:7 (July 1932): 123-125. See also Yasutomi Kunio, "Shōwa shoki kyūnō seisaku no keisei shōmetsu katei ni kansuru jakkan no kōsatsu," pp. 145-146.

107. Between June 1 and August 17, 1932, the *Fukushima minpō* covered at least 32 different rallies and meetings related to rural relief; a third of these were sponsored all or in part by agricultural associations. The Association of Mayors of Towns and Villages and individual villages were responsible for most of the rest.

108. There is no doubt that the prefectural agricultural association was well aware of the depth of the debt crisis, since the *Fukushima ken nōkai hō* had been running articles about just that subject since at least as early as April 1931. See Kageyama Shikazō, "Fusai o seyo!" Kageyama liked to use wordplay to get his points across. In April he made use of the fact that the verb *harau* can mean both "to shovel" and "to pay" in a poem that went (roughly), "The falling of the white snow, the yearly accumulation of debt, the house will be flattened if it is not shoveled / paid off." Ibid., p. 23.

109. For the agricultural association stance in early 1932, see *Fukushima minpō*, January 27, 1932; *Fukushima ken nōkai hō* 129 (January 1932): 24-27, and 130 (February 1932): 37-38. After the early June meeting in Tokyo of the heads of the prefectural agricultural associations, the agricultural association in Fukushima began to incorporate the decisions reached at that conference into their own proposals. The prefectural agricultural association leaders met on June 22, 1932, and drafted a document entitled "Steps to Be Taken in Response to the Crisis" (Jikyoku ni taishite nōkai no toru beki hōhō). The phrasing of the prefectural document mimics that of the one issued at the national meeting earlier that month almost word for word in its requests for state intervention in farm debt, burden reduction, and so on. See Yasutomi Kunio, "Fukushimaken ni okeru keizai kōsei undō," p. 202.

110. *Fukushima minpō*, June 14, 1932.

111. At least one politician took the issues to the farmers instead of the other way around. Sukegawa Keishirō, one of the prefecture's Seiyūkai Diet members, helped organize a Fukushima Farm-Village Policy Association in January 1932. The 200 farmers who attended the initial meeting in Fukushima city decided on resolutions

calling on the Prefectural Agricultural and Industrial Bank and the Japan Industrial Bank to extend repayments on their mortgages. They also sought the establishment of a debt arrangement policy for all farmers and discussed the need to do something about what had caused farmers to fall so deeply into debt. To that end, the group called for the development of policies to promote the "rationalization of production in the villages," and in its final resolution stated that it would press the government to develop "fundamental policies related to debt arrangement and the rationalization of village production" (*Fukushima minpō*, January 25, 1932). It is not clear what became of the group after this meeting, although the Seiyūkai organized a similar type of assembly later in the year. Sukegawa went on to play a role in shaping the farm relief package in the Diet, as discussed above.

112. Yasutomi Kunio, "Fukushimaken ni okeru keizai kōsei undō," p. 202. See also *Fukushima minpō*, July 8, 1932, and July 15, 1932.

113. Within a month, Kodaira would take over leadership of the newly created Economic Revitalization Section within his ministry. "Kengi narabi ketsugi jikō," *Teikoku nōkai hō* 22:9 (September 1932): 8.

114. "Zenkoku nōkai taikai narabi dōjikkō undō no keika," *Teikoku nōkai hō* 22:10 (October 1932): 6–8.

115. On July 10, 1932, Fukuzawa Yasue, the president of the National Association of Mayors of Towns and Villages, met with representatives of the Imperial Agricultural Association and discussed with them that association's relief proposals. "Nōkai kiji," *Teikoku nōkai hō* 22:7 (July 1932), p. 127. For the text of the mayors' appeal, see *Tokkō geppō* (June 1932), pp. 7–9.

116. Kase Kazutoshi, "Nōson fusai seiri seisaku no ritsuan katei," p. 25. The Industrial Cooperative Central Bank program had loaned out 43.1 million yen by the end of September 1936, which was only 43 percent of the amount the state had expected to spend. The program amortized about 50 million yen in otherwise fixed assets. The passage of the 1933 Agricultural Chattel Law (Nōgyō dōsan shinyō hō) gave farmers the right to use tools, livestock, and other "movable assets" as collateral on loans. In one example cited by the Ministry of Agriculture and Forestry, a farmer behind on his other debts to the local industrial cooperative and thus ineligible for more loans under the old rules was able under the new system to borrow enough money to buy a cow by mortgaging the cow to the union. The cow had been a boon to the farmer's family, providing fertilizer for the fields and more efficient plowing, which freed the farmer to start a rope-making business. See Nōrinshō keizai kōseibu, "Sangyō kumiai chūō kinkō tokubetsu yūzu shikin no reiyō to nōson no kaizen, nōgyō dōsan shinyō seido riyō no tebiki," March 1937, in *NSS* 2:5, pp. 241–242, 246.

117. Haley, *Authority Without Power*, esp. pp. 85–96.

118. Kase Kazutoshi, "Nōson fusai seiri seisaku no ritsuan katei," *Tōkyō suisan daigaku ronshū*, no. 14 (March 1979), p. 26.

119. Teikoku gikai shūgiin, *Teikoku gikai shūgiin giji tekiyō* (hereafter TGT) 63, p. 320. The bill was originally supposed to run for three years, but it was renewed and slightly modified in 1934.

120. Ibid., p. 325; The bill was reportedly based, at least in part, on the conclusions of the Nōrin shingikai (Agriculture and Forestry Deliberative Council). See Mori Tokuhisa, *Teikoku gikai nōson mondai kaisetsu*, p. 199.

121. TGT 63, p. 321.

122. Ibid., p. 327.

123. Ibid., p. 330.

124. Ibid., p. 346.

125. Ibid., pp. 335–336. Nōrinshō keizai kōseibu, "Nōson fusai seiri ni kansuru shoan yōryō," August 1936, in *NSS* 2:5, pp. 166–168.

126. Kase Kazutoshi, "Nōson fusai seiri seisaku no ritsuan katei," *Tōkyō suisan daigaku ronshū*, no. 14 (March 1979), p. 26; Nōrinshō keizai kōseibu, "Nōson fusai seiri ni kansuru shoan yōryō," August 1936, in *NSS* 2:5, pp. 166–168; TGT 63, pp. 337–339.

127. TGT 63, p. 344.

128. Ibid., pp. 349–351.

129. Kase Kazutoshi, "Nōson fusai seiri seisaku no ritsuan katei," p. 26. See also Saitō shisaku kinenkai, ed., *Shisaku Saitō Makoto den*, vol. 3, pp. 219–220, and Nōrin daijin kanbō sōmuka, ed., *Nōrin gyōsei shi*, vol. 2, p. 203.

130. Kase Kazutoshi, "Nōson fusai seiri seisaku no ritsuan katei," pp. 29–30; *Tōkyō asahi shinbun*, January 18, 1933.

131. *Tōkyō asahi shinbun*, January 14, 1933.

132. Kase Kazutoshi, "Nōson fusai seiri seisaku no ritsuan katei," p. 30; *Tōkyō asahi shinbun*, January 18, 1933.

133. Kase Kazutoshi, "Nōson fusai seiri seisaku no ritsuan katei," p. 30.

134. Saitō shisaku kinenkai, ed., *Shisaku Saitō Makoto den*, vol. 3, p. 439. The authors of this work take care to note that although the cabinet came to this problem late in its development, the policy it devised should be considered a success.

135. *Tōkyō asahi shinbun*, January 25, 1933.

136. Kase Kazutoshi, "Nōson fusai seiri seisaku no ritsuan katei," p. 31. The state would pay up to 30 million yen in total losses, but once it reached that level, the burden would be split equally between the prefecture and the local government.

137. Teikoku gikai shūgiin, *Dai 64-kai Teikoku gikai shūgiin giji tekiyō*, vol. 2 (Tokyo: Shūgiin jimukyoku, 1933), pp. 1359–1366 (hereafter cited as TGT 64).

138. Ibid., vol. 2, p. 1402.

139. *Tōkyō asahi shinbun*, March 26, 1933.

140. Ishiguro Tadaatsu estimated that only 6.8 percent of all farm debt had been arranged, based on an August 1935 Ministry of Agriculture and Forestry estimate of farm debt of 4.1 billion yen. Nōson kōsei kyōkai, "Fusai seiri kumiai keiri no taiken o kataru," May 1939, in *NSS* 2:5, pp. 366, 402–403.

141. Nōrin keizai kōseibu, "Nōson fusai seiri jimu shumukachō kyōgikai yōroku (secret)," February 1934, in *NSS* 2:5, p. 176.

142. Ibid., p. 197.

143. Kodaira Gonichi and Furuse Denzō, "Nōsangyoson fusai seiri no hōhō to jirei" (Nishinkaku kankō, 1937), in *NSS* 2:5, p. 270.

144. Ibid., pp. 266–267.

145. Ibid., pp. 261–264, 318–319. By the end of September 1936, there were an average of 2.8 unions in those communities with unions. Kase notes that the 4,327 unions established by the end of July 1936 were only 17 percent of the planned number and that funding as of the end of July 1938 was 34 million yen—only 17 percent of the 200 million planned. Kase Kazutoshi, "Nōson fusai seiri seisaku no ritsuan katei," p. 38, fn. 2.

146. Kodaira Gonichi and Furuse Denzō, "Nōsangyoson fusai seiri no hōhō to jirei" (Nishinkaku kankō, 1937), in *NSS* 2:5, p. 259.

147. Nōson kōsei kyōkai, "Fusai seiri kumiai keiri no taiken o kataru," May 1939, in *NSS* 2:5, p. 381.

148. Ibid., pp. 381, 394–395.

## Chapter 5

1. Saitō shisaku kinenkai, ed., *Shisaku Saitō Makoto den*, vol. 3, pp. 162–169. In this same speech, Saitō explained that his cabinet was without party affiliation. Parties are a natural part of the political system, he said, but pointed out that their behavior of late had earned them the mistrust of many. The political world was in need of change, and his cabinet was the result.

2. A series of cabinet-level meetings was held in late 1933 to determine how best to divvy up the budget. The military had made demands for additional spending that Takahashi felt he had to meet, which forced the other ministries to scramble for what remained. Agriculture and Forestry Minister Gotō tried and failed to convince Takahashi to continue to support large-scale funding for the countryside. His failure can be attributed at least in part to the personal animosity between the two men and to Gotō's inability to provide the finance minister with workable policies for rural Japan.

3. Soon after the Sixty-third Diet ended, Saitō and Takahashi both spoke out in favor of cutting back on spending. Both men were apparently under the impression

that an upturn in the prices for silk and rice signaled the return of good times for farmers. Yasutomi Kunio, "Shōwa shoki kyūnō seisaku no keisei shōmetsu katei ni kansuru jakkan no kōsatsu," pp. 160, 169, fn. 3.

4. See *Ōsaka mainichi shinbun*, June 13, 1932, for a list of the items the Seiyūkai wanted to pursue in the Village Relief Diet. See also Saitō shisaku kinenkai, ed., *Shisaku Saitō Makoto den*, vol. 3, pp. 147–149.

5. *Tōkyō asahi shinbun*, June 12, 1932.

6. Teikoku gikai shūgiin, *Teikoku gikai shūgiin giji sokkiroku*, vol. 57, pp. 141–142. Sugiyama Motojirō also commented on the failure of public works to do much for the farmers up to that time and called on the government to ensure that in the future more projects were put under the direct control of the villages. Saitō shisaku kinenkai, ed., *Shisaku Saitō Makoto den*, vol. 3, p. 145. Although the government's entire budget for public works over the three years prior to 1932 was slightly less than the 350 million yen proposed by the Home Ministry, the almost 575 million it spent between 1926 and 1928 was considerably more. Ōkurashō Shōwa zaiseishi henshūshitsu, ed., *Shōwa zaiseishi*, vol. 3, p. 8.

7. For a good description of the development of state-assisted public works, see Tamaki Akira, "Kyūnō doboku jigyō seiritsu e no michi," pp. 45–53.

8. Rōdōshō, *Rōdō gyōsei shi*, pp. 169–170.

9. The relationship between the Imperial Agricultural Association and Agriculture and Forestry Minister Machida Chūji was not an easy one. Yasutomi Kunio, "Shōwa shoki kyūnō seisaku no keisei shōmetsu katei ni kansuru jakkan no kōsatsu," pp. 139–140.

10. Planning took place both within ministries and in inter-ministerial planning sessions.

11. The chronology of relief planning is described in Takahashi Yasutaka, "Nihon fashizumu to nōgyō keizai kōsei undō no tenkai," p. 7.

12. For a lucid discussion of state and local finance, see Ōishi Kaichirō, "Shōwa kyōkō to chihō zaisei."

13. One of the most serious problems associated with the new loan programs was the extent to which the state would provide guarantees to the Industrial Cooperative Central Bank or to other creditors. The draft proposal put limits of 18 million yen (for fertilizer funding) and 40 million yen for the industrial cooperative loans on the state's liability.

14. Nōrinshō, "Nōson kyūsai narabi kōsei taisaku" (draft), in *NSS* 1:2, p. 90.

15. See Hatade Isao, "Shōwa kyōkō to kyūnō doboku," pp. 180–181, and Kusumoto Masahiro, "Shōwa kyōkō ki no kiban seibi jigyō," p. 126, for positive assessments of what the Ministry of Agriculture and Forestry eventually did with public works.

16. Taikakai (Gotō Fumio), ed., *Naimushō shi*, vol. 2, pp. 148, 150–153. A former banker, Yamamoto was well known for his ability both to avoid giving a straight answer to questions in the Diet and to be unable to recognize all but one or two of the people he had appointed to high posts in the ministry. It was the seventy-seven-year-old Yamamoto who insisted that Gotō be included in the cabinet (but only after his first two candidates declined the appointment).

17. Also included were the other Ministry of Agriculture proposals for loan programs, and others for debt arrangement, economic revitalization, village planning, and funding for rice-price supports. Saitō shisaku kinenkai, ed., *Shisaku Saitō Makoto den*, vol. 3, pp. 159, 163–164.

18. For the text of Takahashi's remarks to the Diet, see *TGT 63*, pp. 13–17.

19. "Nōgyosanson kyōkyū shisetsu," *Shimin* 27:10 (October 1932): 23. See also *TGT 63*, pp. 15–17.

20. *TGT 63*, p. 16.

21. Nakajima was joined in his attack by the Seiyūkai's Takeda Tokusaburō (Niigata), Sugiyama Motojirō, and others. See ibid., pp. 161–163, 169–173, 188–191.

22. Takeda Tokusaburō speaking. Nakajima found Takahashi's reply to his questions "absolutely unsatisfactory." Ibid., pp. 164, 166, 181–182, 202–204. The committee that reviewed the bank-funding law attached three nonbinding requests to it when they sent it back to the lower house. The Seiyūkai-sponsored items called on the government to increase the funding in 1932 as necessary, to monitor banks to ensure that they did not refuse requests for loans, and to have the banks that received funding lower their interest rates for borrowers. See ibid., p. 194.

23. From the prime minister's speech on August 25, 1932. Ibid., p. 6.

24. Ibid., pp. 14–15.

25. Yasutomi Kunio, "Shōwa shoki kyūnō seisaku no keisei shōmetsu katei ni kansuru jakkan no kōsatsu," pp. 152–153.

26. Hatade Isao, "Shōwa kyōkō to kyūnō doboku," pp. 180–181. Nōrinshō nōmukyoku, ed., *Jikyoku kyōkyū kōdo kankei nōgyō doboku jigyō no gaikyō narabi sankō jirei*, March 1934, in *NSS* 1:2, pp. 138–139.

27. Nōrinshō, "Dai 63 kai teikoku gikai o chūshin to site okonawaretaru Nōrinshō kankei no nōsangyoson fukyō kyōkyū shisetsu yōroku," November 1932, in *NSS* 1:2, p. 126.

28. Kusumoto Masahiro, "Shōwa kyōkō ki no kiban seibi jigyō," p. 126.

29. Nōrinshō nōmukyoku, ed., *Jikyoku kyōkyū kōdo kankei nōgyō doboku jigyō no gaikyō narabi sankō jirei*, March 1934, in *NSS* 1:2, p. 145. See Kusumoto Masahiro, "Shōwa kyōkō ki no kiban seibi jigyō," p. 125, for employment figures.

30. Kitakata-shi shi hensan iinkai, ed., *Kitakata-shi shi*, vol. 8, p. 651.

31. SMY, *Sonkai giroku 1933–1935*. The 1934 budget was 8,910 yen. *Hōkoku 10*,

December 23, 1935, KST. Spending on mulberry field projects was not part of the village budget because they were sponsored by a private organization.

32. SMY, *Sonkai giroku 1932*. See Gian 32, September 30, 1932, KST.

33. SMY, *Sonkai giroku 1933*. See Gian 35, May 22, 1933, and Gian 38, May 22, 1933, KST. The terms of the new loan were identical to the previous one except for its 3.2 percent interest rate, which was lower.

34. SMY, Report from Satō to the head of the Fukushima-ken gakumubu, "Shōwa 7 nen do ni okeru kyōkyū jigyō shitsugyō ōkyū jigyō sono ta no kōei jigyō ni kansuru ken kaihō," July 27, 1933, KST. This report covered the period from April 1, 1932, to March 31, 1933.

35. Fukushima-ken, "Nōson hihei jōkyō narabi sono taisaku," pp. 603–604. The prefectural report covered wage levels in Date, Shinobu, and Adachi counties.

36. SMY, Satō to the head of the Fukushima-ken gakumubu, July 27, 1933, KST.

37. At least one village in Fukushima did just that, dividing hiring more or less equally among the different hamlets to ensure that no one part of the village benefited more than the others. See Ōishi Kaichirō, "Shōwa kyōkō to chihō zaisei," p. 130.

38. SMY, *Jikyoku kyōkyū jigyō hi, 1932*, vols. 1 and 2, 1933, KST.

39. This assumes, for instance, that everyone who worked on the irrigation and mulberry field projects had worked on road projects. I say "around 500" because there were more women hired to work on the farm practice associations' projects than had done road work.

40. Population figures are from SMY, *Keizai kōsei keikaku chōsa 1934*, KST. Employment figures are from SMY, Report from Satō to the head of the Fukushima-ken gakumubu, July 27, 1933.

41. Relief-project wages were equivalent to about 2.3 percent of the value of the 1932 rice crop.

42. SMY, Report from Satō to the head of the Fukushima-ken gakumubu, July 27, 1933, KST.

43. SMY, *Shūgyōbetsu kensabo, Kyōkyū jigyōhi hyō, Shimoshiba Komatsu sen*, 1934, KST.

44. SMY, "Komatsu buraku kakuko keizai chōsabo," October 1934, KST.

45. Of the names noted above, only Satō Chōta's comes from a household near the lower end of the tax rankings. Were poorer families excluded, or is it possible that the relief jobs were given over to the better-connected within the hamlet? Unfortunately, the nature of the village's recordkeeping makes it hard to answer these questions with any certainty; wage records can be used to establish the presence of certain families but cannot easily be used to establish the absence of one.

46. See, for instance, *Tōkyō asahi shinbun*, September 6, 1932.

47. See *Fukushima minpō*, January 26, 1933, and "Forum: Nōson kyōkyū sho taisaku hihan," paper presented at the Shakai seisaku jihō, May 1933, pp. 99, 114–115. There were a few positive accounts. A tenancy official in Kōchi, for instance, pointed out that residents in the mountainous northern part of the prefecture had used the projects to improve transportation there, with considerable benefits to the local lumber industry. A Nagano tenant reported that, unlike past years, he had been able to work for three or four months during the winter on relief projects, which had made his life much better. Much of the *Nihon nōgyō nenpō* 5 (1934) was devoted to criticism of the state's agricultural policies. See pp. 184–187 for case-by-case examples of the failings of public works programs.

48. "Forum: Nōson kyōkyū sho taisaku hihan," paper presented at the Shakai seisaku jihō, May 1933, pp. 107–109.

49. Inomata Tsunao, *Kyūbō no nōson*, esp. pp. 383–386.

50. See, for example, Inoue Harumaru, *Nihon shihon shugi no hatten to nōgyō oyobi nōsei*, pp. 350–353. Inoue cites some of Inomata's examples to help make his case. See also Teruoka Shūzō, *Nihon nōgyō mondai no tenkai*, vol. 2, p. 210, for a brief description of some of these earlier assessments.

51. Teruoka Shūzō, *Nihon nōgyō mondai no tenkai*, vol. 2, pp. 182–183. For another slightly more favorable assessment, see Nakamura Takafusa, *Meiji Taishō ki no keizai*, pp. 142–146. Based on aggregate figures for overall farm income, Nakamura estimates that the extra cash income created under relief spending would have been enough to boost total farm incomes by around 20 percent.

52. Miwa Ryōichi, "Takahashi zaiseiki no keizai seisaku," esp. pp. 138–139. For the government's own assessment of the value of relief spending as of 1934, see Nihon ginkō chōsakyoku, ed., *Nihon kinyūshi shiryō, Shōwa hen*, vol. 29, pp. 1–12.

53. Both Commerce Minister Nakajima Kumakichi and Rail Minister Mitsuchi Chūzō were charged in the scandal, which began with accusations that Finance Ministry officials had given certain businessmen access to Imperial Rayon stock at bargain-basement prices. The two ministers were eventually acquitted. Tiedemann, "Big Business and Politics in Prewar Japan," pp. 294–295.

54. Tanaka Tokihiko, "Saitō naikaku: 'Hijōji' no chinsei o ninatte," p. 321.

55. Saitō shisaku kinenkai, ed., *Shisaku Saitō Makoto den*, vol. 3, pp. 462, 464–465.

56. Ibid., pp. 473–474.

57. Ōkurashō Shōwa zaiseishi henshūshitsu, ed., *Shōwa zaiseishi*, vol. 3, p. 153.

58. Saitō shisaku kinenkai, ed., *Shisaku Saitō Makoto den*, vol. 3, pp. 483–485. The meetings began on October 3 and ended on October 20, 1932. See also Tanaka Tokihiko, "Saitō naikaku: 'Hijōji' no chinsei o ninatte," pp. 322–324, and Barnhart, *Japan Prepares for Total War*, pp. 34–37.

59. *Chūgai shōgyō*, October 19, 1933. See also Yasutomi Kunio, "Shōwa shoki kyūnō seisaku no keisei shōmetsu katei ni kansuru jakkan no kōsatsu," p. 164.

60. For Takahashi's reasoning behind the cuts, see Harada Kumao, *Saionji Kō to seikyoku*, vol. 3, p. 187.

61. Tanaka Tokihiko, "Saitō naikaku: 'Hijōji' no chinsei o ninatte," p. 326.

62. Saitō shisaku kinenkai, ed., *Shisaku Saitō Makoto den*, vol. 3, pp. 497–498.

63. Weiner, "Bureaucracy and Politics in the 1930's," pp. 114–118.

64. Ōkurashō Shōwa zaiseishi henshūshitsu, ed., *Shōwa zaiseishi*, vol. 3, pp. 149, 154. Calculations are based on requests for new funding. The Ministry of Agriculture and Forestry had been given 30 percent of its initial request for new funding in 1933, the army and the navy 58 and 30 percent, respectively. The average approval rate that year was 45 percent.

65. Saitō shisaku kinenkai, ed., *Shisaku Saitō Makoto den*, vol. 3, pp. 487–488. Takahashi was apparently busy with cabinet-level meetings on the budget.

66. See Minichiello, *Retreat from Reform*, pp. 87–94, and Weiner, "Bureaucracy and Politics in the 1930's," for a discussion of the rise of the reform bureaucrats and their links to the military. For interesting contemporary accounts, see Ikeda Miyoji, *Shin Nihon no tenbō*; Sugihara Masami, "Gunbu no shin shidō seiryoku to naisei kaigi"; idem, "Gunbu to kakushō shinkanryō no ōdanteki ketsugō"; and Kindai Nihon shi kenkyūkai, *Manshū Jihen zengo*, p. 215.

67. Harada Kumao, *Saionji Kō to seikyoku*, vol. 3, p. 188.

68. Ibid., p. 192.

69. Ibid., p. 191.

70. Ibid., pp. 187–188.

71. Ibid., p. 188.

72. Yasutomi Kunio, "Shōwa shoki kyūnō seisaku no keisei shōmetsu katei ni kansuru jakkan no kōsatsu," pp. 160, 169, fn. 3.

73. *Ōsaka mainichi shinbun*, November 8, 1933. An article the same day in the *Chūgai shōgyō* noted that of all the ministers, only Araki and Gotō seemed to have any enthusiasm for the meetings. Education Minister Hatoyama had been more or less asked *not* to attend by Cabinet Secretary Horikiri, which further heightened tensions. Commerce Minister Nakajima left the first meeting early, and the second after only an hour. He told reporters that he didn't see any reason to stay if Takahashi wasn't there; *Ōsaka mainichi shinbun*, November 11, 1933. Nakajima was also reportedly upset with Gotō's emphasis on the industrial cooperatives and demanded that steps be taken to help businesses as well. See Sugihara Masami, "Gunbu no shin shidō seiryoku to naisei kaigi," p. 11. The third session was eventually scheduled for a date in early December 1933, when Takahashi indicated he would be able to attend. He also pointed out that since the 1934 budget was more or less decided, it didn't really matter when they had the conferences because there would be no additional money available for domestic programs. See *Tōkyō asahi shinbun*, November 15, 1933 (evening edition).

74. Ōsaka mainichi shinbun, November 11, 1933.

75. Havens, Farm and Nation in Modern Japan, p. 61. See also T. C. Smith, Political Change and Industrial Development in Japan, pp. 37–41.

76. Ōsaka mainichi shinbun, December 6, 1933. Rail Minister Mitsuchi made comments in support of Takahashi's points.

77. Ibid., December 8, 1933. Mitsuchi added another plank to the local initiative platform, pointing out that since state taxes were a relatively small share of the total rural tax burden, actual burden reduction would have to be the result of lower village, household, or prefectural taxes. Araki was apparently frustrated by the lack of progress in the meetings and called on the participants to do more than just debate.

78. Ibid., December 8, 1933. Army Minister Araki apparently submitted an opinion paper at this session calling in general terms for price stabilization, debt and tax policies, and the need to consider farm policy in the light of the decisions reached on national security in the five ministers' conferences. Araki referred to self-revitalization policies and attempts to rely on spiritual improvement in lieu of budget policies as "muddying the tea" and "absolutely impermissible." Yasutomi Kunio, "Shōwa shoki kyūnō seisaku no keisei shōmetsu katei ni kansuru jakkan no kōsatsu," pp. 166–167.

79. Ōsaka mainichi shinbun, December 13, 1933 (evening). See also Chūgai shōgyō, December 13, 1933.

80. Tōkyō asahi shinbun, December 16, 1933.

81. See Ōsaka mainichi shinbun, November 11, 1933, for a list of the proposals Gotō made at the November 10 second meeting.

82. Saitō shisaku kinenkai, ed., Shisaku Saitō Makoto den, vol. 3, pp. 491–492.

83. Tōkyō nichi nichi shinbun, December 23, 1933.

84. Saitō shisaku kinenkai, ed., Shisaku Saitō Makoto den, vol. 3, pp. 511–512.

85. Azuma Takeshi, "Nōson no san dai mondai," pp. 24–25. Azuma originally gave this speech in the lower house on January 23, 1934.

86. Ibid., p. 26. Azuma of course went on to make a case for increased funding for agricultural association technicians.

87. Den Akira, "Shōwa 9 nen do sōyosan hihan." For more of the Minseitō attitude toward Gotō's farm policy, see Ushiba Keijirō, "Nōson taisaku no jūten o issu."

88. Yagi Hisato, "Hijōji ni taisuru nōshō no ninshiki."

89. Shioda Shōichi, "Takahashi rō Zōsho no kokoro o utta nōkai gishiiin." The Nōkai's emissary was Viscount Aoki Nobumitsu, an influential veteran of the upper house. Similar attempts by Aoki to discuss funding with Cabinet Secretary Horikiri and by Azuma Takeshi and other Seiyūkai members to do so with Finance Ministry officials also failed.

90. Shioda Shōichi, "Takahashi rō Zōsho no kokoro o utta nōkai gishiiin."
91. Ibid., p. 9.
92. Teikoku nōkai shikō hensankai, ed., *Teikoku nōkai shikō*, pp. 774–775. By 1937, assistance funding had risen to 3 million yen.
93. Yasutomi Kunio, "Shōwa shoki kyūnō seisaku no keisei shōmetsu katei ni kansuru jakkan no kōsatsu," p. 168.
94. Nihon nōgyō kenkyūkai, ed., *Nihon nōgyō nenpō* 4:1933, p. 164. Questions had been raised in the Diet about the statement, and Saitō was meeting with the two ministers to hear their explanation. (The navy had apparently issued a statement similar to that of the army.)
95. *Chūgai shōgyō*, October 21, 1933.
96. Ikeda Miyoji, *Shin Nihon no tenbō*; Sugihara Masami, "Gunbu no shin shidō seiryoku to naisei kaigi," p. 10. Sengoku was a long-time industrial cooperative activist, and later agriculture minister in the short-lived Higashikuni cabinet (August-October 1945). Arima was a member of the upper house and part of the Kakushin group and would become agriculture minister in Konoe's first cabinet. He was active in the development of Konoe's New Order and the IRAA. See also Yasutomi Kunio, "Shōwa shoki kyūnō seisaku no keisei shōmetsu katei ni kansuru jakkan no kōsatsu," p. 170, fn. 12.
97. *Chūgai shōgyō*, October 29, 1933. Araki's other policy ideas include crop diversification and rural industrialization, employment to boost cash income, debt burden reduction, and—perhaps because he was speaking in Fukui—unemployment relief projects in fishing villages. See also Kikkawa Manabu, *Arashi to tatakau tesshō Araki*, vol. 2, pp. 276–277, 284.
98. Sugihara Masami, "Gunbu to kakushō shinkanryō no ōdanteki ketsugō," pp. 12–13. For a similar concern ascribed to Araki, see Barnhart, *Japan Prepares for Total War*, p. 35, fn. 42.
99. Yasutomi Kunio, "Shōwa shoki kyūnō seisaku no keisei shōmetsu katei ni kansuru jakkan no kōsatsu," pp. 172–173.
100. Nihon nōgyō kenkyūkai, ed., *Nihon nōgyō nenpō*, p. 475.
101. Ibid.
102. Ibid., p. 480.
103. Berger, *Parties out of Power in Japan, 1931–1941*, esp. pp. 67–74.
104. "Dai 65 gikai teikoku gikai hōkokusho," *Seiyū* 405 (May 1934), p. 14.
105. Nihon nōgyō kenkyūkai, ed., *Nihon nōgyō nenpō*, p. 267. See also "Dai 65 gikai teikoku gikai hōkokusho," *Seiyū* 405 (May 1934), p. 14.
106. Nihon nōgyō kenkyūkai, ed., *Nihon nōgyō nenpō*, pp. 264–265. The Foreign Ministry's 1934 budget was 35 percent smaller than its 1933 budget.

## Chapter 6

1. Kusumoto Masahiro, ed., *Nōsangyoson keizai kōsei undō to Kodaira Gonichi,* p. 15.
2. Ibid., pp. 16–17. See also Teikoku nōkai, "Nōson keikaku jirei," November 1931, in NSS 1:2, pp. 1–21, for detailed descriptions of these plans. Note that Kusumoto's description of the plan in Fukuoka does not agree with the description in the Teikoku nōkai text, which describes that program as being led by the prefectural agricultural association. This is closer to an account given by Matsumoto Gaku below (see note 5 below). See also Nakamura Masanori, "Keizai kōsei undō to nōson tōgō," pp. 197–262, for a description of early planning efforts in Nagano.
3. Teikoku nōkai, "Nōson keikaku jirei," November 1931, in NSS 1:2, pp. 3–4; see also Kusumoto Masahiro, ed., *Nōsangyoson keizai kōsei undō to Kodaira Gonichi,* pp. 15–16.
4. Kodaira Gonichi to kindai nōsei henshū shuppan iinkai, ed., *Kodaira Gonichi to kindai nōsei,* pp. 118–119.
5. Matsumoto Gaku, "Nōson no keizai kaizen," pp. 5–14.
6. For an example of agricultural-association encouragement of planning efforts outside Hyōgo, see *Fukushima-ken nōkai hō* 125 (September 1931): 28–29, and 126 (October 1931): 24–25, and Shōji Kichinosuke, "Fukushima-ken nōkai shi," pp. 289, 292–293. The Fukushima Agricultural Association had been active since early in the 1920s in attempts to use long-term planning with a small number of model communities and families.
7. Teikoku nōkai shikō hensankai, ed., *Teikoku nōkai shikō,* p. 526.
8. Kusumoto Masahiro, ed., *Nōsangyoson keizai kōsei undō to Kodaira Gonichi,* pp. 23, 27–28. Born in Hyōgo, Yamawaki (1875–1941) briefly attended Tokyo University before entering the prefectural assembly and serving at one point as the president of the assembly. In 1921 he became the secretary of the Hyōgo Prefecture Agricultural Association and later president, a post he kept until his death in 1941. Nagashima (1879–1951) was also a Hyōgo native, and a graduate of Tokyo University Agricultural School. In 1914 he served as a technician for the prefectural agricultural association and as secretary, and later as head of the Prefectural Agricultural Affairs Section. He became president of the Hyōgo Prefecture Agricultural Association when Yamawaki left. Ishihara (1901– ), an Okayama native, is also a graduate of Tokyo University's Agricultural School. In 1941 he entered the Ministry of Agriculture and Forestry, where he worked on land-opening and land development, and retired in 1964. As of 1983, he was a supervisor of the Nōson kōsei kyōkai (Farm Village Revitalization Association).
9. Shōji Shunsaku, *Kindai Nihon nōson shakai no tenkai,* pp. 462–463. See also Nagashima Sadashi, "Warera ga teishō suru jiriki kōsei no shingi," p. 28.

10. Nagashima, quoted in Shōji Shunsaku, *Kindai Nihon nōson shakai no tenkai*, pp. 462-463.

11. Nagashima Sadashi, "Warera ga teishō suru jiriki kōsei no shingi," pp. 28-29.

12. Quoted in Shōji Shunsaku, *Kindai Nihon nōson shakai no tenkai*, pp. 508-509. For the full text of Okada's speech, see Kusumoto Masahiro, ed., *Nōsangyoson keizai kōsei undō to Kodaira Gonichi*, pp. 239-246. The speech was given during the May 1932 Jiriki kōsei matsuri (Self-revitalization Festival). For more information on Okada's views on farm policy, see Havens, *Farm and Nation in Modern Japan*, pp. 155-160.

13. Shōji Shunsaku, *Kindai Nihon nōson shakai no tenkai*, p. 465, and Nagashima Sadashi, "Shōwa 7 nendo Hyōgo-ken nōkai narabi ni gun nōkai shisetsu jigyō no taiyō," p. 31. Through 1934 more than half of the villages designated in Hyōgo by the Ministry of Agriculture as *keizai kōsei* communities had already been designated *jiriki kōsei* communities by the prefectural agricultural association. In 1935, the ratio fell to nine out of twenty.

14. Shōji Shunsaku, *Kindai Nihon nōson shakai no tenkai*, pp. 465-466.

15. Ibid., p. 463. See also Hyōgo-ken nōkai, *Nōson jiriki kōsei setsumei shiryō*, 1932, in NSS 1:1, p. 431, for the original data.

16. Shōji Shunsaku, *Kindai Nihon nōson shakai no tenkai*, p. 464. The first five categories applied to individuals, the remainder to families.

17. Ibid., pp. 488-490; see p. 492, table 9-9, for a list of contest results and landholding in Kitatachibana village, Gumma ken, a participant in the Economic Revitalization Campaign. Shōji has argued that despite the different time frames and sponsors, there was little difference in the "mechanisms" of the two movements. See especially ibid., p. 490.

18. See Okada Atsushi, "Nōson jiriki kōsei no seishin to mokuhyō," p. 6. His speech offered listeners a synopsis of Okada's thinking on life, farming, and the importance of self-revitalization to both. Okada also made specific reference to the similarities between Ninomiya Sontoku's teachings and the spirit of self-revitalization.

19. Hyōgo-ken nōkai, *Nōson jiriki kōsei setsumei shiryō* 1932, reprinted in Kusumoto Masahiro, ed., *Nōsangyoson keizai kōsei undō to Kodaira Gonichi*, p. 251.

20. See also Kusumoto Masahiro, ed., *Nōsangyoson keizai kōsei undō to Kodaira Gonichi*, pp. 249-250.

21. The figures are from 1930. The Morikawa family and the "regular" family they were compared to were both residents of Kansaki county. The Takada family lived in Taka county, the other anonymous farm family lived in Asago county. See Hyōgo-ken nōkai, *Nōson jiriki kōsei setsumei shiryō* 1932, in NSS 1:1, p. 426.

22. The Morikawa family had a total of 0.9805 *chō*, while the anonymous family they were compared with had 1.224 *chō*. The Morikawa family consisted of a couple and one set of parents; the other family was made up of a couple and a son and

daughter (ibid.). The Takada family had 1.2 *chō* of land, and a husband, wife, and elderly mother to work it. Their anonymous counterparts had 1.05 *chō* of land, a couple and one set of parents as labor.

23. Kusumoto Masahiro, ed., *Nōsangyoson keizai kōsei undō to Kodaira Gonichi*, p. 252.

24. Ibid., p. 27.

25. Teikoku nōkai shikō hensankai, ed., *Teikoku nōkai shikō*, p. 526.

26. Roughly 11,000 copies went to local recipients, the remainder to national ones. Kusumoto Masahiro, ed., *Nōsangyoson keizai kōsei undō to Kodaira Gonichi*, p. 24.

27. Ibid.

28. Ishiwara described how careful the Hyōgo Agricultural Association was to make sure that the addressees actually read the material. If it was sent in a less expensive, brown envelope, reasoned Ishiwara, the maids probably wouldn't pass it on to the head of the household. To make sure it got past the maid and into the right hands, the material was put in a nice, white envelope and addressed in the best script that association members could muster. Ibid., p. 25.

29. There were also encouraging signs within the Imperial Agriculture Association. Meetings of that body in April 1932, and then again in June and August, produced resolutions calling for "the self-revitalization of the village." Takahashi Yasutaka, "Nihon fashizumu to nōgyō keizai kōsei undō no tenkai," p. 4, table 1.

30. Kusumoto Masahiro, ed., *Nōsangyoson keizai kōsei undō to Kodaira Gonichi*, p. 27.

31. Kodaira Gonichi, "Nōson jiji no shin kenkyū." p. 141.

32. Ibid., pp. 144, 147–149, 151. He made a similar point about debt. It was fiscally impossible, Kodaira argued, for the state to provide low-interest loans to cover every existing debt. Other measures were necessary.

33. Nagashima Sadashi, "Warera ga teishō suru jiriki kōsei no shingi," pp. 25–26. It should be noted that by the time this issue of *Nōsei kenkyū* was published, the Hyōgo Agricultural Association was only one of many farm organizations on the self-revitalization bandwagon. The entire August 1932 issue of that journal was devoted to articles written by representatives of groups from around the country describing their experiences with and advocacy of self-revitalization.

34. Saitō shisaku kinenkai, ed., *Shisaku Saitō Makoto den*, vol. 3, p. 170.

35. Ibid., p. 171. For instance, Saitō met with petitioners from Nagano on June 15, 1932, with another group on June 28, and with more on June 30. The next month, he met with petitioning groups on July 2, 5, 6, 19 (three groups), 23 (three groups), 25, 26, 27, and 28. He was ill in early August but met with a group of small businessmen on August 17 before beginning preparations for the opening of the Diet. See ibid., pp. 188–191.

36. Ibid., p. 171.

37. Ibid., p. 173.

38. Self-revitalization entered the popular lexicon as well. For satirical depictions of revitalization, see, for example, "Aki no seisaku," which originally appeared in *Asahi gurafu* (1933) and "Jiriki kōsei," which appeared in *Manga nenkan* (1933). The latter depicts an older man (identified as "the Saitō cabinet") carrying parcels labeled "Recognition of Manchuria," "Unemployment Prevention," "China Policy Problem," "Arms Reduction Problem," and "Dangerous Finances"; he turns to speak to a young boy (identified as "the village") who has fallen into a deep hole. The caption reads "Father, I've fallen in!" The father replies, "Well, get yourself out! Do it yourself!" Both are reprinted in Harada Katsumasa, "Fashizumu e no michi," pp. 75, 77.

39. Yasutomi Kunio, "Shōwa shoki kyūnō seisaku no keisei shōmetsu katei ni kansuru jakkan no kōsatsu," p. 157. See Saitō shisaku kinenkai, ed., *Shisaku Saitō Makoto den*, vol. 3, pp. 175–177, for a text of the speech.

40. Yasutomi Kunio, "Shōwa shoki kyūnō seisaku no keisei shōmetsu katei ni kansuru jakkan no kōsatsu," p. 157.

41. *Tōkyō asahi shinbun*, July 20, 1932.

42. Kusumoto Masahiro, ed., *Nōsangyoson keizai kōsei undō to Kodaira Gonichi*, pp. 25, 27. The prefectural agricultural association was moved, too, and designated July 20, 1932, as *jiriki kōsei* commemoration day in honor of the emperor's kindness. The incident is also mentioned in an August 1932 agricultural association report entitled "The Glory of the Nōson jiriki kōsei Movement." See *NSS* 1:1, p. 433.

43. Kodaira Gonichi, "Nōson taisaku no kichō," pp. 1–3.

44. Takahashi Yasutaka, "Nihon fashizumu to nōgyō keizai kōsei undō no tenkai," pp. 7–8.

45. Nōrinshō, "Nōson kyūsai narabi kōsei taisaku," July 10, 1932, draft, in *NSS* 1:2, pp. 91–92. See also the explanatory document that accompanies the policy proposal, "Nōson kyūsai narabi kōsei taisaku setsumeisho," July 19, 1932, draft, in *NSS* 1:2, pp. 96–107.

46. Takahashi points out that this revision to the law was mentioned in both the 6.27 and 7.10 drafts, but that an emphasis on the role of the unions in providing funding to small farmers appears only in the later draft. See Takahashi Yasutaka, "Nihon fashizumu to nōgyō keizai kōsei undō no tenkai," p. 7.

47. Nōrinshō, "Nōson kyūsai narabi kōsei taisaku setsumeisho," in *NSS* 1:2, p. 107.

48. Nōrinshō, "Nōson kōsei keikaku shisetsu yōkō," July 1932, in *NSS* 1:2, pp. 111–113.

49. Ibid., pp. 112–113.

50. Takahashi argues that the new outline reflects a shift by the government away from the "positive" and expensive spending program outlined in the 6.27 and 7.20 drafts and toward a much less expensive *jiriki kōsei* program. See Takahashi Yasutaka, "Nihon fashizumu to nōgyō keizai kōsei undō no tenkai," p. 9.

51. *TGT* 63, p. 7.
52. Ibid., p. 9.
53. Nōrinshō nōmukyoku, "Nōson keizai kōsei shisetsu yōkō," August 24, 1932, in *NSS* 1:2, pp. 117–122. There were fourteen survey categories in total. See pp. 118–119.
54. *TGT* 63, p. 97.
55. Ibid., p. 55.
56. See ibid., pp. 215–259, for details of the bills. During discussion of these bills, Kurihara Kikosaburō (Tochigi, Kokumin dōmei) accused the government of shifting all the responsibility onto the backs of the villages and small communities and assuming none itself. He suggested as well that the state had failed to understand the severity of the problems confronting the farm community. He said, "There used to be a saying about 'breaking a butterfly upon a wheel,' but what you are doing to cope with the current crisis is like trying to break a wheel on a butterfly." Ibid., p. 240.
57. Farm practice associations were small local organizations of farmers built around a shared interest in farming and the need for cooperation at the hamlet level. The new law made it relatively simple for any practice association to become a legal organization (*hōjin*) and join the industrial cooperative in that form. See Nōrinshō, "Dai 63 kai teikoku gikai o chūshin to shite okonowaretaru Nōrinshō kankei nōsangyoson fukyō kyōkyū shisetsu yōroku," November 1932, in *NSS* 1:2, pp. 128–129. For Kodaira's thinking on the important role of the farming associations, see Kusumoto Masahiro, ed., *Nōsangyoson keizai kōsei undō to Kodaira Gonichi*, pp. 40–42, fn. 48.
58. Saitō shisaku kinenkai, ed., *Shisaku Saitō Makoto den*, vol. 3, p. 222.
59. Ibid., p. 224.
60. Kamei Kanichirō (Fukuoka), who spoke against the budget, argued that *jiriki kōsei* wouldn't come to much, relying as it did solely on the spirit of mutual assistance. Yamazaki Tatsunosuke (Seiyūkai, Fukuoka) used the program as part of an argument against the excessive concentration of power in the central government. *TGT* 63, pp. 130, 134, 136.
61. Tago Ichimin, "Nōson kōsei ni tsuite," pp. 24–36.
62. Ibid., pp. 24–30.
63. Azuma Takeshi, "Nōsei mondai ni kansuru shitsumon," p. 47. Originally from comments in the lower house, January 24, 1933.
64. Ibid., pp. 47–48. Azuma also commented on the need for rice, silk, fertilizer, and debt policies. Satō Nobuhiro was a late-Tokugawa-era reformer and scholar who wrote extensively on agricultural economics, among other topics. His ideas were much less benign than Ninomiya's, and included plans both for sweeping changes in the structure of the state and for the creation of a global Japanese empire. See Totman, *Early Modern Japan*, pp. 453–456, for a synopsis of his career and thought.

65. "Nōson kyūjō dankai zadankai," *Minsei* 6:7 (July 1932): 17. See especially comments by Murakami Kuniyoshi. Seimu chōsa kai, "Wagatō no nōgyosanson taisaku," *Minsei* 6:8 (August 1932): 49–54. In the same issue see "Seiji keizai jihō," pp. 74–75, for support of the Saitō cabinet against charges that it was promoting *jiriki kōsei* to hide a lack of real relief policies.

66. Wakatsuki Reijirō, "Hijōjikyoku kōkyū no wagatō no seisaku," p. 5. Originally from an August 20, 1932, speech in the lower house.

67. Arakawa Gorō, "Jiriki shinkō keikaku ni tsuite," pp. 62–68.

68. Ibid., p. 64.

69. The party magazine devoted a special issue to "village revitalization policies" in July 1933, featuring articles by Kodaira and Nasu Hiroshi, as well as descriptions of villages that had implemented recovery plans. See *Minsei* 7:7 (July 1933). Descriptions of village economic revitalization were printed in other issues as well. Kodaira also wrote articles that appeared in *Seiyū*, as befit a politically neutral state bureaucrat.

70. Baba Eiichi, "Nōson keizai no shinkō to jiriki kōsei undō."

71. Yamamoto Tatsuo, "Jikyoku ni kangami kokumin no jikaku funki o nozomu." Yamamoto's address took place on September 5, 1932.

72. Ibid., p. 6.

73. Yamamoto appears to be following this document closely in his September speech. Taikakai (Gotō Fumio), ed., *Naimushō shi*, vol. 2, pp. 509–510.

74. Tomita Aijirō, "Kokumin kōsei undō no gaikan," pp. 12–14. Tomita was head of the Social Bureau's Social Section. For a broader interpretation of the importance of spiritual development within the revitalization movement, and for comments on the relatively good state of "spirit" in Denmark and the United States, see Yoshida Shigeru, "Kokumin kōsei no seishin," pp. 1–16.

75. Yamamoto Tatsuo, "Jikyoku ni kangami kokumin no jikaku funki o nozomu," p. 8. See also *Ōsaka mainichi shinbun*, September 21, 1932 (evening edition), for a discussion of the prime minister's September 20, standing-room-only speech at the Shisei Kaikan in Hibiya Park.

76. Moriya Hideo, "Jikyoku kyōkyū no dai issen ni tatsu nōgyosanson no tokyokusha ni yosu," pp. 20–21. See also Tōgō Makoto, "Nōson no kōsei to kyōiku no kakushin," pp. 1–8, for more on the Ministry of Education's attitude toward the revitalization movement.

77. Sekiya Ryūkichi, "Kokumin kōsei undō no kontei," p. 15. Sekiya was head of the Shakai kyōikukyoku (Social Education Department) in the Ministry.

78. Kusumoto Masahiro, ed., *Nōsangyoson keizai kōsei undō to Kodaira Gonichi*, p. 42.

79. For a full discussion of this conflict and its implications, see Ushiyama Kenji, "Shōwa nōgyō kyōkō," pp. 181–182; and idem, "Nōson keizai kōsei undōka no 'mura' no kinō to kōsei," pp. 27–28.

80. Kusumoto Masahiro, ed., *Nōsangyoson keizai kōsei undō to Kodaira Gonichi*, p. 35. Between Kodaira's departure and the Economic Revitalization Section's demise in 1941, there were six directors. As Kusumoto notes, this early period under Kodaira thus has a focus that the section later lacked.

81. Ibid., p. 46.

82. Nōrinshō, *Nōsangyoson keizai kōsei keikaku juritsu hōshin*, in NSS 1:2, pp. 151–173.

83. See Nōrinshō keizai kōseibu, ed., "Dai ikkai nōson keizai kōsei chūō iinkai yōroku," February 1933, in NSS 1:2, pp. 189–190, and idem, ed., "Dai nikai nōson keizai kōsei chūō iinkai yōroku," July 1934, in NSS 1:2, pp. 231–232, for lists of members.

84. Kusumoto Masahiro, ed., *Nōsangyoson keizai kōsei undō to Kodaira Gonichi*, p. 33.

85. Nōrinshō order number 2, October 6, 1932, "Nōsangyoson keizai kōsei keikaku ni kansuru ken," in Nōrinshō, *Nōsangyoson keizai kōsei keikaku juritsu hōshin*, December 1932, in NSS 1:2, p. 154.

86. Nōrinshō, *Nōsangyoson keizai kōsei keikaku juritsu hōshin*, in NSS 1:2, pp. 151–173.

87. In the first few years of the Economic Revitalization Campaign, designation was not an especially tasty carrot to dangle in front of recalcitrant communities; by 1937, as discussed in Chapter 7 below, designation brought with it potential access to a large pool of funding from the state. Incentives to conform were therefore much greater.

88. Nōrinshō nōmukyoku, "Nōson keizai kōsei shisetsu no keika gaiyō," April 1943, in NSS 1:7, pp. 286–287.

89. Note that these categories apply to farming villages, and that mountain and fishing communities are covered separately. The plan also discussed the types of funding that the Ministry of Agriculture and Forestry would provide, which were limited to assistance for the establishment of prefectural committees, subsidies for the salaries of prefectural officials working on self-revitalization, and extremely small subsidies for revitalization planning at the village level.

90. Nōrinshō, *Nōsangyoson keizai kōsei keikaku juritsu hōshin*, in NSS 1:2, p. 161.

91. Ibid., pp. 170–172.

92. The industrial cooperatives were so important to the success of the overall recovery plan that they had a whole section to themselves in the Ministry of Agriculture and Forestry's guidelines.

93. Nōrinshō, *Nōsangyoson keizai kōsei keikaku juritsu hōshin*, in NSS 1:2, pp. 151–173, esp. p. 156.

94. Nishiyama has already been mentioned in connection with farm debt; see also Nishiyama Kōichi et al., *Nishiyama Kōichi nikki*.

95. Both Kinmonth, *The Self-Made Man in Meiji Japanese Thought*, and Gluck, *Japan's Modern Myths*, touch on this.

96. See Kinmonth, *The Self-Made Man in Meiji Japanese Thought*, chap. 8.

97. Ōkado Masakatsu, "Review of *Nishiyama Kōichi nikki*," p. 50.

98. Radio was also significant. Kasza, *The State and the Mass Media in Japan, 1918–1945*, pp. 88, 94–97; Iwasaki Akira, "Atarashii media no tenkai," pp. 240, 244.

99. Kano Masanao, *Taishō Demokurashii no teiryū*; Waswo, "The Transformation of Rural Society, 1900–1950"; Wilson, "Angry Young Men and the Japanese State." See also Mariko Tamanoi, *Under the Shadow of Nationalism*.

100. Dai Nihon rengō seinendan chōsabu, *Nōson jitsujō hōkokusho*, September 1932, in NSS 1:2, p. 83.

101. Itagaki Kuniko, *Shōwa senzen, senchūki no nōson seikatsu*, pp. 54–56; Adachi Ikitsune, "Jiriki kōsei undōka no Ie no hikari," p. 106.

102. For more detailed analyses of the magazine's content and approach, see Itagaki Kuniko, *Shōwa senzen, senchūki no nōson seikatsu*; Adachi Ikitsune, "Ie no hikari no rekishi," pp. 59–76; idem, "Ie no hikari no sengo tekiō," pp. 79–96; and idem, "Jiriki kōsei undōka no Ie no hikari."

103. See, for example, "(Tochigi ken ni okeru) Nōson seinendan no koe o kiku zadankai," Ie no hikari (November 1932), pp. 34–48. For more general comments, see Adachi Ikitsune, "Ie no hikari no rekishi," p. 71; Itagaki Kuniko, *Shōwa senzen, senchūki no nōson seikatsu*, p. 169; and Tasaki Nobuyoshi, "Toshi bunka to kokumin ishiki," pp. 167–198.

104. Itagaki Kuniko, *Shōwa senzen, senchūki no nōson seikatsu*, p. 52.

105. For just one example, see "Nōmin no koe o kiku zadankai," Ie no hikari (March 1932), pp. 59–67.

106. Gordon, "Managing the Japanese Household," pp. 248–251; Garon, *Molding Japanese Minds*, pp. 11–13; idem, "Fashioning a Culture of Diligence and Thrift"; Mariko Tamanoi, *Under the Shadow of Nationalism*.

107. Newspapers put out by young men's associations in Nagano in the late 1920s and early 1930s make this point as well; see Mariko Tamanoi, *Under the Shadow of Nationalism*, and Itagaki Kuniko, *Shōwa senzen, senchūki no nōson seikatsu*, p. 32.

108. Armstrong, *Just Before the Dawn*, pp. 232–234; see also Havens, "Religion and Agriculture in Nineteenth Century Japan." Kodaira Gonichi, "Hōtoku shisō to nōson kōsei," is just one example of the links that bureaucrats and Hōtoku advocates alike drew between revitalization and Ninomiya's teachings.

109. Sasai was a native of Hyōgo prefecture with a background in teaching and administration, having served as the head of the Kanagawa Prefecture Social Department for several years. He became the vice president of the Dai Nihon Hōtoku Society in 1927 and held that post for the next two decades. He was also the author of a number of books on Hōtoku-ism and, between 1927 and 1932, was the editor of the 36-volume edition of *Ninomiya Sontoku zenshū*. Unno Fukuju, "Nōson keizai kōsei undō to sonraku sangyō kumiai" (August 1980), p. 119, fn. 13.

110. Hijikata was designated in 1933 and received special designation in 1938. In 1935, the Home Ministry's Shakaikyoku (Social Bureau) published Sasai's com-

ments on village planning as "Chōson ni okeru kōsei keikaku o jitsugen suru ni tsuite." For an analysis of the Hōtoku recovery effort in Hijikata, see Yagi Shigeki, *Hōtoku undō 100 nen no ayumi*, pp. 258–266; Ogawa Nobuo, "Shōwa kyōkōka ni okeru 'Jiriki kōsei' to Hōtokusha undō"; Unno Fukuju, "Nōson keizai kōsei undō to sonraku sangyō kumiai" (August 1980); and idem, "Shōwa kyōkōka no nōson saihensei katei (1)."

111. Sasai Shintarō, "Hōtokushiki hijōji kyōkyū hōsaku," Parts 1 and 2, pp. 4–8. See also Wilson, "Bureaucrats and Villagers in Japan."

112. See Sasai's comments in *Shimin*, "Nōson taisaku zadankai," 27:7 (July 1932), pp. 2–50.

113. Garon, *Molding Japanese Minds*, p. 7.

114. See Sasai's comments in *Shimin*, "Nōson taisaku zadankai," 27:7 (July 1932), pp. 16–18, under a section entitled "The Basis of Crisis Relief is *Kyōka*."

115. Tasaki Nobuyoshi, "Toshi bunka to kokumin ishiki," pp. 167–198.

116. Sasai didn't reserve his scorn for the West. His comments about the Chinese include references to them as "especially selfish" (in "Hōtokushiki hijōji kyōkyū hōsaku," part 1, p. 7) and as "the ones with the most selfishness," or "the Chinese are the ones with the most developed persistence in the search for profit" (in "Hōtokushiki hijōji kyōkyū hōsaku," part 2, p. 10). For earlier examples of very favorable assessments of foreign practices, see Higashinari Tetsugorō, ed., *Hōtoku Ninomiya ō kyōkun dōwa*, pp. 220–223.

117. Sasai, "Hōtokushiki hijōji kyōkyū hōsaku," part 1, pp. 7–8. Sasai applied a similar argument on a broader scale when he discussed the most recent development in thinking—the conflict between the proletariat and the bourgeoisie. Where the Western approach emphasized only conflicts over rights, the Hōtoku approach was to improve the lot of the poor through vigorous and steady growth. See Sasai, "Hōtokushiki hijōji kyōkyū hōsaku," part 2, pp. 10–11.

118. Ibid., part 2, p. 10.

## Chapter 7

1. Nōrinshō keizai kōseibu, ed., "Dai nikai nōson keizai kōsei chūō iinkai yōroku," July 1934, in *NSS* 1:2, p. 236.

2. Kodaira Gonichi, "Keizai kōsei dai san nen ni mukau no kakugo," pp. 17–18.

3. See *Fukushima minpō*, April 18 and 23, 1934, for coverage of the meetings and ceremonies marking Sekishiba's designation as a campaign village.

4. Other categories include land, population and employment, fertilizer use, production and sales, the cost of living, finances, local organizations, and a balance sheet of income and expenditure from farming. See SMY, *Keizai kōsei keikaku kihon chōsa*, 1934, KST.

5. All comparisons are based on data gathered in 1923. See SMY, *Tahata jisaku kōsaku tanbetsu chō*, 1923, KST. See SMY, *Komatsu buraku kakuko keizai chōsabo*, October 1934, KST. Komatsu's plans were written on standardized forms that could easily have been employed throughout the village.

6. I have relied on Watanabe's draft when referring to the hamlet-level plan. In some categories, like population, for instance, he seems to have gone directly from the information provided in the individual reports to an estimate for the hamlet. In others the link may be less exact, in that I have been unable to arrive at the same figures that Watanabe did by simply adding up the data provided in each of the 18 individual reports. His results and mine are usually close, though, and his are certainly more trustworthy. Another fact to bear in mind is that not all households reported in every category, especially when it came to planning five years down the road, something that Watanabe must have compensated for.

7. Unlike the village's Economic Revitalization Plan, the one drawn up in Komatsu focuses not on the size of crop yields but on their worth in yen. Individual household plans, however, do include estimates of crop sizes.

8. SMY, *Komatsu buraku kakuko keizai chōsabo*, October 1934, KST. The rice crop was reportedly worth 6,294 yen when the plan was drafted, and residents proposed increasing its value to 7,863 yen by 1938.

9. This figure is obtained by adding the subtotals in each production-related subcategory of the hamlet's plan and comparing them. Excluded from the calculation are amounts entered under the "other" category. These seem to involve rent payments, pensions, and the like, which came to almost 4,800 yen in 1933 and which were expected to fall to just over 2,700 by 1938. If included in the above calculation, the increase in total income over that period falls to around 10 percent.

10. SMY, *Komatsu buraku kakuko keizai chōsa bo*, October 1934, KST.

11. The plan for silk does not involve any major cuts in production, so Utsumi may have been taking into account the relatively good market for cocoons in 1933, and have expected prices to stay low for the next several years.

12. Since the Kobiyama family planned to go on renting the same amount of land, it is possible either that it expected to face a rent increase or that it was going to rent the same amount of land from a different landlord, which would help account for the higher rent.

13. As explained in Chapter 3, here I counted Hara Masaru's family as being in the black. Note also that Hara Yoshitomi's deficit fell from 70 yen in 1933 to a predicted loss of only 7 yen; a more generous definition of a balanced budget might put him in the black as well, in which case the total number of households breaking even or better at the end of the planning period would be 11.

14. Landownership and rental figures are from each household's Economic Revitalization Plan. Here are some other comparisons. Five households owned a total

of less than 1 *chō* of paddy and upland, three owned between 1 and 2 *chō*, and eight owned more than 2 *chō*. Their average expected increases in income were 51, 11, and 10 percent, respectively. The three households with less than 1 *chō* of paddy land under cultivation (rented or owned) had average planned income increases of 81 percent; the average for everyone else was a 4 percent decline in income.

15. On average, the five households that owned a total of less than 1 *chō* of paddy and upland predicted a spending increase of about 12 percent; the three that owned between 1 and 2 *chō* expected a drop of about 10 percent, and the eight with more than 2 *chō* projected a cut in total spending of more than 20 percent.

16. See Totman, *Early Modern Japan*, pp. 6–7, for a discussion of Japan's climate and the introduction of rice to the northeast.

17. For a detailed description of Tōhoku's climate in 1934, see Teikoku nōkai, *Tōhoku chihō nōson ni kansuru chōsa, Kyōsaku hen*, p. 47. Note that many farmers in the region were reportedly two weeks behind schedule even before July's bad weather, having been delayed by late snowfalls and low temperatures in April. Officials in nearby Toyokawa recorded several thousand yen in damage from three consecutive days of rain in mid-July; Sekishiba was almost certainly hit just as hard. See Kitakata-shi shi hensan iinkai, ed., *Kitakata-shi shi*, vol. 8, p. 877. Reports from Fukushima show that the temperature in July was 1.4° C lower than normal, and that there were 13 percent fewer sunny days than normal. In August the temperature was just under a degree lower than normal, and there were 4 percent fewer sunny days. Conditions elsewhere in the region were much worse. Morioka (in Iwate prefecture) reported receiving 67 more centimeters of rain per month (on average) than in a normal year and a 15 percent reduction in sunny days. Ishinomaki (Miyagi prefecture) had 93 centimeters more rain than normal, and almost 10 percent fewer days with sun. Nihon ginkō Fukushima shiten, "Kannai Tōhoku yon-ken kyōsaku jitsujō," pp. 669–670.

18. H. Arakawa, "Three Great Famines in Japan," p. 211; Totman, *Early Modern Japan*, p. 6.

19. *Tōkyō asahi shinbun*, October 16, 1934.

20. Teikoku nōkai, *Tōhoku chihō nōson ni kansuru chōsa, Kyōsaku hen*, p. 108.

21. The 1.5 million *koku* estimate for Fukushima was 24 percent less than normal and 36 percent smaller than the 1933 harvest. The comparable figures for Iwate are 48 percent and 56 percent, respectively. The second crop estimate for Miyagi was actually slightly higher than the first. Teikoku nōkai, *Tōhoku chihō nōson ni kansuru chōsa, Kyōsaku hen*, pp. 22–23, and foldout table, pp. 34–35.

22. Of course, rice crops were not the only ones to be damaged in 1934. Other grains, as well as fruits, greens, potatoes, and silk-cocoon production, were also harmed by the inclement weather. However, their yen value to the average Tōhoku

farmer was relatively insignificant compared to that of the rice crop, and they can be safely omitted from most discussions of the famine. For more information on nonrice crops in 1934, refer to either Nihon ginkō Fukushima shiten, "Kannai Tōhoku yon-ken kyōsaku jitsujō," or Teikoku nōkai, Tōhoku chihō nōson ni kansuru chōsa, Kyōsaku hen.

23. Those two counties were the hardest hit of any in the prefecture and experienced drops in the size of the harvest that were comparable with those found in Miyagi and Yamagata. See Nihon ginkō Fukushima shiten, "Kannai Tōhoku yon-ken kyōsaku jitsujō," pp. 670–672. The total value of all farm production in Yama county fell by 55 percent between 1933 and 1934; officials estimated that the combination of cold and wind damage cost farmers there almost 2.8 million yen. Fukushima-ken keizaibu, "Kyōsaku taisaku gaikyō," 1934, in Fukushima-ken shi, vol. 13, pp. 68, 70, 534–535.

24. Tōkyō asahi shinbun, October 26, 1934.

25. For the village's own report on crop damage, see SMY, "Nōsakubutsu no genshū jōkyō chōsa ni kansuru ken," November 15, 1934, in Kitakata-shi shi hensan iinkai, ed., Kitakata-shi shi, vol. 6, pp. 462–463.

26. There were 420 households listed in the village's Special Household tax records in 1934; 373 appear in tables labeled "Beisaku sono hoka ni yoru genshūsha chō," which are part of the "Kyōsaku jōkyō chōsa" (Survey of Farm Conditions) conducted in December 1934. These records may be found in SMY, Kyōsaku kankei shorui tsuzuri, 1934, KST. The difference between the taxpaying population (420 households) and the number of families (373) appearing in the survey comes about because not all residents of the village were farmers and not all of Sekishiba's farmers experienced the 50 percent reduction in the value of farm production necessary for inclusion in the report. In a small number of cases, it was impossible to match the names on the survey records with those that appear in the tax assessments. Those cases were omitted. The missing or non-surveyed households run the gamut of high and low taxpayers, suggesting that the omissions probably do not skew the results significantly one way or the other. The 373 surveyed households represent 94 percent of all farming households in the community (based on a 1933 figure of 396 farming families).

27. Geography also played a role. Only two of the sixty-three surveyed households in Kamitakahitai, for instance, suffered losses greater than 75 percent, while half the households in Komatsu and a third of those in Sosogi and Kyōde did. Sekishiba and Higashi-nakamei also had a relatively high number of households with large losses. And three of the four families with more than 3 chō of paddy land in cultivation and with losses in excess of 75 percent were from the latter hamlet; eleven of the thirteen households reporting total crop failures were in Sekishiba.

28. See SMY, "Shokuryō fusoku jokyōchō ni kansuru ken kaihō," November 12, 1934, in *Kyōsaku kankei shorui tsuzuri, 1934*, KST, for details on survey methods and terminology.

29. Village officials estimated that 175 households would run out of rice by the end of May, involving 1,190 individuals. See SMY, "Shokuryō fuzoku jōkyōchō ni kansuru ken," November 17, 1934, in Kitakata-shi shi hensan iinkai, ed., *Kitakata-shi shi*, vol. 6, pp. 466–467. For the results of the hamlet-level surveys, see "Shokuryō fuzoku jōkyō chō ni kansuru ken," November 12, 1934, in *Kyōsaku kankei shorui tsuzuri, 1934*, KST. For the later, larger estimate of needed rice supplies, see SMY, "Sonkai giin, kuchō, keizai kōseiiin gōdō kyōgikai teishutsu jikō," December 27, 1934, KST. See also SMY, Mayor Satō to the Governor, "Seifumai kōfu ni kansuru chinjōsho," January 16, 1935, *Kangyō kankei 1935* documents, 1935, KST. A separate survey identified more than 300 people in 75 households who met the prefecture's definition of those particularly vulnerable to the famine's effects: those sixty-five and older unable to work, those fifteen and under unable to work, the sick and injured, expectant and nursing mothers, the physically or mentally disabled, and mothers caring for infants less than a year old. See notice from the Fukushima-ken gakumu buchō, "Kyōsaku risaishachū seikatsu konkyūsha chōsa no ken," November 13, 1934, in SMY, *Kyōsaku kankei shorui tsuzuri, 1934*, KST.

30. Teikoku nōkai, *Tōhoku chihō nōson ni kansuru chōsa, Kyōsaku hen*.

31. This is from the second of the *Tōkyō asahi shinbun*'s "Tōhoku no kyōsakuchi o miru" series, in the October 13, 1934 edition. Other major papers, such as the *Tōkyō nichi nichi shinbun* (see its "Kyōsaku no Tōhoku o mite" of November 2, 1934) and the *Ōsaka mainichi shinbun*, ran their own articles on local conditions.

32. Nihon ginkō Fukushima shiten, "Kannai Tōhoku yon-ken kyōsaku jitsujō," pp. 680–681. The data from Fukushima are as of the end of December 1934; Yamagata's survey is from the end of October, as were those in Miyagi and Iwate, where the share of hungry children was 6 percent. The estimate of 1 million hungry children is from the *Tōkyō nichi nichi*, November 2, 1934.

33. *Tōkyō asahi shinbun*, October 12, 1934.

34. *Fukushima minpō*, November 29, 1934.

35. In at least one community in Minami Aizu, residents could attend lectures on how to prepare bark and grasses for consumption. *Tōkyō asahi shinbun*, October 26, 1934.

36. In *Return to Tsugaru*, pp. 64–65, Dazai Osamu presents the following conversation between himself and a friend:

> "This is too much," I said. "They tell us all those beautiful stories about how this is the age of science, and they can't even teach the farmers how to prevent such bad harvests. They're a useless lot!"

"But the agronomists are doing all sorts of research. They've come up with improved varieties that are more resistant to the cold and with new planting techniques, so we no longer have complete harvest failures as we did in the past. But still, you know, despite all that, we have a bad time of it every five years or so."

"A useless lot!" I spat out, my anger directed at no one in particular.

37. For a contrary opinion, see Smethurst, *Agricultural Development and Tenancy Disputes in Japan, 1870–1940*, pp. 96, 98.

38. Totman, *Early Modern Japan*, pp. 236–245.

39. H. Arakawa, "Three Great Famines in Japan," p. 212.

40. On a related theme, at least one report issued by Fukushima prefecture concluded that the famine may have benefited the region indirectly by attracting so much attention to its problems. The establishment by the government of the Tōhoku Development Investigation Group (Tōhoku shinkō chōsakai) was done in part to reassure people in the region that the state took their problems seriously, even if it would be years before any benefits were seen locally. See Fukushima-ken keizaibu, "Kyōsaku taisaku gaikyō," p. 547.

41. *Fukushima minpō*, September 29 and November 29, 1934, March 13, 1935.

42. Kitakata-shi shi hensan iinkai, ed., *Kitakata-shi shi*, vol. 8, p. 653.

43. Nihon ginkō Fukushima shiten, "Kannai Tōhoku yon-ken kyōsaku jitsujō," p. 689.

44. Kitakata-shi shi hensan iinkai, ed., *Kitakata-shi shi*, vol. 8, p. 652. Others were added later, so that by 1940 there was a storage building in eleven of the village's fourteen hamlets.

45. Kusumoto Masahiro, ed., *Nōsangyoson keizai kōsei undō to Kodaira Gonichi*, p. 38. Takahashi also suggests that concerns about the failures of the program prompted a review that led to the development of special funding. See Takahashi Yasutaka, "Nihon fashizumu to nōgyō keizai kōsei undō no tenkai" pp. 16–17.

46. Kodaira Gonichi, "Nōson keizai kōsei undō o kentō shi," pp. 83–84. Kodaira appears to have paraphrased the text of the Nōrinshō keizai kōseibu, "Nōson keizai kōsei tokubetsu josei shisetsu an yōkō," November 1935 (secret), p. 2, in Kusumoto Masahiro, ed., *Nōsangyoson keizai kōsei undō to Kodaira Gonichi*, p. 408.

47. The funding process had to change significantly to allow the Economic Revitalization Plans to proceed. Grants would be made on a village-by-village, not project-by-project, basis. Central control over the funds and over the projects were necessarily loose, and local discretion was allowed if not encouraged. See, for example Takeyama, quoted in Kusumoto Masahiro, ed., *Nōsangyoson keizai kōsei undō to Kodaira Gonichi*, p. 47.

48. The printing shop responsible for producing the materials was located in the middle of a Shinbashi street, and the constant noise from the presses was so loud

that Takeyama was summoned to the police to explain and to apologize for depriving the shop's neighbors of their sleep. It worked, but he remembers, "I was worried for a while that work would be stopped. It was a near thing." Quoted in ibid., p. 45.

49. Agriculture and Forestry Minister Yamazaki reportedly thought very highly of Kodaira. Both he and Takahashi were favorably impressed with Kodaira's commitment to rural reform. See ibid., p. 48.

50. Kodaira Gonichi, "Nōson keizai kōsei undō o kentō shi," p. 87. In 1884, Takahashi was already thirty years old.

51. Kusumoto Masahiro, ed., *Nōsangyoson keizai kōsei undō to Kodaira Gonichi*, p. 47.

52. Takeyama, quoted in ibid., p. 46.

53. Ibid.

54. Two documents outline the Economic Revitalization Section's approach—"Nōson keizai kōsei tokubetsu josei shisetsu an yōkō," and "Nōson keizai kōsei tokubetsu josei shidō kantoku seidoan yōkō," both "secret" and both written in November 1935.

55. Kodaira Gonichi, "Nōson keizai kōsei undō o kentō shi," p. 84.

56. Takahashi Yasutaka, "Nihon fashizumu to nōgyō keizai kōsei undō no tenkai," p. 17, quoting Nōrinshō keizai kōseibu, *Nōson keizai kōsei tokubetsu shisetsu setsumei sho tsuika*, 1935.

57. These are repeated in "Nōsangyoson keizai kōsei tokubetsu josei kin kōtai yōkō ni kansuru ken," June 27, 1936. Kodaira also refers to these conditions. See Kodaira Gonichi, "Nōson keizai kōsei undō o kentō shi," p. 84; Nōrinshō keizai kōseibu, "Nōson keizai kōsei tokubetsu josei shisetsu an yōkō," November 1935 (secret), pp. 6–7, in Kusumoto Masahiro, ed., *Nōsangyoson keizai kōsei undō to Kodaira Gonichi*, pp. 412–413.

58. Kodaira Gonichi, "Nōsangyoson keizai kōsei tokubetsu josei shisetsu," p. 8. The wages would be accordingly low, "no more than enough to get a box lunch."

59. Kodaira Gonichi, "Nōson keizai kōsei undō o kentō shi," p. 85. The state would subsidize the interest on the loans for the first five years.

60. Ibid., pp. 101, 120. Annual levels are as follows: 1936, 350; 1937, 403; 1938, 407; 1939, 235; 1940, 131; 1941, 69.

61. Ibid., pp. 119–120.

62. Tōjima village, the fourth Yama county community, was selected in 1936. Nōrinshō nōseikyoku, "Nōsangyoson keizai kōsei tokubetsu josei chōson mei ichiran," March 1942, reprinted in Kusumoto Masahiro, ed., *Nōsangyoson keizai kōsei undō to Kodaira Gonichi*, p. 596.

63. See *Fukushima minpō*, June 26, 1937; *Sekishiba sonpō*, no. 6, June 1938.

64. See Fukushima-ken, "Shōwa 9 nendo keikaku juritsu nōsangyoson keizai kōsei keikaku gaiyō," for abridged versions of the plans that were established that year. Sekishiba's plan appears on pp. 123–126.

65. The other six crops are rice, barley, soybeans, potatoes, vegetables, and persimmons.

66. Inomata Tsunao, "Kyūbō no nōson," contains a good discussion of the risks associated with diversification from the point of view of the farmer. See esp. pp. 353–363.

67. This latter topic is covered under Section 6 of the plan, which deals with land expansion and improvements.

68. The pigs were expected to produce fertilizer that farmers could use to reduce their dependence on the store-bought variety.

69. In addition to the role outlined for the usual farm groups, the local Young Women's Association was expected to help make tofu, homespun cloth, and silk floss.

70. The village was encouraging people to make more compost and using publicly staged competitions before the Economic Revitalization program got under way. An April 13, 1934, *Fukushima minpō* article described Sekishiba's twenty-day-long Fertilizer Fair and reported that the village had produced much more than the previous year's amount.

71. The part of the plan that covers debt arrangement includes a reference to the Debt Arrangement Union Law, but that section of the text has been crossed out, leaving only the industrial cooperative and not a new debt-arrangement union as the focus of village debt policies. See Section 10 of the recovery plan.

72. See Section 12, "Seikatsu kaizen ni kansuru keikaku."

73. Better nutrition is something that surfaces in many Economic Revitalization Plans, and in Sekishiba it seems to have involved making more use of pickles, proper seasoning methods, and the use of different foods in recipes. Funding for kitchen reform would be available when necessary, and eventually the village hoped to improve half the kitchens in Sekishiba.

74. The best discussions in English of these texts and the topics they explore is T. C. Smith, "Peasant Time and Factory Time in Japan"; see also idem, "Ōkura Nagatsune and the Technologists."

75. SMY, Satō Sakichi to ku chō, "Keizai kōsei keikaku jisshi ni kansuru ken," September 9, 1935, *Keizai kōsei, 1934*, KST.

## Chapter 8

1. Fukushima-ken, ed., *Sangyō keizai 1*, vol. 18 of *Fukushima-ken shi*, pp. 97–100. Factory and employment figures are for workplaces of five or more people. Textiles and other light industries, which had traditionally employed many from the countryside, grew much less quickly in Fukushima. See also Nakamura Masanori, *Shōwa no kyōkō*, vol. 2, pp. 272–273.

2. Mataji Umemura et al., *Agriculture and Forestry*, vol. 9 in *Estimates of Long-Term*

*Economic Statistics of Japan Since 1868*, p. 161. If, instead of 1929, the period 1925–1927 is used as a baseline, then the recovery of farm prices must be pushed back even farther. Rice prices took until 1938 to return to 1925–1927 levels, while the average for all farm product prices did not recover until 1939. For an example of a scholar who uses this approach, see Shimizu Yōji, "Nōgyō to jinushi sei," pp. 256–258.

3. Satō used this phrase in a directive sent to all the heads of the hamlets in late 1935. See SMY, Satō Sakichi to ku chō, "Keizai kōsei keikaku jisshi ni kansuru ken," September 9, 1935, *Keizai kōsei, 1934*, KST.

4. For an example of the types of projects the farming associations were supposed to undertake, see SMY, "Keizai kōsei keikaku juritsu jikkō jōkyō ni kansuru chōsa (seisan keikaku o nozoku)," March 1936, in *Keizai kōsei keikaku jikkō jōkyō hōkoku, 1935*, KST.

5. SMY, "Tokubetsu josei no taishō to naru keikaku jikō o hōgan suru keizai kōsei keikaku jikkō hichō," n.d., KST. Village hamlet meetings also received small sums.

6. See *Fukushima minpō*, December 4, 1935, for a description of a farm products fair and contest in Sekishiba sponsored by the agricultural association.

7. Adachi Ikitsune, "Jiriki kōsei undōka no *Ie no hikari*," p. 110; Teruoka Shūzō, *Nihon nōgyō mondai no tenkai*, vol. 2, p. 172.

8. Teruoka Shūzō, *Nihon nōgyō mondai no tenkai*, vol. 2, p. 173.

9. Coverage in the northeast expanded even more dramatically, from only 53.9 percent of households to 76 percent in 1936. In Fukushima, the rates were 54.9 percent and 75.1 percent, respectively. Mori Takemaro, *Senji Nihon nōsonshakai no kenkyū*, p. 217.

10. Itagaki Kuniko, *Shōwa senzen, senchūki no nōson seikatsu*, p. 56; Teruoka Shūzō, *Nihon nōgyō mondai no tenkai*, vol. 2, p. 173.

11. An excerpt from one of the *Kumiai geppō* (Cooperative Monthly Report) appears in Kitakata-shi shi hensan iinkai, ed., *Kitakata-shi shi*, vol. 6, pp. 520–521. For others, see SMY, *Sangyō kumiai shorui*, KST.

12. Teruoka Shūzō, *Nihon nōgyō shi*, pp. 176–177. Japan's fertilizer use on a per-hectare basis was among the highest in the world in the late 1930s. Farmers in the Netherlands used the most; Japan ranked fifth. Johnston, *Japanese Food Management in World War II*, p. 12.

13. Teruoka Shūzō, *Nihon nōgyō mondai no tenkai*, vol. 2, p. 173.

14. The 1933 figure comes from the village recovery plan and represents cooperative sales of combined fertilizer, sulfuric acid, nitrogenous fertilizer, and other varieties, which at the time were the only four items handled by the union. The plan called on the union both to sell more of those fertilizers and to start selling other varieties. The 1937 and 1939 figures are from SMY, "Keizai kōsei keikaku juritsu jikkō

jōkyō ni kansuru chōsa (seisan keikaku o nozoku)," *Keizai kōsei keikaku jikkō jōkyō hōkoku, 1935, 1938–1940*, KST, and refer only to "fertilizer" sales.

15. Teruoka Shūzō, *Nihon nōgyō mondai no tenkai*, vol. 2, p. 173.

16. See SMY, "Nōsangyoson keizai kōsei tokubetsu joseison keizai kōsei seiseki hōkoku sho," May 1, 1939, and May 14, 1940, *Keizai kōsei, 1938*, KST.

17. The village started reporting rice sales in terms of bales instead of *koku* after 1937. Although the bale figures rise between 1938 and 1939, it is not clear how they compare with what came before. Attempts to calculate backward, based on the normal ratio of 2.5 bales of rice for every *koku*, yields figures that are not compatible with the estimates of market share appearing in the 1936 and 1937 reports. In any case, the question is less one of whether or not the cooperative was doing better than of how much better. SMY, "Keizai kōsei keikaku juritsu jikkō jōkyō ni kansuru chōsa (seisan keikaku o nozoku)," *Keizai kōsei keikaku jikkō jōkyō hōkoku, 1935, 1939–1940*, KST. In what appears to be a rough draft of a report to the prefecture, the village reported in late 1937 that the cooperative had a 40 percent share of both sales and purchases, but offers no other evidence in support. See SMY, report following a directive from the head of the Fukushima-ken keizaibu to designated villages entitled "Nōsangyoson keizai kōsei keikaku jikkō chōsa no ken," October 18, 1937, *Keizai kōsei, 1938*, KST.

18. SMY, "Nōsangyoson keizai kōsei tokubetsu joseison keizai kōsei seiseki hōkoku no ken," May 1, 1939, *Keizai kōsei, 1938*, KST.

19. See "Gyōgura kankei," April 1935, KST.

20. Kitakata-shi shi hensan iinkai, ed., *Kitakata-shi shi*, vol. 8, p. 652. See any of the "Keizai kōsei keikaku juritsu jikkō jōkyō ni kansuru chōsa (seisan keikaku o nozoku)" (e.g., in note 14 above) for reports on the use of the work sites.

21. These and other projects are described in SMY, "Tokubetsu josei no taishō to naru keikaku jikō o hōgan suru keizai kōsei keikaku jikkō hichō," n.d., KST.

22. Two hulling devices alone were budgeted at 5,560 yen in 1937. Ibid.

23. Teruoka Shūzō, *Nihon nōgyō mondai no tenkai*, vol. 2, pp. 245–246.

24. Teruoka Shūzō, *Nihon nōgyō shi*, p. 176. The number of kerosene or electric-powered motors in use in farming rose from just 2,500 in 1920 to 50,000 in 1927 and 300,000 in 1939; Johnston, *Japanese Food Management in World War II*, p. 11. For anecdotal accounts of the spread of farm machinery in the Niigata area, see Nishiyama Kōichi et al., *Nishiyama Kōichi nikki*. One of Nishiyama's many non-farm sources of income was small-engine repair, which kept him tremendously busy.

25. As Teruoka points out, there were limits to what mechanization could accomplish; shortages of parts, of fuel, and eventually of the machines themselves greatly reduced their utility to farmers after 1939. It is also interesting to note that even with the sharp rise in tractor use, in 1941 there were still only 1.4 tractors for

every thousand farm families. Given that in 1980 the ratio was 906 tractors for every thousand families, there was clearly room to grow. Teruoka Shūzō, *Nihon nōgyō mondai no tenkai*, vol. 2, p. 246.

26. New technology and organization, argues Penelope Francks, did not get rid of the need for cooperation; rather, "it changed the functions which made cooperation necessary, and it made the relationships within the group less those between patron and client and more those of a cross between business partners and trade union members, but in many ways it did not lessen the unity of the village group." Francks, *Technology and Agricultural Development in Pre-War Japan*, pp. 275–276.

27. SMY, "Zōsan keikaku juritsu jikkō ni kansuru chōsa," 1936–1940, KST.

28. This is not to say that the idea of increasing the rice yield by about 20 percent over five years, which the plan said they could do, was far-fetched. The 1930–1933 harvests were, on average, about 20 percent more than the 1925–1928 rice harvests. (Data are not available for 1929.) See Kitakata-shi shi hensan iinkai, ed., *Kitakata-shi shi*, vol. 6, pp. 796–797.

29. See Kitakata-shi shi hensan iinkai, ed., *Kitakata-shi shi*, vol. 8, pp. 670–671, and SMY, "Zōsan keikaku juritsu jikkō ni kansuru chōsa," 1940–1941, KST. Sekishiba's yields were consistently higher than those for Yama county as a whole.

30. Snow damage cut into the harvest of purple vetch in 1938, 1939, and 1940. Farmers had better luck with a form of soybean used as fertilizer; harvests between 1937 and 1939 were, on average, almost five times the 1933 level.

31. See SMY, report following a directive from the head of the Fukushima-ken keizaibu to designated villages entitled "Nōsangyoson keizai kōsei keikaku jikkō chōsa no ken," October 18, 1937, *Keizai kōsei, 1938*, KST.

32. Teruoka Shūzō, *Nihon nōgyō shi*, p. 172.

33. Based on the village's own figures, the value of the rice crop was calculated using a price of about 15 yen per *koku* in 1931 and about 29 yen per *koku* in 1937. The price in 1938 was 31 yen, compared to 41 yen in 1939.

34. Consumer prices are based on figures appearing in Kazushi Ōkawa, Miyohei Shinohara, and Larry Meissner, *Patterns of Japanese Economic Development*, p. 388. For fertilizer prices, see Nōrinshō nōmukyoku, *Hiryō yōran, 1939*, p. 52.

35. The 1935 figure is from SMY, "Keizai kōsei keikaku oyobi sono jikkō hi," date unknown, in *Keizai kōsei, 1937*, vol. 1. Figures for 1938–1940 are from Satō to Governor of Fukushima, "Nōsangyoson keizai kōsei tokubetsu joseison keizai kōsei seiseki hōkoku no ken," May 1, 1939; Satō to Governor of Fukushima, "Nōsangyoson keizai kōsei tokubetsu joseison keizai kōsei seiseki hōkokushi," May 14, 1940; and a document of the same title dated May 6, 1941, KST.

36. Teruoka Shūzō, *Nihon nōgyō shi*, p. 184.

37. SMY, "Nōsangyoson keizai kōsei tokubetsu joseison keizai kōsei seiseki hōkoku no ken," May 1, 1939, May 14, 1940, May 6, 1941, *Keizai kōsei, 1938*, KST.

38. Nōrinshō keizai kōseibu, "Jūgo nōsangyoson jijō shisatsu hōkokuki." For comments on conditions in Fukushima and Aizu in late 1938, see esp. pp. 295–298.

## Chapter 9

1. Kodaira Gonichi, "Keizai kōsei dai san nen ni mukau no kakugo," p. 15.
2. See Nōrinshō keizai kōseibu, ed., "Dai nikai nōson keizai kōsei chūō iinkai yōroku," in NSS 1:2, p. 288. For Home Ministry efforts to work with village mainstays during the Local Improvement campaign, see Pyle, "The Technology of Japanese Nationalism," pp. 61, 65.
3. Nōrinshō keizai kōseibu, ed., "Dai nikai nōson keizai kōsei chūō iinkai yōroku," in NSS 1:2, p. 285.
4. Exchange between Kodaira and committee member Niwa Shichirō, Nōrinshō keizai kōseibu, ed., "Dai nikai nōson keizai kōsei chūō iinkai yōroku," in NSS 1:2, p. 287.
5. This was committee member Sekiya Ryūkichi speaking.
6. Nōsangyoson keizai kōsei keikaku jikkō shōrei hōshin, in NSS 1:2, p. 182.
7. Ibid., pp. 182–183.
8. Nōrinshō keizai kōseibu, ed., "Dai nikai nōson keizai kōsei chūō iinkai yōroku," in NSS 1:2, p. 292. Honjo and Fukagawa were two of Tokyo's poorer wards. Until the city's expansion in 1932, they were the only two east of the Sumida River. Arima also wanted steps taken to warn people about records and movies, while committee member Kawagoe (from the Finance Ministry's Deposit Bureau) commented on the evils of radio broadcasting.
9. There are signs that rural communities were at least aware of the cultural and spiritual issues that had been raised by planners in Tokyo. A report from a regional inspector on the effects of the Economic Revitalization Campaign noted a "tendency for women and young people to flee the influence of city civilization (*bunmei*) and to 'love the soil' and 'return to the soil.'" Quoted by Kodaira Gonichi, "Nōson keizai kōsei undō o kentō shi," p. 106.
10. Between 1942 and 1947, the council had sixteen members; council elections were held on May 29 in 1929, 1933, and 1937. Kitakata-shi shi hensan iinkai, ed., *Kitakata-shi shi*, vol. 8, p. 664.
11. Ibid., pp. 314–316, 586–587, 661–662, 746–747, 820–821, 897–899.
12. SMY, Abe Tadashi to Fukushima-ken keizaibuchō, "Nōsangyoson kōsei kōrōsha hyōshō no ken," May 30, 1936, *Keizai kōsei, 1937*, vol. 1, KST. See also Kitakata-shi shi hensan iinkai, ed., *Kitakata-shi shi*, vol. 8, p. 702. There were only eighteen households in Satō's hamlet, so a ranking of fifth is not as spectacular as it might sound.
13. SMY, Abe Tadashi to Fukushima-ken keizaibuchō, "Nōsangyoson kōsei

kōrōsha hyōshō no ken," May 30, 1936, *Keizai kōsei, 1937*, vol. 1, KST. Note that this document is Abe's nomination of Satō for an award from the prefecture and may well exaggerate Satō's role. For examples of how Sekishiba was described as a model community, see *Fukushima minpō*, June 1, 1937, and April 17, 1938.

14. Although what happened in 1928 and 1932 is unclear, by 1936 no one was willing to challenge Satō for the position of mayor. A newspaper report entitled "Will the Mayor of Sekishiba Be Re-elected?" stated that although a majority of village council members were opposed to Satō "in principle," there was no one who could match his skill at creating one of the prefecture's model villages, and that therefore it looked as if he would be re-elected. Tōjō Genbei and vice headman Abe Tadashi were among those mentioned as possible candidates, but Satō was returned to office. *Fukushima minpō*, January 13, 1936.

15. SMY, *Chisō meikichō, ta chōson no ichi*, KST. The family owned roughly 22 *chō* of paddy land in Kamitakahitai, 1 *chō* in Toyoashi, and less than 1 *chō* each in Mitsui and Hirabayashi in 1931. Yabe owned about one-fifth of the paddy land in Kamitakahitai.

16. As of 1928, only one other non-resident individual reported landholdings worth more than Yabe's. Kitakata-shi shi hensan iinkai, ed., *Kitakata-shi shi*, vol. 6, p. 480.

17. Biographic material is from Watanabe Eiichi and Yabe Tsuneko, eds., *Yabe Zenbei den*, pp. 96–97. See also Kitakata-shi shi hensan iinkai, ed., *Kitakata-shi shi*, vol. 8, pp. 412–413, for information on Yabe's father.

18. Yabe Zenbei, "Hōtokushiki shōten keiei no taiken ni motozuku wagakuni keizai seikatsu no hihan," part 1, p. 125. This article and its sequel are apparently the text of a speech Yabe gave to the Hōtoku keizaigaku kenkyūkai in 1937. They are reprinted in Watanabe Eiichi and Yabe Tsuneko, eds., *Yabe Zenbei den*, pp. 429–474, as are some of Yabe's other pieces for *Shimin*.

19. Yabe Zenbei, "Hōtokushiki shōten keiei no taiken ni motozuku wagakuni keizai seikatsu no hihan," part 1, pp. 120–121.

20. Kihara, for instance, began his career as Japan's preeminent scholar of Hegel, and in 1915 published the country's first research into epistemology before developing his own school devoted to the study of a particularly Japanese philosophy. Kakei also had a long career as a legal scholar before turning to Shinto studies and the promotion of an emperor-centric nationalism.

21. Yabe Zenbei, *Haha no omoide*, pp. 56–58.

22. Yabe also made quite an impression on his fellow attendees. A person who sat next to him at the lectures remembers how hard it was to listen as seriously as Yabe did, and having the strong impression that he was no "ordinary person." See Ono Jinsuke's recollections in Watanabe Eiichi and Yabe Tsuneko, eds., *Yabe Zenbei den*, pp. 215–216.

23. SMY, "Sekishiba mura keizai kōsei iinkai kitei," *Keizai kōsei, 1934,* KST.

24. SMY, Satō to ku chō, "Keizai kōsei keikaku jisshi ni kansuru ken," September 9, 1935, *Keizai kōsei, 1934,* KST. The heads of each section were appointed to their five-year terms by Satō.

25. SMY, "Keizai kōsei iinkai hi jōseikin kōfu seigansho," July 20, 1934, *Keizai kōsei, 1934,* and SMY, "Sekishiba mura keizai kōsei iinkai kitei," *Keizai kōsei, 1934,* both KST.

26. If we take Endō Gengō's 476-yen payment out of the calculation, as it was by far the largest in the village and seven times larger than anyone else's on the committee, the committee average falls only to 23 yen, which is still twice the village average that year.

27. The exceptions to this include Anazawa Masayasu and Endō Dentarō (both village clerks), Igarashi Shoki, and Utsuki Taichi. Anazawa worked about half a *chō* of paddy land and was clearly not a full-time farmer; the others reported using even less land.

28. Members reported farming, on average, just under half of a *chō* of upland in 1934, compared to an average for Sekishiba as a whole of about a third of a *chō*. A member's average farm income was 1,190 yen a year; the village average was 845 yen.

29. They are Endō Gengō, Odagiri Yōgo, and Anazawa Kisohachi. See Satō to the head of the Fukushima-ken keizaibu, "Jisakunō sōsetsu iji shikin kashitsuke ni kansuru ken," July 11, 1936, in *Jisakunō shorui, 1935–1937,* KST. Tōjō Genbei and Maruyama Sakuma also show up in land tax records as having holdings in excess of 4 *chō*.

30. On the issue of landlords and tenants, information is scarce. Of the 17 members whose records I have been able to locate in the village's 1923 land survey, 9 reported renting at least some land to another person, and 8 reported borrowing land in 1923. Only one person, Igarashi Shoki, reported that all the land he was using at the time of the survey was borrowed. SMY, *Tahata jisaku kosaku tanbetsu chō,* 1923, KST.

31. There are indications, however, that many communities were less enthusiastic about the committees than the Ministry of Agriculture and Forestry might have hoped. The head of Fukushima's Economics Section felt compelled to write to all the designated villages in the prefecture in mid-1936 to point how their committees ought to be strengthened. He was quite concerned, he wrote, about the number of villages in which the committees had been found to exist in name only and to have no real activities. One of the things that he suggested to the mayors of designated villages was that they pay less attention to the importance of official position in deciding who they selected for committee membership. In a very roundabout way, he hinted that while it might be well and good to have the heads of the industrial cooperative, agricultural association, and women's groups on the committee, there should

also be some people with less prestige and more leadership ability active in the Economic Revitalization program. Notice from the Fukushima-ken keizaibuchō to Keizai kōsei shitei chōson chō, "Keizai kōsei iinkai no kyōka ni kansuru ken," May 16, 1936, *Keizai kōsei, 1934,* KST.

32. See Yabe Zenbei, "Hōtokushiki shōten keiei no taiken ni motozuku wagakuni keizai seikatsu no hihan," parts 1 and 2; idem, "Shitsumon ōmon"; and idem, "'Kuni nimei ronkō' shokan," parts 1 and 2. Yabe's articles appeared in the same issues as ones by people like Admiral and then Home Minister Suetsugu Nobumasa ("Long-Term War and the Resolution of the Citizens") and Finance Minister Kaya Okinori ("Hoping for the Arousal of the People as We Pass Through the Spring of the First Year of the Victorious War.")

33. Yabe was not the only person interested in this topic. The task of creating a new economics involved people like Sasai, Gotō Fumio, the Ministry of Agriculture and Forestry's Ishiguro Tadaatsu, and Tokyo University's Nasu Hiroshi, all of whom might be expected to have something to say on the subject. They were joined by almost a hundred other members of the bureaucracy, academia, and business (including Yabe Zenbei) in what became known as the Hōtoku keizaigaku kenkyūkai (Research Group on Hōtoku Economics). Although the research group did not manage to replace Adam Smith overnight, *Shimin* printed some of the speeches that members made and, in doing so, helped generate at least some wider discussion about what "Japanese-style economics" might involve.

34. Yabe, "Hōtokushiki shōten keiei no taiken," part 1, p. 128.

35. Ibid., pp. 128–129. Like Sasai, Yabe also identified China as an important non-Western source of trouble. See p. 129 for his explanation of how "selfishness and the pursuit of the private good" arrived from China long ago and plunged "the harmonious and united country of Greater Japan" into conflict and, ultimately, the Warring States period.

36. For some earlier examples of the use of "standstill" (*ikizumari*) to describe conditions in Japan, see Wilson, "Bureaucrats and Villagers in Japan."

37. Yabe, "Hōtokushiki shōten keiei no taiken," part 2, pp. 107–108.

38. Note that the end of the Russo-Japanese War was about the time that officials began to employ the Hōtokusha to stabilize the countryside as part of the Local Improvement campaign.

39. Yabe, "Hōtokushiki shōten keiei no taiken," part 1, pp. 126–127.

40. Ibid., part 1, p. 127; part 2, pp. 117–118. Yabe also reported that the ratio of costs to sales had fallen by half between 1930 and 1936.

41. Ibid., part 1, p. 134, part 2, p. 115.

42. Ibid., part 2, pp. 115–117. For a brief discussion of the *kyōka* (moral suasion) villages in Fukushima, see Yasutomi Kunio, "Fukushima-ken ni okeru keizai kōsei undō," pp. 219–221. The other four villages were Ōmori, Shinobu county; Nakasato,

Tamura county; Narahara, Minami-Aizu county; and Nozawa machi, Kawanuma county.

43. Yabe, "Hōtokushiki shōten keiei no taiken," part 2, p. 117. Sasai Shintarō was similarly insistent on combining economic revitalization planning and the Hōtoku movement. See his Sasai Shintarō, *Kokumin kōsei to hōtoku*, p. 38.

44. Yabe, "Hōtokushiki shōten keiei no taiken," part 1, p. 124; part 2, pp. 120–121. Yabe's optimism about the rest of Kitakata was linked to growing state efforts in the National Spiritual Mobilization movement.

45. Ibid., part 1, p. 124.

46. Yabe Zenbei, *Haha no omoide*, pp. 62–63. Personal communication, Tsuneko Yabe, March 2, 1993.

47. Aizu Hōtokusha nenpyō henshū iinkai, *Aizu Hōtokusha nenpyō*, pp. 10–13. A Sekishiba village document announcing the "Dai-ni kokumin kōsei hōtoku kōshūkai," to be held September 6–8, 1934, spoke of the importance of the lectures to an understanding of the revitalization of the village and urged members of the Economic Revitalization Committee to attend. See SMY, "Dai nikai kokumin kōsei hōtoku kōshūkai ni kansuru ken," *Keizai kōsei, 1934*, KST.

48. Kitakata-shi shi hensan iinkai, ed., *Kitakata-shi shi*, vol. 8, pp. 654–655, and Aizu Hōtokusha nenpyō henshū iinkai, *Aizu Hōtokusha nenpyō*, pp. 10–13. Komatsu hamlet's society is described as participating in early 1939 in a meeting of affiliated societies in Aizu. References to a Komatsu Hōtoku Society first appear in hamlet record meetings in May 1939. See SMY, *Buraku jōkai nisshi*, vol. 4, KST.

49. Five hamlets reported rates in excess of 100 percent, which means that more than the required two persons per household attended. Both Sekishiba and Kamitakahitai, which at 70 percent also had a low attendance rate, pointed out that residences in their hamlets were quite scattered and that the "spirit of unity" was somewhat lacking as a result. See SMY, Satō to Governor of Fukushima, "Shichōson shinkō iinkai oyo(bi) buraku jōkai nado ni kansuru chōsa menkai no ken," February 7, 1937, in *Keizai kōsei, 1937*, KST.

50. SMY, Satō to ku chō, "Keizai kōsei keikaku jisshi ni kansuru ken," September 9, 1935, *Keizai kōsei, 1934*, KST. See "Buraku jōkai kitei."

51. Ibid.

52. All comments referring to the contents of the hamlet assemblies are based on Sekishiba's four-volume *Buraku jōkai nisshi* (Record of Hamlet Assemblies). There were originally five volumes; vol. 2, which would have covered the period from August 1936 to December 1937, is missing.

53. See SMY, *Kamitakahitai Hōtokusha nisshi*, vol. 3, p. 105, KST, for the minutes of a meeting held on January 10, 1935.

54. This period is even longer if one counts the meetings from 1941 to 1945. No diary has been found for those meetings, but other records suggest that the meetings

were still being held. See Kitakata-shi shi hensan iinkai, ed., *Kitakata-shi shi*, vol. 8, p. 654.

55. SMY, Satō to the Governor of Fukushima, "Shichōson shinkō iinkai oyo(bi) buraku jōkai nado ni kansuru chōsa kaihō no ken," February 7, 1937, *Keizai kōsei, 1937*, KST. He also reported a hundred-percent attendance rate for Komatsu's meetings since they began. Sekishiba had the lowest rate, at 69 percent, while small Sanjōnome reported 150 percent attendance.

56. SMY, Satō to the Governor of Fukushima, "Shichōson shinkō iinkai oyo(bi) buraku jōkai nado ni kansuru chōsa kaihō no ken," February 7, 1937, *Keizai kōsei, 1937*, KST.

57. Handbills and other materials, all from SMY, *Senkyō shusei kankei shoruizuri*, (from) July 1935, KST.

58. For an example of Sasai Shintarō's advice to local leaders in a Niigata village on how to rid their community of partisan strife, see Yagi Shigeki, *Hōtoku undō 100 nen no ayumi*, pp. 246–250. Three of Sekishiba's hamlets had voter turnout rates of 100 percent in April 1937 and were therefore eligible for an Election Purification award; so was Komatsu, where 97 percent of those eligible to vote had done so. SMY, *Senkyō shusei kankei shoruizuri*, (from) July 1935, KST. Voting patterns in Sekishiba were not noticeably affected by the Election Purification Campaign. Residents cast 36 percent of their votes for Seiyūkai candidates, 41 percent for Minseitō. Such shares are well within the range of past election results. Seisen kinenshi kankōkai, *Seisen no ato*, pp. 55, 56, 58. Shūgiin jimukyoku, *Dai 18 kai shūgiin giin sōsenkyo ichiran* (1932); *Dai 19* (1936); *Dai 20* (1937); *Dai 21* (1943), various pages.

59. Or "Sekishiba mura keizai kinshuku oyo(bi) kyōfū kiyaku," which appears as part of SMY, Satō to ku chō, "Keizai kōsei keikaku jisshi ni kansuru ken," September 9, 1935, *Keizai kōsei, 1934*, KST.

60. Mariko Tamanoi, *Under the Shadow of Nationalism*, also touches on *seikatsu kaizen* (the improvement of daily life).

61. T. C. Smith, "Peasant Time and Factory Time in Japan," pp. 199–235, suggests that Tokugawa-era peasants were already well aware of the value of time.

62. Garon, *Molding Japanese Minds*; idem, "Fashioning a Culture of Diligence and Thrift."

63. In *The Land of Milk and Honey*, Tanaka Tōsuke is almost as upset by the extravagance surrounding his father's funeral as he is by his death; the cost of the ceremony and associated events wipes out Tōsuke's savings.

64. The list of education-related topics covered in the revitalization plan includes the establishment of a national ideal and a sound national spirit; instilling reverence for the gods and respect for ancestors; fostering public spiritedness; knowledge about employment and a love for work; economic thought and morals; making education practical; and improving physical standards.

65. Another aspect of reform connected to education was the selection and training of village mainstays, discussed in detail in Chapter 10 below.

66. "Seishin sakkō shisetsu jisshi seiseki," n.d., *Keizai kōsei 1938*, KST. SMY, report following a directive from the head of the Fukushima-ken keizaibu to designated villages entitled "Nōsangyoson keizai kōsei keikaku jikkō chōsa no ken," October 18, 1937, *Keizai kōsei, 1938*, KST. That same report also mentions that although 350 households were using a bookkeeping system, most of them were not getting as much out of the recordkeeping system as they should. Similar comments appear in "Keizai kōsei keikaku juritsu jikkō jōkyō ni kansuru chōsa (seisan keikaku o nozoku)," 1936, KST.

67. *Fukushima minpō*, February 11, 1937. In 1938 the national government bestowed an even higher honor on Sekishiba, by choosing it as one of two Fukushima communities to receive an award on the fiftieth anniversary of the promulgation of the local system of self-government. *Fukushima minpō*, April 17, 1938.

68. Itagaki Kuniko, *Shōwa senzen, senchūki no nōson seikatsu*, traces these developments in detail. See below for references to specific articles.

69. See, for more information, the *Fukushima minpō*, January 17 and February 19, 1936. For a copy of the Fujinkai's bylaws, see Kitakata-shi shi hensan iinkai, ed., *Kitakata-shi shi*, vol. 6, part 2, p. 436. The Dai Nihon kokubō fujinkai (Greater Japan National Defense Women's Association), which was more concerned with support for soldiers and their families, was formed soon afterward. A rival body, the Aikoku fujinkai (Patriotic Women's Association), was also created. The three existed side by side until their merger in 1942.

70. "Nōson fujin no koe o kiku zadankai" (June 1932), pp. 104–114; "(Josei seinendanchō to shōgakkō jokyōin kara) Nōson seikatsu no fuhei to kibō o kiku" (June 1936), pp. 72–78; "Warera no fuhei fuman o hakidasu zadankai" (September 1937), pp. 56–64; "Machi ya mura o mamoru watakushidomo fujin no katsudō zadankai" (July 1940), pp. 82–89.

71. Uno, "Women and Changes in the Household Division of Labor," pp. 17–41; Mariko Tamanoi, *Under the Shadow of Nationalism*, also touches on this.

72. Mary Neth describes a similar process in the U.S. countryside during the New Deal, in which the state's attempts to create businesslike, male-run farms were resisted by rural communities. Neth, *Preserving the Family Farm*.

73. For examples, see Itagaki Kuniko, *Shōwa senzen, senchūki no nōson seikatsu*, and "(Tochigi ken ni okeru) Nōson seinendan no koe o kiku zadankai" (November 1932), pp. 34–48; "Nōka no seikatsu kaizen ni kansuru zadankai" (July 1933), pp. 54–62; "Seishin kōsei keizai kōsei—dochira ga saki ka" (June 1934), pp. 52–58; "Kōsei keikaku wa dore dake jitsugen shita ka" (March 1935), pp. 60–69; "Keizai kōsei no ayumi to shōrai wo kataru zadankai" (March 1936), pp. 46–57; "(Josei seinendanchō to shōgakkō jokyōin kara) Nōson seikatsu no fuhei to kibō o kiku" (June 1936), pp. 72–78.

## Chapter 10

1. The village officially lost 124 soldiers and sailors to the war. As of the end of 1941, there had been only ten reported deaths in uniform. Almost 70 percent of the servicemen from Sekishiba killed in the war died after January 1, 1944, and more than two-fifths did so after January 1, 1945. Kitakata-shi shi hensan iinkai, ed., *Kitakata-shi shi*, vol. 6, pp. 766–769.

2. A useful account of planning and strategic thinking appears in Barnhart, *Japan Prepares for Total War*; see also Peattie, *Ishiwara Kanji and Japan's Confrontation with the West*.

3. Akira Iriye, *The Origins of the Second World War in Asia and the Pacific*.

4. Johnson, *MITI and the Japanese Miracle*; Dower, *Japan in War and Peace*.

5. Thomas R. H. Havens describes the IRAA as "a giant organizational sponge, wielded at the pleasure of the military-dominated state. Its cumbersome sogginess is doubtless the main reason why the association, having absorbed all the citizen's groups, became almost useless for the authorities after mid-1942"; Havens, *Valley of Darkness*, p. 60.

6. Watanabe Eiichi and Yabe Tsuneko, eds., *Yabe Zenbei den*, pp. 101, 249–250, 418–423; Yabe Zenbei, "Hōtokushiki shōten keiei no taiken," part 1, p. 124. Yabe Zenbei's biography also describes in great detail the process by which his wife Tsuneko (they were married in 1932) was chosen in 1939 to be one of the nursemaids to Princess Suganomiya. That happened in 1939, and the accompanying prestige may have played a role in Yabe's later position in the prefectural Imperial Rule Assistance Association. Watanabe Eiichi and Yabe Tsuneko, eds., *Yabe Zenbei den*, pp. 111–120.

7. Masao Maruyama, *Thought and Behavior in Modern Japanese Politics*, offers a clear exposition of this approach; see also Fletcher, *The Search for a New Order*.

8. Gordon, *Labor and Imperial Democracy in Prewar Japan*, pp. 333–339; Shillony, *Politics and Culture in Wartime Japan*.

9. Havens provides this chronology of the war at home: early mobilization, July 1937 to September 1940; consolidation and regimentation, September 1940 to May 1942; full-scale general participation, mid-1942 to late 1944; destruction and defeat, late 1944 to August 1945. Havens, *Valley of Darkness*, p. 7.

10. Nōrinshō nōseikyoku, "Nōson keizai kōsei shisetsu no keika gaiyō," April 1943, in NSS 1:7, p. 283. See also Nōrinshō, "Nōsangyoson keizai kōsei keikaku setsubi hōshin" (March 1940), in Kusumoto Masahiro, ed., *Nōsangyoson keizai kōsei undō to Kodaira Gonichi*, pp. 437–450.

11. Nōrinshō nōseikyoku, "Nōson keizai kōsei shisetsu no keika gaiyō," in NSS 1:7, p. 290. Also included were similar instructions for fishing and mountain villages. See Nōrinshō, "Nōsangyoson keizai kōsei keikaku setsubi hōshin" (March 1940),

in Kusumoto Masahiro, ed., *Nōsangyoson keizai kōsei undō to Kodaira Gonichi*, pp. 445–449.

12. SMY, "Keizai kōsei tokubetsu josei shisetsu no kekka senji taisaku jō no nobashitaru sōgōteki kekka," *Keizai kōsei, 1938*, KST. This undated document is probably from 1939.

13. Later reports were even more explicit in their assertions that people were abandoning their belief in the primacy of the individual in favor of mutual assistance and absolute cooperation. This development was also attributed to the Economic Revitalization Campaign. SMY, Mayor Satō to the Governor of Fukushima, "Nōsangyoson keizai kōsei tokubetsu joseison keizai kōsei seiseki hōkokusho," May 6, 1941, *Keizai kōsei, 1940*, KST.

14. Teruoka Shūzō, *Nihon nōgyō shi*, p. 185.

15. Umemura Mataji, *Rōdōryoku*, pp. 210–211, 214–215.

16. Mori Takemaro, *Senji Nihon nōson shakai no kenkyū*, p. 206.

17. Teruoka Shūzō, *Nihon nōgyō shi*, pp. 186–190; idem, *Nihon nōgyō mondai no tenkai*, vol. 2, pp. 258–260.

18. SMY, "Keizai kōsei iinkai joseikin kōfu shinseisho," March 17, 1939, *Keizai kōsei, 1938*, KST.

19. Japan relied on imports from China to meet its domestic needs for ammonium sulfate, a key component in manmade fertilizers. Those imports naturally fell after 1937, and were almost completely curtailed by 1940. Chemicals that otherwise would have gone into the manufacture of fertilizer were also increasingly diverted to the production of explosives. Teruoka Shūzō, *Nihon nōgyō mondai no tenkai*, vol. 2, pp. 243–244.

20. These regulations eventually became part of the 1942 Food Management Law (Shokuryō kanri hō). See Teruoka Shūzō, *Nihon nōgyō mondai no tenkai*, vol. 2, pp. 243–244, 270.

21. Johnston, *Japanese Food Management in World War II*, pp. 94–95; Teruoka Shūzō, *Nihon nōgyō mondai no tenkai*, vol. 2, pp. 289–290, 332–366.

22. See, for example, Ishida Takeshi, *Kindai Nihon seiji kōzō no kenkyū*, pp. 35–36.

23. Kodaira Gonichi, "Nōgyōkai no honshitsu to shimei," pp. 540–546.

24. The Nōgyōkai assimilated local agricultural associations, industrial cooperatives, and tea, livestock, and silk unions and was responsible for all their existing services to the community as well as the coordination of all levels of local production with the war effort. As Kodaira Gonichi pointed out, in regulations defining the role of similarly consolidated organizations in industry and manufacturing, the operative phrase always referred to their "cooperation with national policy." In the Nōgyōkai's case, however, policymakers stated that "cooperation" didn't capture the vital nature of agriculture's contributions to the nation, so they decided instead that "complete compliance" was a better choice. Ibid.

25. In one telling anecdote, villagers were encouraged by officials to help themselves to any "illicit" crops growing in nearby fields, in the hope that theft would prevent what regulations could not. B. F. Johnston, *Japanese Food Management in World War II*, p. 118.

26. Havens, *Valley of Darkness*, pp. 11–33; Berger, *Parties out of Power in Japan, 1931–1941*, pp. 149–161, 186–187, 207–208; Teruoka Shūzō, *Nihon nōgyō mondai no tenkai*, vol. 2, pp. 263–264. The National General Mobilization Law, passed in 1938, gave the state powerful tools to control industry, allocate resources (including manpower), and direct the economy as it saw fit during wartime, all with little or no input from the Diet.

27. *Sekishiba sonpō*, no. 20, August 1939.

28. Ibid., no. 12, December 1938.

29. SMY, *Buraku jōkai nisshi*, vols. 1, 3, 4, and 5, KST.

30. Yabe didn't limit himself to Sekishiba; at one speech in nearby Keitoku village, he spoke to an audience of 300 listeners for close to five hours in early 1938. *Fukushima minpō*, April 6, 1938.

31. All comments about the content of the hamlet assemblies are based on the four-volume *Buraku jōkai nisshi* (see note 29 above). There were originally five volumes; vol. 2, which covered the period from August 1936 to December 1937, is missing.

32. The police played a role in overseeing controls on distribution. By late 1940, policemen spoke at the assemblies on topics such as "About the Economic Police." See, for example, the record for Kamisugure's meeting on September 16, 1940, in SMY, *Buraku jōkai nisshi*, vol. 5, KST.

33. There are some gaps in the extant copies of the paper, but the publication schedule on the whole was remarkably consistent.

34. *Ie no hikari* underwent similar changes; from 1941 on, the Ministry of Agriculture used it as a channel to promote farm policies and regulations. With the ministry's support, the magazine retained access to paper supplies until late in the war, so that in late 1944 it still had a circulation of 1.4 million. Itagaki Kuniko, *Shōwa senzen, senchūki no nōson seikatsu*, p. 187.

35. The Home Ministry had similar ideas and had tried them once before under the aegis of the Local Improvement Campaign. See Pyle, "The Technology of Japanese Nationalism," pp. 51–65, esp. pp. 61, 65. For the Nōrinshō's proposal, see Nōrinshō keizai kōseibu, ed., "Dai nikai nōson keizai kōsei chūō iinkai yōroku," in *NSS* 1:2, p. 288.

36. SMY, "Keizai kōsei keikaku juritsu jikkō jōkyō ni kansuru chōsa (seisan keikaku o nozoku)," *Keizai kōsei, 1940*, KST. The year 1939 was the last in which the long-term lectures were offered by the organization.

37. The Aizu Mountain Village Hall (Aizu sanson dōjō) was called the Fukushima Prefectural Mountain Village Hall when it opened in early 1937 but changed its name after only six months to attract more students.

38. The curriculum at the Aizu dōjō was heavily weighted toward practical, hands-on training. Full-time students received more than 3,300 hours of instruction in 21 different subjects over the course of a school year. Classes ranged from physical education to farming-related law. There was also time for spiritual training, but on balance the practical aspects of farming accounted for most class time. The various morale-building and spiritual topics together came to less than 5 percent of annual class time. In 1938 the dōjō had only 40 students, 26 of whom were from Minami-Aizu, and only 2 of whom were from Yama county. See SMY, "Aizu sanson dōjō ichiran," January 1939, *Keizai kōsei, 1938*, KST. There is no comparable description of the curriculum at Yabukigahara available.

39. Mori Takemaro, "Nihon fashizumu no keisei to nōson keizai kōsei undō," pp. 135–152; Nishida Yoshiaki, ed., *Shōwa kyōkōka no nōson shakai undō*; Mori Takemaro, "Nōson no kiki no shinkō," pp. 136–166; Waswo, "The Transformation of Rural Society, 1900–1950," pp. 598–602; for a more recent analysis, see Ōkado Masakatsu, *Kindai Nihon to nōson shakai*.

40. Ōkado Masakatsu, *Kindai Nihon to nōson shakai*, pp. 310–318.

41. SMY, "Keizai kōsei iinkai joseikin kōfu shinseisho," March 17, 1939, *Keizai kōsei, 1938*, KST. See also the notice in the *Sekishiba sonpō*, no. 15 (March 1939), explaining the revisions.

42. See SMY, Satō to head of Fukushima-ken keizaibu, "Shōwa 13 nendo ken oyobi shichōson keizai kōsei iinkai jigyō seiseki hōkoku," June 26, 1939, *Keizai kōsei, 1938*, KST.

43. Although there is really no way to measure how effective the committee was at its new duties, it is worth pointing out that Sekishiba continued to bring in large rice harvests until 1943.

44. For the 1934 committee, I was able to estimate landholdings for 23 of 34 members; in 1939, the estimates cover 23 of the 32 members.

45. SMY, "Keizai kōsei iinkai joseikin kōfu shinseisho," January 17, 1941, *Keizai kōsei, 1940*, KST. See also land tax records, various years. Figures are for both paddy and upland fields.

46. For the 1934 committee, I was able to determine dates of birth (from voting rolls) of 29 of the 34 members; for the 1939 committee, 31 of the 32 are known. The youngest committee member (within the ranks of those whose age can be determined) in 1934 was 35, the oldest 67. In 1939, the youngest was 26, the oldest 70.

47. Nishida Yoshiaki, ed., *Shōwa kyōkōka no nōson shakai undō*, and Nakamura Masanori, "Keizai kōsei undō to nōson tōgō"; several of Mori Takemaro's seminal articles on the Economic Revitalization Campaign have been collected in a single

volume: Mori Takemaro, *Senji Nihon nōson shakai no kenkyū*. Waswo summarizes some of Mori's conclusions in "The Transformation of Rural Society," pp. 599–603. Ōkado's work is the most recent and in some ways the most far-reaching: Ōkado Masakatsu, "Nōson keizai kōsei undō to buraku no tōgō," and idem, *Kindai Nihon to nōson shakai*.

48. Mori Takemaro, *Senji Nihon nōson shakai no kenkyū*, pp. 193–194.

49. My analysis of the program draws heavily on Nishida Yoshiaki, *Kindai Nihon nōmin undōshi kenkyū*, pp. 240–241. See also Nōrin daijin kanbō sōmuka, ed., *Nōrin gyōsei shi*, vol. 2, pp. 187–188.

50. When the Ministry of Agriculture first proposed the law to the Diet, it read in part, "The purpose of this law is to secure the position of producers, develop and maintain the productive power of farming, and preserve the economic revitalization and peace of the villages." The Diet inserted a new clause into the original language, so that it read "The purpose of this law is to, *on a basis of compromise and mutual assistance*, secure the position *of landowners* and producers" (new text italicized). Mori Takemaro, *Senji Nihon nōson shakai no kenkyū*, p. 220.

51. Nishida Yoshiaki, *Kindai Nihon nōmin undōshi kenkyū*, pp. 252–253. See also Shimizu Yōji, "Shokuryō seisan to nōchi kaikaku," pp. 331–368.

52. See Nishida Yoshiaki, ed., *Sengo kaikakuki no nōgyō mondai*.

53. Nishida Yoshiaki, *Kindai Nihon nōmin undōshi kenkyū*, p. 241. Between 1926 and 1941, 7.7 percent of all farm households were involved in the Owner-Cultivation Establishment program; between 1943 and 1946, the national average jumped to 13 percent. Mori Takemaro, *Senji Nihon nōson shakai no kenkyū*, p. 225.

54. For an example of how the Owner-Cultivation Establishment program could be used by tenants, see Nishiyama Kōichi, Nishida Yoshiaki, and Kubo Yasuo, *Nishiyama Kōichi nikki, 1925–1950-nen*, especially the years 1944–1945.

55. Nagano sent 37,859 individuals, Yamagata 17,177, and Fukushima 12,673 as of May 1945. Figures include both groups of settlers and Young Volunteers for the Development of Manchuria and Mongolia (Manmō kaitaku seishōnen giyūgun). See Young, *Japan's Total Empire*; Wilson, "The 'New Paradise'"; and Mori Takemaro, *Senji Nihon nōson shakai no kenkyū*, pp. 160–164, for analyses of the emigration programs.

56. Wilson, "The 'New Paradise,'" pp. 273–274; Takahashi Yasutaka, "Nihon fashizumu to nōgyō keizai kōsei undō no tenkai," pp. 19–25.

57. Wilson, "The 'New Paradise,'" p. 282.

58. Ibid., p. 281.

59. Ibid., pp. 259–261; Kase Kazutoshi, "Keizai seisaku," p. 375.

60. Wilson, "The 'New Paradise,'" pp. 259–261; Young, *Japan's Total Empire*, chap. 7.

61. Mori Takemaro, *Senji Nihon nōson shakai no kenkyū*, p. 162; Young, *Japan's Total Empire*, chap. 7.

62. Or only 3.7 percent of all those farm households cultivating less than half a *chō* of land. Mori Takemaro, *Senji Nihon nōson shakai no kenkyū*, p. 219.

63. Emigrants received a month of training in Fukushima, discounts on the cost of travel to Manchuria, free train tickets in Manchuria, and a variety of subsidies in support of their relocation. Ōishi Kaichirō, *Fukushima-ken no hyakunen*, p. 238.

64. Kitakata-shi shi hensan iinkai, ed., *Kitakata-shi shi*, vol. 6, p. 609; figures originally appeared in *Fukushima minpō*, July 8, 1937. This was fewer than nearby villages like Kamisanmiya and Atsushio had offered; at 50 and 75 households, respectively, their commitment seemed greater.

65. Speeches on emigration were given at hamlet assemblies in January 1938, December 1938, and January 1939; Yabe's report on Manchuria was in July 1940. SMY, *Buraku jōkai nisshi*, vols. 4–5, KMT. See Watanabe Eiichi and Yabe Tsuneko, eds., *Yabe Zenbei den*, p. 105.

66. Kitakata-shi shi hensan iinkai, ed., *Kitakata-shi shi*, vol. 6, pp. 609–610; Wilson, "The 'New Paradise,'" pp. 281–282.

67. Kamisanmiya sent only seven families, Atsushio three. Kitakata-shi shi hensan iinkai, ed., *Kitakata-shi shi*, vol. 6, p. 610.

68. The Central Federation of Moral Suasion Groups (Chūō kyōka dantai rengōkai) was also involved in the selection process. See Kitakata-shi shi hensan iinkai, ed., *Kitakata-shi shi*, vol. 6, part 2, pp. 334–338.

69. *Fukushima minpō*, March 28, 1939. Originally the prefecture had planned to designate only five communities, but added Sekishiba and one other to the list.

70. For a report on the village's progress, see Kitakata-shi shi hensan iinkai, ed., *Kitakata-shi shi*, vol. 6, part 2, pp. 338–341.

71. *Ie no hikari*, June 1940. One young man from Nagano had a slightly different take on the same problem. People left the village, he wrote, because there wasn't enough entertainment. His suggestion was that the industrial cooperative furnish a portable generator and portable movie projector to provide the necessary access to modern media. Man, he pointed out, cannot live on bread alone. *Ie no hikari*, July 1938, pp. 202–203.

72. Itagaki Kuniko, *Shōwa senzen, senchūki no nōson seikatsu*, p. 281.

73. Where Maruyama argues for a middle class that supported authoritarianism because it feared change and modernity, this study, like Itagaki and, more recently, Garon, suggests that it was possible to embrace both authoritarianism and modernity. See Masao Maruyama, *Thought and Behavior in Modern Japanese Politics*; Itagaki Kuniko, *Shōwa senzen, senchūki no nōson seikatsu*, p. 282; and Garon, "Rethinking Modernization and Modernity in Japanese History."

## Chapter 11

1. Nishiyama Kōichi, Nishida Yoshiaki, and Kubo Yasuo, *Nishiyama Kōichi nikki, 1925–1950-nen*; see especially 1944–1945.

2. In discussions with Occupation officials, farmers often spoke proudly of their wartime experiences of becoming landowners via the Owner-Cultivator Establishment program. Napier, *The Japanese Village in Transition*, pp. 162–163.

3. Wolf I. Ladejinsky, one of those who helped draft the American land reform proposals, was familiar with the writings of Nasu Hiroshi and Yagi Yoshinosuke. E. H. Norman and John F. Embree's work on agriculture and village life also informed policymakers. Chira, *Cautious Revolutionaries*, pp. 25, 31, 54–55; Walinsky, ed., *Agrarian Reform as Unfinished Business*.

4. The classic study of these policies and their implementation is Dore, *Land Reform in Japan*.

5. General Douglas MacArthur eventually came to share this perception, seeing similarities between his own efforts on behalf of land reform and those of Tiberius Sempronius Gracchus and his brother Gaius, whose reforms had limited landownership in favor of farmers. Chira, *Cautious Revolutionaries*, p. 38.

6. Ōishi Kaichirō, "Nōchi kaikaku no rekishiteki igi," p. 5.

7. Dore, *Land Reform in Japan*, pp. 186–187.

8. Ibid., p. 174; Ōishi Kaichirō, "Nōchi kaikaku no rekishiteki igi," p. 34.

9. Dore, *Land Reform in Japan*, pp. 139–141. Neutral parties could also be added.

10. Kitakata-shi shi hensan iinkai, ed., *Kitakata-shi shi*, vol. 8, pp. 657–659; Ōishi Kaichirō, "Nōchi kaikaku no rekishiteki igi," p. 30; idem, *Fukushima-ken no hyakunen*, p. 237.

11. There still are, of course, considerable variations within rural communities in terms of access to basic services and important non-farm sources of income. My use of the term "countryside" does not seek to impose a homogeneity that does not in fact exist.

12. Nishida Yoshiaki, *Kindai Nihon nōmin undōshi kenkyū*, pp. 262–263.

13. Williamson, "Agricultural Programs in Japan, 1945–51," p. 103.

14. Takeshi Ishida, "Nōchi kaikaku to nōson ni okeru seiji shidō no henka," p. 230.

15. Napier, *The Japanese Village in Transition*, p. 201.

16. Yabe's postwar activities are recalled in Watanabe Eiichi and Yabe Tsuneko, eds., *Yabe Zenbei den*.

17. American observers commented on these fears but noted that people were generally optimistic about the future. Napier, *The Japanese Village in Transition*, pp. 78–79.

18. See, for example, Yujiro Hayami, *Japanese Agriculture Under Siege*, p. 27. Farmers in Korea and Taiwan, which underwent land reforms informed by some of the

same ideas (and people) as did Japan, have similarly small farms, on average. The average farm size in Taiwan decreased slightly from 1.3 hectares in 1952 to 1.03 hectares in 1990. Ai-Ching Yen, "The Effects of Land Reform on Changes in the Structure of Agriculture in Taiwan in the 1950s," p. 373.

19. Nishida also observes that postwar rural support for Japan's conservative political parties stems at least in part from this tremendous increase in the value of land and from farmers' reluctance to see that challenged. Nishida Yoshiaki, *Kindai Nihon nōmin undōshi kenkyū*, p. 267.

20. Yujiro Hayami, *Japanese Agriculture Under Siege*, pp. 88–89.

21. Yujiro Hayami, *Japanese Agriculture Under Siege*, p. 47.

22. Teruoka Shūzō, *Nihon nōgyō shi*, p. 288. The Basic Law was modeled in part after European legislation, namely the 1955 Landwirtschaft Recht in Germany, the 1957 Agricultural Act in the United Kingdom, and France's 1960 Loi d'orientation agricole; Yujiro Hayami, *Japanese Agriculture Under Siege*, p. 77.

23. Yujiro Hayami, *Japanese Agriculture Under Siege*, pp. 20, 48–49.

24. Waswo, *Modern Japanese Society, 1868–1994*, p. 138.

25. Aurelia George, *The Politics of Agriculture in Japan*, provides thorough coverage of this topic.

26. Nōrin suisan gyōsei kenkyūkai, *Nōrin suisan*, p. 286.

27. Yamamoto Osamu, ed., *Nōgyō seisaku to tenkai no genjō*, pp. 105–106.

28. Kodaira was responsible for 396 publications in his lifetime, 313 of which were published before 1946. Kusumoto Masahiro, ed., *Nōsangyoson keizai kōsei undō to Kodaira Gonichi*, end pages 1–18.

29. Ibid., pp. 688, 692.

30. Kodaira Gonichi, "Nōson keizai kōsei undō o kentō shi, hyōjun nōson kakuritsu undō ni oyobu," in Kusumoto Masahiro, ed., *Nōsangyoson keizai kōsei undō to Kodaira Gonichi*, pp. 65–66.

31. Ibid., pp. 82–83. Kodaira went on to note that "the movements to expand the industrial cooperatives and the cooperative unions were [also] absolutely democratic ones." He remained active and influential in a large number of farm-related organizations until his death in 1976, at the age of ninety-two.

32. Garon, "Rethinking Modernization and Modernity in Japanese History," p. 357.

33. Gordon, "Managing the Japanese Household." Note, too, the importance attached more generally to science and rationality as key elements in the reconstruction of defeated Japan; see Dower, *Embracing Defeat*, pp. 494–495.

34. Garon, "Rethinking Modernization and Modernity in Japanese History," p. 358.

35. Tanino Akira, *Kokudo to nōson no keikaku*, pp. 128–132.

36. Kelly, "Rationalization and Nostalgia," p. 605. See also idem, "Finding A Place in Metropolitan Japan," pp. 189–216.

37. The postwar Ie no hikari has reflected these changes. Although it continues to stress the advantages of community life built around the Nōkyō, its articles promote a lifestyle that is essentially the same as that of the urban salaryman. Adachi Ikitsune, "Ie no hikari no sengo tekiō," pp. 91–95.

38. Ryohei Kada and Junko Goto, "Present Issues of Sustainable Land Use Systems and Rural Communities in Japan," p. 43.

39. For an interesting discussion of one community's successful efforts to resist a proposed merger, see Bailey, *Ordinary People, Extraordinary Lives*; Steiner, *Local Government in Japan*, pp. 187–189.

40. Steiner, *Local Government in Japan*, p. 192. Note, too, that the absence of strict rules about land use and zoning in Japan have meant that the borders between farm and non-farm areas are much less clear than in Europe, making it that much more difficult to tell where one begins and the other leaves off. Nishida Yoshiaki, "From a Train Window."

41. Of course, the fact that a household lies within a city's administrative boundaries tells us very little about how "urban" a setting it occupies. The expansion and amalgamation of the 1950s and early 1960s led to a blurring of the rural and urban, so that since 1960 census figures have reported on the relative population density of a community (including those within larger administrative units) to determine its status more clearly. In 1960, more than half of the population lived outside a densely inhabited district (those with a population density of more than 4,000 people per square kilometer), but by 1970 just under 47 percent did so. Ryohei Kada and Junko Goto, "Present Issues of Sustainable Land Use Systems and Rural Communities in Japan," pp. 43–44.

42. Kitakata-shi shi hensan iinkai, ed., *Kitakata-shi shi*. vol. 8, pp. 247, 643.

43. Nishida Yoshiaki, *Kindai Nihon nōmin undōshi kenkyū*, p. 1.

44. Nishida Yoshiaki, "From a Train Window."

45. In 1965, 35 percent of farm households were full-time; in 1975, 13 percent were. See Kitakata-shi shi hensan iinkai, ed., *Kitakata-shi shi*, vol. 7, p. 635. Japan is not unique in having had a drop-off in farmers and in farming's importance to the economy. The number of farms in the United States dropped by about 40 percent between 1930 and 1959 and by two-thirds between 1930 and 1987. The U.S. experience differs from that of Japan in that the amount of land under cultivation has tended to remain more or less constant since the 1930s, and more and more of that acreage is operated as part of very large farms. By 1959, more than a fifth of all farms in the U.S. were 105 hectares or larger. In Japan, in contrast, the average area under cultivation per farm has remained almost constant at 1.2 hectares. Stanton, "Structural Change in American Agriculture into the Next Century," pp. 118, 121.

46. Knight, "Rural Revitalization in Japan," offers a rich analysis of how some rural communities have marketed themselves and their special qualities to urbanites; see also Bailey, *Ordinary People, Extraordinary Lives*.

47. As Ann Waswo points out, the realities of farm life were too well understood by previous generations of Japanese for it to be idealized; only recently has the public's removal from farming been sufficient to allow for a successful idealization. Waswo, *Modern Japanese Society, 1868–1994*, p. 135.

48. A growing body of work explores the meaning of *furusato* (native place) in contemporary Japan; see especially Ivy, "Formations of Mass Culture"; Kelly, "Rationalization and Nostalgia"; and Robertson, "It Takes a Village."

49. Kitakata's 1995 population of 37,532 was only slightly larger than the number who lived in the area at the end of the 1920s, and considerably smaller than the 43,273 area residents reported in 1953. Kitakata-shi shi hensan iinkai, ed., *Kitakata-shi shi*, vol. 8, p. 256; Sōmucho tōkei kyoku, ed., *Nihon tōkei nenkan*.

50. The phrase "Kura no machi Kitakata" (City of Storehouses, Kitakata) is the standard slogan on local brochures, maps, and tourist literature.

51. Kitakata-shi shi hensan iinkai, ed., *Kitakata-shi shi*, vol. 7, pp. 848–849.

# Works Cited

Adachi Ikitsune. "Ie no hikari no sengo tekiō." *Shisō no kagaku* 21 (September 1960): 79–96.

———. "Ie no hikari no rekishi: aru nōhon shugi to sono baitai." *Shisō no kagaku* 18 (June 1960): 59–76.

———. "Jiriki kōsei undōka no Ie no hikari." *(Kikan) Gendai shi* 2 (May 1973): 105–114.

Aizu Hōtokusha nenpyō henshū iinkai. *Aizu Hōtokusha nenpyō*. Bange-machi: Suzuki insatsu, 1981.

Aizu-Wakamatsu-shi shuppankai, ed. *Aizu no rekishi*. Aizu-Wakamatsu-shi: Aizu-Wakamatsu-shi shuppankai, 1969.

Arai Masao. "Jiriki kōsei o kataru." *Minsei* 6 (November 1932): 24–28.

Arakawa Gorō. "Jiriki shinkō keikaku ni tsuite." *Minsei* 6 (October 1932): 62–68.

Arakawa, H. "Three Great Famines in Japan." *Weather* 12, no. 7 (1957): 211–217.

Armstrong, Robert Cornell. *Just Before the Dawn: The Life and Work of Ninomiya Sontoku*. New York: Macmillan, 1912.

Asahi shinbunsha. *Asahi jinbutsu jiten: gendai Nihon*. Tokyo: Asahi shinbunsha, 1990.

Azuma Takeshi. "Nōsei mondai ni kansuru shitsumon." *Seiyū*, no. 390 (February 1933): 38–48.

———. "Nōson no san dai mondai." *Seiyū*, no. 402 (February 1934): 24–26.

Baba Eiichi. "Nōson keizai no shinkō to jiriki kōsei undō." *Shimin* 28 (February 1933): 1–3.

Bailey, Jackson H. *Ordinary People, Extraordinary Lives: Political and Economic Change in a Tōhoku Village*. Honolulu: University of Hawai`i Press, 1991.

Barnhart, Michael. *Japan Prepares for Total War: The Search for Economic Security, 1919–1941*. Ithaca, N.Y.: Cornell University Press, 1987.

Bashō, Matsuo. *The Narrow Road to Oku*. Translated by Donald Keene. Tokyo, New York, and London: Kodansha, 1996.

Berger, Gordon. *Parties out of Power in Japan, 1931–1941.* Princeton, N.J.: Princeton University Press, 1977.

Bowen, Roger W. *Rebellion and Democracy in Meiji Japan: A Study of the Commoners in the Popular Rights Movement.* Berkeley: University of California Press, 1980.

Brinkley, Alan. *Voices of Protest.* New York: Vintage-Random House, 1982.

Case, H. C. M. "Farm Debt Adjustment During the Early 1930s." *Agricultural History* 34 (October 1960): 173–181.

Chira, Susan Deborah. *Cautious Revolutionaries: Occupation Planners and Japan's Post-War Land Reform.* Tokyo: Agricultural Policy Research Center, 1982.

Crawcour, E. Sydney. "Industrialization and Technological Change, 1885-1920." In *The Economic Emergence of Modern Japan*, ed. Kozo Yamamura, 50–115. Cambridge, Eng., and New York: Cambridge University Press, 1997.

*Dai Nihon teikoku tōkei nenkan.* 1920–1937.

Dazai, Osamu. *Return to Tsugaru.* Translated by James Westerhoven. Tokyo, New York, and San Francisco: Kodansha, 1985.

Den Akira. "Shōwa 9 nendo sōyosan hihan." *Minsei* 8 (January 1934): 24–25.

Dore, Ronald P. *Land Reform in Japan.* New York: Schocken Books, 1985.

———. *Shinohata: A Portrait of a Japanese Village.* 1st American ed. New York: Pantheon Books, 1978.

Dore, Ronald P., and Tsutomu Ōuchi. "Rural Origins of Japanese Fascism." In *Dilemmas of Growth in Prewar Japan*, ed. James W. Morley, 181–209. Princeton, N.J.: Princeton University Press, 1971.

Dower, John W. *Embracing Defeat: Japan in the Wake of World War II.* New York: W. W. Norton, New Press, 1999.

———. *Japan in War and Peace: Selected Essays.* New York: New Press; distributed by W. W. Norton, 1993.

Downard, Jack Douglas. "Tokyo: The Depression Years, 1927–1933." Ph.D. dissertation, Indiana University, 1976.

Duus, Peter. "Introduction, Japan's Informal Empire in China, 1895–1937: An Overview." In *The Japanese Informal Empire in China, 1895–1937*, ed. Peter Duus, Ramon Hawley Myers, and Mark R. Peattie, xi–xxix. Princeton, N.J.: Princeton University Press, 1989.

Duus, Peter, Ramon Hawley Myers, and Mark R. Peattie, eds. *The Japanese Informal Empire in China, 1895–1937.* Princeton, N.J.: Princeton University Press, 1989.

*Economisuto.* 1930.

Farquharson, John E. *The Plough and the Swastika: The NSDAP and Agriculture in Germany, 1928–45.* Sage Studies in Twentieth Century History, vol. 5. London and Beverly Hills, Calif.: Sage Publications, 1976.

Fletcher, William Miles, III. *The Search for a New Order: Intellectuals and Fascism in Prewar Japan.* Chapel Hill: University of North Carolina Press, 1982.

Francks, Penelope. *Technology and Agricultural Development in Pre-War Japan.* New Haven and London: Yale University Press, 1984.
Fukushima-ken. *Fukushima-ken tōkei sho.* Vol. 1. Fukushima-shi: Fukushima-ken, 1931.
——, ed. *Sangyō keizai 1.* Vol. 18 of *Fukushima-ken shi.* Fukushima: Kohama insatsu, 1969.
——, ed. *Seiji 1.* Vol. 15 of *Fukushima-ken shi.* Fukushima: Kohama insatsu, 1968.
——, ed. *Seiji 2.* Vol. 16 of *Fukushima-ken shi.* Fukushima: Kohama insatsu, 1969.
Fukushima-ken keizaibu. *Shōwa 9 nendo nōsangyoson keizai kōsei keikaku gaiyō: keikaku juritsu.* Fukushima-shi: Fukushima-ken keizaibu, 1935.
*Fukushima minpō.* 1930–1939.
Fukutake, Tadashi. *Japanese Rural Society.* Translated by Ronald P. Dore. Tokyo, London, and New York: Oxford University Press, 1967.
Garon, Sheldon. "Fashioning a Culture of Diligence and Thrift: Savings and Frugality Campaigns in Japan, 1900–1931." In *Japan's Competing Modernities: Issues in Culture and Democracy, 1900–1930,* ed. Sharon A. Minichiello, 312–334. Honolulu: University of Hawai'i Press, 1998.
——. *Molding Japanese Minds: The State in Everyday Life*: Princeton, N.J.: Princeton University Press, 1997.
——. "Rethinking Modernization and Modernity in Japanese History: A Focus on State-Society Relations." *Journal of Asian Studies* 53, no. 2 (May 1994): 346–366.
George, Aurelia. *The Politics of Agriculture in Japan.* Nissan Institute / Routledge Japanese Studies Series. New York: Routledge, 2000.
Gluck, Carol. *Japan's Modern Myths: Ideology in the Late Meiji Period.* Princeton, N.J.: Princeton University Press, 1985.
Gordon, Andrew. *Labor and Imperial Democracy in Prewar Japan.* Berkeley: University of California Press, 1991.
——. "Managing the Japanese Household: The New Life Movement in Postwar Japan." *Social Politics* (Summer 1997): 245–283.
Haley, John Owen. *Authority Without Power: Law and the Japanese Paradox.* Oxford and New York: Oxford University Press, 1991.
Hall, John Whitney. "Changing Conceptions of the Modernization of Japan." In *Changing Japanese Attitudes Towards Modernization,* ed. Marius B. Jansen, 7–41. Princeton, N.J.: Princeton University Press, 1965.
Hanes, Jeffrey E. "Media Culture in Taishō Osaka." In *Japan's Competing Modernities: Issues in Culture and Democracy, 1900–1930,* ed. Sharon A. Minichiello, 267–287. Honolulu: University of Hawai'i Press, 1998.
Hara Akira. "Keiki junkan." In *Sekai daikyōkōki,* ed. Ōishi Kaichirō, vol. 2 of *Nihon teikokushugishi,* 367–410. Tokyo: Tōkyō daigaku shuppankai, 1987.
Harada Katsumasa. *Manga irasuto Shōwa no rekishi.* Vol. 2. Tokyo: Kodansha, 1984.

Harada Kumao. *Saionji Kō to seikyoku*. Vol. 3. Tokyo: Iwanami shoten, 1950.
Hastings, Sally Ann. *Neighborhood and Nation in Tokyo, 1905–1937*. Pitt Series in Policy and Institutional Studies. Pittsburgh: University of Pittsburgh Press, 1995.
Hatade Isao. "Shōwa kyōkō to kyūnō doboku." In *Tochi kairyō hyakunenshi*, ed. Zenkoku tochi kairyō jigyō dantai rengōkai nijū shūnen kinenshi henshū iinkai, 177–190. Tokyo: Heibonsha, 1977.
Havens, Thomas R. H. *Farm and Nation in Modern Japan: Agrarian Nationalism, 1870–1940*. Princeton, N.J.: Princeton University Press, 1974.
———. "Religion and Agriculture in Nineteenth Century Japan: Ninomiya Sontoku and the Hōtoku Movement." *Japan Christian Quarterly* 38, no. 2 (Spring 1972): 100–102.
———. "Two Popular Views of Rural Self-Rule in Modern Japan." *Studies on Japanese Culture* 2 (1973): 249–256.
———. *Valley of Darkness: The Japanese People and World War Two*. New York: Norton, 1978.
Hayami, Yujiro. *Japanese Agriculture Under Siege: The Political Economy of Agricultural Policies*. New York: St. Martin's Press, 1988.
Higashinari Tetsugorō, ed. *Hōtoku Ninomiya ō kyōkun dōwa*. Tokyo: Aizensha, 1907.
Hokushin fukyō taisakukai daihyōsha. "Nōson kyūsai no chinjō o kiku." *Tōyō keizai shinpō*, June 18, 1932.
Holt, John Bradshaw. *German Agricultural Policy, 1918–1934: The Development of a National Philosophy Toward Agriculture in Postwar Germany*. Chapel Hill: University of North Carolina Press, 1936.
Hosaka Masayasu. *Go-ichigo jiken: Tachibana Kōzaburō to Aikyōjuku no kiseki*. Tokyo: Sōshisha, 1974.
*Ie no hikari*. 1932–1940.
Iinuma Jirō. "Seitō seiji to Shōwa nōgyō kyōkō." *Shisō*, no. 624 (June 1976): 155–173.
Ikeda Miyoji. *Shin Nihon no tenbō*. Tokyo: Kokumin kyōikukai, 1936.
Inamura Ryūichi. *Inamura Ryūichi shi danwa (dai ni) sokkiroku*. Naiseishi kenkyū shiryō, no. 188. Tokyo: Naiseishi kenkyūkai, 1974.
Inomata Etsuzō. "Shūsen zengo no kiroku kara." In Kitakata-shi shi hensan junbi iinkai, ed., *Kitakata-shi shi nenpō*, no. 4. Kitakata-shi: Kitakata-shi shi hensan junbi iinkai, 1987, 1–73.
Inomata Tsunao. *Kyūbō no nōson*. In *Shōwa zenki nōsei keizai meichoshū*, ed. Kondō Michio, vol. 1, 279–438. Tokyo: Nōsangyoson bunka kyōkai, 1978.
Inoue Harumaru. *Nihon shihon shugi no hatten to nōgyō oyobi nōsei*. Tokyo: Chūō kōron sha, 1957.
Iriye, Akira. *The Origins of the Second World War in Asia and the Pacific*. London and New York: Longman, 1987.
Ishida Takeshi. *Kindai Nihon seiji kōzō no kenkyū*. Tokyo: Miraisha, 1956.

———. "Nōchi kaikaku to nōson ni okeru seiji shidō no henka." In *Nōchi kaikaku*, ed. Tōkyō daigaku shakai kagaku kenkyūjo, vol. 6 of *Sengo kaikaku*, 217–250. Tokyo: Tōkyō daigaku shuppankai, 1975.

Itagaki Kuniko. *Shōwa senzen, senchūki no nōson seikatsu*. Tokyo: Mitsumine shobō, 1992.

Ivy, Marilyn. "Formations of Mass Culture." In *Postwar Japan as History*, ed. Andrew Gordon, 239–258. Berkeley: University of California Press, 1993.

Iwasaki Akira. "Atarashii media no tenkai." *Shisō*, no. 624 (June 1976): 240–255.

Johnson, Chalmers A. *MITI and the Japanese Miracle: The Growth of Industrial Policy, 1925–1975*. Stanford, Calif.: Stanford University Press, 1982.

Johnston, B. F. *Japanese Food Management in World War II*. Stanford, Calif.: Stanford University Press, 1953.

Kada, Ryohei, and Junko Goto. "Present Issues of Sustainable Land Use Systems and Rural Communities in Japan." In *Japanese and American Agriculture: Tradition and Progress in Conflict*, ed. Luther Tweeten, Cynthia L. Dishon, Wen S. Chern, Naraomi Imamura, and Masaru Morishima, 31–50. Boulder, Colo.: Westview Press, 1993.

Kagawa, Toyohiko. *The Land of Milk and Honey*. Translated by Marion Romer Draper. London: Hodder & Stoughton, 1937.

Kagawa Toyohiko. *Chichi to mitsu no nagaruru sato*. In *Kagawa Toyohiko zenshū*, ed. Kagawa Toyohiko zenshū kankōkai, vol. 17. Tokyo: Kirisuto shinbunsha, 1935 (1982).

Kageyama Shikazō. "Fusai o seyo!" *Fukushima-ken nōkai hō* (April–June 1931): 120–122.

*Kaizō*. 1932–1933.

Kano Masanao. *Taishō demokurashii no teiryū*. Tokyo: Nihon hōsō shuppan kyōkai, 1973.

Kase Kazutoshi. "Keizai seisaku." In *1920 nendai no Nihon shihon shugi*, ed. 1920 nendai shi kenkyūkai, 373–411. Tokyo: Tōkyō daigaku shuppankai, 1983.

———. "Nōson fusai seiri seisaku no ritsuan katei—Manshū jihenki nōgyō seisaku taikei no ichisokumen." *Tōkyō suisan daigaku ronshū*, no. 14 (March 1979): 11–38.

———. "Senzen Nihon ni okeru shitsugyō kyūsai jigyō no tenkai katei." 2 pts. *Shakai kagaku kenkyū* 43, no. 3 (October 1991): 159–229; 43, no. 5 (January 1992): 201–288.

Kasza, Gregory J. *The State and the Mass Media in Japan, 1918–1945*. Berkeley and Los Angeles: University of California Press, 1988.

Kayo Nobufumi. *Nihon nōgyō kiso tōkei*. Tokyo: Nōrin tōkei kyōkai, 1977.

Kazahara Yasoji. *Nihon shakai seisaku shi*. Tokyo: Nihon hyōronsha, 1937.

*Keizai ōrai*. 1932–1935.

Kelly, William W. *Deference and Defiance in Nineteenth-Century Japan*. Princeton, N.J.: Princeton University Press, 1985.

———. "Finding A Place in Metropolitan Japan: Ideologies, Institutions, and Everyday Life." In *Postwar Japan as History*, ed. Andrew Gordon, 189–216. Berkeley: University of California Press, 1992.

———. "Rationalization and Nostalgia: Cultural Dynamics of New Middle-Class Japan." *American Ethnologist* 13, no. 4 (1986): 603–618.

Kenmochi Seiichi. "Shōwa kyōkō ki to hoppō no kyōshi-tachi." In *Minshū to shite no Tōhoku*, ed. Makabe Jin and Nozoe Kenji, 205–224. Tokyo: Nihon hōsō shuppan kyōkai, 1976.

Kikkawa Manabu. *Arashi to tatakau tesshō Araki*. Vol. 2. Tokyo: Araki Sadao shōgun denki hensan kankōkai, 1955.

Kindai Nihon shi kenkyūkai. *Manshū Jihen zengo*. Tokyo: Hakuyōsha, 1943.

Kinmonth, Earl H. *The Self-Made Man in Meiji Japanese Thought*. Berkeley: University of California Press, 1981.

Kitakata no ayumi henshū iinkai, ed. *Aizu Kitakata no ayumi*. Aizu-Wakamatsu shi: Kitakata no ayumi hensan iinkai, 1966.

Kitakata-shi shi hensan iinkai, ed. *Kitakata-shi shi*. Vol. 6. Kitakata City: Kita Nihon insatsu, 1993.

———, ed. *Kitakata-shi shi*. Vol. 7. Kitakata City: Kita Nihon insatsu, 1998.

———, ed. *Kitakata-shi shi*. Vol. 8. Kitakata City: Kita Nihon insatsu, 1991.

Knight, John. "Rural Revitalization in Japan: Spirit of the Village and Taste of the Country." *Asian Survey* 34, no. 7 (1994): 634–646.

Kodaira Gonichi. "Hōtoku shisō to nōson kōsei." *Shimin* 30 (October 1935): 1–4.

———. "Keizai kōsei dai san nen ni mukau no kakugo." *Shimin* 29 (January 1934): 5–18.

———. *Nōgyō kinyūron*. Tokyo: Iwamatsudō shoten, 1930.

———. "Nōgyōkai no honshitsu to shimei." February 1944. In *Senji nōgyō seisaku shiryōshū*, ed. Kusumoto Masahiro and Hiraga Akihiko, pt. I, vol. 6, 540–546. Tokyo: Kashiwa shobō, 1988.

———. "Nōsangyoson keizai kōsei tokubetsu josei shisetsu." *Shimin* 31, no. 6 (1936): 8.

———. "Nōson jiji no shin kenkyū." *Shimin* 25 (October 1930): 141–154.

———. "Nōson keizai kōsei undō o kentō shi, hyōjun nōson kakuritsu undō ni oyobu." January 1948. In *Nōsangyoson keizai kōsei undō to Kodaira Gonichi*, ed. Kusumoto Masahiro, 57–168. Tokyo: Fuji shuppan, 1983.

———. "Nōson taisaku no kichō." *Shimin* 27 (August 1932): 1–3.

———. *Saikin ni okeru naigai nōgyō kinyū jijō no kōsatsu*. Tokyo: Privately published, 1931.

Kodaira Gonichi to kindai nōsei henshū shuppan iinkai, ed. *Kodaira Gonichi to kindai nōsei*. Tokyo: Nihon hyōronsha, 1985.

Kusumoto Masahiro. "Shōwa kyōkō ki no kiban seibi jigyō—nōsei to nōmin." *Gendai nōgyō* (April 1979).

Kusumoto Masahiro, ed. *Nōsangyoson keizai kōsei undō shi shiryō shūsei.* Pt. II. 6 vols. Tokyo: Kashiwa shobō, 1988.

———, ed. *Nōsangyoson keizai kōsei undō to Kodaira Gonichi.* Tokyo: Fuji shuppan, 1983.

Kyōchōkai. *Tōhoku nōgyō no kenkyū.* Tokyo: Kyōchōkai, 1933.

———. *Tōhoku chihō ni okeru shakai narabi ni keizai jō no tokuisei.* Tokyo: Kyōchōkai, 1935.

Lee, Hye Kyung. "Development of Social Welfare Systems in the United States and Japan: A Comparative Study." Ph.D. dissertation, University of California, 1982.

Levine, Lawrence W. "American Culture and the Great Depression." *Yale Review* 74, no. 2 (1985): 196–223.

Lewis, Michael. *Rioters and Citizens: Mass Protest in Imperial Japan.* Berkeley: University of California Press, 1990.

Martin, Harris I. "Popular Music and Social Change in Prewar Japan." *Japan Interpreter: A Journal of Social and Political Ideas* 7, no. 3–4 (1974): 332–352.

Maruyama, Masao. *Thought and Behavior in Modern Japanese Politics,* ed. Ivan Morris. Oxford: Oxford University Press, 1963.

Matsumoto Gaku. "Nōson no keizai kaizen." *Shimin* 26 (October 1931): 5–14.

Mertz, Paul E. *New Deal Policy and Southern Rural Poverty.* Baton Rouge and London: Louisiana State University Press, 1978.

Minichiello, Sharon. *Retreat from Reform: Patterns of Political Behavior in Interwar Japan.* Honolulu: University of Hawai`i Press, 1984.

———, ed. *Japan's Competing Modernities: Issues in Culture and Democracy, 1900–1930.* Honolulu: University of Hawai`i Press, 1998.

*Minsei.* 1932–1935.

Miwa Ryōichi. "Takahashi zaiseiki no keizai seisaku." In *Senji Nihon keizai,* ed. Tōkyō daigaku shakai kagaku kenkyūjo, vol. 2 of *Fashizumuki no kokka to shakai,* 111–172. Tokyo: Tōkyō daigaku shuppankai, 1979.

Miyazaki Rikuji. "Taishō demokurashii ki no nōson to seitō." *Kokka gakkai zasshi* 93, no. 11 (1980): 77–145.

Mizunuma Tomokazu. "Shōwa kyōkō." In *Shōwa kyōkō,* ed. Sumiya Mikio, 81–196. Tokyo: Yūhikaku, 1974.

Mori Takemaro. "Nihon fashizumu no keisei to nōson keizai kōsei undō." *Rekishi gaku kenkyū bessatsu tokushū* (1971): 135–152.

———. "Nōson no kiki no shinkō." In *Kōza Nihon rekishi,* ed. Rekishigaku kenkyūkai, vol. 10, 135–166. Tokyo: Tōkyō daigaku shuppankai, 1985.

———. *Senji Nihon nōson shakai no kenkyū.* Tokyo: Tōkyō daigaku shuppankai, 1999.

Mori Takemaro and Ōkado Masakatsu. *Chiiki ni okeru senji to sengo: shōnai chihō no nōson, toshi, shakai undō.* Tokyo: Nihon keizai hyōronsha, 1996.
Mori Tokuhisa. *Teikoku gikai nōson mondai kaisetsu.* Tokyo: Nōson keizai chōsakyoku, 1933.
Mori Yoshizō. "Shōwa shōki no nōson keizai kōsei undō ni tsuite, Yamagata-ken no baai." *Keizai gaku* 29, no. 1–2 (1968): 91–116.
Moriya Hideo. "Jikyoku kyōkyū no dai issen ni tatsu nōgyosanson no tōkyokusha ni yosu." *Shimin* 27 (October 1932): 15–23.
Nagahara Yutaka. "1932 nen 'Nōson kyūsai seigan undō' no tokushitsu, Jichi nōmin kyōgikai—Nihon nōmin kyōkai no Nagano-ken ni okeru undō o megutte." *Nōgyō keizai kenkyū* 52, no. 1 (1980): 1–12.
Nagano Akira. "Genjitsu ni sokuseru Nihon no kaizō." *Keizai ōrai* (July 1932), 53–54.
———. "Hijōji haigo no hito—Gondō Seikyō shi to sono gakusetsu." *Kaizō* 15 (October 1933): 190–197.
———. "Nōson no jissō to sono kyūsai saku." *Tōyō,* vol. 37 (February 1934), 54–60.
———. "Nōson seigan undō no keika." *Kaizō* 14 (October 1932): 90–96.
———. *Shōwa nōmin sōkekki roku.* Tokyo: Jichi kenkyūkai, 1966.
———. "Takahashi zaisei to nōmin mondai." *Keizai ōrai* 10 (February 1935): 47–54.
Nagashima Sadashi. "Shōwa 7 nendo Hyōgo-ken Nōkai narabi ni gun Nōkai shisetsu jigyō no taiyō." *Nōsei kenkyū* 11 (April 1932): 23–37.
———. "Warera ga teishō suru jiriki kōsei no shingi to nōson jiriki kōsei no kakushin o suru jūyō shisetsu ni tsuite." *Nōsei kenkyū* 11 (August 1932): 25–29.
Naikaku tōkeikyoku, *Shōwa 10 nen kokusei chōsa hōkoku,* vol. 1, zenkoku hen. Tokyo: Naikaku tōkeikyoku, 1939.
Naimushō keihōkyoku. *Shakai undō no jōkyō,* vols. 4–5. Tokyo: Naimushō keihōkyoku, 1932–1933.
———. *Shuppan mono o tsūjite mitaru Nihon kakushinron no genjō.* Vol. 6 of *Shuppan keisatsu shiryō shūsei.* Tokyo: Fuji shuppan, 1933 (1986).
Nakamura Masanori. "Keizai kōsei undō to nōson tōgō—Nagano-ken Chisagata-gun Urazato-mura no baai." In *Shōwa kyōkō,* ed. Tōkyō daigaku shakai kagaku kenkyūjo, vol. 1 of *Fashizumuki no kokka to shakai,* 197–262. Tokyo: Tōkyō daigaku shuppankai, 1979.
———. *Shōwa no kyōkō.* Vol. 2 of *Shōwa no rekishi.* Tokyo: Shōgakukan, 1988.
Nakamura Takafusa. *Meiji Taishō ki no keizai.* Tokyo: Tōkyō daigaku shuppankai, 1985.
Nanto, Dick K., and Shinji Takagi. "Koreikiyo Takahashi and Japan's Recovery from the Great Depression." *American Economic Review* 75 (May 1985): 369–374.
Napier, Arthur. *The Japanese Village in Transition.* Tokyo: General Headquarters, Supreme Commander for the Allied Powers, Natural Resources Section, 1950.

Neth, Mary. *Preserving the Family Farm: Women, Community, and the Foundations of Agribusiness in the Midwest, 1900–1940.* Baltimore and London: Johns Hopkins University Press, 1995.

Nihon ginkō chōsakyoku, ed. *Senji kinyū kankei shiryō,* vol. 29, *Nihon kinyūshi shiryō, Shōwa hen.* Tokyo: Ōkurashō insatsukyoku, 1971.

Nihon ginkō Fukushima shiten. *Fukushima-ken nōson jōkyō.* Tokyo: Ōkurashō insatsukyoku, December 1934.

———. "Kannai Tōhoku yon-ken kyōsaku jitsujō." 1935. In *Nihon kinyūshi shiryō, Shōwa zokuhen, furoku,* ed. Nihon ginkō kinyū kenkyūjo, vol. 1. Tokyo: Ōkurashō insatsukyoku, 1986.

*Nihon keizai nenpō.* 1931–1932.

Nihon nōgyō kenkyūkai, ed. *Nihon nōgyō nenpō.* Tokyo: Kaizōsha, 1933–1934.

Nishida Yoshiaki. "From a Train Window: Why Is Japanese Farmland So Different from That in Europe?" *Social Science Japan,* no. 3 (April 1995).

———. "Growth of the Meiji Landlord System and Tenancy Disputes After World War I: A Critique of Richard Smethurst, *Agricultural Development and Tenancy Disputes in Japan, 1870–1940." Journal of Japanese Studies* 15, no. 2 (Summer 1989): 389–415.

———. *Kindai Nihon nōmin undōshi kenkyū.* Tokyo: Tōkyō daigaku shuppankai, 1997.

———. "Nōmin keiei no tenkai." In *Nishikinbara tochi kairyō shi,* ed. Nishikinbara tochi kairyō ku, vol. 1, 943–990. Niigata City: Niigata nippō jigyō sha, 1981.

———. "Nōmin undō to nōgyō seisaku." In *Sekai daikyōkōki,* ed. Ōishi Kaichirō, vol. 2 of *Nihon teikokushugishi,* 295–330. Tokyo: Tōkyō daigaku shuppankai, 1987.

———. "Senzen Nihon ni okeru rōdō undō nōmin undō no seishitsu." In *Rekishi teki zentei,* vol. 4 of *Gendai Nihon shakai,* ed. Tōkyō daigaku shakai kagaku kenkyūjo. Tokyo: Tōkyō daigaku shuppankai, 1991.

———, ed. *Sengo kaikakuki no nōgyō mondai: Saitama-ken o jirei to shite.* Tōkyō daigaku shakai kagaku kenkyūjo kenkyū hōkoku, dai 51-shū. Tokyo: Nihon keizai hyōronsha, 1994.

———, ed. *Shōwa kyōkōka no nōson shakai undō: yōsanchi ni okeru tenkai to kiketsu.* Tōkyō daigaku shakai kagaku kenkyūjo kenkyū hōkoku, dai 27-shū. Tokyo: Ochanomizu shobō, 1978.

Nishiyama Kōichi, Nishida Yoshiaki, and Kubo Yasuo. *Nishiyama Kōichi nikki, 1925–1950-nen: Niigata-ken ichi kosakunō no kiroku.* Tokyo: Tōkyō daigaku shuppankai, 1991.

Nōchi seido shiryō shūsei hensan iinkai, ed. *Nōchi seido shiryō shūsei.* Vol. 2. Tokyo: Ochanomizu shobō, 1969.

Nōrin daijin kanbō sōmuka, ed. *Nōrin gyōsei shi.* Vols. 2–4. Tokyo: Nōrin kyōkai, 1957–1959.

Nōrin daijin kanbō tōkeika. *Nōrinsho tōkei hyō.* Vols. 2–14. 1925–1937.

Nōrin suisan gyōsei kenkyūkai. *Nōrin suisan.* Tokyo: Gyōsei, 1983.

Nōrinshō keizai kōseibu. "Jūgo nōsangyoson jijō shisatsu hōkokuki." In *Senji nōgyō seisaku shiryōshū*, ed. Kusumoto Masahiro and Hiraga Akihiko, pt. I, vol. 1, 257–319. Tokyo: Kashiwa shobō, 1988.

Nōrinshō nōmukyoku. *Hiryō yōran, 1939.* Tokyo: Nōrinshō, 1941.

Nōrinshō nōseikyoku, *Kosaku nenpō.* 1930, 1939.

Nōrinshō sanshikyoku. *Kenshi-ka teiraku no yōsan nōmin ni oyoboshitaru eikyō.* Tokyo: Nōrinshō sanshikyoku, September 15, 1934. Handwritten report.

Nornes, Abé Mark. "Forest of Pressure: A History of Japanese Documentary to 1946." Ph.D. dissertation, University of Southern California, 1996.

Ōe Shinobu, ed., *"Hijōji" Nihon: Shōwa no rekishi.* Tokyo: Shūeisha, 1980.

Ogawa Nobuo. "Shōwa kyōkōka ni okeru 'Jiriki kōsei' to Hōtokusha undō." *Shundai shigaku* 40 (March 1977): 60–91.

Ohkawa Kazushi, Miyohei Shinohara, and Larry Meissner. *Patterns of Japanese Economic Development: A Quantitative Appraisal.* New Haven, Conn.: Yale University Press, 1979.

Ohkawa Kazushi, Tsutomu Noda, Nobukiyo Takamatsu, Saburo Yamada, Minoru Kumazaki, Yuichi Shionoya, and Ryoshin Minami. Prices. Vol. 8 of *Estimates of Long-Term Economic Statistics of Japan Since 1868*, ed. Kazushi Ohkawa, Miyohei Shinohara, and Mataji Umemura. Tokyo: Tōyō keizai shinpōsha, 1967.

Ohkawa Kazushi, Nobukiyo Takamatsu, and Yuzo Yamamoto. National Income. Vol. 1 of *Estimates of Long-term Economic Statistics of Japan since 1868*, ed. Kazushi Ohkawa, Miyohei Shinohara, and Mataji Umemura. Tokyo: Tōyō keizai shinpōsha, 1974.

Ōishi Kaichirō. *Fukushima-ken no hyakunen.* Tokyo: Yamakawa shuppansha, 1992.

———. "Nōchi kaikaku no rekishiteki igi." In *Nōchi kaikaku*, ed. Tōkyō daigaku shakai kagaku kenkyūjo, vol. 6 of *Sengo kaikaku*, 3–48. Tokyo: Tōkyō daigaku shuppankai, 1975.

———. "Sekai daikyōkō to Nihon shihon shugi." In *Sekai daikyōkōki*, ed. Ōishi Kaichirō, vol. 2 of *Nihon teikokushugishi*, 3–37. Tokyo: Tōkyō daigaku shuppankai, 1987.

———. "Shōwa kyōkō to chihō zaisei, nōson zaisei o chūshin to shite." In *Shōwa kyōkō*, ed. Tōkyō daigaku shakai kagaku kenkyūjo, vol. 1 of *Fashizumuki no kokka to shakai*, 81–148. Tokyo: Tōkyō daigaku shuppankai, 1979.

Ōishi Kaichirō and Nishida Yoshiaki, eds. *Kindai Nihon no gyōseison: Nagano-ken Hanishina-gun Gokamura no kenkyū.* Tokyo: Tōkyō keizai hyōronsha, 1991.

Okada Atsushi. "Nōson jiriki kōsei no seishin to mokuhyō." *Teikoku nōkai jihō*, no. 57 (August 1932), 6–8.

Ōkado Masakatsu. *Kindai Nihon to nōson shakai: nōmin sekai no henyō to kokka.* Tokyo: Nihon keizai hyōronsha, 1994.

———. "Nōson keizai kōsei undō to buraku no tōgō." *Shinano* 34, no. 3 (1982): 202–228.

———. "Review of *Nishiyama Kōichi nikki*, Nishida Yoshiaki and Kubo Yasuo." *Rekishigaku kenkyū*, no. 662 (September 1994): 46–51.

Ōkurashō Shōwa zaisei shi henshūshitsu, ed. *Shōwa zaisei shi.* 18 vols. Tokyo: Tōyō keizai shinpōsha, 1951–1965.

Ōmameuda Minoru. "1920 nendai ni okeru shokuryō seisaku no tenkai." *Shigaku zasshi* 91, no. 10 (October 1982): 40–73.

Ono Seiichirō. "Shōwa kyōkō to nōson kyūsai seisaku." In *Nihon keizai seisakushi-ron*, ed. Andō Yoshio, vol. 2, 3–96. Tokyo: Tōkyō daigaku shuppankai, 1976.

Ouchi Tsutomu. *Nōka keizai.* Vol. 6 of *Keizai bunseki shirizu.* Tokyo: Chūō keizaisha, 1957.

Patrick, Hugh. "The Economic Muddle of the 1920s." In *Dilemmas of Growth in Prewar Japan*, ed. James William Morley, 211–266. Princeton, N.J.: Princeton University Press, 1971.

Peattie, Mark R. *Ishiwara Kanji and Japan's Confrontation with the West.* Princeton, N.J.: Princeton University Press, 1975.

Pyle, Kenneth B. "The Technology of Japanese Nationalism: The Local Improvement Movement, 1900–1918." *Journal of Asian Studies* 33 (November 1973): 51–65.

Rōdōshō. *Rōdō gyōsei shi.* Tokyo: Rōdō hōrei kyōkai, 1961.

Roberts, Luke S. "The Petition Box in Eighteenth-Century Tosa." *Journal of Japanese Studies* 20, no. 2 (Summer 1994): 423–458.

Robertson, Jennifer. "It Takes a Village: Internationalization and Nostalgia in Postwar Japan." In *Mirror of Modernity*, ed. Stephen Vlastos, 110–129. Berkeley: University of California Press, 1998.

Saitō shisaku kinenkai, ed. *Shisaku Saitō Makoto den.* Vol. 3. Tokyo: Kyōdō insatsu, 1941.

Sakata Masatoshi. "Kaisetsu." In *Zasshi "Shimin" mokuji sōran, 1906–1944*, ed. Nihon kindai shiryō kenkyūkai Naiseishi kenkyūkai, 1–17. Tokyo: Nihon kindai shiryō kenkyūkai Naiseishi kenkyūkai, 1972.

Sasai Shintarō. "Hōtokushiki hijōji kyōkyū hōsaku," Parts 1 and 2. *Shimin* 28 (August–September 1933): 4–13, 9–17.

———. *Kokumin kōsei to hōtoku.* Tokyo: Heibonsha, 1936.

Scheiner, Irwin. "Benevolent Lords and Honorable Peasants: Rebellion and Peasant Consciousness in Tokugawa Japan." In *Japanese Thought in the Tokugawa Period*, ed. Tetsuo Najita and Irwin Scheiner, 39–62. Chicago: University of Chicago Press, 1978.

Seisen kinenshi kankōkai. *Seisen no ato.* Fukushima-shi: Seisen kinenshi kankōkai, 1934.
*Seiyū.* 1932–1934.
Sekishiba village documents, Office for the Compilation of Municipal History, Kitakata Municipal Library, Fukushima prefecture.
Sekiya Ryūkichi. "Kokumin kōsei undō no kontei." *Shimin* 27 (September 1932): 14–16.
*Shimin.* 1930–1939.
Shōji Kichinosuke. "Chihō ni okeru Shōwa kyōkō to nōmin-rōdōsha no undō." *Shōgaku ronshū* 40 (June 1972): 175–241.
———. "Fukushima-ken nōkai shi." In *Nōgyō hattatsushi chōsakai shiryō*, no. 51. Tokyo: Nōgyō hattatsu shi chōsakai, 1951.
Shōji Shunsaku. *Kindai Nihon nōson shakai no tenkai.* Tokyo: Minerba shobō, 1991.
Shillony, Ben-Ami. *Politics and Culture in Wartime Japan*: Oxford: Clarendon Press; New York: Oxford University Press, 1981.
Shimizu Yōji. "Nōgyō to jinushi sei." In *Sekai daikyōkō ki*, ed. Ōishi Kaichirō, vol. 2 of *Nihon teikokushugishi*, 255–294. Tokyo: Tōkyō daigaku shuppankai, 1987.
———. "Shokuryō seisan to nōchi kaikaku." In *Dai niji taisenki*, ed. Ōishi Kaichirō, vol. 3 of *Nihon teikokushugishi*, 331–368. Tokyo: Tōkyō daigaku shuppankai, 1994.
Shioda Shōichi. "Takahashi rō Zōsho no kokoro o utta nōkai gishiiin." *Mizuho*, no. 76 (March 1934): 5.
Shūgiin jimukyoku. *Shūgiin giin sōsenkyo ichiran.* Vols. 18–21. Tokyo: Shūgiin jimukyoku, 1932–1943.
Silberman, Bernard S., and Harry D. Harootunian, eds. *Japan in Crisis: Essays on Taishō Democracy.* Princeton, N.J.,: Princeton University Press, 1974.
Silverberg, Miriam. "The Cafe Waitress Serving Modern Japan." In *Mirror of Modernity: Invented Traditions of Modern Japan*, ed. Stephen Vlastos, 208–225. Berkeley: University of California Press, 1998.
———. "Remembering Pearl Harbor, Forgetting Charlie Chaplin, and the Case of the Disappearing Western Woman: A Picture Story." *Positions: East Asian Cultures Critique* 1, no. 1 (1993): 24–76.
Smethurst, Richard J. *Agricultural Development and Tenancy Disputes in Japan, 1870–1940.* Princeton, N.J.: Princeton University Press, 1986.
———. "A Challenge to Orthodoxy and Its Orthodox Critics: A Reply to Nishida Yoshiaki." *Journal of Japanese Studies* 15, no. 2 (Summer 1989): 417–437.
———. *A Social Basis for Prewar Japanese Militarism:The Army and the Rural Community.* Berkeley: University of California Press, 1974.
Smith, Robert John. *Kurusu: The Price of Progress in a Japanese Village, 1951–1975.* Stanford, Calif.: Stanford University Press, 1978.
Smith, Thomas C. *Native Sources of Japanese Industrialization, 1750–1920.* Berkeley: University of California Press, 1988.

———. *Political Change and Industrial Development in Japan: Government Enterprise, 1868–1880*. Stanford, Calif.: Stanford University Press, 1955.
Sōmucho tōkeikyoku, ed. *Nihon tōkei nenkan*. Tokyo: Ōkurashō insatsukyoku, 1997.
Stanton, Bernard F. "Structural Change in American Agriculture into the Next Century." In *Japanese and American Agriculture: Tradition and Progress in Conflict*, ed. Luther Tweeten, Cynthia L. Dishon, Wen S. Chern, Naraomi Imamura, and Masaru Morishima, 117–139. Boulder, Colo.: Westview Press, 1993.
Steiner, Kurt. *Local Government in Japan*. Stanford, Calif.: Stanford University Press, 1965.
Sugihara Masami. "Gunbu no shin shidō seiryoku to naisei kaigi." *Kaibō jidai* 4, no. 1 (January 1934): 6–16.
———. "Gunbu to kakushō shinkanryō no ōdanteki ketsugō." *Kaibō jidai* 4, no. 3 (March 1934): 6–20.
Sumiya Mikio. "Kyōkō to kokumin shōkaikyū." In *Shōwa kyōkō*, ed. Sumiya Mikio, 247–314. Tokyo: Yūhikaku, 1974.
———, ed. *Shōwa kyōkō*. Tokyo: Yūhikaku, 1974.
Sumiya Yoshiharu. "Nōson kyōkyūsaku to shakai seisaku no genkai." *Shakai seisaku jihō*, no. 146 (November 1932): 283–295.
Tago Ichimin. "Nōson kōsei ni tsuite." *Shimin* 27 (November 1932): 24–36.
Taikakai (Gotō Fumio). ed. *Naimushō shi*. 4 vols. Tokyo: Chihō zaimu kyōkai, 1970.
Taira, Koji. "Public Assistance in Japan: Development and Trends." *Journal of Asian Studies* 27 (November 1967): 95–109.
Takahashi Yasutaka. "Nihon fashizumu to nōgyō keizai kōsei undō no tenkai: Shōwa ki 'kyūnō' seisaku ni tsuite no kōsatsu." *Tochi seido shigaku* 65 (October 1974): 1–26.
Takamura, Kōtarō. *Chieko and Other Poems of Takamura Kōtarō*. Translated by Hiroaki Sato. Honolulu: University of Hawai`i Press, 1980.
Takeda Tsutomu and Kusumoto Masahiro, eds. *Nōsangyoson keizai kōsei undō shi shiryō shūsei*. Pt. I. 7 vols. Tokyo: Kashiwa shobō, 1985.
Takisawa Makoto. *Gondō Seikyō*. Tokyo: Kinokuniya shoten, 1971.
Tamaki Akira. "Kyūnō doboku jigyō seiritsu e no michi." *Nōson kenkyū* 40 (March 1973): 45–53.
Tamanoi, Mariko. *Under the Shadow of Nationalism: Politics and Poetics of Rural Japanese Women*. Honolulu: University of Hawai`i Press, 1998.
Tamura Kō. "Aomori-ken no nōson kyōkō jijō taisaku fusai chōsa." *Shakai seisaku jihō* 145 (October 1932): 134–143.
Tanaka Tokihiko. "Saitō naikaku: 'Hijōji' no chinsei o ninatte." In *Nihon naikaku shiroku*, ed. Hayashi Shigeru and Tsuji Kiyoaki, 287–341. Tokyo: Daiichi hōki shuppan, 1981.

Tanino Akira. *Kokudo to nōson no keikaku: sono shiteki tenkai*. Tokyo: Nōrin tōkei kyōkai, 1994.
Tasaki Nobuyoshi. "Toshi bunka to kokumin ishiki." In *Kōza Nihon rekishi*, ed. Rekishigaku kenkyū kai, vol. 10, 167–198. Tokyo: Tōkyō daigaku shuppankai, 1989.
Teikoku gikai shūgiin. *Dai 62 rinji teikoku gikai shūgiin hōkoku*. Tokyo: Shūgiin jimukyoku, 1932.
———. *Dai 63 rinji teikoku gikai shūgiin hōkoku*. Tokyo: Shūgiin jimukyoku, 1933.
———. *Dai 63 teikoku gikai shūgiin giji tekiyō*. Tokyo: Shūgiin jimukyoku, 1932.
———. *Dai 64 teikoku gikai shūgiin giji tekiyō*. Tokyo: Shūgiin jimukyoku, 1933.
———. *Teikoku gikai shūgiin giji sokkiroku*. Vols. 57–58. Tokyo: Tōkyō daigaku shuppankai, 1983.
Teikoku nōkai. *Tōhoku chihō nōson ni kansuru chōsa*, vol. 1, *Kyōsaku hen*. Tokyo: Teikoku nōkai, 1935.
Teikoku nōkai shikō hensankai, ed. *Teikoku nōkai shikō*. Tokyo: Nōmin kyōiku kyōkai, 1972.
Teruoka Shūzō. *Nihon nōgyō mondai no tenkai*. Vol. 2. Tokyo: Tōkyō daigaku shuppankai, 1984.
———. *Nihon nōgyō shi*. Tokyo: Yūhikaku, 1981.
Tiedemann, Arthur E. "Big Business and Politics in Prewar Japan." In *Dilemmas of Growth in Prewar Japan*, ed. James W. Morley, 267–316. Princeton, N.J.: Princeton University Press, 1971.
Tōgō Makoto. "Nōson no kōsei to kyōiku no kakushin." *Shimin* 27 (September 1932): 1–8.
*Tōkyō asahi shinbun*. 1932–1940.
Tōkyō daigaku shakai kagaku kenkyūjo, ed. *Shōwa kyōkō*, vol. 1 of *Fuashizumuki no kokka to shakai*. Tokyo: Tōkyō daigaku shuppankai, 1978.
Tōkyō nichi nichi shinbun keizaibu, ed. *Ikaga ni site nōson o sukūbeki ka*. Tokyo: Sōzōsha, July 1932.
Tomita Aijirō. "Kokumin kōsei undō no gaikan." *Shimin* 27 (October 1932): 12–14.
Totman, Conrad. *Early Modern Japan*. Berkeley: University of California Press, 1993.
Toyoda Takeshi. *Tōhoku no rekishi*. Vol. 2. Tokyo: Yoshikawa kōbunkan, 1973.
Turner, Victor. *Dramas, Fields, and Metaphors: Symbolic Action in Human Society*. Ithaca, N.Y.: Cornell University Press, 1974.
Umemura Mataji. *Rōdōryoku*. Vol. 2 of *Chōki keizai tōkei*. Tokyo: Tōyō keizai shinpōsha, 1988.
Umemura, Mataji, Saburo Yamada, Yujiro Hayami, Nobukiyo Takamatsu, and Minoru Kumazaki. *Agriculture and Forestry*, Vol. 9 of *Estimates of Long-Term Economic Statistics of Japan Since 1868*, ed. Kazushi Ohkawa, Miyohei Shinohara, and Mataji Umemura. Tokyo: Tōyō keizai shinpōsha, 1966.

Unno Fukuju. "Shōwa kyōkōka no nōson saihensei katei (1)." *Meiji daigaku jinbun kagaku kenkyūjo kiyō*. Extra number 1 (1981): 69–99.

———. "Nōson keizai kōsei undō to sonraku sangyō kumiai." *Kyōdō kumiai shōrei kenkyū hōkoku* 6 (August 1980): 109–133.

Uno, Kathleen S. "Women and Changes in the Household Division of Labor." In *Recreating Japanese Women, 1600–1945*, ed. Gail Lee Bernstein, 17–41. Berkeley: University of California Press, 1991.

Ushiba Keijirō. "Nōson taisaku no jūten o issu." *Minsei* 8, no. 3 (March 1934): 50–53.

Ushiyama Kenji. "Nōson keizai kōsei undōka no 'mura' no kinō to kōsei." *Rekishi hyōron*, no. 435 (July 1986): 19–31.

———. "Shōwa nōgyō kyōkō." In *Kindai Nihon keizaishi o manabu*, ed. Ishii Kanji, Unno Fukuju, and Nakamura Masanori, vol. 2, 171–188. Tokyo: Yūhikaku, 1977.

Vaporis, Constantine Nomikos. *Breaking Barriers: Travel and the State in Early Modern Japan*. Harvard East Asia Monographs, no. 163. Cambridge, Mass.: Harvard University, Council on East Asian Studies, 1994.

Vlastos, Stephen. "Agrarianism Without Tradition: The Radical Critique of Prewar Japanese Modernity." In *Mirror of Modernity: Invented Traditions of Modern Japan*, ed. Stephen Vlastos, 79–94. Berkeley: University of California, 1998.

———. *Peasant Protests and Uprisings in Tokugawa Japan*. Berkeley: University of California Press, 1986.

———. "Tradition: Past/Present Culture and Modern Japanese History." In *Mirror of Modernity: Invented Traditions of Modern Japan*, ed. Stephen Vlastos, 1–16. Berkeley: University of California Press, 1998.

Wakatsuki Reijirō. "Hijōjikyoku kōkyū no wagatō no seisaku." *Minsei* 6 (September 1932): 2–5.

Walinsky, Louis J., ed. *Agrarian Reform as Unfinished Business: The Selected Papers of Wolf Ladejinsky*. New York: Oxford University Press, 1977.

Walthall, Anne. *Social Protest and Popular Culture in Eighteenth Century Japan*. Tucson: University of Arizona Press, 1986.

———, ed. *Peasant Uprisings in Japan: A Critical Anthology of Peasant Histories*. Chicago: University of Chicago Press, 1991.

Waswo, Ann. *Japanese Landlords: The Decline of a Rural Elite*. Berkeley: University of California Press, 1977.

———. *Modern Japanese Society, 1868–1994*. Oxford and New York: Oxford University Press, 1996.

———. "Review of *Agricultural Development and Tenancy Disputes in Japan, 1870–1940*." *Monumenta Nipponica* 42, no. 3 (Autumn 1987): 364–366.

———. "The Transformation of Rural Society, 1900–1950." In *Twentieth Century*, ed. Peter Duus, vol. 6 of *The Cambridge History of Japan*, 541–605. Cambridge, Eng.: Cambridge University Press, 1988.

Watanabe Eiichi and Yabe Tsuneko, eds. *Yabe Zenbei den*. Ishikawa-shi: Nihon ekonomisuto gurūpu sha, 1976.

Weiner, Susan Beth. "Bureaucracy and Politics in the 1930's: The Career of Goto Fumio." Ph.D. dissertation, Harvard University, 1984.

Weir, Margaret, Ann Shola Orloff, and Theda Skocpol, eds. *The Politics of Social Policy in the United States*. Princeton, N.J.: Princeton University Press, 1988.

Williamson, Mark B. *Agricultural Programs in Japan, 1945–51*. Tokyo: General Headquarters, Supreme Commander for the Allied Powers, Natural Resources Section, 1951, 148.

Wilson, Sandra. "Angry Young Men and the Japanese State: Nagano Prefecture, 1930–1933." In *Society and the State in Interwar Japan*, ed. Elise K. Tipton, 100–125. London and New York: Routledge, 1997.

———. "Bureaucrats and Villagers in Japan: Shimin and the Crisis of the Early 1930s." *Social Science Japan Journal* 1, no. 1 (1998): 121–140.

———. "The 'New Paradise': Japanese Emigration to Manchuria in the 1930s and 1940s." *International History Review* (August 1995): 249–286.

Yabe Zenbei. *Haha no omoide*. Tokyo: Kaimeidō, 1940.

———. "Hōtokushiki shōten keiei no taiken ni motozuku wagakuni keizai seikatsu no hihan," 2 pts. *Shimin* 33 (January 1938), 119–135; (February 1938), 105–122.

———. "Kuni nimei ronkō shokan," 2 pts. *Shimin* 34 (March 1939), 117–125; (April 1939): 115–124.

———. "Shitsumon ōmon." 2 pts. *Shimin* 33 (March 1938): 113–124; (August 1938): 119–122.

Yagi Hisato. "Hijōji ni taisuru nōshō no ninshiki." *Teikoku nōkai hō*, vol. 23 (December 1933): 44.

Yagi Shigeki. *Hōtoku undō 100 nen no ayumi*. Tokyo: Ryūkei shosha, 1980.

Yama gunyakusho, ed., *Fukushima-ken Yama-gun shi*. Tokyo: Meicho shuppan, 1972.

Yamamoto Osamu, ed. *Nōgyō seisaku no tenkai to genjō*. Tokyo: Ie no hikari kyōkai, 1988.

Yamamoto Tatsuo. "Jikyoku ni kangami kokumin no jikaku funki o nozomu." *Shimin* 27 (October 1932): 5–8.

Yamamura, Kozo. "The Japanese Economy, 1911–1930: Concentration, Conflicts, and Crises." In *Japan in Crisis: Essays on Taisho Democracy*, ed. Bernard S. Silberman and Harry D. Harootunian, 299–328. Princeton, N.J.: Princeton University Press, 1974.

Yano, Christine R. "Defining the Modern Nation in Japanese Popular Song, 1914–1932." In *Japan's Competing Modernities: Issues in Culture and Democracy, 1900–1930*, ed. Sharon A. Minichiello, 247–264. Honolulu: University of Hawai'i Press, 1998.

Yasuda Tsuneo. *Nihon fashizumu to minshū undō*. Tokyo: Renga shobō shinsha, 1979.

Yasutomi Kunio. "Fukushima-ken ni okeru keizai kōsei undō." In *Fukushima no kenkyū*, ed. Kobayashi Seiji, vol. 4, 196–223. Osaka: Kiyobundo shuppan, 1986.

———. *Shōwa kyōkōki kyūnō seisaku shiron*, vol. 5. Tokyo: Hassakusha, 1994.

———. "Shōwa shoki kyūnō seisaku no keisei shōmetsu katei ni kansuru jakkan no kōsatsu." *Shōgaku ronshū* 40, no. 3–4 (1972): 131–174.

Yen, Ai-Ching. "The Effects of Land Reform on Changes in the Structure of Agriculture in Taiwan in the 1950s." In *Land Policy Problems in East Asia: Toward New Choices*, ed. Bruce Koppel and D. Young Kim. Honolulu: East-West Center; and Seoul: Korea Research Institute for Human Settlements, 1993.

Yoshida Shigeru. "Kokumin kōsei no seishin." *Shimin* 29 (March 1934): 1–16.

Young, Louise. *Japan's Total Empire: Manchuria and the Culture of Wartime Imperialism*. Berkeley: University of California Press, 1998.

# Index

Abe Tadashi, 299, 314, 316, 341
Activists, rural causes, 44, 80–83, 90–110. *See also individual activists by name*
Agrarianism, 44, 81–82, 94
Agrarianist campaigns for rural reform, 86–87, 94–113, 288
Agrarianist Federation (Nōhon renmei), 98, 104
Agricultural Adjustment Act, 13
Agricultural Association Law, 89
Agricultural Basic Law, 359–360
Agricultural Organization (Nōgyōkai), 333–334
Agricultural policies, 47–50, 79, 88
Agricultural Production Control Ordinance (Nōgyō seisen tōsei rei), 332–333
Agricultural Recovery Act, 164
Agriculture, 40, 53; decline in importance of, 16–17, 44–45; depression-era policy, 110–112; early Meiji policy, 87–91; modern economy and, 5, 365–366; post–World War I growth, 44–50; post–World War I policy, 47–50, 79, 91–93; post–World War II policy, 40, 353–357, 359–360; productivity, 53, 281–284; Tōhoku region, characteristics of, 20, 22
Agriculture and Forestry Deliberative Council (Nōrin shingikai), 175
Agriculture and Forestry Planning Committee (Nōrin keikaku iinkai), 330
Agriculture, Forestry, and Fishing Fundamental Problem Research Group, 359
Aizu, 6, 10, 19, 24–27, 34, 366–367
Aizu Bank, 30
Aizu Mountain Village Hall, 340
Akutagawa Shinkichi, 84–85, 135
Amalgamation of towns and villages, 35–36, 96–97, 364
Anazawa Masayasu, 301
Araki Sadao, 157–159, 162–163; rural relief and, 161, 167–168, 170
Arima Yoriyasu, 291
Azuma Takeshi, 163–164, 166

Baba Eiichi, 202–203
Banetsu rail line, 26
Banking Crisis, 1927, 30, 50
Banks, 30–32, 50

Basic Agricultural Law, 364
Basic Survey (Kihon chōsa), 60–62, 225–227
Bookkeeping, 17, 60
Budget debates and rural relief, 136–138, 141, 143, 157
Buraku jōkai, *see* Hamlet Assemblies
Bureaucrats and policy making, 4, 15

Campaign to Improve Daily Life (Seikatsu kaizen undō), 218
Central Association of Industrial Co-operatives, 207
Central Committee for Farm Village Economic Revitalization, 207, 330
Central Federation of Moral Suasion Groups (Chūō kyōka dantai rengōkai), 190–191
Central Hōtoku Association (Chūō Hōtokukai), 91–92, 219
Central Union of Cooperative Societies, 89
Charity campaigns, 253, 278
*Chichi to mitsu no nagaruru sato*, *see* *Land of Milk and Honey, The*
Chihō kairyō undō, *see* Local Improvement Campaign
China, Japan and, 3; war with, 287, 325–327, 329, 335–336, 348
*Chōson-ze* (local economic planning), 91
Chūō Hōtokukai (Central Hōtoku Association), 91–92, 219
Chūzenji Temple, 37–38
Citizen's Revitalization Campaign (Kokumin kōsei undō), 204
Climate: 1934 famine and, 225, 241–243; Tōhoku region, 20
Colonial rice production, 47–48
Contests and competitions, 179–180
Cooperative work sites, 264, 278–281

Credit, 30–31; rural relief and, 139–141; Sekishiba, 64
Crises in the countryside, 2, 5–6, 15, 40–41, 43–44, 57, 69, 269, 287; causes explained, 188–189; postwar, 358; similarities to wartime, 333, 335
Crop diversification, *see* Diversification

Dai Nihon Hōtokusha, 90–91, 219–220, 296, 312, 315
Dan Takuma, 96
Debt arrangement, 12, 85, 115, 119–120, 129, 140; Economic Revitalization Campaign and, 130, 175, 210–211, 257; Sekishiba, 66, 131, 263–264
Debt arrangement policies, 114–116, 119, 121, 124, 132–134, 139; Diet and, 117; difficulties associated with, 125–126, 129, 131; Imperial Agricultural Association and, 114; unions, 116–119, 122, 129–131, 285
Debt Arrangement Union Central Treasury Law, 124
Debt Arrangement Union Law, 115, 198–199, 206
Den Akira, 164
Depression, 225; community life and, 68–80, 92–93, 277–281, 286–291, 303–304, 319–324, 335–336; comparison with the United States, 1; effects, 8–9, 11–12, 15, 57–58, 63, 70, 72, 209; modern Japan and, 1–6; policies to address, 12; recovery from, 171, 224, 269; rural response to, 8–9, 174
Diet legislators: debt arrangement policies and, 115; rural revitalization and, 143, 199–203
Diet response to petitioners, 110

Diligence (*kinrō shugi*), 177–179; and rural revitalization, 185, 303, 323–324
Discipline and rural revitalization, 303, 323–324
Diversification, 8, 53, 56, 281–282, 284
Domestic Policy Conferences (Naisei kaigi), 158, 160–164, 170, 411*n*73
Dore, Ronald P., 358

Economic revitalization and hamlet assemblies, 314–315
Economic Revitalization Campaign Central Committee, 290
Economic Revitalization Committee, 208, 270, 289; membership of, 208, 213, 435*n*31; Sekishiba, 226–228, 259, 270, 291–292, 297
Economic revitalization planning, 60–61, 210–213, 228, 241, 261–262; diversification and, 261, 281, 283; Economic Revitalization Committee and, 212; family strategies, 240–241; fertilizer use, 262, 283; finances, 210, 262, 285–286; goals, 209–210, 228, 259–260; household, 231–234, 239–240; Hyōgo Prefecture Agricultural Association and, 211; industrial cooperatives and, 210–211, 261; Komatsu hamlet, 260; productivity and, 260–261; reforms of daily life, 265; Sekishiba, 227–231, 281–284, 286–287
Economic Revitalization Section: Special Assistance program, 255–256
Education, 16, 23, 31, 36, 38–39, 70, 72, 85, 163, 319–321; Dai Nihon Hōtokusha lectures and seminars, 219–220; funding, 69, 163; postwar, 39

Election Purification Campaign, 318, 335
Elections, 29
Electric lighting, 23–24, 44
Emergency relief, 12–16, 82, 85–86, 114, 136–145, 152–154, 171, 252; budget debates, 15, 136, 143, 170; compared to Germany and the United States, 13–14, 164; petitions for, 2, 84–85
Emigration, 95, 99–100, 134; and rural revitalization, 345–348; and village mainstays, 347
Endō Dentarō, 301
Endō Gengō, 78, 301, 317
Exports, decline in value of, 51

Factory workers and wages, 45
Famine, 1934, 8, 20, 53, 59–60, 75, 151, 171, 241, 251–253; countermeasures, 242–243, 252; crop damage, 242–248; effects on farm households, 225, 243, 247–252, 269; emergency assistance, 249–250, 252–253; landownership and land use, 245–248; media accounts, 250–252; Sekishiba, 225, 241–243, 245–246, 249, 252–253, 268; Tokugawa era, 251
Farmers, 22, 45; as share of population, 16, 40, 365
Farmers' Self-Revitalization Festivals (Nōjin jiriki kōsei matsuri), 172, 176, 180–181, 183–185, 187
Farmers' Training Centers (Nōmin dōjō), 340
Farm Household Surveys, 56–57
Farmlands Adjustment Law (Nōchi chōsei hō), 344
Farm machinery, 278, 280
Farm, Mountain, and Fishing Village Economic Revitalization Cam-

paign, 12–14, 17–18, 133–134, 139, 169, 171–172, 187, 192, 198, 204, 206, 208, 225, 263, 267–270, 289, 323, 329–331, 352; 1934 famine and, 241, 252; alternatives to, 12–14, 266; assessments of, 267, 362, 382n29; concludes, 328–329; emigration and, 345–348; indebtedness and, 198–199, 263; Komatsu hamlet, 228–231; legislation and, 192, 198, 206; local leadership and, 297–299, 339–340; mobilization and, 270, 287, 352; modifications to, 253–258, 329–332, 382n29; shortcomings, 253–254, 353–354
Farm Practice Associations (Nōji jikkō kumiai); and rural revitalization, 199, 213, 271; industrial cooperatives and, 199, 213, 272; Sekishiba, 262–263, 271
Farm Tenancy Conciliation Law, 121
Farm Village Debt Arrangement Union Law (Nōson fusai seiri kumiai hōan), 119, 122, 127–128
Farm Village Policy Federation Conference (Nōson taisaku rengō kyōgikai), 167
Fascism, 14, 17–18, 327–328
Fertilizer use, 56, 262–263, 332; Sekishiba, 262, 283; trends, 275–276
Finance Ministry, 50; budget debates and, 138, 141, 157–159, 197–198, 255; debt arrangement policies and, 125–128, 131–132
Food, Agriculture, and Rural Areas Basic Law, 360
Food Control Act, 344
Foucault, Michel, 323–324
Freedom and People's Rights movement, 28

Frugality, 14, 17, 185, 320; reform of daily life and, 319–320, 322
Fukushima Commercial Bank, 30
Funerals, 42, 72–74, 319, 335
Furu hamlet, 36, 148, 312
*Furusato* (native place), 367
Furuse Denzō, 131
Furuya Keiji, 190–191
*Fusai seiri, see* Debt arrangement

Garon, Sheldon, 319, 363
Gold Standard, 51–52, 388n34
Gondō Seikyō, 81, 94, 96–99, 103–104
Gotō Fumio, 64, 103, 105, 115, 117, 120, 128, 133, 137, 158, 162–164, 167–168, 170, 175, 219; budget debates and, 160–161, 253; criticized, 158–159, 162–164; debt arrangement policies and, 122–126; economic revitalization and, 197, 200, 207
Greater Japan Federation of Young Men's Associations, 207
Greater Japan Hōtoku Society, *see* Dai Nihon Hōtokusha

Haga village, Gumma prefecture, 343
Hamaguchi cabinet, 51, 139
Hamlet assemblies, 221–222, 312–314, 316–317, 348–349; benefits attributed to, 317–318; mobilization and, 336–337, 351; participation, 312–315; rural revitalization and, 221, 226, 314–315, 324
Hamlets, 36–37, 133–134, 312–318; rural revitalization and, 133–134
Hara Kei, 47
Haru Haruji, 150
Haru Masaru, 61–62
Hatta Sōkichi, 29, 120, 166
Hayashi Senjūrō, 167–168

Higashi-nakamei hamlet, 36
Highway 121, 34
Hijikata village, Shizuoka prefecture, 219, 308
Hirabayashi hamlet, 36, 38, 264
Hirata Tōsuke, 88–89, 91
*History of Kitakata City, The*, 368–370
Hokushin fukyō taisakukai, 104–106, 113
Home Ministry, 36, 91–92, 127, 133, 143, 155, 175; Citizen's Revitalization Campaign, 204, 206
Hoshi Tozaburō, 131–132
Hōtoku societies, 88–90, 303, 309–310, 312; rural revitalization and, 222; Sekishiba, 303, 310, 312
Hōtoku teachings; *kyōka* (moral suasion), 220; rural revitalization and, 90, 219–222
Household savings, 285–286
Household spending, 23; Komatsu hamlet, 61–62; local differences, 56–62, 73–74
Hyōgo Prefecture Agricultural Association, 172–173, 176, 180, 183, 185, 191, 211, 214; self-revitalization campaign and, 177–178, 183–185, 188, 190–191

Ichiki Kitokurō, 91
*Ie no hikari*, 6, 9, 94–95, 217–218, 265, 353; readership, 216–217, 222, 273; rural revitalization and, 218, 275, 321, 350
Igarashi Shoki, 301
"Imagined communities," and *The History of Kitakata City*, 369
Imperial Agricultural Association, 31, 48, 62–63, 87, 89, 93–95, 110, 116, 120, 133, 170, 178, 188, 191, 207, 242; budget debates and, 139, 164–166; debt arrangement policies and, 114–115, 118–120; reports on 1934 famine, 242, 250; rural revitalization and, 87, 137, 161, 175–176
Imperial Rule Assistance Association (IRAA), 327–328, 358
Inamura Ryūichi, 99
Income, 53, 58, 284–286, 358–359; adjusted for inflation, 284–285; farming, 40, 45–46, 53, 56–62; local differences, 56–62, 245–249; national trends, 285, 358; relief projects, 149–155; return to pre-depression levels, 53; Sekishiba, 60–61, 284–285; silk cocoons, 49
Income and spending, planning for, 185–187
Indebtedness, 43, 58, 62–68, 116–117, 150; depression and, 63, 68; effects on farm families, 113–114; estimates of, 62–64, 113, 128, 263; Imperial Agriculture Association and, 114, 116, 118–120; interest rates and, 64, 67; Ministry of Agriculture and Forestry, 114–117, 121–123, 126–128; moratorium on, 86–87, 100; petitions campaigns and, 63, 98–113; policies to address, 63, 113–132; political parties and, 117, 120, 122–126; reasons for borrowing, 65–67; Sekishiba, 58, 65, 67, 263, 285
Industrial Cooperative Central Bank, 121, 139
Industrial cooperatives, 6–7, 88, 272–273; membership, 222–223, 273; mobilization and, 332; rural revitalization and, 199, 210–211, 213, 264; Sekishiba, 92, 261–264, 272; ties to

Ministry of Agriculture and Forestry, 199
Industrial Cooperatives Law, 89
Industrialization, 16, 44
Infant mortality, 23, 287
Inflation, 284–285, 287
Inomata Tsunao, 153
Inoue Junnosuke, 51, 96
Inukai Tsuyoshi, 80, 82, 86
Ishiguro Tadaatsu, 103, 115–116, 207
Ishiwara Jirō, 176, 181
Iwatsuki village, 32, 365

*Japan in a Time of Crisis*, film, 380n10
Japan National Higher Level School (Nihon kokumin kōtō gakkō), 95
Japan Village Rule Alliance (Nihon sonjiha dōmei), 97–98, 104
Jichi nōmin kyōgikai (Local Autonomy Farmers' Conference), 99–100
*Jiriki kōsei, see* Self-revitalization
Journalism and the rural crisis, 57–58

Kagawa Toyohiko, 6–9, 217
Kaizō, 6, 215
Kamei Kaichirō, 105
Kamisanmiya village, 32, 258, 365
Kamisugure hamlet, 36
Kamitakahitai hamlet, 36–37, 310–311, 315
Katō Kanji, 94–95, 98, 115, 346, 348
Kawahara Saburō, 165
Kazami Akira, 97, 105, 108, 110–111, 142
Keitoku village, 32, 258, 365
keizai kaizen (economic improvement), 175
Keizai kōsei iinkai, *see* Economic Revitalization Committee
Kelly, William, 364
*Kihon chōsa, see* Basic Survey

Kinmonth, Earl, 215
Kinsen saimu rinji chōtei hōan (Monetary Claims Temporary Conciliation Law), 121
Kita Ikki, 96
Kitakata, 10–11, 24, 27–32, 353, 365–366; 1934 famine, 251; as tourist destination, 367–368, 370; characteristics, 28–32; 1918 Rice Riots, 46
Kitakata Incident, 28–29, 38
Kitakata Middle School, 31
Kitashiobara village, 353
Kobiyama Zenhachi, 238–239
Kodaira Gonichi, 95, 115, 120, 134, 140, 189, 219, 254; assessments of Economic Revitalization, 224–225; debt arrangement policies and, 115–117, 123, 130–131; Hyōgo Prefecture Agricultural Association and, 189–190; postwar career, 362; Revitalization Section, director, 206–207; rural revitalization and, 199, 288–290; self-revitalization campaign and, 189–191, 194; Special Assistance program, 255, 257; Takahashi Korekiyo and, 207, 256
*Kōgyō iken* (Advice on Promoting Enterprise), 161, 255–256
Komatsu hamlet, 36–37, 62, 150–152, 227, 233, 312, 317; 1934 famine, 245; Economic Revitalization Campaign and, 239–240, 267–268; economic revitalization planning in, 228–231; effects of the depression on, 60–62; household revitalization plans, 231–234
Kōno Ichirō, 361–362
Korea, rice production in, 48
Kosūwari, 61

Kumagura village, 32, 365
Kura (storehouses), 37, 367–368
Kwantung Army, 3, 42, 345–346
Kyōde hamlet, 36
Kyōhō famine, 251
*Kyōka, see* Moral suasion
*Kyūbō no nōson* (The Impoverished Village), 153

Labor disputes, 2, 4
Lake Inawashiro, 19
Landlords: decline in support for, 344–345, 354; in Sekishiba, 78
Landlord-tenant conflict, 46–47, 74–75
Landlord-tenant relations, 22; northeastern Japan, 22, 75–76; Sekishiba, 75–79
*Land of Milk and Honey, The,* 6–9, 324, 353
Landownership and land use, 74, 76–79, 245–248, 344–345, 393n104
Land reform, 39, 345, 355–359
Law for Credit on Immovables and Indemnification for Losses, 121
Law for Special Financing of the Industrial Cooperative Central Bank, 121
League of Nations, 155–156
Legal protection for tenants, 79
Local Autonomy Farmers' Conference (Jichi nōmin kyōgikai), 99, 102, 104, 108, 110
Local economic planning, 174–175, 183–185
Local elites and campaigns for rural reform, 104–106
Local Improvement Campaign (Chihō kairyō undō), 91–92, 339; Hōtoku movement and, 91–92, 219

Local initiatives for rural reform, 1930s, 2, 14–15, 84–87, 99–110, 132–134, 172–188, 288, 291–312
Local leadership, 44, 93, 215, 302; changing face of, 93, 215, 289, 302, 352; Economic Revitalization Campaign and, 297, 299, 302
London Naval Conference, 81
Lytton Commission, 155

Maeda Masana, 161, 255
Manchuria, 81, 325–326; emigration and, 345–349; petition campaigns and, 100–101, 108
Manchurian Incident, 3, 42–43, 155–156
Matsudaira clan, 24, 26
Matsukata deflation, 47
Matsumoto Gaku, 175
Matsuyama village, 32, 365
May 15 Incident, 43–44, 80, 82, 86, 103; trials, 80–83, 170
Mechanization, 39, 331
Media and the rural crisis, 5, 11, 57, 112, 215–216, 218, 250
Medical care, 16, 23, 44, 73; rural revitalization and, 303, 319
Meiji Restoration, 3, 24, 26
Microhistory and rural Japan, 2, 5–12; and the 1930s, 17–18, 368–370
Military, 14–15; budget debates and, 156–159; relief spending and, 4, 12, 166–170; rural Japan and, 136–137, 166
Ministry of Agriculture and Commerce, 115
Ministry of Agriculture and Forestry, 12, 56–57, 62, 105, 113, 137, 155, 160, 174–175; budget debates and, 138, 141, 143, 158–159, 164–165, 170–171,

195–196; debt arrangement policies and, 114–115, 125–127, 129; friction with Home Ministry, 205; public works and, 137, 155; rural revitalization and, 160, 194–195, 197–198
Ministry of Commerce and Industry, 167–168
Ministry of Education, 72, 205–206
Minseitō, 4, 29, 51, 202; budget debates and, 164; debt arrangement policies and, 117–118, 125–126; rural relief and, 82, 85–86, 107
Miwa Ryōichi, 154
Miyagi Shinichirō, 98–99
Miyasaki Hajime, 123–124
Mobilization, 11–12, 286, 326–327, 331–332; compared to Germany and Italy, 327–328; fascism and, 327–328; local leadership and, 340, 343; rural revitalization and, 17–18, 270–271, 287, 328, 330, 332–335, 337, 345; Sekishiba, 270–271, 287, 328–329, 352; Sekishiba Village Economic Revitalization Committee, 341
Modernity, 4–5, 17, 352; agrarianism and, 87, 94
Monetary Claims Temporary Conciliation Law (Kinsen saimu rinji chōtei hōan), 121–122
Moral suasion, 220; postwar, 363; rural revitalization and, 220–221, 309, 349–350
Mori Takemaro, 343
Mount Bandai, 19, 34

Nagano Akira, 94, 96–104, 107–113, 134–135
Nagashima Sadashi, 176–178, 181, 187–188, 190

Naisei kaigi, *see* Domestic Policy Conferences
Nakamura Masanori, 343
Nakamura Takafusa, 154
Nakazato hamlet, 36, 312
Nankō Agricultural Association, 119
Nasu Hiroshi, 13–14, 95, 115, 207, 346
National Association of Mayors of Towns and Villages, 118, 120, 207
National campaigns for rural relief and reform, 86
National Spiritual Mobilization Campaign; rural revitalization and, 335–336
New Life Campaign (Shin seikatsu undō), 361–363
New Village Development Campaign, 361–363
Nihon kokumin kōtō gakkō (Japan National Higher Level School), 95
Nihon sonjiha dōmei (Japan Village Rule Alliance), 97–98
Ninomiya Sontoku, 185–186, 219, 288, 291; teachings of, 92, 291, 296, 313, 315
Nishida Yoshiaki, 343–344, 359
Nishikata Toshima, 128
Nishi-nakamei hamlet, 36
Nishi-shioda village, Nagano prefecture, 343
Nishiyama Kōichi, 68, 214–215, 354
*Nōgu benriron* (On the Efficacy of Farm Implements), 267
Nōhon renmei (Agrarianist Federation), 98
Nōhonshugi, *see* Agrarianism
Nōjin jiriki kōsei matsuri, *see* Farmers' Self-Revitalization Festivals
Nōkaihō, 89

Nōka keizai chōsa, see Farm Household Surveys
Nōkyō (Association of Agricultural Cooperatives), 40, 357–358, 363
Non-farm employment, 22, 58, 331
Nōrin shingikai (Agriculture and Forestry Deliberative Council), 175
Nōrinshō, see Ministry of Agriculture and Forestry
Northeastern Japan, see Tōhoku region
Northern Shinano Depression-Policy Association, 104–106, 113
Nōsangyoson keizai kōsei undō, see Farm, Mountain, and Fishing Village Economic Revitalization Campaign
Nōson taisaku rengō kyōgikai (Farm Village Policy Federation Conference), 167
Nutrition, 72, 287; changes in, 58–59; children's diet and, 72, 250–251; rural revitalization and, 303, 319

Occupation-era rural reforms, 354–355, 357–358
Odagiri Yōgo, 342
Office for the Compilation of Municipal History, 368, 370
Oguchi Kiroku, 124–125
Ōishi Kaichirō, 50
Okada Atsushi, 94–95, 120, 174–175, 177–178
Okada Ryōhei, 91
Ōkado Masakatsu, 340, 343
Ōkawa Shūmei, 96
Ōkura Nagatsune, 267
107th Bank, 30
Ōshio village, 6–10, 353
Ōta village, 309–310

Owner-cultivator promotion policies, 79, 344–345, 356

Patriotic Women's Association (Aikoku Fujinkai), 92
Petition campaigns, 2, 57, 63, 82, 84–85, 99–106, 108–112, 252, 288
Police, 31, 38
Political parties, 3–4, 28–29, 107, 115, 136, 156, 163, 170. See also specific parties by name
Popular culture, 4–5; rural revitalization and, 214–216
Postwar agricultural productivity, 358–359
Power, shifts in rural balance of, 44, 79–80, 289, 343–345, 352
Prices, 43, 52–53; farm goods, 45, 47; fertilizer, 62, 284–285; rice, 43, 45, 47–48, 52, 284, 359–360
Productivity, 53, 330–331
Prostitution and the rural crisis, 113
Public works projects, 70, 134, 136–140, 143, 145, 152, 252; beneficiaries of, 140, 145, 147–149, 151; budgets, 12, 137, 141; burden on villages, 143, 146–147; criticism of, 152–155; Sekishiba, 146–148, 150–151; value to farmers of, 149–152, 154; wages, 147, 149–150; women and, 148

Radio, 44
Ramen, 368
Recession, 1920s, 47–50
Reform of daily life, 266, 321; Sekishiba, 265, 303, 319–322
Reservist organizations, 88, 92
Revitalization Section, Ministry of Agriculture and Forestry, 206–207

478  Index

Rice; as diet staple, 58–60, 72, 249–251; production, 52–53
Rice imports, 48
Rice Law, 48
Rice riots, 1918, 28, 46–48, 52, 139
Rural and urban cultures, 16, 43–44; compared, 290–291
Rural communities, variations across households, 61, 73–74
Rural Japan; qualities attributed to, 2, 361
Rural medical facilities, 163
Rural poverty, 181–182
Rural readership, 215
Rural revitalization, 7–8, 11–12, 17–18, 85, 91, 133–134, 179, 206, 219, 226; case studies of, 219; debt arrangement and, 130; Imperial Agricultural Association and, 87; mobilization and, 286, 328, 350–351; modern countryside and, 361; popular cultures of, 214–223; postwar developments, 360; Satō Sakichi and, 291–294; wartime developments, 354; Yabe Zenbei and, 291
Rural revitalization advocates, *see* Hyōgo Prefecture Agricultural Association; Imperial Agriculture Association; Ministry of Agriculture and Forestry; National Association of Mayors of Towns and Villages; *and specific individuals by name*
Rural revitalization campaigns, *see* Campaign to Improve Daily Life; Farm, Mountain, and Fishing Village Economic Revitalization Campaign; Local Improvement Campaign; New Village Development Campaign
Rural youth, 93, 216

Rural-urban differences, 5, 16, 43–44, 134, 290–291; described, 361, 364
Russo-Japanese War, 3, 91

Saionji Kinmochi, 156
Saitō cabinet, 106, 155–156
Saitō Makoto, 107, 120, 127, 135, 143, 156–157, 160, 163, 166–167; emergency relief and, 135–137; enthusiasm for self-revitalization campaign, 190–191, 193, 195–197; petitioners and, 191–192; rural revitalization and, 160, 171, 173, 187, 200, 203
Sakura Sōgorō, 101
*Sangyō kumiai*, *see* Industrial cooperatives
Sanjōnome hamlet, 36
Sasai Shintarō, 219–222, 296, 315, 421n109; visits to Kitakata area, 311–312; Yabe Zenbei and, 307–308
Satō Chōta, 62, 151
Satō Sakichi, 10, 61, 68, 71, 227, 268–270, 312–313, 330, 336, 358; career, 292–294; economic revitalization and, 234–236, 291–292, 296, 303, 318, 321, 330–331, 334; hamlet assemblies and, 313–316; IRAA and, 327; reform of daily life, 319–320; Sekishiba Village Economic Revitalization Committee and, 299, 301–302, 341
Savings rates, 224
Sawayanagi Masatarō, 91
Schools, 70
Seikatsu kaizen undō, 218
Seinendan, 88, 92, 216, 222
Seiyūkai, 4, 29, 156, 165; budget debates and, 164, 166; debt arrangement policies and, 115, 117–118, 122–126,

128; emergency relief and, 82, 85–86, 107; rural revitalization and, 200–202

Sekishiba, 9–12, 29, 32–40, 69, 225–226, 242, 265, 268, 270–271, 277, 291–292, 312, 357, 365, 367, 370; 1934 famine, 225, 241–243, 245, 249, 268; Basic Survey, 225, 263; community life and the depression, 68–80, 92–93, 277–281; cooperative work sites, 264, 278, 280–281; Economic Revitalization Campaign and, 259, 269, 291–292, 297–299; emigration and, 348–349; household savings, 285–286; income from farming, 284–285; indebtedness and, 64, 285; local leadership, 297–299; mobilization, 326–329; public works projects in, 146, 148–149; results of economic revitalization planning, 281–284, 286–287; storage facilities, 277–278, 280–281

Sekishiba Elementary School, 38
Sekishiba hamlet, 36–37, 148, 264, 317
Sekishiba Industrial Cooperative, 271–277
Sekishiba Industrial Cooperative Newsletter, 274
*Sekishiba sonpō*, 337–339
Sekishiba Village Agricultural Association, 92
Sekishiba Village Economic Revitalization Committee, 298, 301, 303, 343; and changes in local leadership, 340–342; and mobilization, 332, 341; membership, 299–301, 341–343; structure, 298–299; women, 300
Sekishiba Village Women's Association (Fujinkai), 322

Sekishiba Village Young Men's Association, 299
Sekishiba Youth School, 39
Self-revitalization, 85, 109, 134, 136, 160, 176–177, 179–181, 187
Self-sufficiency, as component of Economic Revitalization, 203
Sericulture, 43, 45, 48–49, 51–52
Shimada Toshio, 107
*Shimin*, 194, 219, 396n20; Yabe Zenbei in, 304–305, 307, 310
Shimizu Ginzō, 199
Shimoshiba hamlet, 36–37, 150–151, 264, 325
Shimosugure hamlet, 36, 312
Shinagawa Yajirō, 88
*Shinano mainichi shinbun*, 102
Shōji Shunsaku, 176, 179
Showa Emperor, 194
Sino-Japanese War, 3
Sixty-fifth Diet, 158, 163, 169–170
Sixty-fourth Diet, 156, 201
Sixty-second Diet, 102, 106, 175
Sixty-third Diet, 102, 106–107, 121, 135, 143, 175, 196; rural revitalization and, 196–197, 206, 254
Smethurst, Richard, 39, 56
Smiles, Samuel, 214–215
Social policy and reform, initiatives for, 14–16, 84–87, 99–110, 132–134, 172–188, 288, 361–364
Social unrest, 4, 10–11
Social welfare programs, 70
Sonobe Shukei, 299, 316
Sosogi hamlet, 36, 317
Special Assistance funding, 321–322, 339–340, 351
Special Assistance program, 254–257, 275, 278–280
Special Household Tax, 61

Spending, 60–61, 73–74; farming costs, 47, 56; household, 45–47, 56–62
Spiritual revitalization, Home and Education ministries, 205
Standards of living, 40, 74, 359–360; depression's effects and, 56, 287
Stock Market Crash, 1929, 50–51
Sugiyama Motojirō, 105
Suicide and the rural crisis, 113
Sukegawa Keishirō, 124–125, 403n111

Tachibana Kōzaburō, 80–83, 86, 94, 97–99, 350; and petition campaigns, 103–104
Tadashi Fukutake, 36
Tago Ichimin, 200–201
Taiwan, rice production in, 48
Takahashi Korekiyo, 86, 103, 125–127, 137, 142, 156–158, 161–162, 164, 200, 256; budget debates and, 138, 155, 157–159, 161, 163, 165–166, 170, 224, 253, 255; petitioners and, 193; rural revitalization and, 136, 160, 171, 173, 187, 195–197; Special Assistance program, 255–256; views on rural relief, 159–160
Takeshita Fumi, 103–104, 106, 110
Tanaka Gorō, 43
Tanaka Tōsuke, 6–10, 324
Tatsuki River, 32
Tax burdens, 16, 69
Tax collection, 70–72, 317–318
Teachers' salaries, 69–72
Teikoku nōkai, *see* Imperial Agricultural Association
Teishirogi Chiyoichi, 317
Tenancy, 56, 69, 79; land reforms and, 355–357, 359; Sekishiba, 40, 76–79
Tenancy disputes, 2, 4, 10, 74–76, 255

Tenant movement, 22, 75–76
Tenmei famine, 251
Tenpō famine, 251
Terrorism, domestic, 43–44, 80–83, 86, 103, 170
Teruoka Shūzō, 154
Textile industry, 51–52
Tōhoku region, 20–24; famine, 241–244; landlord-tenant relationships in, 75–76; meteorological conditions, 241–243
Tōjō Genbei, 312
Tokugawa era, 24, 26–27, 32, 101
Tokugawa Mitsukuni, 188
*Tōkyō asahi shinbun*: 1934 famine and, 250–251, 253; coverage of rural crisis, 112–113
*Tōkyō nichi nichi shinbun*: 1934 famine and, 253; coverage of rural crisis, 113
Tokyo stock market, 51
Tokyo University Faculty of Agriculture, 95
Tourism, 26, 366–367
Toyokawa village, 32, 365
*Tōyō keizai shimpō*, 105
Transportation: rail service, 11, 19, 26–27, 29; roads and highways, 26, 34–35

Uda Seiichi, 28, 292–293
Umeyama Ichirō, 217
Unemployment, 51, 389n52
United States Department of Agriculture, 13
University of Aizu, 366
Urazato village, Nagano prefecture, 7, 343
Urbanization, 43, 364–365
Utsumi Haruki, 151–152, 236–238, 315, 317

Village-level planning, 17, 161, 208–209
Village mainstays, 339–343, 352; local leadership and, 289, 343; rural revitalization and, 256–257, 270, 289; Sekishiba, 339–340, 349
Vlastos, Stephen, 26, 80, 94
Vocabulary of rural reform, 203

Wagō Tsuneo, 98–99, 101–103, 108
Wakamatsu, 11, 24, 26–27
Wakatsuki Reijirō, 202
Waswo, Ann, 44, 74
Watanabe Hikoe, 62, 150
Watanabe Kyūgo, 299, 315–316, 336
Watanabe Masaichi, 151
Watanabe Shinta, 151, 228, 300
Wilson, Sandra, 346
Women: public life and, 4, 44; public works projects and, 149; rural revitalization and, 322–323; textile workers, 7–8, 29
Women's Association (Fujinkai), 92
World War I, 45, 48
World War II, 1–2

Yabe Tsuneko, 295
Yabe Zenbei, 30, 78, 270, 294–295, 301, 358; career, 294, 327; hamlet assemblies and, 314–316; IRAA and, 327; mobilization and, 336; origins of rural crisis explained, 306–307; personal philosophy, 295–296, 304–309; publications, 304–305, 307, 310; reform strategies, 307–312; revitalization in Sekishiba, 291, 296, 302–303, 309, 311; Sasai Shintarō and, 296, 304–305, 307
Yabukigahara Training Farm, 340
Yahagi Eizō, 346
Yama County Association of Mayors of Towns and Villages, 84–85
Yama County Depression-Policy People's General Meeting, 84
Yamada village, Hyōgo prefecture, 185
Yamagata Aritomo, 88
Yamamoto Tatsuo, 203–205
Yamawaki Nobukichi, 176, 178, 181, 189, 194
Yamazaki Masami, 42–43
Yamazaki Naokichi, 217
Yamazaki Nobuyoshi, 94–95
Young Men's Association, 88, 92, 216, 222
Young Volunteers for the Development of Manchuria and Mongolia, 346, 348
Young Women's Association, 92

Zaigō gunjinkai (Reservists' Association), 88

## Harvard East Asian Monographs
(* out-of-print)

- *1. Liang Fang-chung, *The Single-Whip Method of Taxation in China*
- *2. Harold C. Hinton, *The Grain Tribute System of China, 1845–1911*
- 3. Ellsworth C. Carlson, *The Kaiping Mines, 1877–1912*
- *4. Chao Kuo-chün, *Agrarian Policies of Mainland China: A Documentary Study, 1949–1956*
- *5. Edgar Snow, *Random Notes on Red China, 1936–1945*
- *6. Edwin George Beal, Jr., *The Origin of Likin, 1835–1864*
- 7. Chao Kuo-chün, *Economic Planning and Organization in Mainland China: A Documentary Study, 1949–1957*
- *8. John K. Fairbank, *Ching Documents: An Introductory Syllabus*
- *9. Helen Yin and Yi-chang Yin, *Economic Statistics of Mainland China, 1949–1957*
- *10. Wolfgang Franke, *The Reform and Abolition of the Traditional Chinese Examination System*
- 11. Albert Feuerwerker and S. Cheng, *Chinese Communist Studies of Modern Chinese History*
- 12. C. John Stanley, *Late Ching Finance: Hu Kuang-yung as an Innovator*
- 13. S. M. Meng, *The Tsungli Yamen: Its Organization and Functions*
- *14. Ssu-yü Teng, *Historiography of the Taiping Rebellion*
- 15. Chun-Jo Liu, *Controversies in Modern Chinese Intellectual History: An Analytic Bibliography of Periodical Articles, Mainly of the May Fourth and Post–May Fourth Era*
- *16. Edward J. M. Rhoads, *The Chinese Red Army, 1927–1963: An Annotated Bibliography*
- 17. Andrew J. Nathan, *A History of the China International Famine Relief Commission*
- *18. Frank H. H. King (ed.) and Prescott Clarke, *A Research Guide to China-Coast Newspapers, 1822–1911*
- 19. Ellis Joffe, *Party and Army: Professionalism and Political Control in the Chinese Officer Corps, 1949–1964*
- *20. Toshio G. Tsukahira, *Feudal Control in Tokugawa Japan: The Sankin Kōtai System*
- 21. Kwang-Ching Liu, ed., *American Missionaries in China: Papers from Harvard Seminars*
- 22. George Moseley, *A Sino-Soviet Cultural Frontier: The Ili Kazakh Autonomous Chou*
- 23. Carl F. Nathan, *Plague Prevention and Politics in Manchuria, 1910–1931*

# Harvard East Asian Monographs

*24. Adrian Arthur Bennett, *John Fryer: The Introduction of Western Science and Technology into Nineteenth-Century China*

25. Donald J. Friedman, *The Road from Isolation: The Campaign of the American Committee for Non-Participation in Japanese Aggression, 1938–1941*

26. Edward LeFevour, *Western Enterprise in Late Ching China: A Selective Survey of Jardine, Matheson and Company's Operations, 1842–1895*

27. Charles Neuhauser, *Third World Politics: China and the Afro-Asian People's Solidarity Organization, 1957–1967*

28. Kungtu C. Sun, assisted by Ralph W. Huenemann, *The Economic Development of Manchuria in the First Half of the Twentieth Century*

*29. Shahid Javed Burki, *A Study of Chinese Communes, 1965*

30. John Carter Vincent, *The Extraterritorial System in China: Final Phase*

31. Madeleine Chi, *China Diplomacy, 1914–1918*

*32. Clifton Jackson Phillips, *Protestant America and the Pagan World: The First Half Century of the American Board of Commissioners for Foreign Missions, 1810–1860*

33. James Pusey, *Wu Han: Attacking the Present through the Past*

34. Ying-wan Cheng, *Postal Communication in China and Its Modernization, 1860–1896*

35. Tuvia Blumenthal, *Saving in Postwar Japan*

36. Peter Frost, *The Bakumatsu Currency Crisis*

37. Stephen C. Lockwood, *Augustine Heard and Company, 1858–1862*

38. Robert R. Campbell, *James Duncan Campbell: A Memoir by His Son*

39. Jerome Alan Cohen, ed., *The Dynamics of China's Foreign Relations*

40. V. V. Vishnyakova-Akimova, *Two Years in Revolutionary China, 1925–1927*, tr. Steven L. Levine

*41. Meron Medzini, *French Policy in Japan during the Closing Years of the Tokugawa Regime*

42. Ezra Vogel, Margie Sargent, Vivienne B. Shue, Thomas Jay Mathews, and Deborah S. Davis, *The Cultural Revolution in the Provinces*

*43. Sidney A. Forsythe, *An American Missionary Community in China, 1895–1905*

*44. Benjamin I. Schwartz, ed., *Reflections on the May Fourth Movement.: A Symposium*

*45. Ching Young Choe, *The Rule of the Taewŏngun, 1864–1873: Restoration in Yi Korea*

46. W. P. J. Hall, *A Bibliographical Guide to Japanese Research on the Chinese Economy, 1958–1970*

47. Jack J. Gerson, *Horatio Nelson Lay and Sino-British Relations, 1854–1864*

48. Paul Richard Bohr, *Famine and the Missionary: Timothy Richard as Relief Administrator and Advocate of National Reform*

49. Endymion Wilkinson, *The History of Imperial China: A Research Guide*

50. Britten Dean, *China and Great Britain: The Diplomacy of Commercial Relations, 1860–1864*

51. Ellsworth C. Carlson, *The Foochow Missionaries, 1847–1880*

52. Yeh-chien Wang, *An Estimate of the Land-Tax Collection in China, 1753 and 1908*

53. Richard M. Pfeffer, *Understanding Business Contracts in China, 1949–1963*

# Harvard East Asian Monographs

54. Han-sheng Chuan and Richard Kraus, *Mid-Ching Rice Markets and Trade: An Essay in Price History*
55. Ranbir Vohra, *Lao She and the Chinese Revolution*
56. Liang-lin Hsiao, *China's Foreign Trade Statistics, 1864–1949*
*57. Lee-hsia Hsu Ting, *Government Control of the Press in Modern China, 1900–1949*
58. Edward W. Wagner, *The Literati Purges: Political Conflict in Early Yi Korea*
*59. Joungwon A. Kim, *Divided Korea: The Politics of Development, 1945–1972*
*60. Noriko Kamachi, John K. Fairbank, and Chūzō Ichiko, *Japanese Studies of Modern China Since 1953: A Bibliographical Guide to Historical and Social-Science Research on the Nineteenth and Twentieth Centuries, Supplementary Volume for 1953–1969*
61. Donald A. Gibbs and Yun-chen Li, *A Bibliography of Studies and Translations of Modern Chinese Literature, 1918–1942*
62. Robert H. Silin, *Leadership and Values: The Organization of Large-Scale Taiwanese Enterprises*
63. David Pong, *A Critical Guide to the Kwangtung Provincial Archives Deposited at the Public Record Office of London*
*64. Fred W. Drake, *China Charts the World: Hsu Chi-yü and His Geography of 1848*
*65. William A. Brown and Urgrunge Onon, translators and annotators, *History of the Mongolian People's Republic*
66. Edward L. Farmer, *Early Ming Government: The Evolution of Dual Capitals*
*67. Ralph C. Croizier, *Koxinga and Chinese Nationalism: History, Myth, and the Hero*
*68. William J. Tyler, tr., *The Psychological World of Natsume Sōseki*, by Doi Takeo
69. Eric Widmer, *The Russian Ecclesiastical Mission in Peking during the Eighteenth Century*
*70. Charlton M. Lewis, *Prologue to the Chinese Revolution: The Transformation of Ideas and Institutions in Hunan Province, 1891–1907*
71. Preston Torbert, *The Ching Imperial Household Department: A Study of Its Organization and Principal Functions, 1662–1796*
72. Paul A. Cohen and John E. Schrecker, eds., *Reform in Nineteenth-Century China*
73. Jon Sigurdson, *Rural Industrialism in China*
74. Kang Chao, *The Development of Cotton Textile Production in China*
75. Valentin Rabe, *The Home Base of American China Missions, 1880–1920*
*76. Sarasin Viraphol, *Tribute and Profit: Sino-Siamese Trade, 1652–1853*
77. Ch'i-ch'ing Hsiao, *The Military Establishment of the Yuan Dynasty*
78. Meishi Tsai, *Contemporary Chinese Novels and Short Stories, 1949–1974: An Annotated Bibliography*
*79. Wellington K. K. Chan, *Merchants, Mandarins and Modern Enterprise in Late Ching China*
80. Endymion Wilkinson, *Landlord and Labor in Late Imperial China: Case Studies from Shandong by Jing Su and Luo Lun*
*81. Barry Keenan, *The Dewey Experiment in China: Educational Reform and Political Power in the Early Republic*

# Harvard East Asian Monographs

*82. George A. Hayden, *Crime and Punishment in Medieval Chinese Drama: Three Judge Pao Plays*

*83. Sang-Chul Suh, *Growth and Structural Changes in the Korean Economy, 1910–1940*

84. J. W. Dower, *Empire and Aftermath: Yoshida Shigeru and the Japanese Experience, 1878–1954*

85. Martin Collcutt, *Five Mountains: The Rinzai Zen Monastic Institution in Medieval Japan*

86. Kwang Suk Kim and Michael Roemer, *Growth and Structural Transformation*

87. Anne O. Krueger, *The Developmental Role of the Foreign Sector and Aid*

*88. Edwin S. Mills and Byung-Nak Song, *Urbanization and Urban Problems*

89. Sung Hwan Ban, Pal Yong Moon, and Dwight H. Perkins, *Rural Development*

*90. Noel F. McGinn, Donald R. Snodgrass, Yung Bong Kim, Shin-Bok Kim, and Quee-Young Kim, *Education and Development in Korea*

91. Leroy P. Jones and Il SaKong, *Government, Business, and Entrepreneurship in Economic Development: The Korean Case*

92. Edward S. Mason, Dwight H. Perkins, Kwang Suk Kim, David C. Cole, Mahn Je Kim et al., *The Economic and Social Modernization of the Republic of Korea*

93. Robert Repetto, Tai Hwan Kwon, Son-Ung Kim, Dae Young Kim, John E. Sloboda, and Peter J. Donaldson, *Economic Development, Population Policy, and Demographic Transition in the Republic of Korea*

94. Parks M. Coble, Jr., *The Shanghai Capitalists and the Nationalist Government, 1927–1937*

95. Noriko Kamachi, *Reform in China: Huang Tsun-hsien and the Japanese Model*

96. Richard Wich, *Sino-Soviet Crisis Politics: A Study of Political Change and Communication*

97. Lillian M. Li, *China's Silk Trade: Traditional Industry in the Modern World, 1842–1937*

98. R. David Arkush, *Fei Xiaotong and Sociology in Revolutionary China*

*99. Kenneth Alan Grossberg, *Japan's Renaissance: The Politics of the Muromachi Bakufu*

100. James Reeve Pusey, *China and Charles Darwin*

101. Hoyt Cleveland Tillman, *Utilitarian Confucianism: Chen Liang's Challenge to Chu Hsi*

102. Thomas A. Stanley, *Ōsugi Sakae, Anarchist in Taishō Japan: The Creativity of the Ego*

103. Jonathan K. Ocko, *Bureaucratic Reform in Provincial China: Ting Jih-ch'ang in Restoration Kiangsu, 1867–1870*

104. James Reed, *The Missionary Mind and American East Asia Policy, 1911–1915*

105. Neil L. Waters, *Japan's Local Pragmatists: The Transition from Bakumatsu to Meiji in the Kawasaki Region*

106. David C. Cole and Yung Chul Park, *Financial Development in Korea, 1945–1978*

107. Roy Bahl, Chuk Kyo Kim, and Chong Kee Park, *Public Finances during the Korean Modernization Process*

108. William D. Wray, *Mitsubishi and the N.Y.K, 1870–1914: Business Strategy in the Japanese Shipping Industry*

109. Ralph William Huenemann, *The Dragon and the Iron Horse: The Economics of Railroads in China, 1876–1937*

# Harvard East Asian Monographs

110. Benjamin A. Elman, *From Philosophy to Philology: Intellectual and Social Aspects of Change in Late Imperial China*
111. Jane Kate Leonard, *Wei Yüan and China's Rediscovery of the Maritime World*
112. Luke S. K. Kwong, *A Mosaic of the Hundred Days:. Personalities, Politics, and Ideas of 1898*
113. John E. Wills, Jr., *Embassies and Illusions: Dutch and Portuguese Envoys to K'ang-hsi, 1666–1687*
114. Joshua A. Fogel, *Politics and Sinology: The Case of Naitō Konan (1866–1934)*
*115. Jeffrey C. Kinkley, ed., *After Mao: Chinese Literature and Society, 1978– 1981*
116. C. Andrew Gerstle, *Circles of Fantasy: Convention in the Plays of Chikamatsu*
117. Andrew Gordon, *The Evolution of Labor Relations in Japan: Heavy Industry, 1853–1955*
*118. Daniel K. Gardner, *Chu Hsi and the "Ta Hsueh": Neo-Confucian Reflection on the Confucian Canon*
119. Christine Guth Kanda, *Shinzō: Hachiman Imagery and Its Development*
*120. Robert Borgen, *Sugawara no Michizane and the Early Heian Court*
121. Chang-tai Hung, *Going to the People: Chinese Intellectual and Folk Literature, 1918–1937*
* 122. Michael A. Cusumano, *The Japanese Automobile Industry: Technology and Management at Nissan and Toyota*
123. Richard von Glahn, *The Country of Streams and Grottoes: Expansion, Settlement, and the Civilizing of the Sichuan Frontier in Song Times*
124. Steven D. Carter, *The Road to Komatsubara: A Classical Reading of the Renga Hyakuin*
125. Katherine F. Bruner, John K. Fairbank, and Richard T. Smith, *Entering China's Service: Robert Hart's Journals, 1854–1863*
126. Bob Tadashi Wakabayashi, *Anti-Foreignism and Western Learning in Early-Modern Japan: The "New Theses" of 1825*
127. Atsuko Hirai, *Individualism and Socialism: The Life and Thought of Kawai Eijirō (1891–1944)*
128. Ellen Widmer, *The Margins of Utopia: "Shui-hu hou-chuan" and the Literature of Ming Loyalism*
129. R. Kent Guy, *The Emperor's Four Treasuries: Scholars and the State in the Late Chien-lung Era*
130. Peter C. Perdue, *Exhausting the Earth: State and Peasant in Hunan, 1500–1850*
131. Susan Chan Egan, *A Latterday Confucian: Reminiscences of William Hung (1893–1980)*
132. James T. C. Liu, *China Turning Inward: Intellectual-Political Changes in the Early Twelfth Century*
133. Paul A. Cohen, *Between Tradition and Modernity: Wang T'ao and Reform in Late Ching China*
134. Kate Wildman Nakai, *Shogunal Politics: Arai Hakuseki and the Premises of Tokugawa Rule*
135. Parks M. Coble, *Facing Japan: Chinese Politics and Japanese Imperialism, 1931–1937*
136. Jon L. Saari, *Legacies of Childhood: Growing Up Chinese in a Time of Crisis, 1890–1920*
137. Susan Downing Videen, *Tales of Heichū*

# Harvard East Asian Monographs

138. Heinz Morioka and Miyoko Sasaki, *Rakugo: The Popular Narrative Art of Japan*
139. Joshua A. Fogel, *Nakae Ushikichi in China: The Mourning of Spirit*
140. Alexander Barton Woodside, *Vietnam and the Chinese Model.: A Comparative Study of Vietnamese and Chinese Government in the First Half of the Nineteenth Century*
141. George Elision, *Deus Destroyed: The Image of Christianity in Early Modern Japan*
142. William D. Wray, ed., *Managing Industrial Enterprise: Cases from Japan's Prewar Experience*
143. T'ung-tsu Ch'ü, *Local Government in China under the Ching*
144. Marie Anchordoguy, *Computers, Inc.: Japan's Challenge to IBM*
145. Barbara Molony, *Technology and Investment: The Prewar Japanese Chemical Industry*
146. Mary Elizabeth Berry, *Hideyoshi*
147. Laura E. Hein, *Fueling Growth: The Energy Revolution and Economic Policy in Postwar Japan*
148. Wen-hsin Yeh, *The Alienated Academy: Culture and Politics in Republican China, 1919–1937*
149. Dru C. Gladney, *Muslim Chinese: Ethnic Nationalism in the People's Republic*
150. Merle Goldman and Paul A. Cohen, eds., *Ideas Across Cultures: Essays on Chinese Thought in Honor of Benjamin L Schwartz*
151. James Polachek, *The Inner Opium War*
152. Gail Lee Bernstein, *Japanese Marxist: A Portrait of Kawakami Hajime, 1879–1946*
153. Lloyd E. Eastman, *The Abortive Revolution: China under Nationalist Rule, 1927–1937*
154. Mark Mason, *American Multinationals and Japan: The Political Economy of Japanese Capital Controls, 1899–1980*
155. Richard J. Smith, John K. Fairbank, and Katherine F. Bruner, *Robert Hart and China's Early Modernization: His Journals, 1863–1866*
156. George J. Tanabe, Jr., *Myōe the Dreamkeeper: Fantasy and Knowledge in Kamakura Buddhism*
157. William Wayne Farris, *Heavenly Warriors: The Evolution of Japan's Military, 500–1300*
158. Yu-ming Shaw, *An American Missionary in China: John Leighton Stuart and Chinese-American Relations*
159. James B. Palais, *Politics and Policy in Traditional Korea*
160. Douglas Reynolds, *China, 1898–1912: The Xinzheng Revolution and Japan*
161. Roger Thompson, *China's Local Councils in the Age of Constitutional Reform*
162. William Johnston, *The Modern Epidemic: History of Tuberculosis in Japan*
163. Constantine Nomikos Vaporis, *Breaking Barriers: Travel and the State in Early Modern Japan*
164. Irmela Hijiya-Kirschnereit, *Rituals of Self-Revelation: Shishōsetsu as Literary Genre and Socio-Cultural Phenomenon*
165. James C. Baxter, *The Meiji Unification Through the Lens of Ishikawa Prefecture*
166. Thomas R. H. Havens, *Architects of Affluence: The Tsutsumi Family and the Seibu-Saison Enterprises in Twentieth-Century Japan*
167. Anthony Hood Chambers, *The Secret Window: Ideal Worlds in Tanizaki's Fiction*
168. Steven J. Ericson, *The Sound of the Whistle: Railroads and the State in Meiji Japan*

## Harvard East Asian Monographs

169. Andrew Edmund Goble, *Kenmu: Go-Daigo's Revolution*
170. Denise Potrzeba Lett, *In Pursuit of Status: The Making of South Korea's "New" Urban Middle Class*
171. Mimi Hall Yiengpruksawan, *Hiraizumi: Buddhist Art and Regional Politics in Twelfth-Century Japan*
172. Charles Shirō Inouye, *The Similitude of Blossoms: A Critical Biography of Izumi Kyōka (1873–1939), Japanese Novelist and Playwright*
173. Aviad E. Raz, *Riding the Black Ship: Japan and Tokyo Disneyland*
174. Deborah J. Milly, *Poverty, Equality, and Growth: The Politics of Economic Need in Postwar Japan*
175. See Heng Teow, *Japan's Cultural Policy Toward China, 1918–1931: A Comparative Perspective*
176. Michael A. Fuller, *An Introduction to Literary Chinese*
177. Frederick R. Dickinson, *War and National Reinvention: Japan in the Great War, 1914–1919*
178. John Solt, *Shredding the Tapestry of Meaning: The Poetry and Poetics of Kitasono Katue (1902–1978)*
179. Edward Pratt, *Japan's Protoindustrial Elite: The Economic Foundations of the Gōnō*
180. Atsuko Sakaki, *Recontextualizing Texts: Narrative Performance in Modern Japanese Fiction*
181. Soon-Won Park, *Colonial Industrialization and Labor in Korea: The Onoda Cement Factory*
182. JaHyun Kim Haboush and Martina Deuchler, *Culture and the State in Late Chosŏn Korea*
183. John W. Chaffee, *Branches of Heaven: A History of the Imperial Clan of Sung China*
184. Gi-Wook Shin and Michael Robinson, eds., *Colonial Modernity in Korea*
185. Nam-lin Hur, *Prayer and Play in Late Tokugawa Japan: Asakusa Sensōji and Edo Society*
186. Kristin Stapleton, *Civilizing Chengdu: Chinese Urban Reform, 1895–1937*
187. Hyung Il Pai, *Constructing "Korean" Origins: A Critical Review of Archaeology, Historiography, and Racial Myth in Korean State-Formation Theories*
188. Brian D. Ruppert, *Jewel in the Ashes: Buddha Relics and Power in Early Medieval Japan*
189. Susan Daruvala, *Zhou Zuoren and an Alternative Chinese Response to Modernity*
190. James Z. Lee, *The Political Economy of a Frontier: Southwest China, 1250–1850*
191. Kerry Smith, *A Time of Crisis: Japan, the Great Depression, and Rural Revitalization*